I0296368

Anual Report

Annual Report of the Comptroller of the Currency

Anual Report

Annual Report of the Comptroller of the Currency

ISBN/EAN: 9783741151576

Manufactured in Europe, USA, Canada, Australia, Japa

Cover: Foto ©ninafisch / pixelio.de

Manufactured and distributed by brebook publishing software
(www.brebook.com)

Anual Report

Annual Report of the Comptroller of the Currency

ANNUAL REPORT

OF THE

COMPTROLLER OF THE CURRENCY

TO THE

FIRST SESSION OF THE FIFTIETH CONGRESS

OF

THE UNITED STATES.

DECEMBER 1, 1887.

TABLE OF CONTENTS.

(A full index will be found at page 365 of this volume.)

REPORT.

	Page.
Report submitted to Congress	1
Requirements of section 333, Revised Statutes of the United States, in detail, as to Comptroller's report	1
Summary of the state and condition of every national bank reporting during the year	2
Statement of national banks closed during the year	3
Suggestions as to amendments to the laws by which the system may be improved	4
New national-bank code	12
Legal decisions affecting organization, operations, and dissolution of national banks	38
Reference to digest of national-bank cases in the Appendix	38
Suggestion as to interstate commercial code	38
State banks, savings banks, private banks, and loan and trust companies	38
Resources, liabilities, and condition thereof	40-44
Distribution, number, and average par value of shares of stock	45
Names and compensation of officers and clerks in the office of the Comptroller of the Currency	46
Organization and expenses of the office	47, 48
Number and value of items representing clerical work in the office	49
Comparative statement of the number of banks organized, and number and compensation of officers and clerks	50
Number of national banks organized in each State and Territory during the year, with capital, bonds, and circulation	51
Statement of banks failed during the year, their capital, surplus, and liabilities	52
Causes of failure	52-55
Organization of national banks	55
Conversion of State banks	56, 57
Number of national banks of primary organization, number in voluntary liquidation, and number insolvent	58
Extension of corporate existence of national banks	59-61
Table showing distribution of national-bank stock	62-65
Circulating notes	66
Minimum of bonds required by going banks	66
Minimum of bonds and maximum of circulation	66
Bonds deposited and minimum required, and percentage of excess deposited by banks organized since July 1, 1882	66
Interest-bearing funded debt of the United States, and amount held by national banks	67, 68
Course of redemption of 3 per cent. bonds	69-72
Security for circulating notes	73
United States bonds of all classes held	73
Comparison of amounts for five years	73
Decrease in national-bank circulation	74
Number and capital of national banks by geographical divisions, bonds deposited, minimum, excess, and percentages	75
Increase and decrease in capital and circulation	76
Banks without circulation	76
Dissolution	77
Number of banks which have passed into voluntary liquidation and into the hands of receivers	77
Banks closed during the year	77
Inactive receiverships	77, 78
Dividends paid to creditors of insolvent national banks during past year	79
Amounts collected from assessments on shareholders	79

Page.

Issues and redemptions during the year 80
Additional circulation on bonds 81
Issues of national-bank notes 82
Process of redemption of national-bank notes 82
Five per cent. redemption fund 83
Receipts and deliveries by national-bank redemption agency 84, 85
Amount and mode of payment of national-bank notes redeemed 86
Redemption of circulation of insolvent national banks 87
Lawful money deposited 88
National-bank notes received monthly for redemption by Comptroller of the Currency 89
Amount destroyed yearly since establishment of the system 89
Supervision of national banks 90
Powers of the Comptroller of the Currency, and recommendations 90-92
Examinations of national banks, and areas covered by individual examiners 92
Reports of national banks, and treatment by office 93
Compendium of capital, surplus, undivided profits, circulation, bonds, deposits, loans and discounts, specie, etc., 1866-1887 93
Classification of loans in reserve cities 94
In New York City for five years 95
Twenty-five cities having largest amount of capital 96
Provisions of law governing reserve 96-100
Amount of reserve, and ratio of deposits, New York City, reserve cities, and States and Territories 100, 101
Clearing-house transactions 102
Kinds of money, and amount used in settlement of balances 104
New York Clearing-House transactions for thirty-four years 103
Clearing-house transactions of the assistant treasurer of the United States in New York 103
Comparative statements of clearing-houses in the United States 104, 105
Movement of reserve, weekly, in New York City 106
Increase and decrease in exchanges and balances of the clearing-houses of the United States. 107
Duties, assessments, and redemption charges 107
State taxation of national banks 108
Recent decision of the Supreme Court of the United States 109-118
Conclusion 118-128

APPENDIX.

Contents of digest of national-bank cases 131
Digest 133
Digest of recent decisions in banking law 155
Propositions to amend existing law for improvement in system received from various sources.. 165
Estimated population of each State and Territory, aggregate capital, surplus, undivided profits, and individual deposits of national and other banks June 1, 1887, and per-capita averages of resources 175
Number of banks organized, in liquidation and in operation, capital, bonds, circulation issued, redeemed, and outstanding 176
National-bank currency issued, redeemed, and outstanding 177
Number and denominations of national-bank notes issued and redeemed 178
Increase or decrease of national-bank circulation 180
Additional circulation issued and lawful money deposited to retire circulation 181
National-bank notes outstanding, and lawful money on deposit with the Treasurer of the United States 182
National banks in States, Territories, and reserve cities, their capital, minimum amount of bonds required by law, bonds held, and circulation outstanding 183
National banks in each State, Territory, and reserve city, with capital of $150,000 and under, and with capital exceeding $150,000 185
Number of national banks in each State, Territory, and reserve city, with a capital of $250,000 and under, and those with a capital exceeding $250,000 187-189
National banks in voluntary liquidation under sections 5220 and 5221, Revised Statutes 191-199
National banks in voluntary liquidation under sections 5220 and 5221, Revised Statutes, for the purpose of organizing new associations 200
National banks in liquidation under section 7 of the act of July 12, 1882 202
National banks in liquidation under section 7 of the act of July 12, 1882, succeeded by associations with the same or different title 203
National banks in the hands of receivers 204-216
Liabilities of national banks, and reserve required 217-228

	Page.
Average weekly deposits, circulation, and reserve of national banks in New York City	229
State of the lawful-money reserve	230
Dividends and earnings of national banks	234-243
Ratios of dividends and earnings to capital and to capital and surplus	244
Classification of loans and discounts of national banks	246
Clearings and balances of banks in New York City	247
Abstract of reports of condition of State banks, savings banks, private banks, loan and trust companies, official and unofficial	249
Report of condition of the National Savings Bank of the District of Columbia	295
Distribution by States, Territories, and geographical divisions, number and average par value of shares of stock of State, savings, private banks, and loan and trust companies	296
Aggregate resources and liabilities of national banks from 1863 to 1887	299
Summary of the state and condition of national banks on dates of reports during the past year.	319
General index	365
Condition of each national bank at close of business October 5, 1887	Vol. II

REPORT

OF

THE COMPTROLLER OF THE CURRENCY.

TREASURY DEPARTMENT,
OFFICE OF COMPTROLLER OF THE CURRENCY,
Washington, December 1, 1887.

SIR: In obedience to law, I have the honor to submit a report for the year ending October 31, 1887, exhibiting—

First. A summary of the state and condition of every association from which reports have been received the preceding year, at the several dates to which such reports refer, with an abstract of the whole amount of banking capital returned by them, of the whole amount of their debts and liabilities, the amount of circulating notes outstanding, and the total amount of means and resources, specifying the amount of lawful money held by them at the times of their several returns.

Second. A statement of the associations whose business has been closed during the year, with the amount of their circulation redeemed and the amount outstanding.

Third. Suggestions as to amendments to the laws relative to banking by which it is thought the system may be improved.

Fourth. A statement exhibiting under appropriate heads the resources and liabilities and condition of the banks, banking companies, and savings banks organized under the laws of the several States and Territories, such information being obtained by the Comptroller from the reports made by such banks, banking companies, and savings banks, to the legislatures or officers of the different States and Territories, and where such reports could not be obtained, the deficiency has been supplied from such other authentic sources as were available.

Fifth. The names and compensation of the clerks employed in the office of the Comptroller of the Currency, and the whole amount of the expenses of the banking department during the year.

This is the twenty-fifth annual report of the Comptroller of the Currency.

FIRST.

SUMMARY OF THE STATE AND CONDITION OF EVERY NATIONAL BANK REPORTING DURING THE YEAR ENDING OCTOBER 31, 1887.

	December 28.	March 4.	May 13.	August 1.	October 5.
	2,875 banks.	2,909 banks.	2,955 banks.	3,014 banks.	3,049 banks.
RESOURCES.					
Loans and discounts	$1,464,360,246.61	$1,500,261,355.97	$1,533,768,029.65	$1,553,751,437.12	$1,580,045,647.14
Overdrafts	5,907,434.52	6,273,318.70	6,523,781.08	6,020,303.93	7,503,486.62
U. S. bonds to secure circulation	228,184,350.00	211,537,150.00	200,452,300.00	189,032,050.00	189,083,100.00
U. S. bonds to secure deposits	21,010,000.00	22,976,000.00	24,890,500.00	26,402,000.00	27,757,000.00
U. S. bonds on hand	10,576,200.00	9,721,450.00	8,157,250.00	7,808,000.00	6,914,350.00
Other stocks, bonds, and mortgages	81,431,000.66	87,441,034.86	88,031,124.15	88,374,837.99	88,831,000.96
Due from approved reserve agents	142,117,979.28	163,161,181.37	148,007,874.43	140,270,155.75	140,873,587.98
Due from other national banks	88,271,097.96	86,460,829.09	105,570,841.90	90,487,767.80	93,302,413.94
Due from State banks and bankers	21,465,427.08	21,725,805.90	22,746,190.43	20,952,187.83	22,103,677.18
Real estate, furniture, and fixtures	54,763,530.37	55,128,600.78	55,729,098.76	56,951,022.58	57,968,150.71
Current expenses and taxes paid	10,283,097.79	8,061,292.40	7,781,151.97	5,158,910.86	8,253,890.72
Premiums paid	15,160,621.67	15,537,721.22	16,806,431.83	17,353,130.17	17,288,771.35
Checks and other cash items	13,218,073.44	13,308,520.04	13,065,663.79	13,014,070.02	14,691,373.38
Exchanges for clearing-house	70,525,126.02	89,230,194.59	86,820,303.73	128,211,628.48	88,775,457.09
Bills of other banks	20,132,330.00	22,235,206.00	25,188,137.00	22,962,737.00	21,937,881.00
Fractional currency	447,833.09	577,878.03	556,180.75	564,260.72	540,594.50
Trade dollars	1,827,364.20	1,603,661.40	164,253.08	63,671.97	509.25
*Specie, viz:					
Gold coin	72,855,405.48	73,503,961.60	73,864,674.63	74,093,439.47	73,782,480.62
Gold Treasury certificates	55,259,200.00	59,245,100.00	56,387,010.00	51,274,940.00	53,961,690.00
Gold clearing-house cert's	24,926,000.00	24,590,000.00	21,489,000.00	24,044,000.00	23,981,000.00
Silver coin, dollars	7,403,152.00	7,517,343.00	7,139,180.00	6,343,213.00	6,683,368.00
Silver coin, fractional	2,780,513.53	3,154,893.55	3,314,612.99	2,813,138.81	2,715,526.76
Silver Treasury certificates	3,000,225.00	3,667,608.00	5,121,188.00	3,535,479.00	3,961,380.00
Legal-tender notes	67,739,828.00	66,228,158.00	79,505,068.00	74,477,342.00	73,751,255.00
U. S. certificates of deposit for legal-tender notes	6,195,000.00	7,645,000.00	8,025,000.00	7,810,000.00	6,190,000.00
Five per cent. redemption fund with Treasurer	10,050,128.39	9,289,755.33	8,810,585.35	8,341,968.77	8,310,442.35
Due from Treasurer other than redemption fund	975,376.96	1,856,195.13	1,113,554.81	900,818.42	985,410.14
Aggregate	2,507,753,012.05	2,581,143,115.05	2,620,314,022.42	2,637,276,167.72	2,620,193,475.59
*Total specie	166,083,536.01	171,678,906.15	167,315,665.62	165,104,210.28	165,085,454.38
LIABILITIES.					
Capital stock paid in	$550,698,675.00	$555,351,765.00	$565,629,068.45	$571,648,811.00	$578,462,765.00
Surplus fund	159,573,479.21	164,337,132.72	167,411,521.03	172,348,308.99	173,913,440.97
Other undivided profits	79,298,286.13	67,248,949.16	70,153,368.11	62,291,634.02	71,451,167.02
National-bank circulation outstanding	202,078,287.00	183,231,498.00	176,771,539.00	166,625,658.00	167,283,343.00
State-bank notes outstanding	115,352.00	106,100.00	98,716.00	98,607.00	98,609.00
Dividends unpaid	1,500,345.06	1,111,628.17	1,077,314.40	2,239,029.46	2,495,127.83
Individual deposits	1,169,716,413.13	1,221,925,698.26	1,296,570,537.67	1,285,070,978.58	1,249,477,126.05
U. S. deposits	13,705,700.73	15,239,009.91	17,556,185.93	19,186,712.77	20,392,284.03
Deposits of U. S. disbursing officers	4,276,257.85	4,277,187.61	3,779,735.14	4,074,903.62	4,831,066.14
Due to other national banks	223,812,270.46	240,337,482.40	241,575,545.12	235,966,022.46	227,491,984.15
Due to State banks and bankers	91,251,533.23	103,012,572.48	102,089,438.63	103,003,598.14	102,094,625.68
Notes and bills rediscounted	9,159,345.79	7,536,897.10	10,132,799.61	11,125,230.08	17,312,806.39
Bills payable	2,444,958.36	2,082,371.21	2,567,953.30	2,985,987.60	4,888,430.43
Aggregate	2,507,753,012.05	2,581,143,115.05	2,620,314,022.42	2,637,276,167.72	2,620,193,475.59

SECOND.

Statement of National Banks Closed During the Year.

Name and location of bank.	Date of authority to commence business.	Date of closing.	Capital stock.	Circulation.		
				Issued.	Redeemed	Outstanding.
National Bank of Kingwood, W. Va	Nov. 14, 1865	Oct. 21, 1886	$125,000	$96,140	$20,230	$75,910
Commercial National Bank, Marshalltown, Iowa	June 9, 1883	Oct. 25, 1886	100,000	22,500	4,200	18,300
First National Bank, Indianapolis, Ind	Sept. 1, 1881	Nov. 11, 1886	500,000	162,325	30,295	132,030
First National Bank, Pine Bluff, Ark	Sept. 18, 1882	Nov. 15, 1886	50,000	26,280	7,305	18,975
First National Bank, Concord, Mich	Sept. 15, 1884	Nov. 27, 1886	50,000	11,250	2,700	8,550
Jamestown National Bank, Jamestown, Dak	Apr. 10, 1885	Nov. 20, 1886	50,000	11,250	1,500	9,750
First National Bank, Berea, Ohio	June 27, 1872	Dec. 1, 1886	50,000	45,000	9,909	35,091
First National Bank, Allerton, Iowa	Sept. 29, 1874	Dec. 6, 1886	50,000	11,250	3,380	7,870
Second National Bank, Hillsdale, Mich	July 20, 1865	Dec. 18, 1886	50,000	13,892	3,228	10,664
Topton National Bank, Topton, Pa	June 26, 1885	Dec. 28, 1886	50,000	18,000	2,960	15,040
First National Bank, Warsaw, Ill	Aug. 16, 1864	Dec. 31, 1886	50,000	38,250	3,470	34,780
First National Bank, Hamburgh, Iowa	June 28, 1877	Dec. 31, 1886	50,000	13,500	3,425	10,075
Darlington National Bank, Darlington, S. C	Mar. 26, 1881	Feb. 10, 1887	100,000	22,500	5,940	16,560
Union National Bank, Cincinnati, Ohio	Aug. 6, 1881	Feb. 14, 1887	500,000	237,230	49,052	188,178
Roberts National Bank, Titusville, Pa	Dec. 12, 1882	Feb. 28, 1887	100,000	75,610	12,300	63,310
National Bank of Rahway, N. J	Mar. 16, 1865	Mar. 9, 1887	100,000	42,500	6,184	36,316
Olney National Bank, Olney, Ill	Feb. 14, 1882	Mar. 11, 1887	60,000	27,000	4,630	22,370
Metropolitan National Bank, Leavenworth, Kans	May 26, 1884	Mar. 15, 1887	100,000	22,500	2,590	19,910
Ontario County National Bank, Canandaigua, N. Y	Aug. 11, 1882	Mar. 23, 1887	50,000	11,250	1,100	10,150
Winsted National Bank, Winsted, Conn	Mar. 15, 1879	Apr. 12, 1887	50,000	11,250	2,120	9,130
Council Bluffs National Bank, Council Bluffs, Iowa	Dec. 30, 1883	May 5, 1887	100,000	22,500	1,130	21,370
Palatka National Bank, Palatka, Fla	Nov. 20, 1884	May 30, 1887	50,000	19,210	1,595	17,615
Fidelity National Bank, Cincinnati, Ohio	Feb. 27, 1886	June 20, 1887	1,000,000	90,000	2,235	87,765
First National Bank, Homer, Ill	June 2, 1883	June 22, 1887	50,000	11,250	5,130	6,120
First National Bank, Beloit, Wis	Aug. 4, 1874	June 30, 1887	50,000	11,250	1,350	9,900
Mystic National Bank, Mystic, Conn	June 14, 1865	July 7, 1887	52,450	47,205	3,166	44,039
Exchange National Bank, Louisiana, Mo	Jan. 7, 1884	July 12, 1887	50,000	11,250	1,130	10,120
Henrietta National Bank, Henrietta, Tex	Aug. 8, 1883	July 25, 1887	50,000	11,250	....	11,250
Exchange National Bank, Downs, Kans	Sept. 30, 1886	Aug. 1, 1887	50,000	11,250	550	10,700
National Bank of Sumter, S. C	Nov. 26, 1883	Aug. 22, 1887	50,000	11,250	....	11,250
First National Bank, Dansville, N. Y	Sept. 4, 1863	Aug. 23, 1887	50,000	11,250	....	11,250
First National Bank, Corry, Pa	Dec. 6, 1884	Sept. 16, 1887	100,000	44,450	....	44,450
Stafford National Bank, Stafford Springs, Conn	Jan. 7, 1865	Oct. 12, 1887	200,000	94,048	....	94,048
Total	....	....	4,087,450	1,315,640	192,804	1,122,836

Of the above banks, twenty-five went into voluntary liquidation and eight failed.

THIRD.

SUGGESTIONS AS TO AMENDMENTS TO THE LAWS RELATING TO BANKING BY WHICH THE SYSTEM MAY BE IMPROVED AND THE SECURITY OF THE HOLDERS OF ITS NOTES AND OTHER CREDITORS MAY BE INCREASED.

The views expressed in the Report of 1886 as to the sufficiency of the security now provided for the circulating notes of national banks are respectfully reaffirmed, and the suggestions then made for improving the general features of the national banking system are renewed. These suggestions, with others drawn from enlarged experience, have been embodied in a bill for a national-bank code, incorporated herewith, and respectfully commended to the early attention of Congress. Every material change proposed to be made by the adoption of this code, and the reasons for it, will appear in the statement appended to it. In order that due preparation may be made for the early consideration of this important measure, the explanatory statement, the bill, and a codification of all existing laws, arranged in sections parallel with those of the bill, have been sent in advance to the Senators, Representatives, and Delegates in Congress, in order that each may satisfy himself of the fidelity and accuracy of the codification of the laws now in force, and by means of this medium of comparison may conveniently compare with those laws the provisions of the proposed code.

Upon scrutiny it will be found that the proposed code conforms to the existing law, with some variation in phraseology and some unimportant modification of import, except in the following instances:

Sections 4, 5, and 6 increase the salary of the Deputy Comptroller of the Currency, enlarge his duties, and state in a more comprehensive manner the prohibition against the Comptroller or Deputy Comptroller having any interests inconsistent with their official positions.

Section 33 provides against such a constitution of the board of directors as makes the officers of the bank a majority of the board.

Section 42 incorporates into the oath which directors are required to take an obligation to inform themselves at all times as to the business and condition of the association. This addition to the law is, in my judgment, necessary, because in a recent case submitted to the courts it has been decided that directors who do not keep themselves informed as to the business of their association can not be held responsible for the mismanagement of its affairs.

Sections 44 and 45 are new matter. They provide a formal method by which directors may resign their positions and be discharged from further accountability.

Section 51 forbids the organization of national banks with branches. When the system was first established there were some State banks with branches, and as it was desired that these should be induced to become national banks, provision was made for their retaining their branches after conversion. This reason no longer exists, and it would appear to be in the line of public policy to take precaution in advance against any future development of the national banking system in the direction of combination and agglomeration similar to the development among railroad and other corporations controlling interests upon which the business and convenience of whole communities depend. In section 127 of the proposed code provision is made for national banks having more than one office under certain conditions.

Section 59 supplements existing law as to the extension of the corporate existence of national banks, by providing adequate relief to shareholders who do not assent to the extension of the bank, and who do not concur with the directors as to the appraisement of its stock.

Section 62 states in more precise language, and with some modification, the existing restrictions upon national banks as to holding real estate.

Sections 67 to 71, inclusive, provide a method by which the stockholders of national banks may substitute for their contingent liability a surplus fund to be held by the bank. In this connection I respectfully refer to the recommendations presented to Congress in the Comptroller's Report for 1886, and to what is said on the subject in the appropriate place in the Report of this year.

Section 75 makes an important change in the amount of bonds required to be deposited by the banks.

The acts of 1863 and 1864 required a deposit of bonds not less in amount than one-third of the capital; the act of 1874 made $50,000 the minimum for banks of which the capital exceeded $150,000; the act of 1882 fixed the amount at one-fourth the capital in cases where the capital does not exceed $150,000, and at $50,000 for all banks of which the capital exceeds $150,000.

The proposed code divides the banks into two classes, those with a capital of $250,000 and less, and those of which the capital exceeds $250,000, and reduces the amount to be deposited by the smaller banks from one-fourth to one-tenth of their capital, and that to be deposited by the larger banks from $50,000 to $25,000.

The reason for the change is, that the bond requirement is a serious impediment to the absorption into the national-bank system of the State banks, which are still numerous in those sections which were more or less excluded from early participation in the privileges of the acts of 1863 and 1864; and it is also an impediment to the formation of new banks of large capital. While the change may induce some banks to withdraw a portion of their bonds, it may reasonably be expected that the deposit of bonds made by new banks and by banks increasing their capital will offset such withdrawals to some extent.

The danger of a spasmodic contraction of the national-bank circulation is obviated by the retention of the clause in section 9 of the act of July 12, 1882, which provides that not more than $3,000,000 of lawful money shall be deposited in any one calendar month for the purpose of withdrawing such circulation; but there seems no reason to retain the other clause of that section, which prohibits banks that have reduced circulation from again increasing it until after an interval of six months. Among all the objections that have been made to the national-bank currency, none seems so well founded, and at the same time so serious, as the charge that it is inelastic in volume, and therefore devoid of one of the prime requisites of a bank currency. The clause referred to manifestly tends to aggravate this defect, and it should, therefore, be discarded from the law.

Sections 89 to 94, inclusive, provide for the custody and periodical examination of the plates and dies used in the printing of national-bank notes and for the destruction of material no longer in use. Under the existing law, the Comptroller of the Currency is responsible for the safe-keeping and proper use of these plates and dies, but since the enactment of that provision the Bureau of Engraving and Printing has been removed from the Treasury building, and it is now a physical impossibility for the Comptroller of the Currency to have any knowledge of or supervision over the keeping or the handling of these plates and dies.

Section 97 modifies the existing law as to national-bank notes, so as to permit them to be counted as a part of the cash reserve of the banks. This feature is introduced rather to settle a doubt than to make a change, because there seems to be good reason to believe that these notes may be so counted under the existing law.

Section 98 provides that the cashier's signature to the circulating notes of the bank may be affixed by an agent appointed with due formality. This provision, it is believed, will relieve many banks from an inconvenience which at times is quite serious.

Section 114 repeals the requirement that banks extending their corporate existence shall after three years deposit lawful money to the amount of their outstanding circulation.

Section 115 extends to the entire national-bank circulation the provision in section 6, act of July 12, 1882, which reserves to the United States whatever profit arises from the failure to redeem the notes of banks extending their corporate existence; and in this connection it should be observed that the other provisions in section 6 of that act are omitted from this code. The omitted clauses provide that the circulating notes of extended banks shall be retired, and that notes of a different and readily distinguishable design shall be issued in place of them.

The purpose of the provision now omitted is not obvious, especially as the act declares that the bank after extension "shall continue to be in all respects the identical association it was before the extension of its period of succession."

The debate on the bill (see Congressional Record, pages 2534 to 5878, volume 13, parts 3 to 6, inclusive, Forty-seventh Congress, first session) shows that the change in the design of the notes was connected with the provision reserving to the United States any profit arising from the non-presentation for redemption of the old issue of notes.*

It seems to have been intended that the notes of new design, now known as the series of 1882, should be issued only to banks extending their period of succession, whereas it appears that all banks that have been organized since the passage of the act in question have received notes of the series of 1882, and therefore the distinction has now been lost, which was presumably intended to be preserved, between the circulation of extended banks and of those still operated under their original certificates of organization. It is impracticable at this late day to re-establish this distinction, because of 2,263 banks issuing notes of the series of 1882 only 1,217 have been extended.

While the act of 1882 contains the only express provision in the statutes reserving to the Treasury the profit arising from the non-presentation of national-bank notes, yet under the operation of the act of June 20, 1874, all profits from that source must necessarily remain in the

*The bill was reported from committee by Mr. Crapo, of Massachusetts, who, in the course of his remarks, May 13, 1882, while it was under discussion in the House, said:

"There can be no doubt, while all the burdens attending the issue and circulation of bank notes fall upon the banks, that all the gain from loss of bank notes inures to the Government. To avoid any delay in receiving this gain the sixth section of the bill provides for a new issue of bank notes, and a redemption of the present issue, as summarily and effectually as is possible by the liquidation of the banks. The bill under consideration disposes of all doubts, if any exist, as to who shall receive the profits resulting from lost bank notes." (Page 3904, vol. 13, part 4, Cong. Record.)

Treasury, because the Treasury is the depositary of the ultimate redemption fund of every bank, and it is certain that the moment will never come within the period of succession of any bank when it can be determined whether or not at some time thereafter its still outstanding notes may not be presented for redemption at the Treasury.

For these reasons it is considered no departure from existing law, and no infringement upon the rights which any bank can establish or enjoy, to embody in a code framed for continuous application to a permanent system the distinct provision that all uncalled-for moneys in the various redemption funds shall ultimately belong to the United States, while it is a distinct gain to get rid of the obligation to keep up an unnecessary and confusing distinction between circulating notes issued by banks organized prior to July 12, 1882, but not yet extended, and those issued by banks organized or extended after that date.

If these views prevail with Congress, it will, no doubt, also seem expedient to adopt the series of 1882 as a uniform design for the entire national-bank currency, and in that case it will be no more than just to provide by an appropriation from the Treasury for the expense of preparing new plates for the 797 banks now entitled to the notes of the old design.

Section 127 is that to which allusion is made in explaining section 51. There seems to be in some large cities, especially where the banks are concentrated in one part of the city, out of the reach of many of their customers, a growing need for some such provision as is made in this section.

Sections 134 and 135 preserve all existing provisions as to reserve, except that which allows the 5 per cent. fund in the hands of the Treasurer of the United States for the redemption of circulating notes to be counted as a part of the lawful-money reserve against deposits.

It seems barely possible that the intent of section 3, act of June 20, 1874, in this regard may have been misapprehended, but in any case it is anomalous in law and misleading in practice to count as a part of the reserve against deposits a fund wholly devoted to the redemption of circulation and not to any, even the least, extent available for paying depositors.

Except in the cases of some few banks of which the circulation is large and the deposits small, no material inconvenience is likely to be caused by the omission of the redemption fund from the items of reserve, especially if the recommendation is adopted to count national-bank notes on hand as part of the lawful-money reserve against deposits. On October 5, 1887, the banks held in the aggregate in their cash $21,937,884 national-bank notes, while the total amount on deposit in the redemption fund was only $8,310,442.25.

Section 136 relieves banks of the obligation of keeping a cash reserve against Government deposits. The existing statute requires a reserve on all deposits, and its language admits of no exception, but it is probable that this was not meant to include deposits of public money, because the Secretary of the Treasury is authorized by law to determine, in his own discretion, the security for, and the regulations applicable to, such deposits. It is believed that the proposed amendment will facilitate the operations of the Treasury. It will certainly relieve the depositary banks of a needless and an expensive requirement.

Section 146 is intended to remedy an inconsistency in the present law, which gives the Comptroller of the Currency power to place a receiver in charge of a bank of which any impairment of capital is not made up within three months after notice from him, while under the same circumstances the directors can not enforce assessments against stockholders until four months after such notice.

Sections 147 to 150, inclusive, contain what is believed to be a very salutary check upon the managers of national banks in respect to investments in real-estate securities. Since the liabilities of banks are payable on demand, the fundamental principle of good banking is that the assets should be readily convertible into money. Real estate and real-estate securities are hardly ever readily convertible, while under conditions often arising they become inconvertible and remain so for long periods of time. Experience teaches that these conditions are sure to arise just when the exigencies of the community demand from banks the largest and readiest money accommodation.

Dealing in real estate and in bonds and debentures secured by real estate is of course an entirely legitimate employment for private or corporate capital, and there seems no lack of capital seeking such employment; it is generally safe, and often profitable; but commercial banks should be restrained from investing their deposits in such forms, lest their depositors should be exposed to the danger of finding that the cash upon which they depend for their current transactions has become locked up in investments, which, however safe and profitable for the bank, can not be made to reproduce the cash at the moment at which it is most urgently needed. Statistics presented in the Report of this year show that real-estate investments are responsible wholly or in part for the failure of 16 out of the 100 national banks of which the causes of failure have been ascertained.

While the general principle here stated is indisputable, and admits of but few exceptions in its application to settled communities where real-estate investments constantly tend to increased permanence, yet it should not be overlooked that in some sections of the country a very large amount of active capital is always seeking employment in real-estate securities, which tends to make such securities exceptionally convertible, and it is no doubt difficult for the banks situated in those localities to keep themselves entirely free from this business. To meet these cases, section 148 has been framed in such a way as to afford to such banks an opportunity to accommodate their customers and promote the general business around them without too much risk of becoming embarrassed with locked-up funds.

Sections 151 and 152 are designed to give more elasticity to the present provision of law which limits to one-tenth of the capital of the bank, loans of money to any individual, firm, or corporation. This is a perplexing subject, and it is difficult to regulate it by statute satisfactorily; yet experience proves that existing restraints have been on the whole salutary in their character, for in many cases disaster has followed the disregard of them.

The statistics of failures already referred to show that excessive loans (which are generally made to officers and directors of the banks, or to firms or companies in which they are interested) have caused wholly or in part 18 out of 100 failures.

Section 153 provides a penalty for making loans contrary to law. Heretofore the only penalty attaching to a violation of such restraints was the forfeiture of the franchise of the bank and the dissolution of the corporation, a punishment quite out of proportion to the offense, except under circumstances of concealment and aggravation rarely occurring, and still more rarely discovered before the failure of the bank renders the penalty superfluous.

Sections 155 to 160, inclusive, are intended to throw some additional safeguards around the administration of the banks, and to impress upon the directors a more definite sense of responsibility by indicating to them practical methods for discharging their trusts.

Section 161 embodies, with slight modifications, the prohibition contained in section 5208 of the Revised Statutes, against certifying checks not drawn against actual money. I respectfully submit that it would be well to strike this provision out of the law altogether, because experience shows that it has failed to prevent the practice of certifying checks representing stock operations, against which it is understood to have been aimed, while it has excluded national banks from very valuable business which State institutions, which are not subject to the same prohibition, carry on free from the wholesome supervision to which national banks are subjected.

If, however, the provision is to be retained in the law, I earnestly recommend the adoption of the modification herein submitted, so as to relieve from its operation legitimate and well-recognized methods of accommodation that materially facilitate the commercial business of the country.

Section 163 embodies the present usury law, except that it permits of special contracts as to rate of interest in the States and Territories where no usury law exists.

In this connection I make bold to say that, in my judgment, it would be a decided step toward emancipating industry from the trammels of antiquated notions of governmental guidance to omit from this code all reference to usury and to leave only a provision fixing the rate of interest in the absence of special stipulation between lender and borrower. No one of experience can doubt that money would be cheaper and more accessible to all borrowers if there were no usury laws in force anywhere in the United States.

Section 172 reduces the penalty from $100 a day to $10 a day in cases where the banks fail to transmit reports within the period prescribed in the statutes. The present law has never been fully enforced, and probably can not be; the penalty is excessive.

Sections 174 to 176, inclusive, enlarge the provisions of law applying to examiners of national banks and define their duties and responsibilities. The effect of these sections is mainly to incorporate into the statute what has heretofore been practiced by the best examiners.

Section 177 establishes a new scale for reckoning the assessment of examination fees upon national banks.

From many points of view it would be expedient for the examiners to be paid out of the tax upon the national banks, and not by fees. The present system establishes relations between the bank and the examiner which are inconsistent with the functions of that officer and with what ought to be his attitude toward the bank.

Sections 179 and 180 relieve banks of the obligation to pay fees for preliminary examination, and provide for these fees and the expenses of special examinations being paid out of such appropriation as Congress may make for that purpose.

In the Report for 1886 I recommended the employment of supervising examiners, to be paid by the Government, and the views then entertained as to the value of such an addition to the inspection machinery of the system have been confirmed in the highest degree by the additional experience and observation of the last twelve months.

The advantages to be secured may be briefly stated as follows:

1. That banks may be specially examined at any point of time between the dates of ordinary examination without exciting alarm in the community and without reflecting upon the management of the bank.

Such intermediate examinations are often very desirable in order to clear up doubtful inferences from reports of examiners and reports of condition, and to set at rest apprehensions excited by communications reaching the Comptroller's office. Banks are sometimes clandestinely assailed by local enemies, and sometimes a truthful warning comes from an obscure or a doubtful source. It is impossible for the Comptroller to discriminate between the true and the false in such charges, while their simple existence places him under a responsibility from which the present system of examination provides no method of relief. If he orders a special examination and the charges prove to be false, the mere examination, by discrediting the bank, inflicts upon it unmerited and often irreparable injury. If the apprehension of these consequences should deter the Comptroller from ordering an examination in a case where the charges afterward turn out to have been true, he will find it difficult to escape censure from the community which has apparently had its losses aggravated by what seems to be indifference or something worse.

2. The visits of a supervising examiner will afford to the banks, especially those in remote localities, a protection which they can not now receive against arbitrary or otherwise improper conduct on the part of the local examiner, and will also protect both the banks and the public against injury in case the local examiner proves to be inattentive, incompetent, or corrupt.

3. Supervising examiners will carry with them all over the Union a knowledge of correct and uniform methods of business, and, if properly selected, will possess the capacity of instructing both the local examiners and the officials of the banks in respect to these matters. Statistics show that out of 100 failures of national banks, 27 are due wholly to bad management, and in 36 other cases bad management contributed to the failure. Sixty-three per cent. of failures thus appear attributable in whole or in part to ignorance and to loose methods of business.

4. Supervising examiners will have circuits beginning and ending with the office of the Comptroller, and they will supply a means by which this officer can obtain definite and comprehensive information about banking interests in remote sections and about the local examiners. Such information is very important to a proper administration of the office at Washington; but it is still more important to the banks that the Comptroller should understand their circumstances and their needs, varying, as these do, according to the peculiarities of different sections, and that he should have trustworthy information as to the character, methods, and personal bias of the local examiners.

Sections 185 and 186 give to the Comptroller of the Currency a reasonable degree of supervision over national banks that have gone into voluntary liquidation. It appears to have been held in former years that after associations had, in accordance with law, made some progress in voluntary liquidation, the Comptroller might lawfully interpose and appoint a receiver to wind up their affairs. As the law now stands, it does not appear to me to justify action in accordance with these precedents, and, if this is the case, there is obviously a gap in the completeness of the protection which the law aims to extend to the creditors and stockholders of national banks.

Sections 188 and 189 prescribe the duties of the directors and officers of national banks that are in a position of insolvency. They embody existing provisions and the decisions of the courts in respect to matters not now provided for by statute.

Sections 195 to 197, inclusive, provide for the discharge of receivers of national banks in cases not provided for in the existing law. Justice seems to require some such enactments as are here proposed, and without them it may reasonably be expected that the difficulty now experienced of obtaining the best men for receivers will constantly increase.

Sections 198 and 199 supplement the present law for the selection of an agent of stockholders by supplying certain details now required by the Comptroller but which should have statutory force.

Section 206 affords to agents of stockholders the means of obtaining their discharge, no such means now existing.

Sections 207 to 209, inclusive, provide for the case of a bank which has been restored to solvency during the receivership, and which the stockholders desire to revive under its old name. Such a case was lately presented when, within thirty days of the appointment of a receiver for the Abington National Bank, of Abington, Mass., the creditors were paid in full, with interest, and sufficient assets remained to justify resumption of business upon a capital above the minimum limited to the locality. The name and reputation of this bank were regarded by its stockholders as of material value, and, being desirous that that value should not be lost to them by a change of name, they made application to be allowed to resume business. After careful examination of the laws, I could find nothing either permitting or forbidding compliance with this application; it appeared to be a matter not provided for either way, and therefore I could reply only that if the stockholders unanimously agreed to resume, I would recognize the bank as again in operation.

Section 213 re-enacts section 380 of the Revised Statutes, with a proviso which is intended to obviate the claim made by some district attorneys that the statute permits them to force upon receivers of national banks services which are neither required nor desired. I assume that it was not the intention of Congress to confer upon these officers a statutory right to act as counsel to receivers of national banks, irrespective of their qualifications or of their local interests and connections.

Section 217 amends the provision as to a semi-annual tax upon circulation by relieving banks from the tax on so much of their circulation as is predicated upon the minimum deposit of bonds required by law. While for more than one reason it may be well to tax circulation voluntarily taken out or maintained, neither reason nor justice appears to justify a tax on circulation represented by a compulsory deposit of bonds.

Section 223 re-enacts section 5219 of the Revised Statutes, with a change of phraseology aimed at securing to national banks adequate protection against such State and municipal assessment and taxation as places them at a disadvantage in competition with corporations which are doing the same business but which call their operations by special names.

It is only reasonable to believe that there was no intention on the part of Congress to make the discrimination, which has in some cases been inferred from the language of the present statute, between moneyed capital in the hands of individuals and moneyed capital managed by corporations.

Sections 227, 228, and 229 re-enact the provisions of section 5209 of the Revised Statutes, with some changes suggested by experience, others prompted by precaution, and some additions applying to persons appointed to be examiners of national banks.

Section 232 extends the general provisions for the punishment of forgers and other like offenders to persons who, without authority of law, affix signatures to the blank circulating notes printed for national banks, or who issue or circulate such notes knowing that they have not been duly signed by the proper officers of the association for which they were printed. The present law contains no provision for this offense, which is a manifest omission.

Section 235 re-enacts section 5243 of the Revised Statutes, and provides for its enforcement. In the last Report of the Comptroller of the Currency the attention of Congress was called to several instances of violation of section 5243 which have been of long standing, and of which no judicial notice has been taken, either before that report was made or since.

An act relating to national-banking associations.

Be it enacted by the Senate and House of Representatives of the United States of America, in Congres assembled, as follows:

CHAPTER I.—THE BUREAU OF THE CURRENCY.

SECTION 1. There shall be in the Department of the Treasury a bureau charged with the execution of all laws passed by Congress relating to national banking associations; the chief officer of which bureau shall be called the Comptroller of the Currency, and shall perform his duties under the general direction of the Secretary of the Treasury. (Sec. 324, R. S.)

SEC. 2. The Comptroller of the Currency shall be appointed by the President, on the recommendation of the Secretary of the Treasury, by and with the advice and consent of the Senate, and shall hold his office for the term of five years unless sooner removed by the President, upon reasons to be communicated by him to the Senate; and he shall be entitled to a salary of five thousand dollars a year. (Sec. 325, R. S.)

SEC. 3. The Comptroller of the Currency shall, within fifteen days from the time of notice of his appointment, take and subscribe the oath of office, and he shall give to the United States a bond in the penalty of one hundred thousand dollars, with not less than two responsible sureties, to be approved by the Secretary of the Treasury, conditioned for the faithful discharge of the duties of his office. (Sec. 326, R. S.)

SEC. 4. There shall be in the Bureau of the Comptroller of the Currency a Deputy Comptroller of the Currency, to be appointed by the Secretary, who shall be entitled to a salary of three thousand five hundred dollars a year, and who shall possess the power and perform the duties attached by law to the office of Comptroller during a vacancy in the office or during the absence or inability of the Comptroller. The Deputy Comptroller shall also take the oath of office prescribed by the Constitution and laws of the United States, and shall give a like bond in the penalty of fifty thousand dollars. (Sec. 327, R. S.)

SEC. 5. The Comptroller of the Currency, when present and acting, may delegate to the Deputy Comptroller of the Currency such part of the powers and duties pertaining to the office of the Comptroller of the Currency as he may consider proper and expedient for the speedy and systematic performance of public business.

SEC. 6. It shall not be lawful for the Comptroller or for the Deputy Comptroller, of the Currency, either directly or indirectly, to be a stockholder or otherwise pecuniarily interested in any national banking association, or in any other institution, corporation, or firm engaged in any banking operations. (Sec. 329, R. S.)

SEC. 7. The seal devised by the Comptroller of the Currency for his office, and approved by the Secretary of the Treasury, shall continue to be the seal of office of the Comptroller, and may be renewed when necessary. A description of the seal, with an impression thereof, and a certificate of approval of the Secretary shall be filed in the office of the Secretary of State. (Sec. 330, R. S., as amended by an Act February 18, 1875.)

SEC. 8. There shall be assigned from time to time to the Comptroller of the Currency by the Secretary of the Treasury suitable rooms in the Treasury building for conducting the business of the Currency Bureau, containing safe and secure fireproof vaults, in which the Comptroller shall deposit and safely keep all valuable things belonging to his office; and the Comptroller shall from time to time furnish the necessary furniture, stationery, fuel, lights, and other proper conveniences for the transaction of the business of his office. (Sec. 331, R. S.)

SEC. 9. The Comptroller of the Currency shall employ from time to time the necessary clerks, to be appointed and classified by the Secretary of the Treasury, to discharge such duties as the Comptroller shall direct. (Sec. 328, R. S.)

SEC. 10. The Comptroller of the Currency shall make an annual report to Congress at the commencement of its session, exhibiting—

(1) A summary of the state and condition of all the associations from which reports have been received the preceding year, at the several dates to which such reports refer, with an abstract showing the whole amount of banking capital returned by them, the whole amount of their debts and liabilities, the amount of circulating notes outstanding, and the total amount of their means and resources, specifying the amount of lawful money held by them at the times of their several returns, and such other information in relation to such associations as, in his judgment, may be useful.

(2) A statement of the associations which have withdrawn from business during the year, with the amount of their circulation redeemed and the amount outstanding

(3) A statement of the associations which have failed during the year, or which for any other reason have been placed in the hands of a receiver, together with a special report in each case as to the cause of failure, and the liabilities, assets, and so forth.

(4) A statement exhibiting under appropriate heads the resources and liabilities and the condition of the banks, banking companies, and savings banks, organized under the laws of the several States and Territories, which information shall be obtained by the Comptroller from the reports made by such banks, banking companies, and savings banks to the legislatures or officers of the different States and Territories, and, where such reports cannot be obtained, the deficiency shall be supplied from such other authentic sources as may be available.

(5) The names and compensation of the clerks employed by him, and the whole amount of the expenses of the Bureau of the Currency during the year.

(6) Such suggestions as he may deem proper for the amendment and improvement of the laws relating to national banking associations. (Sec. 333, R. S.)

SEC. 11. The expenses necessarily incurred in executing the laws respecting the procuring of circulating notes, and all other expenses of the Bureau of the Currency, except as otherwise provided, shall be paid out of the proceeds of the taxes or duties assessed and collected on the circulation of national banking associations under this act. (Sec. 5173, R. S.)

CHAPTER II.—ORGANIZATION OF ASSOCIATIONS.

SEC. 12. Associations for carrying on the business of banking under this act may be formed by any number of natural persons, not less in any case than five. (Sec. 5133, R. S.)

SEC. 13. The persons forming the associations shall enter into articles of association, which shall specify in general terms the object for which the association is formed, and may contain any other provisions, not inconsistent with law, which the association may see fit to adopt for the regulation of its business and the conduct of its affairs. These articles shall be signed by the persons uniting to form the association, and a copy of them shall be forwarded to the Comptroller of the Currency, to be filed and preserved in his office. (Sec. 5133, R. S.

SEC. 14. The persons uniting to form such association shall, under their hands make an organization certificate, which shall specifically state—

(1) The name assumed by such association, which name shall be subject to the approval of the Comptroller of the Currency.

(2) The place where its operations of discount and deposit are to be carried on, designating the State, Territory, or District, and the particular county, and the city, town or village.

(3) The amount of capital stock, and the number of shares into which the same is to be divided.

(4) The names and places of residence of the shareholders, and the number of shares held by each of them.

(5) The fact that the certificate is made to enable such persons to avail themselves of the advantages of this act. (Sec. 5134, R. S.)

SEC. 15. The organization certificate shall be acknowledged before a judge of some court of record, or notary public, and, together with the acknowledgment thereof, authenticated by the seal of such court or notary, shall be transmitted to the Comptroller of the Currency, who shall record and carefully preserve the same in his office. (Sec. 5135, R. S.)

SEC. 16. Upon duly making and filing articles of association and an organization certificate, the association shall become, as from the date of the execution of its organization certificate, a body corporate. (Sec. 5136, R. S.)

SEC. 17. The capital stock of associations organized under this act shall not be less than the amounts following:

(1) Every association in a city having more than fifty thousand inhabitants, two hundred thousand dollars.

(2) Every other association, one hundred thousand dollars, except that, with the approval of the Secretary of the Treasury, associations with a capital stock of not less than fifty thousand dollars each may be organized in any place having not more than six thousand inhabitants. (Sec. 5138, R. S.)

SEC. 18. The capital stock of each association shall be divided into shares of one hundred dollars each and be deemed personal property, and shall be transferable on the books of the association in such manner as may be prescribed in the by-laws or articles of association. Every person becoming a shareholder by such transfer shall, in respect to the shares thus acquired, succeed to all the rights and liabilities of the prior holder of such shares. (Sec. 5139, R. S.)

SEC. 19. At least fifty per centum of the capital stock of every association shall be paid in money within thirty days from the execution of the organization certificate and before the association shall be authorized to commence business; and the remainder of the capital stock shall be paid in installments of at least ten per centum each on the whole amount of the capital as frequently as one installment at the end of each succeeding month from the time the association shall be authorized by the Comptroller of the Currency to commence business. The payment of each installment shall be certified to the Comptroller, under oath, by the president or cashier of the association. (Sec. 5140, R. S.)

SEC. 20. Whenever any shareholder, or his assignee, fails to pay any installment on the stock when the same is required by the preceding section to be paid, the directors of such association may sell the stock of such delinquent shareholder at public auction to any person who will pay the highest price therefor, to be not less than the amount then due thereon, with the expenses of advertisement and sale; and the excess, if any, shall be paid to the delinquent shareholder. Three weeks' previous notice of such sale shall be given in a newspaper of general circulation published in the city or county where the association is located. (Sec. 5141, R. S.)

SEC. 21. If no bidder can be found who will pay for such stock the amount due thereon to the association, and the cost of advertisement and sale, the amount previously paid shall be forfeited to the association, and such stock shall be sold as the directors may order, within six months from the time of such forfeiture, and if not sold it shall be canceled and deducted from the capital stock of the association. (Sec. 5141, R. S.)

SEC. 22. If such cancellation and reduction shall reduce the capital of the association below the minimum of capital required by law, the capital stock shall, within thirty days from the date of such cancellation, be increased to the required amount; in default of which a receiver may be appointed by the Comptroller of the Currency to close up the business of the association. (Sec. 5141, R. S.)

SEC. 23. Whenever a certificate is transmitted to the Comptroller of the Currency, as provided in this act, and the association transmitting the same notifies the Comptroller that at least fifty per centum of its capital stock has been duly paid in, and that such association has complied with all the provisions of this act required to be complied with before an association shall be authorized to commence the business of banking, the Comptroller shall examine into the condition of such association, ascertain especially the amount of money paid in on account of its capital, the name and place of residence of each of its directors, the amount of the capital stock of which each is the owner in good faith, and generally whether such association has complied with all the provisions of this act required to entitle it to engage in the business of banking; and he shall cause to be made and attested by the oaths of a majority of the directors, and by the president or cashier of the association, a statement of all the facts necessary to enable him to determine whether the association is lawfully entitled to commence the business of banking. (Sec. 5168, R. S.)

SEC. 24. If, upon a careful examination of the facts so reported, and of any other facts which may come to his knowledge, whether by means of a special commission appointed by him for the purpose of inquiring into the condition of such association or otherwise, it appears that such association is lawfully entitled to commence the business of banking, the Comptroller of the Currency shall give to such association a certificate, under his hand and official seal, that such association has complied with all the provisions required to be complied with before commencing the business of banking, and that such association is authorized to commence such business. But the Comptroller may withhold from any association his certificate authorizing the commencement of business, whenever he has reason to suppose that the shareholders have formed the same for any other than the legitimate objects contemplated by this act. (Sec. 5169, R. S.)

SEC. 25. The association shall cause the certificate issued under the preceding section to be published for at least sixty days next after the receipt thereof in some newspaper published in the city or county where the association is located. (Sec. 5170, R. S.)

SEC. 26. Any association, after filing notice in the office of the Comptroller of the Currency, may, by the vote of shareholders owning two-thirds of the shares, increase its capital stock, in accordance with the provisions of this act, to any sum, notwithstanding the limit fixed in its original articles of association and determined by the Comptroller. No increase of capital shall be valid until the whole amount of such increase is paid in, and notice thereof has been transmitted to the Comptroller of the Currency, and his certificate obtained specifying the amount of such increase of capital stock, and that it has been duly paid in as part of the capital of such association; but failure to notify the Comptroller and to obtain his certificate shall not exempt subscribers to such increase of capital from any obligation or responsibility undertaken by them or arising out of such subscription. No increase of the capital stock of any association, either within or beyond the limit fixed in its original articles of association, shall be made except in the manner herein provided. (Act May 1, 1886, sec. 1, and sec. 5142, R. S.)

SEC. 27. Any association, by the vote of shareholders owning two-thirds of the stock may reduce its capital stock to any sum not below the amount required by section seventeen of this act, and not below the amount required for its outstanding circulation. But no such reduction shall take effect and no payments shall be made on account thereof until the action of the shareholders has been duly certified to the Comptroller of the Currency, and his approval has been obtained. (Sec. 5143, R. S.)

SEC. 28. Any association, with the approval of the Comptroller of the Currency, may change its title by vote of shareholders owning two-thirds of the stock. (Act May 1, 1886.)

SEC. 29. Any association, by a vote of shareholders owning two-thirds of the stock, and with the approval of the Comptroller of the Currency, may change its location to any place within the same State not more than thirty miles distant. But if the capital stock of the association is less than the amount prescribed for associations to be established in the place to which the association is to remove, it must be increased to the required amount before such removal; and if the increase of capital involves an increase in the amount of bonds to be deposited with the Treasurer of the United States, the additional bonds shall be deposited before the removal. (Act May 1, 1886.)

SEC. 30. A duly authenticated notice of the new title or location selected, and of the vote authorizing the change, shall be sent to the office of the Comptroller of the Currency; and no change of title or location shall be made or claimed until the Comptroller shall have issued his certificate of approval of the same. (Act May 1, 1886.)

SEC. 31. All rights, privileges, and powers, and all debts and liabilities of the association under its old title or at its old location shall devolve upon and inure to the association under its new title and at its new location. No change of title or location shall release any association from any liability incurred previous to such change, or affect any action or proceeding in law to which it is a party, or in which it is interested. (Act May 1, 1886.)

SEC. 32. No association shall make any change in its articles of association by which the rights, remedies, or security of existing creditors of the association shall be impaired. (Sec. 5139, R. S.)

SEC. 33. The affairs of each association shall be managed by a board of directors, not less than five in number, exclusive of the vice-president, cashier, assistant cashier, or any other officer, except the president, who may be a member of the board. (Sec. 5145, R. S.)

SEC. 34. The directors shall be elected by the shareholders at a meeting to be held at any time before the association is authorized by the Comptroller of the Currency to commence the business of banking, and afterward at meetings to be held on such day in January of each year as is specified in the articles of association. They shall hold office for one year, and until their successors are elected and have qualified. (Sec. 5145, R. S.)

SEC. 35. If the articles of association do not fix the day on which the election shall be held, the day for the election shall be designated by the board of directors in their by-laws, or otherwise; or if the directors fail to fix the day, shareholders representing two-thirds of the shares may do so. (Sec. 5149, R. S.)

SEC. 36. If, from any cause, an election of directors is not made at the time appointed, the association shall not be dissolved on that account, but an election may be held on any subsequent day. Thirty days' notice of such election shall be given in all cases in a newspaper published in the city, town, or county in which the association is located. (Sec. 5149, R. S.)

SEC. 37. In all elections of directors, and in deciding all questions at meetings of shareholders, each shareholder shall be entitled to one vote on each share of stock held by him. Shareholders may vote by proxies duly authorized in writing; but no officer or employee of such association shall act as proxy. No vote shall be allowed on any share of which the certificate is held by or for the association as collateral security, or otherwise, or on which there is any installment or assessment due and unpaid, in whole or in part. (Sec. 5144, R. S.)

SEC. 38. Any vacancy in the board shall be filled by appointment by the remaining directors, and any director so appointed shall hold his place until the next election. (Sec. 5148, R. S.)

SEC. 39. The directors shall choose one of their number to be the president of the board. (Sec. 5150, R. S.)

SEC. 40. Every director must, during his whole term of service, be a citizen of the United States, and at least three-fourths of the directors must have resided in the State, Territory, or District in which the association is located, for at least one year immediately preceding their election, and three-fourths of every board must at all times consist of permanent residents in such State, Territory, or District. Every director during his continuance in office must own in his own right, free from any lien, at least ten shares of the capital stock of the association of which he is a director. (Sec. 5146, R. S.)

SEC. 41. Any director who ceases to be the owner of ten shares of the capital stock of the association, or who becomes in any other manner disqualified, shall thereby vacate his place. Notice of any vacancy so arising shall at once be given to the Comptroller of the Currency by the president or cashier. (Sec. 5146, R. S.)

SEC. 42. Each director, when appointed or elected, shall take an oath that he will at all times inform himself as to the business and condition of such association, and so far as the duty devolves on him will diligently and honestly administer its affairs; that he will not knowingly violate, or willingly permit to be violated, any of the laws relating to national banking associations; and that he is the owner, in good faith and in his own right, of the number of shares of stock required by this act, subscribed by him, or standing in his name on the books of the association, and that the same is not hypothecated, or in any way pledged as security for any loan or debt. Such oath, subscribed by the director making it and certified by the officer before whom it is taken, shall be immediately transmitted to the Comptroller of the Currency, and shall be filed and preserved in his office. (Sec. 5147, R. S.)

SEC. 43. If any person elected or appointed a director shall fail to qualify, by taking the prescribed oath, within thirty days from the date of such election or appointment, his place in the board shall be deemed to be vacant and shall be filled as in other cases of vacancy.

SEC. 44. Any director may resign from the board upon serving upon the president, vice-president, or cashier written notice of his intention so to do. But such resignation shall not take effect until an acknowledgment or proof of such service shall have been filed with the Comptroller of the Currency, and his certificate to that effect shall have been obtained, and shall have been published for at least thirty days in every issue of the newspaper in which the association is accustomed to publish its statements of condition. A like certificate must be obtained by the association and similarly published whenever a vacancy occurs in the board by the death, removal, or disqualification of a director.

SEC. 45. Any director may request the Comptroller of the Currency at any time, upon a written statement of his reasons therefor, to cause an examination to be made into the affairs of the association; and the Comptroller, if he is satisfied that the request is made in good faith and upon reasonable grounds, may order such examination to be made. But the Comptroller may require the director making the request to enter into a stipulation to pay the cost of such examination, if it shall prove to have been unnecessary, and to deposit beforehand a sufficient sum of money for that purpose.

SEC. 46. If the directors of any national banking association shall knowingly violate or knowingly permit any of the officers, agents, or servants of the association to violate any of the provisions of this act, all the rights, privileges, and franchises of the association shall be thereby forfeited. But before the association shall be declared dissolved such violation shall be determined and adjudged by a proper circuit, district, or Territorial court of the United States, in a suit brought for that purpose by the Comptroller of the Currency, in his own name. In case of such violation, every director who participated in or assented to the same shall be held liable in his personal and individual capacity for all damages which the association, its shareholders, or any other person shall have sustained in consequence thereof. (Sec. 5239, R. S.)

SEC. 47. Any bank incorporated by special law, or any banking institution organized under a general law of any State, may become a national banking association under this act by the name prescribed in its organization certificate; and in such case the articles of association and the organization certificate may be executed by a majority of the directors of the bank or banking institution; and the certificate shall declare that the owners of two-thirds of the capital stock have authorized the directors to make such certificate and to change and convert the bank or banking institution into a national banking association. A majority of the directors, after executing the articles of association and organization certificate, shall have power to execute all other papers, and to do whatever may be required to make the organization perfect and complete as a national banking association. (Sec. 5154, R. S.)

SEC. 48. The shares of any such association may continue to be for the same amount each as they were before the conversion; and any State bank which is a stockholder in any other bank by authority of State laws, may continue to hold its stock, although either bank, or both, may be organized under, and may have accepted the provisions of this act. (Sec. 5154, R. S.)

SEC. 49. When the Comptroller of the Currency has given to such association a certificate, under his hand and official seal, that the provisions of this act have been complied with, and that it is authorized to commence the business of banking, the association shall have the same powers and privileges and shall be subject to the same duties, responsibilities, and rules, in all respects, as are prescribed for other associations originally organized as national banking associations, and shall be held and regarded as such an association. But no such association shall have a less capital than the amount prescribed for associations organized under this act. (Sec. 5154, R. S.)

SEC. 50. The directors at the time of the conversion may continue to be the directors of the association until others are elected or appointed in accordance with the provisions of this chapter. (Sec. 5154, R. S.)

SEC. 51. No bank having branches shall continue to operate such branches after being converted into a national banking association.

SEC. 52. Associations may be organized under this act for the purpose of issuing notes payable in gold; and, except as specially provided, such associations shall be subject to all the provisions of law to which the other associations organized under this act are subject. (Sec. 5185, R.S.)

SEC. 53. Any association organized for the purpose of issuing notes payable in gold may be converted into an association with the same powers and obligations in all respects as the other associations organized under this act. Such conversion shall be effected in the same manner in which banks organized under State laws are converted into national banking associations. But the organization certificate shall bear the date of the original organization of the association. (Act February 14, 1880.)

SEC. 54. Nothing in this act shall affect any appointments made, acts done, or proceedings had or commenced in or toward the organization of any national banking association under any laws previously in force; but all associations which were organized or in process of organization under any such law, shall enjoy all the rights and privileges granted, and be subject to all the duties, liabilities, and restrictions imposed by this act. (Sec. 5156, R. S.)

CHAPTER III.—EXTENSION OF PERIOD OF SUCCESSION.

SEC. 55. Any association at any time within two years next previous to the date of the expiration of its original period of corporate existence, and with the approval of the Comptroller of the Currency, may, by amending its articles of association, extend its period of succession for a term of not more than twenty years from the expiration of the period of succession named in the articles of association, and shall have succession for such extended period. But such amended articles of association shall not be valid until the Comptroller shall have given to the association a certificate as hereinafter provided. (Act July 12, 1882, secs. 1 and 2.)

SEC. 56. Such amendment of the articles of association shall be authorized by the consent in writing of shareholders owning not less than two-thirds of the capital stock of the association; and the board of directors shall cause such consent to be certified under the seal of the association, by its president or cashier, to the Comptroller of the Currency, accompanied by an application made by the president or cashier for the approval of the amended articles of association by the Comptroller. (Act July 12, 1882, sec. 2.)

SEC. 57. Upon the receipt of the certificate and application provided for in the preceding section, the Comptroller of the Currency shall cause a special examination to be made, at the expense of the association, to determine its condition, and if after such examination, or otherwise, the condition of the association shall appear to him to be satisfactory, he shall give to such association a certificate under his hand and seal that the association has complied with all the provisions required to be complied with, and is authorized to have succession for the extended period named in the amended articles of association; but if the condition of the association appears to be unsatisfactory, he shall withhold such certificate of approval. (Act July 12, 1882, secs. 2 and 3.)

SEC. 58. Any association so extending the period of its succession shall continue to enjoy all the rights, privileges, and immunities granted to, and shall continue to be subject to all the duties, liabilities, and restrictions imposed upon national banking associations; and it shall continue to be in all respects the identical association it was before the extension of its period of succession. (Act July 12, 1882, sec. 4.)

SEC. 59. If any shareholder not assenting to the amendment extending the period of succession shall, within thirty days from the date of the Comptroller's certificate of approval, give to the directors notice in writing of his desire to withdraw from the association, he shall be entitled to receive from the association the value of the shares so held by him. Such value shall be ascertained by an appraisal made by a committee of three persons, one to be selected by the dissenting shareholder, one by the directors, and the third by these two. If the directors refuse or unnecessarily delay to appoint an appraiser to act for them, the Comptroller of the Currency may make the appointment. In case the value fixed by the committee shall not be satisfactory to the shareholder or to the association, either may appeal to the Comptroller, who shall cause a reappraisal to be made, which shall be final and binding; and if the reappraisal shall change the value fixed by the committee, the expense of reappraisal shall be paid by the party against whom such change is made. The value so ascertained and determined shall be deemed to be a debt due to the shareholder from the association, and shall be forthwith paid by it; and the shares so surrendered and appraised shall be sold at public sale, after due notice, within thirty days after the final appraisal provided for in this section. (Act July 12, 1882, sec. 5.)

SEC. 60. In the organization of any association intended to replace another association, and retaining the name thereof, the holders of stock in the expiring association, in proportion to their shares, respectively, shall be entitled to preference in the allotment of the shares of the new association. (Act July 12, 1882, sec. 5.)

CHAPTER IV.—POWERS AND OBLIGATION

SEC. 61. Every national banking association, in the name designated in its organization certificate, shall have power—

(1) To adopt and use a corporate seal.

(2) To have succession for the period of twenty years from its organization, unless it is sooner dissolved according to the provisions of its articles of association, or by the act of its shareholders owning two-thirds of its stock, or unless its franchise becomes forfeited by some violation of law.

(3) To make contracts.

(4) To sue and be sued, complain and defend, in any court of law or equity, as fully as natural persons.

(5) To elect or appoint directors, and by its board of directors to appoint a president, vice-president, cashier, and other officers, define their duties, require bonds of them and fix the penalty thereof, dismiss such officers or any of them at pleasure, and appoint others to fill their places.

(6) To prescribe, by its board of directors, by-laws not inconsistent with law, regulating the manner in which its stock shall be transferred, its directors elected or appointed, its officers appointed, its property transferred, its general business conducted, and the privileges granted to it by law exercised and enjoyed.

(7) To exercise, by its board of directors, or duly authorized officers or agents, subject to law, all such incidental powers as shall be necessary to carry on the business of banking; by discounting and negotiating promissory notes, drafts, bills of exchange, and other evidences of debt; by receiving deposits; by buying and selling exchange, coin, and bullion; by lending money on personal security; and by obtaining and issuing circulating notes according to the provisions of this act.

But no association shall transact any business, except such as is incidental and necessarily preliminary to its organization, until it has been authorized by the Comptroller of the Currency to commence the business of banking. (Sec. 5136, R. S.)

SEC. 62. A national banking association may purchase, hold, and convey real estate for the following purposes, and for no others:

(1) Such as shall be necessary for its adequate accommodation and protection in the transaction of its business.

(2) Such as shall be mortgaged to it as security for debts previously contracted.

(3) Such as shall be conveyed to it in satisfaction of debts previously contracted in the course of its dealings.

(4) Such as it shall purchase at sales under judgments, decrees, or mortgages held by the association, or shall purchase in order to secure debts due to it.

But no loan shall be made upon any understanding that the association is afterward to receive a mortgage or lien upon real estate as security therefor, or to take any conveyance of real estate in payment thereof, in whole or in part. And no association shall hold for a longer period than five years the possession of any real estate upon which there is any mortgage or lien, or the title and possession of any real estate or any interest therein, otherwise than for the purpose specified in subdivision one of this section. (Sec. 5137, R. S.)

SEC. 63. All associations designated for that purpose by the Secretary of the Treasury shall be depositaries of public money, under such regulations as may be prescribed by the Secretary; and they may also be employed as financial agents of the Government; and they shall perform all such reasonable duties, as depositaries of public moneys and financial agents of the Government, as may be required of them. The Secretary shall require the associations thus designated to give satisfactory security, by the deposit of United States bonds and otherwise, for the safe keeping and prompt payment of the public money deposited with them, and for the faithful performance of their duties as financial agents of the Government. Every association so designated as receiver or depositary of the public money shall take and receive at par all of the national currency bills, by whatever association issued, which may form part of the public money deposited with it. (Sec. 5153, R. S.)

SEC. 64. The president and cashier of every association shall cause to be kept at all times in the office where its business is transacted a full and correct list of the names and residences of all the shareholders in the association, and the number of shares held by each. Such list shall be subject to the inspection of all the shareholders and creditors of the association, and of the officers authorized to assess taxes under State authority, during business hours of each day in which business may be legally transacted. A copy of such list, as the same shall be on the first Monday of July of each year, verified by the oath of the president or cashier, shall be transmitted to the Comptroller of the Currency within five days from that date, under penalty of ten dollars for each day of delay thereafter. (Sec. 5210, R. S.)

SEC. 65. The shareholders of every association shall be held individually responsible, equally and ratably, and not one for another, for all contracts, debts, and engagements of such association, to the extent of the amount of their stock therein, at the par value thereof, in addition to the amount invested in such shares. (Sec. 5151, R. S.)

SEC. 66. The provisions of the preceding section shall not apply to shareholders of any banking association now existing under State laws, having not less than five millions of dollars of capital actually paid in, and a surplus of twenty per centum on hand, both to be determined by the Comptroller of the Currency; but such shareholders shall be liable only to the amount invested in their shares. Such surplus of twenty per centum shall be kept undiminished and be in addition to the surplus provided for in this act, and if at any time there is a deficiency in such surplus of twenty per centum, the association shall not pay any dividends to its shareholders until the deficiency is made good, and in case of such deficiency the Comptroller of the Currency may compel the association to close its business and wind up its affairs under the provisions of chapter VIII. of this act. (Sec. 5151, R. S.)

SEC. 67. Whenever the surplus fund of any association shall exceed by twenty per centum the amount of its capital stock, the shareholders of such association may be relieved of the individual liability imposed by section sixty-six of this act; and the shareholders of every association may be relieved of such liability in the proportion which the surplus, after deducting an amount equal to twenty per centum of the capital, bears to the whole amount of the capital stock. But no exemption from individual liability shall be obtained through any process by which any portion of the capital stock of an association may be, or may have been, converted into surplus, and in no case shall the shareholders of any association be relieved of any proportion of their individual liability until all the conditions of the two succeeding sections are complied with.

SEC. 68. Whenever the shareholders of an association shall become entitled to any exemption from individual liability, the directors of such association, if they deem advisable, and at such times as shall seem to them proper, may cause the president or cashier to certify to the Comptroller of the Currency the amount of the surplus fund accumulated by the association; and upon the receipt of such certificate the Comptroller shall cause to be made, at the expense of the association, a special examination of its affairs; and if, after such examination had, the Comptroller shall be satisfied that the association is solvent, and that its capital and surplus are represented by good and adequate assets, he shall give to the association a certificate, under his hand and seal, setting forth that the association has complied with all the provisions required to be complied with by this and the preceding section, and specifying the proportion of the exemption from liability on each share of the capital stock.

SEC. 69. The association shall cause the certificate of the Comptroller of the Currency issued under the preceding section to be printed in each issue of a newspaper published in the city or county where the association is located for at least sixty days next after the issuing thereof.

SEC. 70. If any association, of which the shareholders have become exempt from any portion of their individual liability, shall have its surplus reduced, by losses or otherwise, below the amount required for such exemption, such association, within three months after receiving notice thereof from the Comptroller of the Currency, shall make good the deficiency in the surplus by assessment upon the shareholders pro rata for the amount of capital stock held by each; and, upon notice from the Comptroller, the Treasurer of the United States shall withhold the interest upon all bonds which the association has on deposit with him until otherwise notified by the Comptroller. If any association shall not make good its surplus as herein required, and shall fail to go into liquidation within three months after receiving notice from the Comptroller, a receiver may be appointed by the Comptroller to close up the business of the association.

SEC. 71. If any shareholder shall neglect or refuse to pay within two months any assessment made by the directors for the purpose of restoring reduced surplus, the directors shall cause a sufficient amount of the capital stock of such shareholder to be sold at public auction to make good the deficiency, and the balance, if any, shall be returned to such delinquent shareholder or shareholders. Ten days' notice of such sale shall be posted in the office of the association and shall be published in a newspaper of the city or town where the association is located.

SEC. 72. Persons holding stock as executors, administrators, guardians, or trustees shall not be personally subject to any liabilities as stockholders; but the estates and funds in their hands shall be liable in like manner and to the same extent as the testator, intestate, ward, or person interested in such trust-funds would be, if living and competent to act and hold the stock in his own name. (Sec. 5152, R. S.)

SEC. 73. All savings banks or other banks now organized, or which shall hereafter be organized in the District of Columbia, under any act of Congress, shall be subject to all the laws of the United States applicable to national banking associations, so far as those laws may be applicable to such savings banks or other banks. But no savings bank now established and which has a capital stock paid up in whole or in part shall be required to have a paid-in capital exceeding one hundred thousand dollars. (Act June 30, 1876, sec. 6.)

CHAPTER V.—ISSUE AND REDEMPTION OF CIRCULATING NOTES.

SEC. 74. The term "United States bonds," as used throughout this chapter, shall be construed to mean registered bonds of the United States bearing interest; and any reference to the value of such bonds shall be construed to mean the par value, unless the market value is specified. (Sec. 5158, R. S.)

SEC. 75. Every association, before it shall be authorized to commence banking business, shall transfer and deliver to the Treasurer of the United States United States registered bonds, bearing interest, in the amounts following:

(1) Every association having a capital not exceeding two hundred and fifty thousand dollars, an amount equal to not less than one-tenth of the capital stock.

(2) Every association having a capital in excess of two hundred and fifty thousand dollars, an amount not less than twenty-five thousand dollars.

The deposit of bonds made by each association shall be increased as its capital may be increased, so that every association shall at all times have on deposit with the Treasurer United States bonds to the amount herein prescribed. (Secs. 5159 and 5160, R. S.; Act July 12, 1882, sec. 8, and Act June 20, 1874, sec. 4. Sec. 5160, R. S.)

SEC. 76. The bonds transferred to the Treasurer of the United States under the requirements of the preceding section shall be received by him upon deposit, and shall be by him safely kept in his office, until they shall be otherwise disposed of, in pursuance of the provisions of this act; and such bonds shall be held exclusively as security for the circulating notes of the association by which they were transferred, until such notes are redeemed, except as otherwise provided. (Secs. 5159 and 5167, R. S.)

SEC. 77. To facilitate a compliance with section seventy-five of this act, the Secretary of the Treasury is authorized to receive from any association, and cancel, any United States coupon bonds, and to issue in lieu thereof registered bonds of like amount, bearing a like rate of interest, and having the same time to run. (Sec. 5161, R. S.)

SEC. 78. All transfers of United States bonds made by any association under the provisions of this act shall be made to the Treasurer of the United States in trust for the association, with a memorandum written or printed on each bond, and signed by the cashier, or some other officer of the association making the deposit. A receipt shall be given to the association by the Comptroller of the Currency, or by a clerk appointed by him for that purpose, stating that the bond is held in trust for the association on behalf of which the transfer is made, and as security for the redemption and payment of any circulating notes that have been or may be delivered to such association. (Sec. 5162, R. S.)

SEC. 79. No assignment or transfer by the Treasurer of the United States of any bond deposited with him under the provisions of this act shall be valid unless countersigned by the Comptroller of the Currency. Every such transfer or assignment, immediately after it is so countersigned, shall be entered in a book to be kept by the Comptroller in his office for that purpose. The Comptroller shall state in such entry the name of the association from the account of which the transfer is made, the name of the party to whom it is made, the par value, and the numerical designation and the denomination of each bond transferred. (Secs. 5162 and 5163, R. S.)

SEC. 80. The Comptroller of the Currency, immediately upon countersigning and entering any transfer or assignment by the Treasurer of the United States of any bonds belonging to a national banking association, shall advise by mail the association from the account of which the transfer is made of the kind and numerical designation of the bonds and the amount thereof so transferred. (Sec. 5164, R. S.)

SEC. 81. The Comptroller of the Currency shall have at all times, during office hours, access to the books of the Treasurer of the United States for the purpose of ascertaining the correctness of any transfer or assignment of bonds presented for his countersignature; and the Treasurer shall have the like access to the book mentioned in section seventy-nine of this act, to ascertain the correctness of the entries in the same. The Comptroller shall also have like access to the bonds on deposit with the Treasurer, to ascertain their amount and condition. (Sec. 5165, R. S.)

SEC. 82. Every association having bonds deposited in the office of the Treasurer of the United States shall, once or oftener in each fiscal year, examine and compare the bonds pledged by the association with the books of the Comptroller of the Currency and with the accounts of the association, and, if they are found correct, shall execute to the Treasurer a certificate setting forth the different kinds and the amounts thereof, and that the same are in the possession and custody of the Treasurer at the date of the certificate. Such examination shall be made at such time or times, during the ordinary business hours, as the Treasurer and the Comptroller, respectively, may select. It may be made by an officer or agent of such association, duly appointed in writing for that purpose; and the certificate before mentioned, when made by such officer or agent, shall be of the same force and validity as if executed by the president or cashier. A duplicate of such certificate, signed by the Treasurer, shall be retained by the association. (Sec. 5166, R. S.)

SEC. 83. If any association fail to appoint one of its officers or an agent to make the examination required by the preceding section, or if such officer or agent fail to attend at the time designated, or to make the examination, or to execute the certificate specified, the examination may be made and the certificate may be executed by some person designated for the purpose by the Secretary of the Treasury. And such person, upon a faithful performance of such duties, shall be entitled to recover from the association reasonable compensation therefor, to be fixed by the Comptroller of the Currency.

SEC. 84. The Comptroller of the Currency shall give to each association powers of attorney to receive and appropriate to its own use the interest on the bonds which it has so transferred to the Treasurer. But such powers of attorney shall not apply to any portion of such interest withheld in pursuance of any provision of this act; and they shall become wholly inoperative whenever such association fails to redeem its circulating notes, or is placed in the hands of a receiver or other agent of the Comptroller in accordance with law. (Sec. 5167, R. S.)

SEC. 85. Whenever the market or cash value of any bonds deposited with the Treasurer by any association is reduced below the rate of one hundred dollars for ninety dollars of the circulation issued for the same, the Comptroller of the Currency may demand of the association and receive from it the amount of such depreciation in other United States bonds at cash value, or in money, to be deposited with the Treasurer as long as such depreciation continues. (Sec. 5167, R. S.)

SEC. 86. The Comptroller of the Currency, upon the terms prescribed by the Secretary of the Treasury, may permit an exchange to be made of any bonds deposited with the Treasurer by any association for other bonds of the United States authorized to be received as security for circulating notes, if he is of the opinion that such an exchange can be made without prejudice to the United States. (Sec. 5167, R. S.)

SEC. 87. Upon a deposit of bonds as prescribed by section seventy-five of this act, the association making the same shall be entitled to receive from the Comptroller of the Currency circulating notes of different denominations, in blank, registered and countersigned as hereinafter provided, equal in amount to ninety per centum of the current market value, not exceeding par, of the United States bonds so transferred and delivered; but at no time shall the total amount of circulating notes supplied to any association exceed ninety per centum of its capital stock at such time actually paid in. (Sec. 5171, R. S., and Act July 12, 1882, sec. 10.)

SEC. 88. In order to furnish suitable notes for circulation, the Comptroller of the Currency, under the direction of the Secretary of the Treasury, shall cause plates and dies to be engraved, in the best manner to guard against counterfeiting and fraudulent alterations, and shall have printed therefrom and numbered, such quantity of circulating notes, in blank, of the denominations of five dollars, ten dollars, twenty dollars, fifty dollars, one hundred dollars, five hundred dollars, and one thousand dollars, as may be required to supply the associations entitled to receive the same. Such notes shall bear upon their face the statement that they are secured by United States bonds deposited with the Treasurer of the United States, which statement shall be attested by the written or engraved signatures of the Treasurer and Register and by the imprint of the seal of the Treasury. They shall likewise express upon their face the promise of the association to which they are supplied to pay the amount thereof on demand; and for the proper attestation of this promise blank spaces shall be left for the signatures of the president or vice-president and the cashier. There shall also be printed upon such notes, under such regulations as the Secretary shall prescribe, the charter number of the association to which they are supplied; and they shall bear such devices and statements other than those herein specified, and shall be in such form as the Secretary shall, by regulation, direct. (Sec. 5172, R. S., and Act June 20, 1874, sec. 5.)

SEC. 89. The plates, dies, bed-pieces, and other appliances prepared for the printing of the national-bank notes, together with the original engraved plates, the cylinders and other material used in the preparation thereof, shall be kept in suitable vaults in the building of the Bureau of Engraving and Printing. They shall be at all times, when not in actual use, under the control and direction of the Comptroller of the Currency, but in the special charge of a custodian, who shall be responsible for the safe keeping of such appliances as come into his charge, and for the proper issue and due return, the same day, of every piece taken out for use. The custodian shall keep an accurate record of every such issue and return, and at the end of each calendar month he shall transmit to the Comptroller of the Currency a report in such form as that officer may prescribe. (Secs. 5173 and 5174, R. S.)

SEC. 90. The custodian shall be appointed by the Secretary of the Treasury, and shall be entitled to a salary of three thousand dollars a year. He shall give to the United States a bond in the penalty of twenty-five thousand dollars, with not less than two responsible sureties to be approved by the Secretary, conditioned for the faithful discharge of his duties.

SEC. 91. Once in each year the Secretary of the Treasury shall cause to be examined all the plates, dies, bed-pieces, cylinders, and other appliances used in the preparation of the national-bank notes, and a correct list to be taken thereof, and such list to be compared with the list made the previous year, and all differences to be noted and accounted for, and a full report made to him of such examination and the results.

SEC. 92. All material prepared for or used in the printing of the notes of associations which are in liquidation, or have closed business, and all other material not required for present or future use, shall be destroyed, under such regulations as shall be prescribed by the Comptroller of the Currency and approved by the Secretary of the Treasury.

SEC. 93. The examination and destruction provided for by the two preceding sections shall be conducted by a committee of three persons, one to be selected by the Comptroller of the Currency, one by the Treasurer of the United States, and one by the Register of the Treasury, all subject to the approval of the Secretary of the Treasury. Such committee shall perform its duties under regulations to be established by the Secretary, and each member thereof shall be entitled to such compensation as may be provided by such regulations. But no person appointed for this duty shall hold any position or office under either of the officers charged with the selection of the committee, nor shall the same person be twice appointed upon the committee.

SEC. 94. The expenses of such examinations and destructions shall be paid out of any appropriation made by Congress for the special examination of national banking associations and bank-note plates.

SEC. 95. Every association shall reimburse the Treasury the cost of engraving the plates required for printing its circulating notes. (Act June 20, 1874, sec 3, and Act June 12, 1882, sec. 6.)

SEC. 96. Upon deposit with the Treasurer of the United States of any United States bonds, bearing interest, payable in gold, in the manner prescribed for other associations, it shall be lawful for the Comptroller of the Currency to furnish to any association organized under section fifty-two of this act circulating notes of different denominations, but none of them of less than five dollars, and not exceeding in amount ninety per centum of the par value of the bonds deposited, which notes shall express the promise of the association to pay them, upon presentation at the office at which they are issued, in gold coin of the United States, and they shall be so redeemable. (Sec. 5185, R. S.)

SEC. 97. After any association receiving circulating notes under this act has caused its promise to pay such notes on demand to be signed by its president or vice-president and cashier, in such manner as to make them obligatory promissory notes payable on demand, at its place of business, such association may issue and circulate the same as money. And the same shall be received at par in all parts of the United States in payment of taxes, excises, public lands, and all other dues to the United States, except duties on imports; and also for all salaries and other debts and demands owing by the United States to individuals, corporations, and associations within the United States, except interest on the public debt, and in redemption of the national currency. They may also be counted as a part of the lawful-money reserve which any association is required to keep on hand against its deposits; but they shall not be available for deposit with the Treasurer of the United States in the redemption fund of five per centum upon circulation. (Sec. 5182, R. S.)

SEC. 98. The cashier, with the approval of the board of directors, which approval shall be entered upon the directors' minutes, and certified to the Comptroller of the Currency, may appoint a deputy to affix the cashier's signature to the circulating notes of the association. But such notes shall not be signed by any assistant or acting cashier.

SEC. 99. No national banking association shall issue any notes or other obligations to circulate as money, except the circulating notes authorized by this act. (Sec. 5183, R. S.)

SEC. 100. The Comptroller of the Currency shall receive, when delivered to him in sums of one hundred dollars or any multiple thereof, worn or mutilated circulating notes issued by any association, and shall furnish to the association other blank circulating notes to an equal amount in place thereof; and, also, upon due proof of the destruction of any circulating notes, he shall deliver to the association by which such notes were issued other blank circulating notes to an equal amount. (Sec. 1584, R. S.)

SEC. 101. The Comptroller of the Currency shall establish regulations for registering in proper books all worn or mutilated notes received by him and all notes which have been redeemed or surrendered to be canceled, and he shall cause all such notes, after identification and registration, to be destroyed by maceration, under regulations to be prescribed by the Secretary of the Treasury, and in the presence of four persons, one to be appointed by the Secretary of the Treasury, one by the Comptroller of the Currency, one by the Treasurer of the United States, and one by the association interested in such destruction. A certificate of such destruction, signed by the parties witnessing the same, shall be made in the books of the Comptroller, and a duplicate thereof shall be by him forwarded to the association the notes of which are thus destroyed. If any association shall fail to appoint some person to witness the destruction of its notes, the Comptroller may designate some person to act as witness for it; and the person so appointed shall be entitled to reasonable compensation for such services. (Sec. 5184, R. S., and Act June 23, 1874.)

SEC. 102. The Comptroller of the Currency may direct any bonds to be returned, in sums of not less than one thousand dollars, to the association which transferred the same, upon the surrender to him and the cancellation of a proportionate amount of its circulating notes. But no such return of bonds shall be made if thereby the remaining bonds which the association has on deposit would be reduced below the amount required by section seventy-five of this act, or below the amount required, either at par or in cash value, to secure the unsurrendered circulating notes of the association. (Sec. 5167, R. S.)

SEC. 103. Any association may take up the bonds deposited by it with the Treasurer of the United States, in excess of the amount it is required to keep on deposit, if no circulating notes have been issued thereon, or when notes have been issued thereon, if a proportionate amount of such notes are surrendered to the Comptroller of the Currency for cancellation without replacement. Any association closing up its business and dissolving its organization may take up, in sums of not less than one thousand dollars, the bonds deposited by it, upon surrendering to the Comptroller a proportionate amount of its circulating notes; and in like manner any association which reduces its capital stock may take up the bonds it has on deposit in excess of the amount required by section seventy-five of this act. (Sec. 5160, R. S.)

SEC. 104. Every association shall at all times keep and have on deposit in the Treasury of the United States, in lawful money of the United States, a sum equal to five per centum of its circulating notes, to be held and used for the redemption of such notes. And when the circulating notes of any associations, assorted or unassorted, shall be presented for redemption to the Treasurer of the United States, in sums of one thousand dollars or any multiple thereof, the same shall be redeemed in United States notes, or, at the option of the Treasurer, in coin of equal current value with such United States notes. Upon the request of the person presenting any national-bank notes for redemption, the Treasurer may, if convenient, pay the same in gold or silver coin certificates. (Act June 20, 1874, sec. 3.)

SEC. 105. All notes redeemed by the Treasurer of the United States under the preceding section shall be charged by him to the respective associations issuing the same, and he shall notify them severally, on the first day of each month, or oftener, at his discretion, of the amount of such redemptions; and whenever such redemptions for any association shall amount to the sum of five hundred dollars, such association so notified shall forthwith deposit with the Treasurer in United States notes, or in such coin or coin certificates as the Treasurer may accept as equivalent thereto, a sum equal to the amount of its circulating notes so redeemed. (Act June 20, 1874, sec. 3.)

SEC. 106. When such redemptions have been reimbursed as required, the circulating notes redeemed shall be forwarded to the respective associations by which they were issued; but if any of such notes are worn, mutilated, defaced, or otherwise unfit for use, they shall be forwarded to the Comptroller of the Currency to be destroyed and replaced. (Act June 20, 1874, sec. 3.)

SEC. 107. Any association desiring to withdraw any of its circulating notes, may, upon the deposit of lawful money with the Treasurer of the United States, in sums of not less than four thousand five hundred dollars, take up the bonds which it has transferred to the Treasurer for the security of such circulating notes, in the order in which it makes such deposit of lawful money; and the outstanding notes of such association, to an amount equal to the lawful money deposited, shall be redeemed at the Treasury of the United States, and destroyed, as prescribed in this chapter. But the bonds on deposit to secure the circulating notes of such association shall not be reduced below the amount required by section seventy-five of this act. (Act June 20, 1874, sec. 4, and Act July 12, 1882, sec. 8.)

SEC. 108. Not more than three millions of dollars of lawful money shall be deposited during any calendar month for the purpose of withdrawing circulating notes as provided in the preceding section. But this provision shall not apply where bonds on deposit with the Treasurer are called by the Secretary of the Treasury for redemption. (Act July 12, 1882, sec. 9.)

SEC. 109. Every association which shall go into voluntary liquidation shall, within six months from the date of the vote to liquidate its affairs, deposit with the Treasurer of the United States lawful money of the United States sufficient to redeem all its outstanding circulation. The Treasurer shall execute duplicate receipts for money thus deposited, stating the amount received by him and the purpose for which it has been received, and shall deliver one to the association and the other to the Comptroller of the Currency; and the money shall be paid into the Treasury of the United States and placed to the credit of such association upon redemption account. (Sec. 5222, R. S.)

SEC. 110. Whenever a sufficient deposit of lawful money to redeem the outstanding circulation of an association proposing to close its business has been made, the bonds deposited by the association to secure payment of its notes shall be reassigned to it. And thereafter the association and its shareholders shall stand discharged from all liabilities upon the circulating notes, and those notes shall be redeemed at the Treasury of the United States. If any such association shall fail to make the deposit and take up its bonds for thirty days after the expiration of the time specified, the Comptroller of the Currency shall have power to sell, at public auction in New York City, the bonds pledged to secure the circulating notes of such association, and, after providing for the redemption and cancellation of such notes, and the necessary expenses of the sale, to pay over any balance remaining to the association or its legal representative. (Sec. 5224, R. S., as amended by Act February 18, 1875.)

SEC. 111. Whenever the Treasurer of the United States has redeemed any of the notes of an association which has commenced to close its affairs, he shall cause the notes to be mutilated and charged to the redemption account of the association; and all notes so redeemed by the Treasurer shall, every three months, be certified to and destroyed by maceration, in the manner prescribed in section one hundred and one of this act. (Sec. 5225, R. S.)

SEC. 112. The provisions of the three preceding sections shall apply also to associations of which the corporate existence expires, and which do not extend their succession, the deposit of lawful money to be made within six months from the expiration of such corporate existence. (Act July 12, 1882, sec. 7.)

SEC. 113. An association which is in good faith winding up its business for the purpose of consolidating with another association shall not be required to deposit lawful money for its outstanding circulation; but its bonds on deposit and its outstanding circulating notes shall be reported by the association with which it is in process of consolidation. (Sec. 5223, R. S.)

SEC. 114. When any association shall extend the period of its succession, the circulating notes issued to it prior to such extension shall be redeemed at the Treasury of the United States, as provided in section one hundred and four of this act; and such notes when redeemed shall be forwarded to the Comptroller of the Currency and destroyed. From time to time as such notes are redeemed new circulating notes shall be supplied to the association. (Act July 12, 1882, sec. 6.)

SEC. 115. Any gain that may arise from the failure to present for redemption the circulating notes of any association shall inure to the benefit of the United States. (Act July 12, 1882, sec. 6.)

SEC. 116. All notes of national banking associations redeemed at the Treasury of the United States shall be canceled, except when returned to the association by which they were issued, as provided by section one hundred and six of this act. (Sec. 5223, R. S.)

SEC. 117. All notes of national banking associations, worn, defaced, mutilated, or otherwise unfit for circulation, when received by an assistant treasurer, or by any designated depositary of the United States, shall be forwarded to the Treasurer of the United States for redemption as provided in section one hundred and four of this act. (Act June 20, 1874, sec. 3.)

SEC. 118. Whenever any association fails to redeem in the lawful money of the United States any of its circulating notes, upon demand of payment duly made during the usual hours of business, at the office of such association, the holder may cause the same to be protested, in one package, by a notary public, unless the president or cashier of the association offers to waive demand and notice of the protest, and, in pursuance of such offer, makes, signs, and delivers to the party making such demand an admission in writing, stating the time of the demand, the amount demanded, and the fact of the non-payment thereof. The notary public, on making such protest, or upon receiving such admission, shall forthwith forward such admission or notice of protest to the Comptroller of the Currency, retaining a copy thereof. If, however, satisfactory proof is produced to the notary public that the payment of the notes demanded is restrained by order of any court of competent jurisdiction, he shall not protest the same. (Sec. 5226, R. S.)

SEC. 119. All fees for protesting the notes of any association shall be paid by the person procuring the protest to be made, and such association shall be liable therefor; but no part of the proceeds of any bonds deposited by such association shall be applied to the payment of such fees, nor shall such fees be preferred to other claims against an insolvent association. When the holder of any notes causes more than one note or package to be protested on the same day he shall not acquire a claim for more than one protest fee; and no fees shall in any case be allowed for protesting the notes of any association after it has closed its doors in consequence of insolvency. (Secs. 5526 and 5238, R. S.)

SEC. 120. On receiving notice that any national banking association has failed to redeem any of its circulating notes the Comptroller of the Currency, with the concurrence of the Secretary of the Treasury, may appoint a special agent, of whose appointment immediate notice shall be given to such association, who shall immediately proceed to ascertain whether it has refused to pay its circulating notes in the lawful money of the United States, when demanded, and shall report to the Comptroller the fact so ascertained. (Sec. 5227, R. S.)

SEC. 121. If from the protest, and from the report made by the agent appointed under the preceding section the Comptroller of the Currency is satisfied that such association has refused to pay its circulating notes and is in default, he shall, within thirty days after he has received such report, declare the bonds deposited by such association forfeited to the United States, and they shall thereupon be so forfeited. (Sec. 5227, R. S.)

SEC. 122. Immediately upon declaring the bonds of an association forfeited for non-payment of its notes the Comptroller of the Currency shall give notice, in such manner as the Secretary of the Treasury, by general rules or otherwise, shall direct, to the holders of the circulating notes of such association to present them for payment at the Treasury of the United States, and the same when presented shall be paid in lawful money of the United States; whereupon the Comptroller shall cause the bonds pledged by such association, or so much of them as may be necessary to redeem its outstanding notes, to be sold at public auction in the city of New York, after giving thirty days' notice of such sale to the association. (Secs. 5229 and 5230, R. S.)

SEC. 123. When all the bonds of an association have been sold, as provided in the preceding section, and the proceeds thereof are insufficient for the payment of the outstanding notes of the association, the United States shall have a paramount lien upon all the assets of the association for the amount of the deficiency; and such deficiency shall be made good out of such assets in preference to any and all claims whatsoever, except the necessary costs and expenses of administering the same. (Sec. 5230, R. S.)

SEC. 124. The Comptroller of the Currency, if he deems it for the interest of the United States, may sell at private sale any of the bonds of an association shown to have made default in paying its notes, and receive therefor either money or the circulating notes of the association. But no such bonds shall be sold by private sale for less than par, nor for less than the market value thereof at the time of sale; and no sales of any such bonds, either public or private, shall be complete until the transfer of the bonds shall have been made with the formalities prescribed by section seventy-nine of this act. (Sec. 5231, R. S.)

SEC. 125. Every association the circulating notes of which shall be redeemed by the Treasurer of the United States, as provided in section one hundred and four of this act, and every association making any deposit of lawful money with the Treasurer for reducing its circulation, shall be assessed the cost of transporting and assorting its notes, and such assessment shall be in proportion to the circulating notes redeemed, and shall be charged to the fund deposited with the Treasurer under the requirement of said section one hundred and four, and every association which shall make a deposit of lawful money for retiring its circulation in full shall, at the time of such deposit, be assessed, for the cost of transporting and redeeming its notes then outstanding, a sum equal to the average cost of the redemption of national-bank notes during the preceding year, and shall thereupon pay such assessment. (Act June 20, 1874, sec. 3, and Act July 12, 1882, sec. 8.)

SEC. 126. The Secretary of the Treasury may from time to time make such regulations respecting the perpetuation of the evidence of the payment of circulating notes presented at the Treasury of the United States for redemption as may seem to him proper. (Sec. 5232, R. S.)

CHAPTER VI.—THE BANKING BUSINESS.

SEC. 127. The usual business of each association shall be transacted at an office or banking house located in the place specified in its organization certificate. But, with the approval of the Comptroller of the Currency first obtained, any association may have in such place more than one office for receiving deposits, paying checks, and buying and selling exchange; and in every such case the association shall conform to the requirements of the Comptroller as to the clerical force to be employed and the accounts to be kept at and for each such office, and as to the extra compensation for examinations thereof. (Sec. 5190, R. S.)

SEC. 128. For the purposes of this act the cities of Albany, Baltimore, Boston, Cincinnati, Cleveland, Detroit, Kansas City, Louisville, Milwaukee, New Orleans, Omaha, Philadelphia, Pittsburgh, Saint Joseph, San Francisco, and Washington shall be known as reserve cities; and the cities of Chicago, New York, and Saint Louis shall be known as central reserve cities. (Sec. 5191, R. S.)

SEC. 129. Upon the application, in writing, of three-fourths in number of the associations located in any city of the United States having fifty thousand inhabitants, the Comptroller of the Currency shall have authority to designate such city a reserve city. (Act March 3, 1887.)

SEC. 130. Upon the application, in writing, of three-fourths in number of the associations located in any city of the United States having two hundred thousand inhabitants, the Comptroller of the Currency shall have authority, with the approval of the Secretary of the Treasury, to designate such city a central reserve city. But if any city named in section one hundred and twenty-eight of this act as a reserve city shall be designated a central reserve city, it shall thereafter be known only as a central reserve city. (Act March 3, 1887.)

SEC. 131. Every association in a reserve city, or in a central reserve city, shall at all times have on hand lawful money of the United States equal to at least twenty-five per centum of its deposits and other liabilities payable on demand, and every other association shall at all times have on hand lawful money of the United States equal to at least fifteen per centum of its deposits and its liabilities so payable. But no association is required to keep on hand lawful money on account of Government deposits, except as provided in section one hundred and thirty-six of this act. (Sec. 5191, R. S., and Act March 3, 1887.)

SEC. 132. Whenever the lawful money of any association shall be below the amount required by the preceding section, such association shall not impair its cash resources by making any new loans or discounts, otherwise than by discounting or purchasing bills of exchange payable at sight or on demand, nor make any dividend of its profits until the required proportion between its deposits and its lawful money of the United States has been restored. (Sec. 5191, R. S.)

SEC. 133. Whenever the lawful-money reserve of any association is found to be below the amount required, the Comptroller of the Currency may notify the association to make good its reserve; and if the association shall fail so to do for thirty days after such notice, the Comptroller, with the concurrence of the Secretary of the Treasury, may appoint a receiver to wind up its business. (Sec. 5191, R. S.)

SEC. 134. Three-fifths of the reserve of fifteen per centum required by section one hundred and thirty-one of this act may consist of cash balances due from associations in reserve cities or in central reserve cities; and one-half of the lawful money reserve of associations in reserve cities may consist of cash balances due from associations in central reserve cities. But every association with which any part of the lawful-money reserve of any other association is kept shall first be approved for that purpose by the Comptroller of the Currency. (Secs. 5192 and 5195, R. S.: Act June 20, 1874, and Act March 3, 1887, sec. 2.)

SEC. 135. Certificates representing specie or lawful money specially deposited by the members of any clearing-house association for the purpose of settling balances between them shall, when owned and held by any association which is a member of such clearing-house, be deemed to be lawful money within the meaning of section one hundred and thirty-one of this act. (Sec. 5192, R. S.)

SEC. 136. Any association designated by the Secretary of the Treasury as a depositary of public money may be required by the Secretary to keep on hand on account of such deposits such reserve fund as he may deem expedient. But such deposits shall not be counted in estimating the reserve required under section one hundred and thirty-one of this act.

SEC. 137. The Secretary of the Treasury may receive, at the Treasury or at any sub-treasury, from any national banking association United States notes on deposit, without interest, in sums of not less than ten thousand dollars, and issue certificates therefor in such form as he may prescribe, in denominations of not less than five thousand dollars, payable on demand in United States notes at the place where the deposits were made. The notes so deposited shall not be counted as part of the lawful-money reserve of the association; but the certificates issued therefor may be counted as such, and may be deposited with the Treasurer of the United States as a part of the five per cent. fund for the redemption of the circulating notes of the association. (Sec. 5193, R. S.)

SEC. 138. The power conferred on the Secretary of the Treasury by the preceding section shall not be exercised so as to create any expansion or contraction of the currency. And United States notes for which the certificates are issued under that section, or other United States notes of like amount, shall be held as special deposits in the Treasury and used only for the redemption of such certificates. (Sec. 5194, R. S.)

SEC. 139. No association shall be a member of any clearing-house in which gold certificates issued under the authority of the act of July twelfth, eighteen hundred and eighty-two, and silver certificates shall not be receivable in the settlement of clearing-house balances. (Act July 12, 1882, sec. 12.)

SEC. 140. Every association shall take and receive at par, for any debt or liability to it, any and all notes or bills issued by any lawfully organized national banking association. This provision shall not apply to any association organized for the purpose of issuing notes payable in gold; but every such association shall receive at par in the payment of debts the gold notes of every other such association which at the time of such payment is redeeming its circulating notes in gold coin of the United States. (Secs. 5186 and 5196, R. S.)

SEC. 141. No association shall at any time, or for any purpose, pay out or put in circulation the notes of any bank or banking association which are not at such time receivable, at par, on deposit, and in payment of debts by the association so paying out or circulating them; nor shall any association knowingly pay out or put in circulation any notes issued by any bank or banking association which at the time of such paying out or putting in circulation is not redeeming its circulating notes in lawful money of the United States. (Sec. 5206, R. S.)

SEC. 142. No association shall, either directly or indirectly, pledge or hypothecate any of its notes of circulation, for the purpose of procuring money to be paid in on its capital stock, or to be used in its banking operations, or otherwise; nor shall any association use its circulating notes, or any part thereof, in any manner or form, to create or increase its capital stock. (Sec. 5203, R. S.)

SEC. 143. No association shall make any loan or discount on the security of the shares of its own capital stock, nor be the purchaser or holder of any such shares, unless such security or purchase shall be necessary to prevent loss upon a debt previously contracted in good faith; and stock so purchased or acquired shall be sold at public or private sale within six months from the time of such purchase or acquisition or, in default thereof, a receiver may be appointed by the Comptroller of the Currency to close up the business of the association. (Sec. 5201, R. S.)

SEC. 144. No association shall, during the time it shall continue its banking operations, withdraw, or permit to be withdrawn, either in the form of dividends or otherwise, any portion of its capital stock. But nothing herein shall prevent the reduction of the capital stock of the association under section twenty-seven of this act. (Sec. 5204, R. S.)

SEC. 145. Every association of which the capital stock is not paid up as required by law, and every association of which the capital stock may become impaired by losses or otherwise, shall, within three months after receiving notice thereof from the Comptroller of the Currency, pay the deficiency in the capital stock, by assessment upon the shareholders in proportion to the shares held by each; and the Treasurer of the United States, upon notice from the Comptroller, shall withhold the interest upon all bonds held by him in trust for any such association until otherwise notified by the Comptroller. If any such association shall fail to pay up its capital stock and shall refuse to go into liquidation, for three months after receiving notice from him, the Comptroller may appoint a receiver to close up its business. (Sec. 5205, R. S.)

SEC. 146. If any shareholder shall neglect or refuse to pay within two months any assessment made by the directors for the purpose of restoring impaired capital, the directors shall cause a sufficient amount of the capital stock of such shareholder to be sold at public auction to make good the deficiency, and the balance, if any, shall be returned to such delinquent shareholder. Ten days' notice of such sale shall be posted in the office of the association, and shall be published in a newspaper of the city or town where the association is located. (Act June 30, 1876.)

SEC. 147. No association shall take, either in its own name, or in the name of any person or corporation for its benefit, any mortgage or lien upon real estate as security for a contemporaneous loan or for future advances made or to be made by it; nor shall any association purchase or hold any bond, note, or evidence of debt so secured, or the shares or debentures of any company or corporation dealing in real-estate securities.

SEC. 148. The provisions of the preceding section shall not apply in either of the following cases:

(1) The discount for an indorser in the ordinary course of business of a bona fide bill of exchange or negotiable promissory note having not more than four months to run, which is deemed by the board of directors a good asset without reference to any mortgage or lien collateral thereto.

(2) The taking of a bill or note so secured which has not more than four months to run, when the same is assigned to the association, in good faith, for the purpose of procuring the extension of a debt previously incurred.

(3) The taking of a mortgage or lien on real estate, or any obligation secured thereby, for the purpose of securing a debt previously contracted in good faith.

But in all the cases specified in this section a full record of the transaction, and of the reasons therefor, shall be entered upon the directors' minutes, and shall be attested by the signatures of a majority of the board.

SEC. 149. Nothing in this act shall be held to invalidate the title of any association to any bonds, debentures, or stocks acquired by it, or to any bill, note, or evidence of debt discounted by it, nor to render any mortgage or lien upon real estate invalid, nor to deprive any association or its assigns of the title to or possession of any real estate, or of any of the remedies to which mortgagees or persons holding liens upon real estate are entitled by the laws of the State, Territory, or District in which the property is situated.

SEC. 150. Every association offending against the provisions of section one hundred and forty-seven of this act shall be liable to a penalty for each infraction at the rate of one per centum per month upon the amount involved therein during the entire period that such obligations or securities are held by it, or by any person or corporation for its benefit.

SEC. 151. The total liabilities to any association, of any person, firm, company, or corporation, for money borrowed, including in the liabilities of a firm or company the liabilities of the several members thereof, shall at no time exceed one-tenth part of the capital stock actually paid in. But the discount of bills of exchange drawn in good faith against actually existing values, shall not be considered as money borrowed by the drawers or indorsers thereof; nor shall the discount of commercial paper actually owned by the persons for whom such discount is made be regarded as money borrowed by the makers of such paper; but in all such cases the limitation herein specified shall apply to the person, firm, company, or corporation, for whose use or benefit, directly or indirectly, any such loans or discounts are made. (Sec. 5200, R. S.)

SEC. 152. The prohibition of the preceding section shall not apply to loans made upon convertible collateral security, of which the cash market value is not less than the amount borrowed thereon, if neither the value nor the convertibility of the security is dependent upon the solvency or the success of any party to the loan. But the total liabilities of any person, firm, or corporation to an association, including loans on collaterals, shall at no time exceed twenty per centum upon the aggregate of its paid-in capital stock and surplus fund.

SEC. 153. Any association which shall make any loan contrary to the provisions of section one hundred and fifty-one of this act shall be subject to a penalty at the rate of one per centum per month on the entire amount of such loan for the period for which it shall have been made, and during which it shall continue.

SEC. 154. No association shall at any time be indebted, or in any way liable, to an amount exceeding the amount of its capital stock at such time actually paid in and remaining undiminished by losses or otherwise, except on account of demands of the nature following:

(1) Notes of circulation.

(2) Moneys deposited with or collected by the association.

(3) Bills of exchange or drafts drawn against money actually on deposit to the credit of the association or due thereto.

(4) Liabilities to the stockholders of the association for dividends and reserved profits. (Sec. 5202 R. S.)

SEC. 155. All losses sustained by any association shall be promptly charged against its undivided profits, and like charge shall be made of all bad debts; and no association shall at any time make or publish any statement of its condition which does not reflect the deduction from its undivided profits of all losses incurred up to that time, and of all bad debts.

SEC. 156. The directors of any association, at stated periods, to be fixed by the by-laws and reported to the Comptroller of the Currency, may declare dividends out of its net earnings, or any portion thereof, except the portion required by section one hundred and fifty-eight of this act to be passed to surplus account; but no dividend shall be made by any association, while it continues its banking operations, to an amount greater than its net profits then on hand, after deducting all losses and bad debts.

SEC. 157. In all cases before any dividend is declared or paid the directors shall ascertain by personal examination that all losses and bad debts have been charged off and that the association otherwise is in a good condition to make such distribution of net earnings; and every director shall be held to have assented to any dividend declared by the board, unless he shall at once notify the Comptroller of the Currency of his dissent.

SEC. 158. Every association shall accumulate a surplus fund equal to at least twenty per centum of its capital stock, by appropriating thereto ten per centum or more of its net profits as ascertained by deducting from the gross earnings and profits all bad debts as defined in section one hundred and sixty-six of this act, and all losses, expenses, and taxes.

SEC. 159. The ascertainment of net profits shall be made by the officers and accountants of the association, under the supervision of the board of directors, at half-yearly intervals, and every time a dividend is to be declared. And whenever the surplus fund of any association is less than twenty per centum of its capital stock, the association shall not declare or pay any dividend until after the ascertainment herein required shall have been made, and until at least ten per centum of the net profits of the last half year or shorter period, if dividends are oftener paid, has been carried to the credit of surplus-fund account.

SEC. 160. No part of the surplus fund shall be withdrawn, in the form of dividends or otherwise, except so much thereof as may be in excess of the amount specified in section one hundred and fifty-eight of this act.

SEC. 161. It shall be unlawful for any officer, clerk, or agent of any national banking association to certify, accept, or otherwise render the bank liable for any check drawn upon the association, unless the person or company drawing the check has on deposit with the association, at the time such check is certified, an amount of money equal to the amount specified therein. Any check so certified by a duly authorized officer shall be a good and valid obligation against the association; but for any act of any officer, clerk, or agent, in violation of this section, the Comptroller of the Currency may assess a penalty upon such association not exceeding one per centum of the amount so unlawfully certified. (Sec. 5208, R. S.)

SEC. 162. The prohibition of the preceding section shall not apply to the certification of checks drawn by regular customers of an association to meet drafts upon them to which bills of lading or transportation receipts for produce or marketable commodities or securities are attached, if these, or other securities equally valuable and convertible, are held by the certifying bank until the overdraft is made good.

SEC. 163. Any association may take, receive, reserve, and charge, on any loan or discount made, or upon any note, bill of exchange, or other evidence of debt, interest at the rate allowed by the laws of the State, Territory, or District where the bank is located, and no more, except that where by the laws of any State a different rate is limited for banks of issue organized under State laws, the rate so limited shall be allowed for associations organized or existing in any such State under this act: When no rate is fixed by the laws of the State, Territory, or District, and no agreement is made in advance with the borrower, an association may take, receive, reserve, or charge a rate not exceeding seven per centum, and such interest may be taken in advance, reckoning the days for which the note, bill, or other evidence of debt has to run. The purchase, discount, or sale of a bona fide bill of exchange, payable at another place than the place of such purchase, discount, or sale, at not more than the current rate of exchange for sight drafts in addition to the interest, shall not be considered as taking or receiving a greater rate of interest. (Sec. 5197, R. S.)

SEC. 164. The taking, receiving, reserving, or charging a rate of interest greater than is allowed by the preceding section, when knowingly done, shall be deemed a forfeiture of the entire interest which the note, bill, or other evidence of the debt carries with it, or which has been agreed to be paid thereon. (Sec. 5198, R. S.)

SEC. 165. In case a rate of interest greater than is allowed by this act has been paid, the person by whom it has been paid, or his legal representatives, may recover back from the association taking or receiving the same, in an action in the nature of an action of debt, twice the amount of the interest thus paid. But such action must be commenced within two years from the time the usurious transaction occurred. (Sec. 5198, R. S.)

SEC. 166. All debts due to any association, on which interest is past due and unpaid for a period of six months, shall be considered bad debts within the meaning of this act, unless the same are well secured or are in process of collection.

SEC. 167. The penalties authorized to be imposed by sections one hundred and fifty, one hundred and fifty-three, and one hundred and sixty-one of this act shall be assessed against the offending association by the Comptroller of the Currency, subject to an appeal to the Secretary of the Treasury; and in default of payment, the amount thereof shall be withheld by the Treasurer from the interest on the United States bonds deposited by such association to secure its circulating notes. In case any penalty in default shall amount to more than the interest due to such association at the next quarterly payment of interest on such bonds, the excess thereof, and the amount of other penalties in default, may be recovered from the association by suit instituted by the Comptroller, in his own name in the United States district court for the district in which the association is located.

CHAPTER VII.—REPORTS AND EXAMINATIONS.

SEC. 168. Every association shall make to the Comptroller of the Currency, according to the form which may be prescribed by him, not less than five reports during each year, each verified by the oath or affirmation of the president, vice-president, or cashier of such association, and attested by the signatures of at least three other directors. Each such report shall exhibit, in detail and under appropriate heads, th resources and liabilities of the association making the same at the close of business on any past day specified by the Comptroller; and it shall be transmitted to the Comptroller within five days after the receipt of a request or requisition therefor from him. (Sec. 5211, R. S.)

SEC. 169. Each report made to the Comptroller of the Currency under the requirements of the preceding section shall, in the same form in which it is made to the Comptroller, be published, at the expense of the association by which it was made, in a newspaper published in the place where such association is established; and such proof of publication shall be furnished as may be required by the Comptroller. (Sec. 5211, R. S.)

SEC. 170. The Comptroller of the Currency shall have power to call for special reports from any particular association whenever, in his judgment, the same are necessary in order to a full and complete knowledge of its condition. (Sec. 5211, R. S.)

SEC. 171. In addition to the other reports required by this act each association shall report to the Comptroller of the Currency, within ten days after declaring any dividend, the amount of such dividend, the amount of net earnings in excess thereof, and such other facts touching the declaration of such dividend as the Comptroller shall prescribe. Such reports shall be attested by the oath of the president, vice-president, or cashier of the association. (Sec. 5212, R. S.)

SEC. 172. Any association failing to make and transmit any report required by this chapter shall be subject to a penalty of ten dollars for each day it delays so to do after the periods respectively mentioned, which penalty shall be assessed by the Comptroller of the Currency. Whenever any association delays or refuses to pay the penalty so assessed, the amount thereof shall be retained by the Treasurer of the United States, upon the order of the Comptroller, out of the interest, as it may become due to the association, on the bonds deposited to secure circulation. (Sec. 5213, R. S.)

SEC. 173. All savings banks or savings and trust companies organized under authority of any act of Congress shall make to the Comptroller of the Currency, and shall publish all the reports which national banking associations are required to make and publish under the provisions of this chapter, and shall be subject to the same penalties for failure to make or publish such reports as are herein provided; which penalties may be collected by suit before any court of the United States in the district in which such savings banks or savings and trust companies may be located. (Act June 30, 1876, sec. 6.)

SEC. 174. The Comptroller of the Currency, with the approval of the Secretary of the Treasury, shall, as often as shall be deemed necessary or proper, appoint a suitable person or persons to make an examination of the affairs of every national banking association and of every savings bank or savings and trust company organized under authority of any act of Congress. Such persons shall be known as examiners of national banks, and each such examiner shall have power to make a thorough examination into all the affairs of the association, and, in doing so, to examine any of the officers and agents thereof, on oath, and shall make to the Comptroller a full and detailed report of the condition of the association. But no person shall be appointed to examine the affairs of any association in which, or adversely to which, he has any interest, personal or pecuniary. (Sec. 5240, R. S.)

SEC. 175. The Comptroller of the Currency may from time to time assign examiners of national banks to certain cities or districts, and require them to reside at some convenient place therein, or at a point readily accessible thereto, and to exercise a general inspection over all national banking associations therein. But no examiner shall visit or examine any bank except by direction, either general or special, of the Comptroller.

SEC. 176. Every person appointed an examiner of national banks shall take an oath that he will perform faithfully all the duties of his office, and preserve inviolate all confidences reposed in him by the Comptroller of the Currency, or by the officers or agents of any association; and that he will not divulge any information obtained by examination of any bank, except in his official reports or when called to testify in some competent court, nor use, directly or indirectly, such information or his official position or opportunities in any manner not authorized by this act.

SEC. 177. The compensation of persons appointed to examine associations not located in a reserve city or in a central reserve city, or in either of the States of Colorado, Oregon, California, and Nevada, or in any Territory, shall be an annual salary equal to two cents on every thousand dollars of aggregate liabilities of the associations examined during the year, and for each examination an additional sum as follows:

(1) For examining an association having a capital not exceeding one hundred and fifty thousand dollars, twenty dollars.

(2) For examining an association having a capital exceeding one hundred and fifty thousand dollars and not exceeding three hundred thousand dollars, twenty-five dollars.

(3) For examining an association having a capital exceeding three hundred thousand dollars and not exceeding five hundred thousand dollars, thirty dollars.

(4) For examining an association having a capital exceeding five hundred thousand dollars and not exceeding seven hundred and fifty thousand dollars, forty dollars.

(5) For examining an association having a capital exceeding seven hundred and fifty thousand dollars and not exceeding one million dollars, fifty dollars.

(6) For examining an association having a capital of over one million dollars, sixty dollars, and one dollar additional for every one hundred thousand dollars of capital in excess of one million dollars. (Sec. 5240, R. S., as amended by Act February 19, 1875.)

SEC. 178. The compensation of persons appointed to examine associations located in any reserve city, or in any central reserve city, or in either of the States of Colorado, Oregon, California, and Nevada, or in any Territory, shall be fixed by the Secretary of the Treasury, upon the recommendation of the Comptroller of the Currency. (Sec. 5240, R. S., as amended by Act February 19, 1875.)

SEC. 179. The fees for examining associations shall be assessed by the Comptroller of the Currency upon the respective associations so examined; and shall be paid by such associations. (Secs. 5283 and 5240, R. S.)

SEC. 180. The Comptroller of the Currency is authorized, whenever he may deem it useful, to cause examination to be made into the condition of any bank in the District of Columbia organized under act of Congress. The Comptroller, at his discretion, may report to Congress the results of such examination. The expense necessarily incurred in any such examination, and all expenses of any preliminary or other special examination into the condition of any association, wherever situated, shall be paid out of any appropriation made by Congress for special bank examinations; but this provision does not include special examinations of associations in liquidation. (Sec. 332, R. S.)

SEC. 181. No association shall be subject to any visitorial powers other than such as are authorized by this act, or are vested in the courts of justice. (Sec. 5241, R. S.)

CHAPTER VIII.—LIQUIDATION AND RECEIVERSHIP.

SEC. 182. When the corporate existence of an association, as fixed in section sixty-one of this act, expires, and is not extended, such corporate existence shall continue for the sole purpose of liquidating the affairs of the association until such affairs are finally closed. (Act July 12, 1882, sec. 7.)

SEC. 183. Any association may go into liquidation and be closed by the vote of shareholders owning two-thirds of its stock. (Sec. 5220, R. S.)

SEC. 184. Whenever a vote to go into liquidation is taken the board of directors shall cause such fact to be certified, under the seal of the association, by its president or cashier, to the Comptroller of the Currency, and shall cause notice to be published that the association is closing up its affairs, and that all its circulating notes and all other claims against it are to be presented for payment. Such publication shall be made for a period of two months in a newspaper published in the city of New York, and also in a newspaper published in the city or town in which the association is located. Like publication shall be made whenever an association is to be wound up by reason of the expiration of its corporate existence. (Sec. 5221, R. S., and Act July 12, 1882, sec. 7.)

SEC. 185. Every association in liquidation shall, on the first of January and first of July of each year, report the progress of such liquidation to the Comptroller of the Currency, in such form as he may require; and the Comptroller, if he deems it expedient, may cause such reports to be verified by a special examination at the expense of the association. The reports required by this section shall be made upon the oath or affirmation of the president, vice-president, or cashier of the association, and shall be attested by the signatures of at least three directors.

SEC. 186. Upon the request of any of the creditors or shareholders of an association in liquidation, the Comptroller of the Currency, after due hearing and inquiry, may appoint a receiver to wind up the affairs of such association. Such receiver, in addition to his other powers, shall have power to inquire into the doings of the persons previously conducting the liquidation, and to proceed against them for damages in case they shall appear to have wasted or misappropriated the assets, or to have failed in any other way to administer the affairs of the association prudently and equitably.

SEC. 187. When any association has gone into liquidation the individual liability of the shareholders may be enforced by any creditor of such association by bill in equity, in the nature of a creditor's bill, brought by such creditor on behalf of himself and of all other creditors of the association against the shareholders thereof in any court of the United States having original jurisdiction in equity for the district in which such association was located. (Act June 30, 1886, sec. 2.)

SEC. 188. Whenever an association has failed to pay its circulating notes on demand or to pay the current demands of its depositors, or is otherwise in a position of insolvency, it shall not be lawful for such association or any of its directors, officers, clerks, or agents to pay out any of its notes or other moneys, to receive deposits, to discount or purchase any notes or bills, or in any other way, directly or indirectly, to prosecute the business of banking. But nothing herein shall forbid an association to receive and safely keep money and other property belonging to it, or to redeem its circulating notes. (Sec. 2228, R. S.)

SEC. 189. All transfers of the property or credits of any association, and all acts which prevent or are intended to prevent the application of its assets in the manner prescribed in this chapter shall be utterly void, when made or done after an act of insolvency committed by such association, or in contemplation of insolvency, and with intent to defeat the pro-rata distribution of the assets of the association, or with intent to give any creditor preference over others. No attachment, injunction, or execution shall be issued against an insolvent association or its property before final judgment in any suit, action, or proceeding in any State, county, or municipal court; and where such process shall have been issued, it shall be immediately quashed or dissolved upon proof that the association was insolvent at the time of the issue thereof. (Sec. 5242, R. S.)

SEC. 190. In addition to the cases where the appointment of a receiver is especially provided for, a receiver of a national banking association may be appointed by the Comptroller of the Currency in either of the following cases:

(1) Whenever the Comptroller shall become satisfied, as specified in sections one hundred and eighteen and one hundred and twenty of this act, that the association has failed to pay its circulating notes and is in default.

(2) Whenever after due examination the Comptroller shall become satisfied that the association is insolvent.

(3) Whenever the association is dissolved, and its rights, privileges, and franchises are declared forfeited, as provided in section forty-six of this act.

(4) Whenever any creditor of the association who has obtained a judgment against it in any court of record makes application for the appointment of a receiver, and furnishes the certificate of the clerk of the court that such judgment has been rendered, and has remained unpaid for thirty days after the expiration of the time for taking an appeal or a writ of error. (Sec. 5234, R. S., and Act June 30, 1876, sec 1.)

SEC. 191. The Comptroller of the Currency may require of the receiver appointed by him such bond and security as he may deem proper. (Sec. 5234, R. S.)

SEC. 192. The receiver appointed by the Comptroller of the Currency shall, under the direction of the Comptroller, take possession of the books, records, and assets of every description of the association, collect all debts, dues, and claims belonging to it, and, upon the order of a court of record of competent jurisdiction, may sell or compound all bad or doubtful debts, and, on a like order, may sell all the real and personal property of the association, on such terms as the court shall direct, and may, if necessary to pay the debts of the association, enforce the individual liability of the stockholders. The receiver shall pay over all money so obtained to the Treasurer of the United States, subject to the order of the Comptroller; and he shall make report to the Comptroller of all his acts and proceedings. (Sec. 5234, R. S.)

SEC. 193. The Comptroller of the Currency, upon appointing a receiver, shall cause notice to be given, by advertisement in such newspapers as he may direct, for three consecutive months, calling on all persons who may have claims against the association to present the same, and to make legal proof thereof. (Sec. 5235, R. S.)

SEC. 194. From time to time, after full provision has been first made for refunding to the United States any deficiency in the funds specially devoted to redeeming the notes of the association, the Comptroller of the Currency shall make a ratable dividend of the money so paid over to him by the receiver on all such claims as may have been proved to his satisfaction or adjudicated in a court of competent jurisdiction; and, as the proceeds of the assets of the association are paid over to him, he shall make further dividends on all claims previously proved or adjudicated. But all expenses of any receivership shall be paid out of the assets of the association before final distribution of the proceeds thereof. (Secs. 5236 and 5238, R. S.)

SEC. 195. Whenever the assets of an insolvent association are exhausted and its affairs are wound up, the receiver, under instructions from the Comptroller of the Currency, may apply to the United States circuit court for the district in which the association was located, for a final discharge from further accountability; and if it shall appear that he has well and faithfully administered the trust, and that there are no further assets to be realized, the court shall have power to grant him a discharge and to require the cancellation and surrender of his bond or bonds; and thereupon both the receiver and the Comptroller of the Currency shall stand forever discharged from all further accountability for the debts and obligations of such association.

SEC. 196. When any person appointed receiver of an association is removed from such receivership by the Comptroller of the Currency, he may apply to the circuit court of the United States for the district in which such association was located to grant him a discharge from further accountability, and to cause his bond, or bonds, to be canceled and surrendered; and thereupon such court shall have power to summon the Comptroller of the Currency to show cause why such petition should not be granted and, after due hearing and investigation, the court may make such order as shall be deemed proper.

SEC. 197. If any person appointed receiver of an association shall die, or shall permanently absent himself from the country, or if he shall become in any other way unable to make a petition for discharge, or if he shall refuse or neglect to make such petition, such petition may be made in his behalf by his sureties, or by either of them.

SEC. 198. Whenever, after any association has been placed in the hands of a receiver by the Comptroller of the Currency, all claims against such association which have been proved and allowed, and all expenses of the receivership have been paid in full, and lawful money of the United States has been deposited for the redemption of the circulating notes of the association, the Comptroller shall call a meeting of the shareholders for the purpose of electing an agent to receive the remaining assets of the association. Such meeting shall be called by publishing notice for thirty days in a newspaper published in the place where the business of the association was carried on. (Act June 30, 1876, sec. 3.)

SEC. 199. No person shall be allowed to vote at such meeting upon any share of stock upon which the assessment has not been paid in full, or upon any share which has been surrendered to the receiver in compromise or settlement of debts to the association, but all such shares of stock shall be deducted from the whole number of shares, and a majority of such reduced number shall prevail in the election of an agent and in determining all other questions. (Act June 30, 1876, sec. 3.)

SEC. 200. The agent shall be elected by ballot; and he must receive votes representing at least a majority of the stock upon which votes can be cast. (Act June 30, 1876, sec. 3.)

SEC. 201. In selecting an agent, administrators or executors of deceased shareholders may act and sign as the decedent might have done if living, and guardians may so act and sign for their wards. (Act June 30, 1876, sec. 3.)

SEC. 202. Before any of the assets of the association are delivered to the agent some of the shareholders of the association shall execute and file a bond to the satisfaction of the Comptroller of the Currency, conditioned for the payment and discharge in full of any and every claim against the association that may thereafter be proved, before, and allowed by any competent court, and also for the faithful performance of all the duties of the trust. (Act June 30, 1876, sec. 3.)

SEC. 203. When the bond required by the preceding section has been filed, the Comptroller of the Currency and the receiver shall transfer to the agent all the undivided or uncollected or other assets and property of the association then remaining in their hands, or subject to their order or control; whereupon the Comptroller and the receiver shall be discharged and released from any and all liability to such association, and to each and all of the creditors and shareholders thereof. (Act June 30, 1876, sec. 3.)

SEC. 204. For the purpose of enabling them to make the transfer provided for by the preceding section, the Comptroller of the Currency and the receiver are severally empowered to execute any deed, assignment, or other instrument that may be necessary and proper. (Act June 30, 1876, sec. 3.)

SEC. 205. The agent selected by the shareholders is authorized to sell, compromise, or compound the debts due to the association upon the order of the United States circuit court for the district where the business of the association was carried on, or other competent court. He shall hold, control, and dispose of the assets and property of the association which he may receive for the benefit of the shareholders of such association as they, or a majority of them in value or number of shares, may direct, distributing such assets and property among such shareholders in proportion to the shares held by each, discriminating equitably between those who have paid assessments in full, those who have paid in part, and those who have not paid at all; and he may in his own name, or in the name of such association, sue and be sued, and do all other lawful acts and things necessary to finally settle and distribute the assets and property in his hands. (Act June 30, 1876, sec. 3.)

SEC. 206. Whenever the agent of the shareholders has collected and distributed all the assets of the association, he may apply to the United States circuit court for the district in which the association was located for a final discharge from further accountability; and if it shall appear that he has well and faithfully administered his trust, and that there are no further assets to be collected and distributed, the court shall grant him a discharge from all further accountability for the debts and obligations of such association. And thereafter all claims against the association shall be forever barred.

SEC. 207. When the assets of any association which has been adjudged to be insolvent by the Comptroller of the Currency, and for which a receiver has been appointed, shall prove sufficient to pay all the creditors in full, with interest, such association shall not be deemed to be dissolved; but after the receiver shall have so paid such creditors, and shall have transferred and delivered to an agent of the shareholders the undivided or uncollected assets and property of the association, the association shall be entitled to resume the business of banking, if the shareholders owning two-thirds of the capital stock shall desire so to do. Before resuming business the association shall restore the entire amount of its capital stock. But, with the approval of the Comptroller, the capital stock may be reduced in the manner prescribed in section twenty-seven of this act before it is restored.

SEC. 208. Where any association has determined to resume business as provided in the preceding section, the agent elected by the shareholders shall certify such fact to the Comptroller of the Currency, and the Comptroller, when he shall be satisfied that the association has complied with all the requirements of the preceding section, and that the shareholders have reorganized the administration thereof by the election of a board of directors, shall issue his certificate that such association is entitled to resume the business of banking.

SEC. 209. The association shall cause the certificate of the Comptroller of the Currency, issued under the preceding section, to be printed in each issue of some paper published in the place where the association is located, for at least sixty days after the issuing thereof.

CHAPTER IX.—JURISDICTION, SUITS, AND EVIDENCE.

SEC. 210. All national banking associations established under the laws of the United States shall, for the purpose of all actions by or against them, real, personal, or mixed, and all suits in equity, be deemed citizens of the States in which they are respectively located; and in such cases the circuit and district courts of the United States shall not have jurisdiction other than such as they would have in cases between the individual citizens of the same State. But the provisions of this section shall not be held to affect the jurisdiction of the courts of the United States in cases commenced by the United States, or by the direction of any officer thereof, or in cases for winding up the affairs of any such association. (Act March 3, 1887, sec. 4.)

SEC. 211. The jurisdiction for suits brought by or against any national banking association in any State, county, or municipal court, except suits between an association and the United States, or the officers and agents of the United States, shall be the same as, and not other than, the jurisdiction for suits by or against banks not organized under any law of the United States, which do or might do banking business where such national banking association may be doing business when such suits are commenced. (Act July 12, 1874, sec. 4.)

SEC. 212. All proceedings by any national banking association to enjoin the Comptroller of the Currency, under the provisions of any law relating to national banking associations, shall be had in the district where such association is located. (Sec. 736, R. S.)

SEC. 213. All suits and proceedings arising out of the provisions of law governing national banking associations, in which the United States or any of its officers or agents shall be parties, shall be conducted by the district attorneys of the several districts under the direction and supervision of the Solicitor of the Treasury. Nothing herein shall be construed to confer upon any district attorney the right to conduct any suits or proceedings on behalf of a receiver; but he may be employed by such receiver, with the approval of the Comptroller of the Currency, and, in such case, shall receive for his services the same compensation as would be paid to other counsel out of the funds of the trust. (Sec. 380, R. S.)

SEC. 214. Whenever an association against which proceedings have been instituted, on account of any alleged refusal to redeem its circulating notes, denies having failed to do so, it may, at any time within ten days after it has been notified of the appointment of an agent, as provided in section one hundred and twenty of this act, apply to the nearest circuit, district, or territorial court of the United States to enjoin further proceedings in the premises; and such court, after citing the Comptroller of the Currency to show cause why further proceedings should not be enjoined, and after the decisions of the court or finding of a jury that such association has not refused to redeem its circulating notes, when legally presented, in the lawful money of the United States, shall make an order enjoining the Comptroller, and any receiver acting under his direction, from all further proceedings on account of such alleged refusal. (Sec. 5237, R. S.)

SEC. 215. Every certificate, assignment, and conveyance executed by the Comptroller of the Currency, in pursuance of law, and sealed with his seal of office, shall be received in evidence in all places and courts; and all copies of papers in his office, certified by him and authenticated by his official seal, shall in all cases be evidence equally with the originals. An impression of such seal directly on the paper shall be as valid as if made on wax or wafer. (Sec. 884, R. S.)

SEC. 216. Copies of the organization certificate of any national banking association, duly certified by the Comptroller of the Currency, and authenticated by his seal of office, shall be evidence in all courts and places within the jurisdiction of the United States of the existence of the association, and of every matter which could be proved by the production of the original certificate. (Sec. 885, R. S.)

CHAPTER X.—TAXATION.

SEC. 217. Every association shall pay to the Treasurer of the United States, in the months of January and July, a duty of one-half of one per centum each half-year upon the average amount of its notes in circulation, after deducting the amount of such notes represented by the minimum amount of bonds which such association is required to keep on deposit with the Treasurer. (Sec. 5214, R. S.)

SEC. 218. In order to enable the Treasurer to assess the duties imposed by the preceding section, each association shall, within ten days from the first days of January and July of each year, make a return, under the oath of its president or cashier, to the Treasurer, in such form as that officer may prescribe, of the average amount of its notes in circulation for the six months next preceding the most recent first day of January or July. (Sec. 5215, R. S.)

SEC. 219. Every association which fails to make the return required by the preceding section shall be liable to a penalty of two hundred dollars, to be collected either out of the interest as it may become due such association on the bonds deposited with the Treasurer, or, at his option, in the manner in which penalties are to be collected of other corporations under the laws of the United States. (Sec. 5215, R. S.)

SEC. 220. Whenever any association fails to make the required half-yearly return, the duties to be paid by such association shall be assessed upon the amount of notes delivered to such association by the Comptroller of the Currency, after making the deduction specified in section two hundred and seventeen of this act. (Sec. 5216, R. S.)

SEC. 221. Whenever an association fails to pay the duties imposed herein, the sums due may be collected in the manner provided for the collection of United States taxes from other corporations; or the Treasurer may reserve the amount out of the interest as it may become due on the bonds deposited with him by such defaulting association. (Sec. 5217, R. S.)

SEC. 222. In all cases where an association pays in excess of what is found due from it, on account of the duty required to be paid to the Treasurer of the United States, the association may state an account therefor, which, on being certified by the Treasurer, and found correct by the First Comptroller of the Treasury, shall be refunded in the ordinary manner by warrant on the Treasury. (Sec. 5218, R. S.)

SEC. 223. Nothing in this act shall prevent all the shares in any association from being included in the valuation of the personal property of the owner or holder of such shares, in assessing taxes imposed by authority of the State within which the association is located; but the legislature of each State may determine and direct the manner and place of taxing all the shares of national banking associations located within the State, subject only to the two restrictions: first, that the taxation shall not be at a greater rate in proportion to their real value than is assessed upon the shares of other corporations engaged in receiving deposits, negotiating loans, or transacting any other business similar to that which national banks are authorized to transact, or at any rate which will amount on the aggregate of all the shares to more than is assessed upon a like amount of other capital similarly employed, whether in the hands of individuals or under the control of corporations; secondly, that the shares of any national banking association owned by non-residents of any State shall be taxed in the city or town where the association is located, and not elsewhere. Nothing herein shall be construed to exempt the real property of associations from either State, county, or municipal taxes, to the same extent, according to its value, as other real property is taxed. (Sec. 5219, R. S.)

SEC. 224. Whenever any national banking association has ceased to do business by reason of insolvency or bankruptcy, no tax shall be assessed or collected, or paid into the Treasury of the United States, on account of such association, which will diminish the assets thereof necessary for the full payment of all its depositors. (Act March 1, 1879, sec. 22.)

CHAPTER XI.—PENAL PROVISIONS.

SEC. 225. No officer acting under the provisions of this act shall countersign or deliver to any association, or to any other company or person, any circulating notes contemplated by this act, except in accordance with the true intent and meaning of its provisions. Every officer who violates this section shall be deemed guilty of a high misdemeanor, and shall be fined not more than double the amount so countersigned and delivered, and imprisoned not less than one year and not more than fifteen years. (Sec. 5187, R. S.)

SEC. 226. No association shall offer or receive United States notes or national-bank notes as security or as collateral security for any loan of money, or for a consideration agree to withhold the same from use, or offer or receive the custody or promise of custody of such notes as security or as collateral security or consideration for any loan of money. Any association offending against the provisions of this section shall be deemed guilty of a misdemeanor, and shall be fined not more than one thousand dollars and a further sum equal to one-third of the money so loaned. The officer or officers of any association who shall make any such loan shall be liable for a further sum equal to one-quarter of the money loaned. Any fine or penalty incurred by a violation of this section shall be recoverable for the benefit of the party bringing the suit. (Sec. 5207, R. S.)

SEC. 227. Every director, and every other person employed in or by any association who embezzles, abstracts, or willfully misapplies any of the moneys, funds, or credits of the association; or who, without authority from the directors, issues or puts in circulation any of the notes of the association; or who, without such authority, issues or puts forth any certificate of deposit, draws any order or bill of exchange, makes any acceptance, assigns any note, bond, draft, bill of exchange, mortgage, judgment, or decree; or who makes any false representation as to the business or resources of the association or makes any false entry in any book, report, or statement of the association, with intent, in either case, to injure or defraud the association or any other company, body politic or corporate, or any individual person, or to deceive the public, any officer of the association, or the Comptroller of the Currency, or any person appointed to examine the affairs of any such association; and every person who with like intent aids or abets any other person in any violation of this section shall be deemed guilty of a misdemeanor and shall be imprisoned not less than five years nor more than ten. (Sec. 5209, R. S.)

SEC. 228. If any person appointed or directed by the Comptroller of the Currency to examine into the affairs of any association shall make any false entry in any report or statement made by him to the Comptroller, or shall suppress or conceal any material fact, with intent to deceive that officer, such person shall be deemed guilty of a misdemeanor, and shall be imprisoned not less than five nor more than ten years.

SEC. 229. Every examiner of national banks who shall knowingly violate any confidences reposed in him by the Comptroller of the Currency, or by the officers or agents of any association, or who shall use his official position, or the information acquired in the discharge of his official duties, for any purpose not authorized by this act, shall be deemed guilty of a misdemeanor, and shall be fined not less than one thousand, and not more than five thousand, dollars, and shall be imprisoned not less than one, and not more than five, years.

SEC. 230. It shall not be lawful to design, engrave, print, or in any manner make or execute, or to utter, issue, distribute, circulate, or use, any business or professional card, notice, placard, circular, hand-bill, or advertisement, in the likeness or similitude of any circulating note or other obligation or security of any banking association organized or acting under the laws of the United States which has been or may be issued under this act, or any act of Congress, or to write, print, or otherwise impress upon any such note, obligation, or security any business or professional card, notice, or advertisement, or any notice or advertisement of any matter or thing whatever. Every person who violates this section shall be liable to a penalty of one hundred dollars, recoverable one-half to the use of the informer. (Sec. 5188, R. S.)

SEC. 231. Every person who falsely makes, forges, or counterfeits, or causes or procures to be made, forged, or counterfeited, or willingly aids or assists in falsely making, forging, or counterfeiting any note in imitation of, or purporting to be in imitation of, the circulating notes issued by any banking association now or hereafter authorized and acting under the laws of the United States; or who passes, utters, or publishes, or attempts to pass, utter, or publish, any false, forged, or counterfeited note, purporting to be issued by any such association doing a banking business, knowing the same to be falsely made, forged, or counterfeited, or who falsely alters, or causes or procures to be falsely altered, or willingly aids or assists in falsely altering, any such circulating notes, or passes, utters, or publishes, or attempts to pass, utter, or publish, as true any falsely altered or spurious circulating note issued, or purporting to have been issued, by any such banking association, knowing the same to be falsely altered or spurious, shall be imprisoned at hard labor not less than five years nor more than fifteen years, and fined not more than one thousand dollars. (Sec. 5415, R. S.)

SEC. 232. Every person, who, without authority of law, affixes any signature to any blank circulating note printed for any national banking association, or, who issues or puts in circulation any such note, knowing that the same has not been duly signed by the proper officers of the association for which it was printed, shall be imprisoned at hard labor for not less than five, and not more than fifteen years, and shall be fined not more than one thousand dollars.

SEC. 233. Every person who mutilates, cuts, defaces, disfigures, or perforates with holes, or unites or cements together, or does any other thing to any bank bill, draft, note, or other evidence of debt issued by any national banking association, or who causes or procures the same to be done, with intent to render such bank bill, draft, note, or other evidence of debt unfit to be reissued by such association, shall be liable to a penalty of fifty dollars, recoverable by the association. (Sec. 5189, R. S.)

SEC. 234. Any officer, clerk, or agent of any national banking association who shall willfully violate the provisions of section one hundred and sixty-one of this act, or who shall resort to any device, or receive any fictitious obligation, direct or collateral, in order to evade the provisions thereof, or who shall certify or accept checks before the amount thereof shall have been regularly entered to the credit of the dealer upon the books of the banking association, shall be deemed guilty of a misdemeanor, and shall, on conviction thereof in any circuit or district court of the United States, be fined not more than five thousand dollars, or shall be imprisoned not more than five years, or both, in the discretion of the court. (Act July 12, 1882, sec. 13.)

SEC. 235. All banks not organized and transacting business under the national banking laws, and all persons or corporations doing the business of bankers, brokers, or savings institutions, except savings banks authorized by Congress to use the word "national" as a part of their corporate name, are prohibited from using the word "national" as a portion of the name or title of such bank, corporation, firm, or partnership; and any violation of this prohibition shall subject the party chargeable therewith to a penalty of fifty dollars for each day during which it is permitted or repeated. And it is hereby made the duty of the United States district attorney for the judicial district in which such bank is located, or such business carried on to proceed against all persons or corporations violating this section. (Sec. 5243, R. S.)

CHAPTER XII.—GENERAL PROVISIONS.

SEC. 236. The provisions of this act, which are expressed without restrictive words as applying to "national banking associations," or to "associations," apply to all associations organized to carry on the business of banking under any act of Congress. And the word "association" means national banking association, unless otherwise specially indicated. (Sec. 5157, R. S.)

SEC. 237. Any oath required by this act may be taken before any officer who is authorized, either by the laws of the United States or by the local municipal laws, to administer oaths in the State, Territory, or District where the oath may be administered; but when any such oath is taken before an officer not using an official seal, proper evidence of the authority of such officer to administer oaths shall be filed in the office of the Comptroller of the Currency. When taken in any foreign country, any such oath may be administered by any diplomatic or consular representative of the United States.

SEC. 238. All sums of money collected for penalties under this act shall be paid into the Treasury of the United States, except as otherwise provided.

SEC. 239. In the absence or disability of the cashier all certificates and verifications required by this act to be made by him may be made by the assistant cashier, if the association has such an officer, and if it has no such officer, then by some one appointed by the directors to perform the duties of cashier.

SEC. 240. Where by this act publication is required to be made in a newspaper, it shall be made in a newspaper among those of most frequent issue and largest circulation in the place. If no newspaper is published in such place, the publication shall be made in some newspaper among those of the largest general circulation therein.

SEC. 241. This act shall be known as the National-Bank Code.

SEC. 242. All laws and parts of laws re-enacted herein are repealed; but such repeal shall not extend to any matters other than those relating to national banking associations.

SEC. 243. Congress may at any time amend, alter, or repeal this act.

LEGAL DECISIONS.

The "Digest of National-Bank Cases" presented in the Report of 1886 is reproduced in the Appendix, page 133, enlarged by the incorporation of decisions announced during the last twelve months. There will also be found in the Appendix, page 155, a digest of decisions determining questions arising in practical banking. An examination of this digest will bring out very clearly how wide apart, and even contradictory, are the decisions which have been rendered in different States in respect to substantially the same question. Considering how active and extended the interstate commercial relations now are, and how much of the business of the national banks consists of operations in exchange, arising out of transactions between the citizens of different States, it may not be out of place for the Comptroller to draw attention to the confusion and friction caused by these local differences of judicial construction.

The time may not yet be ripe for the enactment by Congress of an interstate commercial code, but such legislation appears to be in logical sequence to the establishment and extension of the national banking system and to the regulation by Congress of interstate transportation, and it would certainly be a great convenience to banks and merchants.

FOURTH.

STATE, SAVINGS, AND PRIVATE BANKS, AND LOAN AND TRUST COMPANIES.

In order to comply with the fourth requirement of section 333 of the Revised Statutes of the United States, the Comptroller has obtained, through the courtesy of the authorities of 21 States, which exact returns of this nature, all the information received by them. This information, transmitted sometimes in detail and sometimes compiled by the State officers, embraces the affairs of 1,620 incorporated institutions and 182 private banking concerns, making 1,802 in all.

In order to obtain the information about the institutions of like character in States and Territories where no returns are made to local authorities, resort was had to an extended and laborious correspondence. The names and addresses of over 4,000 concerns were collected, and to each a circular was sent asking for the information desired, and inclosing blank forms to be filled and returned. Out of the total number thus approached less than 1,400 have returned answers available for the purpose in view, and in many of these cases further correspondence was necessary in order to elicit all the information desired. In addition to this correspondence, each bank reporting its condition through the medium of State officials was written to individually, and requested to report the distribution of its stock.

The returns of 1,620 institutions obtained from the State authorities embrace a statement of the condition of 914 banks operated under State charters: aggregate capital, $114,830,660; surplus and undivided profits, $44,043,984; deposits, $390,821,688; of 42 loan and trust companies, capital, $21,858,797; surplus and undivided profits, $18,308,324; deposits, $109,799,370; of 664 savings banks, of which 580 report no capital, and 84 report capital aggregating $6,991,166. The aggregate surplus and undivided profits of the 664 savings banks is $120,187,883, and their aggregate deposits amount to $1,157,867,483. One hundred and eighty-two private banks report capital to the amount of $5,896,144, surplus and undivided profits of $1,720,192, and deposits of $18,843,930.

In response to circulars sent directly, reports of condition have been received from 1,354 concerns in States and Territories where no reports are required to be made to local authorities, viz, from 499 State banks having an aggregate capital of $26,169,717, surplus and undivided profits of $8,028,226, and deposits of $55,738,334; from 16 loan and trust companies, with capital of $14,496,972, surplus and undivided profits of $8,884,995, and deposits of $40,391,341; from 20 savings banks, with capital of $3,099,700, surplus and undivided profits of $6,712,360, and deposits of $77,868,586; and from 819 private banks with capital of $34,183,294, surplus and undivided profits of $16,443,708, and deposits of $77,736,527.

The 1,471 incorporated banks and loan and trust companies, reporting their condition officially and unofficially, have an aggregate capital of $177,356,146, and of these 1,120 furnished statements as to the distribution of their stock, aggregating $151,587,705 in par value. From examination of the details of those statements, it appears that the par value of the share ranges from $10 to $1,000, and the average par value of all the shares is $79.53.*

It was desired to make a classified report of the holdings of gold, silver, legal tenders, and national-bank notes, but as only a comparatively small number of associations outside of the national-bank system separate the items composing "cash on hand," and as the majority of the State reports simply show "cash on hand" and "cash in bank," the result is not as satisfactory as was hoped for. From the reports in which "cash on hand" is classified, it appears that the amount held by 1,360 such associations in gold coin is $27,015,952; in gold certificates, $937,710; in silver coins, $1,824,657; in silver certificates, $598,313; in specie (not classified), $13,744,873; and in legal tenders and national-bank notes, $35,462,589.

For purposes of comparison, reference is made to the following table:

STATEMENT SHOWING THE AMOUNT OF GOLD, SILVER, ETC., HELD BY NATIONAL BANKS, AND OTHER BANKING ASSOCIATIONS, AT DATE OF LATEST RETURNS.

Classification.	National banks.	1,360 other banking associations.	Total.
Gold coins	$73,782,489	$27,015,952	$100,798,441
Gold certificates	53,961,690	937,710	54,899,400
Gold clearing-house certificates	23,981,000	....	23,981,000
Silver dollars	6,683,308	} 1,824,657	} 11,223,55[illegible]
Silver, fractional	2,715,520		
Silver certificates	3,961,380	598,313	4,559,69[illegible]
National-bank notes	21,937,884	} 35,462,589	} 131,151,72[illegible]
Legal tenders	73,751,255		
Specie (not classified)	....	13,744,873	13,744,873
Total	260,774,592	79,584,094	340,358,686

* In one case shares are reported at the par value of 33⅓ cents.

In the Appendix tables will be found showing by States and Territories the condition of these banks as obtained from official sources and from banks direct (classified as unofficial returns); aggregate resources and liabilities of each class and from both sources; comparative statements of condition 1882 to 1887; distribution of shares of stock, by States and geographical divisions, and deposits in savings banks, number of depositors and average amount due each, by States, in 1885–'86, and 1886–'87.

The following tables present summaries of these matters:

AGGREGATE RESOURCES, LIABILITIES, AND CONDITION OF STATE BANKS, LOAN AND TRUST COMPANIES, AND SAVINGS AND PRIVATE BANKS, ORGANIZED UNDER STATE AND TERRITORIAL LAWS. (FROM OFFICIAL SOURCES.)

	State banks.	Loan and trust companies.	Savings banks.	Private banks.	Total.
	914 banks.	42 banks.	664 banks.	182 banks.	1,802 banks.
RESOURCES.					
Loans on real estate	$23,053,410	$11,067,315	$446,624,258	$2,089,374	$483,434,357
Loans on personal and collateral security	79,141,632	204,756	122,631,426	9,771,504	211,839,318
Loans and discounts	269,897,676	141,607,100	31,612,743	5,777,353	448,894,872
Overdrafts	1,348,583	1,318	77,357	352,393	1,779,651
United States bonds	2,292,013	28,403,836	166,219,198	89,600	197,005,547
State, county, municipal, etc., bonds	1,029,683	45,607	209,038,864	....	210,114,154
Railroad bonds and stocks	351,472	75,931	58,992,053	....	59,419,456
Bank stocks	56,910	13,301	39,778,238	....	39,848,449
All other bonds, stocks, etc	22,652,256	30,648,205	47,150,157	1,101,358	101,551,976
Due from other banks	54,184,825	14,516,239	53,139,067	4,159,814	125,999,945
Real estate, furniture, and fixtures	16,365,170	7,648,811	27,848,385	1,450,839	53,313,205
Current expenses and taxes	1,141,024	132,778	1,633,313	26,182	2,933,297
Cash and cash items	100,182,861	11,218,823	12,842,682	3,767,071	128,011,437
All other resources	13,950,459	2,383,681	70,425,624	367,535	87,136,299
Total	586,257,874	248,057,701	1,288,013,365	28,953,023	2,151,281,963
LIABILITIES.					
Capital stock	114,830,060	21,858,707	6,991,166	5,896,144	149,576,767
Surplus	34,115,460	9,594,192	114,091,457	1,681,523	159,482,632
Other undivided profits	10,828,524	8,714,132	6,096,426	38,669	25,677,751
State-bank notes	138,973	....	....	....	138,973
Dividends unpaid	473,416	525,979	122,308	....	1,121,703
Deposits	390,821,688	199,799,370	1,157,867,483	18,843,930	1,767,332,471
State, county, and municipal deposits	....	....	....	....	....
Deposits of State, county, and municipal disbursing officers	88,193	....	....	....	88,193
Due to other banks	28,949,795	1,136,023	88,588	871,897	31,046,303
Other liabilities	6,011,165	6,429,208	2,755,937	1,620,860	16,817,170
Total	586,257,874	248,057,701	1,288,013,365	28,953,023	2,151,281,963

AGGREGATE RESOURCES, LIABILITIES, AND CONDITION OF STATE BANKS, LOAN AND TRUST COMPANIES, AND SAVINGS AND PRIVATE BANKS, ORGANIZED UNDER STATE AND TERRITORIAL LAWS. (FROM UNOFFICIAL SOURCES).

	State banks.	Loan and trust companies.	Savings banks.	Private banks.	Total.
	499 banks.	16 banks.	20 banks.	819 banks.	1,354 banks.
RESOURCES.					
Loans on real estate	$5, 613, 963	$5, 202, 678	$10, 817, 408	$15, 499, 166	$37, 133, 215
Loans on personal and collateral security	41, 053, 200	36, 249, 262	22, 921, 709	54, 003, 430	154, 227, 601
Loans and discounts	16, 494, 483	1, 675, 719	6, 292, 074	18, 587, 909	43, 050, 185
Overdrafts	1, 047, 027	11, 492	12, 768	1, 506, 385	2, 577, 672
United States bonds	237, 243	383, 881	14, 029, 556	4, 265, 056	18, 915, 736
State, county, municipal, etc., bonds	612, 720	132, 541	6, 725, 951	356, 234	7, 827, 446
Railroad bonds and stocks	459, 257	7, 324, 417	15, 416, 878	2, 904, 872	26, 105, 424
Bank stocks	324, 555	119, 350	289, 442	592, 991	1, 326, 338
All other bonds, stocks, etc	5, 057, 846	5, 780, 673	3, 534, 070	5, 641, 692	20, 014, 281
Due from other banks	10, 590, 056	4, 279, 264	1, 970, 660	18, 066, 251	34, 906, 231
Real estate, furniture, and fixtures	4, 109, 932	3, 438, 461	1, 791, 365	8, 306, 977	17, 646, 735
Current expenses and taxes	982, 648	300, 731	128, 137	725, 365	2, 136, 881
Cash and cash items	10, 662, 857	5, 603, 401	5, 162, 553	11, 896, 653	33, 325, 464
All other resources	1, 278, 184	566, 026	554, 788	3, 172, 335	5, 571, 393
Total	98, 523, 971	71, 067, 956	89, 647, 359	145, 525, 316	404, 764, 602
LIABILITIES.					
Capital stock	26, 169, 717	14, 496, 972	3, 099, 700	34, 183, 294	77, 949, 683
Surplus	4, 404, 260	6, 247, 601	5, 603, 853	10, 556, 542	26, 812, 256
Other undivided profits	3, 623, 966	2, 637, 394	1, 108, 507	5, 887, 166	13, 257, 033
State bank notes	89, 983	....	....	2, 155	92, 138
Dividends unpaid	276, 333	55, 276	71, 078	170, 055	572, 742
Deposits	55, 738, 334	40, 391, 341	77, 868, 586	77, 736, 527	251, 734, 788
State, county, and municipal deposits	1, 132, 109	38, 084	....	946, 192	2, 116, 385
Deposits of State, county, and municipal disbursing officers	408, 278	....	....	1, 158, 905	1, 567, 183
Due to other banks	3, 495, 619	4, 470, 874	2, 200	4, 941, 254	12, 909, 947
Other liabilities	3, 185, 372	2, 730, 414	1, 893, 435	9, 943, 226	17, 752, 447
Total	98, 523, 971	71, 067, 956	89, 647, 359	145, 525, 316	404, 764, 602

AGGREGATE RESOURCES, LIABILITIES, AND CONDITION OF ALL STATE BANKS, LOAN AND TRUST COMPANIES, AND SAVINGS AND PRIVATE BANKS, ORGANIZED UNDER STATE AND TERRITORIAL LAWS.

	Official.	Unofficial.	Total.
	1,802 banks.	1,354 banks.	3,156 banks.
RESOURCES.			
Loans on real estate	$483, 434, 357	$37, 133, 215	$520, 567, 572
Loans on personal and collateral security	211, 839, 318	154, 227, 601	366, 066, 919
Loans and discounts	448, 894, 872	43, 050, 185	491, 945, 057
Overdrafts	1, 779, 651	2, 577, 672	4, 357, 323
United States bonds	197, 005, 547	18, 915, 736	215, 921, 283
State, county, municipal, etc., bonds	210, 114, 154	7, 827, 446	217, 941, 600
Railroad bonds and stocks	59, 419, 456	26, 105, 424	85, 524, 880
Bank stocks	39, 848, 449	1, 326, 338	41, 174, 787
All other bonds, stocks, etc	101, 551, 976	20, 014, 281	121, 566, 257
Due from other banks	125, 999, 945	34, 906, 231	160, 906, 176
Real estate, furniture, and fixtures	53, 313, 205	17, 646, 735	70, 959, 940
Current expenses and taxes	2, 933, 297	2, 136, 881	5, 070, 178
Cash and cash items	128, 011, 437	33, 325, 464	161, 336, 901
All other resources	87, 136, 299	5, 571, 393	92, 707, 692
Total	2, 151, 281, 963	404, 764, 602	2, 556, 046, 565
LIABILITIES.			
Capital stock	149, 576, 767	77, 949, 683	227, 526, 450
Surplus	150, 482, 632	26, 812, 256	186, 294, 888
Other undivided profits	25, 677, 751	13, 257, 033	38, 934, 784
State bank notes	138, 973	92, 138	231, 111
Dividends unpaid	1, 121, 703	572, 742	1, 694, 445
Deposits	1, 767, 332, 471	251, 734, 788	2, 019, 067, 259
State, county, and municipal deposits	....	2, 116, 385	2, 116, 385
Deposits of State, county, and municipal dis. officers	88, 193	1, 567, 183	1, 655, 376
Due to other banks	31, 046, 303	12, 909, 947	43, 956, 250
Other liabilities	16, 817, 170	17, 752, 447	34, 569, 617
Total	2, 151, 281, 963	404, 764, 602	2, 556, 046, 565

NUMBER, CAPITAL STOCK, SURPLUS AND UNDIVIDED PROFITS, AND DEPOSITS OF STATE BANKS, 1886-'87.

States, etc.	Number.	Official.		
		Capital.	Surplus and undivided profits.	Deposits.
New Hampshire	1	$50,000	$15,216	$35,342
Rhode Island	10	1,766,685	160,775	1,177,883
Connecticut	8	2,390,000	497,508	3,407,182
New York State	71	8,428,000	5,235,075	37,688,748
New York City	31	14,712,700	8,937,631	112,699,172
New Jersey	8	1,209,350	492,120	3,284,201
Pennsylvania	80	7,888,473	2,662,600	29,117,308
Maryland	8	1,979,390	460,072	3,799,136
North Carolina	11	691,410	228,706	1,424,783
Kentucky	71	11,555,686	2,891,327	16,832,350
Missouri	212	11,626,403	6,596,349	49,173,704
Ohio	46	3,079,695	585,859	10,314,788
Indiana	32	1,676,600	379,510	3,126,840
Michigan	62	4,556,150	1,380,101	26,069,050
Wisconsin	56	3,350,340	1,121,834	19,960,417
Iowa	65	3,570,843	694,799	5,747,280
Minnesota	54	5,228,000	1,193,125	14,429,516
California	88	31,061,935	11,402,287	52,513,971
Total	914	114,830,660	44,943,984	390,821,688

States.	Number.	Unofficial.		
		Capital.	Surplus and undivided profits.	Deposits.
Delaware	2	$356,000	$51,143	$497,427
Virginia	39	1,900,255	650,713	5,956,769
West Virginia	14	819,855	304,169	2,897,123
South Carolina	10	788,704	365,767	4,121,254
Georgia	16	2,738,850	1,257,002	4,958,365
Florida	6	290,100	376,590	830,108
Alabama	7	735,000	228,142	934,260
Mississippi	9	759,650	97,534	1,102,906
Louisiana	5	2,017,300	548,693	5,000,873
Texas	9	761,098	212,761	976,851
Arkansas	6	265,000	51,433	593,264
Tennessee	27	2,924,254	633,688	5,590,552
Illinois	48	1,655,500	890,495	5,178,069
Kansas	149	6,618,545	1,370,121	9,151,026
Nebraska	140	2,864,606	795,997	4,836,266
Colorado	8	505,000	168,555	2,270,135
Oregon	4	170,000	25,423	173,390
Total	499	26,169,717	8,028,226	55,738,334

NUMBER, CAPITAL STOCK, SURPLUS AND UNDIVIDED PROFITS, AND DEPOSITS OF LOAN AND TRUST COMPANIES, 1886-'87.

NUMBER, CAPITAL STOCK, SURPLUS AND UNDIVIDED PROFITS, AND DEPOSITS OF LOAN AND TRUST COMPANIES, 1886-'87.—Continued.

States, etc.	Number.	Unofficial.		
		Capital.	Surplus and undivided profits.	Deposits.
Philadelphia	10	$12,241,972	$8,524,447	$40,244,593
Missouri	2	1,200,000	50,850	42,536
Nebraska	4	1,055,000	309,698	104,212
	16	14,496,972	8,884,995	40,391,341

NUMBER, CAPITAL STOCK, SURPLUS AND UNDIVIDED PROFITS, AND DEPOSITS OF SAVINGS BANKS, 1886-'87.

States, etc.	Number.	Official.		
		Capital.	Surplus and undivided profits.	Deposits.
Maine	54	....	$2,199,862	$37,215,072
New Hampshire	66	....	4,604,080	50,822,762
Vermont	28	$400,000	776,112	15,587,050
Massachusetts	172	....	12,928,350	291,107,900
Rhode Island	37	....	2,797,248	53,284,821
Connecticut	85	....	4,845,631	97,424,820
New York	115	....	85,633,329	482,486,730
New Jersey	25	....	2,412,877	27,482,135
Maryland	2	30,105	14,879	204,125
District of Columbia	1	....	11,464	834,524
North Carolina	1	5,991	374	11,307
Ohio	4	....	388,326	15,065,059
Indiana	6	....	212,550	2,312,013
Iowa	37	2,128,693	492,204	9,909,019
Minnesota	7	150,000	138,908	3,891,053
California	24	4,216,377	2,731,089	70,077,893
Total	664	*6,991,166	120,187,883	1,157,867,483

States, etc.	Number.	Unofficial.		
		Capital.	Surplus and undivided profits.	Deposits.
Philadelphia	5	$444,700	$3,811,224	$42,219,099
Delaware	2	....	269,740	2,771,392
Maryland	8	....	1,142,697	18,816,837
Chicago	5	2,655,000	1,488,699	14,061,258
Total	20	3,099,700	6,712,360	77,868,586

* Only 84 savings banks report capital.

NUMBER, CAPITAL STOCK, SURPLUS AND UNDIVIDED PROFITS, AND DEPOSITS OF PRIVATE BANKS, 1886-'87.

NUMBER, CAPITAL STOCK, SURPLUS AND UNDIVIDED PROFITS, AND DEPOSITS OF PRIVATE BANKS, 1886-'87—Continued.

States.	Number.	Unofficial.		
		Capital.	Surplus and undivided profits.	Deposits.
Massachusetts	5	$231,000	$200,068	$827,880
Connecticut	4	78,000	43,821	387,378
New York	41	1,218,272	843,811	6,013,485
New Jersey	3	169,325	102,125	754,489
Pennsylvania	46	1,571,351	690,000	8,990,050
Maryland	3	16,000	1,254	47,859
District of Columbia	1	33,000	13,118	79,490
North Carolina	2	40,000	22,090	112,535
South Carolina	3	87,850	31,330	51,161
Georgia	12	740,770	179,050	372,785
Florida	2	53,000	5,381	228,129
Alabama	5	312,000	2,514,632	1,471,209
Mississippi	2	120,000	50,976	129,957
Louisiana	2	33,000	8,925	52,285
Texas	18	1,709,809	220,458	1,916,563
Kentucky	15	631,700	173,063	1,406,540
Ohio	77	2,949,975	1,213,579	11,039,045
Indiana	44	2,371,142	419,443	6,319,457
Illinois	99	4,246,028	4,233,693	15,128,207
Michigan	55	994,077	259,466	2,914,008
Iowa	139	5,130,606	1,265,206	6,143,252
Minnesota	40	2,895,615	348,551	2,642,758
Kansas	55	2,852,934	676,101	2,426,726
Nebraska	34	1,256,262	267,652	1,538,131
Colorado	8	221,300	20,095	990,961
Nevada	2	108,150	22,215	93,247
Oregon	3	186,282	413,409	818,181
Dakota	77	2,019,189	364,920	1,155,693
Idaho	2	127,660	156,751	54,016
New Mexico	2	130,000	26,936	194,919
Utah	7	995,907	1,125,391	1,818,718
Washington	2	225,000	300,039	513,310
Wyoming	7	338,000	92,916	730,874
Arizona	2	90,000	108,329	344,229
Total	810	34,183,204	16,443,708	77,736,527

NUMBER, CAPITAL STOCK, SURPLUS AND UNDIVIDED PROFITS, AND DEPOSITS OF STATE, ETC., BANKS, 1886-'87.

	Number.	Official.		
		Capital.	Surplus and undivided profits.	Deposits.
State banks	914	$114,830,660	$44,943,984	$390,821,688
Loan and trust companies	42	21,858,797	18,308,324	199,799,370
Savings banks	664	6,991,166	120,187,883	1,157,867,483
Private banks	182	5,896,144	1,720,192	18,843,930
Total	1,802	149,576,767	185,160,383	1,767,332,471

	Number.	Unofficial.		
		Capital.	Surplus and undivided profits.	Deposits.
State banks	499	$26,169,717	$8,028,226	$55,738,334
Loan and trust companies	16	14,406,972	8,884,995	40,391,341
Savings banks	20	3,099,700	6,712,360	77,868,586
Private banks	810	34,183,204	16,443,708	77,736,527
Total	1,354	77,919,683	40,069,289	251,734,788

DISTRIBUTION, NUMBER, AND AVERAGE PAR VALUE OF SHARES OF STOCK OF 1,120 INCORPORATED BANKS IN THE UNITED STATES ON JUNE 30, 1887.

	Number.
Number of shares of stock held by—	
State residents	1,669,070 15/16
Non-State residents	237,062 9/16
Same, in detail, held by—	
Natural persons	1,839,886
Religious, charitable, and educational institutions	9,472
Municipal corporations	1,625
Savings banks, loan and trust and insurance companies	41,389½
All other corporations	18,761
Total issued	1,906,133½
Average par value of share	$79.53
Number of shareholders—	
Natural persons	46,553
Corporations	824

	Number.
Number of shareholders—	
Resident	39,477
Non-resident	7,900
Total	47,377
Number of shareholders owning specific amounts—	
Owning shares to the par value of $1,000 and less	24,609
Owning shares to the par value of over $1,000 and less than $5,000	14,812
Owning shares to the par value of $5,000 and less than $30,000	7,397
Owning shares to the par value of $30,000 and over	559
Total	47,377

A table in the Appendix, page 175, shows, by States and Territories, the estimated population of each, and the aggregate capital, surplus, undivided profits, and individual deposits of national and State banks, loan and trust companies, and savings and private banks in the United States on June 1, 1887; the average of these per capita of population, and the per capita averages of such resources in each class of banks, from which it appears that the estimated population of the United States, June 1, 1887, is 59,893,000; total banking funds amount to $4,563,192,203, which is an average of $76.19. The per capita averages of such resources in each class of banks are: National banks, $34.91; State banks, $10.69; loan and trust companies, $5.07; savings banks, $22.92; and private banks, $2.58.

The Comptroller is indebted for the estimates of population to Mr. E. B. Elliott, Government Actuary, whose national reputation for skill and accuracy in reaching conclusions by mathematical methods is the surest guaranty that the figures given are as nearly correct as possible.

The following table, stating, by geographical divisions, the number of private banks in the United States, with the aggregate amount of their capital, deposits, and investments in United States bonds, for the six months ending May 31, 1882, has appeared in previous Reports. It is repeated for the reason that it has been impossible to obtain similar information from any official source since the date above mentioned:

Geographical divisions.	No. of banks.	Capital.	Deposits.	Invested in U. S. bonds.
New England States	94	$6,215,637	$6,568,310	$963,958
Middle States	967	62,418,206	112,690,636	9,227,728
Southern States	289	6,334,090	20,675,301	107,167
Western States and Territories	2,062	30,308,300	149,023,311	3,298,990
United States	3,412	105,276,233	288,957,578	13,597,843

FIFTH.

NAMES AND COMPENSATION OF OFFICERS AND CLERKS IN THE OFFICE OF THE COMPTROLLER OF THE CURRENCY, OCTOBER 31, 1887.

Names.	Grade.	Salary.
William L. Trenholm	Comptroller	$5,000
Jesse D. Abrahams	Deputy Comptroller	2,800
George M. Coffin	Chief of division	2,200
John J. Crawford	do	2,200
Alonzo B. Dickerson	do	2,200
Robert P. Mayfield	do	2,200
David L. Perkins	Superintendent	2,000
Finis E. Marshall	Teller	2,000
Theodore O. Ebaugh	Book-keeper	2,000
Charles J. Stoddard	Assistant book-keeper	2,000
Charles E. Brayton	Fourth-class clerk	1,800
Edward A. Demaray	do	1,800
Watson W. Eldridge	do	1,800
John A. Hebrew	do	1,800
George T. May	do	1,800
Edmund E. Schreiner	do	1,800
Walter Taylor	do	1,800
Charles McC. Taylor	do	1,800
Thomas P. Kane	Stenographer	1,600
Harriet M. Black	Third-class clerk	1,600
Fernando C. Cate	do	1,600
Sarah F. Fitzgerald	do	1,600
Willis J. Fowler	do	1,600
William H. Heald	do	1,600
Washington K. McCoy	do	1,600
Isaac C. Miller	do	1,600
Joseph K. Miller	do	1,600
William D. Swan*	do	1,600
Ephraim S. Wilcox	do	1,600
George H. Wood	do	1,600
William E. Colladay	Second-class clerk	1,400
Julia R. Donoho	do	1,400
R. LeRoy Livingston	do	1,400
Edward S. May	do	1,400
Mary L. McCormick	do	1,400
Morris M. Ogden	do	1,400
Margaretta L. Simpson	do	1,400
Arthur M. Wheeler	do	1,400
Eveline C. Bates	First-class clerk	1,200
Willard E. Buell	do	1,200
Eliza R. Hyde	do	1,200
Carrie L. Pennock	do	1,200
Eliza M. Peters	do	1,200
Charles A. Stewart	do	1,200
Therese E. Tilley	do	1,200
Frederick Widdows	do	1,200
Eliza M. Barker	Clerk	1,000
Alice M. Kennedy	do	1,000
Lafayette J. Garner	Engineer	1,000
Thomas H. Austin	Clerk	900
Margaret L. Browne	do	900
Louisa Campbell	do	900
Sarah M. Cartwright	do	900
Virginia H. Clarke	do	900
Sarah G. Clemens	do	900
Geraldine Clifford	do	900
Richard W. Comly	do	900
Mary L. Conrad	do	900
Talma Drew	do	900
Amanda W. Doty	do	900
Henry S. Goodall	do	900
Margaret E. Gooding	do	900
Lucretia W. Knowlton	do	900
Emma Lafayette	do	900
Edward H. Latch	do	900
Annie W. Lockhart	do	900
Maggie B. Miller	do	900
James D. Moler	do	900
Mary E. Oliver	do	900
Carrie B. Pumphrey	do	900
Marie Richardson	do	900
Francis M. Richardson	do	900
Hannah Sanderson	do	900
Eliza A. Saunders	do	900
Fayette C. Snead	do	900

* Additional as bond clerk, $200.

NAMES AND COMPENSATION OF OFFICERS AND CLERKS IN THE OFFICE OF THE COMPTROLLER OF THE CURRENCY, OCTOBER 31, 1887—Continued.

Names.	Grade.	Salary.
Mathilda C. Stoffregen	Clerk	$900
Elise K. Taylor	do	900
Sarah A. W. Tiffey	do	900
Caius E. Triplet	do	900
Julia C. Townsend	do	900
Anna M. Whiteside	do	900
Glendie B. Young	do	900
Morris A. Moore	Messenger	840
Philo L. Bush	Assistant messenger	720
William Griffiths	do	720
Silas Holmes	do	720
Langston W. Allen	Watchman	720
W. Frank Robey	do	720
John A. McDonald	Fireman	720
Bessie P. Cowell	Laborer	600
Harry C. Derby	do	600
Lambert A. Whiteley	do	600

EXPENSES OF THE OFFICE OF THE COMPTROLLER OF THE CURRENCY FOR THE YEAR ENDING JUNE 30, 1887.

For special dies, plates, printing, etc	$31,454.10
For salaries	97,653.00
For salaries, reimbursable by national banks	15,047.97

The contingent expenses of the office are not paid by the Comptroller, but from the general appropriation for contingent expenses of the Treasury Department; no separate account of them is kept.

ORGANIZATION AND EXPENSES OF THE BUREAU OF THE CURRENCY.

One subject of material importance to the banks and to the public is the more complete organization and better equipment of the office of the Comptroller of the Currency.

Each year greater numbers of new banks are organized, involving increased correspondence, explanation, and book-keeping, and more packages of currency to be kept safely; each year the number of banks in operation grows larger, calling for a wider scope of supervision, more reports to be examined, corrected, and compiled, more letters from banks to be received, more letters to be written to banks, more examiners to be employed, and more correspondence maintained with them.

The number of receiverships also increases annually, causing more work, more correspondence, and more book-keeping. The labor and anxiety of continuous and simultaneous attention to twenty-eight active receiverships can not be described. Almost every one of them is involved in serious litigation, while in many of the cases pending not only large amounts of money and great interests, but important principles, are at stake.

On the other hand, no relief comes from the reduction of circulation, for the work in the divisions of issue and redemption varies with the number of banks and not with the amount of bonds deposited or of circulation issued, while every change in either bonds or circulation increases the work in these or other divisions. Changes of bonds and circulation become more frequent annually.

Without entering into wearisome details, it must be obvious that the growth of the national-bank system must impose upon the Comptroller and the officers and clerks who assist him labors and responsibilities which increase year by year, and if the annual reports made to Congress are compared with each other it will be found that they are constantly becoming not only more voluminous but more complex in their contents, and more exacting upon those charged with their preparation. Not only is this the case, but the growing complexity and amplitude both of mass and of detail which mark the annual Reports also reflect a corresponding augmentation of mass and differentiation of detail in the daily work of the Bureau.

The volume and the minute particularity of the contents of these Reports imply antecedent operations of investigation, collocation, arrangement, analysis, compilation, and statistical interpretation, which were not possible when the national-bank system was less fully developed, and which can not be adequately described.

In order that the present work of the Bureau may be properly performed the following changes are essential:

1. The Deputy Comptroller should have a salary of $3,500. No less sum can be depended upon to secure or to permanently retain any one entirely qualified for the position.

2. There should be provided for the Bureau a responsible legal adviser, with such clerks and books as may be necessary to the proper examination of the questions that are daily presented in almost every branch of commercial law.

3. There should be added to the four divisions now existing a division of archives and statistics.

Provision should be made by appropriation for an annual conference in Washington of all examiners of national banks, for the employment of supervising examiners, as recommended elsewhere, for such traveling expenses as may be incurred by the Comptroller or Deputy Comptroller in visiting different sections of the country in connection with the banks and banking interests there, and for the accumulation of a library of standard books of reference on subjects related to banking and financial legislation and administration.

In order that some measure of justice may be done to the officers and clerks of the Bureau for the assiduity and intelligence by which alone it has been possible to accomplish the constantly increasing tasks devolved upon them, the subjoined tables are respectfully submitted.

The first table has been made up from a report lately prepared for a select committee of the Senate, and it shows the number of letters and papers handled, and the value of circulating notes and of incomplete currency passing in and out of the Bureau during each of the last three years.

The second table shows the number and compensation of officers, clerks, messengers, and laborers employed in the Bureau, and the total salaries during each year from 1863 to 1887, inclusive.

NUMBER AND VALUE OF ITEMS REPRESENTING CLERICAL WORK IN THE OFFICE OF THE COMPTROLLER OF THE CURRENCY DURING EACH OF THE YEARS 1884, 1885, AND 1886.

Number of—	1884.	1885.	1886.
Papers and letters received and filed	161,021	163,818	174,826
Papers and letters examined	46,088	50,237	49,154
Papers and letters copied	6,564	5,271	5,143
Papers prepared and issued	195,113	246,313	278,602
Papers prepared for Bureau use	151,347	192,040	209,292
Letters written, copied, and indexed	74,701	80,187	74,754
Certificates issued under seal	4,963	7,740	4,903
Packages of mutilated currency received, contents counted, and certified for destruction	42,815	63,878	90,259
Packages of incomplete currency on hand at the end of each year	4,449	4,610	4,814
Packages of incomplete currency received from Bureau of Engraving and Printing, examined, and counted	3,552	3,960	2,250
Packages of incomplete currency counted for issue, strapped, and labeled	31,914	42,127	53,003
Packages of incomplete currency withdrawn from vault, opened, resealed, and replaced	33,066	43,332	53,506
Packages of incomplete currency made up for shipment, sealed, addressed, and delivered to mail or express	27,419	30,408	43,009
Packages of bonds received, counted, and disposed of	1,345	451	1,189
Packages of bonds made up, sealed, and delivered to mail or express	1,005	210	930
Entries in ledgers, journals, and other books of record	523,879	657,228	758,319
Total	1,312,304	1,597,840	1,813,955

Value of—	1884.	1885.	1886.
Packages of mutilated currency received, contents counted, and certified for destruction	$110,529,684.50	$104,266,700.00	$78,375,583.50
Packages of incomplete currency on hand at the end of each year	70,384,220.00	75,125,200.00	59,405,780.00
Packages of incomplete currency received from Bureau of Engraving and Printing, examined and counted	83,496,110.00	102,360,620.00	40,759,460.00
Packages of incomplete currency withdrawn from vault, opened, resealed, and replaced*	523,104,120.00	701,545,080.00	660,261,040.00
Packages of incomplete currency made up for shipment, counted, strapped, sealed, addressed, and delivered to mail or express	80,325,920.00	83,666,300.00	55,518,170.00
Packages of bonds received, counted, and disposed of	114,711,250.00	47,311,700.00	145,736,000.00
Bonds on deposit with United States Treasurer to secure circulation December 31, each year	318,655,050.00	306,008,750.00	220,438,350.00
Bonds deposited to secure circulation during each year	43,450,050.00	17,333,000.00	35,582,500.00
Bonds withdrawn from deposit each year	72,333,200.00	29,979,300.00	112,152,900.00
Total	1,416,989,604.50	1,467,605,740.00	1,417,232,783.50

*Estimated by number of packages withdrawn and deposited, as compared with average value per package at time of vault-test by committee.

COMPARATIVE STATEMENT OF NUMBER OF BANKS ORGANIZED AND NUMBER UNDER SUPERVISION, UP TO THE END OF EACH FISCAL YEAR FROM 1863 TO 1887, TOGETHER WITH THE NUMBER AND COMPENSATION OF THE OFFICERS, CLERKS, ETC., IN THE BUREAU OF THE CURRENCY FOR EACH YEAR.

Years.	Number of banks organized up to October 31 in each year.	Number of banks in operation and in the hands of receivers on October 31 of each year.	Number of officers, clerks, messengers, etc.	Amount of salaries for fiscal years.	Additional salaries 20 per cent., and reimbursed by national banks.	Total.
1863	117	117	8	$1,991.17	....	....
1864	561	561	42	26,792.89	....	....
1865	1,001	1,600	85	58,374.16	....	....
1866	1,665	1,652	73	86,826.01	....	....
1867	1,673	1,649	68	109,600.00	$14,749.28	$124,349.28
1868	1,685	1,643	74	89,335.20	....	....
1869	1,694	1,635	68	97,404.20	....	....
1870	1,731	1,657	78	86,940.12	....	....
1871	1,886	1,801	87	101,400.00	....	....
1872	2,061	1,965	84	101,140.00	....	....
1873	2,129	2,012	94	112,800.00	....	....
1874	2,200	2,063	98	118,500.00	....	....
1875	2,307	2,132	130	120,680.00	12,410.80	133,090.80
1876	2,343	2,136	130	122,605.95	33,675.76	156,281.71
1877	2,372	2,130	99	109,391.93	25,457.22	134,849.15
1878	2,400	2,127	101	104,820.00	22,297.28	127,117.28
1879	2,438	2,131	99	103,280.00	22,219.97	125,499.97
1880	2,495	2,181	91	101,400.00	22,205.20	123,105.20
1881	2,581	2,155	96	101,383.64	16,745.80	118,129.44
1882	2,808	2,304	93	101,398.88	16,641.50	118,040.38
1883	3,070	2,620	93	102,397.08	16,792.56	119,189.64
1884	3,201	2,771	92	102,151.01	16,567.48	118,718.49
1885	3,406	2,831	90	101,674.47	16,756.43	118,430.90
1886	3,581	2,981	80	96,494.67	13,742.99	110,237.66
1887	3,805	3,180	92	97,653.00	15,047.97	112,700.97

No words can add force to the testimony of these figures, and yet they represent only imperfectly the annually growing disparity between the work accomplished in the Bureau and the number and compensation of those upon whom the burdens and the responsibilities rest.

If the considerations here presented should be deemed insufficient to justify more liberal appropriations, there is the further reason that without more enlarged facilities the valuable information continually accumulating will soon get beyond the present overtaxed capacity of the Bureau, and its value will become lost.

INFORMATION.

Section 333 of the Revised Statutes of the United States, in prescribing the scope of the annual Report to be made by the Comptroller of the Currency, imposes upon that officer the further duty of submitting to Congress such other information in relation to the banks as in his judgment may be useful. The following information is accordingly submitted:

The following table gives the number of national banks organized in each State and Territory during the year ending October 31, 1887, with their aggregate capital, bonds, and circulation:

States and Territories.	Number of banks.	Capital.	Bonds.	Circulation.
Maine	2	$100,000	$25,000	$22,500
Massachusetts	1	100,000	25,000	22,500
Connecticut	2	200,000	50,000	45,000
Division No. 1	5	400,000	100,000	90,000
New York	8	4,065,000	191,500	172,350
New Jersey	7	825,000	206,250	185,625
Pennsylvania	12	2,135,000	373,800	336,400
Division No. 2	27	7,025,000	771,550	694,375
Delaware	1	50,000	12,500	11,250
Maryland	3	150,000	37,500	33,750
District of Columbia	1	250,000	50,000	45,000
West Virginia	1	50,000	15,000	13,500
Division No. 3	6	500,000	115,000	103,500
North Carolina	1	50,000	12,500	11,250
South Carolina	1	50,000	12,500	11,250
Georgia	4	400,000	100,000	90,000
Florida	2	100,000	25,000	22,500
Alabama	8	1,409,000	252,500	227,250
Mississippi	4	300,000	75,000	67,500
Louisiana	4	400,000	100,000	90,000
Arkansas	2	150,000	37,500	33,750
Texas	18	2,140,000	400,000	414,000
Tennessee	6	1,200,000	187,500	168,750
Division No. 4	50	6,199,000	1,202,500	1,136,250
Ohio	11	2,030,000	382,500	344,250
Indiana	2	100,000	25,000	22,500
Illinois	12	1,500,000	304,500	274,050
Michigan	4	800,000	102,500	92,250
Wisconsin	8	580,000	145,000	130,500
Division No. 5	37	5,010,000	959,500	863,550
Iowa	5	350,000	87,500	78,750
Minnesota	4	1,450,000	162,500	146,250
Missouri	7	3,100,000	212,500	191,250
Kansas	41	3,392,000	760,500	684,450
Nebraska	13	710,000	177,500	159,750
Division No. 6	70	9,002,000	1,400,500	1,260,450
Colorado	4	350,000	87,500	78,750
Arizona	1	100,000	25,000	22,500
California	7	750,000	187,500	168,750
Oregon	5	310,000	77,500	69,750
Division No. 7	17	1,510,000	377,500	339,750
Dakota	9	500,000	125,000	112,500
Montana	1	50,000	12,500	11,250
Washington	2	250,000	62,500	56,250
Wyoming	1	100,000	25,000	22,500
Division No. 8	13	900,000	225,000	202,500
Grand total	225	30,546,000	5,211,550	4,690,375

Eight national banks, with an aggregate capital of $1,550,000, failed and were placed in the hands of receivers during the year, as is shown in the following tabulated statement, to which is appended an account of the chief cause of failure in each case:

STATEMENT OF BANKS FAILED DURING THE YEAR, THEIR CAPITAL, SURPLUS, AND LIABILITIES ACCORDING TO LAST REPORT OF CONDITION.

Name and location of bank.	Date of authority to commence business.	Date of failure.	Receiver appointed.	As shown at date of last report of condition in each case.			
				Capital.	Surplus and undivided profits.	Other liabilities.*	Date of last report of condition.
First National Bank, Pine Bluff, Ark	Sept. 18, 1882	1886. Nov. 15	1886. Nov. 20	$50,000	$22,864	$184,697	1886. Oct. 7
Palatka National Bank, Palatka, Fla	Nov. 20, 1884	1887. May 30	1887. June 3	50,000	1,882	14,051	1887. May 13
Fidelity National Bank, Cincinnati, Ohio	Feb. 27, 1886	June 20	June 27	1,000,000	129,283	5,867,064	May 13
Henrietta National Bank, Henrietta, Tex	Aug. 8, 1883	July 25	Aug. 17	50,000	12,328	99,598	May 13
National Bank of Sumter, S. C	Nov. 26, 1883	Aug. 22	Aug. 24	50,000	10,774	112,763	Aug. 1
First National Bank, Dansville, N. Y†	Sept. 4, 1863	Aug. 25	Sept. 8	50,000	23,863	87,852	Aug. 1
First National Bank, Corry, Pa†	Dec. 6, 1864	Sept. 16	Oct. 11	100,000	10,314	172,857	Aug. 1
Stafford National Bank, Stafford Springs, Conn†	Jan. 7, 1865	Oct. 12	Oct. 17	200,000	25,048	293,476	Aug. 1
Total				1,550,000	236,356	6,832,358	

* Total, as per report, except capital, surplus, circulation, undivided profits, and unpaid dividends.
† Extended.

The First National Bank of Pine Bluff, Ark., failed because of the failure of its president, who was engaged in buying and shipping cotton on a scale too extensive for his means. To handle this business he made use of the bank, and at the date of failure he was maker or indorser of more than two-thirds of its bills receivable, the only security for which consisted of mortgages on land, crops, and plantation chattels. He had also undertaken a railroad enterprise which he was unable to carry through, and the bank had a great deal of money locked up in the stock and bonds of the railroad company. A large amount of bills receivable having been rediscounted, and the president being unable, through lack of railroad transportation, to make prompt shipments of cotton to meet their maturities, the bank suspended. No run was made by the depositors. A dividend of 25 per cent. was paid to the creditors of the bank, about five months after date of failure, on claims aggregating $64,956.08.

The Palatka National Bank, of Palatka, Fla., suffered an impairment of capital through losses attributable mainly to the gradual withdrawal of deposits by customers who were moving out of the locality, general stagnation of business, and a marked decline in the enterprises of the town. The directors made an abortive effort to place the bank in voluntary liquidation, but the requisite stockholders' vote could not be obtained. In less than sixty days after appointment of the receiver the creditors were paid principal and interest in full on claims aggregating $9,379.69, and the remaining assets of the bank have been turned over to an agent of the stockholders, under the provisions of the act approved June 30, 1876.

The Fidelity National Bank of Cincinnati, Ohio, was reduced to insolvency through the reckless management of its board of directors, who suffered certain of their number to divert its funds and to prostitute its credit in support of a speculation in wheat in Chicago during the months of March, April, May, and June of this year. In the progress of this nefarious enterprise many provisions of the national banking laws were violated, and the public was deceived by false statements as to the capital, surplus, and business of the association. While entertaining grave apprehensions as to the management of this bank, the Comptroller had no evidence, either from its reports of condition or from an examination made in March, to justify any measure on his part likely to discredit it, or to embarrass its directors in the conduct of its affairs.

On June 20 the Comptroller received notice of the protest in New York of $200,000 of its drafts, and immediately notified the examiner, who had been waiting in Cincinnati and the vicinity for several weeks to act upon any information which should justify a re-examination. He entered the bank immediately, and finding it insolvent took possession under instructions. The doors were not opened on the morning of the 21st, and on June 27 a receiver was appointed and took charge of its affairs. Upon obtaining evidence sufficient for the purpose, the Comptroller caused proceedings to be taken under section 5239, Revised Statutes, to dissolve the corporation and to have its franchises declared forfeited. A decree to this effect was made July 12 in the United States circuit court for the southern district of Ohio. No appeal was taken. Upon the basis thus prepared suit has been brought by the receiver against every director implicated in the violations of law, and such damages as the courts will grant, and the personal means of the directors can be made to supply, will be collected and applied to the relief of those who have suffered loss or damage. A dividend was declared on October 31 of 25 per cent. on all claims proved and allowed, amounting to $2,386,569.20.

A very large number of accounts with corresponding banks are still unadjusted, and claims are in dispute aggregating about $1,000,000 of which it is feared the larger part can be settled only by litigation. Both the examiner and the receiver were early instructed to supply to the United States district attorney for the southern district of Ohio all evidence they could find indicating criminal misconduct on the part of any of the directors or officers of the bank, and arrests were promptly made upon the evidence furnished by them. The Attorney-General joined with the Comptroller in the employment of special means for detecting the persons implicated in the misappropriation of the bank's funds, and the Solicitor of the Treasury, the district attorney, the Chief of the Secret Service Division of the Treasury, and the officers detailed for the work entered heartily and efficiently into all measures for discovering and establishing their guilt. Indictments have been found against several persons, and their trials will shortly take place. It is to be hoped that this conspicuous instance of fraudulent conduct and lax administration may furnish occasion for establishing a just degree of responsibility on the part of directors.

The Henrietta National Bank of Henrietta, Tex., became involved in the cattle business of its president and four other directors, who constitute a majority of the board, and own more than half the capital stock of the bank. In the names of their several firms these five directors had each borrowed from the bank amounts largely in excess of the limit prescribed by law, and their aggregate indebtedness exceeded the entire capital stock. The drought in Texas last summer caused heavy losses in the cattle trade, and as soon as the firms referred to became embarrassed their property was attached, and this precipitated the failure of the bank. While the management is to be condemned, it must be said that the principal debtors of the bank had been men of large means, and that its other assets were fairly sound. Within sixty days of its suspension a dividend of 50 per cent. was paid to the creditors on claims aggregating $64,784.31.

The National Bank of Sumter, S. C., closed its doors on August 20. Two days before the cashier had absconded, carrying with him a considerable amount of money belonging to the bank. This person performed the duties of cashier, teller, and book-keeper, and was thus in a position to conceal his embezzlements until they exceeded in amount the capital stock of the bank. The president seems to have been often absent and habitually negligent, and although a committee was appointed quarterly by the board of directors to examine the affairs of the bank, the members of it must have been incompetent or neglectful of the trust thus confided to them. No evidence has been as yet obtained sufficient to justify proceedings under section 5239, United States Revised Statutes, and in presence of the decision in the case of Movius, receiver, *v.* Directors of the First National Bank of Buffalo, the Comptroller has not felt justified in subjecting this impoverished trust to the expenses of a suit against the directors at common law. The assets are estimated to be good, and a dividend of 75 per cent. will probably be paid before the end of this year.

The First National Bank of Dansville, N. Y., was wrecked by its president, who telegraphed to the Comptroller August 26 that the bank had closed its doors, and immediately absconded to Canada. When the national-bank examiner took possession of the bank the most important books and papers were missing, and those which remained contained little that was true. Nothing but a judicial investigation will unravel the tangle of falsehood and chicanery by which the public has been deceived and robbed, and a once honored family disgraced. The stock of the bank belonged almost wholly to a single family, and all its losses are chargeable to the operations of the president and one of his brothers. Evidence sufficient to justify a criminal investigation has been laid before the district attorney of the United States for the western district of New York, by whom proceedings have been commenced against the only parties within the jurisdiction of the court.

The First National Bank of Corry, Pa., was crippled by mismanagement several years ago. Its stockholders have had no dividends since 1881. In 1883 a change was made in the officers and directors, but the new men proved unequal to the exigency. It appears that the president lived several miles away from Corry, and that the cashier was negligent, and a poor business man, while the directors were weak or inattentive. In consequence of general neglect the bank went from bad to worse, and the cashier is particularly censured for not fully informing the directors of the true condition of a large amount of paper which was thus allowed to become entirely worthless. Added to the effects of weak management there was a constant shrinkage in the value of the old assets, and recently adverse decisions were rendered in important litigation, and the losses on current business proved to be large.

The bank suspended on September 16, and upon examination it appeared that about 80 per cent. of the capital was lost. Ample time was allowed the stockholders to make this good, in accordance with section

5205 United States Revised Statutes, but their efforts proving unsuccessful, a receiver was appointed, who qualified and took possession on October 11. The assets as at present estimated should pay the creditors in full, but no dividend has yet been declared owing to slow collections.

The Stafford National Bank of Stafford Springs, Conn., lost upward of $100,000 by its cashier, who is now under arrest, charged with embezzlement and misappropriation of the funds of the bank. It appears that he was intrusted with the entire management of the bank's affairs, and was successful in deceiving the president and directors by means of fictitious notes and cash items, and the manipulation of the accounts of correspondent banks. His operations extended over a considerable period of time, and involve very large amounts of money lent to a lumber company, of which he was treasurer. The true condition of this bank was ascertained by a special examination ordered in September, out of the regular term, and the arrest of the cashier was the first notice the public had of the bank's being in trouble. The loss to the bank is nearly equal to the amount of its capital, but it is expected that enough will be realized from the assets to nearly or quite pay the creditors in full.

Tables will be found in the Appendix, pp. 206–212, showing the amount of capital, nominal assets, amounts collected, claims proved, and dividends paid, according to the facts in each of these cases, and other statistical information in relation to all insolvent national banks.

A table, Appendix, p. 212, has been prepared with great care and minute accuracy, showing every item of public interest connected with each bank that has been placed in the hands of a receiver since January 1, 1877. It was desired to embrace in this table similar information as to all failed national banks, but it appears that prior to 1877 the various items in the reports of receivers were not always classified, as they have been since that date, and their uniform classification involved so much labor that it could not be completed in time for this Report. In some of the earliest cases the information on file seems to be very meager.

THE ORGANIZATION OF NATIONAL BANKS.

As the laws now stand a national banking association may be formed by any number (not less than five) of natural persons, and any banking corporation having a State or Territorial charter may be converted into a national banking association. Every person applying for information as to the formation of a national bank, or the conversion of a State bank, is supplied with a copy of the national bank laws and a book of instructions as to the practical steps to be taken in effecting either of these purposes. He is also requested to cause a formal notice to be filed, setting forth the name of the place at which the bank is to be located, the title selected, and the names of at least five among those who intend to subscribe for the capital stock. After notice has been filed the person or persons acting in the matter are furnished with blank forms to be used in effecting an organization, and the title which they have selected, if it is approved, is reserved for them for a reasonable period. The forms sent include articles of association, organization certificate, certificate upon which officers and directors are to set forth the facts which it is necessary for the Comptroller to know before authorizing the bank to begin business, oaths of directors, and a blank order for circulating notes. As soon as these papers are returned, duly executed, and all the requirements of the law have been complied with by the corporators, the Comptroller's certificate to that effect is issued. The requirements of law for the formation of new banks are simple and reasonable, the only one appearing onerous being that which requires the bank to deposit in the Treasury certain amounts of United States registered bonds bearing interest.

Under the act of February 25, 1863, national banking associations were required to deposit with the Treasurer United States bonds to the amount of one-third their paid-in capital. In 1864 this provision was amended by fixing $30,000 as the minimum amount of bonds for any bank.

The act of June 20, 1874, permitted associations to withdraw any bonds they might have on deposit in excess of $50,000. Obviously this affected only banks of which the capital exceeded $150,000.

The act of July 12, 1882, specified that banks of which the capital does not exceed $150,000 should be required to keep on deposit bonds to the amount of one-fourth of their capital.

By a special provision of law banks and banking corporations having State charters may be converted into national banks upon satisfying the Comptroller of the Currency that they are in sound financial condition, and upon complying with such of the general requirements of the law as are applicable to them.

CONVERTED AND ORIGINAL BANKS.

It will be seen from the foregoing statement that banks that enter the national system are of two classes, viz, institutions already organized under State laws, converted to national banks under section 5154, Revised Statutes of the United States, and national banking associations primarily organized as such under various acts of Congress:

The following tables show the history of these two classes:

WHOLE NUMBER OF STATE BANKS CONVERTED TO NATIONAL BANKING ASSOCIATIONS, THEIR CAPITAL AT DATE OF CONVERSION, PRESENT CAPITAL AND SURPLUS; SPECIFYING SUCH AS HAVE SINCE GONE INTO VOLUNTARY LIQUIDATION, AND SUCH AS HAVE BECOME INSOLVENT.

Years.	Existing.					Voluntary liquidation.				Insolvent.		
	Whole number converted.	Number in existence.	Capital at date of conversion.	Present capital.	Surplus.	Number.	Capital at date of conversion.	Capital at date of liquidation.	Surplus at date of liquidation.	Number.	Capital at date of conversion.	Capital at date of failure.
1863	12	12	$6,110,000	$9,710,000	$2,504,300							
1864	150	145	66,589,500	72,580,200	26,910,700	2	$200,000	$250,000	$38,900	3	$117,000	$367,000
1865	264	223	59,176,000	58,904,000	27,501,900	47	11,715,200	10,101,200	1,772,000	14	4,401,100	4,371,100
1866	6	3	860,300	3,100,000	92,000	2	275,000	250,000	52,200	1	3,410,200	2,500,000
1867	1					1	50,000	100,000	11,100			
1868	3	1	250,000	250,000	10,000	2	200,000	200,000	29,700			
1869												
1870	1	1	1,000,000	1,500,000	259,000							
1871	5	2	1,378,000	1,225,000	159,000	3	278,000	300,000	35,000			
1872	5	3	1,110,000	830,000	195,000	2	150,000	150,000	13,500			
1873	4	4	855,000	605,000	155,000							
1874	11	9	2,244,000	2,560,000	479,100	2	250,000	250,000	15,500			
1875	7	5	850,000	860,000	197,500	2	200,000	120,000	12,000			
1876	2	2	161,000	141,000	26,500							
1877	5	3	680,000	980,000	320,000	1	50,000	50,000	4,500	1	130,000	130,000
1878	7	7	710,000	769,000	198,000							
1879	10	10	1,285,000	1,435,000	417,500							
1880	6	6	1,147,600	1,340,000	311,500							
1881	11	11	1,445,700	2,213,100	468,300							
1882	13	13	1,190,300	1,790,300	311,600							
1883	16	12	980,000	1,000,000	136,100	4	250,000	250,000	11,200			
1884	1	1	50,000	50,000	25,000							
1885	5	5	850,000	850,000	152,700							
1886*	10	9	2,152,000	2,400,000	179,000	1	50,000	50,000	500			
1887†	11	11	1,350,000	1,350,000	144,100							
Total	586	498	152,423,800	166,442,600	61,273,800	69	13,668,200	12,061,200	1,936,100	19	8,[illegible]8,400	[illegible],368,100

*To November 1. †From November 1, 1886, to November 1, 1887.

Percentage of capital of national banks, organized as such, that went into voluntary liquidation	14.3
Percentage of capital of national banks, organized as such, that went into insolvency	3.3
Percentage of capital of national banks, organized as such, that are in existence	82.4
Percentage of capital of converted banks that went into voluntary liquidation	6.5
Percentage of capital of converted banks that went into insolvency	3.9
Percentage of capital of converted banks that are still in existence	89.6
Percentage of increase of capital of national banks, organized as such	18.8
Percentage of increase of capital of converted banks	9

WHOLE NUMBER OF NATIONAL BANKS OF PRIMARY ORGANIZATION UNDER THE NATIONAL-BANK LAWS, CAPITAL AT DATE OF ORGANIZATION, AND PRESENT CAPITAL AND SURPLUS, SPECIFYING SUCH AS HAVE SINCE GONE INTO VOLUNTARY LIQUIDATION AND SUCH AS HAVE BECOME INSOLVENT.

Years.	Whole number organized.	Existing.				Voluntary liquidation.				Insolvent.		
		Number.	Capital at date of organization.	Present capital.	Surplus.	Number.	Capital at date of organization.	Capital at date of liquidation.	Surplus at date of liquidation.	Number.	Capital at date of organization.	Capital at date of failure.
1863	474	296	$40,588,900	$58,654,800	$25,923,400	147	$14,981,200	$25,424,600	$7,839,300	31	$3,460,000	$5,119,500
1864	104	69	11,848,100	15,370,100	6,682,800	31	4,310,000	6,166,000	1,558,900	4	450,000	500,000
1865	603	440	107,777,400	111,014,700	35,540,900	144	19,592,300	18,490,000	4,913,500	19	2,475,000	3,560,000
1866	33	7	2,730,000	4,385,000	2,384,900	8	800,000	775,300	176,200	2	100,000	150,000
1867	9	23	850,000	1,800,000	746,000	2	150,000	150,000	14,300	......	......	......
1868	10	8	710,000	1,150,000	311,500	2	200,000	200,000	7,500	......	......	......
1869	8	4	850,000	650,000	200,000	2	260,000	310,000	48,500	2	350,000	350,000
1870	62	40	4,298,000	5,160,500	1,558,900	20	2,401,000	2,880,000	375,300	2	300,000	350,000
1871	148	109	11,668,000	14,478,900	4,981,800	34	3,010,000	3,000,000	656,000	5	1,000,000	1,300,000
1872	156	97	9,074,700	12,471,100	3,868,800	48	4,255,000	3,843,100	585,100	11	1,450,000	1,485,000
1873	53	38	4,635,000	4,463,000	1,178,100	13	925,000	1,125,000	116,700	3	370,000	350,000
1874	72	46	3,726,500	4,345,000	1,338,800	22	1,350,000	1,320,000	86,900	4	350,000	350,000
1875	94	79	10,012,000	11,044,000	2,697,800	14	1,000,000	1,010,000	75,800	1	50,000	50,000
1876	27	23	2,020,800	2,377,800	679,300	4	250,000	250,000	11,400	......	......	......
1877	26	21	1,864,000	2,564,000	1,141,700	3	150,000	150,000	21,000	2	300,000	1,011,300
1878	23	18	1,625,000	1,870,000	600,000	5	250,000	250,000	21,400	......	......	......
1879	30	25	2,550,000	3,105,000	631,800	4	200,000	200,000	13,200	1	60,000	60,000
1880	47	43	5,222,100	6,147,100	1,385,100	3	250,000	250,000	32,400	1	50,000	50,000
1881	97	87	8,335,000	10,181,000	2,522,200	9	1,720,000	1,770,000	80,000	1	50,000	50,000
1882	230	212	28,318,000	35,039,000	8,529,100	14	1,380,000	1,380,000	76,200	4	225,000	225,000
1883	236	214	22,962,000	26,403,000	3,770,300	16	2,135,000	2,135,000	53,700	6	550,000	350,000
1884	179	171	17,269,000	20,086,100	3,161,600	7	450,000	450,000	3,000	1	50,000	50,000
1885	142	139	13,593,000	14,203,000	1,589,800	3	200,000	200,000	5,500	......	......	......
1886*	142	140	15,453,000	16,215,000	693,700	1	100,000	100,000	500	1	1,000,000	1,000,000
1887†	214	214	29,196,000	29,096,000	521,400	......	......	......	......	......	......	......
Total	3,219	2,563	347,216,500	412,474,100	112,639,700	556	60,352,500	71,829,000	16,772,300	100	12,640,000	16,360,800

*To November 1.

†From November 1, 1886, to November 1, 1887.

SUMMARY OF NATIONAL BANKS ORGANIZED AND DISSOLVED SINCE FEBRUARY 25, 1863, AND THE NUMBER EXISTING NOVEMBER 1, 1887.

Banks organized.	Number.	Dissolved.					Now existing.		Remarks.
		In liquidation, voluntary or by expiration.		Failed.		Total number dissolved.	Number.	Per cent.	
		Number.	Per cent.	Number.	Per cent.				
Converted from State system	586	69	12	19	3	88	498	85	Of 625 banks which have gone into voluntary liquidation, 471 took that step for the purpose of winding up their affairs, 79 for the purpose of reorganization, and 75 went into liquidation by reason of expiration of charter, 38 of them having since been reorganized.
Other banks	3,219	556	17	100	3	656	2,563	80	
Total	3,805	625	16	119	3	744	3,061	80	

EXTENSION OF THE CORPORATE EXISTENCE OF NATIONAL BANKS.

The act of July 12, 1882, contains the only provision made for the extension of the corporate existence of national banks, and 1,234 associations have availed themselves of this privilege. Annexed is a table brought down to October 31, 1887, showing the capital of these extended banks and their geographical distribution.

TABLE SHOWING, BY STATES, THE NUMBER AND CAPITAL OF NATIONAL BANKS, THE CORPORATE EXISTENCE OF WHICH WAS EXTENDED PRIOR TO NOVEMBER 1, 1887.

States and Territories.	No. of banks.	Capital.	States and Territories.	No. of banks.	Capital.
Alabama	2	$350,000	Montana	1	$500,000
Arkansas	1	250,000	Nebraska	3	750,000
Colorado	3	400,000	New Hampshire	35	4,005,000
Connecticut	73	22,450,820	New Jersey	48	9,783,350
Delaware	11	1,503,185	New York	222	72,672,400
District of Columbia	2	500,000	North Carolina	3	650,000
Georgia	6	1,450,000	South Carolina	2	750,000
Illinois	48	6,210,000	Ohio	82	11,854,000
Indiana	32	4,157,000	Oregon	1	250,000
Iowa	25	2,095,000	Pennsylvania	165	44,479,390
Idaho	1	100,000	Rhode Island	59	19,050,800
Kansas	3	300,000	Tennessee	6	1,750,000
Kentucky	11	3,150,000	Texas	4	625,000
Louisiana	2	1,300,000	Vermont	29	5,256,000
Maine	53	8,630,000	Virginia	10	2,016,000
Maryland	20	12,069,000	West Virginia	11	1,341,000
Massachusetts	199	85,712,500	Wisconsin	10	1,085,000
Michigan	19	1,575,000			
Minnesota	6	2,100,000	Total	1,234	340,069,505
Missouri	8	3,150,000			

The following table accounts for all banks organized, and shows how many of these have been extended, and how many are still in operation under the original organization certificates:

TOTAL NUMBER OF BANKS ORGANIZED UNDER THE NATIONAL CURRENCY ACT OF FEBRUARY 25, 1863, AND THE NATIONAL-BANK ACT OF JUNE 3, 1864, THE NUMBER EXTENDED UNDER THE ACT OF JULY 12, 1882, AND STILL IN OPERATION UNDER THEIR ORIGINAL CERTIFICATES OF ORGANIZATION, AND THE TOTAL NUMBER IN OPERATION OCTOBER 31, 1887.

	Act February 25, 1863.		Act June 3, 1864. Before 1882.		Act June 3, 1864. Since 1882.		Total.
Originally organized		488		2,278			
Out of existence July 12, 1882		146		347			
In operation July 12, 1882		342		1,931			2,273
Organized since July 12, 1882						1,039	
Since passed into voluntary liquidation to wind up affairs	7		97		37		141
Since in voluntary liquidation by expiration of corporate existence	20		55				75
Placed in hands of receivers	1		20		9		30
		28		172		46	
Extended under act July 12, 1882		314		920			1,234
To reach the term of corporate existence				849			
Passed into voluntary liquidation since extension	3						
Placed in hands of receivers since extension	3	6					
Still in operation under original organization certificate		308		1,759			2,067
Restored to solvency and resumed business				1			
Total number in operation October 31, 1887		308		1,760		993	3,061

The figures in the table as to the number of banks organized under these two acts, respectively, conform to the records of the office, but are not in conformity with the Comptroller's reports of previous years.

The discrepancy is attributable to the fact that certain banks originally organized under the act of 1863 afterward went into voluntary liquidation and were reorganized under the act of 1864. In the records of the office they stand among the banks organized under the latter act, while in the reports they have been included with banks organized under the act of 1863. It is perhaps a matter of but little consequence, but upon principle it seems best that the report should reflect accurately the records as they are.

From the foregoing table it will be found that all of the banks organized under the national currency act of 1863 have either ceased to exist or have had their corporate existence extended, while of those organized prior to July 12, 1882, under the national-bank act of 1864, 1,760 are still in operation under their original certificates of organization.

The following table shows how many of these 849 banks will reach the expiration of their corporate existence during each year from 1888 to 1901, inclusive, with their capital and circulation:

Years.	No. of banks.	Capital.	Circulation.	Years.	No. of banks.	Capital.	Circulation.
1888	10	$1,250,000	$321,750	1896	23	$2,173,800	$980,650
1889	3	600,000	184,500	1897	24	3,419,000	1,171,205
1890	61	9,560,500	364,000	1898	25	2,679,000	1,198,350
1891	97	12,358,900	4,040,085	1899	39	4,905,000	2,270,700
1892	100	13,815,100	4,562,760	1900	50	7,807,100	2,153,330
1893	38	4,701,000	1,082,925	1901	108	14,609,150	3,702,350
1894	63	7,628,000	2,812,720				
1895	76	11,250,000	4,431,610	Total	717	96,915,550	30,183,625

The number, capital, and circulation of the national banks of which the periods of succession terminated between October 31, 1886, and October 31, 1887, are shown by the following table, which also indicates the number of which the corporate existence has been extended:

Date.	No. of banks that have expired.	Capital.	Circulation.	No. of banks that have extended.	Capital.	Circulation.
1886.						
December	1	$150,000	$135,000	1	$150,000	$135,000
1887.						
March	3	700,000	162,000	3	700,000	162,000
May	1	100,000	90,000	1	100,000	90,000
Total	5	950,000	387,000	5	950,000	387,000

The corporate existence of one national bank, with a capital of $250,000, will expire in November of this year, and the corporate existence of ten national banks, with an aggregate capital of $1,250,000, will expire during the year 1888.

NATIONAL BANKS OF WHICH THE CORPORATE EXISTENCE WILL EXPIRE DURING THE YEAR 1888, WITH THE DATE OF THE EXPIRATION, THE AMOUNT OF CAPITAL STOCK OF EACH BANK, THE UNITED STATES BONDS ON DEPOSIT WITH THE TREASURER, AND THE AMOUNT OF CIRCULATION ISSUED THEREON.

Charter number.	Title of bank.	State.	Expiration of corporate existence.	Capital stock.	United States bonds.	Circulation.
			1888.			
1676	The First National Bank of Honeybrook	Pa	Jan. 1	$100,000	$68,000	$61,200
1677	The Greene County National Bank of Springfield	Mo	Jan. 8	100,000	25,000	22,500
1678	The Union Stock-Yard National Bank of Chicago (Lake)	Ill	Feb. 20	500,000	50,000	45,000
1680	The Carolina National Bank of Columbia	S. C	Mar. 14	100,000	25,000	22,500
1683	The First National Bank of Mankato	Minn	May 20	75,000	20,000	18,000
1682	The State National Bank of Raleigh	N. C	June 2	100,000	25,000	22,500
1685	The First National Bank of Sharon	Pa	Aug. 31	125,000	32,000	28,800
1688	The First National Bank of Hillsborough	N. H	Sept. 2	50,000	50,000	45,000
1690	The First National Bank of Austin	Minn	Oct. 27	50,000	12,500	11,250
1686	The First National Bank of Faribault	Minn	Nov. 21	50,000	50,000	45,000

SHAREHOLDERS IN BANKS.

In the report of last year tables were given by which a comparison could be made between the distribution of the shares of national banks in 1886 and the distribution as shown by tables reproduced from the Comptroller's Report of 1876.

The tables subjoined hereto afford a comparison between the distribution of national-bank stock and that of the stock of State banks and loan and trust companies, so far as the latter can be ascertained.

DISTRIBUTION, BY STATES, ETC., NUMBER, AND PAR VALUE AT $100 EACH, OF SHARES

	State, etc.	No. of banks.	Number of shares held by—		Same, in detail, held by—				
			State residents.	Non-State residents.	Natural persons.	Religious, charitable, and educational institutions.	Municipal corporations.	Savings banks, loan and trust and insurance companies.	All other corporations.
1	Maine	72	96, 984	5, 116	82, 702	2, 237		10, 101	
2	New Hampshire	49	57, 101	4, 940	51, 848	258	5	9, 934	10
3	Vermont	49	67, 426	7, 734	72, 181	51	102	2, 826	
4	Massachusetts	198	411, 750	35, 155	373, 782	4, 833	661	67, 618	11
5	Boston	54	475, 571	33, 020	264, 320	19 000	231	225, 275	68
6	Rhode Island	61	191, 264	12, 136	172, 519	4, 458	1, 052	25, 366	5
7	Connecticut	83	224, 368	22, 325	183, 325	7, 026	363	55, 466	513
	Division No. 1	566	1, 526, 464	121, 344	1, 200, 678	38, 403	2, 414	405, 646	607
8	New York	269	333, 320	13, 977	346, 126	391		780	
9	New York City	46	326, 061	162, 439	457, 853	3, 067	190	27, 087	298
10	Albany	6	16, 583	915	17, 098	39		363	
11	New Jersey	80	119, 535	10, 748	129, 116	514	60	593	
12	Pennsylvania	237	319, 874	19, 520	337, 461	541	25	1, 158	218
13	Philadelphia	43	218, 670	7, 910	223, 760	528	20	2, 272	
14	Pittsburgh	23	99, 060	2, 740	100, 192	223		1, 385	
	Division No. 2	704	1, 433, 105	218, 258	1, 611, 611	5, 303	295	33, 038	516
15	Delaware	17	17, 426	3, 414	20, 435	145	229	31	
16	Maryland	30	26, 724	943	26, 526	342	228	571	
17	Baltimore	17	112, 080	5, 033	103, 305	6, 350	61	7, 203	63
18	Washington	7	11, 766	3, 984	15, 304	13		373	
19	District of Columbia	1	2, 040	480	2, 435	66	10		
20	Virginia	25	30, 139	7, 824	36, 320	408	65	1, 071	
21	West Virginia	20	15, 903	3, 207	17, 891	9	500	410	300
	Division No. 3	117	216, 078	24, 905	222, 345	7, 432	1, 102	9, 749	353
22	North Carolina	18	21, 750	2, 510	24, 232	7		21	
23	South Carolina	15	16, 253	1, 227	17, 233	92	87	68	
24	Georgia	19	19, 125	10, 235	27, 213	33	1	2, 113	
25	Florida	8	4, 110	890	5, 000				
26	Alabama	20	31, 269	3, 671	31, 820		20	100	
27	Mississippi	11	6, 965	2, 285	9, 175			75	
28	Louisiana	5	4, 865	135	4, 953	16		31	
29	New Orleans	8	20, 775	8, 475	28, 220	2		1, 018	10
30	Texas	87	79, 271	18, 329	97, 292	20	75	203	
31	Arkansas	7	7, 724	1, 276	9, 000				
32	Kentucky	59	93, 420	4, 169	96, 971	414		177	27
33	Louisville	9	31, 465	4, 030	35, 099	100		194	62
34	Tennessee	40	67, 074	7, 101	73, 930	65		100	
	Division No. 4	306	404, 066	64, 353	463, 138	830	182	4, 160	99
35	Ohio	190	213, 122	12, 818	224, 058	128		854	
36	Cincinnati	15	95, 087	8, 913	99, 646	40		4, 314	
37	Cleveland	9	60, 384	6, 616	66, 031	275			91
38	Indiana	92	108, 798	9, 617	118, 281	54		110	
39	Illinois	160	132, 366	9, 149	141, 209	61		245	
40	Chicago	18	131, 143	19, 357	149, 950			550	
41	Michigan	99	96, 700	10, 086	106, 826			20	
42	Detroit	8	36, 963	2, 037	39, 000				
43	Wisconsin	53	41, 170	3, 180	44, 325	10		15	
44	Milwaukee	3	4, 366	2, 134	6, 500				
	Division No. 5	647	920, 150	83, 937	997, 326	568		6, 108	94
45	Iowa	127	82, 582	19, 218	101, 379			421	
46	Minnesota	57	96, 582	38, 818	132, 152	252		2, 900	96
47	Missouri	35	23, 590	1, 720	25, 270			40	
48	Saint Louis	5	21, 385	5, 615	26, 772	44		184	
49	Kansas City	6	16, 770	21, 230	35, 558	25		2, 417	
50	Saint Joseph	2	2, 322	678	3, 000				
51	Kansas	123	66, 036	21, 255	86, 462			829	
52	Nebraska	91	48, 737	11, 168	59, 838			67	
53	Omaha	8	16, 573	7, 427	24, 000				
	Division No. 6	457	377, 577	130, 120	500, 431	321		9, 858	96

OF STOCK OF NATIONAL BANKS ON THE FIRST MONDAY OF JULY, 1887.

Total shares issued.	Number of shareholders.					Number of shareholders owning specific amounts.				
Number reduced to par value of $100 each.	Natural persons.	Corporations.	Resident.	Non-resident.	Total.	Owning shares to the par value of $1,000 and less.	Over $1,000 and less than $5,000.	Over $5,000 and less than $30,000.	Over $30,000.	
104,100	6,965	539	6,985	519	7,504	5,335	1,790	367	12	1
62,050	3,896	145	3,573	468	4,041	2,858	970	199	14	2
75,100	3,903	44	3,514	405	3,919	2,506	1,140	284	19	3
446,905	31,120	794	28,965	2,949	31,914	22,031	7,409	1,450	64	4
509,500	17,236	3,235	18,203	2,268	20,471	11,309	6,459	2,578	125	5
203,400	12,482	457	11,631	1,308	12,939	7,888	4,205	720	30	6
246,093	13,454	910	12,831	1,533	14,364	9,706	3,696	795	77	7
1,647,808	89,058	6,124	85,732	9,450	95,182	62,023	25,819	6,399	341	
347,297	15,156	43	14,253	946	15,199	8,099	5,408	1,528	74	8
488,500	14,629	442	8,516	6,555	15,071	7,012	5,439	2,445	175	9
17,500	611	7	576	42	618	290	226	96	6	10
130,283	9,054	47	8,309	792	9,101	5,926	2,675	488	12	11
330,403	22,964	83	22,102	945	23,047	14,695	7,047	1,243	62	12
220,580	10,976	93	10,438	631	11,069	6,503	3,476	1,047	43	13
101,800	3,992	37	3,972	57	4,0[illegible]9	2,085	1,431	483	30	14
1,631,363	77,382	752	68,166	9,968	78,134	44,610	25,792	7,330	402	
20,840	1,682	21	1,347	356	1,703	1,186	440	76	1	15
27,007	1,963	27	1,924	66	1,990	1,209	503	96	2	16
117,133	5,237	186	5,114	309	5,423	3,005	1,913	480	25	17
15,730	608	7	525	90	615	339	208	67	1	18
2,520	151	4	39	116	155	77	69	9	....	19
37,963	1,561	15	1,326	250	1,576	980	387	201	8	20
19,110	929	6	778	157	935	506	340	83	6	21
240,983	12,131	266	18,053	1,344	12,397	7,392	3,950	1,012	43	
24,260	893	3	765	133	898	401	202	104	41	22
17,480	1,034	25	1,008	51	1,059	721	271	63	4	23
20,300	876	22	719	179	898	480	231	100	12	24
5,000	123	....	101	22	123	64	34	24	1	25
34,040	869	2	757	114	871	383	285	189	14	26
9,250	299	3	235	67	302	151	90	50	2	27
5,000	99	4	99	4	103	47	25	28	3	28
20,250	841	5	669	177	846	341	293	197	15	29
97,600	1,974	10	1,573	411	1,984	898	576	520	50	30
9,000	238	....	198	40	238	106	84	46	2	31
97,580	3,807	41	3,697	151	3,848	1,913	1,401	516	18	32
35,515	1,147	10	1,073	84	1,157	539	432	178	8	33
74,175	2,320	7	2,122	205	2,327	1,024	855	426	22	34
408,410	14,522	132	13,016	1,638	14,654	7,077	4,869	2,516	192	
225,940	8,144	31	7,708	467	8,175	4,302	2,614	1,205	54	35
104,000	1,538	50	1,467	121	1,588	421	529	381	57	36
67,000	839	2	764	77	841	163	274	368	36	37
118,445	2,304	5	2,062	247	2,309	782	823	646	58	38
14[illegible],515	4,162	8	3,846	324	4,170	2,097	1,324	701	48	39
150,500	1,545	4	1,344	205	1,549	351	443	690	95	40
106,840	3,218	1	2,899	320	3,219	1,450	1,109	638	23	41
39,000	597	....	554	43	597	139	188	245	25	42
44,350	1,201	2	1,055	148	1,203	535	304	271	13	43
6,500	145	....	39	106	145	68	57	15	5	44
1,004,090	23,693	103	21,738	2,058	23,796	10,328	7,725	5,330	413	
101,800	3,244	6	2,390	860	3,250	1,670	1,016	531	33	45
135,400	2,807	35	1,966	876	2,842	1,079	896	816	51	46
25,310	885	1	831	55	886	455	281	139	11	47
30,000	800	6	607	259	866	371	322	164	9	48
38,000	930	29	836	123	959	443	295	205	16	49
3,000	46	....	25	21	46	20	10	16	....	50
90,291	2,745	15	1,932	828	2,760	1,502	729	503	20	51
50,905	1,361	2	1,014	349	1,363	627	354	355	27	52
24,000	171	....	114	57	171	49	24	73	25	53
507,706	13,049	94	9,715	3,428	13,143	6,216	3,927	2,802	198	

DISTRIBUTION BY STATES, ETC., NUMBER, AND PAR VALUE AT $100 EACH OF SHARES OF

	State, etc.	No. of banks.	Number of shares held by— State residents.	Number of shares held by— Non-State residents.	Same in detail, held by— Natural persons.	Religious, charitable, and educational institutions.	Municipal corporations.	Savings banks, loan and trust and insurance companies.	All other corporations.
54	Colorado	20	22,307	3,953	26,350	....	....	....	....
55	Nevada	2	1,092	408	1,500	....	....	....	....
56	California	28	35,149	3,351	38,478	22	....	....	....
57	San Francisco	3	17,796	9,204	26,593	....	....	407	....
58	Oregon	22	15,281	2,369	17,565	....	....	85	....
	Division No. 7	84	91,715	19,285	110,486	22	....	492	....
59	Dakota	62	20,681	16,369	36,768	15	....	267	....
60	Idaho	6	2,620	880	3,500	....	....	....	....
61	Montana	17	13,592	5,658	19,250	....	....	....	....
62	New Mexico	9	6,[illegible]00	2,300	8,350	....	....	150	....
63	Utah	7	7,686	814	8,500	....	....	....	....
64	Washington	18	7,345	4,455	11,725	....	50	25	....
65	Wyoming	8	6,037	4,713	10,620	....	50	80	....
66	Arizona	1	1,000	....	1,000	....	....	....	....
	Division No. 8	128	65,161	35,180	99,713	15	100	522	....
	United States	3,009	5,034,325	697,400	5,205,728	52,963	4,094	467,173	1,767

STOCK OF NATIONAL BANKS ON THE FIRST MONDAY OF JULY, 1887—Continued.

Total shares issued.	Number of shareholders.					Number of shareholders owning specific amounts.				
Number reduced to par value of $100 each.	Natural persons.	Corporations.	Resident.	Non-resident.	Total.	Owning shares to the par value of $1,000 and less.	Over $1,000 and less than $5,000.	Over $5,000 and less than $30,000.	Over $30,000.	
26, 350	443	....	359	84	443	173	129	128	13	54
1, 500	25	....	20	5	25	3	8	14	....	55
38, 500	678	2	639	41	680	230	243	187	20	56
27, 000	140	2	130	12	142	14	43	68	17	57
17, 650	282	1	257	26	283	89	82	100	12	58
111, 000	1, 568	5	1, 405	168	1, 573	509	505	497	62	
37, 050	1, 124	8	628	504	1, 132	589	315	224	4	59
3, 500	57	....	40	17	57	19	13	25	....	60
19, 250	252	....	185	67	252	118	57	66	11	61
8, 500	205	4	140	69	209	86	71	51	1	62
8, 500	235	....	219	16	235	130	61	41	3	63
11, 800	251	2	165	88	253	115	56	79	3	64
10, 750	147	2	66	83	149	28	45	69	7	65
1, 000	6	....	4	2	6	3	....	1	2	66
100, 350	2, 277	16	1, 447	846	2, 293	1, 088	618	550	31	
5, 731, 725	233, 680	7, 492	212, 272	28, 900	241, 172	139, 843	73, 205	20, 442	1, 082	

NOTE.—The difference in the amount of capital stock as shown by this table and by the reports of condition on August 1 is accounted for by the fact that a number of banks organized during the five months just preceding that date had not paid up their capital stock.

CIRCULATING NOTES.

Upon the security of its bonds, deposited with the Treasurer, each bank is entitled to receive, and the Comptroller of the Currency is by law required to issue to it upon demand of its officers, circulating notes to the amount of 90 per cent. of the market value, and not more than 90 per cent. of the par value, of the bonds. Any bank may deposit more than the minimum of bonds, and may take out circulating notes for 90 per cent. of its deposit, provided its entire outstanding circulation against bonds does not exceed 90 per cent. of its capital stock actually paid in. The circulating notes when issued by the Comptroller are in sheets, and are not valid until signed by the bank officers designated by the statute.

Under the present law the minimum deposit of bonds required to be made by the 3,049 national banks in operation in the United States on October 5, 1887, amounts to $89,912,347.

A table in the Appendix, p. 185, shows by States and geographical divisions the national banks in operation on October 5, 1887, separated into two classes, namely, banks of which the capital does not exceed $150,000, and banks of which the capital exceeds $150,000. The first class contains 2,150 banks, with an aggregate capital of $179,849,390; the second, 899 banks, with an aggregate capital of $398,613,375. The minimum of bonds required to be kept on deposit by the entire body of banks in the first class is $44,962,347; the minimum for the 899 banks of the second class is $44,950,000. If all banks held only the minimum of bonds, the total national-bank circulation could not exceed $80,921,113, while the possible maximum of circulation, namely, 90 per cent. of the aggregate of the national-bank capital, would be $520,616,489.

The actual circulation on October 5, 1887, was $272,387,176, inclusive of $102,719,440 still outstanding, but which, having been surrendered by the banks that issued it, is no longer represented by bonds, but by that amount of lawful money deposited with the Treasurer of the United States to redeem the notes as they are presented.

The $169,667,736 of circulation for which the banks are responsible consists of $71,536,500 secured by the bonds deposited by the 2,150 banks having $150,000 capital and less, and $98,131,236 secured by the bonds belonging to the 899 banks of which the capital exceeds $150,000. The first class of banks have, therefore, $31,070,387 more than their minimum and $90,327,951 less than their possible maximum circulation, while the larger banks have $57,676,236 more than their minimum and $260,620,802 less than their maximum.

The following table shows the number of banks organized from July 1, 1882, to July 1, 1887, their capital stock, amount of bonds deposited, and the circulation issued thereon:

Year.	Number of banks.	Capital.	Minimum bonds required.	Bonds actually deposited.	Percentage of excess.	Circulation issued.
					Per cent.	
July 1, 1882, to July 1, 1883 ..	251	$26,552,300	$5,155,500	$7,116,400	28	$6,404,760
July 1, 1883, to July 1, 1884 ..	218	19,941,000	4,016,000	4,676,100	11	4,208,490
July 1, 1884, to July 1, 1885 ..	142	15,205,000	3,061,250	3,332,800	8	2,999,520
July 1, 1885, to July 1, 1886 ..	163	17,553,000	3,401,500	3,715,500	8	3,343,950
July 1, 1886, to July 1, 1887 ..	217	31,444,000	4,986,000	5,051,500	1	4,538,390

From the foregoing table it appears that 991 banks have been organized between the dates given, with a capital of $110,698,300; that they have received circulation to the amount of $21,495,110 on bonds deposited to the amount of $23,892,100, and that the minimum deposit of bonds required by law for these banks is $20,623,250.

The actual deposit of bonds during the whole period exceeds the minimum by about 15 per cent. only, and taken year by year the percentage of excess has decreased from 28 per cent. in 1882–'83 to less than 1½ per cent. in 1886–'87.

Of the 217 national banks organized during the past fiscal year, 102 have a capital of $50,000 each, amounting to $5,100,000; 76 have a capital of over $50,000 and not exceeding $150,000, amounting to $7,044,000; and 39 have a capital of $10,300,000. The 39 largest banks deposited the exact amount of bonds required by law, and out of 178 banks of which the capital does not exceed $150,000 only 8 have deposited bonds in excess of the requirement.

Tables will be found in the Appendix, pp. 183, etc., showing for the national banks in each State, Territory, and reserve city the minimum amount of bonds required by law, the bonds actually held, and the circulation thereon outstanding October 5, 1887; also all other information deemed useful as to circulation.

Banks are privileged to change their deposited bonds from time to time, to increase and to reduce the amount, within limits, and are required to inspect once a year the bonds held for them in trust by the Treasurer. The Comptroller of the Currency is the agent and medium of all such changes; his indorsement on the bonds establishes their ownership and alone validates their transfer. Section 5163 of the Revised Statutes requires him to record every act of deposit, transfer, and withdrawal, and to keep a set of books for the purpose, all of which has been carefully complied with.

INTEREST-BEARING FUNDED DEBT OF THE UNITED STATES, AND THE AMOUNT HELD BY NATIONAL BANKS.

The connection between the banks and the distribution of the funded debt of the United States renders the following statement appropriate:

The public debt at its maximum, on August 31, 1865, amounted to $2,844,649,626, of which obligations not bearing interest amounted to $461,616,311, leaving interest-bearing debt $2,383,033,315. On October 31, 1887, the interest-bearing debt amounted to $1,041,770,742.

The following table shows the class of bonds, authorizing act, date of maturity, rate of interest, and intermediate changes:

BONDED DEBT AT DATES NAMED.

Date.	6 per cent.	5 per cent.	4½ per cent.*	4 per cent.†	6 per cent.‡	Total.
Aug. 31, 1865	$908,518,091	$199,792,100			$1,258,000	$1,109,568,191
June 30, 1866	1,008,388,469	198,528,435			6,042,000	1,212,958,904
June 30, 1867	1,421,110,719	198,533,435			14,762,000	1,634,406,154
June 30, 1868	1,841,521,800	221,588,400			29,089,000	2,092,199,200
June 30, 1869	1,886,341,300	221,589,300			58,638,320	2,166,568,920
June 30, 1870	1,764,932,300	221,589,300			64,457,320	2,050,978,920
June 30, 1871	1,613,897,300	274,236,450			64,618,832	1,952,752,582
June 30, 1872	1,374,883,800	414,567,300			64,623,512	1,854,074,612
June 30, 1873	1,281,238,650	414,567,300			64,623,512	1,760,429,462
June 30, 1874	1,213,624,700	510,628,050			64,623,512	1,788,876,262
June 30, 1875	1,100,865,550	607,132,750			64,623,512	1,772,621,812
June 30, 1876	984,999,650	711,685,800			64,623,512	1,761,308,962
June 30, 1877	854,621,850	703,266,650	$140,000,000		64,623,512	1,761,512,012
June 30, 1878	738,619,000	703,266,650	240,000,000	$98,850,000	64,623,512	1,845,359,162
June 30, 1879	310,932,500	646,905,500	250,000,000	679,878,110	64,623,512	1,952,339,622
June 30, 1880	235,780,400	484,864,900	250,000,000	739,347,800	64,623,512	1,774,616,612
June 30, 1881	196,378,600	439,841,350	250,000,000	739,347,800	64,623,512	1,690,191,262
	Continued at 3½ per cent.	Continued at 3½ per cent.				
June 30, 1882	58,957,150	401,503,900	250,000,000	739,349,350	64,623,512	1,514,433,912
June 30, 1883		32,082,600 Funded into 3 per cents, act July 12, 1882. 304,204,350	250,000,000	737,942,200	64,623,512	1,388,852,662
June 30, 1884		224,612,150	250,000,000	737,661,700	64,623,512	1,276,897,362
June 30, 1885		194,190,500	250,000,000	737,719,850	64,623,512	1,246,533,862
June 30, 1886		144,046,600	250,000,000	737,759,700	64,623,512	1,196,429,812
June 30, 1887		19,716,500	250,000,000	737,800,600	64,623,512	1,072,140,612
Oct. 31, 1887			230,544,600	732,447,550	64,623,512	1,027,615,662

* Funded loan 1891; authorizing act, July 14, 1870, and January 20, 1871; date of maturity, 1891.
† Funded loan 1907; authorizing act, July 14, 1870, and January 20, 1871; date of maturity, 1907.
‡ Pacific railroad bonds; authorizing act, July 1, 1862, and July 2, 1864; date of maturity, 1895 to 1899.
The Navy pension fund, amounting to $14,000,000 in 3 per cents, the interest upon which is applied to the payment of naval pensions exclusively, and $155,060 of refunding certificates are not included in the table.

The act approved July 12, 1882, authorized the Secretary of the Treasury to receive at the Treasury any bonds of the United States bearing 3½ per cent. interest, and to issue in exchange therefor an equal amount of registered bonds of the United States bearing interest at the rate of 3 per cent. per annum—

Provided, That the bonds herein authorized shall not be called in and paid so long as any bonds of the United States heretofore issued bearing a higher rate of interest than three per centum, and which shall be redeemable at the pleasure of the United States, shall be outstanding and uncalled.

Under this act $305,581,250 of 3 percents were issued, but the largest amount outstanding at any time was $305,529,000, on August 7, 1883, $52,250 having been redeemed before the last issue was made.

The largest amount of 3 percents held by the national banks on deposit as security for circulation was $202,386,750, on August 16, 1883.

On October 31, 1886, there was outstanding $95,850,050 3 per cent. bonds, of which $31,607,400 had been called. The $64,242,550 then remaining uncalled have been called during the past year, except that bonds amounting to $605,150 were voluntarily presented for redemption under Treasury circulars dated August 30, 1886, and September 15, 1886. Of the $63,637,400 called, $1,448,400 was still outstanding October 31, 1887.

Of this amount the national banks on that date held $144,500, deposited with the Treasurer of the United States as security for circulation, and $550,000 was held by him for them as security for public deposits.

REDEMPTION OF LOAN OF JULY 2, 1882, KNOWN AS THREE PER CENT. BONDS.

Since the last annual report the whole amount of 3 per cent. bonds then outstanding has been called in for redemption.

The following tables show the general progress of this redemption, and its effect upon national-bank circulation, from September 15, 1886, to July 1, 1887.

The first table relates to the entire mass of 3 per cent. bonds outstanding September 15, 1886, including both those held by the Treasurer for the banks and those held by others. It gives the date and maturity of each call since August 1, 1886, the amount of bonds embraced in each, the bonds then outstanding, and those thereafter redeemed.

The second table shows the amount of 3 per cent. bonds held by the Treasurer as security for national-bank circulation on September 15, 1886, the amount of such bonds included in each call for redemption since August 1, 1886, the total amount so held at each date at which interest ceased under any call for redemption, the amounts redeemed at those dates, and the amounts held on which interest had ceased.

STATEMENT SHOWING CHANGES IN THREE PER CENT. LOAN OF JULY 12, 1882, FROM AUGUST 1, 1886, TO JULY 1, 1887.

Call No. 140 to 149.			Amount of bonds outstanding at maturity of each call.			Amount of bonds redeemed between the maturity of each call and maturity of succeeding call.		
Date of call.	Maturity of call.	Amount called.	Amount previously called.	Amount not yet called.	Total amount outstanding.	Redeemed under last call.	Redeemed under previous calls.	Voluntarily surrendered under special calls.
1886.	1886.							
Aug. 12	Sept. 15	$10,003,050	$36,337,150	$91,133,050	$127,470,200	....	$177,270,800	$788,000
19	Oct. 1	15,005,000	40,575,300	75,450,200	116,025,500	$11,600	10,758,550	674,550
Sept. 13	16	15,122,400	29,669,900	74,484,700	104,154,600	822,900	10,094,100	965,500
27	Nov. 1	15,008,200	26,043,500	64,222,450	90,265,950	40,000	14,414,650	256,000
Oct. 29	Dec. 1	10,005,350	12,270,900	64,017,600	76,288,500	4,845,000	8,957,600	204,850
	1887.							
Dec. 28	Feb. 1	10,010,900	23,205,350	39,958,400	63,163,750	155,900	17,052,550	161,300
1887.								
Jan. 22	Mar. 1	13,887,000	20,481,050	29,921,350	50,402,400	....	12,887,950	29,300
Feb. 21	Apr. 1	10,007,750	15,636,200	19,814,600	35,450,800	162,500	14,606,000	93,500
Mar. 23	May 1	10,014,250	7,258,300	19,774,000	27,032,300	6,832,300	1,708,100	40,600
May 20	July 1	10,717,500	8,851,050	....	8,851,050	14,929,100	10,027,950	56,500
							278,478,850	3,270,000

RECAPITULATION OF REDEMPTIONS.

Amount redeemed under last call	$14,929,100
Amount redeemed under previous calls	278,478,850
Amount redeemed uncalled	3,270,000
Bonds of Lewis legacy redeemed	52,250
Total redemptions	296,730,200
Outstanding July 1, 1887	8,851,050
Amount of original issue of loan	305,581,250

STATEMENT SHOWING CHANGES IN THREE PER CENT. LOAN OF JULY 12, 1862—Continued.

Calls No. 140 to No. 149.			Amount of 3 per cent. bonds held by the Treasurer as security for national-bank circulation at maturity of each call.			Amount of 3 per cent. bonds withdrawn by banks in the interval between the maturity of each call and the maturity of the succeeding call.		
Date of call.	Maturity of call.	Amount of bonds included in call held as security for national-bank circulation.	Amount included in previous calls.	Amount not previously called.	Total amount held by the Treasurer.	Redeemed under last call.	Redeemed under previous calls.	Voluntarily surrendered under special calls.
1886.	1886.							
Aug. 12	Sept. 15	$7,045,200	$14,644,000	$80,238,800	$94,882,800	....	....	....
19	Oct. 1	11,188,000	29,826,050	57,222,400	87,048,450	$2,179,100	$4,978,250	$677,000
Sept. 15	16	10,795,200	21,873,650	57,180,400	79,034,050	3,682,200	4,056,700	255,500
27	Nov. 1	12,067,650	19,881,600	49,156,450	69,038,050	5,557,500	4,194,000	264,500
Oct. 29	Dec. 1	7,925,500	8,861,450	48,464,000	57,325,450	3,774,400	7,085,400	852,800
	1887.							
Dec. 28	Feb. 1	8,440,250	18,131,950	29,000,300	47,132,250	3,637,350	5,930,750	605,100
1887.								
Jan. 22	Mar. 1	10,613,750	13,975,500	22,919,300	36,894,800	4,945,550	5,188,000	103,000
Feb. 21	Apr. 1	5,989,500	10,408,300	17,677,600	27,085,900	4,111,500	5,328,900	368,500
Mar. 23	May 1	7,818,700	5,006,950	15,221,600	20,228,550	5,115,950	1,455,900	285,500
May 20	July 1	15,221,600	5,205,950	....	5,205,950	12,245,150	2,565,450	212,000
						45,248,700	40,804,250	3,023,900

RECAPITULATION.

Amount held by the Treasurer September 15, 1886	$94,882,800
Amount redeemed from September 15 to October 1, 1886	7,834,350
October 1 to October 16, 1886	7,994,400
October 16 to November 1, 1886	10,016,000
November 1 to December 1, 1886	11,712,600
December 1, 1886, to February 1, 1887	10,193,200
February 1 to March 1, 1887	10,237,450
March 1 to April 1, 1887	9,808,900
April 1 to May 1, 1887	6,857,350
May 1 to July 1, 1887	15,022,600
Amount unredeemed July 1, 1887	5,205,950
	94,882,800

It will be seen by reference to foregoing tables that call No. 140 was dated August 12, 1886. On that day the Treasurer held as security for circulation of national banks 3 per cent. bonds amounting to $103,351,650, of which $1,720,000 had ceased to bear interest, having matured under previous calls.

Upon the assumption that it would be found practicable and desirable to continue the redemption of these bonds, it became a matter of solicitude with a great many banks holding only 3 percents to ascertain whether their bonds could remain on deposit with the Treasurer as a basis for circulation after interest on them had ceased. Singular as it may seem, some strong and ordinarily well managed banks left large amounts of called bonds on deposit for months, preferring to forego all interest rather than to replace them with other bonds at the then prevailing premium, but as a rule the banks that resisted the replacement of called bonds were those of small capital in sections where money was scarce and dear.

The language of the statute makes it clear that only interest-bearing registered bonds can be deposited, but in the clause requiring the deposit to be maintained up to a certain minimum, registered bonds only are mentioned, nothing being said about their being also interest-bearing.

Taking advantage of this ambiguity in the law, it was contended on behalf of certain banks, that when a deposit was once made of interest-bearing registered bonds of the United States, the requirement of the statute was fulfilled, and that banks could not be compelled against their will to replace those bonds, or to retire the circulation issued upon them, because without any action on their part, and even without their consent, the Government had called the bonds for redemption, and had thereby acquired the right to cease paying interest.

On the other hand, it has always been maintained in the Treasury Department, that bonds upon which interest has ceased are not such bonds as the statute requires national banks to keep on deposit as a basis for circulation.

The controversy at one time became very serious, as it was represented that banks in all parts of the country were resolved to go out of the system if they should be compelled to withdraw their called bonds.

With a view of terminating the controversy as to the meaning of the law, the Secretary of the Treasury was requested to submit the question to the Attorney-General, and this being done the Attorney-General decided that bonds on which interest had ceased could not be lawfully held by the Treasurer as security for national-bank circulation.

If at any time within six months after August 12, 1886, the true position of the banks had been known, especially how many of them held no bonds but 3 per cents, or if peremptory measures had been taken to compel the immediate replacement of called bonds, a speculation in the 4 and 4½ per cent. bonds would no doubt have been precipitated, and in that event the formation of new banks would have been arrested, and many of those already in the system would have been forced into liquidation.

If by accident or inadvertence the magnitude of the necessary bond replacements had got out, or if the ambiguity of the law had not afforded opportunity for temporizing with the reluctant banks, there is little doubt that the banks would have been cornered for available bonds, and while the corner lasted no new banks could have been formed, and a greater or less number of the several hundred which held only 3 per cent. bonds would have been forced into liquidation.

It is needless to specify the steps taken to avert these consequences, and at the same time to bring about an acquiescence in the requirement of the law without having recourse to coercive measures, but it is, perhaps, proper to state that between August 12, 1886, and July 1, 1887, nearly $102,000,000 of 3 per cent. bonds were surrendered by the banks for redemption, and that replacements were made in 4 and 4½ per cent. bonds to the amount of upward of $20,000,000, while during the same time new banks deposited 4 and 4½ per cent. bonds to the amount of $4,532,300, and the amounts of these bonds held to secure deposits of public moneys increased by over $12,000,000. Thus fully $37,000,000 of 4 and 4½ per cent. bonds were obtained by the banks and transferred to the Treasury within less than twelve months, without exciting any speculative advance in the premium of either loan, as will appear from the subjoined table.

OPENING, HIGHEST, AND LOWEST PRICES OF UNITED STATES REGISTERED FOUR AND FOUR AND A HALF PER CENT. BONDS IN NEW YORK FOR EACH WEEK FROM AUGUST 14, 1886, TO JULY 2, 1887, BOTH DATES INCLUSIVE.

[Compiled from the "Commercial and Financial Chronicle."]

Week ending—	4 per cent. bonds, registered.			4½ per cent. bonds, registered.		
	Opening.	Highest.	Lowest.	Opening.	Highest.	Lowest.
1886.						
Aug. 14	126⅞	126⅞	126¾	110⅝	110⅝	110¼
21	126¾	126⅞	125⅞	110⅛	110⅛	109⅞
28	126⅛	126¼	126¼	109⅞	109⅞	109⅞
Sept. 4	126⅛	126¼	125	110⅛	110⅛	109⅞
11	125	125¾	125	110	110⅛	110
18	125⅞	126¾	125⅞	110½	111⅛	110½
25	126⅝	127	126⅞	111⅛	112	111⅛
Oct. 2	127	128¾	127	111⅞	112¼	111⅞
9	129¼	129¼	128⅝	112⅝	112⅝	111¾
16	128¼	128¾	127⅞	111⅜	111⅞	111⅜
23	128⅝	128¾	128½	111⅞	112	111⅞
30	128⅞	128⅝	128⅛	111⅝	111¾	111⅛
Nov. 6	128⅛	128⅝	128⅛	110⅝	110⅝	110⅜
13	128¼	128¼	127⅞	110⅜	110⅜	109⅞
20	128⅛	128⅛	127	109⅞	110	109⅝
27	127⅝	128⅝	127⅝	109⅞	110⅜	109⅞
Dec. 4	129	129¼	128⅞	110⅜	110⅛	110¼
11	128⅝	128⅝	128¾	110⅜	110⅜	110⅜
18	128⅛	128½	127½	110¾	110¾	110⅛
25	127¼	127½	127½	110⅝	110½	110¼
1887.						
Jan. 1	127½	128	127½	110½	110½	110¼
8	127½	127⅝	126½	110⅛	110⅛	109¾
15	127¼	127¾	127¼	110	110¼	110

Week ending—	4 per cent. bonds, registered.			4½ per cent. bonds registered.		
	Opening.	Highest.	Lowest.	Opening.	Highest.	Lowest.
1887.						
Jan. 22	127⅞	127⅞	127⅝	110	110½	110
29	128¼	128⅜	128¼	110⅜	110⅜	110⅛
Feb. 5	128¼	128⅛	128½	110¼	110¼	109⅞
12	128⅝	128¾	128⅝	109⅞	109¼	109⅞
19	128⅝	128⅝	128⅜	109⅛	109⅞	108¾
26	128½	128¾	128¾	109	109¼	109
Mar. 5	128⅝	128⅝	127½	109⅛	109½	108⅞
12	127½	127⅞	127⅞	108⅞	109⅛	108¾
19	127⅝	127⅝	127⅜	109⅛	109⅛	108⅞
26	127½	127¾	127½	108⅞	109⅜	108⅞
Apr. 2	128⅛	128¼	128⅛	109⅞	110	109⅜
9	128¾	129	128¼	109⅞	110	109¾
16	129¼	129¼	129⅛	110	110¼	110
23	129	129½	129	110	110¼	110
30	129½	129½	129¼	110¼	110¼	110⅛
May 7	129	129	128¾	109	109	108¾
14	128⅞	129	128⅞	108⅞	109½	108⅞
21	129⅛	129¼	129	109⅛	109⅜	109⅛
28	129⅜	129½	129⅜	109⅛	109¼	109⅛
June 4	129½	129½	128¾	109¾	109¾	109¼
11	128⅞	128⅞	128½	109⅛	109⅞	109⅛
18	128⅝	128½	128⅜	109⅞	109⅞	109¾
25	128⅜	128¾	128	109¾	109¾	109⅜
July 2	128¼	128¼	128¼	109⅜	109½	109⅜

It is of grave importance for Congress to observe the perilous contingencies involved in the existence of the present relations between the public debt and the national-bank circulation.

It is neither wise nor prudent to maintain a condition of things which makes the possession of official information, necessarily accessible even to clerks in the Departments, an incentive or a temptation to speculation in public securities, nor should the natural and healthy growth of the national-bank system be exposed to the danger of being suddenly arrested by legitimate and discreet operations of the Treasury, directed to the reduction of the public debt.

During the year ending October 31, 1887, $5,379,250 of 4 percents and $19,455,400 of 4½ percents were purchased for sinking-fund purposes, making a total of $24,834,650. Of this amount $297,500 of 4 percents and $687,500 of 4½ percents were withdrawn by the national banks from deposit to secure circulation, making total withdrawals from this cause $985,000, while the replacement by deposits of 4 percents amounted to only $279,650.

Changes in the debt have induced corresponding changes in the bonds held by the national banks. In January 1866, 1,582 banks, with a capital, surplus, and undivided profits of $475,330,204, held $440,380,350 of United States bonds. On October 5, 1887, 3,049 banks, with a capital, surplus, and undivided profits of $823,827,373, held only $223,754,450 of bonds. The total bank circulation on January 1, 1866, was $213,239,530, and on October 5, 1887, that which was secured by bonds was $167,283,343.

The amount and classes of United States bonds owned by the banks, including those pledged as security for circulation and for public deposits, on June 30 in each year since 1865, are exhibited in the following table:

Years.	United States bonds held as security for circulation.					United States bonds held for other purposes at nearest date.	Grand total.
	6 per cent. bonds.	5 per cent. bonds.	4½ per cent. bonds.	4 per cent. bonds.	Total.		
1865 ..	$170,382,500	$65,576,600	....	....	$235,959,100	$155,785,750	$391,744,850
1866 ..	241,083,500	86,226,850	....	....	327,310,350	121,152,950	448,463,300
1867 ..	251,430,400	89,177,100	....	....	340,607,500	84,002,650	424,610,150
1868 ..	250,726,950	90,768,950	....	....	341,495,900	80,922,500	422,418,400
1869 ..	255,190,350	87,661,250	....	....	342,851,600	55,102,000	397,953,600
1870 ..	247,355,350	94,923,200	....	....	342,278,550	43,980,600	386,259,150
1871 ..	220,497,750	130,387,800	....	....	350,885,550	39,450,800	390,336,350
1872 .	173,251,450	207,189,250	....	....	380,440,700	31,868,200	412,308,900
1873 ..	160,923,500	229,487,050	....	....	390,410,550	25,724,400	416,134,150
1874 ..	154,370,700	236,800,500	....	....	391,171,200	25,347,100	416,518,300
1875 ..	136,955,100	239,359,400	....	....	376,314,500	26,900,200	403,214,700
1876 ..	109,313,450	232,081,300	....	....	341,394,750	45,170,300	386,565,050
1877 ..	87,690,300	206,651,050	$44,372,250	....	338,713,600	47,315,050	386,028,650
1878 ..	82,421,200	199,514,550	48,448,650	$19,162,000	349,546,400	68,850,900	418,397,300
1879 ..	56,042,800	144,616,300	35,056,550	118,538,950	354,254,600	76,603,520	430,858,120
1880 ..	58,056,150	139,758,650	37,760,950	126,076,300	361,652,050	42,831,300	404,483,350
1881 ..	61,901,800	172,348,350	32,600,500	93,637,700	360,488,400	63,849,950	424,338,350
	Continued at 3½ per cent.:	Continued at 3½ per cent.:					
1882 ..	25,142,600	202,487,650	32,752,650	97,429,800	357,812,700	43,122,550	400,935,250
1883 ..	385,700	7,402,800 } 3 per cents: 200,877,850 }	39,408,500	104,954,650	353,029,500	34,094,150	387,123,650
1884 ..	....	172,412,550	46,546,400	111,690,900	330,649,850	31,203,000	361,852,850
	Pacifics.						
1885 ..	3,520,000	142,240,850	48,483,050	117,901,300	312,145,200	32,195,800	344,341,000
1886 ..	3,505,000	107,782,100	50,484,200	114,143,500	275,974,800	31,345,550	307,320,350
1887 ..	3,175,000	5,205,050	67,743,100	115,842,650	191,966,700	33,147,750	224,814,450

SECURITY FOR CIRCULATING NOTES.

The following table shows the amount of bonds held by the Treasurer as security for the circulating notes of the national banks on October 31 of each year from 1882 to 1887, inclusive, the amount held by the banks for all other purposes, and the total of these two:

Year.	Number of banks.	United States bonds held as security for circulation.					United States bonds held for other purposes at nearest date.	Total.
		4½ per cent. bonds.	4 per cent. bonds.	3 per cent. bonds.	Pacific 6 per cent. bonds.	Total.		
1882.......	2,301	$33,754,650	$104,927,500	*$40,621,950 / 179,675,550	$3,526,000	$362,505,650	$37,563,750	$400,069,400
1883.......	2,522	41,319,700	106,164,850	*602,000 / 201,327,750	3,463,000	352,877,300	30,674,050	383,551,350
1884.......	2,671	49,537,450	116,705,450	155,601,400	3,469,000	325,316,300	30,419,600	355,735,900
1885.......	2,727	40,547,250	116,391,650	138,920,650	3,505,000	303,364,550	31,780,100	340,144,650
1886.......	2,868	57,436,850	115,383,150	69,038,050	3,586,000	245,444,050	32,431,400	277,875,450
1887.......	3,061	69,696,100	115,731,400	114,500	3,256,000	188,828,000	34,671,350	223,499,350

* Three and one-half per cent.

The foregoing tables show how the banks have shifted their investments from one class of bonds to another, and the following table exhibits especially the steady decrease in the amount of bonds held for and by the banks, and in connection with other tables in this report it tends to establish the proposition that the banks are gradually reducing their investments in these securities.

Table showing the decrease of national-bank circulation during each of the years ending October 31, from 1884 to 1887, inclusive, and the amount of lawful money on deposit at the end of each year:

National-bank notes outstanding October 31, 1883, including notes of national gold banks	$352,013,787	
Less lawful money on deposit at same date, including deposits of national gold banks	35,993,461	
		$316,020,326
National-bank notes outstanding October 31, 1884, including notes of national gold banks	333,559,813	
Less lawful money on deposit at same date, including deposits of national gold banks	41,710,163	
		291,849,650
Net decrease of circulation		24,170,676
Net outstanding as above, October 31, 1884		291,849,650
National-bank notes outstanding October 31, 1885, including notes of national gold banks	315,847,168	
Less lawful money on deposit at same date, including deposits of national gold banks	39,542,979	
		276,304,189
Net decrease of circulation		15,545,461
Net outstanding as above, October 31, 1885		276,304,189
National-bank notes outstanding October 31, 1886, including notes of national gold banks	301,529,889	
Less lawful money on deposit at same date, including deposits of national gold banks	81,819,233	
		219,710,656
Net decrease of circulation		56,593,533
Net outstanding as above, November 1, 1886		219,710,656
National-bank notes outstanding October 31, 1887, including notes of national gold banks	272,041,203	
Less lawful money on deposit at same date, including deposits of national gold banks	102,826,136	
		169,215,067
Net decrease of circulation		50,495,589

The following table shows the diminishing scale on which banks organized during each of the past five years have availed themselves of the privilege of issuing circulation upon bonds in excess of the minimum which the law obliges them to keep on hand.

For the sake of conciseness in the table the circulation is omitted, but as every bank has received circulation to the amount of 90 per cent. of the bonds deposited, the proportions of the table reflect faithfully the features of the circulation.

NUMBER AND CAPITAL OF NATIONAL BANKS ORGANIZED IN EACH GEOGRAPHICAL DIVISION OF THE UNITED STATES FROM OCTOBER 31, 1882, TO OCTOBER 31, 1887, SHOWING THE AMOUNT OF BONDS DEPOSITED TO SECURE THEIR CIRCULATION, THE MINIMUM AMOUNT OF BONDS REQUIRED BY THE ACT OF JULY 12, 1882, AND THE EXCESS DEPOSITED OVER REQUIREMENTS BOTH IN AMOUNT AND PERCENTAGE.

Divisions.*	Number of banks.	Capital.	United States bonds.			
			Deposited.	Minimum.	Excess.	Per cent. of excess over minimum.
1883.						
First	7	$1,275,000	$995,000	$312,500	$682,500	218.40
Second	38	2,975,200	1,854,500	743,800	1,110,700	149.32
Third	5	295,000	155,500	73,700	81,800	110.99
Fourth	43	3,643,650	1,238,100	748,400	489,700	65.43
Fifth	61	11,210,000	2,578,000	1,765,000	813,000	46.06
Sixth	71	7,085,500	1,729,250	1,246,400	482,850	38.73
Seventh	11	620,000	268,400	155,000	113,400	73.16
Eighth	26	1,550,000	556,800	375,000	181,800	48.48
Total	262	28,654,350	9,375,550	5,419,800	3,955,750	72.987
1884.						
First	10	810,000	313,000	190,000	123,000	64.73
Second	22	1,662,250	718,000	340,500	377,500	110.86
Third	6	280,000	166,500	70,000	96,500	137.85
Fourth	27	2,861,100	693,600	627,700	65,900	10.49
Fifth	34	3,413,100	927,000	570,700	356,300	62.43
Sixth	68	5,492,780	1,239,750	1,135,600	104,150	9.17
Seventh	5	380,000	120,000	95,000	25,000	26.31
Eighth	19	1,143,000	309,250	285,700	23,550	8.24
Total	191	16,012,230	4,487,100	3,315,200	1,171,900	35.349
1885.						
First	4	400,000	100,500	100,000	500	.5
Second	18	2,635,000	1,037,500	543,700	493,800	90.822
Third	3	660,000	112,500	112,500	....	....
Fourth	20	2,025,000	561,500	506,100	55,400	10.946
Fifth	35	7,123,000	1,963,500	1,218,200	745,300	61.172
Sixth	41	2,350,000	759,800	587,500	172,300	29.329
Seventh	8	725,000	169,000	168,700	300	.177
Eighth	10	1,020,000	255,000	255,000	....	....
Total	145	16,938,000	4,959,300	3,491,700	1,467,000	42.031
1886.						
First	5	500,000	125,000	125,000	....	....
Second	15	4,000,000	525,000	525,000	....	....
Third	4	450,000	112,500	112,500	....	....
Fourth	23	1,658,000	404,750	402,000	2,750	.684
Fifth	27	5,465,000	843,000	743,750	99,250	13.344
Sixth	58	5,830,000	982,500	982,500	....	....
Seventh	18	2,100,000	367,500	360,000	7,500	2.083
Eighth	24	1,355,000	353,250	313,750	39,500	12.589
Total	174	21,358,000	3,713,500	3,564,500	149,000	4.18
1887.						
First	5	400,000	100,000	100,000	....	....
Second	27	7,025,000	771,550	743,750	27,800	3.74
Third	6	500,000	115,000	112,500	2,500	2.22
Fourth	50	6,199,000	1,262,500	1,262,250	250	.02
Fifth	37	5,010,000	959,500	952,500	7,000	.74
Sixth	70	9,002,000	1,400,500	1,400,500	....	....
Seventh	17	1,510,000	377,500	377,500	....	....
Eighth	13	900,000	225,000	225,000	....	....
Total	225	30,546,000	5,211,550	5,174,000	37,550	.72

*See page 183.

The following table exhibits in detail the changes which have occurred during the past year in the amount of national-bank circulation, so arranged as to illustrate the process by which the circulation steadily decreases concurrently with the accession of new banks and an increase in the aggregate national-bank capital:

CAPITAL AND CIRCULATION.

	Paid in capital.	Circulation represented by bonds.
Increase by banks existing November 1, 1886	$3,868,005	$3,957,175
Increase caused by formation of new banks	32,416,770	4,592,090
Increase by banks organized during the year	610,000	....
Total increase	36,894,775	8,549,265
Decrease by banks still in operation November 1, 1887	2,235,000	57,770,475
Decrease by banks going into voluntary liquidation and failed	4,087,450	1,274,380
Total decrease	6,322,450	59,044,855
Net increase of capital	30,572,325	....
Net decrease of circulation	....	50,495,590

STATEMENT BY MONTHS, SHOWING THE AMOUNT OF UNITED STATES BONDS TRANSFERRED FROM THE SECURITIES HELD IN TRUST BY THE TREASURER OF THE UNITED STATES FOR NATIONAL-BANK CIRCULATION TO THE SECURITIES SO HELD FOR PUBLIC DEPOSITS DURING THE YEAR ENDING OCTOBER 31, 1887, AND THE METHODS BY WHICH SUCH TRANSFER WAS MADE.

Date.	Exchanged.	Substituted.	Transferred by retirement of circulation.
1886.			
November	....	....	$70,000
December	$100,000	....	100,000
1887.			
January	....	....	530,000
February	....	....	220,000
March	....	....	145,000
April	....	....	40,000
May	....	....	155,000
June	....	....	60,000
July	....	$50,000	80,000
August	30,000	....	....
September	140,000	....	62,500
October	115,000	100,000	500,000
Total	385,000	150,000	1,962,500

BANKS WITHOUT CIRCULATION.

As reported last year, some national banks have not availed themselves of the privilege of taking out circulating notes, and others have surrendered their entire circulation. The following list is unchanged since October 31, 1886:

Title of bank.	Capital.	Bonds.
Chemical National Bank, New York, N. Y	$300,000	$50,000
Fulton National Bank, New York, N. Y	300,000	50,000
National City Bank, New York, N. Y	1,000,000	50,000
American Exchange National Bank, New York, N. Y	5,000,000	50,000
Third National Bank, New York, N. Y	1,000,000	50,000
National Bank, Washington, D. C	200,000	50,000
Chestertown National Bank, Chestertown, Md	50,000	12,500
First National Bank, Houston, Tex	100,000	25,000
Mechanics' National Bank, New York, N. Y	2,000,000	50,000
Total	9,950,000	387,500

DISSOLUTION.

The total number of national banks organized since February 25, 1863, is 3,805, of which there are now in operation, as shown elsewhere, 3,061; passed out of the system, 744, accounted for thus:

Passed into voluntary liquidation to wind up their affairs	480
Less number afterward placed in hands of receivers	9
	471
Passed into liquidation for purpose of reorganization	79
Passed into liquidation upon expiration of corporate existence	*75
Placed in hands of receivers	120
	745
Less restored to solvency and resumed business	1
Total passed out of system	744

The corporate existence of five national banks expired during the year ending October 31, 1887, and in each case an extension has been obtained in accordance with the provisions of the act of July 12, 1882.

There were eight failures of national banks during the year ending October 31, 1887, and, as has been shown, in one case the creditors have been paid in full, principal and interest, in another they have received 50 per cent., and in two others 25 per cent. on account of the claims proved.

The affairs of five failed banks have been closed during the past year, and final dividends have been paid to their creditors. These banks, with the total dividends paid in each case, are given below:

Name and location of bank.	Date of appointment of receiver.	Total dividends on principal.	Proportion of interest paid.
		Per cent.	*Per cent.*
Abington National Bank of Abington, Mass	Aug. 2, 1886	100	100
First National Bank of Blair, Nebr	Sept. 8, 1886	100	100
City National Bank of Williamsport, Pa	May 4, 1886	100	100
Palatka National Bank of Palatka, Fla	June 3, 1887	100	100
First National Bank of Butler, Pa	July 23, 1879	81	....

INACTIVE RECEIVERSHIPS.

There still remain in the hands of receivers a small number of banks of which the affairs have been liquidated as far as possible, but the receiverships are kept open by matters pending in the courts. In these cases the expenses of the receivership are reduced to a minimum, and the compensation of the receiver is made dependent as far as practicable upon services rendered and results obtained.

The following table shows the receiverships that are in this condition:

Name and location of bank.	Date of appointment of receiver.	Dividends paid.
		Per cent.
First National Bank of Anderson, Ind	Nov. 23, 1873	30.
National Bank of the State of Missouri, Saint Louis, Mo	June 23, 1877	†100
Third National Bank of Chicago, Ill	Nov. 24, 1877	†100
Central National Bank of Chicago, Ill	Dec. 1, 1877	60
People's National Bank of Helena, Mont	Sept. 13, 1878	40
German American National Bank of Washington, D. C	Nov. 1, 1878	50
First National Bank of Union Mills, Union City, Pa	Mar. 24, 1883	65

* Thirty-eight of these have been reorganized.

† And interest.

By reference to the Report of 1886 it will be seen that the number of these inactive receiverships has been reduced during the past year by two, viz, that of the New Orleans National Banking Association, and the First National Bank of Butler, Pa.

The New Orleans National Banking Association was interested in the case No. 897, Supreme Court of the United States, New Orleans National Banking Association, appellant, *v.* E. D. Le Breton, appellee, which was decided on March 21, 1887, adversely to the receiver. When the last dividend was declared, there was reserved only money enough to defray the expenses of this litigation, so that when the decision was rendered the trust was closed. Out of the amount reserved, however, a small sum was applied to publishing in New Orleans a list of creditors who had not drawn dividends, and by this means unclaimed dividend checks to the amount of $511.83 have since been delivered.

The First National Bank of Butler, Pa., was kept open because of the unadjusted accounts of the receiver. An adjustment was reached during the past year, and a final dividend was declared of 11 per cent., making 81 per cent. in all, and closing the trust.

The receivership of the National Bank of the State of Missouri in Saint Louis seems to have been placed in an anomalous position by reason of the assets proving more valuable than they were supposed to be.

The receiver was appointed June 23, 1877, and on October 2, 1879, an assessment of 25 per cent. was ordered on the stock of the bank.

This assessment, which amounted to $510,025, yielded only $245,108, and although the creditors were paid in full before October 31, 1882, the receivership seems to have been continued because of apprehended disagreements among shareholders as to the relative rights of those who had paid their assessments in full, those who had paid in part, and those who had not paid.

In order to comply with the law the Comptroller caused a meeting of shareholders to be called on June 16, 1887, at which an agent was duly elected, but up to the present time he has failed to give the requisite bond.

There is some litigation in progress of immense importance to the interests involved in this trust, and it is necessary, therefore, that its affairs should be looked after. The stockholders have shown very little concern about the matter.

On March 1, 1882, a final dividend for balance due on principal and interest was declared and paid to the creditors of the Third National Bank of Chicago, Ill. No assessment upon the shareholders had been levied. On June 7, 1882, in pursuance of instructions from the Comptroller, a meeting of the shareholders was held for the purpose of selecting an agent to receive the remaining assets of the bank. In consequence of the failure of the shareholders to select such agent, the receivership was continued. During the past year another meeting was called, in accordance with instructions from the Comptroller, with the same result. A resolution distinctly refusing to elect an agent was adopted by shareholders representing 5,828 shares out of a total of 7,500, being based upon statements entered in the records of the meeting that grave complications would arise in the sale and disposition of the remaining assets of the trust, to the financial injury of the shareholders.

The law affords no means by which shareholders can be coerced into availing themselves of the privilege of taking charge of their own affairs.

DIVIDENDS PAID TO CREDITORS OF INSOLVENT NATIONAL BANKS DURING THE PAST YEAR, WITH TOTAL DIVIDENDS IN EACH CASE UP TO NOVEMBER 1, 1887.

Name and location of bank.	Dividends paid during the past year.		Total dividends paid to depositors.	Proportion of interest paid to depositors.
	Total amount.	*Per cent.*	*Per cent.*	*Per cent.*
Pacific National Bank of Boston, Mass	$691,874.96	30	50	....
First National Bank of Blair, Nebr	82,945.82	100	100	100
Richmond National Bank of Richmond, Ind	73,172.39	29	56	....
Lancaster National Bank of Clinton, Mass	34,147.64	20	70	....
City National Bank of Williamsport, Pa	70,442.34	50	100	100
First National Bank of Pine Bluff, Ark	16,238.24	25	25	....
Exchange National Bank of Norfolk, Va	291,973.33	10	40	....
Schoharie County National Bank of Schoharie, N. Y	14,932.52	10	40	....
First National Bank of Angelica, N. Y	15,518.79	10	85	....
First National Bank of Wahpeton, Dak	11,011.18	10	10	....
Palatka National Bank of Palatka, Fla	9,491.70	100	100	100
First National Bank of Butler, Pa	12,787.24	11	81	....
First National Bank of Livingston, Mont	21,262.54	75	75	....
Middletown National Bank of Middletown, N. Y	102,876.81	15	70	....
Henrietta National Bank of Henrietta, Tex	32,391.89	50	50	....
Fidelity National Bank of Cincinnati, Ohio	596,042.30	25	25	....
Logan National Bank of West Liberty, Ohio	8,108.66	10	30	....
First National Bank of Leadville, Colo	20,385.06	10	40	....
Total	2,106,203.41	....	....	....

Out of 3,805 national banks organized since February, 1863, only 120, or about 3 per cent., have been placed in the hands of receivers; this includes 9 which had been previously placed in liquidation by their stockholders, but upon their failing to pay their depositors the Comptroller appointed receivers to wind up their affairs. Out of the above total of 120 failed banks, 41 have paid their creditors in full, while 23 have besides paid interest, 18 in full and 5 in part. The affairs of 85 banks of the 120 have been finally closed, leaving 35 in process of settlement, of which, as has been seen, 7 are virtually closed with the exception of pending litigation, leaving 28 receiverships only in active operation.

The total amount so far paid to creditors of insolvent national banks has been $29,434,986, upon proved claims amounting to $46,938,388. The amount paid during the year has been $2,135,878, which includes $29,675 paid in dividends declared prior to November 1, 1886, on claims proved since that date. Assessments amounting to $9,945,250 have been made upon stockholders of insolvent national banks under section 5151 of the Revised Statutes of the United States. From this source the gross collections amount to $4,682,563, of which there has been received during the past year $636,755. Suits are pending in some cases.

It will be observed that the gross collections from stockholders of insolvent banks amount to only about 47 per cent. of the assessments. Unfortunately the cost of the litigation attending such collections cannot be accurately ascertained from the records in this office, but it has been very great, and should be deducted from gross collections. The Comptroller is disposed to think the net amount actually realized to creditors from this source has been under, rather than over, 40 per cent. of the total assessments. In any case the figures show that the security afforded to creditors by subjecting shareholders to liability beyond the loss of their stock is quite disproportionate to the damage inflicted upon solvent shareholders. This personal-liability feature tends to discourage prudent business men from investing in national-bank stock, while contested assessments generally develop an amount of chicanery and fraud which must exercise an injurious influence upon morals.

ISSUES AND REDEMPTIONS.

The following table exhibits the number and amount of national-bank notes of each denomination which have been issued and redeemed since the organization of the system, and the number and amount outstanding on October 31, 1887:

Denominations.	Number of notes.			Amount.		
	Issued.	Redeemed.	Outstanding.	Issued.	Redeemed.	Outstanding.
Ones	23,167,677	22,776,403	391,274	$23,167,677	$22,776,403	$391,274.00
Twos	7,747,519	7,646,720	100,799	15,495,038	15,293,440	201,598.00
Fives	100,455,524	85,170,819	15,284,705	502,277,620	425,854,095	76,423,525.00
Tens	42,762,799	33,799,928	8,962,871	427,627,990	337,999,280	89,628,710.00
Twenties	13,301,145	10,091,941	3,209,204	266,022,900	201,838,820	64,184,080.00
Fifties	1,849,613	1,536,143	313,470	92,480,650	76,807,150	15,673,500.00
One hundreds	1,375,140	1,127,452	247,694	137,514,000	112,745,200	24,769,400.00
Five hundreds	23,924	23,293	631	11,962,000	11,646,500	315,500.00
One thousands	7,369	7,305	64	7,369,000	7,305,000	64,000.00
Fractions outstanding						23,742.60
Totals	190,690,716	162,180,004	28,510,712	1,483,917,475	1,212,265,888	271,675,329.60

Notes of gold banks are not included in this table.

A table showing the number and denomination of national-bank notes issued and redeemed, and the number of each denomination outstanding on October 31, for the last twenty years, will be found on page 178 in the Appendix.

Distinct accounts are kept for the incomplete currency issued to banks in replacement of notes redeemed and destroyed under the provisions of the act of June 20, 1874, to banks taking out new circulation upon an extension of their corporate existence under the act of July 12, 1882, and to old and new banks increasing the volume of their circulation by adding to the amount of bonds deposited. The notes issued in the three latter cases have heretofore been designated (on the books of this office and in previous reports) "additional circulation," but this term applies properly only to the two cases last above mentioned.

In order that the following table, showing by States the amount of "additional circulation" issued during the year ending October 31, 1887, and the total amount of such circulation issued since June 20, 1874, may conform to previous reports, the three classes of issue are distributed into two columns, one showing amounts issued under the act of 1882 and the other the issues which are properly additional. This table also shows the amount of circulation retired during the year and the total amount retired since June 20, 1874.

TABLE SHOWING BY STATES THE AMOUNT OF "ADDITIONAL CIRCULATION" ISSUED DURING THE YEAR ENDING OCTOBER 31, 1887, AND TOTAL AMOUNT ISSUED SINCE JUNE 20, 1874.

States and Territories.	Circulation issued under act of July 12, 1882.	Additional circulation issued.	Total.	Circulation retired. Under act of June 20, 1874.	Insolvent and liquidating banks.	Total.
Maine	$46,220	$11,250	$57,470	$429,204	$433,197	$862,401
New Hampshire	49,940	45,000	94,940	208,673	198,942	407,615
Vermont	51,590	56,250	107,840	500,257	337,939	838,196
Massachusetts	1,113,805	940,320	2,054,125	4,341,101	3,869,189	8,210,290
Rhode Island	2,950	13,050	16,000	796,280	1,112,291	1,908,577
Connecticut	178,465	45,000	223,465	1,107,930	1,195,343	2,303,273
New York	217,510	1,041,030	1,258,540	1,973,799	2,780,776	4,754,575
New Jersey	19,000	203,270	222,270	588,602	456,091	1,044,693
Pennsylvania	597,940	806,290	1,404,230	3,598,189	2,920,249	6,518,438
Delaware	....	11,240	11,240	38,160	33,343	71,503
Maryland	3,000	67,500	70,500	650,448	752,486	1,402,934
District of Columbia	....	45,000	45,000	61,982	881	62,863
Virginia	....	11,250	11,250	140,320	147,059	287,379
West Virginia	....	25,650	25,650	73,114	146,032	219,146
North Carolina	....	11,250	11,250	112,052	27,202	139,254
South Carolina	....	11,240	11,240	135,102	35,050	170,152
Georgia	....	90,000	90,000	211,640	110,073	321,713
Florida	....	1,930	1,930	3,340	1,595	4,935
Alabama	....	249,750	249,750	127,450	18,622	146,072
Mississippi	....	96,740	96,740	11,730	15	11,745
Louisiana	....	302,480	302,480	281,372	170,077	451,449
Texas	....	468,675	468,675	108,636	16,801	125,437
Arkansas	....	71,010	71,010	10,097	10,355	20,452
Kentucky	....	....	....	1,154,197	288,240	1,442,437
Tennessee	....	227,340	227,340	253,335	108,890	362,225
Missouri	20	253,975	254,005	216,441	130,161	346,600
Ohio	110,250	439,955	550,205	1,730,530	1,242,340	2,972,872
Indiana	30,310	249,680	279,990	649,186	503,567	1,152,753
Illinois	128,450	310,025	438,475	666,927	419,580	1,086,507
Michigan	18,600	93,420	112,020	281,533	287,942	569,475
Wisconsin	420	181,120	181,540	163,603	156,736	320,339
Iowa	3,850	94,580	98,430	437,826	169,517	607,343
Minnesota	32,750	180,035	212,785	124,323	89,817	214,140
Kansas	....	877,420	877,420	107,461	23,011	130,472
Nebraska	....	225,000	225,000	153,688	51,547	205,235
Nevada	....	11,250	11,250	5,960	....	5,960
Oregon	....	92,240	92,240	20,650	....	20,650
Colorado	....	78,900	78,900	63,437	67,845	131,282
Utah	....	10	10	32,530	841	33,371
Idaho	....	....	....	12,851	4,015	16,866
Montana	....	15,000	15,000	13,000	....	13,000
Wyoming	....	22,505	22,505	140	3,560	3,700
New Mexico	....	13,520	13,520	80,840	20,350	101,190
Dakota	....	133,265	133,265	37,326	....	37,326
Washington	....	82,510	82,510	38,750	7,612	46,362
California	....	318,850	318,850	104,740	8,370	113,110
Arizona	....	22,500	22,500	....	8,070	8,070
Total	2,614,080	8,549,265	11,163,345	21,957,758	18,366,519	40,324,277
Surrendered to this office and retired	....	....	....	....	....	290,769
From June 20, 1874, to October 31, 1886	....	....	196,704,902	171,775,021	58,347,227	230,122,248
Surrendered and retired same dates	....	....	....	....	....	15,246,964
Grand total October 31, 1887	....	....	207,878,247	193,732,779	76,713,746	285,984,258

Notes of gold banks are not included in the above table.

Of the above $8,549,265 there was issued to banks organized during the year $4,690,375, and to already existing banks increasing their circulation $3,858,890.

ISSUES.

The total issues of incomplete currency during the year are shown by the vault account, as follows:

National-bank currency in vaults October 31, 1886		$62, 486, 660
Amount received from Bureau of Engraving and Printing during the year ending October 31, 1887		25, 413, 750
Total		87, 900, 410
Amount issued to banks during the year	$36, 756, 100	
Amount canceled during the year, not having been issued	934, 060	
		37, 690, 160
Balance in vaults		50, 210, 250

The duties devolving upon the clerical force in the division of issue of this office are of great responsibility, requiring absolute accuracy and promptness on the part of those to whom these duties are assigned. The records of receipts and issues are balanced daily with the vault accounts, and the work of each day is completed before that of another day is begun. During the past year 29,993 packages of currency were forwarded to banks by express, the same number of receipts prepared for signature and return by the banks, and a large amount of correspondence was conducted.

REDEMPTION.

The provisions of law relating to the redemption of the circulating notes of national banks have undergone many changes, but no change has at any time been made in the only two provisions contained in the act of February, 1863.

These are, first, that every bank must redeem on demand at its place of business any of its circulating notes presented there for redemption during business hours; and second, that the medium of redemption must be "lawful money of the United States."

By the act of June 3, 1864, every association located in Saint Louis, Louisville, Chicago, Detroit, Milwaukee, New Orleans, Cincinnati, Cleveland, Pittsburgh, Baltimore, Philadelphia, Boston, New York, Albany, Leavenworth, San Francisco, or Washington City was required to select, subject to the approval of the Comptroller of the Currency, some national bank in the city of New York, "at which it will redeem its circulating notes at par;" and each association not organized within any of the cities named had likewise to select as its redemption agent some association in one of these cities.

The Comptroller was required to give public notice of the redemption agent of every association, and of any changes made in such agents, and in case any bank failed to select an agent, or to redeem its notes, as provided by the act, the Comptroller, with the concurrence of the Secretary of the Treasury, might appoint a receiver to wind up its affairs.

The act of June 20, 1874, established the National Bank Redemption Agency of the Treasury at Washington, repealed all requirements as to redemption agents elsewhere, relieved the banks of the obligation to keep a reserve upon their circulating notes, and substituted therefor the requirement that every bank should keep up a redemption fund in the hands of the Treasurer of the United States equal to 5 per cent. of its outstanding circulation.

The following table, compiled from the Treasurers' reports, shows the practical working of the law as to the 5 per cent. redemption fund:

TABLE SHOWING MODE OF REIMBURSEMENT OF FIVE PER CENT. REDEMPTION FUND BY NATIONAL BANKS, BY FISCAL YEARS, FROM 1875 TO 1887, INCLUSIVE.

Years.	Deposits of lawful money with assistant treasurers, United States.	Deposits with Treasurer, United States.			Total.
		Deposits received at counter.	Remittances of lawful money by express.	Proceeds of national-bank notes redeemed.	
1875	$88, 834, 653. 12	$989, 646. 63	$32, 308, 100. 78	$18, 742, 163. 00	$140, 874, 563. 53
1876	105, 134, 528. 37	664, 989. 45	19, 042, 491. 62	52, 643, 065. 00	177, 485, 074. 44
1877	116, 044, 751. 34	(*)	7, 678, 750. 57	91, 856, 769. 92	215, 580, 271. 83
1878	100, 819, 824. 50	(*)	5, 935, 806. 89	98, 552, 739. 98	205, 308, 371. 37
1879	101, 194, 261. 04	(*)	4, 894, 393. 06	50, 581, 484. 09	156, 670, 138. 19
1880	46, 960, 242. 06	(*)	2, 627, 861. 16	6, 924, 097. 88	56, 512, 201. 10
1881	41, 411, 436. 87	(*)	3, 106, 187. 40	4, 313, 702. 36	48, 831, 326. 63
1882	50, 531, 496. 68	(*)	2, 975, 682. 27	4, 534, 598. 69	58, 041, 777. 64
1883	113, 726, 801. 90	(*)	2, 939, 882. 01	5, 248, 120. 14	121, 914, 804. 05
1884	89, 338, 255. 34	(*)	3, 801, 957. 46	5, 727, 786. 37	98, 867, 999. 17
1885	106, 264, 901. 13	(*)	4, 503, 141. 79	6, 376, 897. 26	117, 144, 940. 18
1886	92, 363, 184. 15	1, 787, 241. 84	3, 433, 468. 78	5, 775, 408. 84	103, 359, 303. 61
1887	46, 254, 760. 76	2, 077, 837. 82	2, 000, 214. 04	2, 189, 546. 65	52, 522, 359. 27
Total	1,098,879,037.26	5, 519, 715. 74	95, 247, 997. 83	353, 466, 470. 18	1,553,113,221.01
Average	70.75	0. 13	6. 13	22. 76	100.00

* No record.

The following tables, compiled from the Treasurers' reports, show for the fiscal years 1874–'75 to 1886–'87—

1. The amounts of national-bank currency received annually at the redemption agency, and the disposition made of it.
2. The points from which this currency was forwarded, and the percentage of the whole received from each point.
3. The total amount of notes redeemed, and the mode of redemption.
4. The cost of redemption.

TABLE SHOWING RECEIPTS AND DELIVERIES OF MONEYS BY THE NATIONAL-BANK REDEMPTION AGENCY (UNITED STATES TREASURER'S OFFICE) FOR EACH FISCAL YEAR FROM 1875 TO 1887, INCLUSIVE.

Year ending June 30—	Cash balance on hand at close of previous year.	To national-bank notes received for redemption.	To "overs" reported in national-bank notes received for redemption.	Aggregates.	By national-bank notes, fit for circulation, deposited in the Treasury, and forwarded to national banks by express.	By national-bank notes, unfit for circulation, delivered to the Comptroller of the Currency.	By notes of failed and liquidating national banks, deposited in the Treasury of the United States.
1875		$155, 520, 880. 48	$24, 644. 85	$155, 545, 525. 33	$26, 166, 291. 00	$115, 109, 445. 00	$6, 579, 217. 00
1876	$6, 031, 022. 32	209, 036, 854. 94	16, 491. 42	215, 086, 368. 68	102, 478, 700. 00	78, 643, 155. 00	24, 927, 900. 00
1877	7, 942, 539. 60	242, 885, 375. 14	24, 956. 58	250, 852, 910. 72	151, 070, 300. 00	62, 518, 600. 00	24, 439, 700. 00
1878	11, 505, 312. 52	213, 151, 458. 56	37, 649. 20	224, 694, 420. 28	152, 437, 300. 00	51, 585, 400. 00	11, 852, 100. 00
1879	8, 410, 848. 33	157, 656, 644. 96	22, 148. 42	166, 089, 641. 71	112, 411, 800. 00	40, 204, 700. 00	8, 354, 250. 00
1880	3, 785, 389. 29	61, 585, 675. 68	6, 461. 30	65, 377, 526. 27	24, 980, 500. 00	29, 861, 700. 00	6, 671, 700. 00
1881	3, 097, 983. 77	59, 650, 259. 43	13, 231. 38	62, 761, 474. 58	6, 763, 600. 00	40, 080, 700. 00	12, 435, 400. 00
1882	2, 844, 107. 37	76, 089, 327. 48	11, 222. 13	78, 944, 656. 98	3, 801, 500. 00	53, 838, 500. 00	16, 953, 730. 00
1883	3, 630, 989. 32	102, 699, 676. 73	8, 032. 09	106, 338, 758. 14	15, 572, 100. 00	78, 664, 758. 00	4, 667, 600. 00
1884	6, 672, 963. 85	126, 152, 572. 34	6, 056. 20	132, 838, 602. 49	26, 255, 500. 00	95, 616, 064. 00	3, 507, 950. 00
1885	6, 910, 452. 03	150, 209, 129. 01	17, 060. 07	157, 136, 641. 11	45, 634, 800. 00	98, 598, 170. 00	5, 591, 730. 00
1886	6, 791, 087. 93	130, 296, 606. 82	25, 528. 97	137, 113, 223. 72	46, 701, 100. 00	82, 256, 713. 50	3, 910, 573. 00
1887	3, 840, 402. 05	87, 689, 687. 15	16, 404. 07	91, 546, 493. 27	20, 786, 640. 00	66, 841, 550. 00	1, 133, 215. 50
Total	71, 463, 097. 78	1, 772, 626, 148. 72	229, 996. 78	1, 844, 320, 243. 28	735, 060, 131. 00	893, 819, 435. 50	131, 025, 125. 50

Year ending June 30—	By United States notes deposited in the Treasury of the United States.	By packages referred and moneys returned.	By express charges deducted.	By counterfeit notes rejected and returned.	By national-bank notes—less than three-fifths, lacking signatures, and stolen—rejected and returned, and discount on United States currency.	By "shorts" reported in national-bank notes received for redemption.	Cash on hand at close of year.
1875		$1, 620, 557. 39		$3, 741. 00	$15, 028. 12	$20, 223. 50	$6, 031, 022. 32
1876		1, 065, 002. 20		5, 188. 00	7, 709. 22	16, 175. 26	7, 942, 539. 00
1877		1, 278, 903. 86		5, 634. 00	4, 755. 91	29, 704. 43	11, 505, 312. 52
1878		384, 372. 22		4, 008. 00	3, 997. 13	16, 394. 60	8, 410, 848. 33
1879	$959, 132. 00	329, 323. 34	$25, 812. 15	3, 016. 00	6, 282. 58	9, 906. 35	3, 785, 389. 29
1880	428, 686. 00	305, 432. 14	9, 938. 41	3, 846. 75	7, 870. 23	9, 868. 97	3, 097, 983. 77
1881	30, 645. 00	569, 971. 06	3, 345. 03	4, 324. 50	22, 763. 37	6, 618. 25	2, 844, 107. 37
1882	24, 970. 00	672, 427. 09	1, 152. 09	4, 151. 00	3, 832. 35	13, 405. 13	3, 630, 989. 32
1883	7, 267. 00	727, 282. 98	725. 84	4, 559. 50	4, 337. 62	10, 103. 35	6, 672, 963. 85
1884	81, 858. 00	455, 333. 05	523. 54	3, 770. 50	3, 365. 77	3, 785. 60	6, 910, 452. 03
1885	177, 350. 00	319, 219. 19	612. 25	3, 560. 00	3, 636. 49	6, 445. 25	6, 791, 087. 93
1886	111, 924. 50	277, 194. 78	526. 96	2, 720. 00	3, 822. 28	8, 246. 65	3, 840, 402. 05
1887	126, 727. 10	464, 413. 45	573. 58	2, 924. 00	2, 554. 23	22, 356. 00	2, 165, 539. 41
Total	1, 918, 559. 60	8, 479, 462. 75	43, 239. 85	51, 443. 25	89, 955. 30	173, 233. 34	73, 628, 637. 19

TABLE SHOWING, BY FISCAL YEARS, FROM 1875 TO 1887, THE AMOUNTS OF NATIONAL-BANK NOTES RECEIVED AT THE UNITED STATES TREASURY FOR REDEMPTION FROM THE PRINCIPAL CITIES AND OTHER PLACES, AND THE PROPORTION OF EACH AMOUNT TO THE WHOLE.

Year.	New York.		Boston.		Philadelphia.		Chicago.		Cincinnati.		Saint Louis.	
	Amounts.	Per cent.	Amounts.	Per cent.	Amounts.	Per cent.	Amounts.	Per cent.	Amounts.	Per cent.	Amounts.	Per cent.
1875	$30,925,000	52.07	$17,598,000	11.32	$9,096,000	5.85	$6,824,000	4.39	$3,676,000	2.37	$1,384,000	.89
1876	78,389,000	38.37	55,878,000	27.35	9,778,000	4.79	10,006,000	4.89	3,085,000	1.51	1,019,000	.50
1877	76,693,000	32.47	75,212,000	31.84	20,988,000	8.89	4,162,000	1.76	2,781,000	1.18	1,292,000	.55
1878	66,273,000	31.48	80,527,000	38.26	10,836,000	5.15	3,194,000	1.52	2,268,000	1.08	999,000	.47
1879	54,170,000	35.00	59,375,000	38.36	7,052,000	4.56	1,719,000	1.11	1,219,000	.79	1,487,000	.96
1880	26,460,000	42.96	11,701,000	19.00	3,358,000	5.45	1,673,000	2.72	819,000	1.33	392,000	.64
1881	23,319,000	39.09	5,565,000	9.33	4,919,000	8.25	2,655,000	4.45	996,000	1.67	673,000	1.13
1882	28,012,000	36.82	7,370,000	9.69	5,939,000	7.81	3,545,000	4.66	1,188,000	1.56	1,061,000	1.39
1883	36,042,000	35.10	16,631,000	16.19	7,333,000	7.14	6,146,000	5.98	1,774,000	1.73	1,372,000	1.34
1884	54,327,000	43.07	19,971,000	15.83	6,830,000	5.41	5,794,000	4.59	1,822,000	1.45	1,155,000	.92
1885	75,409,000	50.20	27,473,000	18.29	7,220,000	4.81	4,558,000	3.03	1,910,000	1.27	977,000	.65
1886	49,487,000	37.98	30,031,000	23.05	7,323,000	5.62	5,493,000	4.22	2,269,000	1.74	3,422,000	2.63
1887	31,314,583	35.71	13,219,269	15.08	6,972,856	7.95	5,315,319	6.06	2,244,310	2.55	3,421,698	3.90

Year.	Baltimore.		New Orleans.		Providence.		Pittsburgh.		Other places.		Totals.	
	Amounts.	Per cent.	Amounts.	Per cent.	Amounts.	Per cent.	Amounts.	Per cent.	Amounts.	Per cent.	Amounts.	Per cent.
1875	$1,902,000	1.22			$1,388,000	.89	$1,449,000	.93	$31,189,000	20.07	$155,421,000	100.00
1876	3,265,000	1.60			3,247,000	1.59	1,425,000	.70	38,108,000	18.70	204,300,000	100.00
1877	1,821,000	.77			5,653,000	2.39	1,322,000	.56	46,286,000	19.59	236,213,000	100.00
1878	1,085,000	.52			4,989,000	2.37	1,141,000	.54	39,179,000	18.61	210,491,000	100.00
1879	694,000	.45			3,772,000	2.44	635,000	.41	24,647,000	15.92	154,709,000	100.00
1880	415,000	.67			1,451,000	2.36	547,000	.89	14,767,000	23.98	61,586,000	100.00
1881	673,000	1.13			1,419,000	2.38	606,000	1.01	18,825,000	31.56	59,650,000	100.00
1882	947,000	1.24			1,426,000	1.87	880,000	1.16	25,721,000	33.80	76,089,000	100.00
1883	1,626,000	1.58			1,666,000	1.62	917,000	.89	29,191,000	28.43	102,709,000	100.00
1884	2,853,000	2.26			1,820,000	1.44	819,000	.65	30,761,000	24.38	126,152,000	100.00
1885	3,705,000	2.47	$2,063,000	1.37	2,293,000	1.53	681,000	.45	23,918,000	15.92	150,309,000	100.00
1886	3,546,000	2.72	1,423,000	1.09	1,731,000	1.32	526,000	.40	25,051,000	19.23	130,296,000	100.00
1887	3,102,500	3.54	1,316,036	1.50	1,615,131	1.16	527,800	.60	19,240,185	21.91	87,689,687	100.00

TABLE SHOWING TOTAL AMOUNT AND MODE OF PAYMENT FOR NATIONAL-BANK NOTES REDEEMED, BY FISCAL YEARS, COMMENCING WITH YEAR ENDING JUNE 30, 1875.

Year.	Transfer checks.	United States notes.	Fractional silver coin.	Standard silver dollars.	Redeemed at counter.	Credits to assistant treasurers and United States depositaries in general account.	Credits in redemption accounts.	Notes fit for circulation and of failed, liquidating, and reducing banks, deposited in Treasury in payment of notes redeemed by Treasury prior to July 1, 1875.	Total.
1875 ..	$83,872,954.00	$19,977,719.00	....	....	$100,000.00	$12,667,011.00	$18,742,163.00	$17,532,008.00	$152,891,855.00
1876 ..	92,374,801.00	40,120,338.00	....	....	4,738,979.00	19,078,209.00	52,613,065.00	....	208,955,392.00
1877 ..	95,212,713.45	34,588,129.15	$468,974.00	....	6,675,000.00	12,789,757.00	91,856,769.92	....	241,591,373.52
1878 ..	75,361,427.23	23,046,418.44	549,615.40	....	2,661,021.00	12,609,083.76	98,552,739.98	....	212,780,335.81
1879 ..	51,718,253.06	14,617,649.41	52,178.90	$96,683.32	5,089,222.80	35,148,181.38	50,581,484.09	....	157,303,622.96
1880 ..	10,852,505.53	21,171,826.66	28,230.59	174,831.85	3,883,417.60	18,218,070.37	6,924,097.88	....	61,255,980.48
1881 ..	22,415,972.28	19,567,744.21	85,164.56	215,045.27	3,522,607.00	8,936,232.92	4,313,702.36	....	59,056,468.60
1882 ..	32,992,144.72	23,222,831.83	246,447.42	269,918.44	4,033,402.40	10,106,238.45	4,534,598.69	....	75,405,581.95
1883 ..	56,018,417.71	24,068,064.66	296,257.79	242,518.37	3,941,638.00	12,426,692.86	5,248,120.14	....	101,843,739.53
1884 ..	77,991,916.83	24,080,304.62	158,127.60	1,015,519.10	3,826,293.00	12,960,221.66	5,727,786.37	....	125,760,169.18
1885 ..	105,8[illegible]	19,236,730.27	135,773.22	182,500.35	3,818,090.50	13,944,370.50	6,443,697.26	....	149,931,396.90
1886 ..	74,149,555.26	9,204,752.76	103,843.62	451,194.22	8,385,485.00	31,007,087.30	6,727,706.96	....	130,029,625.12
1887 ..	39,906,984.07	15,657,298.62	97,670.41	248,970.92	4,200,654.50	24,708,344.79	2,243,346.65	....	87,213,269.96

TABLE SHOWING, BY FISCAL YEARS FROM 1875 to 1887, EXPENSES INCURRED IN THE REDEMPTION OF NATIONAL-BANK NOTES AT THE UNITED STATES TREASURY.

Year.	Charges for transportation.	Costs for assorting notes.						
		Salaries.	Printing and binding.	Stationery.	Postage.	Contingent and other expenses.	Furniture.	Total.
1875	$88,098.31	$158,227.39	....	*$12,290.72	$3,298.80	$16,131.47	$12,918.68	$290,965.37
1876	159,142.84	188,018.94	....	*9,174.68	3,391.00	1,993.01	3,472.84	365,193.31
1877	180,362.05	150,695.68	$6,604.30	3,818.10	3,716.66	2,869.31	....	357,066.10
1878	173,420.60	136,580.63	2,660.32	3,090.00	....	2,190.93	....	317,942.48
1879	98,298.75	133,956.27	2,894.60	2,507.22	....	3,203.11	....	240,949.95
1880	34,764.24	104,350.08	2,632.69	1,034.29	....	947.09	....	143,728.39
1881	33,843.86	89,564.72	1,220.60	1,051.27	....	531.67	....	126,212.12
1882	39,203.31	87,593.56	1,535.42	896.51	....	390.58	....	129,529.38
1883	57,190.86	86,213.35	2,401.54	890.41	....	896.11	....	147,592.27
1884	68,684.11	88,426.79	1,935.91	1,133.84	....	716.00	....	160,896.65
1885	85,255.48	93,371.82	1,670.77	1,114.19	....	444.90	....	181,857.16
1886	74,490.52	89,665.18	3,190.89	1,163.65	....	333.11	....	168,243.35
1887	48,020.53	87,450.54	1,430.93	1,053.39	....	1,011.61	....	138,967.00

* In 1875 and 1876 "Printing and binding" was included with item "Stationery."

REDEMPTION OF CIRCULATION OF BANKS IN THE HANDS OF RECEIVERS, OF THOSE IN VOLUNTARY LIQUIDATION, AND OF THOSE REDUCING CIRCULATION UNDER THE ACT OF JUNE 20, 1874.

The redemption of the circulating notes of failed banks at the United States Treasury was provided for originally as it is now, by giving the Comptroller power to cancel or to sell the bonds of the banks, and in case of deficiency in the proceeds to make it good out of the assets of the corporation; but before the act of 1874 went into effect the notes of such banks were called in by public advertisement, whereas now they are left in circulation until they are brought by the ordinary currents of redemption into the office of the Treasurer or of one of the assistant treasurers, or into the hands of a designated depositary of public moneys, or one of the national-bank depositaries.

Section 8 of the act of June 20, 1874, requires the Treasurer, assistant treasurers, designated depositaries, and national-bank depositaries to assort and return to the Treasury for redemption the notes of such national banks as have failed, or have gone into voluntary liquidation, and of all such as shall thereafter fail or go into such liquidation.

The following table, compiled from the records of the Bureau of the Currency, shows the course of redemption of the notes of failed banks:

Total circulation of all failed banks, $14,818,276; amount redeemed, $13,392,311; balance outstanding or lost, $1,425,965.

TABLE SHOWING, BY YEARS, FROM OCTOBER 1, 1865, TO NOVEMBER 1, 1887, THE TOTAL CIRCULATION OF BANKS FAILED, THE AMOUNT REDEEMED, AND THE BALANCE OUTSTANDING AT CLOSE OF EACH YEAR. (COMPILED FROM REPORTS OF COMPTROLLER OF THE CURRENCY.)

Year ending—	Total circulation outstanding at end of previous year.	Total circulation of banks failed during the year.	Aggregate of two previous columns.	Amount of circulation of failed banks redeemed during year.	Balance of circulation of failed banks outstanding at close of year.
October 1, 1865	....	$44,000	$44,000.00	None.	$44,000.00
October 1, 1866	$44,000.00	265,000	309,000.00	$5,320.00	303,680.00
October 1, 1867	303,680.00	748,900	1,052,580.00	163,288.00	889,292.00
October 1, 1868	889,292.00	321,800	1,211,092.00	648,533.00	562,559.00
October 1, 1869	562,559.00	45,000	607,559.00	274,820.55	332,738.45
October 1, 1870	332,738.45	129,700	462,438.45	143,602.60	318,835.85
October 1, 1871	318,835.85	None.	318,835.85	110,284.25	208,551.60
November 1, 1872	208,551.60	1,388,393	1,596,944.60	1,095,581.00	501,363.00
November 1, 1873	501,363.00	2,522,100	3,023,463.00	720,915.00	2,302,548.00
November 1, 1874	2,302,548.00	230,000	2,532,548.00	494,910.00	2,037,638.00
November 1, 1875	2,037,638.00	638,676	2,676,314.00	1,279,346.50	1,396,967.50
November 1, 1876	1,396,967.50	540,609	1,937,576.50	961,279.80	976,296.70
November 1, 1877	976,296.70	2,349,114	3,325,410.70	2,299,785.25	1,025,625.45
November 1, 1878	1,025,625.45	1,385,068	2,410,693.45	859,239.45	1,551,454.00
November 1, 1879	1,551,454.00	516,825	2,068,279.00	919,600.00	1,148,679.00
November 1, 1880	1,148,679.00	506,143	1,654,822.00	322,546.00	1,332,276.00
November 1, 1881	1,332,276.00	None.	1,332,276.00	382,534.00	949,742.00
November 1, 1882	949,742.00	999,500	1,949,242.00	547,610.00	1,401,632.00
November 1, 1883	1,401,632.00	108,200	1,509,832.00	648,704.00	861,128.00
November 1, 1884	861,128.00	850,120	1,711,248.00	612,960.00	1,098,288.00
November 1, 1885	1,098,288.00	486,550	1,584,838.00	451,424.00	1,133,414.00
November 1, 1886	1,133,414.00	434,840	1,568,254.00	110,228.00	1,458,026.00
November 1, 1887	1,458,026.00	307,738	1,765,764.00	339,799.00	1,425,965.00
Total	....	14,818,276	....	13,392,311.00	....

Before the act of June 20, 1874, banks reducing their circulation could withdraw their bonds from the Treasury only upon surrendering there for cancellation an amount of their circulating notes proportioned to the amount of bonds to be withdrawn, and up to July 14, 1870, banks for one year after going into voluntary liquidation had to resort to the same means in order to withdraw their bonds, but after the expiration of the year such banks might deposit lawful money for the difference between the whole amount of circulation issued to them and the amount surrendered, and thereupon get back the rest of their bonds. The amount of such deposits and the time at which they should be made were left to the voluntary choice of the bank. The act of July 14, 1870, made the deposit of lawful money obligatory upon liquidating banks, and the act of June 20, 1874, fixed six months after notice of liquidation as the limit of time allowed for making such deposits.

The act of June 20, 1874, provided also that any national banking association might withdraw its circulating notes upon the deposit of lawful money with the Treasurer of the United States in sums of not less than $9,000. Under this act, and on account of liquidating and insolvent banks, and under section 6 of the act of July 12, 1882, which provides for a deposit of lawful money to retire the old circulation of national banks whose corporate existence has been extended, $371,882,780 of lawful money has been deposited with the Treasurer. This includes $2,663,720 for redemption of the notes of national gold banks and $75,806,357 for the redemption of national-bank notes under section 6 of the act of July 12, 1882.

During the year ending October 31, 1887, lawful money to the amount of $61,387,320 was deposited with the Treasurer to retire circulation, of which $1,169,472 was deposited by banks in liquidation, $36,664,668 by banks reducing circulation under the act of June 20, 1874, and $23,553,180 by banks retiring old circulation under the act of July 12, 1882. The amount previously deposited under the acts of June 20, 1874, and July 12, 1882, was $260,463,378; by banks in liquidation, $64,276,892; making a total of $386,127,590. Deducting from the total the amount of circulating notes redeemed and destroyed without re-issue, which was $283,301,453, there remained in the hands of the Treasurer on October 31, 1887, $102,826,137 of lawful money for the redemption and retirement of national bank circulation, including $239,929 for the redemption of the circulating notes of national gold banks.

Prior to June 20, 1874, there were redeemed and destroyed $10,431,-135, and since that date $272,870,317 of bank notes have been redeemed, destroyed, and retired. This latter amount includes $2,423,-791 of the notes of national gold banks, and $30,728,515 of the notes of national banks whose corporate existence has been extended under the act of July 12, 1882.

There are at present no national gold banks in existence. Of those which had been organized, three went into voluntary liquidation and the others became currency banks, under the provisions of the act approved February 14, 1880.

Under all the laws now in operation the Treasurer has received for redemption up to November 1, 1887, national-bank notes aggregating in amount $1,795,093,803.

During the past year the receipts at the Treasury amounted to $83,243,-017, of which amount $30,052,077, or 36 per cent., was received from the banks in the city of New York, and $11,006,900, or 13 per cent., from banks in the city of Boston. The amount received from Philadelphia was $6,896,189; from Chicago, $5,220,200; from Cincinnati, $2,650,868; from Saint Louis, $3,219,086; from Baltimore, $2,708,500; from New Orleans, $1,350,647; from Providence, $948,631, and from Pittsburgh, $600,889

The following table exhibits the amount of national-bank notes received monthly for redemption by the Comptroller of the Currency during the year ending October 31, 1887, and the amount received during the same period at the redemption agency of the Treasury, together with the total amount received since the passage of the act of June 20, 1874:

Months.	Received by the Comptroller of the Currency—					Received at United States Treasury redemption agency.
	From national banks in connection with reduction of circulation and replacement with new notes.	From the redemption agency—			Total.	
		For replacement with new notes.	For reduction of circulation under act June 20, 1874.	Insolvent and liquidating national banks.		
1886.						
November	$72, 840	$2, 200, 310	$1, 150, 583	$1, 827, 553	$5, 251, 286	$5, 954, 011
December	6, 515	2, 304, 475	1, 646, 230	1, 566, 826	5, 524, 046	7, 940, 494
1887.						
January	13, 940	3, 231, 160	2, 379, 512	1, 851, 451	7, 467, 063	11, 513, 904
February	80	2, 845, 340	2, 390, 118	1, 775, 167	7, 010, 705	7, 769, 081
March	40, 700	2, 096, 630	1, 754, 554	1, 549, 566	5, 441, 450	5, 943, 971
April	40	1, 901, 125	1, 682, 552	1, 510, 087	5, 093, 804	6, 908, 850
May	10, 690	2, 263, 050	2, 133, 914	1, 743, 237	6, 150, 891	7, 866, 911
June	103, 970	2, 440, 760	2, 434, 653	1, 856, 924	6, 836, 307	6, 878, 141
July	26, 210	1, 512, 110	1, 686, 679	1, 253, 260	4, 478, 259	5, 903, 291
August	690	1, 541, 705	1, 827, 235	1, 289, 870	4, 659, 569	5, 921, 000
September	3, 905	1, 562, 075	1, 690, 764	1, 307, 548	4, 564, 292	5, 101, 627
October	40	1, 536, 715	1, 094, 064	835, 021	3, 465, 840	5, 541, 736
Total	279, 620	25, 435, 515	21, 861, 858	18, 366, 519	65, 943, 512	83, 243, 017
Received from June 20, 1874, to October 31, 1886	16, 065, 805	740, 273, 100	171, 865, 151	58, 222, 236	986, 426, 292	1, 711, 850, 786
Grand total	16, 345, 425	765, 708, 615	193, 727, 009	76, 588, 755	1, 052, 369, 804	1, 795, 093, 803

Notes of gold banks are not included in the above table.

The following table, compiled from the books of the Comptroller of the Currency, exhibits the amount of national-bank notes received at this office and destroyed yearly since the establishment of the system:

Prior to November 1, 1865	$175, 490	During year ended October 31—	
During year ended October 31—		1879	$41, 101, 830
1866	1, 050, 382	1880	35, 539, 660
1867	3, 401, 423	1881	54, 941, 130
1868	4, 602, 825	1882	74, 917, 611
1869	8, 603, 729	1883	82, 913, 766
1870	14, 305, 689	1884	93, 178, 418
1871	24, 344, 047	1885	91, 048, 723
1872	30, 211, 720	1886	69, 989, 810
1873	36, 433, 171	1887	47, 720, 083
1874	49, 939, 741	Additional amount of insolvent and liquidating national banks	87, 144, 882
1875	137, 697, 696		
1876	98, 672, 716	Total	1,212,240,754
1877	76, 918, 963		
1878	57, 381, 249		

Notes of gold banks are not included in the above table.

There was in the vault of the redemption division of this office, awaiting destruction, at the close of business October 31, 1886	$287, 240
Received during the year ended October 31, 1887	65, 997, 812
Total	66, 285, 052
Withdrawn and destroyed during the year	66, 148, 742
Balance in vault October 31, 1887	136, 310

There was received from the United States Treasurer $65,718,192, contained in 89,288 packages, and from banks direct, $279,620, contained in 64 packages. The work in this division, in handling this vast amount of mutilated notes, requires great accuracy, skill, and precision.

SUPERVISION.

The law imposes upon the Comptroller of the Currency the duty of exercising a supervision over the national banks, and to that end requires him to exact reports from them as to their condition on at least five days in each year, and reports of the dividends and earnings of each bank as often as dividends are declared.

The act of 1864 required reports of earnings to be made every six months, whether dividends were declared or not, and although this provision was omitted from the Revised Statutes, these reports have been continuously required by the Comptroller under the general authority to call for reports at his discretion.

The Comptroller is also authorized to cause examination of banks to be made from time to time by persons selected for that purpose by him and approved by the Secretary of the Treasury.

The acts of 1863 and of 1864 seemed to contemplate only occasional examinations, and these by persons employed specially for the occasion. The compensation for each examination was $5 a day and mileage.

Afterwards experience appears to have led to the employment of regular examiners, and to their assignment to special districts; then followed periodical examinations, which in time arranged themselves at intervals of about twelve months.

The Revised Statutes adopted in 1874 changed the compensation of examiners from a per diem allowance and mileage to fees, graded in amount according to the capital of the bank examined, but this scale of fees was not made applicable to the examination of banks in reserve cities, in certain States named in the Statutes, and in the then Territories. In these excepted cases the Secretary of the Treasury was empowered, upon the recommendation of the Comptroller, to fix the compensation of examiners.

The act of February 19, 1875, readjusted the scale of fees.

From the beginning of the system, however, until now all examinations have been at the expense of the examined bank, which appears to be a sacrifice of principle to governmental economy.

It would appear that the supervision of the national banks by the Comptroller of the Currency was intended originally only to protect the revenue from being defrauded and the public from suffering loss through improper issues of circulating notes, but in process of time the supervision came to be extended so as to serve as a protection to depositors against the maladministration of directors; and quite recently it has been assumed that examiners are expected to discover the defalcations of cashiers and tellers, fraudulent entries in the books of banks, and false statements of assets and liabilities in cases where the president and directors, or some of them, have failed to make such discoveries.

However desirable it may be that examiners should be encouraged to fulfill this extreme expectation, yet no one of practical experience would rely upon an examiner who comes only once a year and who can afford to stay but a single day, to discover thefts or false entries that have been successfully concealed from directors who are always present and whose own money is being stolen.

All efforts must be futile that are directed to supplying by means of official examination an effective substitute for the vigilance and personal accountability of directors. Legislative or administrative force applied to such efforts will be misapplied and wasted.

The only reasonable theory of accountability and supervision is this: The officers of the bank should be accountable to the directors for the honesty and efficiency of its interior administration; the president and directors should be responsible to the public for such an organization as tends to prevent fraud and to detect irregularities. To this end they should especially be required to satisfy themselves personally that all the officers are of good character and reputable conduct; that they receive sufficient compensation to lift them above undue temptation; that the books of the bank are accurately kept and always up to date; that every statement and report emanating from the bank conforms to the books and the facts, and that no laxity of internal administration induces to fraud by displaying opportunities for its perpetration and concealment.

Only banks thus organized and administered are in condition to undergo official examination, which strictly should not be extended beyond the ascertainment, first, that the bank really is thus organized and administered; second, that no law has been violated in respect to loans, reserve, investments, bad debts, or dividends; and, third, that the assets are really worth the amounts representing them on the books of the bank.

Finally it should be the aim and duty of the Comptroller of the Currency to bring every national bank into the condition of organization and administration described, and he should labor to keep every bank in such condition by a scrutiny of its reports, by correspondence, and by means of examinations.

It is probable that the great majority of banks are properly organized and administered, but it is unfortunately certain that quite too many are not so, and among these arise from time to time the scandals that divert public attention from the general honesty and excellence of national-bank administration to sporadic cases of fraud or imbecility.

While the present system of examinations and reports has no doubt contributed materially to the general improvement of the banks, there are two things which seem to me essential to its completeness: first, a stern enforcement through the courts of the responsibilities of officers and directors, both criminal and pecuniary; and secondly, the assumption by the Government of the expense attending examinations.

Section 5209 of the Revised Statutes of the United States seems broad enough to cover most cases of misappropriation by directors and officers, and section 5239 subjects directors to pecuniary responsibility for all violations of law causing damages to depositors, stockholders or others.

When the capital of a bank is found to have been impaired by losses or otherwise, the Comptroller of the Currency is compelled to decide among the following:

1. He may permit a reduction of capital.
2. He may approve of voluntary liquidation.
3. He may require and empower the directors to assess the shareholders.
4. He may proceed against the corporation under section 5239 and subject the directors to damages for any losses to stockholders or to others by violations of law knowingly committed or permitted by them.

Manifestly the Comptroller can choose the latter course only when the losses can be shown to be fairly due to violations of law known to the directors as a body, and it is difficult to prove such knowledge, because the necessary evidence is generally controlled by the directors themselves. On the other hand, it is obviously unjust that stockholders should lose their investments, or be subjected to assessment, when the losses are due to violation of law committed within range of every director's scrutiny and often with the knowledge and for the benefit of one or more members of the board, but of which personal knowledge can not be specifically established in a sufficient number of cases.

It would appear from this point of view to be very important that the law should be so framed as to establish against all directors an antecedent presumption that they know and consent to whatever is done in the bank habitually, and to whatever else goes on there that an ordinarily intelligent business man would discover by the use of reasonable diligence.

If this were done, stockholders of national banks would come in for their due share of protection, and directors would attend to their duties more faithfully than many of them now do, while both the examinations, and the reports made to the Comptroller directly by the banks would be more trustworthy.

EXAMINATIONS.

It is of the highest importance to the banks as a body, as well as to the public, that examiners should be expert, vigilant, and trustworthy, and that the examinations should be frequent and unexpected.

While the examiners now employed are generally competent, and many of them are excellent, yet in some cases the territory to be covered is too large to permit of anything like sustained observation by the examiners, and the pay is too small to secure the best men for the work. Examiners must be considered as of two classes, those whose supervision is confined to comparatively a few banks in proximity to each other, and those who have to travel over a great area, visiting a number of solitary banks, each of limited resources.

In most of the large cities the banks are numerous enough to permit of an examiner being employed for each city exclusively, and the compensation is sufficient to secure thoroughly competent men.

Again, in the South and West the banks are so sparsely scattered over great areas that it takes a great deal of time and costs a great deal in traveling expenses to make the rounds of a district, while the capital of each bank is so small that a great many must be assigned to one man, in order that the aggregate fees may amount to enough to compensate him. For example, one examiner has to travel all over South Carolina, Georgia, Florida, Alabama, Mississippi, Louisiana, and Arkansas to examine ninety banks.

If all the State banks in the West and South were in the national system, the examination districts in those sections could be subdivided to the great improvement of the supervision in thoroughness and effectiveness.

As has already been said, it would be a great improvement if the examiners could be paid by the Government, and I feel constrained to repeat the recommendation that provision be made for inspectors or supervising examiners. I also respectfully recommend that provision be made for periodical conferences of examiners.

REPORTS.

The reports made by banks upon the requisition of the Comptroller are of two classes, those intended to inform the public as to each bank's condition and those intended for the information of the Comptroller only.

The reports intended for the public are required to be published, and it is the duty of the Comptroller to see that this requirement is complied with. To this end a copy of each publication has to be filed in the Bureau, together with the affidavit of the publisher, verifying the bank's compliance with the law as to the number of insertions.

During the past year 14,802 reports of condition, about 6,000 reports of dividends and earnings, and 2,833 reports from examiners have been received at the office of the Comptroller of the Currency, and fully 13,000 letters and circulars have been sent out in connection with them. The reports received are all carefully examined, compared with one another, and abstracts are made from them.

From these various reports, after examination and verification, the subjoined tables have been compiled, and other tables compiled from the same sources will be found in the Appendix, showing the condition of the reserve of national banks, their loans and discounts, abstract of reports of dividends and earnings, ratios to capital and to capital and surplus, and other valuable information as to the condition of the national banks on the date of the last report.

A large table, on folded sheet, appended hereto, exhibits for October 5, 1887, in aggregate, every detail embraced in the tabulated reports required of the banks. Similar tables are made up for the information of the Comptroller from the reports gathered from all banks five times each year. The amounts are given separately for each State, reserve city, and Territory.

DIAGRAM.

With the report of 1886 a diagram was submitted grouping graphically the main features of the national banking system, and showing by continuous lines the variations occurring between January 1, 1866, and October 7, 1886. It has not been considered necessary to reproduce this diagram, because any one interested in the subject can extend the lines by means of the figures contained in the summary of the condition of the banks, given on page 2 of this report.

The following table groups in a compendious form the most important facts shown in the diagram, extended to October 5, 1887. The exact figures in each case are given in the table; in the diagram they had to be abridged into round millions.

	January 1, 1866.	October 5, 1887.	Highest point touched.		Lowest point touched.	
			Amount.	Date.	Amount.	Date.
Capital	$403,357,346	$578,402,705	$578,402,705	Oct. 5, 1887	$403,357,346	Jan. 1, 1866
Capital, surplus, and undivided profits	475,330,204	823,827,373	823,827,373	Oct. 5, 1887	475,330,204	Jan. 1, 1866
Circulation	213,239,530	167,283,343	341,320,256	Dec. 26, 1873	166,625,658	Aug. 1, 1887
Total investments in United States bonds	440,380,350	223,754,450	712,437,900	Apr. 4, 1879	223,242,050	Aug. 1, 1887
Deposits	520,212,174	1,249,477,126	1,285,076,978	Aug. 1, 1887	501,407,586	Oct. 8, 1870
Loans and discounts	500,650,109	1,580,045,647	1,580,045,647	Oct. 5, 1887	500,650,109	Jan. 1, 1866
Cash:						
National-bank notes	20,406,442	21,937,884	28,809,009	Dec. 31, 1883	11,841,104	Oct. 7, 1867
Legal-tender notes	187,846,548	73,751,255	205,793,579	Oct. 1, 1866	52,156,439	Mar. 11, 1881
Specie	16,909,363	165,085,454	177,612,402	July 1, 1885	8,050,330	Oct. 1, 1875

An examination of this table shows that the aggregate capital, surplus, undivided profits, circulation, and deposits have increased from $1,208,781,908 in January, 1866, to $2,240,587,843 in October, 1887, which is less than double, while the loans and discounts have gone up from $500,650,109 to $1,580,045,647, which is more than treble, showing how much more widely the banks are now identified with the general business of the country than they were twenty-two years ago.

The investments in bonds have taken an opposite course. Amounting to $440,380,350 in 1866, increasing to $712,437,900 in April, 1879, they had subsided by October 5 last to $223,754,450, almost exactly half what they were in 1866, and considerably less than a third of what they momentarily amounted to in 1879.

The specie, which at the beginning of the period was but $16,909,363, had got down in October, 1875, to $8,050,330, is now $165,085,454, and in July, 1885, was $177,612,492. In October, 1886, the specie amounted to $156,387,696.

It is interesting to see how these changes appear when reduced to percentages.

The capital, surplus, undivided profits, circulation, and deposits constitute together the fund upon which a bank does its business.

Loans and discounts, United States bonds, specie, etc., are different forms in which this fund is invested. Taking the fund at $1,208,731,908 in 1866, and at $2,240,587,843 in 1887, these investments represent the following proportions of those amounts, viz:

	1866.	1887.
	Per ct.	*Per ct.*
Loans and discounts	41 32	70.52
United States bonds	36.36	9.98
Specie	1.57	7.37
Total	79.25	87.87

Another striking fact is that in 1866 the circulation was $213,239,530, and in 1887 it is only $167,283,343. At the former period, therefore, the circulation was nearly 45 per cent. of the capital, surplus, and undivided profits, while now it is only about 20 per cent.

LOANS.

The following table gives a classification of the loans of the national banks in each of the cities of New York, Chicago, and Saint Louis, and in the three cities of Boston, Philadelphia, and Baltimore, in the other reserve cities, and in the rest of the country, at nearly the same dates in each of the last three years:

OCTOBER 1, 1885.

Classification.	No. of banks.	On United States bonds on demand.	On other stocks, bonds, etc., on demand.	On single-name paper without other security.	All other loans.	Total.
New York	41	$3,286,124	$80,687,265	$25,331,820	$127,518,380	$236,823,598
Chicago	12	33,400	10,967,875	10,226,583	21,761,567	45,989,425
Saint Louis	6	398,010	1,197,060	123,570	7,473,788	9,182,417
Three cities	105	199,195	33,157,319	31,806,251	150,270,593	218,424,271
Other cities	80	163,735	13,256,157	8,130,100	74,713,601	96,263,590
Country	2,467	501,134	31,036,931	92,873,780	567,057,152	694,471,997
Total	2,711	4,565,607	173,302,607	171,492,087	951,795,003	1,301,155,304

OCTOBER 7, 1886.

Classification.	No. of banks.	On United States bonds on demand.	On other stocks, bonds, etc., on demand.	On single-name paper without other security.	All other loans.	Total.
New York	45	$2,002,551	$91,636,791	$24,616,007	$135,447,027	$253,732,376
Chicago	15	85,900	10,663,000	12,703,921	32,058,515	55,401,342
Saint Louis	5	....	1,028,430	355,373	8,291,968	9,675,771
Three cities	111	202,355	35,741,645	37,315,993	156,201,282	229,581,275
Other cities	86	460,198	16,336,793	12,539,705	86,900,964	116,177,680
Country	2,590	563,717	41,008,812	110,677,534	626,849,753	779,099,816
Total	2,852	3,314,721	196,415,477	198,128,533	1,045,809,509	1,443,668,240

OCTOBER 5, 1887.

Classification.	No. of banks.	On United States bonds on demand.	On other stocks, bonds, etc., on demand.	On single-name paper without other security.	All other loans.	Total.
New York	47	$1,445,900	$95,075,844	$17,585,496	$143,906,941	$258,014,181
Chicago	18	500	10,821,735	15,498,986	34,754,972	61,076,193
Saint Louis	5	......	1,182,214	279,603	8,920,956	10,382,753
Three cities	114	50,225	35,081,531	36,078,453	162,346,995	233,557,204
Other cities	109	122,910	19,551,230	18,598,269	115,167,352	153,439,761
Country	2,756	1,413,918	44,335,893	124,035,463	693,790,281	863,575,555
Total	3,049	3,033,453	206,048,447	212,076,270	1,158,887,477	1,580,045,647

In the table below is given a full classification of the loans in New York City alone for the last five years:

Loans and discounts.	October 2, 1883.	September 30, 1884.	October 1, 1885.	October 7, 1886.	October 5, 1887.
	48 banks.	44 banks.	44 banks.	45 banks.	47 banks.
On indorsed paper	$121,044,201	$110,010,062	$114,013,775	$121,381,380	$115,316,625
On single-name paper	19,147,051	82,559,443	25,331,820	24,646,098	17,585,496
On U. S. bonds on demand	2,003,527	2,933,785	3,286,124	2,002,550	1,445,900
On other stocks, etc., on demand	94,321,605	69,805,215	80,687,265	91,630,791	95,075,844
On real-estate security	184,683	163,397	215,285	211,432	146,885
All other loans	7,717,265	3,881,375	13,289,229	13,854,215	28,443,431
Total	245,108,332	205,353,277	230,823,598	253,732,376	258,014,181

The following table exhibits, in the order of capital, the twenty-five States (exclusive of reserve cities) having the largest amount of national-bank capital, together with the amount of circulation, loans and discounts, and individual deposits of the banks in each on October 5, 1887:

States, etc.	No. of banks.	Capital.	Circulation.	Loans and discounts.	Individual deposits.
Massachusetts	198	$44,790,500	$21,450,692	$91,561,545.60	$53,872,217.39
New York	269	34,724,260	17,406,466	98,792,326.88	87,269,212.02
Pennsylvania	237	33,551,140	13,379,865	80,206,011.08	72,564,898.01
Connecticut	83	24,505,410	8,698,093	43,001,299.86	24,478,665.09
Ohio	192	22,796,020	9,008,926	50,833,330.24	41,268,742.33
Rhode Island	61	20,340,050	4,642,913	34,486,234.78	13,918,046.52
Illinois	160	14,341,500	4,219,305	35,655,100.86	35,161,306.04
Minnesota	58	13,740,000	1,675,725	37,857,045.49	27,037,970.02
New Jersey	81	13,024,220	6,000,523	40,429,717.10	38,044,239.13
Indiana	93	11,894,500	4,217,870	27,785,325.99	25,254,102.80
Michigan	100	10,674,600	2,673,585	29,418,596.69	23,315,420.44
Kansas	139	10,530,800	2,205,210	21,001,450.42	17,741,267.53
Maine	72	10,440,700	4,875,561	19,125,655.89	10,116,282.26
Iowa	128	10,150,000	2,713,623	23,728,940.64	19,284,697.83
Texas	91	9,919,750	2,107,535	20,157,203.67	13,710,426.47
Kentucky	59	9,758,900	3,655,890	17,464,746.62	10,476,083.07
Vermont	49	7,566,000	3,478,100	12,832,309.34	6,627,080.66
Tennessee	40	7,460,000	1,326,895	18,918,301.93	11,759,221.25
New Hampshire	49	6,205,000	3,588,015	9,651,606.49	6,123,423.51
Nebraska	95	6,006,100	1,345,220	13,619,256.37	9,964,472.02
Wisconsin	53	4,442,000	1,225,623	13,340,531.69	12,970,629.95
California	30	4,170,000	939,000	14,295,166.47	19,515,186.09
Virginia	25	3,796,300	1,204,380	10,786,627.63	9,786,470.26
Dakota	62	3,720,000	861,925	6,694,081.52	5,848,810.67
Alabama	20	3,485,100	782,330	8,366,324.95	5,925,317.72

RESERVE.

The act of February 25, 1863, contained the following provision:

SEC. 41. *And be it further enacted*, That every such association shall at all times have on hand, in lawful money of the United States, an amount equal to at least twenty-five per centum of the aggregate amount of its outstanding notes of circulation and its deposits; and whenever the amount of its outstanding notes of circulation and its deposits shall exceed the above-named proportion for the space of twelve days, or whenever such lawful money of the United States shall at any time fall below the amount of twenty-five per centum of its circulation and deposits, such association shall not increase its liabilities by making any new loans or discounts otherwise than by discounting or purchasing bills of exchange, payable at sight, nor make any dividend of its profits, until the required proportion between the aggregate amount of its outstanding notes of circulation and its deposits and lawful money of the United States shall be restored: *Provided, however*, That clearing-house certificates, representing specie or lawful money specially deposited for the purpose of any clearing-house association, shall be deemed to be lawful money in the possession of any association belonging to such clearing-house holding and owning such certificates, and considered to be a part of the lawful money which such association is required to have, under the foregoing provisions of this section: *Provided, further*, That any balance due to any association organized under this act in other places from any association in the cities of Boston, Providence, New York, Philadelphia, Baltimore, Cincinnati, Chicago, Saint Louis, or New Orleans, in good credit, subject to be drawn for at sight, and available to redeem their circulating notes and deposits, may be deemed to be a part of the lawful money which such association in other places than the cities of Boston, Providence, New York, Philadelphia, Baltimore, Cincinnati, Chicago, Saint Louis, and New Orleans are required to have by the foregoing provisions of this section, to the extent of three-fifths of the said amount of twenty-five per centum required. And it shall be competent for the Comptroller of the Currency to notify any such association whose lawful money reserve, as aforesaid, shall fall below said proportion of twenty-five per centum, to make good such reserve; and if such association shall fail for thirty days thereafter so to make good its reserve of lawful money of the United States, the Comptroller may, with the concurrence of the Secretary of the Treasury, appoint a receiver to wind up the business of such association, as provided in this act.

The corresponding clauses of the act of June 3, 1864, are as follows:

SEC. 31. That every association in the cities hereinafter named shall, at all times, have on hand, in lawful money of the United States, an amount equal to at least twenty-five per centum of the aggregate amount of its notes in circulation and its deposits; and every other association shall, at all times, have on hand, in lawful money of the United States, an amount equal to at least fifteen per centum of the aggregate amount of its notes in circulation, and of its deposits. And whenever the lawful money of any association in any of the cities hereinafter named shall be below the amount of twenty-five per centum of its circulation and deposits, and whenever the lawful money of any other association shall be below fifteen per centum of its circulation and deposits, such association shall not increase its liabilities by making any new loans or discounts otherwise than by discounting or purchasing bills of exchange payable at sight, nor make any dividend of its profits until the required proportion between the aggregate amount of its outstanding notes of circulation and deposits and its lawful money of the United States shall be restored: *Provided*, That three-fifths of said fifteen per centum may consist of balances due to an association available for the redemption of its circulating notes from associations approved by the comptroller of the currency, organized under this act, in the cities of Saint Louis, Louisville, Chicago, Detroit, Milwaukee, New Orleans, Cincinnati, Cleveland, Pittsburg, Baltimore, Philadelphia, Boston, New York, Albany, Leavenworth, San Francisco, and Washington City: *Provided, also*, That clearing-house certificates, representing specie or lawful money specially deposited for the purpose of any clearing-house association, shall be deemed to be lawful money in the possession of any association belonging to such clearing-house holding and owning such certificate, and shall be considered to be a part of the lawful money which such association is required to have under the foregoing provisions of this section: *Provided*, That the cities of Charleston and Richmond may be added to the list of cities in the national associations of which other associations may keep three-fifths of their lawful money, whenever, in the opinion of the comptroller of the currency, the condition of the southern states will warrant it. And it shall be competent for the comptroller of the currency to notify any associations, whose lawful money reserve, as aforesaid, shall be below the amount to be kept on hand, as aforesaid, to make good such reserve; and if such association shall fail for thirty days thereafter so to make good its reserve of lawful money of the United States, the Comptroller may, with the concurrence of the Secretary of the Treasury, appoint a receiver to wind up the business of such association, as provided in this act.

SEC. 32. That each association organized in any of the cities named in the foregoing section shall select, subject to the approval of the comptroller of the currency, an association in the city of New York at which it will redeem its circulating notes at par. And each of such associations may keep one-half of its lawful money reserve in cash deposits in the city of New York. And each association not organized within the cities named in the preceding section shall select, subject to the approval of the comptroller of the currency, an association in either of the cities named in the preceding section, at which it will redeem its circulating notes at par, and the comptroller shall give public notice of the names of the associations so selected at which redemptions are to be made by the respective associations, and of any change that may be made of the association at which the notes of any association are redeemed. If any association shall fail either to make the selection or to redeem its notes as aforesaid, the comptroller of the currency may, upon receiving satisfactory evidence thereof, appoint a receiver in the manner provided for in this act to wind up its affairs: *Provided*, That nothing in this section shall relieve any association from its liability to redeem its circulating notes at its own counter at par, in lawful money on demand; *And provided, further*, That every association formed or existing under the provisions of this act shall take and receive at par, for any debt or liability to said association, any and all notes or bills issued by any association existing under and by virtue of this act.

Sections 5191, 5192, and 5195 of the Revised Statutes preserved substantially the provisions of the act of 1864.

The act of June 20, 1874, evidently drafted before the adoption of the Revised Statutes, although not approved until afterward, made the following amendment of the act of June 3, 1864, which it enacts shall be hereafter known as the "National Bank Act":

SEC. 2. That section thirty-one of the "National Bank Act" be so amended that the several associations therein provided for shall not herafter be required to keep on hand any amount of money whatever by reason of the amount of their respective circulations; but the moneys required by said section to be kept at all times on hand shall be determined by the amount of deposits in all respects as provided for in the said section.

SEC. 3. That every association organized, or to be organized, under the provisions of the said act, and of the several acts amendatory thereof, shall at all times keep and have on deposit in the Treasury of the United States, in lawful money of the United States, a sum equal to five per centum of its circulation, to be held and used for the redemption of such circulation; which sum shall be counted as a part of its lawful reserve, as provided in section two of this act; and when the circulating notes of any such associations, assorted or unassorted, shall be presented for redemption, in sums of one thousand dollars or any multiple thereof, to the Treasurer of the United States, the same shall be redeemed in United States notes. All notes so redeemed shall be charged by the Treasurer of the United States to the respective associations issuing the same, and he shall notify them severally, on the first day of each month, or oftener, at his discretion, of the amount of such redemptions; and whenever such redemptions for any association shall amount to the sum of five hundred dollars, such association so notified shall forthwith deposit with the Treasurer of the United States a sum in United States notes equal to the amount of its circulating notes so redeemed. And all notes of national banks, worn, defaced, mutilated, or otherwise unfit for circulation, shall, when received by any assistant treasurer, or at any designated depository of the United States, be forwarded to the Treasurer of the United States for redemption as provided herein. And when such redemptions have been so reimbursed, the circulating notes so redeemed shall be forwarded to the respective associations by which they were issued; but if any of such notes are worn, mutilated, defaced, or rendered otherwise unfit for use, they shall be forwarded to the Comptroller of the Currency and destroyed, and replaced as now provided by law: *Provided*, That each of said associations shall reimburse to the Treasury the charges for transportation, and the costs for assorting such notes; and the associations hereafter organized shall also severally reimburse to the Treasury the cost of engraving such plates as shall be ordered by each association respectively; and the amount assessed upon each association shall be in proportion to the circulation redeemed, and be charged to the fund on deposit with the Treasurer: *And provided further*, That so much of section thirty-two of said national-bank act requiring or permitting the redemption of its circulating notes elsewhere than at its own counter, except as provided for in this section, is hereby repealed.

It will be observed that a strict construction of the act of June 3, 1864, and of subsequent legislation, would exclude any association organized under the act of February 25, 1863, from acting as a reserve agent. This was probably not intended, but it should be corrected in justice to the older associations.

The act of March 3, 1887, is as follows:

That whenever three-fourths in number of the national banks located in any city of the United States having a population of fifty thousand people shall make application to the Comptroller of the Currency, in writing, asking that the name of the city in which such banks are located shall be added to the cities named in sections fifty-one hundred and ninety-one and fifty-one hundred and ninety-two of the Revised Statutes, the Comptroller shall have authority to grant such request, and every bank located in such city shall at all times thereafter have on hand, in lawful money of the United States, an amount equal to at least twenty-five per centum of its deposits, as provided in sections fifty-one hundred and ninety-one and fifty-one hundred and ninety-five of the Revised Statutes.

SEC. 2. That whenever three-fourths in number of the national banks located in any city of the United States having a population of two hundred thousand people shall make application to the Comptroller of the Currency, in writing, asking that such city may be a central reserve city, like the city of New York, in which one-half of the lawful-money reserve of the national banks located in other reserve cities may be deposited, as provided in section fifty-one hundred and ninety-five of the Revised Statutes, the Comptroller shall have authority, with the approval of the Secretary of the Treasury, to grant such request, and every bank located in such city shall at all times thereafter have on hand, in lawful money of the United States, twenty-five per centum of its deposits, as provided in section fifty-one hundred and ninety-one of the Revised Statutes.

SEC. 3. That section three of the act of January 14, 1875, entitled "An act to provide for the resumption of specie payments," be, and the same is, hereby amended by adding after the words "New York" the words "and the city of San Francisco, California."

A review and comparison of the course of legislation as to "reserve" shows that originally all associations, wherever located, were required to keep, either in cash or subject to sight draft, funds in hand equal to at least 25 per cent. of all obligations payable on demand. Subsequently a distinction was made between associations in certain named cities and those located elsewhere, and the latter were required to keep only 15 per cent. reserve upon the aggregate of deposits and circulation. The amount that might be kept with redemption agents was limited to three-fifths of 15 per cent. for associations generally, and to one-half of 25 per cent. for those in reserve cities, and in the latter case New York was the only place in which the banks in other redemption cities might have redemption agents.

At a later period the fund to be kept for the redemption of circulation was separated from the remaining reserve to be held against deposits; it was fixed at 5 per cent. of the outstanding circulation, and was required to be kept on deposit with the Treasurer of the United States. Besides being specifically devoted to the redemption of circulation, this fund is also authorized to be counted as part of the reserve against deposits.

Simultaneously with this provision as to the amount and location of the redemption fund the banks were relieved of the obligation to keep a reserve on circulation, but were required to keep in reserve funds to the amounts represented by 15 per cent. and 25 per cent. respectively upon their deposits.

The new regulation as to redemption of circulation dispensed with redemption agents, but the act of June 20, 1874, re-enacted the provision as to the proportion of reserve that might consist of balances due from approved associations in the cities formerly named as cities of redemption. These cities thus came to be called "reserve cities," and during the present year the term has been incorporated formally into the law, and provision has been made for central reserve cities as well, and also for an increase in the number of both reserve cities and central reserve cities.

Tables will be found in the Appendix, pages 000 to 000, showing by States, Territories, central reserve cities, and reserve cities the state of the reserve of the national banks therein at each report of condition during the years 1882 to 1887, both inclusive. These tables are worthy of careful examination, because they show that banks generally keep reserves in excess of the statutory requirement, and that banks remote from money centers keep not only nearly double the amount required, but that they habitually have in cash more than the 15 per cent. total requirement.

As some banks included in these tables are known to be often short of reserve, it is manifest that the majority must be habitually stronger than the averages here shown, and from this fact it may be inferred that the requirement of the law is in no degree excessive, and that banks that do not conform to it are not prudently managed.

These tables should be especially instructive to the managers of banks, encouraging and confirming as they do the wisdom of those who keep always strong, and rebuking and warning as they also do those who, too eager for gain, allow their reserves to fall below the line of prudence and of safety.

The including of the 5 per cent. redemption fund on deposit with the Treasurer at Washington in the reserve against deposits seems to be either a misconstruction of the act of June 20, 1874, or an anomaly in that act.

The language seems to admit of a strained construction opposite to that placed upon it, but if the most obvious construction is the correct one, then the provision should be repealed.

The money held by the Treasurer is never available for paying depositors, and it bears no constant ratio to the amount of deposits.

Several banks have so large a circulation and have such small deposits that the 5 per cent. redemption fund with the Treasurer fulfills the entire requirement as to reserve against deposits, and while these are extreme cases they serve to show the practical result of this provision of the law.

On the other hand, there is an anomaly in the assumption which appears to have been made heretofore that national-bank notes on hand should not be counted in the reserve.

They are specifically made receivable by all national banking associations, and for all dues to the Government (except customs duties), and they are certainly current all over the country.

It is in the line of public policy to maintain the monetary function of these circulating notes upon the general plane on which the law places all the rest of the currency.

For these reasons these notes should obviously be no longer discriminated against by being excluded from a function to which all the other constituents of the currency are now admitted on equal terms.

On October 5, 1887, the total 5 per cent. fund amounted to $8,310,442 while the national bank currency held by all banks amounted to $21,937,884.

It would, therefore, be a relief to banks generally to be allowed to count in their reserve the latter instead of the former amount.

The subjoined table brings forward to the latest date the usual summary of information as to the course of deposits and reserves since the act of June 20, 1874, went into effect. It shows the amount of deposits and the state of the reserve at about October 1 of each year, in each central reserve city, in all the reserve cities, and in the States and Territories, together with a general summary embracing all banks.

NEW YORK CITY.

Dates.	No. of banks.	Net deposits.	Reserve required (25 per cent.*).	Reserve held.		Classification of reserve.			
				Amount.	Ratio to deposits.	Specie.	Other lawful money.	Due from agents.	Redemption fund.
		Millions.	*Millions.*	*Millions.*	*Per cent.*	*Millions.*	*Millions.*	*Millions.*	*Millions.*
Oct. 2, 1874	48	201.6	51.2	68.3	33.4	14.4	52.4	....	1.5
Oct. 1, 1875	48	202.3	50.7	60.5	29.9	5.0	54.4	....	1.1
Oct. 2, 1876	47	197.9	49.5	60.7	30.7	11.6	45.3	....	0.8
Oct. 1, 1877	47	174.9	43.7	48.1	27.5	13.0	34.3	....	0.8
Oct. 1, 1878	47	189.8	47.4	50.9	26.8	13.3	36.5	....	1.1
Oct. 2, 1879	47	210.2	52.6	53.1	25.3	19.4	32.6	....	1.1
Oct. 1, 1880	47	268.1	67.0	70.6	26.4	58.7	11.0	....	0.9
Oct. 1, 1881	48	268.8	67.2	62.5	23.3	50.6	10.9	....	1.0
Oct. 3, 1882	50	254.0	63.5	64.4	25.4	44.5	18.9	....	1.0
Oct. 2, 1883	48	266.9	66.7	70.8	26.5	50.3	19.7	....	0.9
Sept. 30, 1884	44	255.0	63.7	90.8	35.6	63.1	27.0	....	0.7
Oct. 1, 1885	44	313.9	78.2	115.7	37.0	91.5	23.7	....	0.5
Oct. 7, 1886	45	282.8	70.7	77.0	27.2	64.1	12.5	....	0.4
Oct. 5, 1887	47	284.3	71.1	80.1	28.2	63.6	16.1	....	0.4
Average for 14 years...	47	240.9	60.2	69.5	28.8	40.4	28.2	....	0.9

CHICAGO.

Oct. 5, 1887	18	61.6	16.2	19.7	30.5	12.9	6.7	....	.05

SAINT LOUIS.

Oct. 5, 1887	5	10.3	2.6	2.7	26.4	1.3	1.3	....	.03

* All in cash.

RESERVE CITIES.*‡

Dates.	No. of banks.	Net deposits.	Reserve required (25 per cent.).	Reserve held.		Classification of reserve.			
				Amount.	Ratio to deposits.	Specie.	Other lawful money.	Due from agents.	Redemption fund.
		Millions.	*Millions.*	*Millions.*	*Per cent.*	*Millions.*	*Millions.*	*Millions.*	*Millions.*
Oct. 2, 1874	182	221.4	55.3	76.0	34.3	4.5	36.7	31.1	3.7
Oct. 1, 1875	188	223.9	56.0	74.5	33.3	1.5	37.1	32.3	3.6
Oct. 2, 1876	189	217.0	54.2	76.1	35.1	4.0	37.1	32.0	3.0
Oct. 1, 1877	188	204.1	51.0	67.3	33.0	5.6	34.3	24.4	3.0
Oct. 1, 1878	184	199.9	50.0	71.1	35.6	9.4	29.4	29.1	3.2
Oct. 2, 1879	181	228.8	57.2	83.5	36.5	11.3	33.0	35.7	3.5
Oct. 1, 1880	184	289.4	72.4	105.2	36.2	28.3	25.0	48.2	3.7
Oct. 1, 1881	189	335.4	83.9	100.6	30.0	34.0	21.9	40.6	3.7
Oct. 3, 1882	193	318.8	79.7	89.1	28.0	28.3	24.1	33.2	3.5
Oct. 2, 1883	200	323.9	81.0	100.6	31.1	26.3	30.1	40.8	3.4
Sept. 30, 1884	203	307.9	77.0	99.0	32.2	30.3	33.3	32.3	3.1
Oct. 1, 1885	203	364.5	91.1	122.2	33.5	42.0	34.9	42.4	2.9
Oct. 7, 1886	217	381.5	95.4	114.0	29.9	44.5	26.0	41.3	2.2
Oct. 5, 1887	223	338.5	84.6	100.7	29.7	36.3	23.2	40.0	1.2

STATES AND TERRITORIES.†

Oct. 2, 1874	1,774	293.4	44.0	100.6	34.3	2.4	33.7	52.7	11.9
Oct. 1, 1875	1,831	307.9	46.3	100.1	32.5	1.6	33.7	53.3	11.6
Oct. 2, 1876	1,853	291.7	43.8	99.9	34.3	2.7	31.0	55.4	10.8
Oct. 1, 1877	1,845	290.1	43.6	93.4	32.0	4.2	31.6	48.9	10.7
Oct. 1, 1878	1,822	289.1	43.4	100.1	30.7	8.0	31.1	50.0	11.0
Oct. 2, 1879	1,820	329.9	49.5	124.3	37.7	11.5	30.3	71.3	11.2
Oct. 1, 1880	1,859	410.5	61.6	147.2	35.8	21.2	28.3	86.4	11.3
Oct. 1, 1881	1,895	507.2	76.1	158.3	31.2	27.5	27.1	92.4	11.4
Oct. 3, 1882	2,026	545.8	81.9	150.4	27.5	30.0	30.0	80.1	11.3
Oct. 2, 1883	2,253	577.9	86.7	157.5	27.2	31.2	30.8	84.1	11.3
Sept. 30, 1884	2,417	535.8	80.4	156.3	29.2	35.2	30.9	79.7	10.5
Oct. 1, 1885	2,467	570.8	85.6	177.5	31.1	41.5	29.9	95.9	10.2
Oct. 7, 1886	2,590	637.6	95.6	186.2	29.2	47.8	30.1	99.5	8.7
Oct. 5, 1887	2,756	690.6	103.6	190.9	27.6	50.8	32.6	100.9	6.6

SUMMARY.

Oct. 2, 1874	2,004	719.5	150.1	244.9	34.0	21.3	122.8	83.8	17.1
Oct. 1, 1875	2,087	734.1	152.2	235.1	32.0	8.1	125.2	85.6	16.3
Oct. 2, 1876	2,089	706.6	147.5	236.7	33.5	21.3	113.4	87.4	14.6
Oct. 1, 1877	2,080	669.1	138.3	210.8	31.5	22.8	100.2	73.3	14.5
Oct. 1, 1878	2,053	678.8	140.8	228.1	33.6	30.7	97.0	85.1	15.3
Oct. 2, 1879	2,048	768.9	159.3	269.9	33.9	42.2	95.9	107.0	15.8
Oct. 1, 1880	2,090	968.0	201.0	323.0	33.4	108.2	64.3	134.6	15.0
Oct. 1, 1881	2,132	1,111.6	227.2	321.6	28.9	112.7	59.9	133.0	10.1
Oct. 3, 1882	2,269	1,118.6	225.1	303.9	27.2	102.8	72.0	113.3	15.8
Oct. 2, 1883	2,501	1,168.7	234.4	328.9	28.1	107.8	80.6	124.9	15.6
Sept. 30, 1884	2,664	1,098.7	221.1	340.1	31.0	128.6	91.2	112.0	14.3
Oct. 1, 1885	2,714	1,248.2	254.9	415.4	33.3	175.0	88.5	138.3	13.6
Oct. 7, 1886	2,852	1,301.8	261.7	377.2	29.0	156.4	68.7	140.8	11.4
Oct. 5, 1887	3,019	1,388.4	278.0	394.2	28.4	165.1	79.9	140.9	8.3

* Reserve 25 per cent., one-half in cash.
† Reserve 15 per cent., two-fifths in cash in bank.
‡ Includes Chicago and Saint Louis up to October 5, 1887.

TRANSACTIONS OF THE NEW YORK CLEARING-HOUSE.

The New York Clearing-House Association is composed of 65 members, of which 45 are national banks, 19 are State banks, and the other member is the assistant treasurer of the United States at New York. Two national banks and 15 State banks in the city do not belong to the association, but clear through associate members. Mr. W. A. Camp, the manager of the association, has kindly supplied the data for the following tables, showing the transactions during the year ending October 1, 1887:

COMPARATIVE STATEMENT FOR TWO YEARS OF THE TRANSACTIONS OF THE NEW YORK CLEARING-HOUSE, SHOWING AGGREGATE AMOUNT OF CLEARINGS, AGGREGATE BALANCES, AND THE KINDS AND AMOUNTS OF MONEY PASSING IN SETTLEMENT OF THESE BALANCES.

Year ending—	Aggregate clearings.	Aggregate balances.
October 1, 1886	$33,374,682,216	$1,510,565,385
October 1, 1887	34,872,848,785	1,560,626,324
Increase	1,498,166,569	50,060,939

KINDS OF MONEY AND AMOUNT OF EACH KIND.

Year ending—	U. S. gold certificates.	Bank of America gold certificates.*	Clearing-house loan certificates.	Treasury certificates for legal tenders, sec. 5193, U. S. Revised Statutes.	Legal tenders and minor coin.	Percentages.	
						Gold certificates.	Legal tenders.
October 1, 1886	$645,643,000	$177,673,000	$140,000	$285,795,000	$410,314,385	54.181+	45.809+
October 1, 1887	812,231,000	748,409,000	None.	1,410,000	7,576,325	99+	1−
Increase	166,588,000	570,736,000	....	....	....	....	....
Decrease	....	....	140,000	284,385,000	402,738,060	....	....

*When the Government ceased issuing gold certificates, December 1, 1878, the New York banks agreed to have a common depository for their gold coin, and in that way retain the use of certificates at the clearing-house. This has been found convenient and saves the expense and cost of moving large amounts in specie. The Bank of America performs this function.

Following is a comparative statement of transactions of the New York Clearing-House for thirty-four years, showing for each year the number of banks, aggregate capital, clearings, and balances, average of the daily clearings and balances, and the percentage of balances and clearings:

Years.	No. of banks.	Capital.*	Clearings.	Balances paid in money.	Average daily clearings.	Average daily balances paid in money.	Ratios.
							Per ct.
1854	50	$47,044,000	$5,750,455,987	$297,411,494	$19,104,505	$988,078	5.2
1855	48	48,884,180	5,362,912,098	289,694,137	17,412,052	940,565	5.4
1856	50	52,883,700	6,906,213,328	334,714,489	22,278,108	1,079,724	4.8
1857	50	64,420,200	8,333,226,718	365,313,902	26,968,371	1,182,246	4.4
1858	46	67,146,018	4,756,664,386	314,238,911	15,393,736	1,016,954	6.6
1859	47	67,921,714	5,448,005,956	363,984,683	20,867,333	1,177,944	5.6
1860	50	69,907,435	7,231,143,057	380,693,438	23,401,757	1,232,018	5.3
1861	50	68,900,605	5,915,742,758	353,383,944	19,269,520	1,151,088	6.0
1862	50	68,375,820	6,871,443,591	415,530,331	22,237,682	1,344,758	6.0
1863	50	68,972,508	14,867,597,849	677,626,483	48,428,657	2,207,252	4.6
1864	49	68,586,763	24,097,196,656	885,719,205	77,984,455	2,866,405	3.7
1865	55	80,363,013	26,032,384,342	1,035,765,108	84,796,040	3,373,828	4.0
1866	58	82,370,200	28,717,146,914	1,066,135,106	93,541,195	3,472,753	3.7
1867	58	81,770,200	28,675,159,472	1,144,963,451	93,101,167	3,717,414	4.0
1868	59	82,270,200	28,484,288,637	1,125,455,237	92,182,164	3,642,250	4.0
1869	59	82,720,200	37,407,028,987	1,120,318,308	121,451,393	3,637,397	3.0
1870	61	83,620,200	27,804,539,406	1,036,484,822	90,274,479	3,365,210	3.7
1871	62	84,420,200	29,300,986,682	1,209,721,029	95,133,074	3,927,066	4.1
1872	61	84,420,200	33,844,369,568	1,428,582,707	109,884,317	4,636,632	4.2
1873	59	83,370,200	35,461,052,826	1,474,508,025	115,885,794	4,818,054	4.1
1874	59	81,635,200	22,855,927,636	1,286,753,176	74,692,574	4,205,076	5.7
1875	59	80,435,200	25,061,237,902	1,408,608,777	81,899,470	4,603,297	5.6
1876	59	81,731,200	21,597,274,247	1,295,042,029	70,349,428	4,218,378	5.9
1877	58	71,085,200	23,289,243,701	1,373,996,302	76,358,176	4,504,906	5.9
1878	57	63,611,500	22,508,438,442	1,307,843,857	73,555,988	4,274,000	5.8
1879	59	60,800,200	25,178,770,691	1,400,111,063	82,015,540	4,560,622	5.6
1880	57	60,475,200	37,182,128,621	1,516,538,631	121,510,224	4,956,009	4.1
1881	60	61,162,700	48,565,818,212	1,776,018,162	159,232,191	5,823,010	3.5
1882	61	60,962,700	46,552,846,161	1,595,000,245	151,637,935	5,195,440	3.4
1883	63	61,162,700	40,293,165,258	1,568,983,196	132,543,307	5,161,120	3.9
1884	61	60,412,700	34,092,037,338	1,524,930,994	111,048,982	4,967,202	4.5
1885	64	58,612,700	25,250,791,440	1,295,355,252	82,789,480	4,247,069	5.1
1886	63	59,312,700	33,374,682,216	1,519,565,385	109,067,589	4,965,900	4.5
1887	64	60,862,700	34,872,848,786	1,569,626,325	114,337,209	5,146,316	4.5
		†69,430,325	‡812,942,769,870	‡35,758,018,204	†77,059,820	†3,420,623	4.4

* The capital is for various dates, the amounts at a uniform date in each year not being obtainable.
† Yearly averages for thirty-four years. ‡ Totals for thirty-four years.

The clearing-house transactions of the assistant treasurer of the United States at New York for the year ending October 1, 1887, were as follows:

Exchanges received from clearing-house	$359,788,103.42
Exchanges delivered to clearing-house	111,471,810.74
Balances paid to clearing-house	248,497,702.25
Balances received from clearing-house	181,409.57
Showing that the amount paid by the assistant treasurer to the clearing-house was in excess of the amount received by him	248,316,292.68

The debit balances were paid to the clearing-house as follows:

United States gold certificates	$248,343,000.00
Legal tenders and change	154,702.25
	248,497,702.25

COMPARATIVE STATEMENT OF THE EXCHANGES OF THE CLEARING-HOUSES OF THE UNITED STATES FOR OCTOBER, 1887, AND OCTOBER, 1886.

Clearing-house at—	Exchanges for month of October, 1887.	Exchanges for month of October, 1886.	Comparisons.	
			Increase.	Decrease.
New York	$2,978,940,406	$3,248,318,061	....	$269,377,655
Boston	387,775,488	380,669,570	$7,105,918	....
Philadelphia	272,500,752	271,572,441	928,311	....
Chicago	267,556,120	253,518,831	14,037,289	....
Saint Louis	74,855,031	69,822,165	5,032,866	....
Baltimore	56,795,652	53,856,829	2,938,823	....
San Francisco	74,405,637	56,175,257	18,230,380	....
Pittsburgh	46,775,066	37,612,868	9,162,198	....
New Orleans	42,603,842	31,683,200	10,920,642	....
Cincinnati	47,782,200	45,384,750	2,397,450	....
Providence	23,837,500	22,663,600	1,173,900	....
Louisville	23,210,780	19,093,914	4,116,866	....
Milwaukee	20,123,277	20,183,280	....	60,003
Detroit	18,374,879	14,926,506	3,448,373	....
Cleveland	14,340,059	12,527,278	1,812,781	....
Indianapolis	8,777,900	6,222,279	2,555,621	....
Kansas City	29,702,991	25,903,960	3,799,031	....
Hartford	7,630,018	7,195,784	434,234	....
New Haven	5,360,758	5,175,379	185,379	....
Columbus	10,616,739	8,462,124	2,154,615	....
Memphis	10,725,296	7,686,552	3,038,744	....
Peoria	5,429,418	4,220,702	1,208,716	....
Worcester	4,722,433	4,528,762	193,671	....
Springfield	5,653,280	3,669,715	1,983,565	....
Lowell	3,161,806	2,732,069	429,737	....
Syracuse	3,193,442	2,735,744	463,698	....
Portland	4,607,692	4,694,186	....	86,494
Omaha	12,750,306	9,316,954	3,442,352	....
Saint Joseph	6,659,426	4,447,511	2,211,915	....
Denver	10,812,463	8,351,817	2,460,646	....
Galveston	8,865,282	7,852,246	1,013,036	....
Saint Paul	18,376,835	16,732,700	1,644,135	....
Minneapolis	22,805,030	19,175,451	3,629,579	....
Los Angeles	5,160,514	New.	5,160,514	....
Grand Rapids	2,725,818	2,006,301	719,517	....
Wichita	2,844,645	1,826,202	1,018,443	....
Norfolk	5,817,933	4,465,766	1,352,167	....
Total	4,546,381,714	4,695,480,744 4,546,381,714	120,425,122	269,524,152 120,425,122
Decrease	....	149,099,030	....	149,099,030

COMPARATIVE STATEMENT OF THE EXCHANGES OF THE CLEARING-HOUSES OF THE UNITED STATES FOR WEEKS ENDING OCTOBER 29, 1887, AND OCTOBER 30, 1886.

Clearing-house at—	Exchanges for week ending October 29, 1887.	Exchanges for week ending October 30, 1886.	Comparisons.	
			Increase.	Decrease.
New York	$617,590,720	$625,098,064	$22,492,665	
Boston	83,700,076	77,443,134	6,257,842	
Philadelphia	58,729,071	55,262,510	3,466,561	
Chicago	58,407,000	49,463,000	8,944,000	
Saint Louis	16,057,751	13,428,029	2,629,722	
Baltimore	12,618,840	11,554,889	1,063,951	
San Francisco	17,495,345	14,931,044	2,564,301	
Pittsburgh	11,708,842	8,543,700	3,165,133	
New Orleans	9,863,406	7,861,710	2,001,606	
Cincinnati	9,799,950	9,682,250	117,700	
Providence	5,957,900	5,482,100	475,800	
Louisville	4,800,855	3,980,646	820,209	
Milwaukee	4,702,794	4,741,945		$39,151
Detroit	4,079,159	2,964,573	1,114,586	
Cleveland	3,263,297	2,980,490	282,807	
Indianapolis	2,130,383	1,364,108	766,275	
Kansas City	7,407,620	5,564,678	1,842,942	
Hartford	1,482,341	1,529,645		47,304
New Haven	1,101,904	1,088,433	13,471	
Columbus	2,285,210	1,861,425	423,785	
Memphis	2,532,120	2,039,997	492,123	
Peoria	1,177,411	927,149	250,262	
Worcester	969,381	917,916	51,465	
Springfield	1,007,778	819,206	188,572	
Lowell	650,419	504,913	145,506	
Syracuse	625,190	544,611	80,579	
Portland	1,039,033	1,087,952		48,919
Omaha	2,812,343	2,037,837	774,506	
Saint Joseph	1,702,006	799,574	902,432	
Denver	2,800,391	1,571,233	1,229,158	
Galveston	2,193,758	1,625,986	567,772	
Saint Paul	4,108,446	3,410,580	697,866	
Minneapolis	4,806,272	3,677,381	1,128,891	
Los Angeles	1,133,462	New.	1,133,462	
Total	990,741,383 924,790,717	924,790,717	66,086,040 135,374	135,374
Increase	65,950,666		65,950,666	

The following table, compiled from returns made to the Clearing-House by the national banks in New York City, exhibits the movement of their reserve, weekly, during October, for the last eleven years:

Week ending—	Specie.	Legal tenders.	Total.	Ratio of reserve to—	
				Circulation and deposits.	Deposits.
				Per cent.	*Per cent.*
October 6, 1877	$14,665,600	$36,168,300	$50,833,900	27.0	29.5
October 13, 1877	14,726,500	35,178,900	49,905,400	26.7	29.2
October 20, 1877	14,087,400	35,101,700	49,189,100	26.5	29.0
October 27, 1877	15,209,000	34,367,800	49,576,800	26.8	29.4
October 5, 1878	14,995,800	38,304,900	53,300,700	25.7	28.4
October 12, 1878	12,184,600	37,685,100	49,869,700	24.4	27.0
October 19, 1878	13,531,400	36,576,000	50,107,400	24.7	27.3
October 26, 1878	17,384,200	35,690,500	53,074,700	25.8	28.5
October 4, 1879	18,979,600	34,368,000	53,347,600	23.3	25.8
October 11, 1879	20,901,800	32,820,300	53,722,100	23.4	25.9
October 18, 1879	24,686,500	29,305,200	53,991,700	23.5	26.1
October 25, 1879	25,636,000	26,713,900	52,349,900	23.0	25.5
October 2, 1880	59,823,700	11,129,100	70,952,800	25.4	26.4
October 9, 1880	62,521,300	10,785,000	73,306,300	25.4	27.2
October 16, 1880	62,760,600	10,939,200	73,699,800	25.5	27.1
October 23, 1880	60,888,200	10,988,200	71,876,400	24.8	26.6
October 30, 1880	61,471,600	10,925,000	72,396,600	25.0	26.7
October 1, 1881	54,954,600	12,150,400	67,105,000	23.1	24.8
October 8, 1881	53,287,000	12,153,800	65,441,700	23.1	24.9
October 15, 1881	51,008,300	12,452,700	63,461,000	23.2	25.0
October 22, 1881	54,016,200	12,496,500	66,512,700	24.6	26.6
October 29, 1881	55,961,200	12,947,900	68,909,100	25.6	27.4
October 7, 1882	47,016,000	18,384,500	65,400,500	24.0	26.3
October 14, 1882	48,281,000	18,002,700	66,283,700	24.7	26.6
October 21, 1882	49,518,200	17,023,900	66,542,100	25.0	26.8
October 28, 1882	48,374,200	17,204,700	65,578,900	24.8	26.5
October 6, 1883	51,586,700	20,122,500	71,709,200	25.5	27.0
October 13, 1883	50,894,000	21,145,800	72,039,800	25.4	26.8
October 20, 1883	47,262,900	20,719,700	67,982,600	24.5	25.9
October 27, 1883	46,372,800	20,617,600	66,990,400	24.5	25.9
October 4, 1884	67,470,600	25,817,300	93,287,900	34.5	36.3
October 11, 1884	68,922,500	27,654,100	96,576,600	35.2	36.9
October 18, 1884	67,579,400	27,875,500	95,454,900	34.8	36.5
October 25, 1884	67,638,000	27,354,200	94,992,200	34.6	36.3
October 3, 1885	92,351,600	24,516,600	116,868,200	36.0	37.1
October 10, 1885	93,642,500	23,002,000	116,644,500	35.8	37.0
October 17, 1885	91,945,300	22,221,100	114,166,400	34.9	36.0
October 24, 1885	87,309,100	21,059,800	108,368,900	33.5	34.5
October 30, 1885	84,954,600	21,874,900	106,829,500	33.0	34.1
October 2, 1886	64,111,700	14,607,700	78,719,400	27.1	27.9
October 9, 1886	65,723,800	13,209,100	78,932,900	27.0	27.7
October 16, 1886	65,228,600	13,133,100	78,361,700	26.7	27.4
October 23, 1886	65,668,400	12,803,800	78,472,200	26.9	27.7
October 30, 1886	66,195,100	13,177,200	79,372,300	27.1	27.9
October 1, 1887	64,619,200	15,767,500	80,386,700	27.7	28.5
October 8, 1887	64,317,500	16,229,700	80,587,200	27.4	28.2
October 15, 1887	64,663,100	16,885,400	81,548,500	27.3	28.1
October 22, 1887	64,918,700	16,735,500	81,654,500	27.4	28.2
October 29, 1887	66,005,800	17,542,600	83,848,400	27.8	28.6

The following table exhibits the transactions of the clearing-houses located in 37 cities for the year ending September 30, 1887, from official returns received from the manager of the New York Clearing-House, and a comparison is made with the year ending September 30, 1886, by indicating the increase or decrease in the exchanges and balances:

Clearing-house at—	No. of members.	Exchanges for year ending September 30, 1887.	Balances for year ending September 30, 1887.	Comparison with year ending September 30, 1886.		
				Increase.		Decrease.
				Exchanges.	Balances.	
New York	65	$34,872,848,780	$1,569,026,325	$1,408,106,570	$50,060,940	....
Boston	52	4,408,269,993	510,025,457	399,704,727	17,527,457	....
Philadelphia	40	3,186,188,935	298,701,297	400,313,485	40,694,877	....
Chicago	21	2,887,276,059	301,574,076	326,906,787	10,348,508	....
Saint Louis	18	879,272,738	142,259,972	78,902,128	....	*$6,587,994
Baltimore	23	663,676,756	89,504,281	65,091,763	7,970,677	....
San Francisco	17	800,092,859	124,200,215	200,751,798	17,215,771	....
Pittsburgh	19	490,319,705	81,520,388	104,021,001	7,404,776	....
New Orleans	13	412,231,400	47,805,607	....	805,607	†21,708,600
Cincinnati	19	564,377,200	96,204,200	71,936,700	11,143,200	....
Providence	34	210,838,100	No record.	6,987,400	....	....
Louisville	21	269,780,547	63,564,157	39,652,090	8,923,080	....
Milwaukee	11	240,127,909	40,817,909	46,350,700	6,411,187	....
Detroit	14	188,629,384	31,729,276	40,042,682	6,430,910	....
Cleveland	11	160,010,840	No record.	39,914,003	....	....
Indianapolis	6	87,149,510	18,600,734	17,790,711	8,763,227	....
Kansas City	9	380,407,069	No record.	115,397,901	....	....
Hartford	15	89,871,078	25,689,768	2,893,509	....	*916,181
New Haven	10	63,931,325	15,176,902	7,080,963	1,434,272	....
Columbus	17	53,311,425	8,376,319	10,470,012	....	*4,530,115
Memphis	7	94,241,496	24,020,213	18,890,007	4,621,463	....
Peoria	9	55,006,344	13,074,158	16,674,956	3,865,638	....
Worcester	8	47,197,687	13,466,230	3,640,068	617,142	....
Springfield	10	50,503,291	14,929,388	9,250,560	2,255,028	....
Lowell	7	31,670,050	10,108,362	4,909,878	1,087,183	....
Syracuse	8	28,506,708	6,358,243	1,819,356	210,180	....
Portland	6	49,588,652	9,495,080	2,921,202	659,007	....
Omaha	8	137,220,535	No record.	....	....	†25,075,305
Saint Joseph	7	67,230,133	17,667,401	23,464,120	5,747,999	....
Denver	7	110,240,167	15,866,791	....	3,613,999	†34,031,896
Galveston	7	63,182,537	No record.	....	....	†9,920,239
Saint Paul	15	200,364,307	33,193,845	57,807,724	....	....
Minneapolis	14	184,700,022	30,405,326	24,370,250	5,024,902	....
Los Angeles	7	New.	New.	New.	....	....
Grand Rapids	7	26,229,598	5,070,880	No record 1886	....	....
Duluth	7	New.	New.	New.	....	*315,020
Norfolk	6	40,016,323	6,453,157	253,620	....	....
Total	575	52,126,704,488	3,667,708,563	3,636,978,270	222,267,149	{ 90,706,100 { 12,349,310

* Balances. † Exchanges.

From the above table it will be seen that the exchanges in New York City amounted to 66.9 per cent. of the whole sum, and the balances in that city were nearly 42.8 per cent. of the total balances.

DUTIES, ASSESSMENTS, AND REDEMPTION CHARGES.

National banks are subject to a semi-annual duty of one-half of 1 per cent. upon the average amount of their notes in circulation during the preceding six months. They are also required by the act of June 20, 1874, to pay the cost of the redemption of their notes at the office of the Treasurer of the United States at Washington, and the cost of the plates from which their notes are printed. Banks extending their corporate existence have to pay for new plates. Previously to the act of June 20, 1874, the expense of the plates had been paid out of the tax on the banks, which at that time attached to capital and deposits as well as to circulation.

The banks are further required to pay the fees of the examiners employed to ascertain their condition, under section 5240, Revised Statutes of the United States.

The taxes and assessments collected during the past year were as follows:

Semi-annual duty on circulation	$2,044,922.75
Cost of redemption of notes by United States Treasurer	138,967.00
Assessments for cost of plates, new banks	18,850.00
Assessments for cost of plates, extended banks	1,750.00
Assessments for examiners' fees, sec. 5240, R. S	110,219.88
Total	2,314,709.63

It has not been customary heretofore to include assessments with taxes, but it seems proper to do so.

The following table is a comparative statement of taxes assessed as semi-annual duty on circulation, cost of redemption of notes, cost of plates, and examiners' fees for the past five years:

Years.	Semi-annual duty on circulation.	Cost of redemption of notes by United States Treasurer.	Assessments for cost of plates, new banks.	Assessment for cost of plates, extended banks.	Assessment for examiners' fees (sec. 5240, R. S.).	Total.
1883	$3,132,006.73	$147,502.27	$25,980.00	$34,120.00	$94,606.16	$3,434,305.16
1884	3,024,668.24	160,896.65	18,845.00	1,950.00	99,642.05	3,306,001.94
1885	2,794,584.01	181,857.16	13,150.00	97,800.00	107,781.73	3,195,172.90
1886	2,592,021.33	168,243.35	14,810.00	24,825.00	107,272.83	2,907,172.51
1887	2,044,922.75	138,967.00	18,850.00	1,750.00	110,219.88	2,314,709.63
Total	13,588,203.06	797,536.43	91,635.00	160,445.00	519,522.65	15,157,362.14

The total tax collected on circulation up to July 1, 1887, amounted to $65,841,721.30.

STATE TAXATION OF NATIONAL BANKS.

There has been for some years more or less friction arising out of what is claimed to be discrimination against national banks in the tax laws of some of the States, and in consequence a contention has been going on as to the meaning of so much of section 5219 of the Revised Statutes of the United States as imposes a restriction upon State legislatures in determining and directing the manner of assessing and collecting taxes on national-bank shares. Section 5219 of the Revised Statutes of the United States is as follows:

Nothing herein shall prevent all the shares in any association from being included in the valuation of the personal property of the owner or holder of such shares, in assessing taxes imposed by authority of the State within which the association is located; but the legislature of each State may determine and direct the manner and place of taxing all the shares of national banking associations located within the State, subject only to the two restrictions, that the taxation shall not be at a greater rate than is assessed upon other moneyed capital in the hands of individual citizens of such State, and that the shares of any national banking association owned by non-residents of any State shall be taxed in the city or town where the bank is located, and not elsewhere. Nothing herein shall be construed to exempt the real property of associations from either State, county, or municipal taxes, to the same extent, according to its value, as other real property is taxed.

It will be seen that the only restrictions upon State legislatures in determining and directing the manner and place of taxing all the shares of national banks located within the State are two: first, a restriction as to the manner, viz: "that the taxation shall not be at a greater rate than is assessed upon other moneyed capital in the hands of individual citizens of the State;" and, secondly, a restraint as to the place of taxation, which it is needless to quote, as no doubt seems to have arisen as to its meaning.

The contention over the true interpretation of the clause applying to the rate of taxation has been serious.

In various States the banks have appealed from local assessors and tax collectors to the courts, and during the past year the Supreme Court has finally laid down the meaning and intent of this clause.

The only question now open is whether the clause, as construed by the Supreme Court during the past year, expresses the purpose of Congress, and this question can be answered by Congress alone.

It is claimed by the national banks in many States that the construction placed upon the law deprives them of the full measure of protection which it was the intention of Congress to provide.

Following is the full-text of the decision of the Supreme Court:

Mr. Justice MATTHEWS delivered the opinion of the court.

The bill in this case was filed by the appellant, an association organized as a national bank, in the city of New York, the object and prayer of which were to restrain the collection of taxes assessed upon its stockholders in respect to their shares therein, on the ground that the taxes assessed and sought to be collected by the defendants were illegal and void under section 5219 of the Revised Statutes of the United States, as being at a greater rate than those assessed under the laws of New York upon other moneyed capital in the hands of the individual citizens of that State. The assessment in question was made for the year 1885, by the proper officer, acting in pursuance of section 312 of an act of the legislature of the State of New York, passed July 1, 1882, entitled "An act to revise the statutes of this State relating to banks, banking and trust companies," which reads as follows:

SEC. 312. The stockholders in every bank or banking association organized under the authority of this State, or of the United States, shall be assessed and taxed on the value of their shares of stock therein; said shares shall be included in the valuation of the personal property of such stockholders in the assessment of taxes at the place, city, town, or ward where such bank or banking association is located, and not elsewhere, whether the said stockholders reside in said place, city, town, or ward or not; but in the assessment of said shares each stockholder shall be allowed all the deductions and exceptions allowed by law in assessing the value of other taxable personal property owned by individual citizens of this State, and the assessment and taxation shall not be at a greater rate than is made or assessed upon other moneyed capital in the hands of individual citizens of this State. In making such assessment there shall also be deducted from the value of such shares such sum as is in the same proportion to such value as is the assessed value of the real estate of the bank or banking association, and in which any portion of their capital is invested, in which said shares are held, to the whole amount of the capital stock of said bank or banking association. Nothing herein contained shall be held or construed to exempt the real estate of banks or banking associations from either State, county, or municipal taxes, but the same shall be subject to State, county, municipal, and other taxation to the same extent and rate and in the same manner according to its value, as other real estate is taxed. The local authorities charged by law with the assessment of the said shares shall, within ten days after they have completed such assessment, give written notice to each bank or banking association of such assessment of the shares of its respective shareholders, and no personal or other notice to such shareholders of such assessment shall be necessary for the purpose of this act.

The hearing in the circuit court was had upon an agreed statement of facts, as follows:

"It is hereby stipulated and agreed by and between the parties to the above-entitled suit, that, for the purpose of the trial of this cause, the facts hereinafter stated are true, and that the cause be submitted for trial and decree upon such statement alone, together with the pleadings:

"1. That the complainant, on the second Monday of January, A. D. 1885, and for several months prior thereto, had a capital stock of the par value of $1,000,000 and a surplus fund of $200,000; that nearly the whole of said capital and surplus fund was during that period, invested in bonds of the United States of the par value of $949,000, and of a market value and cost largely exceeding that sum; that its shares of stock were each of the par value of $100 and of the number of 10,000, and were then held by 142 persons and corporations, 50 of whom, owning 1,877 shares, were residents of States other than the State of New York, and the remainder residents of the State of New York.

"2. That, on the second Monday of January, 1885, the proper tax officers of the city of New York, acting under chapter 409 of the Laws of 1882 of the State of New York, did value and assess for taxation the shares of stock of said bank against the individual shareholders thereof, at the rate of $89 per share, after deducting the proportion of the assessed value of the real estate of said bank applicable to each share of stock, as by law required, making the total gross valuation of said shares in the hands of the shareholders the sum of $890,000, from which sum the debts of sundry indebted stockholders, amounting to $89,128, were deducted, as by law allowed, leaving the total valuation of said shares against said stockholders upon which taxes were thereafter assessed the sum of $800,872.

"3. That, on the second Monday of January, 1885, the aggregate actual value of the shares of stock of the incorporated moneyed and stock corporations incorporated by the laws of the State of New York deriving an income or profit from their capital or otherwise (not including life insurance companies, trust companies, banks, or banking associations, organized under the authority of this State or of the United States) amounted to the sum of $755,018,892; that 'Exhibit A,' hereto appended and made a part of this agreement, contains a list of the corporations whose shares of capital stock are embraced in said sum of $755,018,892, and also shows the total par value of the shares of capital stock of each of said corporations.

"4. That, at the period aforesaid, the aggregate actual value of the shares of stock of the life insurance companies incorporated under the laws of this State amounted to the sum of $3,540,000, and at the same period the aggregate value of the personal property of said companies, consisting of mortgages, loans with collateral security, State, county and municipal bonds, and railroad bonds and shares of stock of corporations (but not including the bonds of the United States nor the shares of corporations created by the State of New York), amounted to $195,257,305; all of which is shown in detail in the schedule hereto annexed, marked 'Exhibit B.'

"5. That, at the said period, the aggregate actual value of the shares of the capital stock of the trust companies existing in the State of New York and organized under its laws amounted to $32,018,900, as is shown in detail in the schedule hereto annexed, marked 'Exhibit C,' of which sum the amount of $30,215,900 was of trust companies located in the city of New York.

"6. That, at the same period, the aggregate actual value of the deposits due by the savings banks of this State to depositors was $437,107,501 (not including the surplus accumulated by the said corporations, amounting to $68,669,001).

"7. That the aggregate actual value of the bonds and stocks issued by the city of New York, subject to the provisions of chapter 552 of the Laws of 1880, at the said period, amounted to $13,467,000.

"8. That the aggregate actual value at the same period of the shares of stock of corporations created by States other than the State of New York, owned by the citizens of the State of New York, amounted to at least the sum of $250,000,000.

"9. The assessed valuation of all personal property, after making the deductions allowed by law, in the city of New York (at the said period), as shown by the annual record of the assessed valuation of real and personal estate of the said city for the year 1885, was $202,673,806. This sum included the capital of corporations (after making deductions for investments thereof in real estate, shares of New York corporations, taxable upon their capital stock under the laws of this State, and non-taxable securities), as follows:

Insurance companies	$2,146,379
Trust companies	156,506
Miscellaneous companies	29,234,409
Railroad companies	12,339,871

"It also included:

Shares of national banks	45,046,074
Shares of State banks	15,700,220

"The sum so deducted for the value of the real estate belonging to said trust companies located in the city of New York did not exceed $2,336,572.31.

The assessed value of the real estate in said city for said period is	$1,168,443,137
And in the said State, including the city of New York, is	2,761,973,845
The latter sum including the sum of about	340,000,000

being the assessed value of the real estate located in said State belonging to corporations.

"The 'aggregate amount of the taxable personal estate' within the State of New York, exclusive of said city, after deducting debts due by the owners thereof for the year ending December 31, 1884, as assessed by the assessors and returned to the State comptroller, is $151,632,369.

"This sum included the capital of corporations (after making the deductions for investments thereof in real estate, shares of New York corporations taxable under their capital stock under the laws of this State and non-taxable securities), of the amount of $34,466,612.

The aggregate capital stock, taken at par, of the national banks outside of the city of New York, but within the State of New York, on December 20, 1884, as shown by the report of the Comptroller of the Currency of the United States, was	$36,804,160
And that of State banks, outside of the said city, but within said State, as shown by the report of the bank superintendent of New York, is...	8,128,000
Total (outside of New York City)..........	44,932,160
The total par value of the shares of national banks in said State, including the city of New York, for the period aforesaid, is..........	83,054,160
And of the State banks..........	32,815,700

"10. That it is the intention of the defendants, unless restrained by injunction, to collect the said tax levied by them against the shareholders of the said complainant upon said shares by the use of all needful legal process.

"11. That any statutes of the United States or of the State of New York may be cited and relied upon before the said court as if herein fully set forth."

From a decree dismissing the bill the present appeal is prosecuted.

Section 5219 of the Revised Statutes of the United States is as follows:

"Nothing herein shall prevent all the shares in any association from being included in the valuation of the personal property of the owner or holder of such shares in assessing taxes imposed by authority of the State within which the association is located; but the legislature of each State may determine and direct the manner and place of taxing all the shares of national banking associations located within the State, subject only to the two restrictions that the taxation shall not be at a greater rate than is assessed upon other moneyed capital in the hands of individual citizens of such State, and that the shares of any national banking asssociation owned by non-residents of any State shall be taxed in the city or town where the bank is located and not elsewhere. Nothing herein shall be construed to exempt the real property of associations from either State, county, or municipal taxes to the same extent, according to its value, as other real property is taxed."

In the present case no question is raised by the appellant as to the validity of section 312, chapter 409, of the Laws of New York of 1882, considered by itself, nor in reference to the rule of valuation or assessment which it prescribes. No exception is taken to the form of the assessment, nor is the case based in any degree upon the dereliction of the assessing officers in the discharge of their duties, there being no allegation and no proof that they have not performed their whole duty under the statutes of the State.

The proposition which the appellant seeks to establish is, that the State of New York, in seeking to tax national-bank shares, has not complied with the condition contained in section 5219 of the Revised Statutes, that such taxation shall not be at a greater rate than is assessed upon other moneyed capital in the hands of individual citizens of such State, "in that, it has by its legislation expressly exempted from all taxes in the hands of the individual citizens numerous species of moneyed capital, aggregating in actual value the sum of $1,086,000,000, whilst it has by its laws subjected national-bank shares in the hands of individual holders thereof (aggregating a par value of $83,000,000), and State-bank shares (having a like value of $32,815,700), to taxation upon their full actual value, less only a proportionate amount of the real estate owned by the bank." This exemption, it is claimed, is of a "very material part relatively" of the whole, and renders the taxation of national-bank shares void.

The exemptions thus referred to are classified as follows:

1st. The shares of stock in the hands of the individual shareholders of all incorporated "moneyed or stock corporations deriving an income or profit from their capital or otherwise, incorporated by the laws of New York, not including trust companies and life insurance companies, and State or national banks." The value of such shares, it is admitted, amounts to $755,018,892.

2d. Trust companies and life insurance companies. The actual value of the shares of stock in trust companies amounts to $32,018,900, and the actual value of the shares in life insurance companies amounts to $3,540,000, which life insurance companies, it is admitted, are the owners of personal property consisting of mortgages, loans, stocks, and bonds to the value of $195,257,305.

3d. Savings banks and the deposits therein. The deposits amount to $437,107,501, and an accumulated surplus to $68,069,001.

4th. Certain municipal bonds issued by the city of New York under an act passed in 1880, of the value of $13,467,000.

5th. Shares of stocks in corporations created by States other than New York, in the hands of individual holders, residents of said State, amounting to $250,000,000.

It is argued by the appellant that these exemptions bring the case within the decision of Boyer *v.* Boyer, 113 U. S., 689. In that case, referring to the legislation of Pennsylvania, it was said: "The burden of county taxation imposed by the latter act has at all events been removed from all bonds or certificates of loan issued by any railroad company incorporated by the State; from shares of stock in the hands of stockholders of any institution or company of the State which in its corporate capacity is liable to pay a tax into the State treasury under the act of 1859; from mortgages, judgments, and recognizances of every kind; from moneys due or owing upon articles of agreement for the sale of real estate; from all loans, however made, by corporations which are taxable for State purposes when such corporations pay into the State treasury the required tax on such indebtedness."

This enumeration of exempted property, the amounts of which were stated in the bill and admitted by the demurrer, was held to include such a material portion relatively of the moneyed capital in the hands of individual citizens as to make the tax upon the shares of national banks an unfair discrimination against that class of property, but no attempt was made in the opinion of the court to define the meaning of the words "moneyed capital in the hands of individual citizens" as used in the statute, or to enumerate all the various kinds of property or investments that came within its description, or to show that shares of stock in the hands of stockholders of every institution, company, or corporation of a State, having a capital employed for the purpose of earning dividends or profits for its stockholders, were taxable as moneyed capital in the hands of individual citizens.

It is accordingly contended on behalf of the appellees in the present case, first, that the shares of stock in the various companies incorporated by the laws of New York as moneyed or stock corporations, deriving an income or profit from their income or otherwise, including trust companies, life insurance companies, and savings banks, are not moneyed capital in the hands of the individual citizen within the meaning of the act of Congress; second, that if any of them are, then the corporations themselves are taxed under the laws of New York in such a manner and to such an extent that the shares of stock therein are in fact subject to a tax equal to that which is assessed upon shares of national banks; and third, that if there are any exceptions, they are immaterial in amount and based upon considerations which exclude them from the operation of the rule of relative taxation intended by the act of Congress.

In view of the nature of the contention between the parties to this suit, and the extent and value of the interests involved, it becomes necessary to review with care the previous decisions of this court upon the same subject, and to endeavor to state with precision the rule of relative taxation prescribed to the States by Congress on shares of national banks.

The national-banking act of 1864 (13 Stat., 111), in addition to the restrictions now imposed upon the State taxation of national-bank shares, declared "that the tax so imposed, under the laws of any State, upon the shares of any of the associations authorized by this act, shall not exceed the rate imposed upon the shares in any of the banks organized under the authority of the State where such association is located." In the re-enactment of this statute in 1868 (15 Stat., 34), this proviso was omitted. The case of Van Allen *v.* Assessors, 3 Wallace, 573, was decided under the act of 1864 as originally enacted. In that case the taxing law of New York, which was in question, was held to be invalid, because it levied no taxes upon shares in State banks at all, the tax being assessed upon the capital of the banks after deducting that portion which was invested in securities of the United States; and it was held that this tax on the capital was not a tax on the shares of the stockholders equivalent to that on the shares in national banks. It was also decided in that case that it was competent for the States, under the permission of Congress, to tax the shares of national-bank stock held by individuals, notwithstanding the capital of the bank was invested in bonds of the United States which were not subject to taxation.

It appears, therefore, as the result of the decision in that case, that a tax upon the capital of a State bank, levied upon the value thereof, after deducting such part as was invested in non-taxable Government bonds, was less than an equivalent for a tax upon the shares of national banks from which no such deduction was permitted. Accordingly, in the case of People *v.* The Commissioners, 4 Wallace, 244, the complaint was made on behalf of individual owners of national-bank stock taxed in New York, that no deduction was permitted to them from the value of their shares on account of the capital of the bank being invested in non-taxable Government bonds, while such deduction was allowed in favor of insurance companies and individuals in the assessment for taxation of the value of their personal property; and it was contended, therefore, that the relators in that case were taxed upon their shares of national-bank stock at a greater rate than was assessed upon other moneyed capital in the hands of individual citizens. In reference to this supposed inequality the court said: "The answer is, that, upon a true construction of this clause of the act, the meaning and intent of the law-makers were that the rate of taxation of the shares should be the same or not greater than upon the moneyed capital of the individual citizen, which is subject or liable to taxation. That is, no greater proportion or percentage of tax in the valuation of the shares should be levied than upon other moneyed taxable capital in the hands of the citizens. This rule seems to be as effectual a test to prevent unjust discrimination against the shareholders as could well be devised. It embraces a class which constitutes the body politic of the State, who make its laws and provide for its taxes. They can not be greater than the citizens impose upon themselves. It is known as sound policy that in every well regulated and enlightened state or government, certain descriptions of property and also certain institutions, such as churches, hospitals, academies, cemeteries, and the like, are exempt from taxation; but these exemptions have never been regarded as disturbing the rates of taxation, even where the fundamental law had ordained that it should be uniform." The Court then proceeded to show that the exclusion, as the subject of taxation, of Government securities held by individuals, from their moneyed capital, was by authority of the United States, and hence it would be a contradiction to infer that Congress meant to include the same Government securities as a part of that moneyed capital which it required to be taxed by the States at a rate equal to that imposed by the latter upon the shares held by individuals of national-bank stock.

The other objection taken to the validity of the tax complained of was, that insurance companies created under the laws of the State were authorized to deduct from the amount of their capital and surplus profits, for purposes of taxation, such part as was invested in United States securities. In reference to this the court said: "The answer is, that this clause does not refer to the rate of assessments upon insurance companies as a test by which to prevent discrimination against the shares; that is confined to the rate of assessments upon moneyed capital in the hands of individual citizens. These institutions are not within the words or the contemplation of Congress; but even if they were, the answer we have already given to the deduction of these securities in the assessment of the property of individual citizens is equally applicable to them."

In Lionberger v. Rouse, 9 Wallace, 468, it was held that the proviso originally contained in the act of 1864, and omitted from the act of 1868, expressly referring to State banks, was limited to State banks of issue. The court said (p. 474): "There was nothing to fear from banks of discount and deposit merely, for in no event could they work any displacement of national-bank circulation." Of course, so far as investments in such banks are moneyed capital in the hands of individuals, they are included in the clause as it now stands.

In the case of Hepburn v. School Directors, 23 Wallace, 480, it was decided to be competent for the State to value, for taxation, shares of stock in a national bank at their actual value, even if in excess of their par value, provided thereby they were not taxed at a greater rate than was assessed upon other moneyed capital in the hands of individual citizens of the State. It was a further question in that case whether the exemption from taxation by statute of "all mortgages, judgments, recognizances, and moneys owing upon articles of agreement for the sale of real estate," made the taxation of shares in national banks unequal and invalid. This was decided in the negative on two grounds: first, that the exemption was founded upon the just reason of preventing a double burden by the taxation both of property and of the debts secured upon it; and, second, because it was partial only, not operating as a discrimination against investments in national-bank shares. The court said: "It could not have been the intention of Congress to exempt bank shares from taxation because some moneyed capital was exempt."

The subject was further considered in the case of Adams v. Nashville, 95 U. S., 19. One of the questions in that case had reference to an exemption from taxation by State authority of interest-paying bonds issued by the municipal corporation of the city of Nashville, in the hands of individuals. It was held that the exemption did not invalidate assessment upon the shares of national banks. The court said (p. 22): "The act of Congress was not intended to curtail the State power on the subject of taxation. It simply required that capital invested in national banks should not be taxed at a greater rate than like property similarly invested. It was not intended to cut off the power to exempt particular kinds of property, if the legislature chose to do so. Homesteads to a specified value, a certain amount of household furniture (the six plates, six knives and forks, six teacups and saucers, of the old statutes), the property of clergymen to some extent, school-houses, academies, and libraries, are generally exempt from taxation. The discretionary power of the legislatures of the States over all these subjects remains as it was before the act of Congress of June, 1864. The plain intention of that statute was to protect the corporations formed under its authority from unfriendly discrimination by the States in the exercise of their taxing power."

In People v. Weaver, 100 U. S., 539, it was held that the prohibition against the taxation of national-bank shares at a greater rate than that imposed upon other moneyed capital in the hands of individual citizens could not be evaded by the assessment of equal rates of taxation upon unequal valuations, and that consequently where the State statute authorized individuals to deduct the amount of debts owing by them from the assessed value of their personal property and moneyed capital subject to taxation, the owners of shares of national banks were entitled to the same deduction. The cases of The Supervisors v. Stanley, 105 U. S., 305; Hills v. Exchange Bank, *Ibid.*, 319; Evansville Bank v. Britton, *Ibid.*, 322, and Cummings v. National Bank, 101 U. S., 153, are applications of the same principle.

The rule of decision in Van Allen v. Assessors, 3 Wallace, 573, is not inconsistent with that followed in People v. The Commissioners, 4 Wallace, 244. In the former of these cases the comparison was between taxes levied upon the shares of national banks and taxes levied upon the capital of State banks. In the valuation of the capital of State banks for this taxation, non-taxable securities of the United States were necessarily excluded, while in the valuation of shares of national banks no deduction was permitted on account of the fact that the capital of the national banks was invested in whole or in part in Government bonds. The effect of this was, of course, to discriminate to a very important extent in favor of investments in state banks, the shares in which *eo nomine* were not taxed at all, while their taxable capital was diminished by the subtraction of the Government securities in which it was invested, and against national-bank shares taxed without such deduction at a value necessarily and largely based on the value of the Government securities in which by law a large part of the capital of the bank was required to be invested. In the case of People v. The Commissioners the comparison was not between the taxation of shareholders in national banks and of shareholders in State banking institutions, but between the taxation of national-bank shares and that of personal property held by individuals and insurance companies from the valuation of which the deduction was permitted of the amount of non-taxable Government securities held by them respectively. The general ground of the decision was, that the exemption was not an unfriendly discrimination against investments in national banks in favor of other investments of a similar and competing character. It was held that the exemption, under State authority, of United States securities, which it was not lawful for the State to tax, could not be considered an unwarranted exemption in that case. It was also held that the language of the act of Congress which fixed the rate of taxation upon national-bank shares, by reference to that imposed by the State "upon other moneyed capital in the hands of individual citizens," excluded from the comparison moneyed capital in the hands of corporations, unless the corporations were of that character, such as State banks were held to be in the case of Van Allen v. The Assessors, that shares of stock in them fell within the description of "moneyed capital in the hands of individual citizens." In that way a distinction was established between shares of stock held in banking corporations and those held in insurance companies and other business, trading, manufacturing, and miscellaneous corporations, whose business and operations were unlike those of banking institutions.

It follows, as a deduction from these decisions, that "moneyed capital in the hands of individual citizens" does not necessarily embrace shares of stock held by them in all corporations whose capital is employed, according to their respective corporate powers and privileges, in business carried on for the pecuniary profit of shareholders, although shares in some corporations, according to the nature of their business, may be such moneyed capital. The rule and test of this difference is not to be found in that quality attached to shares of stock in corporate bodies generally whereby the certificates of ownership have a certain appearance of negotiability, so as easily to be transferred by delivery under blank powers of attorney, and to be dealt in by sales at the stock exchange, or used as collateral for loans, as though they were negotiable security for money. This quality, in a greater or less degree, pertains to all stocks in corporate bodies, the facility of their use in this way being in proportion to the estimated wealth and credit, present or prospective, of the corporation itself. Neither is the difference to be determined by the character of the investments in which, either by law or in fact, the bulk of the capital and the accumulated surplus of the corporation is from time to time invested. It does not follow, because these are invested in such a way as properly to constitute moneyed capital, that the shares of stock in the corporations themselves must necessarily be within the same description. Such is the case of insurance companies, in respect to which it was held, in People v. The Commissioners, that shares of stock in them were not taxable as "moneyed capital in the hands of individual citizens;" and that the language of the act of Congress does not include moneyed capital in the hands of corporations.

The true test of the distinction, therefore, can only be found in the nature of the business in which the corporation is engaged.

The key to the proper interpretation of the act of Congress is its policy and purpose. The object of the law was to establish a system of national banking institutions, in order to provide a uniform and secure currency for the people, and to facilitate the operations of the Treasury of the United States. The capital of each of the banks in this system was to be furnished entirely by private individuals; but, for the protection of the Government and the people, it was required that this capital, so far as it was the security for its circulating notes, should be invested in the bonds of the United States. These bonds were not subjects of taxation; and neither the banks themselves, nor their capital, however invested, nor the shares of stock therein held by individuals, could be taxed by the States in which they were located without the consent of Congress, being exempted from the power of the States in this respect, because these banks were means and agencies established by Congress in execution of the powers of the Government of the United States. It was deemed consistent, however, with these national uses, and otherwise expedient, to grant to the States the authority to tax them within the limits of a rule prescribed by the law. In fixing those limits it became necessary to prohibit the States from imposing such a burden as would prevent the capital of individuals from freely seeking investment in institutions which it was the express object of the law to establish and promote. The business of banking, including all the operations which distinguish it, might be carried on under State laws, either by corporations or private persons, and capital in the form of money might be invested and employed by individual citizens in many single and separate operations forming substantial parts of the business of banking. A tax upon the money of individuals, invested in the form of shares of stock in national banks, would diminish their value as an investment and drive the capital so invested from this employment, if at the same time similar investments and similar employments under the authority of State laws were exempt from an equal burden. The main purpose, therefore, of Congress, in fixing limits to State taxation on investments in the shares of national banks, was to render it impossible for the State, in levying such a tax, to create and foster an unequal and unfriendly competition, by favoring institutions or individuals carrying on a similar business and operations and investments of a like character. The language of the act of Congress is to be read in the light of this policy.

Applying this rule of construction, we are led, in the first place, to consider the meaning of the words "other moneyed capital," as used in the statute. Of course it includes shares in national banks; the use of the word "other" requires that. If bank shares were not moneyed capital, the word "other" in this connection would be without significance. But "moneyed capital" does not mean all capital the value of which is measured in terms of money. In this sense, all kinds of real and personal property would be embraced by it, for they all have an estimated value as the subjects of sale. Neither does it necessarily include all forms of investment in which the interest of the owner is expressed in money. Shares of stock in railroad companies, mining companies, manufacturing companies, and other corporations, are represented by certificates showing that the owner is entitled to an interest, expressed in money value, in the entire capital and property of the corporation, but the property of the corporation which constitutes its invested capital may consist mainly of real and personal property, which, in the hands of individuals, no one would think of calling moneyed capital, and its business may not consist in any kind of dealing in money, or commercial representative of money.

So far as the policy of the Government in reference to national banks is concerned, it is indifferent how the States may choose to tax such corporations as those just mentioned, or the interest of individuals in them, or whether they should be taxed at all. Whether property interests in railroads, in manufacturing enterprises, in mining investments, and others of that description, are taxed or exempt from taxation, in the contemplation of the law, would have no effect upon the success of national banks. There is no reason, therefore, to suppose that Congress intended, in respect to these matters, to interfere with the power and policy of the States. The business of banking, as defined by law and custom, consists in the issue of notes payable on demand, intended to circulate as money where the banks are banks of issue; in receiving deposits payable on demand; in discounting commercial paper; making loans of money on collateral security; buying and selling bills of exchange; negotiating loans, and dealing in negotiable securities issued by the Government, State and national, and municipal and other corporations. These are the operations in which the capital invested in national banks is employed, and it is the nature of that employment which constitutes it in the eye of this statute "moneyed capital." Corporations and individuals carrying on these operations do come into competition with the business of national banks, and capital in the hands of individuals thus employed is what is intended to be described by the act of Congress. That the words of the law must be so limited appears from another consideration; they do not embrace any moneyed capital in the sense just defined, except that in the hands of individual citizens. This excludes moneyed capital in the hands of corporations, although the business of some corporations may be such as to make the shares therein belonging to individuals moneyed capital in their hands, as in the case of banks. A railroad company, a mining company, an insurance company, or any other corporation of that description, may have a large part of its capital invested in securities payable in money, and so may be the owners of moneyed capital; but, as we have already seen, the shares of stock in such companies held by individuals are not moneyed capital.

The terms of the act of Congress, therefore, include shares of stock or other interests owned by individuals in all enterprises in which the capital employed in carrying on its business is money, where the object of the business is the making of profit by its use as money. The moneyed capital thus employed is invested for that purpose in securities by way of loan, discount, or otherwise, which are from time to time, according to the rules of the business, reduced again to money and reinvested. It includes money in the hands of individuals employed in a similar way, invested in loans, or in securities for the payment of money, either as an investment of a permanent character, or temporarily with a view to sale or repayment and reinvestment. In this way the moneyed capital in the hands of individuals is distinguished from what is known generally as personal property. Accordingly, it was said in Evansville Bank *v.* Britton, 105 U. S., 322: "The act of Congress does not make the tax on personal property the measure of the tax on the bank shares in the State, but the tax on moneyed capital in the hands of the individual citizens. Credits, money loaned at interest, and demands against persons or corporations are more purely representative of moneyed capital than personal property, so far as they can be said to differ. Undoubtedly there may be said to be much personal property exempt from taxation without giving bank shares a right to similar exemption, because personal property is not necessarily moneyed capital. But the rights, credits, demands, and money at interest mentioned in the Indiana statute, from which bona-fide debts may be deducted, all mean moneyed capital invested in that way."

This definition of moneyed capital in the hands of individuals seems to us to be the idea of the law, and ample enough to embrace and secure its whole purpose and policy.

From this view, it follows that the mode of taxation adopted by the State of New York in reference to its corporations, excluding for the present trust companies and savings banks, does not operate in such a way as to make the tax assessed upon shares of national banks at a greater rate than that imposed upon other moneyed capital in the hands of individual citizens.

This is the conclusion reached on similar grounds by the court of appeals of New York. In the case of McMahon *v.* Palmer, 102 N. Y., 176, that court said:

"Our system of laws, with reference to the taxation of incorporated companies and capital invested therein, has been carefully framed with a view of reaching all taxable property and subjecting it to equality of burden, so far as that object is attainable in a matter so complex. In view of the wide variation in the employable value of such investments and the frequent mutations in their conditions, it is by no means certain that this object has not been attained with reasonable accuracy. It is quite clear, from even this cursory review of the statutes, that if any discrimination is made by our laws in taxing capital invested, it is not to the prejudice of that employed in banking corporations. Even if this were not the result of the statute, we are of opinion that investments in the shares of companies named do not come within the meaning of that clause in the Federal statutes referring to other moneyed capital in the hands of individuals. That phrase, as generally employed, distinguishes such capital from other personal property, and investments in the various manufacturing and industrial enterprises. And this is the sense in which it is used in our tax laws, as appears by reference to the statutes."

The cases of trust companies and saving banks require separate consideration. Section 312 of chapter 409 of the act of 1882 is a re-enactment of section 3 of chapter 596 of the laws of 1880, except that in the latter trust companies were included with banks and banking institutions, so as to subject the stockholders therein to the same rule of assessment and taxation on the value of their shares of stock. The present statute omits them from the corresponding section. The consequence is, that trust companies are taxable, as other corporations, under the act of 1857, for local purposes, upon the actual value of their capital stock. By chapter 361 of the laws of 1881, as amended, they are subjected to a franchise tax, in the nature of an income tax, payable to the State for State purposes. It is argued, from this legislation, in reference to the taxation of trust companies, that it discloses an evident intent to discriminate in favor of the latter as between them and banks, including national banks; and it is argued that, considering the nature of the business in which trust companies are engaged, it is a material and unfriendly discrimination in favor of State institutions engaged to some extent in a competing business with that of national banks. Trust companies, however, in New York, according to the powers conferred upon them by their charters and habitually exercised, are not in any proper sense of the word banking institutions. They have the following powers: To receive moneys in trust and to accumulate the same at an agreed rate of interest; to accept and execute all trusts of every description committed to them by any person or corporation or by any court of record; to receive the title to real or personal estate on trusts created in accordance with the laws of the State, and to execute such trusts; to act as agents for corporations in reference to issuing, registering, and transferring certificates of stock and bonds, and other evidences of debt; to accept and execute trusts for married women in respect to their separate property; and to act as guardian for the estates of infants. It is required that their capital shall be invested in bonds and mortgages on unincumbered real estate in the State of New York worth double the amount loaned thereon, or in stocks of the United States or of the State of New York, or of the incorporated cities of that State.

It is evident, from this enumeration of powers, that trust companies are not banks in the commercial sense of that word, and do not perform the functions of banks in carrying on the exchanges of commerce. They receive money on deposit, it is true, and invest it in loans, and so deal, therefore, in money and securities for money in such a way as properly to bring the shares of stock held by individuals therein within the definition of moneyed capital in the hands of individuals, as used in the act of Congress. But we fail to find in the record any sufficient ground to believe that the rate of taxation, which in fact falls upon this form of investment of moneyed capital, is less than that imposed upon shares of stock in national banks.

It appears from the tax laws of New York applicable to the subject, as judicially construed by the court of appeals of that State, that the capital stock of such a corporation is to be assessed at its actual value. The actual value of the whole capital stock is ascertained by reference, among other standards, to the market price of its shares, so that the aggregate value of the entire capital may be the market price of one multiplied by the whole number of shares. Oswego Starch Factory *v.* Dolloway, 21 N. Y., 449; The People *v.* The Commissioners of Taxes, 95 N. Y., 554. From this are to be deducted, of course, the real estate of the corporation otherwise taxed, and the value of such part of the capital stock as is invested in non-taxable property, such as securities of the United States. In addition to this, the corporation, as already stated, pays to the State, as a State tax, a tax upon its franchise based upon its income; the tax on the capital being for local purposes.

It is evident, we think, that taxation in this mode is at least equal to that upon the shares of individual stockholders, for if the same property was held for the same uses and taxed by the same rule in the hands of individuals, as moneyed capital, it would be subject to precisely the same deductions; in addition to which the individual would be entitled to make a further deduction of any debts he might owe. Upon these grounds, therefore, we are of opinion that this mode of taxing trust companies does not create the inequality which the appellant alleges.

In the case of savings banks, we assume that neither the bank itself nor the individual depositor is taxed on account of the deposits. The language of the statute (section 4, chapter 456, laws of 1857) is as follows:

"Deposits in any banks for savings, which are due to the depositors, . . . shall not be liable to taxation, other than the real estate and stocks which may be owned by such bank or company, and which are now liable to taxation under the laws of this State."

According to the stipulation in this case, the deposits in such banks amount to $437,107,501, with an accumulated surplus of $68,669,001. It can not be denied that these deposits constitute moneyed capital in the hands of individuals within the terms of any definition which can be given to that phrase; but we are equally clear that they are not within the meaning of the act of Congress in such a sense as to require that, if they are exempted from taxation, shares of stock in national banks must thereby also be exempted from taxation. No one can suppose for a moment that savings banks come into any possible competition with national banks of the United States. They are what their name indicates, banks of deposit for the accumulation of small savings belonging to the industrious and thrifty. To promote their growth and progress is the obvious interest and manifest policy of the State. Their multiplication can not in any sense injuriously affect any legitimate enterprise in the community. We have already seen that by previous decisions of this court it has been declared that "it could not have been the intention of Congress to exempt bank shares from taxation because some moneyed capital was exempt" (Hepburn *v.* School Directors, 23 Wallace, 480), and that "the act of Congress was not intended to curtail the State power on the subject of taxation. It simply required that capital invested in national banks should not be taxed at a greater rate than like property similarly invested. It was not intended to cut off the power to exempt particular kinds of property, if the legislature chose to do so." Adams *v.* Nashville, 95 U. S., 19. The only limitation, upon deliberate reflection, we now think it necessary to add, is that these exemptions should be founded upon just reason, and not operate as an unfriendly discrimination against investments in national-bank shares. However large, therefore, may be the amount of moneyed capital in the hands of individuals, in the shape of deposits in savings banks as now organized, which the policy of the State exempts from taxation for its own purposes, that exemption cannot affect the rule for the taxation of shares in national banks, provided they are taxed at a rate not greater than other moneyed capital in the hands of individual citizens otherwise subject to taxation.

It is further objected, on similar grounds, to the validity of the assessment complained of in this case that municipal bonds of the city of New York to the amount of $13,467,000 are also exempted from taxation. The amount of the exemption in this case is comparatively small, looking at the whole amount of personal property and credits which are the subjects of taxation; not large enough, we think, to make a material difference in the rate assessed upon national-bank shares; but, independently of that consideration, we think the exemption is immaterial. Bonds issued by the State of New York, or under its authority by its public municipal bodies, are means for carrying on the work of the government, and are not taxable even by the United States, and it is not a part of the policy of the government which issues them to subject them to taxation for its own purposes. Such securities undoubtedly represent moneyed capital, but as from their nature they are not ordinarily the subjects of taxation, they are not within the reason of the rule established by Congress for the taxation of national-bank shares.

The same considerations apply to what is called an exemption from taxation of shares of stock of corporations created by other States and owned by citizens of New York, which it is agreed amount to at least the sum of $250,000,000. It is not pretended, however, that this exemption is based upon the mere will of the legislature of the State. The courts of New York hold that they are not the proper subjects of taxation in the State of New York, because they have no *situs* within its territory for that purpose. Hoyt *v.* The Commissioners of Taxes, 23 N. Y., 224; People, ex rel. etc., *v.* The Commissioners, 4 Hun, 595. The objection would be equally good if made to the non-taxation of real estate owned by citizens of New York, but not within its limits. Clearly the property to be taxed under the rule prescribed for the taxation of national-bank shares must be property which, according to the law of the State, is the subject of taxation within its jurisdiction.

Upon these grounds, substantially the same as those on which the circuit judge proceeded, 28 Fed. Rep., 776, we are of opinion that the appellant is not entitled to the relief prayed for.

The decree of the circuit court is, therefore, affirmed.

CONCLUSION.

I have the honor to submit in the Appendix, page 165, a summary of communications received from various parts of the country during the last year and a half, suggesting modifications of the laws by which, in the opinion of the writers, the national banking system would be improved and perpetuated.

Upwards of forty plans have been suggested, which are appropriately classed under five propositions, viz:

1. To do away with the note-issuing function of the banks.
2. To increase the inducements for the banks to deposit United States bonds as a basis of national-bank circulation.
3. To provide by a new issue of bonds for a continuance of the present or of some modified system of national-bank circulation based on United States bonds.
4. To substitute some other security for United States bonds deposited in the Treasury as a basis for national-bank circulation.
5. To allow the banks to issue circulation upon their general credit, without requiring specific security to be deposited.

The various suggestions for the deposit of gold and silver as a basis of circulation have been left out of consideration, because, as they contemplate deposits equal in value to the currency to be issued, they contain no inducement either to the public or to the banks to adopt them, and, therefore, they are obviously impracticable. The Treasury now issues gold and silver coin certificates, which answer all the purposes of such currency.

Among the propositions above stated, that which contemplates maintaining the national-bank system without any currency feature is hardly worth considering so long as it is generally conceded that Congress has no certain authority under the Constitution to charter banks that do not issue currency.

The fourth proposition, viz, to substitute State, county, and municipal securities for United States bonds as a basis of circulation, is subject to the fatal objection that the power to accept some and reject others among those securities would have to be lodged somewhere, and as its exercise would incidentally raise and depress the prices of such securities, it would be dangerous to adopt any scheme involving the confiding of such power to any official or any board.

There remain, therefore, but three propositions to be considered as within the range of probable adoption:

I.—Proposition second, to increase the inducements for the banks to deposit United States bonds as a basis of national-bank circulation.

II.—Proposition third, to provide by a new issue of bonds for a continuance of the present or of some modified system of national-bank circulation based on United States bonds.

III.—Proposition fifth, to allow the banks to issue circulation upon their general credit without requiring specific security to be deposited.

Before considering these propositions separately, it is important to observe that the case to be dealt with is that of 3,061 banks now in full operation, with bonds to the aggregate amount of $188,828,000 deposited in the Treasury, on which there is outstanding $169,215,067 of circulation.

It is obvious that this fact must exercise a controlling influence upon the discussion, because it has a paramount bearing upon the two fundamental questions, viz:

First, what is practicable, and, secondly, what is expedient?

A third question may be raised, viz, what is just to the banks? But this question is really merged in the other two, because the relations between the banks and the public are such as to render any unjust measure both inexpedient and impracticable.

It must be obvious, on merely looking at the question from this point of view, that many things that might be practicable or expedient, or both, if we were now initiating a national-bank system, may be impracticable or inexpedient when applied to the existing system.

In discussing the three propositions, therefore, their relative abstract merits must be regarded as subordinate to the effect they will have, severally, upon existing arrangements.

In order to apply this method of inquiry intelligently and effectively we must determine, first, what is sought to be remedied, and, secondly, what is sought to be accomplished beyond merely applying remedial measures.

Speaking broadly, it may be assumed that remedies are sought, first, for the present continual reduction in the volume of national-bank circulation, and, secondly, for the obstacles which the scarcity and high prices of United States bonds present to the formation of new banks, and to the increase of capital on the part of those already existing.

Beyond remedying these defects in the present law, there is a general desire to provide a permanent, safe, and popularly acceptable basis for the continued existence and the future growth of the national-bank system.

To judge properly whether any measure designed to remedy present defects or to accomplish the other ends named is likely to prove both practicable and expedient, as applied to existing conditions, note must be taken of how such a measure will affect banks differently situated, either geographically or financially, or both, because very great differences in these respects really exist among the banks, and what would attract some of them would repel others.

It will be necessary, therefore, to bear in mind that out of the 3,049 banks in operation on October 5 last, 2,150 have $150,000 capital or less, while among the rest there are 107 banks of which the capital is $1,000,000 or over, and 6 of which the capital amounts to $3,000,000 or over.

The 2,150 smaller banks are required by law to hold an amount of bonds equal to 25 per cent. of their capital, while the others, however large their capital, need hold but $50,000 of bonds, which is 10 per cent. on $500,000 capital, 5 per cent. on $1,000,000, and only 1 per cent. on $5,000,000, a discrimination which has become more and more unfavorable to the smaller banks as the bonds have become scarcer and dearer.

If all banks should be required to hold 25 per cent. of their capital in bonds, as the smaller banks are, the larger banks would quit the system, contracting the circulation by nearly $100,000,000, while, on the other hand, if the minimum of the smaller banks is reduced to, say, 10 per cent. of capital, which is about the average now required of the larger banks, it is probable that many more banks would be formed and that some of the small banks would increase their capital.

Having thus before us some of the limitations which encompass the solution of the problem, let us consider the three propositions in the order named:

1. To render the holding of United States bonds more profitable to the banks.

Of course this proposition rests upon the assumption that it is desirable for the banks to be encouraged or enabled to hold United States bonds, but this assumption needs to be substantiated. There was a time when it was important that every possible inducement should be given the banks to take these bonds, but this time is past, and the ability of the banks to do as much for the Government in some future emergency will be greatly increased by their being not only free, but inclined to dispose of all the bonds they now hold in excess of the minimum requirement. From the point of view of the Government, therefore, a very important resource in time of future need is curtailed by the banks being needlessly holders of United States bonds at a time of profound peace, and when the credit of the Treasury is at its zenith.

The proposition presents to the banks an aspect varying according to circumstances. Of course as long as the holding of bonds is obligatory every bank would like to have this holding made more profitable, but all banks are not situated alike in regard to the profitableness of circulation based on bonds. Some banks now hold much larger amounts of bonds than the law requires, while others profess to be excluded from the system because the holding of even the minimum is too great a burden; hence it must be inferred that some banks find a profit in such investments under conditions that inflict loss upon others. If, therefore, the holding of these bonds is rendered profitable to the latter class, the degree of its profitableness to the former class will be proportionately increased. This is stated by way of illustration merely and not as an objection, because, obviously, if a commensurate public advantage is secured by this augmentation of profit the incidental benefit to some banks should not be begrudged.

The most important consideration, however, is as to what the gain would be to the public regarded as distinct from the Government and the banks. Manifestly the only result that can possibly be claimed as a public gain would be a probable increase of bank-note circulation based on bonds, or at least the maintenance of the present volume of such circulation; hence the question as to the public gain involves the precedent question whether increasing the profitableness of bonds as a basis for circulation is likely to increase permanently the volume of national-bank circulation.

In the case of these bonds, as of other securities of stable intrinsic value dealt in by the general public, the market price varies directly and the amount on sale at any given time varies inversely with the number and means of purchasers, while under normal conditions purchasers vary in number and means according to the profitableness of the investment. Now, it is demonstrable that it is only the circulation obtainable upon depositing them in Washington that renders the holding of United States bonds in any degree profitable to national banks, while they are sought for and tenaciously held by other investors, who are excluded from obtaining circulation on them; hence it is probable that the present tendency to contraction of the national-bank currency is due to the scarcity and high price of bonds, resulting from the competition between new banks and outside investors for the few bonds on sale. If this is so, it follows that as the circulation is rendered more profitable the premium should go higher; and since almost all the bonds now offered for sale belong to banks reducing their circulation, the supply on the market will be seriously curtailed by any change of the law that renders it more profitable to the banks to buy these bonds than to sell them.

If this reasoning is correct, new banks can gain nothing by such measures as we are now considering, because, while they will still have to compete for their bonds with outside investors, they will also remain exposed to competition with the existing banks that are now able to get the most profit out of circulation, nor will existing banks generally be benefited, since there will remain the same disparity as now between those more and those less favorably situated for holding bonds. This reasoning carried to its ultimate results, will be found to establish the proposition that should the holding of bonds be rendered more profitable to the banks, the whole benefit will accrue to those which find such investments profitable now, and the only increase of circulation to be relied upon will be such as these banks may take out in addition to what they now have, while, per contra, the higher premium will discourage the formation of new banks and increase the insecurity now felt as to the permanence of the system.

What is desirable from the point of view of those who desire the banks to increase in number and to expand their circulation is that bonds shall decline in price, whereas all these plans tend to elevate their price, because they tend to render the holding of them by banks more profitable than it is now.

This reasoning applies to all those plans which involve raising the amount of note issues in proportion to the face of the bonds, taking the tax off circulation, etc.; but there would seem to be no objection to taking the tax off so much of the circulation as rests on the minimum amount of bonds required by law to be deposited, while such relief would be eminently just, because this being obligatory it should be made as little burdensome as possible, and it will chiefly apply to small banks remote from money centers and which are now required to hold an amount of bonds greatly exceeding in percentage upon capital the amount required of larger banks.

The second of the three practicable propositions contravenes the settled policy of Congress, which is to reduce and ultimately to extinguish the national debt, and therefore not to issue any bonds having remote maturities. The leading authorities of both political parties, the press of the country, and the people generally have approved this policy, and therefore it seems idle to expect legislation to the contrary, even for the purpose of preserving the banks.

If a suspension of this policy were the sole possible condition of preserving the banks there might be a bare possibility of its consideration, but no such argument can be sustained.

The last of the feasible projects, viz, proposition fifth, seems to be the only one containing a general principle under which the national-bank system may possibly be perpetuated. This principle is that while preserving all the other features of the system the main volume of bank currency should rest upon the credit and resources of the banks and not upon the credit of the Government.

All existing banks are entitled to the privilege of issuing circulating notes to the extent of 90 per cent. of the par of the United States bonds deposited, and this privilege can not justly be curtailed in any case without the consent of the bank. It is prudent also, on the part of the Government, to leave the law unchanged in this respect, for an emergency may hereafter arise when it will be very important to resort to the measures of 1863 for rallying the banks to the support of the Treasury, and in such a case it would be convenient to have all the machinery in working order.

On the other hand, there may be good reason why banks which are now being constrained by various influences to bring their circulation on bonds down to the minimum, should be accorded the privilege of issuing currency in addition to that secured by the bonds, if such issues can be subjected to conditions that will preserve the present high credit of the national-bank currency.

With the reservation, therefore, that whatever new legislation is proposed should be additional to, and not in repeal of, existing laws as to the deposit of bonds, whether obligatory or optional, and as to the privilege of issuing currency to 90 per cent. of such deposits, we may proceed to the examination of the plans grouped under proposition fifth.

These plans are ten in number, and they may be arranged in subgroups according to the basis which they propose for the issue of circulation additional to that which is secured by United States bonds. This basis varies in the different plans: First, according to the volume of circulation to be permitted; second, according to the security underlying the bank-notes; third, according to the provision made for their redemption.

The limitation of volume varies in the different plans from 25 per cent. to 100 per cent. upon capital, but no reasons are assigned in any case for the percentage proposed. It seems to be assumed that this is a matter of either fanciful or purely arbitrary selection.

As to security, there are four distinct propositions:

1. To depend solely upon the present provision of the law which makes the circulating notes a first lien upon all the assets of a failed bank.

2. To add to this the requirement that a reserve of 25 per cent. in lawful money shall be kept on hand by each bank.

3. To create a guaranty fund in the Treasury by devoting to that object the profit on lost circulation and the gradual accumulation from an annual tax of 1 per cent.

4. To make the banks mutual guarantors of each other's issues, the notes of each bank, however, to constitute a first lien upon its assets.

The provision for redemption varies in this way:

1. An annual tax of 1 per cent., of which the proceeds shall be used as a redemption fund.

2. The present 5 per cent. redemption deposit.

3. A pro rata assessment on all the issuing banks to whatever amount experience may indicate as sufficient.

Since all these plans embrace the maintenance of the present provision that the notes constitute a first lien upon all the assets of a failed bank, it is proper to consider this feature first.

The law now makes this lien a security for only the deficiency between the proceeds of deposited bonds and the outstanding circulation. No case of such deficiency has, I believe, ever arisen, and in the present state of the market for United States bonds, none is likely to arise; hence the preference thus secured to note-holders over all other creditors of a national bank has never been enforced nor has its existence in the law affected the general credit of these institutions. Never having had any practical significance it is generally lost sight of.

Obviously it will be very different when a currency is issued not specially secured at all, and which in every case of insolvency must be redeemed wholly out of the general assets before these become subject to the claims of depositors.

The national banks owe their present prosperity entirely to the confidence of the general public, and this confidence is manifested in the volume of individual deposits, which in the aggregate amount to $1,250,000,000, or 2½ times the aggregate capital of the banks.

These deposits constitute the chief resource of the banks, and hence it would be a hazardous thing to introduce into the system any feature likely to disturb the confidence of depositors.

The issue of preferred notes to the amount of even 25 per cent. of the capital, the lowest limit proposed, would be a serious matter to depositors, while such issues to the amount of 50, 75, and 100 per cent. of capital, as some suggest, would probably cripple fatally the general credit of the banks with prudent depositors, and in that way their means of accommodation would be curtailed in a ratio greater than the increase of such means derived from the additional issues of currency.

It is much more important to the banks as a body to retain and augment their deposits than to acquire the power to issue more currency, and the public have even a greater interest than the banks in the preservation of this condition of things, because the credit that attracts deposits is always better founded than that which floats currency, and is also more jealously guarded by the banks enjoying it, and is therefore less likely to be abused.

It is, indeed, doubtful whether any really strong and prudent banks would like to risk their credit with depositors by issuing notes as a first lien on their assets, and in that case if the proposition led to the establishment of such a bank currency at all, notes would be issued chiefly by banks having small deposits and their assets might very easily be so handled as to constitute a very poor security, even for the preferred notes. There would certainly be great temptation to a bank to become speculative when once it had floated all the currency allowed and found itself free from the observation of numerous and vigilant local depositors.

If these views are correct, they would seem to be fatal to all schemes of establishing a bank currency secured only by a first lien upon all the assets of the issuing bank, unless some sufficient counterpoise to the objections can be found among the various suggestions as to a 25 per cent. reserve, a sinking fund deposited with the Government, the consolidation of all issuing banks into one association, etc.

While none of these devices appears to me likely to prove practically effective in removing the objections, it is probable that considerable diversity of opinion will arise on the subject, and as individual views can not be anticipated, it seems useless to spread the discussion over the whole field of possible contention. It is important, however, to bear in mind that any computations as to the proper ratios of reserve or redemption funds to the volume of currency, which may be drawn from the history of national-bank circulation, will be misleading, because the conditions heretofore obtaining will all be changed when, on the one hand, banks have every temptation to force out circulation, and, on the other hand, the public acquire the habit of presenting these notes for redemption every time the general credit of the bank is affected.

In times of panic now, banks have to take care of their depositors only, the ordinary process of the redemption of notes is not materially varied, nor is the volume of general currency diminished, but when there is no special security behind these notes, the case will be very different; every rumor of monetary trouble will bring both the noteholders and the depositors clamoring for payment, and just when there is most need of money to pay them with, the currency will be contracted by the discredit of national-bank circulation.

In answer to these general objections to the first lien principle, it may be said, of course, that the assets of the bank will be increased by the whole amount of its issue of notes, while now its assets are actually diminished by the difference between the cost of the bonds and the circulation received from the Government. This is very true; and if those assets were set aside, as the bonds now are, as specific security for the notes, and if, moreover, they could be always maintained in a form as intrinsically valuable and as readily convertible as the bonds are, the force of the objection would be destroyed; but no one familiar with practical banking can really believe that either of these conditions could be maintained in even a single case, while it is more than probable that in most cases they would be disregarded, and the old adage "easy come, easy go" would receive fresh illustration from numerous instances in which the facility of uttering currency would lead, as it did under the old State-bank system, to very lax and speculative methods of employing the resources so obtained.

If the views here submitted are correct, it would appear that no substitute yet proposed for the present basis of national-bank circulation is sufficiently free from objection to be adopted. The 4-per cent. bonds will not mature for twenty years; and, apart from other considerations, there is enough in this fact to justify caution and delay in making any radical change in the basis of circulation. In that time, no doubt, something acceptable will be devised, but at present all that seems practicable is to modify the existing law so as to obviate its inconveniences, and as a first step toward this end it appears both safe and wise to reduce the minimum amount of bonds to be kept on deposit.

This is, no doubt, quite a safe step, because capital is no longer attracted to the system or held in it by any profit derived from circulation, or by the prospect of any profit to be made by holding bonds.

These early inducements have been replaced by others of a much more permanent and satisfactory character. The high credit attaching to national banks, the business-like methods cultivated in their relations with the public, and other similar influences developed within the system itself, constitute a cohesive attraction, which makes it stronger to-day than it has ever been before. Reducing the minimum requirement as to bonds, therefore, can not weaken the system. Concurrently with the progress of this healthful change in the system itself, the bonded debt of the United States has been gradually reduced in amount and refunded at lower rates of interest, while such is the investment demand that the still outstanding bonds of every class are constantly becoming scarcer on the market; indeed, there is hardly any longer a regular market for United States bonds, because they are held almost entirely either by a limited class of investors, who rarely care to sell, or by national banks, which in many cases can not sell.

One effect of this condition of things is to make the obligation to deposit bonds a serious obstacle to the formation of new banks in the sections where they are most needed, and to the increase of capital on the part of those banks of which the capital does not already exceed $150,000.

The public needs and demands a continual increase of banking facilities, and to supply those facilities it is necessary to have not only more banks, but banks in a greater number of localities, and also some increase of capital among banks previously established.

The need of such increased facilities is coextensive with the country, but it is most pressing in those sections where the growth of population and the expansion of industry are year by year outstripping the measure of accommodation afforded by local capital.

To such communities the national-bank system affords opportunities otherwise unobtainable for bringing to the development of their resources supplies of capital from the remote centers of cheap and abundant money; hence, any obstacles to the growth of this system in our newer States and Territories is a more serious matter than it is elsewhere.

Another effect of the laws as they now stand is to deprive the national-bank circulation of the little elasticity possible to it, because the volume of this circulation varies with the amount of bonds held by the banks, and not only are bonds too scarce and dear to be freely bought and sold, but the inducement to banks to reduce their holdings of bonds to the minimum prescribed by law is constant and of growing intensity, while there are no inducements to an increase of such holdings; consequently there is neither elasticity nor steadiness in the volume of bank notes, but only a continuous contraction of circulation that year by year more than overcomes the annual expansion due to the formation of new banks, and keeps the public mind in a state of feverish anxiety, always easily excited into alarm.

Still another effect is to render the banks very sensitive to every step made towards reducing the bonded debt of the Government.

A striking instance of this occurred lately in connection with the redemption of the 3 per cent. bonds. On August 12, 1886, the redemption of these bonds was resumed, and the last call matured July 1, 1887, after which date 3 per cent. bonds were no longer available as a basis of circulation. At the former date the national banks held $103,351,650, on which their outstanding circulation amounted to $93,016,485, so that the redemption of the bonds forced the banks either to surrender circulation to this amount or to replace the 3 percents with bonds obtainable only at a premium.

The progress of this rapid redemption and its effect upon national-bank circulation are elsewhere described in detail. What is material in connection with the topic now under consideration is, that while the unprecedented contraction produced less immediate embarrassment than it might have done, yet it so disturbed public confidence, and rendered the banks so nervous, that the annual autumnal monetary stringency in New York was magnified last September into a portent of impending disaster, and came near seriously interrupting the industries of the entire country.

This effect carries with its recognition considerations as to the future, which are of national importance, because in the autumn of 1891 the 4½ per cent. bonds will become subject to call, and unless precautions are taken in advance to prevent a recurrence of the disquietude we have so lately experienced, the anxieties of this year will have been suffered in vain.

Of those bonds there are now outstanding $230,500,000, and one of the most important problems of the immediate future is how to deal with this indebtedness. The conditions of the problem will be materially simplified if the banks are permitted and induced to gradually reduce their holdings of 4½ percents.

With a view to facilitating the healthy and natural expansion of the national-bank system, to restoring stability and some degree of elasticity to the circulation based on bonds, and to obviating a recurrence, with respect to the 4½ per cent. bonds, of the perilous experience of the last twelve months with respect to the 3 percents, it appears to be wise to reduce the minimum requirement of bonds; and I respectfully recommend that it be hereafter fixed at one-tenth of the capital of all banks of which the capital does not exceed $250,000, and that no bank shall be required to maintain a deposit of more than $25,000 in bonds; also that the banks be relieved of taxation upon so much of the circulation issued to them as is represented by the minimum of bonds which the law requires them to deposit.

This latter recommendation is made chiefly in the interest of the small country banks, to which every expense is a burden, and which, as a rule, deposit only the minimum of bonds.

It would seem to be quite proper to tax circulation in excess of that represented by the minimum of bonds, not for the sake of revenue only, but because such a tax tends to impart elasticity to the entire volume of circulation, and because any bank that likes may escape the tax; but both justice and policy appear to be against a tax on circulation represented by bonds of which the deposit is obligatory.

The recommendation to reduce the minimum amount of bonds to be deposited is supported by the following considerations:

1. As the law now stands, the total amount of bonds required to be deposited by the 3,049 banks in operation on October 5 is $89,912,347, while the amount actually on deposit at that date was $189,083,199, or $99,170,753 more than the minimum requirement.

This excess is distributed as follows: 2,150 banks of $150,000 capital and under, of which the minimum is $44,962,347, hold actually $79,485,000—an excess of $34,522,653; 899 banks of over $150,000 capital, of which the minimum is $44,950,000, hold actually $109,598,100—an excess of $64,648,100.

If the proposed change is made the banks in operation on October 5 will stand thus: 2,552 banks with not over $250,000 capital; minimum, $26,400,309; actual, $116,444,250; excess, $90,043,941; 497 banks with over $250,000 capital; minimum, $12,425,000; actual, $72,638,850; excess, $60,213,850. Total excess, $150,257,791.

Of course it is to be expected that some banks will be prompted by the change in the law to reduce their circulation, but the magnitude of this reduction and the rate at which it can be effected will be controlled by two influences; first, the provision of law which limits to $3,000,000 the amount of lawful money that may be deposited in any calendar month in order to effect the withdrawal of circulation; and, secondly, the decline in the price of the bonds which must attend any sudden and large increase in the amount offered for sale. Banks will not surrender circulation except to realize the premium by selling their bonds.

2. While undoubtedly these two influences will effectually prevent any monetary disturbance, arising from the change in the law, they will not even obstruct but will materially promote such gradual changes in the bonds on deposit as will enable the banks to be practically free from 4½ per cent. bonds by the time these mature in 1891.

The total amount of 4½ per cent. bonds held on October 31 as security for circulation was $69,696,100, and therefore it will only require changes to the extent of about $17,500,000 annually to render the banks entirely independent, in four years, of any policy the Treasury may adopt as to these bonds.

If they are redeemed the national-bank circulation will be undiminished by the process of redemption; if they are refunded on terms admitting of a profit on circulation, the banks will be in a good position to buy the extended bonds.

3. One effect of a gradual shifting of deposits out of 4½ per cent. bonds will probably be, that as the volume of circulation based on these bonds becomes reduced, a corresponding decline will be observed in the sensitiveness of the banks and of the money market to the progress of redemption of the public debt.

This is a very important consideration, because it is desirable that when the time arrives for deciding what is to be done with the 4½ per cent. loan, there shall arise neither the apprehension of financial disturbance nor any strong popular pressure to influence the choice between payment and extension. From every point of view it is desirable that this choice should turn wholly on the position and prospects of the public finances.

4. Throughout the whole period of the existence of the national-bank circulation there never has been a time when the volume of the outstanding notes has been determined by commercial forces only; the operations of the Treasury have always exercised an abnormal and a disturbing influence, and reciprocally the state of the currency has constantly fettered the operations of the Treasury. If the proposed change in the law tends even in the least degree to release the Treasury and the currency from this unnecessary and harassing interdependence, it will be a great public gain.

5. Once free from the disturbing cause referred to, there is no reason why the volume of national-bank currency should not soon find its natural centre of oscillation; that is, the point above and below which its normal movements of increase and decline would conform to the varying needs of the commercial and other industries of the country.

From the stand-point of these industries, elasticity is more important than quantity in the currency; their interests are better subserved by a currency so elastic in volume as to respond immediately to variations in the demand for it, than by a great volume of money rigid in amount. Elasticity in the volume of the currency supplies to commercial operations what springs and a smooth road supply to transportation. In each case more can be accomplished with less wear and tear and less breakage than is possible when these conditions are wanting.

6. A reduction in the amount of bonds which the banks are required to have on deposit will prepare the way for a change in the basis of circulation, in case such change may hereafter seem expedient. As long as the law compels the smaller banks to invest more than one-fourth of their capital in bonds (counting in the premium), it may be unjust to them to permit circulation to be issued upon any other security, for only the large banks could then get the full benefit of such permission; but 10 per cent. of capital invested in bonds will not be a serious impediment even to banks of $50,000 capital getting their fair share of any privileges as to circulation that may hereafter be determined upon.

7. It should be observed, finally, that owing to the two retarding influences already referred to, the results here suggested can be accomplished only during a considerable lapse of time, and of course, in the interval, unforeseen conditions may arise and unexpected influences may modify or reverse the tendencies now existing; but it does not seem possible that any change of conditions or of tendencies can cause embarrassment to the banks or to the public fairly chargeable to the proposed change in the law.

W. L. TRENHOLM,
Comptroller of the Currency.

The SPEAKER OF THE HOUSE OF REPRESENTATIVES.

ABSTRACT OF REPORTS OF THE NATIONAL BANKING ASSOCIATIONS OF THE UNITED STATES, SHOWING THEIR CONDITION AT THE CLOSE OF BUSINESS ON WEDNESDAY, THE 5TH DAY OF OCTOBER 1881.

...stocks, bonds, and mortgages.	Due from approved reserve agents.	Due from other national banks.	Due from State banks and bankers.	Real estate, furniture, and fixtures.	Current expenses and taxes.	Premiums paid.	Checks and other cash items.	Exchanges for clearing house.	Bills of other banks.	Fractional currency.	Specie.	Legal tender notes.	U. S. certificates of deposit.	Five per cent. redemption fund.	Due from U. S. Treasurer.	Trade dollars.	Aggregate of resources and liabilities.	Capital stock paid in.	Surplus fund.	Undivided profits.	National bank circulation...
[illegible]	[illegible]	[illegible]	[illegible]	[illegible]	[illegible]	[illegible]	[illegible]	[illegible]	[illegible]	[illegible]	[illegible]	[illegible]	[illegible]	[illegible]	[illegible]	[illegible]	[illegible]	[illegible]	[illegible]	[illegible]	[illegible]

APPENDIX.

A DIGEST OF NATIONAL-BANK CASES.

CONTENTS.*

I. **Constitutional law.**

(1) Powers of Congress; (2) Powers of the States.

II. **Powers and liabilities of national banking associations.**

(1) Implied powers; (2) As to collateral securities; (3) Special deposits; (4) Government securities; (5) Certified check; (6) Purchasing check; (7) Stocks; (8) Deposits to secure performance of contracts; (9) Loans in excess of one-tenth capital; (10) Real estate; (11) Certificates of deposits; (12) Lien on dividends; (13) Contracts and obligations of old corporation; (14) Place of business; (15) Circulating notes; (16) Business of liquidating association.

III. **Ultra vires.**

(1) Dealing in stocks; (2) Purchasing negotiable paper; (3) Lending credit; (4) Mortgages on real estate; (5) When association can not set up want of power.

IV. **Stock.**

(1) Purchasing its own stock; (2) Liens on stock; (3) May be attached; (4) Capital set free belongs to shareholders; (5) Contracts to give shares for business; (6) Transfer of stock; (7) Subscriptions to increase of capital stock; (8) Specific performance of contract to sell.

V. **Shareholders.**

(1) Estopped to deny incorporations; (2) Individual liability.

VI. **Officers.**

(1) Tenure of office; (2) Bonds of officers; (3) Directors must act as a board; (4) Borrowing of association; (5) Liability for violations of law; (6) Directors of converted banks; (7) Retirement of directors.

VII. **Interest.**

(1) What interest associations may take; (2) On claims against insolvent and liquidating associations; (3) Usury.

VIII. **Insolvent associations.**

(1) Not subject to bankrupt act; (2) What constitutes insolvency; (3) Assets a trust fund; (4) United States has no priority; (5) Claims for torts; (6) Preferences; (7) Basis for estimation of dividends; (8) Set-off.

IX. **Receivers.**

(1) Officer of the United States; (2) Whom he represents; (3) How far subject to Comptroller's orders; (4) Power of courts to appoint; (5) Debtors of association can not question legality of appointments; (6) Receiver's decision not final; (7) Sale by; (8) Contracts of; (9) Expenses of receivership for association which has gone into liquidation.

X. **Taxation.**

(1) What may be taxed; (2) Rate; (3) Valuation; (4) Exemptions; (5) Collection of tax from association; (6) License tax; (7) Powers of taxing officers; (8) Enforcement of taxes; (9) Location of association for taxing purposes.

*Cases which turned upon a peculiar state of facts, and many which but reiterate settled principles, have been omitted; also, a few which are reported so badly or so meagerly that the precise points decided do not clearly appear.

XI. **Jurisdiction.**

(1) Jurisdiction of Federal courts prior to the act of July 12, 1882; (2) Jurisdiction of Federal courts subsequent to act of July 12, 1882; (3) Jurisdiction of State courts; (4) United States can not be subjected to jurisdiction of court; (5) Citizenship.

XII. **Suits.**

(1) By and against associations; (2) By shareholders; (3) By receivers; (4) By creditors of insolvent association; (5) For usury; (6) To enforce liability of shareholders; (7) Execution; (8) Attachments; (9) Abatement; (10) Estoppel; (11) Suits against liquidating associations; (12) Transitory and local suits; (13) Survival of suits.

XIII. **Evidence.**

(1) Certificates of Comptroller; (2) Evidence of insolvency; (3) Necessity for assessment by Comptroller.

XIV. **Crimes.**

(1) Under United States laws; (2) Under State laws; (3) Term "United States currency" in penal statutes.

I. CONSTITUTIONAL LAW.

1. POWERS OF CONGRESS:

(a) Congress has the constitutional power to incorporate banks. (*McCulloch* v. *Maryland*, 4 *Wheat.*, 316; *Osborn* v. *Bank of the United States*, 9 *Wheat.*, 738.)

(b) Congress has power to clothe national banking associations, as to their contracts and dealings with the world, with any special immunities and privileges exempting them, in their trade and intercourse with others, from the laws and remedies applicable in like cases to other citizens. (*The Chesapeake Bank* v. *The First National Bank of Baltimore*, 40 *Md.*, 269.)

(c) Thus, the provision of the banking law that no attachment, injunction, or execution shall issue against a national banking association before final judgment in any suit, action, or proceeding in a State court is constitutional. (*Ibid.*)

(d) The tax imposed on State or national banks paying out the notes of individuals or State banks used for circulation is constitutional. (*Veazie Bank* v. *Fenno*, 8 *Wall.*, 533.)

(e) So is the tax imposed on them for paying out the circulating notes of municipal corporations. (*Merchants' National Bank of Little Rock* v. *United States*, 101 *U. S.*, 1.)

(f) Such a tax is not a direct tax within the meaning of the clause of the Constitution, which declares that "direct taxes shall be apportioned among the several States, according to their respective numbers." (*Veazie Bank* v. *Fenno, and Merchants' National Bank of Little Rock* v. *United States, supra.*)

(g) Congress having, in the exercise of undisputed constitutional powers, undertaken to provide a currency for the whole country, may secure the benefit of it to the people by appropriate legislation. (*Veazie Bank* v. *Fenno, supra.*)

(h) Congress has the power to divest the United States courts of their jurisdiction of suits by or against national banking associations. (*National Bank of Jefferson* v. *Fare et al.*, *U. S. C. C.* (*E. D. Texas*), 25 *Fed. Rep.*, 209.)

2. POWERS OF THE STATES:

(a) National banking associations, being instruments designed to aid the Government in the administration of a branch of the public service, can not be controlled by the States, except in so far as Congress may see proper to permit. (*Farmers and Mechanics' Bank* v. *Dearing*, 91 *U. S.*, 29.)

(b) No authority from the State is necessary to enable a State bank to convert itself into a national banking association. (*Casey* v. *Galli*, 94 *U. S.*, 673.)

(c) National banking associations located outside of a State are subject to its restraining acts prohibiting all corporations, not authorized by the law of the State, from keeping therein offices for the purpose of discount and deposit. (*National Bank of Fairhaven* v. *The Phœnix Warehousing Company*, 6 *Hun*, 71.)

(d) It is competent for a State by penal enactments to protect its citizens in their dealings with national banking associations located within the State. (*State* v. *Fuller*, 34 *Conn.*, 280; see also *Taxation and Jurisdiction.*)

II. POWERS AND LIABILITIES.

1. IMPLIED POWERS:

To the enumerated powers of national banking associations are to be superadded all the powers incidental to the business of banking. (*Pattison* v. *Syracuse National Bank*, 80 *N. Y.*, 82.)

2. AS TO COLLATERAL SECURITIES:

(a) A national banking association may take stock of a corporation as collateral security for a loan. (*Shoemaker* v. *The National Mechanics' Bank*, 2 *Abb. U. S.*, 416; *Canfield* v. *The State National Bank of Minneapolis*, *U. S. C. C.* (*Dist. Minn.*), 1 *Northwestern Reporter*, 173.)

(b) And it may take for such purpose the stock of another national banking association. (*National Bank* v. *Case*, 99 *U. S.*, 628.)

NOTE.—But this point was not necessary to the decision of the case.

2. AS TO COLLATERAL SECURITIES—Continued.

(c) A national banking association may take a pledge of personal chattels as security for a loan. (*Pittsburgh Locomotive and Car Works* v. *State National Bank of Keokuk, U. S. C. C.* (*Eighth Circuit*, 1875), 2 *Cent. L. J.*, 692.)

(d) A national banking association may take as security for a loan the indorsement of a married woman, charging her separate estate. Such security is to be treated as personal security, within the meaning of the banking law, and not as a mortgage. (*Third National Bank* v. *Blake*, 73 *N. Y.*, 260.)

(e) A national banking association may take as collateral security for a loan a warehouse receipt for merchandise. (*Cleveland, Brown & Co.* v. *Shoeman*, 40 *Ohio St.*, 176.)

(f) A national banking association may take as security for a loan the stock of a corporation whose entire capital is vested in real estate. Such a loan does not amount to a lending upon mortgage. (*Baldwin* v. *Canfield*, 26 *Minn.*, 43.)

(g) An agreement by a national banking association to the effect that, in case a note discounted by it shall not be paid, a mortgage given by the maker to his indorser shall inure to the benefit of the association, is not inhibited by the national banking law. (*First National Bank* v. *Haire*, 36 *Iowa*, 443; see also *National Bank* v. *Matthews*, 98 *U. S.*, 621.)

(h) A national banking association having taken a mortgage on real estate to secure a debt previously contracted may, in order to protect itself, pay off a prior lien on the said real estate; and the lien which it thus acquires it may enforce. (*Orna* v. *Merchants' National Bank*, 16 *Kans.*, 341; *Holmes* v. *Boyd*, 90 *Ind.*, 332.)

(i) Where a national banking association has taken collaterals to secure a loan, and, after the loan has been repaid, holds them to secure future advances, it is not a gratuitous bailee; and it is responsible for the loss of such collaterals occasioned by its lack of ordinary care and diligence, though at the time the bailor was not indebted to it. (*Third National Bank of Baltimore* v. *Boyd*, 44 *Md.*, 47.)

3. SPECIAL DEPOSITS:

(a) A national banking association may receive special deposits. The provision in section 5228, Revised Statutes, authorizing an association "to deliver special deposits" implies that it may receive them as a part of its legitimate business; and this implication is as effectual as an express declaration to the same effect would have been. (*National Bank* v. *Graham*, 100 *U. S.*, 699.)

(b) National banking associations have power to receive special deposits either *gratuitously or otherwise*. (*Pattison* v. *Syracuse National Bank*, 80 *N. Y.*, 82.)

(c) But the executive officers of an association can not bind it as a gratuitous bailee, unless they have a special authority from the board of directors so to do, or there exists a general custom or usage to that effect. (*First National Bank of Lyons* v. *Ocean National Bank*, 60 *N. Y.*, 278.)

4. GOVERNMENT SECURITIES:

(a) National banking associations can engage in the business of dealing in and exchanging Government securities. (*Van Leuven* v. *First National Bank*, 54 *N. Y.*, 671; *Yerkes* v. *National Bank of Port Jervis*, 69 *N. Y.*, 383; *Leach* v. *Hale*, 31 *Iowa*, 69.)

(b) And where an association receives United States bonds of one class for the purpose of having them converted into bonds of another class, it is not a mere mandatary, but is responsible for the failure to deliver the bonds on demand. (*Leach* v. *Hale, supra.*)

5. CERTIFIED CHECK:

A national banking association may "certify" a check. A "certified" check is not within the meaning of section 5183, Revised Statutes, which prohibits the issuing of post-notes or any notes to circulate as money other than such as are authorized by the national banking law. (*Merchants' National Bank* v. *State National Bank*, 10 *Wall.*, 604.)

6. PURCHASING CHECK:

A national bank may buy a check drawn upon another bank; and whether the check is payable to order or to bearer is immaterial. (*First National Bank of Rochester* v. *Harris*, 108 *Mass.*, 514.)

7. STOCKS:

(a) A national banking association, in the compromise of a claim growing out of its legitimate business, may take railroad stock. (*First National Bank of Charlotte* v. *National Exchange Bank of Baltimore*, 92 *U. S.*, 122.)

7. STOCKS—Continued.

(*b*) And when necessary to do so, it may pay the difference between the value of the stock and the amount of the claim. (*Ibid.*)

(*c*) A national banking association may take and hold the coupons of municipal bonds, and may maintain actions thereon. (*First National Bank of North Bennington* v. *Town of Bennington*, *U. S. C. C.* (*Dist. Vt.*), *Browne's N. B. Cas.*, 437; see also *Lyons* v. *Lyons National Bank*, 19 *Blatch.*, 279.)

8. DEPOSITS TO SECURE PERFORMANCE OF CONTRACT:

A national banking association may receive a deposit to be held by it as security for the faithful performance of a contract between the depositor and another. (*Bushnell* v. *The Chautauqua County National Bank*, 10 *Hun*, 378.)

NOTE.—But the court put the decision upon the further ground that even were the contract *ultra vires*, the association, having received the deposit, was estopped from setting up its want of power.

9. LOANS IN EXCESS OF ONE-TENTH CAPITAL:

(*a*) Sec. 5200, Revised Statutes, which provides that the total liabilities to any association of any person, etc., shall not exceed one-tenth part of the capital stock paid in, was intended only for the guidance of the association, and, though its franchises may be liable to forfeiture for violation of the law, the association may recover of the borrower the full amount of the loan. (*Gold Mining Company* v. *Rocky Mountain National Bank*, 96 *U. S.*, 640; *O'Hare* v. *Second National Bank of Titusville*, 77 *Penn. St.*, 96; *Shoemaker* v. *The National Mechanics' Bank*, 2 *Abb. U. S.*, 416; *Stewart* v. *National Union Bank of Maryland*, 2 *Abb. U. S.*, 424.)

(*b*) A note is not illegal because at the time it was discounted by the association the maker was indebted to the association in a sum equal to more than one-tenth part of its capital. (*O'Hare* v. *Second National Bank of Titusville*, *supra.*)

(*c*) And a court of equity will not enjoin an association, at the instance of the borrower, from transferring to innocent third persons notes and securities, on the ground that the notes represent part of a loan made in excess of 10 per cent. of the capital of the association. (*Elder* v. *First National Bank of Ottawa*, 12 *Kans.*, 238.)

(*d*) Where a State bank makes a loan to one person of an amount in excess of one-tenth part of its capital, and is afterward converted into a national bank, it may, after conversion, extend the time for payment of such loan without violating section 5200, Revised Statutes. (*Allen* v. *The First National Bank of Xenia*, 23 *Ohio St.*, 97.)

10. REAL ESTATE:

(*a*) Where a national banking association acquires real estate which it is not authorized to take, the conveyance to it is not void, but only voidable. And the title of the association to such real estate is good until assailed in a direct proceeding by the Government. (*Reynolds* v. *Crawfordsville Bank*, 112 *U. S.*, 405; see also *National Bank* v. *Matthews*, 98 *U. S.*, 621; *National Bank* v. *Whitney*, 103 *U. S.*, 99; *Swope* v. *Leffingwell*, 105 *U. S.*, 3; *Fortier* v. *New Orleans Bank*, 112 *U. S.*, 439.)

(*b*) The amount of real estate which a national banking association may purchase to secure a pre-existing debt is not limited to the exact amount of the debt, but as much may be purchased as is necessary to secure the debt due, so long as the security of such debt is the real object of the purchase. (*Upton* v. *National Bank of South Reading*, 120 *Mass.*, 153.)

(*c*) Where the purpose is to secure a debt previously contracted, a national banking association may take a conveyance of real estate worth more than the debt, and pay the difference between the debt and the value of the property. (*Libby* v. *Union National Bank*, 99 *Ill.*, 622.)

(*d*) Where a national banking association sells real estate it may take a mortgage thereon to secure the payment of the purchase-money. (*New Orleans National Bank* v. *Raymond*, 29 *La. Ann.*, 355.)

11. CERTIFICATES OF DEPOSIT:

National banking associations may issue certificates of deposit. Such certificates are not post-notes within the prohibition of section 5183, Revised Statutes. (*Hunt* v. *Appellant*, *Supreme Court of Mass.*, *May* 7, 1886; *Riddle* v. *First National Bank*, *U. S. C. C.* (*W. D. Penn.*), 27 *Fed. Rep.*, 503.)

12. LIEN ON DIVIDENDS:

An association has an equitable lien upon dividends declared for any just debt due to it from the shareholders. (*Hager* v. *Union National Bank*, 63 *Me.*, 509.)

13. CONTRACTS AND OBLIGATIONS OF OLD CORPORATION:

(a) Where a State bank has been converted into a national banking association it may enforce all contracts made with it while a State corporation. (*City National Bank* v. *Phelps*, 97 *N. Y.*, 44.)

(b) And it is liable, after the conversion, for all the obligations of the old institution. (*Coffee* v. *The National Bank of Missouri*, 46 *Mo.*, 140; *Kelsey* v. *The National Bank of Crawford*, 69 *Penn. St.*, 426.)

(c) A national banking association organized as the successor of a State bank may take and hold the assets of the bank whose place it takes, though there was not in form a conversion from a State to a national corporation, but the organization of a new corporation. (*Bank* v. *McIntire*, 40 *Ohio St.*, 528.)

(d) And such association will be liable to the depositors of the former bank. (*Eans* v. *Exchange Bank*, 79 *Mo.*, 182.)

14. PLACE OF BUSINESS:

(a) The provision requiring "the usual business" of the association to be transacted "at an office or banking-house in the place specified in its organization certificate" must be construed reasonably; and a part of the legitimate business of the association which can not be transacted at the banking-house may be done elsewhere. (*Merchants' Bank* v. *State Bank*, 10 *Wall.*, 604.)

(b) Although the general business of a national banking association is to be transacted at its place of business, yet, if the association is fully advised of the facts, and does not object, and there is no fraud, its officers, when acting within the general scope of their authority, may bind it by acts done at another place. (*Burton* v. *Burley*, 9 *Biss.*, 253.)

15. CIRCULATING NOTES:

The circulating notes of a national banking association are valid, though they do not bear the imprint of the seal of the Treasury. Such imprint was intended to be simply evidence of the contract, and forms no part of the contract itself. (*United States* v. *Bennett*, 17 *Blatch.*, 357.)

16. BUSINESS OF LIQUIDATING ASSOCIATION:

After an association goes into liquidation there is no authority on the part of its officers to transact any business in its name so as to bind its shareholders, except that which is implied in the duty of liquidation, unless such authority has been expressly conferred by the shareholders. (*Richmond* v. *Irons*, 121 *U. S.*, 27.)

III. ULTRA VIRES.

1. DEALING IN STOCKS:

(a) A national banking association is not authorized to act as a broker or agent in the purchase of bonds and stocks. (*First National Bank of Allentown* v. *Hoch*, 89 *Penn St.*, 324; *Weckler* v. *The First National Bank of Hagerstown*, 42 *Md.*, 581.)

(b) A national banking association can not deal in stocks. The prohibition is to be implied from the failure to grant the power. (*First National Bank* v. *National Exchange Bank*, 92 *U. S.*, 122.)

NOTE.—But see as to its power to deal in Government securities, Powers, 4.

2. PURCHASING NEGOTIABLE PAPER:

A national banking association can not *purchase* negotiable paper. (*Lazear* v. *National Union Bank of Baltimore*, 52 *Md.*, 78; *First National Bank of Rochester* v. *Pierson*, 24 *Minn.*, 140; see also *Farmers and Mechanics' Bank* v. *Baldwin*, 23 *Minn.*, 198. But see *Smith* v. *The Exchange Bank of Pittsburgh*, 26 *Ohio St.*, 141.)

3. LENDING CREDIT:

(a) A national banking association can not lend its credit. (*Johnston* v. *Charlottesville National Bank*, 3 *Hughes*, 657; *Seligman* v. *Charlottesville National Bank*, 3 *Hughes*, 647.)

(b) A national banking association can not guaranty the paper of a customer *for his accommodation*. (*Seligman* v. *Charlottesville National Bank*, *supra*.)

(c) The accommodation paper of a national banking association is void in the hands of one who takes it with knowledge of its character. (*Johnston* v. *Charlottesville National Bank*, *supra*.)

4. MORTGAGES ON REAL ESTATE:

(a) National banking associations are by implication prohibited from taking mortgages on real estate as security for contemporaneous loans. (*National

4. MORTGAGES ON REAL ESTATE—Continued.

Bank v. *Matthews*, 98 *U. S.*, 621; *Fowler* v. *Scully*, 72 *Penn. St.*, 456; *Kansas Valley National Bank* v. *Rowell*, 2 *Dill.*, 371; *Commonwealth Bank* v. *Clark*, 4 *Mo.*, 59; *Crocker* v. *Whitney*, 71 *N. Y.*, 161; *Fridley* v. *Bowen*, 87 *Ill.*, 151.)

(*b*) But where such security has been taken, no one but the Government can be heard to complain that the association has exceeded its powers. (*National Bank* v. *Matthews*, *supra*; *National Bank* v. *Whitney*, 103 *U. S.*, 99; *Swope* v. *Leffingwell*, 105 *U. S.*, 3; *Reynolds* v. *National Bank*, 112 *U. S.*, 405; *Fortier* v. *National Bank*, 112, *U. S.*, 439.)

NOTE.—These decisions overrule, on this point, *Kansas Valley National Bank* v. *Rowell*, 2 *Dill.*, 371; *Crocker* v. *Whitney*, *supra*; *Fowler* v. *Scully*, *supra*; *Matthews* v. *Skinker*, 62 *Mo.*, 329; *Woods* v. *People's National Bank of Pittsburgh*, 83 *Penn. St.*, 57; *Fridley* v. *Bowen*, *supra*.

5. WHEN ASSOCIATION CAN NOT SET UP WANT OF POWER:

Where a national banking association has entered into a contract which it was not authorized to make, a party who has enjoyed the benefit of such contract can not question its validity. (*Casey* v. *La Société de Credit Mobilier*, 2 *Woods*, 77; *German National Bank* v. *Meadowcroft*, 95 *Ill.*, 124.)

IV. STOCK.

1. PURCHASING ITS OWN STOCK:

Where a national banking association purchases shares of its own stock, and divides them among its directors, to whom the shares are transferred upon the stock books, the transaction is void, and no title passes. (*Meyers* v. *Valley National Bank*, *U. S. D. C.* (*E. Dist. Mo.*), 13 *National Bankruptcy Register*, 34.)

2. LIENS ON STOCK:

(*a*) A national banking association can not acquire a lien on the stock of a shareholder. And a by-law prohibiting a transfer until all liabilities of the shareholder to the association are discharged, or a provision to that effect in the certificates of stock, is void. (*Bullard* v. *National Bank*, 18 *Wall.*, 589; *Bank* v. *Lanier*, 11 *Wall.*, 369; *Conklin* v. *The Second National Bank*, 45 *N. Y.*, 655.)

(*b*) A national banking association can not take a pledge of its stock to secure a deposit made by it with another bank. Such a transaction amounts to a lending upon the security of its own shares. (*Bank* v. *Lanier*, *supra*.)

(*c*) Though a bank is prohibited from lending money upon the security of its own shares, yet if the shares have been sold and the proceeds applied to the payment of the debt, the courts will not aid the shareholder to recover the value of the shares. He can dispute the validity of the transaction only while the contract is executory, and the security still subsists in the possession of the bank. (*National Bank of Xenia* v. *Stewart*, 107 *U. S.*, 676.)

3. MAY BE ATTACHED:

The stock of a shareholder indebted to it may be attached by the association and sold on execution. (*Hagar* v. *Union National Bank*, 63 *Me.*, 509.)

4. CAPITAL SET FREE BELONGS TO SHAREHOLDERS:

When a national banking association reduces its capital stock the amount of capital thus released belongs to the shareholders pro rata, and must be returned to them; and it can not be retained by the association for a surplus. (*Seeley* v. *New York National Exchange Bank*, 8 *Daly*, 400; *s. c.*, 4 *Abb. N. C.*, 61; affirmed, 78 *N. Y.*, 608.)

5. CONTRACTS TO GIVE SHARES FOR BUSINESS:

Where an association has made or ratified a contract to give a person a certain number of the shares of its stock, upon condition that he will continue to do his business with it, and derives the benefit from this contract, the other party may recover of the association the value of the shares. (*Rich* v. *State National Bank of Lincoln*, 7 *Nebr.*, 231.)

6. TRANSFER OF STOCK:

(*a*) The transfer of shares in national banking associations is not governed by different rules from those which are ordinarily applied to the transfer of shares in other corporate bodies. (*Johnson* v. *Laflin*, 103 *U. S.*, 800.)

(*b*) The entry of the transaction in the books of the association is required, not for the translation of the title, but for the protection of the parties, and others dealing with the association, and to enable it to know who are its stockholders. (*Ibid.*)

6. TRANSFER OF STOCK—Continued.

(c) A shareholder in a national bank, while it is a going concern, has the absolute right, in the absence of fraud, to make a bona fide and actual sale and transfer of his shares, at any time, to any person capable in law of purchasing and holding the same, and of assuming the transferrer's liabilities in respect thereto; and this right is not, in such cases, subject to the control of the directors or other stockholders. (*Johnson* v. *Laflin*, 5 *Dill*, 65.)

(d) Under the pretense of prescribing the manner thereof, an association can not clog the transfer with useless restrictions. (*Johnson* v. *Laflin*, *supra*.)

(e) When a shareholder, acting in good faith, delivers his certificates of stock, with a blank power of attorney for making the transfer, and receives the purchase-money, the sale is complete and the title passes. (*Ibid.*)

(f) Where a cashier, who is intrusted by the directors with the duty of transferring the stock of the association, refuses, for insufficient reasons, to transfer shares, and the association subsequently becomes insolvent, the owner of the shares may maintain an action against the receiver for the injury sustained. (*Case* v. *Citizens' Bank*, 100 *U. S.*, 446.)

(g) Where a shareholder who has sold his stock has delivered to the bank the certificates of stock and a power of attorney with the request that the transfer be made upon the books of the bank, and has had no reason to suppose that such transfer was not made, he will not, should the bank afterward become insolvent, be held liable as a shareholder, although he still appears as such on the books of the bank. (*Whitney* v. *Butler*, 118 *U. S.*, 655.)

(h) But where the president of the bank is himself the purchaser of the stock then the delivery of the certificates and power of attorney to him with the request to make the transfer upon the books of the bank would not be sufficient to discharge the seller from liability as a stockholder. (*Richmond* v. *Irons* 121 *U. S.*, 27.)

7. SUBSCRIPTIONS TO INCREASE OF CAPITAL STOCK:

(a) Where one subscribes for shares in the increase of the capital of a national banking association in a certain amount, such subscription and payment are upon the implied condition that the increase shall be in the exact amount so fixed; and if such amount is changed, the subscriber may avoid the subscription and recover the amount paid in. (*Eaton* v. *Pacific Bank*, 144 *Mass.*, 260.)

(b) And the certificate of the Comptroller of the Currency that the amount of the increase in another sum has been paid in, which amount includes what was paid by the dissenting subscriber, will not be conclusive upon such subscriber. (*Ibid.*)

(c) But if such subscriber has assented to or ratified the change he will be held a shareholder. (*Delano* v. *Butler*, 118 *U. S.*, 634.)

8. SPECIFIC PERFORMANCE OF CONTRACT TO SELL:

A specific performance of a contract to sell the stock of a national banking association will not be enforced in favor of a purchaser who places his claim for equitable relief upon the ground that he desires to obtain control of the association. Such an object is contrary to public policy. (*Foll's Appeal*, 81 *Penn. St.*, 434.)

V. SHAREHOLDERS.

1. ESTOPPED TO DENY INCORPORATION:

A shareholder who has held himself out to the world as such is estopped to deny that the association was legally incorporated. (*Casey* v. *Galli*, 94 *U. S.*, 673; *Wheelock* v. *Kost*, 77 *Ill.*, 296.)

2. INDIVIDUAL LIABILITY:

(a) The question whether there is a deficiency of assets, and when it is necessary to enforce the individual liability of shareholders, is for the Comptroller to determine; and his decision in this matter is final and conclusive. (*Kennedy* v. *Gibson*, 8 *Wall.*, 498; *National Bank* v. *Case*, 99 *U. S.*, 628; *Casey* v. *Galli*, 94 *U. S.*, 673.)

(b) The amount contributed by each shareholder should bear the same proportion to the whole amount of the deficit as his own stock bears to the whole amount of the capital stock at its par value. And the solvent shareholders can not be made to contribute more than their proportion to make good the deficiency caused by the insolvency of other shareholders. (*United States* v. *Knox*, 102 *U. S.*, 422.)

2. INDIVIDUAL LIABILITY—Continued.

(c) A shareholder who disposes of his stock will continue to be liable thereon until the transfer is noted on the books of the association. (*Bowdell* v. *Farmers and Merchants' National Bank of Baltimore, U. S. C. C.* (*D. Md.*, 1877), *Browne's N. B. Cas.*, 147.)

(d) The individual liability of a shareholder adheres to his estate after his death until his place as a member of the association is taken by some new shareholder. (*Davis* v. *Weed, U. S. D. C.* (*Dist. Conn.*), *reported* 44 *Conn.*, 569.)

(e) The receiver has a valid claim against the estate generally of a deceased shareholder who died prior to the insolvency of the bank, but whose stock has not been transferred. (*Richmond* v. *Irons*, 121 U. S., 27; *Davis* v. *Weed, supra.*)

(f) And the fact that the title to the stock of a deceased shareholder vests in his administrator does not relieve the estate from the burden of an assessment. (*Davis* v. *Weed, supra.*)

(g) Nor will the fact that the administration is complete, and all the assets have been distributed, defeat an action brought to recover the assessment. (*Ibid.* But see *Witters* v. *Sowles.*)

(h) One who appears on the books of the association as the owner of shares of its stock is individually liable, though he hold the stock merely as collateral security. (*National Bank* v. *Case*, 99 *U. S.*, 628; *Moore* v. *Jones*, 3 *Woods*, 53; *Bowdell* v. *Farmers and Merchants' National Bank of Baltimore, supra*; *Hale* v. *Walker*, 31 *Iowa*, 344; *Wheelock* v. *Kost, supra.*)

(i) But where a pledgee, for the express purpose of avoiding a personal liability, and before the association becomes insolvent, or is in danger of insolvency, transfers the stock to an irresponsible person, he, the pledgee, will not be liable to contribute as a shareholder. (*Anderson* v. *Warehouse Company*, 111 *U. S.*, 479.)

(j) And where stock has been transferred as collateral security for a loan, *with the understanding that in case of default in the payment of the loan the shares shall be sold*, the transferee, upon default made, and before the bank closes its doors, may sell the stock for a nominal consideration, though his purpose be to avoid a personal liability; and such a transaction can not be set aside as a fraud upon the creditors of the association. (*Magruder* v. *Colston*, 44 *Md.*, 349.)

NOTE.—The court put the decision upon the ground that the sale was in pursuance of a stipulation which formed a part of the contract between the original owner and his transferee. See also *Holyoke Bank* v. *Burnham*, 11 *Cush.*, 187, upon the authority of which the Maryland case was decided.

(k) If the trusteeship of one who holds stock in trust does not appear upon the books of the association he will be individually liable. (*Davis* v. *Essex Baptist Society, U. S. D. C.* (*Dist. Conn.*), *reported* 44 *Conn.*, 582.)

(l) A transfer of shares for the purpose of avoiding liability, though made "out and out," is void. (*National Bank* v. *Case, supra*; *Bowden* v. *Santos*, 1 *Hughes*, 158.)

(m) And where a shareholder, who has knowledge of the insolvent condition of the bank, transfers his shares, without consideration, to a person unable to respond to the assessment, the transfer may be set aside and the individual liability of the transferer enforced. (*Bowden* v. *Johnson*, 107 *U. S.*, 251.)

(n) The real owner of the stock is liable as a stockholder, though when he purchased the stock he had it transferred upon the books to another. (*Davis* v. *Stevens*, 17 *Blatch.*, 259.)

NOTE.—The case of the owner of stock is thus different from that of a pledgee. (See *Anderson* v. *Warehouse Company, supra.*)

(o) Where shareholders have assessed themselves to the amount of the par value of the stock for the purpose of restoring impaired capital, the contributions made in pursuance of such assessment, though all used in paying the debts of the association, will not so operate as to discharge the shareholders from their individual liability. (*Delano* v. *Butler*, 118 *U. S.*, 634.)

(p) The individual liability of the shareholders of an insolvent association may be enforced for the purpose of paying all of its liabilities, and not merely for the purpose of paying its "debts," technically so called. (*Stanton* v. *Wilkeson*, 8 *Ben.*, 357.)

(q) The individual liability of the stockholders must be restricted in its meaning to such contracts, debts, and engagements of the association as have been duly contracted in the ordinary course of its business. And, therefore, creditors of an association who make settlements *after the association is put into liquidation* and receive from the president payment of their claims in paper of the association, or the individual notes of the president himself,

2. INDIVIDUAL LIABILITY—Continued.

indorsed or guaranteed in the name of the association, are not to be considered as creditors of the association entitled to subject the stockholders to individual liability; for these are new contracts. (*Richmond* v. *Irons*, 121 *U. S.*, 27.)

VI. OFFICERS.

1. TENURE OF OFFICE:

(*a*) The officers of a national banking association can hold their positions only by the tenure specified in section 5136, Revised Statutes, viz, the pleasure of the board of directors. (*Harrington* v. *First National Bank of Chittenango, S. C. N. Y.*, 1873; *Thomp. N. B. Cas.*, 761; see also *Taylor* v. *Hutton*, 43 *Barb.*, 195.)

(*b*) Directors of national banking associations may remove the president, both under the law of Congress and the articles of association, where the latter so provide. The power exists though the association has adopted no by-laws. (*Taylor* v. *Hutton*, *supra.*)

2. BONDS OF OFFICERS:

(*a*) It is not necessary that national banking associations shall signify their approval of the official bonds of their officers by memoranda entered upon the journals or minutes of the directors. The acceptance is to be presumed from the retention of the bond, and from the fact that the officer is permitted to enter upon or continue in the discharge of his duties. (*Grover* v. *The Lebanon National Bank*, 10 *Bush*, 23.)

(*b*) Where the sureties of an officer can reasonably be presumed to have been deceived by the statement of the condition of the bank published just prior to the execution of the bond, and to have been led to think that there was no deficit, whereas there had been a misapplication of a large part of the funds by the officer whose bondsmen they became, which fact would have been ascertained had the directors exercised ordinary diligence, the sureties are discharged from their liability. (*Grover* v. *The Lebanon National Bank*, *supra.*)

3. DIRECTORS MUST ACT AS A BOARD:

The election of an individual as a director does not constitute him an agent of the corporation with authority to act separately and independently of his fellow members. It is the board duly convened and acting as a unit that is made the representative of the association. The assent or determination of the members of the board acting separately and individually is not the assent of the corporation. The law proceeds upon the theory that the directors shall meet and counsel with each other, and that any determination affecting the association shall be arrived at and expressed only after a consultation at a meeting of the board, attended by at least a majority of its members. (*National Bank* v. *Drake*, 35 *Kans.*, 564.)

4. BORROWING MONEY OF ASSOCIATION:

An officer may, in the ordinary course of business, borrow money of the association. (*Blair* v. *First National Bank of Mansfield, U. S. C. C.* (*N. D. Ohio*, 1877), 10 *Chicago Legal News*, 84.)

5. LIABILITY FOR VIOLATIONS OF LAW:

(*a*) All directors who participate in and assent to a loan in excess of one-tenth of the capital of the bank, in violation of section 5200, Revised Statutes, will be liable to the bank for all damages sustained by it in consequence of such loan. (*Witters* v. *Sowles, U. S. C. C.* (*District of Vermont*), 31 *Fed. Rep.*, 1.)

(*b*) If a cashier, without authority from the directors so to do, makes a loan in excess of one-tenth of the capital of the association, he will be liable, in case of loss, for the amount of the excess. (*Second National Bank of Oswego* v. *Burt*, *XIV. New York Weekly Digest*, 290.)

(*c*) The directors of a national bank will not be held liable for loss occasioned to the bank through the frauds of a co-director in which they had no part, and which were perpetrated without their connivance or knowledge. It is not sufficient to charge them with liability that the frauds might have been prevented by the exercise on their part of a proper degree of supervision over the affairs of the bank. (*Movius* v. *Lee, U. S. C. C.* (*N. D. New York*), 30 *Fed. Rep.*, 298.)

6. DIRECTORS OF CONVERTED BANKS:

(a) When a State bank is converted into a national banking association all of the directors at the time will continue to be the directors of the association until others are appointed or elected, though some of them may not have joined in the execution of the articles of association and organization certificate. (*Lockwood* v. *The American National Bank*, 9 *R. I.*, 308.)

(b) And, *semble*, that the directors of a bank at the time of its conversion into a national banking association are not required to take the oath of directors. (*Ibid.*)

(c) But even were the oath required, a majority of all who were directors at the time of the conversion, and not merely a majority of those who take the oath, are necessary to constitute a quorum. (*Ibid.*)

7. RETIREMENT OF DIRECTORS:

(a) The law providing no particular mode by which a director is to resign from the board, an oral resignation would be as good as any. (*Movius* v. *Lee*, 30 *Fed. Rep.*, 298.)

(b) The president being the head of the board, a resignation to him is a resignation to the board. (*Ibid.*)

(c) A director is not prohibited from resigning during the year. The apparent purpose of the provision in regard to the term of office is to make it conform to the time of the new election, and not to absolutely require every director to serve the full term. (*Ibid.*)

VII. INTEREST.

1. WHAT INTEREST ASSOCIATIONS MAY TAKE:

(a) The provision in section 30 of the act of 1864 "that where, by the law of any State, a different rate is limited for banks of issue organized under State laws, the rate so limited shall be allowed for associations organized in any such State under the act," is enabling, and not restrictive; and, therefore, a national banking association in any State may stipulate for as high a rate of interest as by the laws of such State a natural person may, although State banks of issue are restricted to a less rate. (*Tiffany* v. *National Bank of the State of Missouri*, 18 *Wall.*, 409.)

(b) But it is not to be inferred from Tiffany *v.* National Bank of Missouri that whatever by the laws of the State is lawful for natural persons in acquiring title to negotiable paper by discount is lawful for national banks. (*National Bank* v. *Johnson*, 104 *U. S.*, 271.)

(c) The interest which a national banking association may charge is limited to the rate allowed to the banks of the State generally; and the fact that a few of the State banks are specially authorized to take a higher rate is not a warrant for a national banking association to do so. (*Duncan* v. *First National Bank of Mount Pleasant, U. S. D. C.* (*W. D. Penn.*, 1878), 11 *Bank. Mag.*, 787; *Gruber* v. *First National Bank*, 87 *Penn. St.*, 468.)

(d) Where the State law does not limit the rate of interest which may be charged on loans to corporations, a national banking association located in that State can not charge more than 7 per cent. interest on such loans. (*In re Wild*, 11 *Blatch.*, 243.)

(e) Where by the statutes of the State parties are authorized to contract for any rate of interest, national banking associations in that State may likewise contract for any rate, and are not limited to 7 per cent. (*Hinds* v. *Marmelejo*, 60 *Cal.*, 229; *National Bank* v. *Bruhn*, 64 *Tex.*, 571.)

2. ON CLAIMS AGAINST INSOLVENT AND LIQUIDATING ASSOCIATIONS:

(a) A depositor in a national banking association which has become insolvent is entitled to interest on his deposit. (*National Bank of Commonwealth* v. *Mechanics' National Bank*, 94 *U. S.*, 437.)

(b) He is entitled to interest from the date of the suspension of payments; and no demand upon the association is necessary. (*Chemical National Bank* v. *Bailey*, 12 *Blatch.*, 480.)

(c) Claims, when proved to the satisfaction of the Comptroller, are upon the same footing as if put in judgment, and therefore bear interest; and the fact that, under certain circumstances, there might be thus a compounding of interest will not defeat the right to interest. (*National Bank of Commonwealth* v. *Mechanics' National Bank*, *supra*.)

(d) But where a creditor has obtained judgment against an insolvent national banking association for the full amount of his claim and interest, he is not entitled to interest upon the face of the judgment, but only upon the amount of the claim at the time of the failure. (*White* v. *Knox*, 111 *U. S.*, 784.)

2. ON CLAIMS AGAINST INSOLVENT AND LIQUIDATING ASSOCIATIONS—Continued.

(e) The creditors of an insolvent national banking association in the hands of a receiver are entitled to interest on their claims during the period of administration. (*Chemical National Bank* v. *Bailey*, *supra*.)

(f) The assessments made by the Comptroller upon the shareholders of an insolvent association bear interest from the date of the order. (*Casey* v. *Galli*, 94 *U. S.*, 673.)

(g) In the case of book accounts in favor of depositors, interest begins to run against an association in liquidation from the date of the suspension of business. (*Richmond* v. *Irons*, 121 *U. S.*, 27.)

3. USURY:

(a) The usury laws of the States do not apply to national banking associations. (*Farmers and Mechanics' Bank* v. *Dearing*, 91 *U. S.*, 29; *Central National Bank* v. *Pratt*, 115 *Mass.*, 539; *First National Bank* v. *Gorlinghouse*, 22 *Ohio St.*, 492; *Davis* v. *Randall*, 115 *Mass.*, 547; *Hintermister* v. *First National Bank*, 64 *N. Y.*, 212.)

(b) And the remedies provided by the State for the taking of usury can not be resorted to. (*Farmers and Mechanics' Bank* v. *Dearing*, *supra*; *Wiley* v. *Starbuck*, 44 *Ind.*, 298.)

(c) The taking of illegal interest by a national banking association does not render the contract void. (*Farmers and Mechanics' Bank* v. *Dearing*, *supra*.)

(d) It does not invalidate an indorsement or a guaranty of the notes upon which the usurious interest was paid. (*Oates* v. *First National Bank of Montgomery*, 100 *U. S.*, 239; *Lazear* v. *National Union Bank of Baltimore*, 52 *Md.*, 78.)

(e) But usury destroys the interest-bearing power of the obligation; and there will be no point of time from which it can bear interest. (*Lucas* v. *Government National Bank*, 78 *Penn. St.*, 228.)

(f) The usury works a forfeiture of the entire interest accruing after maturity and before judgment, as well as that which accrues before maturity. (*Shunk* v. *The First National Bank of Galion*, 22 *Ohio St.*, 508.)

(g) The discounting of business paper by a national banking association at a higher than the legal rate is usurious, though the law of the State fixes no limit to the rate which natural persons may take for the discount or purchase of such paper. (*Johnson* v. *National Bank of Gloversville*, 74 *N. Y.*, 329; affirmed in *National Bank* v. *Johnson*, 104 *U. S.*, 271.)

(h) By charging more than legal interest on overdrafts, a national banking association loses the right to recover any interest at all. (*Third National Bank of Philadelphia* v. *Miller*, 90 *Penn. St.*, 241.)

(i) The liabilities of antecedent parties to a note or bill will not be affected by the usurious character of the transaction between the payee and the association; and the association may recover the full amount of the note or bill from the maker or acceptor. (*Smith* v. *The Exchange Bank of Pittsburgh*, 26 *Ohio St.*, 141.)

(j) Usurious interest which has been paid to a national banking association can not be applied by way of payment or set-off in any action by the association to recover the amount of the loan. (*Barnet* v. *Muncie National Bank*, 98 *U. S.*, 555.)

(k) Nor can the penalty for taking the usurious interest be recovered by way of counter-claim in such action, but a separate action must be brought therefor. (*Ibid.*)

NOTE.—This case overrules portions of the decisions in *Lucas* v. *Government National Bank*, *supra*; *Overholt* v. *National Bank*, 82 *Penn. St.*, 490; *Cake* v. *The First National Bank of Lebanon*, 83 *Penn. St.*, 303.

(l) A director is not by reason of his position estopped from setting up the defense of usury in an action brought against him by the association. (*Bank of Cadiz* v. *Slemmons*, 34 *Ohio St.*, 142.)

(m) Where a national banking association has discounted notes for another bank at a usurious rate of interest, the fact that the other bank has charged illegal interest on those notes to its customers will not affect its right to set up the defense of usury in an action by the association. (*Third National Bank of Philadelphia* v. *Miller*, *supra*.)

(n) The amount which may be recovered from the association as a penalty is twice the amount of interest paid, and not simply twice the amount in excess of the legal rate. (*Crocker* v. *First National Bank of Chetopa*, *U. S. C. C.* (*Eighth Circuit*), 3 *Am. L. T.* [N. S.], 350; *Overholt* v. *National Bank of Mount Pleasant*, 82 *Penn. St.*, 490; see also *Barnet* v. *Muncie National Bank*, *supra*.)

VIII. INSOLVENCY.

1. NOT SUBJECT TO BANKRUPT ACT:

National banking associations were not subject to the bankrupt act while that act was in force. (*In re Manufacturers' National Bank*, 5 *Biss.*, 499.)

2. WHAT CONSTITUTES INSOLVENCY:

The term "insolvency," as used in section 5242, Revised Statutes, forbidding transfer of the assets of national banking associations after, or in contemplation of, such insolvency, has the same meaning as it had when applied to traders in the bankrupt act; that is, it does not mean an absolute inability of a debtor to pay his debt at some future time, upon a settlement and winding up of his affairs, but a present inability to pay in the ordinary course of business. (*Case* v. *Citizens' Bank of Louisiana*, 2 *Woods*, 23; *Market Bank* v. *Pacific National Bank*, 30 *Hun*, 50.)

3. ASSETS A TRUST FUND:

Upon the appointment of a receiver all the assets of the association become in his hands a trust fund which the statute of limitations does not touch or affect. (*Riddle* v. *First National Bank*, *U. S. C. C.* (*W. D. Penn.*), 27 *Fed. Rep.*, 503.)

NOTE.—But this point was not necessary to the decision of the case, for suits against insolvent corporations are by a law of Pennsylvania expressly excluded from the operation of the statute.

4. UNITED STATES HAS NO PRIORITY:

(*a*) Section 3466, which gives the United States a priority for all claims it has against insolvent debtors, does not apply to the case of an insolvent national banking association. (*Cook County National Bank* v. *United States*, 107 *U. S.*, 445.)

(*b*) And as against the proceeds of the bonds deposited to secure circulation the United States can set off no claim, except for money advanced to redeem the notes. (*Ibid.*)

(*c*) And upon the failure of an association its five per cent. redemption fund can not be retained by the Treasurer to pay taxes due to the United States, but the fund passes to the Comptroller as an asset of the association. (*Jackson* v. *United States*, 20 *Ct. Cls.*, 298.)

5. CLAIMS FOR TORTS:

Claims arising out of the non-feasance or malfeasance of the association should be paid ratably with the debts, technically so called. (*Turner* v. *The First National Bank of Keokuk et al.*, 26 *Iowa*, 562.)

6. PREFERENCES:

(*a*) A preference, to be within the meaning of section 5242, Revised Statutes, must be given to an existing creditor to secure a pre-existing debt. A transfer by an insolvent bank to secure a contemporaneous loan is not a violation of the law. (*Casey* v. *La Société de Credit Mobilier*, 2 *Woods*, 77.)

(*b*) The insolvency need be in the contemplation of the bank only. It need not be known to the person to whom the transfer is made. (*Case* v. *Citizens' Bank of Louisiana*, *supra*.)

(*c*) After the directors of an insolvent association have voted to close its doors, any transfer of assets whereby a creditor secures a preference must be presumed to be made with an intent to prefer. (*National Security Bank* v. *Price*, 22 *Fed. Rep.*, 697.)

(*d*) Where the officers of an association which is in danger of insolvency, *for the purpose and in the expectation of preventing a failure*, make a pledge of securities to a depositor to induce him not to withdraw his deposit, such a pledge is not a preference within the meaning of section 5242, Revised Statutes, and will not be set aside when the association afterward is declared insolvent. (*Roberts* v. *Hill*, 23 *Fed. Rep.*, 311.)

(*e*) Where an insolvent association receives a deposit a short time before closing its doors, its officers knowing of the insolvency at the time, the receipt of such deposit is a fraud upon the depositor, and no title passes to the association; and, therefore, the depositor may reclaim the whole amount of the deposit; and as he claims under his original title, and not under a transfer from the association, such reclamation does not amount to a preference. (*Cragie et al.* v. *Hadley*, 99 *N. Y.*, 131.)

7. BASIS FOR ESTIMATION OF DIVIDENDS:

In estimating the dividends to be paid out of the assets of an insolvent association, the value of the claims at the time when the insolvency is declared is to be taken as the basis of distribution. (*White* v. *Knox*, 111 *U. S.*, 784.)

8. SET-OFF:

(*a*) A person liable upon a note to an insolvent national bank may set off against his indebtedness the amount of his deposit with the bank. (*Platt* v. *Bentley*, *Thomp. N. B. Cas.*, 758.)

(*b*) But a debtor can not set off the amount of a deposit assigned to him after the act of insolvency committed. (*The Venango National Bank* v. *Taylor*, 56 *Penn. St.*, 14.)

IX. RECEIVERS.

1. OFFICER OF THE UNITED STATES:

A receiver, when appointed by the Comptroller, with the concurrence of the Secretary, is an officer of the United States. (*Stanton* v. *Wilkeson*, 8 *Ben.*, 357.)

2. WHOM HE REPRESENTS:

He represents the bank, its stockholders, and its creditors; but he does not in any sense represent the Government. (*Case* v. *Terrell*, 11 *Wall.*, 199.)

3. HOW FAR SUBJECT TO COMPTROLLER'S ORDERS:

(*a*) The clause of section 50, act of 1864, which prescribes that the receiver shall be "under the direction of the Comptroller," means only that he shall be subject to the Comptroller's direction, not that he shall not act without orders. He may bring suit to collect assets without having been instructed to do so by the Comptroller. (*Bank* v. *Kennedy*, 17 *Wall.*)

(*b*) The receiver of a national bank is the instrument of the Comptroller, and may be removed by him. (*Kennedy* v. *Gibson*, 8 *Wall.*, 505.)

4. POWER OF COURTS TO APPOINT:

(*a*) The power of the Comptroller to appoint a receiver is not exclusive; it does not oust the courts of equity of their authority in the matter; and, therefore, a court of competent jurisdiction may place the bank in the hands of a receiver in cases where, according to the rules of equity, it may pursue such a course with regard to insolvent corporations generally. (*Irons* v. *Manufacturers' National Bank*, 6 *Biss.*, 301; *Wright* v. *Merchants' National Bank*, 1 *Flippin*, 561.)

(*b*) Where a bank has gone into voluntary liquidation, and the Comptroller has no power to appoint a receiver, a proper court, in a case where such action is necessary to protect the interests of a creditor, will appoint a receiver for it. (*Irons* v. *Manufacturers' National Bank*, *supra*.)

5. DEBTORS OF ASSOCIATION CAN NOT QUESTION LEGALITY OF APPOINTMENT:

The legality of the appointment of the receiver can not be questioned by the debtors of the bank when sued by him. The bank may move to have the appointment set aside, but the debtors can not. (*Cadle* v. *Baker*, 20 *Wall.*, 650; see also *Platt* v. *Beebe*, 57 *N. Y.*, 339.)

6. RECEIVER'S DECISION NOT FINAL:

The decision of a receiver rejecting a claim is not final. The claimant still has the right to sue. (*Bank of Bethel* v. *Pahquioque Bank*, 14 *Wall.*, 383.)

7. SALE BY:

(*a*) The receiver can not sell the real or personal property of the bank without an order from a court of competent jurisdiction. (*Ellis* v. *Little*, 27 *Kans.*, 707.)

(*b*) Nor can he sell upon terms in conflict with the order. (*Ibid.*)

(*c*) And under an order permitting him to sell the property of the bank he can not exchange, trade, or barter it for other property. (*Ibid.*)

(*d*) A sale made by a receiver under order of a court is to all intents and purposes a judicial sale. (*In re Third National Bank*, 9 *Biss.*, 535.)

8. CONTRACTS OF:

(*a*) As the power of a receiver of a national bank appointed by the Comptroller is limited, a person dealing with him in his official capacity is bound as a matter of law to have knowledge of his authority to act, and if contracts and agreements are entered into with the receiver in excess of his authority

8. CONTRACTS OF—Continued.

as conferred by law, the parties contract at their own peril, and the estate of the bank can not be charged for the default or inability of a receiver acting outside of his functions as receiver and beyond the duties which it involves. (*Ellis* v. *Little*, 27 *Kans.*, 707.)

(*b*) The receiver can not charge the estate of the bank by any executory contract, unless authorized so to do by the provisions of the national banking law, and the order of a court of competent jurisdiction obtained upon the terms of said law. (*Ibid.*)

9. EXPENSES OF RECEIVERSHIP FOR ASSOCIATIONS WHICH HAVE GONE INTO LIQUIDATION:

Where, after an association bank has gone into liquidation, a receiver is appointed at the instance of the creditors, the expenses of such receivership must be paid by the creditors. The shareholders can not be made individually liable for such expenses. (*Richmond* v. *Irons.*)

X. TAXATION.

1. WHAT MAY BE TAXED:

(*a*) A State can not tax the capital stock of a national bank, as such. The tax must be assessed upon the shares of the different stockholders. (*Collins* v. *Chicago*, 4 *Biss.*, 472.)

(*b*) The entire interests of the shareholders may be taxed without any deduction for that portion of the capital which is invested in United States securities. (*Van Allen* v. *The Assessors*, 3 *Wall.*, 573.)

(*c*) New shares issued by a national banking association can not be taxed until the increase of capital has been approved by the Comptroller of the Currency. (*Charleston* v. *People's National Bank*, 5 *S. C.*, 103.)

(*d*) The undivided surplus of a national banking association, unless invested in Federal securities, may be lawfully taxed by the State. (*North Ward National Bank of Newark* v. *City of Newark*, 10 *Vroom*, 380; *First National Bank* v. *Peterborough*, 56 *N. H.*, 38.)

(*e*) But, of course, if the surplus is taken into consideration in estimating the taxable value of the shares, it is not to be taxed separately. (*North Ward National Bank* v. *City of Newark*, *supra.*)

NOTE.—But it has been held in Maryland that the stock of an association represents its whole property, and where a tax is assessed upon the shares a separate tax upon the real or personal estate amounts to double taxation; and, therefore, where the organic laws of the State prohibit double taxation, such a tax upon the property of an association is void. (*County Commissioners* v. *Farmers and Mechanics' National Bank*, 48 *Md.*, 117; see also *National State Bank* v. *Young*, 25 *Iowa*, 311, wherein it was held that the States could tax only the shares, *eo nomine*, and the real estate.)

(*f*) The surplus fund of a national banking association is not excluded in the valuation of its shares for taxation. (*Strafford National Bank* v. *Dover*, 59 *N. H.*, 316.)

(*g*) Where shares of stock are assessed at their actual cash value without any deduction for the real estate owned by the association the real estate should not be taxed *eo nomine*. (*Commissioners of Rice County* v. *Citizens' National Bank of Faribault*, 23 *Minn.*, 280.)

(*h*) The States can not tax the circulating notes of national banking associations. (*Horne* v. *Greene*, 52 *Miss.*, 452; Contra *Board of Commissioners* v. *Elston*, 32 *Ind.*, 27; see also *Ruffin* v. *Board of Commissioners*, 69 *N. C.*, 498; *Lily* v. *The Commissioners*, 69 *N. C.*, 300.)

2. RATE:

(*a*) Where the State banks are taxed upon their capital, no tax can be imposed upon the shares of national banking associations; for as the capital of the State banks may consist of the bonds of the United States, which are exempt from State taxation, a tax on capital is not equivalent to a tax on shares. (*Van Allen* v. *The Assessors*, 3 *Wall.*, 573; *Bradley* v. *The People*, 4 *Wall.*, 459.)

(*b*) But though the tax upon the State banks is not *eo nomine* a tax on shares, *yet if it is equivalent to such a tax* the shares in the national banking associations located in that State may be taxed. (*Frazer* v. *Seibern*, 16 *Ohio St.*, 614; *Van Slyke* v. *State*, 23 *Wis.*, 656; *Boynoll* v. *State*, 25 *Wis.*, 112.)

(*c*) When by local legislation different rates are prescribed for different classes of moneyed capital, the rate imposed upon shares of national banks should approximate as closely as may be to the rate imposed upon other moneyed capital of the same or similar class, viz, shares of State banks. (*City National Bank* v. *Paducah*, *U. S. C. C.* (*Sixth Circuit*, 1877), 5 *Cent. L. J.*, 347.)

2. RATE—Continued.

(d) Congress meant no more than to require of the States as a condition to the exercise of the power to tax the shares in national banks, that they should, as far as they had the capacity, tax in like manner the shares of banks of issue of their own creation. (*Lionberger* v. *Rouse*, 9 *Wall.*, 468.)

(e) Therefore, where a State has previously contracted with the banks which it has chartered that they shall not be taxed above a certain rate, a tax upon national-bank shares at a greater rate is not invalid, if this rate is not greater than that assessed upon all the moneyed capital within the State, except that of the State banks. (*Ibid.*)

(*f*) Any system of assessment of taxes which exacts from the owner of the shares of a national banking association a larger sum in proportion to the actual value of those shares than it does from other moneyed capital, valued in like manner, taxes the shares at a greater rate, notwithstanding that the percentage of tax on the valuation is the same as that applied to other moneyed capital. (*Pelton* v. *Commercial National Bank*, 101 *U. S.*, 143.)

3. VALUATION:

(a) In estimating the value of the shares for the purpose of taxation reference may be had to all the property and values of the bank. (*Saint Louis National Bank* v. *Papin*, *U. S. C. C.* (*Eighth Circuit*), 3 *Cent. L. J.*, 669.)

(b) If no excessive valuation is complained of, and a correct result is arrived at, equity will not restrain the collection of a tax because the method of computation was erroneous. (*Ibid.*)

(c) The shares may be valued for taxation at an amount exceeding their face value, if this amount is not at a greater rate than the valuation set upon other moneyed capital in the State. (*Hepburn* v. *School Directors*, 23 *Wall.*, 480.)

(d) Under the statute of New York, shares in national banking associations should be taxed at their real or market value. (*People* v. *The Commissioners of Taxes and Assessments*, 94 *U. S.*, 415.)

(e) Where shares in national banking associations are purposely valued proportionally higher than the other moneyed capital in the State, the assessment is void. (*Pelton* v. *National Bank*, 101 *U. S.*, 143.)

(*f*) And the collection of what is in excess of the rate imposed on the other moneyed capital may be enjoined. (*Ibid.*)

4. EXEMPTIONS:

(a) The intention of Congress was that the rate of taxation of the shares should be the same as, or not greater than, the tax upon the moneyed capital of the individual citizen which is *subject and liable to taxation*. (*People* v. *The Commissioners*, 4 *Wall.*, 244.)

(b) Therefore, it is not a ground of objection to the validity of a tax on shares that, while deductions for United States bonds are made from the personal estates of individuals and the capital of State corporations, no deductions are made on account of the capital of national banking associations invested in such bonds. (*Ibid.*)

(c) The fact that by the statutes creating them, which statutes were passed prior to the national banking law, State banks are entirely exempt from taxation, will not render a tax upon the shares of national banking associations void. (*City of Richmond* v. *Scott*, 48 *Ind.*, 568.)

(d) And a State tax upon shares in national banking associations is not rendered invalid by an exemption of the shares of other corporations the capital of which consists of property required to be listed for taxation, as such. (*McIver* v. *Robinson*, 53 *Ala.*, 456.)

(e) Merely a partial exemption of other moneyed capital will not invalidate a tax upon shares in national banking associations. (*Hepburn* v. *School Directors*, 23 *Wall.*, 480.)

(*f*) But though Congress did not contemplate that there should be an absolute equality (which in the nature of things is impossible), yet it did intend that there should be a substantial equality; and, therefore, if the exemptions in favor of other moneyed capital are so palpable as to show that there is a serious discrimination against capital invested in the shares of national banking associations, the tax will be declared unlawful. (*Boyer* v. *Boyer*, 113 *U. S.*, 690.)

(g) A State law which does not permit a deduction to be made from the assessed value of bank shares for all debts due by the holder thereof, while authorizing such a deduction to be made from the assessed value of moneyed capital otherwise invested, is void. (*People ex rel. Williams* v. *Weaver*, 100 *U. S.*, 539, reversing *S. C.*, 67 *N. Y.*, 516, and overruling *People* v. *Dolan*, 36 *N. Y.*, 59.)

4 EXEMPTIONS—Continued.

(*h*) The main purpose of Congress in fixing limits to State taxation on investments in the shares of national banks, was to render it impossible for the State, in levying such a tax, *to create and foster an unequal and unfriendly competition, by favoring institutions or individuals carrying on similar business and operations and investments of a like character;* and the language of the law is to be read in the light of this policy. And, therefore, the exemption of shares of stock in corporations, *the business of which does not come into competition with that of the national banks* (*e. g.*, railroad companies, mining companies, manufacturing companies, and insurance companies) does not invalidate a tax upon national-bank shares. Capital thus employed is not "moneyed capital" within the meaning of the act of Congress. (*Mercantile Bank* v. *New York*, 121 *U. S.*, 138.)

(*i*) Bonds issued by a State, or under its authority by its public municipal bodies, although they undoubtedly represent moneyed capital, yet, as from their nature they are not ordinarily the subject of taxation, are not within the reason of the rule established by Congress for the taxation of national-bank shares, and the fact that the State exempts them from taxation does not deprive it of the right to tax shares of stock of national banks in the State. (*Ibid.*)

(*j*) Although deposits in savings banks constitute moneyed capital in the hands of individuals within the terms of any definition which can be given of that phrase, yet they are not within the meaning of the act of Congress in such a sense as to require that, if they are exempted from taxation, shares of stock in national banks must thereby also be exempted from taxation; for it can not be supposed that savings banks come into any possible competition with national banks. (*Ibid.*)

5. COLLECTION OF TAX FROM THE ASSOCIATION:

(*a*) A State tax upon shares is valid, though the tax is collected from the bank. (*National Bank* v. *Commonwealth*, 9 *Wall.*, 353.)

(*b*) And the State may require the banks to pay a tax rightfully laid upon the shares. (*Ibid.*)

(*c*) And where the tax on shares is payable by the association the collection of the tax may be enforced by distraint of its property. (*First National Bank* v. *Douglas County*, 3 *Dill.*, 330.)

(*d*) But where the tax laws of the State make the bank the *mere agent* for paying the tax on shares, and direct it to retain so much of the dividends as will answer that purpose, other agents being required to pay taxes for their principals only when they have under their control the property, money, or credit of such principals, the bank can not be made liable unless it has the control of the property, etc., of its shareholders, or has dividends in its possession, or has failed to retain them. (*Hershire* v. *The First National Bank*, 35 *Iowa*, 272.)

6. LICENSE TAX:

(*a*) National banking associations can not be subjected to a license or privilege tax. (*Mayor* v. *First National Bank of Macon*, 59 *Ga.*, 648; *City of Carthage* v. *First National Bank of Carthage*, 71 *Mo.*, 508; *National Bank of Chattanooga* v. *Mayor*, 8 *Heiskell*, 814.)

(*b*) A State law prohibiting the establishment of banking companies in the State without authority of the legislature was not intended to apply to banking corporations created by authority of Congress, since such corporations may be legally established in the State without the consent of the legislature. (*Stetson* v. *City of Bangor*, 56 *Me.*, 274.)

7. POWERS OF TAXING OFFICERS:

(*a*) Municipal officers can not assess a tax upon the shares of national banking associations until authorized to do so by some law of the State. (*Stetson* v. *City of Bangor*, 56 *Me.*, 274.)

(*b*) The officers of a national banking association can not be compelled to exhibit to the taxing officers of a State the books of the association showing the deposits of its customers. (*First National Bank of Youngstown* v. *Hughes*, *U. S. C. C.* (*N. D. Ohio*, 1878), *Browne's N. B. Cas.*, 176.)

(*c*) A national banking association is not exempt from examination by internal-revenue officers when it has in its possession any articles subject to an internal-revenue tax. Such an examination is not the exercise of a visitorial power, and, therefore, is not prohibited by the provision of section 5241, Revised Statutes, that the national banks shall not be subject to any visitorial powers except those authorized by the national-bank act or vested in the courts of justice. (*United States* v. *Rhawn*, *U. S. D. C.* (*E. D. Penn.*), *Thomp. N. B. Cas.*, 358.)

7. POWERS OF TAXING OFFICERS—Continued.

(d) Where by the tax laws of a State a perpetual lien for taxes attaches to property only by virtue of a levy thereon, and such levy is not made prior to the insolvency of the bank, the taxing officers of the State will be restrained, at the instance of the receiver, from levying upon the property of an insolvent national bank, and selling it, for the purpose of collecting a tax. (*Woodward* v. *Ellsworth*, 4 *Colo.*, 580.)

(e) A State may require the cashiers of national banking associations located within its territory to transmit lists of the shareholders to the taxing officers of the various towns in which the shareholders reside. (*Waite* v. *Dowley*, 94 *U. S.*, 527.)

8. ENFORCEMENT OF TAXES:

A tax duly assessed upon shares may be enforced in accordance with the general laws of the State on that subject. (*Weld* v. *City of Bangor*, 59 *Me.*, 416.)

9. LOCATION OF ASSOCIATION FOR TAXING PURPOSES:

An association which opens an office for the purpose of receiving deposits in another place than that in which it was organized does not become "located" in that place for purposes of taxation. (*National State Bank of Camden* v. *Pierce*, *U. S. C. C.* (*E. D. Penn.*), 18 *Alb. L. J.*, 16.)

XI. JURISDICTION.

NOTE.—The jurisdiction of the Federal courts in national-bank cases was very materially changed by the proviso to the fourth section of the act of July 12, 1882. The proviso is as follows:

"*Provided, however*, That the jurisdiction for suits hereafter brought by or against any association established under any law providing for national banking associations, except suits between them and the United States, or its officers and agents, shall be the same as, and not other than, the jurisdiction for suits by or against banks not organized under any law of the United States which do or might do banking business where such national banking associations may be doing business when such suits may be begun. And all laws and parts of laws of the United States inconsistent with this proviso be, and the same are hereby, repealed."

1. JURISDICTION OF FEDERAL COURTS PRIOR TO THE ACT OF JULY 12, 1882:

(a) National banking associations may sue in the Federal courts. The word "by" was omitted from section 57 of the act of 1864 by mistake. (*Kennedy* v. *Gibson*, 8 *Wall.*, 505.)

(b) A national banking association may sue and be sued in the circuit court for the district in which the association is located, irrespective of the amount in controversy and the citizenship of the parties. (*County of Wilson* v. *National Bank*, 103 *U. S.*, 770; *Mitchell* v. *Walker*, *U. S. C. C.* (*W. D. Penn.*, 1879), *Browne's N. B. Cas.*, 180; *Commercial Bank of Cleveland* v. *Simmons*, *U. S. C. C.* (*W. D. Ohio*), 10 *Alb. L. J.*, 155.)

(c) But where the amount in controversy does not exceed five hundred dollars, the association can not sue in a Federal court outside of the district in which it is established. (*Saint Louis National Bank* v. *Brinkman*, *U. S. C. C.* (*D. Kans.*), 1 *Fed. Rep.*, 45.)

(d) A national banking association located in one State may bring an action in the circuit court of the United States sitting within another State against a citizen of that State. (*Manufacturers' National Bank* v. *Baack*, 8 *Blatch.*, 147.)

(e) When a national bank is sued in a Federal court the suit must be brought in the district in which the bank is located. And service upon an officer of the bank in another district will not give the court of that district jurisdiction of the cause. (*Maine* v. *Second National Bank of Chicago*, 8 *Biss.*, 26.)

(f) A United States district court has jurisdiction of a suit in equity by or against a national banking association located within the district. (*First National Bank of Pittsburgh* v. *Pittsburgh and Castle Shannon Railroad Company*, 1 *Fed. Rep.*, 190.)

(g) A circuit court has no jurisdiction of a suit by a private person to compel the Comptroller of the Currency and the Treasurer of the United States to disclose what disposition has been made of the United States bonds deposited with the Treasurer by a national banking association, and for a decree directing those officers as to their duty regarding such bonds. (*Van Antwerp* v. *Hulburd*, 7 *Blatch.*, 425; *Van Antwerp* v. *Hulburd*, 8 *Blatch.*, 282.)

1. JURISDICTION OF FEDERAL COURTS PRIOR TO THE ACT OF JULY 12, 1882—Con'td.

(h) Section 380, Revised Statutes, which provides that "All suits and proceedings arising out of the provisions of law governing national banking associations, in which the United States or any of its officers or agents shall be parties, shall be conducted by the district attorneys of the several districts under the direction and supervision of the Solicitor of the Treasury," does not enlarge the jurisdiction of the circuit court, and can not be held to confer jurisdiction in such suits or proceedings upon a court not having, independently of this section, authority to entertain them. (*Van Antwerp* v. *Hulburd*, 7 *Blatch.*, 426.)

(i) National banking associations, being corporations organized under the laws of the United States, are entitled as such to remove into the circuit courts of the United States suits brought against them in the State courts. (*Cruikshank* v. *Fourth National Bank*, 21 *Blatch.*, 322; see also *Removal Cases*, 115 *U. S.*, 1.)

(j) A United States district court has jurisdiction to authorize a receiver to compromise a debt. (*Matter of Platt*, 1 *Ben.*, 534.)

(k) An action at common law to recover a debt due to the bank may be instituted by a receiver in a United States district court, he being an officer of the United States within the meaning of section 563, Revised Statutes. (*Platt* v. *Beach*, 2 *Ben.*, 303; *Stanton* v. *Wilkeson*, 8 *Ben.*, 357.)

(l) The power of a national banking association to take a mortgage upon real estate is a question which the party raising it should be permitted to litigate in a Federal court; and he should not be sent into the State courts to try this question on the distribution of surplus moneys in a foreclosure suit, or in a suit brought by the party holding the alleged invalid mortgage. (*In re Duryea, U. S. D. C.* (*S. D. N. Y.*), 17 *National Bankruptcy Register*, 495.)

2. JURISDICTION OF FEDERAL COURTS SUBSEQUENT TO ACT OF JULY 12, 1882:

(a) The tenth subdivision of section 629, Revised Statutes, which confers upon the circuit court of the United States jurisdiction of all suits by or against any national banking association established in the district for which the court is held, has been repealed by the proviso to section 4 of the act of July 12, 1882. (*National Bank of Jefferson* v. *Fare et al., U. S. C. C.* (*E. D. Tex.*), 25 *Fed. Rep.*, 200.)

(b) The object of this proviso was to deprive the United States courts of jurisdiction of suits by or against national banking associations in all cases where banks organized under State laws could not likewise sue or be sued in such courts. (*National Bank of Jefferson* v. *Fare et al., supra.*)

(c) But the proviso does not affect the right of the receiver of an insolvent association to sue in a Federal court. (*Hendee* v. *Connecticut and P. R. R. Co.*, 26 *Fed. Rep.*, 677.)

(d) Nor would the act of July 12, 1882, take from the circuit court jurisdiction of a suit brought against a director for negligent performance of his duties; for as such suit rests upon the requirements of the United States laws, and by-laws made pursuant thereto, it is a case arising under the laws of the United States. (*Witters v. Foster, U. S. C. C.* (*D. Vt.*), 28 *Fed. Rep.*, 737.)

3. JURISDICTION OF STATE COURTS:

(a) State courts have jurisdiction of suits by and against national banking associations. (*Bank of Bethel* v. *Pahquioque Bank*, 14 *Wall.*, 383; see also *Ordway* v. *Central National Bank*, 47 *Md.*, 217, and *Claflin* v. *Houseman*, 93 *U. S.*, 130.)

(b) Where a national banking association is sued in a State court, the suit must be brought in the city or county in which the bank is located. (*Cadle* v. *Tracy*, 11 *Blatch.*, 101; *Crocker* v. *Maine National Bank*, 101 *Mass.*, 240.)

NOTE.—But the New York court of appeals has held that the provision of the national banking law as to the jurisdiction of State courts is permissive only, and not mandatory, and that a State court, in a proper case, may entertain a proceeding against a national bank located in another State. (*Cooke* v. *The State National Bank of Boston*, 52 *N. Y.*, 96; *Robinson* v. *National Bank of New Berne*, 81 *N. Y.*, 385; see also *Adams* v. *Daunis*, 29 *La. Ann.*, 315.) And in *Talmage* v. *Third National Bank*, 27 *Hun*, 61, the supreme court of New York said: "The words of restriction to the place where said 'association is situated' apply to the county and municipal courts and not to the State courts. In the State courts of general jurisdiction a national banking association can be sued whenever an individual can be for the same cause." In *Cooke* v. *The State National Bank* Chief Judge Church questioned the constitutional right of Congress to deprive the State courts of jurisdiction in such cases.

3. JURISDICTION OF STATE COURTS—Continued.

(c) A State court can entertain an action brought to recover of a national banking association the penalty for taking usury. (*Ordway* v. *The Central National Bank*, 47 *Md.*, 217; *Hade* v. *McVay*, 31 *Ohio St.*, 231; *Bletz* v. *Columbia National Bank*, 87 *Penn. St.*, 87.)

(d) The State courts have jurisdiction of an action brought by a shareholder on behalf of himself and other shareholders to recover of the directors of an insolvent association damages for injuries resulting from their negligence and misconduct. (*Brinckerhoff* v. *Bostwick*, 88 *N. Y.*, 52.)

(e) A State court has no power to make an order directing the receiver of a national bank, who has been appointed by the Comptroller of the Currency, to pay a judgment obtained against the bank before the receiver was appointed. (*Ocean National Bank* v. *Carll*, 7 *Hun*, 237.)

(f) State courts have no jurisdiction of the case of an embezzlement of the funds of the association by one of its officers. (*Commonwealth* v. *Felton*, 101 *Mass.*, 204; *Commonwealth, ex rel. Torrey*, v. *Ketner*, 92 *Penn. St.*, 372.)

(g) The defense of usury may be set up in action brought in a State court. (*National Bank of Winterset* v. *Eyre*, 52 *Iowa*, 114.)

4. UNITED STATES CAN NOT BE SUBJECTED TO JURISDICTION OF COURT:

Neither the Comptroller nor the receiver by putting in an appearance to a suit can subject the United States to the jurisdiction of a court. (*Case* v. *Terrell*, 11 *Wall.*, 199.)

5. CITIZENSHIP:

A national banking association is for jurisdictional purposes a citizen of the State in which it is located. (*Davis* v. *Cook*, 9 *Nev.*, 134.)

XII. SUITS.

1. BY AND AGAINST ASSOCIATIONS:

(a) Suit may be brought against a national banking association though it is in the hands of a receiver. (*Bank of Bethel* v. *Pahquioque Bank*, 14 *Wall.*, 383; *Security National Bank* v. *National Bank of the Commonwealth*, 2 *Hun*, 287; *Green* v. *The Walkill National Bank*, 7 *Hun*, 63.)

(b) Where the tax on shares is collected from the association it may bring a suit to enjoin the collection of an illegal tax. (*Cummings* v. *National Bank*, 101 *U. S.*, 153; *Pelton* v. *Commercial National Bank*, 101 *U. S.*, 143; *Boyer* v. *Boyer*, 113 *U. S.*, 143.)

(c) A State law authorizing national banking associations which have been converted from State banks to use the name of the original corporation for the purpose of prosecuting and defending suits is not in conflict with the national banking law, and, therefore, proceedings based upon a judgment obtained before the conversion may be instituted by such association in its former corporate name. (*Thomas* v. *Farmers' Bank of Maryland*, 46 *Md.*, 43.)

(d) A national banking association is a foreign corporation within the meaning of a State statute requiring corporations created by the laws of any other State or country to give security for costs before prosecuting a suit in the courts of the State. (*National Park Bank* v. *Gunst*, 1 *Abb. N. C.*, 292.)

(e) As a national banking association can acquire no title to *negotiable* paper purchased by it, it can maintain no action thereon in a State where the person suing must be owner of the paper. (*First National Bank of Rochester* v. *Pierson*, 24 *Minn.*, 140.)

(f) But in a State where the holder may sue without respect to the ownership an association may bring suit upon paper so acquired. (*National Pemberton Bank* v. *Porter*, 125 *Mass.*, 333; *Atlas National Bank* v. *Savery*, 127 *Mass.*, 75.)

(g) Suits brought by a receiver can not be settled or compounded upon an order of the Comptroller; this can be done only with the authority of the court. (*Case* v. *Small*, 2 *Woods*, 78.)

2. BY SHAREHOLDERS:

(a) A shareholder of a national banking association can not maintain an action against the directors to recover damages sustained for neglect and mismanagement of the affairs of the association, whereby it became insolvent and its stock was rendered worthless. Such an action can be brought only by the corporation itself. (*Conway* v. *Halsey*, 15 *Vroom*, 462.)

(b) But where the receiver refuses to bring an action against negligent directors to recover the amount which the shareholders have been compelled to contribute to pay the debts of the association, an action against such directors may be brought by a shareholder on behalf of himself and the other shareholders. (*Nelson* v. *Burrows*, 9 *Abb. N. C.*, 280.)

2. BY SHAREHOLDERS—Continued.

(c) And when the receiver is a director, and one of the parties charged with misconduct and against whom a remedy is sought, the action may be brought by a shareholder on behalf of himself and the other shareholders. (*Brinckerhoff* v. *Bostwick*, 88 *N. Y.*, 52.)

3. BY RECEIVERS:

(a) A receiver may sue either in his own name or the name of the bank. (*National Bank* v. *Kennedy*, 17 *Wall.*, 19.)

(b) Suits and proceedings under the act in which the United States or their officers or agents are parties, whether commenced before or after the appointment of a receiver, are to be conducted by the district attorney under the direction of the Solicitor of the Treasury. (*Bank of Bethel* v. *Pahquioque Bank*, 14 *Wall.*, 383.)

(c) But section 380, Revised Statutes, is directory merely, and the employment of private counsel by the receiver can not be made a ground of defense to a suit brought by him. (*Ibid.*)

(d) Receivers may sue in the courts of the United States by virtue of the act, without reference to the locality of their personal citizenship.

(e) The provisions of the codes that every action must be brought in the name of the real party in interest, except in the case of the trustee of an express trust, or of a person authorized by statute to sue, does not apply to the receiver of a national banking association suing in a Federal court held in a State which has adopted the code procedure; for the right of the receiver to sue is derived from the national banking law. (*Stanton* v. *Wilkeson*, 8 *Ben.*, 357.)

(f) Under section 1001 of the Revised Statutes no bond for the prosecution of the suit, or to answer in damages or costs, is required on writs of error or appeals issuing from or brought to the Supreme Court of the United States by direction of the Comptroller of the Currency in suits by or against insolvent national banking associations, or the receivers thereof. (*Pacific National Bank* v. *Mixter*, 114 *U. S.*, 463.)

4. BY CREDITORS OF INSOLVENT ASSOCIATION:

The creditors of an insolvent association must seek their remedy through the Comptroller, in the mode prescribed by the statute; they can not proceed directly in their own names against the stockholders or debtors of the bank. (*Kennedy* v. *Gibson*, 8 *Wall.*, 498.)

5. FOR USURY:

(a) The penalty for all illegal interest paid to a national banking association within two years prior to the commencement of proceedings may be recovered in a single action, whether the amount was in one payment or in several. (*Hintermister* v. *First National Bank*, 64 *N. Y.*, 212.)

(b) Where a bankrupt has paid usurious interest, his assignee may bring an action against the association to recover the penalty. (*Wright* v. *First National Bank of Greensburg*, *U. S. C. C.* (*Dist. Ind.*, 1878); *Crocker* v. *First National Bank of Chetopa*, *U. S. C. C.* (*Eighth Circuit*, 1876); 3 *Am. L. T.*, *N. S.*, 350.)

(c) The party who paid the usurious interest is the only party to the note who is entitled to sue for the penalty. (*Lazear* v. *National Union Bank of Maryland*, 52 *Md.*, 78.)

6. TO ENFORCE LIABILITY OF SHAREHOLDERS:

(a) When the full personal liability of shareholders is to be enforced the action must be at law. (*Kennedy* v. *Gibson*, 8 *Wall.*, 505; *Casey* v. *Galli*, 94 *U. S.*, 673.)

(b) And it may be at law though the assessment is not for the full value of the shares; for, since the sum each shareholder must contribute is a certain, exact sum, there is no necessity for invoking the aid of a court of equity. (*Bailey* v. *Sawyer*, 4 *Dill.*, 463.)

(c) But the suit may be in equity. (*Kennedy* v. *Gibson*, *supra.*)

7. EXECUTION:

A judgment against a national bank in the hands of a receiver only establishes the validity of the claim; the plaintiff can have no execution on such judgment, but must wait pro rata distribution. (*Bank of Bethel* v. *Pahquioque Bank*, 14 *Wall.*, 383.)

8. ATTACHMENTS:

(a) When a creditor attaches the property of an insolvent bank he can not hold such property against the claim of a receiver appointed after the attachment suit was commenced. Such creditor must share pro rata with all others. (*First National Bank of Selma* v. *Colby*, 21 *Wall.*, 609; *Harvey* v. *Allen*, 16 *Blatch.*, 29.)

(b) It was not intended by the national banking law to prohibit attachments against the property of national banking associations, except in cases where an act of insolvency has been committed or is contemplated. (*Robinson* v. *National Bank of New Berne*, 81 *N. Y.*, 385.)

(c) But where the association is insolvent an attachment issued against its property will be void. (*National Shoe and Leather Bank* v. *The Mechanics' National Bank*, 89 *N. Y.*, 467.)

(d) And such attachment will not afterward be rendered valid by the acquisition of new capital by the association and its resumption of business. (*Raynor et al.* v. *Pacific National Bank*, 93 *N. Y.*, 371.)

(e) A State court may issue an attachment against property in the State belonging to a national banking association located in another State. (*Southwick* v. *The First National Bank of Memphis*, 7 *Hun*, 96; Contra, *Central National Bank* v. *Richmond National Bank*, 52 *How. Pr.*, 136.)

(f) The provision of the banking law forbidding attachments in the case of insolvent associations was not repealed by the act of July 12, 1882. (*Raynor et al.* v. *Pacific National Bank*, *supra.*)

9. ABATEMENT:

An action brought by the creditor of a national bank is abated by a decree of a district or circuit court dissolving the corporation and forfeiting its franchises. (*First National Bank of Selma* v. *Colby*, 21 *Wall.*, 609.)

10. ESTOPPEL:

(a) A shareholder against whom suit is brought to recover the assessment made upon him by the Comptroller will not be permitted to deny the existence of the association, or that it was legally incorporated. (*Casey* v. *Galli*, 94 *U. S.*, 673.)

(b) Where one sued by a national bank is accustomed to deal with it, as such, and does so deal with it in respect to the matter in suit, he is estopped from denying its incorporation. (*National Bank of Fairhaven* v. *The Phœnix Warehousing Company*, 6 *Hun*, 71.)

11. SUITS AGAINST LIQUIDATING ASSOCIATIONS:

A national bank which has gone into voluntary liquidation will continue to exist as a body corporate for the purpose of suing and being sued until its affairs are completely settled. (*National Bank* v. *Insurance Company*, 104 *U. S.*, 54; *Ordway* v. *Central National Bank*, 47 *Md.*, 217.)

12. TRANSITORY AND LOCAL SUITS:

The provision of the banking law (section 5198, Revised Statutes) which requires that actions brought against national banking associations in State courts shall be brought in the county or city in which the association is located, applies only to transitory actions; it was not intended to apply to actions local in their character. (*Casey* v. *Adams*, 102 *U. S.*, 66.)

13. SURVIVAL OF SUITS:

Whether a suit against a director for negligent performance of his duties, as required by the statutes of the United States and the by-laws of the association, will survive against the executor or administrator depends upon State laws. (*Witters* v. *Foster*, *U. S. C. C.* (*Dist. Vt.*), 25 *Fed. Rep.*, 737.)

XIII. EVIDENCE.

1. CERTIFICATES OF COMPTROLLER:

(a) The certificate of the Comptroller of the Currency that an association has complied with all the provisions required to be complied with before commencing the business of banking is admissible in evidence upon a plea of *nul tiel corporation*; and such certificate, together with proof that the association has been acting as a national banking association for a long time, is amply sufficient evidence to establish, at least, prima facie, the existence of the corporation. (*Mix* v. *The National Bank of Bloomington*, 91 *Ill.*, 20; see also *Merchants' National Bank of Bangor* v. *Glendon*, 120 *Mass.*, 97.)

1. CERTIFICATES OF COMPTROLLER—Continued.

(b) The certificate of the Comptroller that the association has complied with all the provisions of law touching the organization of associations removes any objection which might otherwise have been made to the evidence upon which he acted. (*Casey* v. *Galli*, 94 *U. S.*, 673; *Thatcher* v. *West River National Bank*, 19 *Mich.*, 196.)

(c) And in a suit against the association or its shareholders such certificate of the Comptroller is conclusive as to the completeness of the organization. (*Casey* v. *Galli*, *supra*.)

(d) A letter from the Comptroller directing the receiver to institute suit, if not objected to at the time, is sufficient evidence that the Comptroller has decided that the enforcement of the individual liability of the shareholders is necessary. (*Bowden* v. *Johnson*, 107 *U. S.*, 251.)

2. EVIDENCE OF INSOLVENCY:

(a) It is not necessary that the facts upon which the Comptroller bases his action in appointing a receiver should be established by what is *competent legal evidence;* but he is left to be satisfied as best he can be, under the peculiar circumstances of each case, of the facts and the necessity for the exercise of his authority. (*Platt* v. *Beebe*, 57 *N. Y.*, 330.)

(b) A return of *nulla bona* upon an execution issued against the property of a national bank is proof of its insolvency. (*Wheelock* v. *Kost*, 77 *Ill.*, 296.)

3. NECESSITY FOR ASSESSMENT BY COMPTROLLER:

It is not essential, in an action to enforce the individual liability of the shareholders of an insolvent national banking association, to aver and prove that the assessment was necessary; for the decision of the Comptroller on this point is conclusive. (*Strong* v. *Southworth*, 8 *Ben.*, 331; *Kennedy* v. *Gibson*, 8 *Wall.*, 505; *Casey* v. *Galli*, 94 *U. S.*, 673.)

XIV. CRIMES.

1. UNDER UNITED STATES LAWS:

(a) The willful misapplication of the moneys and funds of a national banking association, made an offense by section 5209, Revised Statutes, must be for the use or benefit of the party charged or of some person or company other than the association. (*United States* v. *Britton*, 107 *U. S.*, 655.)

(b) The exercise of official discretion in good faith, without fraud, for the advantage or the supposed advantage of the association is not punishable; but if official action be taken in bad faith, for personal advantage and with fraudulent intent, it is punishable. (*United States* v. *Fish*, 24 *Fed. Rep.*, 585.)

(c) It is not necessary that the officer should personally misapply the funds of the association. He will be guilty as a principal offender though he merely procures or causes the misapplication. (*Ibid.*)

(d) A loan in bad faith, with intent to defraud the association, is a willful misapplication within the meaning of the statute. (*Ibid.*)

(e) It is no defense to a charge of embezzlement, abstraction, or misapplication of the funds of a national banking association that the funds were used with the knowledge and consent of the president and some of the directors. The intent to defraud is to be conclusively presumed from the commission of the offense. (*United States* v. *Taintor*, 11 *Blatch.*, 374.)

(f) Where the president charged as a trustee with the administration of the funds of the bank in his hands, converts them to his own use without authority for so doing, he embezzles and abstracts them within the meaning of section 5209, Revised Statutes. (*In the matter of Van Campen*, 2 *Ben.*, 419.)

(g) If, with intent to defraud the association, an officer allows a firm in which he is a member to overdraw its account, he will be guilty of misapplying the funds of the association. (*Ibid.*)

(h) As the national banking law makes the embezzlement, abstraction, or willful misapplication of the funds of a national banking association merely a misdemeanor, a person who procures such an offense to be committed can not be punished under a State statute which provides that a person who procures a felony to be committed may be indicted and convicted of a substantive felony. (*Commonwealth* v. *Felton*, 101 *Mass.*, 204.)

(i) An indictment charging defendants with aiding and abetting a director in a willful misapplication of the money of an association must state facts to show that there has been such misapplication committed by the director. (*United States* v. *Warner*, *U. S. C. C.* (*S. D. N. Y.*), *Feb.* 13, 1886, 26 *Fed. Rep.*, 616.)

1. UNDER UNITED STATES LAWS—Continued.

(j) Allowing the withdrawal of the deposit of one indebted to the association can not be charged as a misapplication of the money of the association. (*United States* v. *Britton*, 108 *U. S.*, 193.)

(k) It is not a willful misapplication of the money of the association within the meaning of section 5209, Revised Statutes, for a president who is insolvent to procure the discounting by the association of his note not well secured. (*Ibid.*)

(l) Prior to the act of February 26, 1881, a notary public holding his commission under a State had no authority to administer the oath required by section 5211, Revised Statutes; and, therefore, a cashier who made oath before such notary to a false statement of the condition of his association was not guilty of perjury. (*United States* v. *Curtis*, 107 *U. S.*, 671.)

(m) Where false entries are made by a clerk at the direction of the president, the latter is a principal. (*In the matter of Van Campen, supra; United States* v. *Fish, supra.*)

2. UNDER STATE LAWS:

(a) An officer of a national banking association can not be punished under State laws for embezzling the funds of the association. (*Commonwealth ex rel. Torrey* v. *Ketner*, 92 *Penn. St.*, 372; *Commonwealth* v. *Felton*, 101 *Mass.*, 204.)

(b) But where the offense committed by an officer is properly a larceny of the funds, and not an embezzlement, he may be indicted under a State law. (*Commonwealth* v. *Barry*, 116 *Mass.*, 1.)

(c) And an officer may be punished under State laws for making false entries in the books of the association with intent to defraud it. (*Luberg* v. *Commonwealth*, 94 *Penn. St.*, 85.)

(d) The officers of a national banking association may be prosecuted under State statutes for fraudulent conversion of the property of individuals deposited with, and in the custody of the association. (*Commonwealth* v. *Tenney*, 97 *Mass.*, 50; *State* v. *Fuller*, 34 *Conn.*, 280.)

3. TERM "UNITED STATES CURRENCY" IN PENAL STATUTE:

The circulating notes of national banking associations are included in the phrase "United States currency" when used in a penal statute. (*State* v. *Gasting*, 23 *La. Ann.*, 1609.)

A DIGEST OF RECENT DECISIONS IN BANKING LAW.

BANKS AND BANKING.

CONSTITUTIONAL PROVISION:

The term "banking powers," as used in the constitution of the State of Ohio, has a restricted meaning, and relates only to the powers of making and issuing paper money, or, at most, to powers exercised by associations organized to deal in money, including the making and issuing of bills and notes intended to circulate as money. (*Dearborn* v. *Bank*, 42 *Ohio State*, 617.)

POWER OF SAVINGS BANK TO BORROW MONEY:

A savings bank having the usual powers of such an institution, may borrow money in the course of its legitimate business, and may make and indorse negotiable paper for the money so borrowed. (*Fifth Ward Savings Bank* v. *First National Bank*, 48 *N. J. Law*, 513.)

WRONGFUL PAYMENT TO AGENT:

S. drew his check for $5,000 on the People's Bank of New York, payable to the order of the United States Trust Company, and delivered it to C. with verbal instructions to deposit it to his (S.'s) credit with the trust company. C. delivered the check to the trust company, but, instead of doing as directed, requested and received from the company a certificate of deposit payable to himself as trustee of S., and shortly thereafter drew the money and converted it to his own use. Held, that the trust company was not authorized in paying the money to C., and was liable to the executors of S. for the amount. The use of the company's name as payee of the check indicated the drawer's intention to lodge the moneys in its custody and place them under its control, and nothing further than this was inferable from the language of the check. (*Sims* v. *United States Trust Company*, 103 *N. Y.*, 472.)

NOTE.—Upon the trial, evidence of a custom to make such payments was submitted to the jury; but the evidence was conflicting, and the jury found against the existence of the custom. (*Id.*)

EVIDENCE OF CUSTOM TO BORROW MONEY:

In order to show that the borrowing of money was within the scope of the ordinary and customary business of a firm doing a banking business, evidence that such is the custom of the banks in the same place is admissible. (*Crain et al.* v. *National Bank*, 114 *Ill.*, 516.)

PAYMENTS THROUGH CLEARING-HOUSE:

(*a*) Where, by the rules of a clearing-house, checks not good are to be returned by the banks receiving them to the banks from which they are received as soon as the fact that they are not good is discovered, *and in no case to be retained after a certain hour*, yet when by mistake as to a matter of fact a bank has delayed to return a check until after the hour so fixed, it may demand repayment of the other bank, *if in the interval between the time fixed by the rule and the time of the actual return the latter bank has not changed its position, as, for instance, by paying over the amount of the check to the person who had deposited it for collection.* (*Merchant's Bank* v. *Bank of Commonwealth*, 139 *Mass.*, 213.

(*b*) But in such case the recovery could be only the difference between the sum which the depositor has to his credit and the amount of the check; notwithstanding that, by the course of dealing between banks in the clearing-house association, the ordinary custom is to return the check as not good when there is not money enough to pay it in full; for the clearing-house rules not having been complied with by the return of the check within the time fixed, these rules can not control in determining how much shall be returned after payment of it has been made. (*Merchants' Bank* v. *Bank of Commonwealth*, 139 *Mass.*, 513.)

PAYMENTS THROUGH CLEARING-HOUSE—Continued.

NOTE.—Under a similar rule of the Chicago clearing-house it has been held by the United States circuit court for the northern district of Illinois that no such mistake could be corrected after the time allowed by the rule. Blodgett, J., said: "If parties competent to contract within what time they may correct mistakes in their dealings with each other have so contracted, it seems to me the courts have no right to override or disregard such an agreement. If a mistake which is discovered within an hour or within ten minutes after the expiration of the time limited by the agreement for its correction may be corrected, I can see no reason why it can not be corrected a week afterwards, or whenever it is discovered." (*Preston* v. *Bank*, 23 *Fed. Rep.*, 179.)

PASS-BOOK:

(*a*) The duty of a depositor in respect to examining his pass-book and reporting any mistake to the bank is such as that which prudent men usually bestow on the examination of such accounts. (*Leather Manufacturers' Bank* v. *Morgan*, 117 *U. S.*, 96.)

(*b*) And by neglecting to make an examination of his pass-book within a reasonable time, a depositor may estop himself from afterwards questioning its correctness. (*Ibid.*)

DUTIES AND LIABILITIES OF BANKS MAKING COLLECTIONS:

(*a*) Where a certified check is left with a bank for collection the collecting bank does not discharge its duty by forwarding that check to the bank on which it is drawn; and if it does so forward the check, and loss results, it will be liable for such loss. (*Drovers' National Bank* v. *Provision Co.*, 117 *Ill.*, 100.)

(*b*) Nor would it in any case be a sufficient discharge of the duty of the collecting bank to forward the check to the bank on which it is drawn. (*Merchants' National Bank* v. *Goodman*, 109 *Penn. St.*, 422.)

NOTE.—In Indig *v.* National City Bank, 80 N. Y., 100, it was said that when there are no indorsers to charge, sending the check through the mail to the bank on which it is drawn is a good presentment. (*See also Heywood* v. *Pickering*, *L. R.*, 93 *B.*, 428.)

(*c*) Where paper is received by a bank in the ordinary course of business for collection, such bank will be responsible for the neglect or misconduct of any sub-agent employed by it in the business of making the collection. (*Simpson* v. *Walby*, *Supreme Ct. Mich.*, 1886, 30 *N. W. Rep.*, 199.)

NOTE.—The same rule has recently been adopted by the Territorial court of Montana. (*Power* v. *First National Bank*, 6 *Mont.*, 251.)

This is now the rule in the Supreme Court of the United States (*Exchange National Bank* v. *Third National Bank*, 112 *U. S.*, 276); in England (*Mackersy* v. *Ramsay*, 9 *Cl. and Fin.*, 818); in New York (*Ayrault* v. *Pacific Bank*, 47 *N. Y.*, 570); in New Jersey (*Titus* v. *Mechanics' Bank*, 35 *N. J. Law*, 588); in Pennsylvania (*Wingate* v. *Mechanics' Bank*, 10 *Penn. St.*, 104); in Ohio (*Reeves* v. *State Bank*, 8 *Ohio St.*, 465); in Indiana (*Tyson* v. *State Bank*, 6 *Blackf.*, 225); in Michigan (*Simpson* v. *Walby*, *supra*), and in Montana.

In other jurisdictions the rule prevails that the bank is only bound to transmit the paper to a suitable agent at the place of payment for that purpose, and when a suitable sub-agent is thus employed, in good faith, the collecting bank is not liable for his neglect or default. This is the rule in Massachusetts. (*Fabens* v. *Mercantile Bank*, 23 *Pick.*, 330; *Dorchester Bank* v. *New England Bank*, 1 *Cush.*, 177); in Maryland (*Jackson* v. *Union Bank*, 6 *Har. and Johns.*, 146); in Connecticut (*Lawrence* v. *Stonington Bank*, 6 *Conn.*, 521; *East Haddam Bank* v. *Scovil*, 12 *Conn.*, 303); in Missouri (*Daly* v. *Butchers and Drovers' Bank*, 56 *Mo.*, 94); in Illinois (*Ætna Insurance Co.* v. *Alton City Bank*, 25 *Ill.* 243); in Tennessee (*Bank of Louisville* v. *First National Bank*, 8 *Baxter*, 101); in Iowa (*Guelich* v. *National State Bank*, 56 *Iowa*, 434); in Wisconsin (*Stacy* v. *Dane County Bank*, 12 *Wis.*, 629; *Vilas* v. *Bryants*, *Id.*, 702).

BANKERS' LIEN AND RIGHT OF SET-OFF:

(*a*) Where a customer deposited with his bankers a policy of life insurance to secure any indebtedness of his to them then due, or which should thereafter become due, not exceeding at any one time the sum of £4,000:—Held, that the bankers had no lien for any indebtedness of the customer in excess of £4,000; for as the express terms of the deposit limited the security to that amount, it would be inconsistent with those terms that the bank should hold the policy for something more. (*Earl of Strathmore* v. *Vane*, *L. R.*, 33 *Ch. Div.*, 586.)

BANKERS' LIEN AND RIGHT OF SET-OFF—Continued.

(*b*) Where agents deposit money in bank for the benefit of their principals, and the purpose of the deposit is known to the bank, the deposit is impressed with a trust, and the bank can not charge against it any indebtedness of the agents, *even with their consent*. (*Baker et al.* v. *New York National Bank*, 100 *N. Y.*, 31.)

(*c*) The general rule is that a bank has the right to set-off as against a deposit only where the person who is both depositor and debtor stands in both these characters alike, in precisely the same relation, and on precisely the same footing toward the bank, and hence an individual deposit can not be set-off against a partnership debt. (*International Bank* v. *Jones*, 119 *Ill.*, 407.)

(*d*) And notwithstanding that it is the duty of a partner to pay the firm's debt to the bank, still, inasmuch as the bank could not set-off the firm debt against his deposit, he could lawfully appropriate such deposit to the payment of a bona fide creditor of his own. (*Id.*)

STATUTE OF LIMITATIONS:

(*a*) Where notes deposited with a bank as collateral security for a line of discounts are paid, it is the duty of the bank to carry the proceeds to the credit of the borrower's account; when he will occupy the position of depositor; and then, as to any part of such proceeds, the rule will apply, that when a deposit is made in bank the statute of limitations does not begin to run until demand is made. (*Humphrey* v. *National Bank of Clearfield*, 113 *Penn. St.*, 417.)

(*b*) Whenever demand is made by presentation of a genuine check in the hands of a person entitled to receive its amount, for a portion of the amount on deposit, and payment is refused, a cause of action immediately arises in favor of the drawer; and as to the amount specified in the check the statute of limitations begins to run from that time. (*Viets* v. *Union National Bank of Troy*, 101 *N. Y.*, 564.)

Although it is a general rule that a bank in accepting and paying a check drawn by a customer is generally held to know the signature, and if a forged check is paid by it it will not be heard to assert a mistake as to the signature, yet where one in whose favor a forged check is drawn *takes it under suspicious circumstances, and gives it credit by indorsing his own name thereon*, and collects the money on it, the bank may recover the amount from him. (*Rouvant* v. *San Antonio National Bank*, 63 *Tex.*, 610.)

BANK OFFICERS.

POWERS OF OFFICERS:

The treasurer of a savings bank is an officer of much more limited powers than the cashier of a commercial bank. His duties more nearly resemble those of the paying and receiving tellers of banks. He can not, simply in virtue of his office as treasurer, create obligations which will be binding upon the bank, as by indorsement of notes, or transfer to a purchaser a promissory note belonging to the bank. (*Fifth Ward Savings Bank* v. *First National Bank*, 48 *N. J.; Law*, 513.)

(*b*) A cashier of a bank may, *without authority from the board of directors*, employ an attorney to collect outstanding debts due the bank; and this though the bank has regularly retained counsel. His authority in this respect is incidental to his duty to collect. (*Root* v. *Olcott*, 49 *Hun.*, 536.)

(*c*) Knowledge acquired by the cashier of a bank *in his capacity as an officer of another corporation* can not be imputed to the bank, unless he communicated that knowledge to some one or more of the other officers of the bank. (*Wilson* v. *Second National Bank of Pittsburgh*, 7 *Atl. Rep.*, 145.)

CASHIER'S BOND:

(*a*) The sureties on a cashier's bond will not be discharged by an increase of the capital stock of the bank when this increase is made under the authority of a provision of the law under which the bank is organized. The bond must be understood and read in the light of the law existing at the time it was made; and the parties must have contemplated that the bank would enlarge its business by all lawful ways and means, not going beyond a banking business. (*Lionberger* v. *Krieger*, 88 *Mo.*, 160.)

(*b*) The cashier's bond will not be invalidated by the fact that he is not a director, though the law under which the bank is organized provides that the cashier shall be chosen from among the directors. (*Id.*)

LIABILITY OF DIRECTOR:

(a) Where a director and member of the finance committee of a savings bank, acting with the president, invests the funds of the institution contrary to the provisions of the law by which it is governed, he will be liable for the loss on such investment. (*Williams* v. *McDonald*, 42 *N. J. Eq.*, 392.)

(b) And in such case it is not essential, in order to charge him with liability for the loss, to show that he acted fraudulently, or that he derived any benefit from the loan; it is sufficient that there was a culpable lack of prudence, or failure to exercise with ordinary care his functions as *quasi* trustee of the funds of the bank, by reason of which loss was sustained. (*Id.*)

BUSINESS PAPER.

CONSTITUTIONAL PROVISIONS:

(a) It is not unconstitutional for a State to enact a law making the liabilities of signers of commercial paper made and payable within its limits entirely different from the laws of other States respecting such liabilities, and by statute change absolutely the operation of the law merchant, so far as it affects contracts made and to be performed within that State. (*Shoe and Leather National Bank* v. *Wood*, 142 *Mass.*, 563.)

(b) A provision in a State law requiring that the words "given for a patent right" shall be inserted in every promissory note executed in consideration of the sale and transfer of a patent right is constitutional. (*New* v. *Walker*, 108 *Ind.*, 365.)

(c) This provision is in the nature of a police regulation. But independent of this consideration it is valid, because it simply prescribes what shall be written in a promissory note given for a particular class of property. (*Id.*)

BILLS DRAWN IN ANOTHER COUNTRY:

Where bills of exchange were drawn in France by a domiciled Frenchman, in the French language, but according to the English form, on an English company, by which they were duly accepted: Held, that the bills were to be regarded as English bills, at least so far as the acceptor was concerned, and that their negotiability could not be attacked by the company on the ground that the indorsement of the drawer was not a good indorsement according to the French law. (*In re Marseilles Extension Railway and Land Company, L. R.* 30 *Ch. Div.*, 598.)

NOTES GIVEN FOR PATENT RIGHTS:

(a) Where a State statute requires that notes for which the consideration is the assignment of a patent right shall contain the words "given for a patent right," notes issued in violation of such provision will be unenforceable as between the parties, and when in the hands of a purchaser with notice of the nature of the consideration. (*New* v. *Walker*, 108 *Ind.*, 365.)

(b) But they will not be void in the hands of an innocent purchaser unless the statute, either expressly or by necessary implication, declares them to be void. But this the Indiana statute (section 6055, R. S.) does not do. (*Id.*)

NOTE.—Similar statutes in Pennsylvania and Ohio have received the same construction. (*Haskell* v. *Jones*, 86 *Penn. St.*, 173; *Tod* v. *Wick*, 36 *Ohio St.*, 370.)

INCOMPLETE INSTRUMENT:

Where one signs and delivers a note in blank to be used as security, the law implies that he means to become liable upon a completed and perfected note, and so far as the same is, at the time of his signature, an incomplete and imperfect instrument, he is held to have authorized the filling of such blank by the agent intrusted with the note for use; but nothing more than this is implied. And, therefore, if a matter of special agreement (*e. g.*, a provision for a special rate of interest) is crowded into it, there being no blank space left for such insertion, the alteration is material, and discharges the indorser. (*Weyerhauser* v. *Dun*, 100 *N. Y.*, 150.)

SUNDAY CONTRACT:

Where a note is signed on Sunday, but not delivered until Monday, it is not open to the objection that it is a Sunday contract; for a promissory note becomes a contract from the time of its delivery. (*Bell* v. *Mohin*, 69 *Iowa*, 408.)

NOTE PAYABLE ON DEMAND;

Although the principle laid down in the case of Merritt *v.* Todd (23 N. Y., 28), has been criticised in later cases, it has been acquiesced in too long as the law of New York to be open to question or dispute. That principle is

NOTE PAYABLE ON DEMAND—Continued.

that a promissory note payable on demand, with interest, is a continuing security; so that the holder may make demand when he pleases, and is not chargeable with neglect if he does not make it within any particular time, *and an indorser on such note remains liable until an actual demand.* (*Parker et al.* v. *Stroud*, 98 *N. Y.*, 379.)

PROMISE TO PAY FORGED NOTE:

An oral promise to pay a note by one whose signature has been forged to the note is nothing more than an oral promise to pay the debt of another, and is ineffectual to bind the promissor. (*Smith* v. *Tramel*, 68 *Iowa*, 488.)

AUTHORITY AND LIABILITY OF AGENT:

(*a*) Where a bill drawn upon him by his principal is accepted by an agent by signing his own name thereto, with the addition of words describing himself as agent and giving the name of his principal, he will be individually liable upon such acceptance; and he will not be allowed to show that the acceptance was intended to charge only his principal. (*Robinson* v. *Kanawha Valley Bank*, 44 *Ohio*, 441.)

(*b*) Where a note ran "we promise to pay," and was signed "Pioneer Mining Company, John E. Mason, sup't," parol evidence was held admissible, in a suit by the payee, to show that the note was given as that of the company, and not as the note of the company *and* Mason. (*Bean* v. *Pioneer Mining Co.*, 66 *Cal.*, 451.)

(*c*) Where a bill of exchange, drawn on a firm, was accepted by one of the partners by signing the name of the firm and adding his own underneath: Held, that the acceptance was that of the firm, and that the individual partner was not separately liable. (*Edwards* v. *Barned*, *L. R.*, 32, *Ch. Div.*, 447.)

(*d*) In the case of a non-trading partnership, in order to subject the firm to liability upon a bill or note executed by one partner in its name, a course of conduct, or usage, or other facts sufficient to warrant the conclusion that the acting partner had been invested by his copartners with the requisite authority must appear, or that the firm has ratified the act by receiving the benefit of it. (*Pearse* v. *Cole*, 53 *Conn.*, 53.)

(*e*) Where a note was made payable to "the order of T. W. Woollen, Attorney-General:" Held, that the words "Attorney-General" were merely descriptive of the individual, and that as the persons in giving the note had executed a commercial instrument, fair on its face and complete in all its parts, they could not, as against a bona fide holder, set up the defense that the payee had no right to transfer it. (*Walke* v. *Kahne*, 109 *Ind.*, 313.)

CONSIDERATION:

(*a*) One dollar is a mere nominal consideration, and therefore not sufficient to constitute the holder of a note a purchaser for value. (*Proctor* v. *Cole*, 104 *Ind.*, 373.)

(*b*) An agreement to pay one-half the proceeds that may be realized upon a note is a venture approaching very near a wagering contract; at all events, it is not such an agreement as will create a right against prior equities. (*Id.*)

(*c*) It is the law of New York that one who takes commercial paper upon a pre-existing debt, without parting with any right or property of value, is not a bona fide holder for value who will be protected against the equities of third persons. (*Webster & Co.* v. *Howe Machine Co.*, 54 *Conn.*, 394.)

NOTE.—See for this the following New York cases: *Coddington* v. *Bay*, 20 *Johns.*, 637; *Stalker* v. *McDonald*, 6 *Hill*, 93; *McBride* v. *Farmers' Bank of Salem*, 26 *N. Y.*, 450; *Comstock* v. *Hier*, 73 *N. Y.*, 269. For the contrary rule see *Swift* v. *Tyson*, 16 *Peters*, 1; *Railroad Company* v. *National Bank*, 102 *U. S.*, 14.

(*d*) An existing debt is a sufficient consideration to constitute a pledgee of a negotiable instrument a holder for value. (*Spencer* v. *Sloan*, 108 *Ind.*, 183.)

(*e*) The pledgee of negotiable securities received by him as collateral security for an antecedent debt is not a holder for value, and is not protected from antecedent equities. (*Appeal of the Leggett Spring and Axle Co.*, 111 *Penn. St.*, 291.)

NOTE.—The rule in the Supreme Court of the United States is in accordance with that in the Indiana case. (*Railroad Company* v. *National Bank*, 102 *U. S.*, 14.)

(*f*) If the compounding of a felony affected the consideration of a note *in any way, or such purpose entered into the consideration, or such motive actuated the maker in any respect*, the contract is illegal. And, therefore, where H. and his wife had given their note to R., the employer of their son, to prevent R.

CONSIDERATION—Continued.

from criminally prosecuting the son for theft, they could not recover from R. the amount which they had been compelled to pay to a bona fide purchaser of the note; and in such case the makers of the note could not set up that it was obtained from them by duress and undue influence; for such a right does not exist when the contract is tainted with a corrupt consideration. (*Haynes* v. *Rudd*, 102 *N. Y.*, 372.)

(*g*) If one becomes a bona fide holder for value of a bill before its acceptance, it is not essential to his right to enforce it against a subsequent acceptor that an additional consideration should proceed from him to the drawee. The holder does not trust wholly to the credit of the drawer. He believes and expects that the drawee will accept, and upon such belief and expectation he acts. (*Heutermatte* v. *Morris*, 101 *N. Y.*, 63; *Credit Company* v. *Howe Machine Co.*, 54 *Conn.*, 357.)

(*h*) The promise of a husband who has borrowed money of his wife to pay it to her children is a consideration sufficient to constitute one of those children a bona fide holder of a note assigned to him by the husband. (*Proctor* v. *Cole*, 104 *Ind.*, 373.)

(*i*) Where the instrument to secure which negotiable securities are deposited as a pledge turns out to be a forgery, this circumstance will not defeat the title of the pledge to the securities; for these having in themselves a negotiable character, the pledgee does not need to make any other title to them than such as springs from a delivery for value. (*Fifth Ward Savings Bank* v. *First National Bank*.)

(*j*) Where a bank has discounted for the drawer drafts to which forged bills of lading are attached, the acceptors can not afterwards defeat the claim of the bank on the ground that they accepted the drafts in the belief that the bills of lading were genuine. (*Goetz* v. *Bank of Kansas City*, 119 *U. S.*, 551.)

(*k*) After discounting the drafts the bank stands towards the acceptors in the position of an original lender, and can not be affected in its claim by the want of a consideration from the drawer for the acceptance or by the failure of such consideration. (*Id.*)

(*l*) To enable one of the makers of a joint note to set up the defense that as to him there was no consideration for it, he is not necessarily obliged to show that it was without consideration as to all the makers; for, though presumably all makers executed it at the same time, and upon ample consideration as to each and all, it is possible that one might have signed the note without any consideration for his contract running to him or to any one else. (*Moyer* v. *Round*, 102 *Ind.*, 301.)

PRESENTMENT AND NOTICE:

(*a*) As to every bill not payable on demand, the day on which payment is to be made to prevent dishonor is to be determined by adding three days of grace, where the bill itself does not otherwise provide, to the time of payment as fixed in the bill. Thus, where the acceptor had stated in his acceptance "Due 21st May," it was held that the bill was not due until three days after the 21st of May. The time named in the acceptance after the word "due" was to be regarded as the time of payment to which days of grace were to be added, and not as a date which included days of grace. (*Bell* v. *First National Bank of Chicago*, 115 *U. S.*, 373.)

(*b*) A draft drawn upon a bank, and purporting to be drawn upon funds deposited, and payable on demand, is to be regarded as a banker's check. And where such a draft is payable at a different place from that in which it is negotiated, the holder should, as a general rule, forward it for presentment on the day on which it is received, or on the next succeeding day; and although this general rule may be varied by the particular circumstances of the case, the presentment must be made, in every instance, with all the dispatch and diligence consistent with the transaction of other commercial matters. Therefore, where the holders retained a draft for several days in their possession, for no other reason than that they chose to send it through a local bank with which they did business, and it did not suit their convenience to deposit it at an earlier date: Held, that they could not recover against the indorsers. (*Northwestern Coal Company* v. *Bowman & Co.*, 69 *Iowa*, 150.)

(*c*) And in such case it makes no difference as between the indorsee and his indorser that the drawer had no funds on deposit with the bank at the time the draft was drawn. (*Id.*)

(*d*) Where notice of the dishonor of a draft was sent by the notary to the indorsers at Boone, Iowa, when their post office address was Odebolt, in a different county: Held, that this was not a sufficient notice to fix their liability. (*The Northwestern Coal Company* v. *Bowman & Co.*, 69 *Iowa*, 150.)

PRESENTMENT AND NOTICE—Continued.

(e) Where there was written upon a note "I hereby acknowledge the receipt of notice of protest on the within note," and this was signed by all the indorsers: Held, that the word "protest" included all acts necessary to hold indorsers, and the legal effect of the acknowledgment was to release the holder from any obligation to make demand or give notice. (*City Savings Bank* v. *Hopson*, 53 *Conn.*, 453.)

BONA FIDE HOLDER:

(a) Mere notice of facts such as would have put a prudent person upon inquiry is not sufficient to impeach the title of the holder of negotiable paper taken for value before maturity, and his right to recover can be defeated only by proof of such circumstances as show that he took the paper with knowledge of some infirmity in it, or with such suspicion with regard to its validity as that his conduct in taking it was fraudulent. (*National Bank of the Republic* v. *Young*, 41 *N. J. Eq.*, 531; *Fifth Ward Savings Bank* v. *First National Bank*, 48 *N. J. Law*, 513; *Credit Co.* v. *Howe Machine Co.*, 54 *Conn.*, 357; *Morton & Bliss* v. *N. O. and Selma Railway Co.*, 79 *Ala.*, 590.)

(b) Therefore, where the vice-president of a bank, who had negotiated a loan upon the paper of a corporation, was advised by one of the officers of the corporation that it had outstanding a large amount of accommodation paper: Held, that this was not sufficient to defeat the claim of the bank as a bona fide holder of paper of the corporation discounted after such notice to the vice-president. (*National Bank of the Republic* v. *Young*, *supra*.)

(c) But in cases of this kind the burden of proof is on the holder to show that he took the instrument before maturity bona fide and for value. The mere possession of it, when it has been obtained or issued under such circumstances, is not enough. (*Id.*)

(d) But when he has shown that he became the holder of it before maturity and for value, in the due course of business, he has established all the facts that are necessary to fulfill the burden of proof laid upon him, and from these facts the law will imply that he is a bona fide holder, unless there should be circumstances from which bad faith may be inferred. (*Id.*)

(e) The bad faith in the taker of negotiable paper which will defeat a recovery by him must be something more than a failure to inquire into the consideration upon which it is made or accepted, because of rumors of general reputation as to the bad character of the maker or drawer. (*Goetz* v. *Bank of Kansas City*, 119 *U. S.*, 551.)

(f) The failure to pay interest on coupon bonds as it becomes due does not dishonor them before maturity so as to subject them to antecedent equities in the hands of otherwise innocent purchasers for value. (*Morton & Bliss* v. *N. O. and Selma Railway Co.*, 79 *Ala.*, 590.)

(g) Where a negotiable bond or other negotiable instrument is taken in such a way that the purchaser is not affected by antecedent equities, a mortgage given to secure payment is likewise protected against such latent defenses. (*Spence* v. *Mobile and Montgomery Railway Co.*, 79 *Ala.*, 576.)

NOTE.—The contrary is held in Ohio and Illinois. (See *Bailey* v. *Smith*, 14 *Ohio St.*, 396; *Kleeman* v. *Frisbie*, 63 *Ill.*, 462.)

(h) Where the condition of a bond is that the principal shall become due and payable upon the failure to pay any of the coupons as they become due, *after demand made*, the fact that the bonds have so become due and payable, as it rests upon an extrinsic matter, foreign to the face of the paper, and which does not dishonor it upon its face, does not of itself operate to charge the purchaser with knowledge that the bonds have been dishonored. The law does not in such case charge him with knowledge of the fact, unless he either knows it, or exhibits bad faith by intentionally avoiding a knowledge of it. And mere neglect to inquire whether there has been a demand made is not evidence conclusive of a fraudulent intent. (*Morton & Bliss* v. *N. O. and Selma Railway Co.*, 79 *Ala.*, 590.)

(i) Where a State repeals the law under which it had become the indorser of the bonds of a corporation, and by which provision was made for the payment of the bonds in the event of a default of payment by the corporation as maker, such action—whether or not it was an open repudiation by the State of its liability as indorser of the bonds, such as to dishonor them *ipso facto*—was at least sufficient to put the purchaser on inquiry, and charge him with notice of the fact that there was something wrong about the bonds, especially when taken in connection with another fact—that, at the time of such repeal, several years of overdue coupons remained unpaid, and were attached to the bonds. (*Morton & Bliss* v. *New Orleans and Selma Railway Company*, *supra*.)

BONA FIDE HOLDER—Continued.

(*j*) By the law of Kentucky, promissory notes in the hands of an indorsee are subject to any defense, discount, or offset that the maker had or might have had against the payee before notice of the assignment. (*Shoe and Leather National Bank* v. *Wood*, 142 *Mass.*, 536. See *Gen. Sts. of Kentucky*, c. 22, secs. 6, 22.)

CHECKS:

(*a*) Where by the law of a State the drawing of a check by a depositor amounts to an assignment of his deposit *pro tanto*, that result will follow where the check is upon a bank in that State, *though the check is drawn in another State in which* this peculiar rule as to the effect of drawing a check does not prevail. (*Bank of America* v. *Indiana Banking Company*, 114 *Ill.*, 483.)

(*b*) A check becomes no valid claim upon the funds against which it is drawn until the bank is notified of its existence. (*Laclede Bank* v. *Schuler*, 120 *U. S.*, 511.)

(*c*) And however the doctrine that a check is an appropriation of the amount for which it is drawn of the funds of the drawer in the possession of the bank may operate to secure an equitable interest in the funds after notice given to the bank (a question which the court expressly stated it did not undertake to decide), yet the bank, so far as concerns itself and its duties and obligations in regard to the fund, remains unaffected by the execution of the check until notice has been given to it, or demand of payment made upon it. (*Id.*)

(*d*) Although the practice of drawing instruments in sets for the payment of money is generally confined to foreign bills of exchange, yet there is nothing in the purpose or effect of that practice which would render it inapplicable under all circumstances to checks. And, therefore, the character of an instrument as a check is not destroyed by the fact that it contains the words "original" and "second unpaid." These words do not make the instrument payable conditionally. (*Merchants' National Bank* v. *Betzinger*, 188 *Ill.*, 484.)

(*e*) Whenever demand is made by presentation of a genuine check in the hands of a person entitled to receive its amount, for a portion of the amount on deposit, and payment is refused, a cause of action immediately arises in favor of the drawer; and as to the amount specified in the check the statute of limitations begins to run from that time. (*Viets* v. *Union National Bank of Troy*, 101 *N. Y.*, 564.)

(*f*) Where by the law of a State the drawing of a check by the depositor operates as the assignment of the deposit *pro tanto*, a bank in such State upon which process of garnishment has been served should be allowed credit for the amount paid upon checks of the depositor drawn *before such service though not presented for payment until after such service*. (*Bank of America* v. *Indiana Banking Co.*, 114 *Ill.*, 483.)

(*g*) But for no credit for checks paid after service, and which do not appear to have been drawn before. (*Id.*)

(*h*) A fraudulent change in the date of a check, whereby the time for its payment is accelerated, is an alteration which vitiates the instrument. (*Crawford* v. *West Side Bank*, 100 *N. Y.*, 50.)

(*i*) If a bank pay a check so altered, it can not charge the amount against the account of the drawer. (*Id.*)

(*j*) And holding the check until its true date will not entitle the bank to charge it to the drawer, for the possibility that the check could ever become a legal liability in the hands of any person was destroyed by the fraudulent alteration. (*Id.*)

PAPER OF CORPORATIONS:

(*a*) A corporation engaged in business has implied power to make negotiable paper for use within the scope of its business, but it has no power, express or implied, to become a party to bills or notes for the accommodation of others, and such paper is valid and enforceable only in the hands of a holder taking the same before maturity bona fide and without notice. (*National Bank of Republic* v. *Young*, 41 *N. J. Eq.*, 531.)

(*b*) The general doctrine of the law is that where a corporation has powers under any circumstances to issue negotiable paper, a bona-fide holder has a right to presume that the paper was issued under the circumstances which give the requisite authority, and such paper is no more liable to be impeached for any infirmity in the hands of such a holder than any other commercial paper. And this doctrine is applied to commercial paper made by a corporation for the accommodation of a third person when in the hands of a bona-fide holder who has discounted it before maturity on the faith of its being business paper. (*Id.*)

PAPER OF CORPORATIONS—Continued.

(c) As corporations may accept drafts for some purposes, and as the purpose for which a draft is drawn does not ordinarily appear on its face, the question as to all parties with notice is, Was it drawn for a legitimate purpose? As to all others the implied inquiry is, Is the holder a bona-fide holder for value? (*Credit Company* v. *Howe Machine Co.*, 54 *Conn.*, 357.)

(d) Although it is a correct proposition that persons dealing in the commercial paper of a corporation are bound to take notice of the limits of the corporate power in this respect, yet a distinction is to be observed *between the terms of the power and the circumstances under which it is exercised.* Parties must take notice of the former, but they are not required to have knowledge of the latter. And, therefore, a purchaser of such paper, when the same has been accepted by the proper officer of the corporation, is not bound to inquire whether it was issued in the legitimate exercise of the officer's power to so bind the corporation, for this he has the right to presume. (*Credit Company* v. *Howe Machine Co.*, 54 *Conn.*, 357.)

(e) The fact that bonds of a private corporation were sold in violation of a restriction in the charter as to the price can not be set up to defeat the claim of a bona-fide holder of such bonds. (*Ellsworth* v. *St. L., A. & T. R. R. Co.*, 98 *N. Y.*, 553.)

(f) When a corporation gives its promissory note in pursuance of a contract, which is afterwards performed on his part by the payee, the corporation can not, in a suit upon the note, set up that the contract was *ultra vires.* (*Main* v. *Casserly*, 67 *Cal.*, 127.)

PROVISIONS WHICH DESTROY NEGOTIABILITY:

(a) Where a note was made payable twelve months after date, but contained a further provision "that the payee or his assigns may extend the time of payment thereof from time to time indefinitely, as he or they may see fit": Held, that the later provision, as it made the time of payment uncertain and indefinite, destroyed the negotiable character of the instrument. (*Gidden* v. *Henry*, 104 *Ind.*, 278.)

(b) Where a note contained the following stipulation: "This note is given in consideration of, and is subject to one certain contract existing between S. B. J. Bryant and Jacob Haas, of even date with this": Held, that this provision destroyed the negotiable character of the instrument, and that the assignee took it subject to all existing equities. (*McComas* v. *Haas*, 107 *Ind.*, 512.)

(c) A note containing a power of attorney, which, in effect, authorizes a confession of judgment *at any time* after date is not negotiable. (*Richards* v. *Barlow*, 140 *Mass.*, 218.)

(d) A provision in a note for the payment of an attorney's fee in case suit should be brought thereon destroys the negotiability of the instrument. (*Chase* v. *Whitmore*, 68 *Cal*, 545.)

(e) But an agreement inserted in a note to pay "all costs of collection, including 10 per cent. attorney's fees," does not render the note non-negotiable. This stipulation does not make the amount which the maker is to pay uncertain, for the promise to pay a fee of 10 per cent. excludes the possibility that the makers could be compelled to pay a fee more or less than that amount, and as to the costs, as they must necessarily fall upon the losing party, the stipulation as to them is to be regarded as mere surplusage. (*Schlesinger* v. *Arline* (*U. S. C. C. S. D. Georgia*), 31 *Fed. Rep.*, 648.)

NOTE.—As to whether a provision for the payment of an attorney's fee will render a note non-negotiable, the authorities are conflicting. That it will have this effect has been decided in Pennsylvania (*Woods* v. *North*, 84 *Penn. St.*, 407); Missouri (*First National Bank* v. *Gay*, 63 *Mo.*, 33); Minnesota (*Jones* v. *Radatz*, 27 *Minn.*, 240); Wisconsin (*First National Bank* v. *Larsen*, 60 *Wis.*, 206); North Carolina (*First National Bank* v. *Bynum*, 84 *N. C.*, 24); and in the United States circuit court for the district of Minnesota, 14 *Fed. Rep.*, 705. The contrary rule prevails in Indiana (*Stoneman* v. *Pyle*, 35 *Ind.*, 103; *Wyant* v. *Pattorf*, 37 *Ind.*, 512); Iowa (32 *Iowa*, 184); Kansas (*Seaton* v. *Scoville*, 18 *Kans.*, 433); Louisiana (*Dietrich* v. *Baylie*, 23 *La. Ann.*, 767); Nebraska (*Heard* v. *Dubuque Bank*, 8 *Nebr.*, 10).

In neither class of cases is any distinction taken between provisions for a fee at a fixed percentage and a provision to pay a "reasonable attorney's fee", or simply "an attorney's fee". The courts which sustain the negotiability of notes containing such provisions, rest their decisions in the main upon the ground that so long as the amount payable is certain up to the time of maturity and dishonor, it is not essential that after that time, when the instrument has for other reasons become non-negotiable, the certainty

PROVISIONS WHICH DESTROY NEGOTIABILITY—Continued.

as to the amount should continue (see *Stoneman* v. *Pyle, supra*, and *Wyant* v. *Pottorf, supra*). The courts which hold that such provisions destroy the certainty essential to commercial instruments follow the reasoning of Sharswood, J., in *Woods* v. *North, supra*. In that case the stipulation was to pay "five per cent. collection fee if not paid when due". In the course of his opinion Judge Sharswood said: "It is a mistake to suppose that if this note was unpaid at maturity the five per cent. would be payable to the holder by the parties. It must go into the hands of an attorney for collection. It is not a sum necessarily payable. The phrase "collection fee" necessarily implies this. Not only so, but this amount of percentage can not be arbitrarily determined by the parties. It must be only what would be a reasonable compensation to an attorney for collection. This, in reason and usage of the legal profession, depends upon the amount of the note. * * * How then can this note be said to be certain as to its amount, or an amount unaffected by any contingency? Interest and cost of protest, after non-payment at maturity, are necessary legal incidents of the contract, and the insertion of them in the body of the note, would not affect its negotiability. But a collateral agreement, as here, depending, too, as it does, upon its reasonableness, to be determined by the verdict of a jury, is entirely different. * * * If this collateral agreement may be introduced with impunity, what may not be?"

DEFENSES:

(*a*) In a suit upon a promissory note evidence is not admissible to show that the note was given upon an understanding between the parties that it should not be of any force. (*Dary* v. *Kelly*, 66 *Wis.*, 452.)

(*b*) The drawer of a bill of exchange will not be permitted to show that at the time the instrument was drawn there was verbal agreement that he should not be held liable thereon as drawer. (*Cummings* v. *Kent*, 44 *Ohio St.*, 92.)

(*c*) Although it is the rule in Iowa that when there is a blank indorsement of a promissory note, a different contract from that which in such case is implied by law may be established by parol evidence, yet this rule will not be extended further so as to allow it to be shown by parol that no contract of any description was entered into or intended by such indorsement. (*Genoser* v. *Wissner*, 69 *Iowa*, 119.)

(*d*) Where the payee of a promissory note is sued as indorser thereon, he may show by parol evidence that when he wrote his name on the note the note had already been paid, and that he put his name thereto at the request of the holder merely as evidence of the payment. (*Spencer* v. *Sloan*, 108 *Ind.*, 183.)

(*e*) Where a promissory note has been given in part payment of a house, the maker of the note may, as against the purchaser of the note with notice of the facts, set up as defense to it the damages sustained by him by reason of the false and fraudulent representations of the vendor as to the condition of one of the walls. (*Applegarth* v. *Robertson*, 65 *Md.*, 493.)

(*f*) The rule early established in Pennsylvania, that an indorser of a negotiable instrument is not a competent witness to invalidate it, is still adhered to in that State. It has not been changed by legislation. (*John's Adm'r* v. *Pardee*, 109 *Penn. St.*, 545.)

INDICIA OF OWNERSHIP:

Where by the laws of the State a married woman can not transfer *without the written or oral assent of her husband*, shares of stock held by her in a corporation, and she delivers to her husband the certificates of stock and a power of attorney in blank, and such stock is pledged by the husband, but the power of attorney *is not accompanied by written evidence of the assent of the husband*, a transferee from the pledgee is put upon inquiry, and his title to the stock can be no better than that which by the assent of the husband the pledgee had; for in such case, all the indicia of ownership are not conferred upon the pledgee. (*Leiper's Appeal*, 109 *Pa.*, 377.

AMOUNT WHICH PLEDGEE MAY RECOVER:

Where negotiable instruments have been transferred as collateral security by one who is not a bona-fide holder for value, the pledgee, if he has taken the instruments in good faith for value before maturity, will still be allowed to prove against the maker of the instruments for the full amount thereof; but the amount of his recovery can not exceed the debt for the security of which the instruments were pledged, and interest. (*Morton & Bliss* v. *New Orleans and Selma Railway Company*, 79 *Ala.*, 590.)

PROPOSITION I.

To eliminate from the national-bank laws the note-issuing function of the banks.

1. WISCONSIN—BANK.

Favors retention of the present charter, annual examination of banks, and the repeal of the law requiring banks to own bonds and to take out currency.

2. WISCONSIN—BANK.

Favors the repeal of the provision requiring a deposit of United States bonds as security for notes, and the banks to give up circulation and to continue in the system.

3. MINNESOTA—BANK.

Suggests that if the banks can not make a small profit on circulation they should not be required to furnish circulation at a loss, and states that with the present rates of interest and the premium on bonds any circulation produces loss.

Favors the repeal of the law requiring the deposit of United States bonds. If the deposit of bonds is left optional with the banks, such as make a profit on circulation can still take advantage of it, and others will not be compelled to maintain a circulation at a loss.

Favors the retiring of all the circulation of his bank and the sale of their bonds, if his bank could remain in the national-bank system.

4. MICHIGAN—CLEARING-HOUSE.

While he favors plan No. I, proposition No. V, and thinks its enactment into a law would cause all banks to become national banks, and thousands of new banks to be organized, he fears it would bring about a tremendous expansion of the currency and an era of wild speculation, and it would be doubtful if paper and gold currency could be maintained on an interchangeable basis.

Thinks it would be wiser to seek relief in a less dangerous way, and in a manner to modify the prejudices against the banks.

When the national-bank act was passed the Government was pressed for funds, and the banks were compelled to buy bonds before they could be authorized to commence business. Now the conditions are reversed, and the necessity for compelling the banks to buy bonds has passed. For this reason the simple repeal of the sections of the national-bank law requiring the banks to hold bonds would give all the relief needed.

Suggests, with this exception, that the act be left as it is, and banks with long-time bonds can still be banks of issue, and new banks could elect to be banks of deposit only.

Thinks the supervision of the banks by the Government, the protection of the depositors, public statements, annual statistics, etc., would render national banks superior to State banks.

If the banks should, as they may, cease to be banks of issue, there would be some danger of a large contraction of the currency, caused by deposits of legal-tenders to redeem circulation, but suggests that surplus silver coinage might be made available.

If the demand for bonds as a basis for circulation ceases, the prices of United States bonds might fall to a point at which the Government could buy them with its surplus revenue.

5. COLORADO.

That as banking is a business carried on for purposes of gain, like mercantile and manufacturing businesses, thinks it is equally as sensible and reasonable for the Government to issue bonds to form a permanent basis for any and all businesses as for the banking business.

6. CALIFORNIA—JOURNALIST.

Currency and its proper management is a matter of abstract fixed science. All changes entail loss to some, gain to others. The shrewd and capable secure the gain; the loss falls on those least able to bear it.

True money is an article of some intrinsic value, as gold, silver, etc., stamped as to quality, fineness, and weight, and worth the face value of the stamp, less the cost of coinage. Every piece, whether gold or silver, must maintain its relative value. If not fixed in relative value, or nearly so, one of them must be the standard and remain fixed, and the other must follow it continually.

6. California—Journalist—Continued.

If in 1880 a grain of gold is worth 20 in silver, the coin must be made on that basis; and if in 1890 it be worth 25, the silver must be that much larger. No sensible man will lay up a silver dollar worth only 90 cents, when he can get a gold one worth 98 cents.

Would coin all the gold that could be bought at such figures as to pay for coinage, and keep all in circulation save a needful reserve for the use of the Treasury.

Would coin all the silver in like manner, of such weight that the silver dollar will have all the intrinsic value of the gold dollar, less cost of coinage.

A commercial people need paper money as well as gold and silver. This paper money should be a promise to pay of the nation, a legal tender for all purposes whatsoever, and maintained at par, as nearly as possible, by the following machinery:

Whenever the legal tender is at par all Government salaries to be paid therein; when 1 per cent. below par, one-tenth of the issue to be cut off, and as they went down 1 per cent. more, two-tenths. Should they reach 3 per cent. discount, the issue should cease.

In every great commercial center there should be a sub-treasury, where the legal tender could be exchanged at pleasure for coin or bonds. No national banks. Let banks, like churches, be clear of the State.

This system would develop these things, to wit:

Just how much paper money the people need and will absorb without discount.

An automatic adjustment, depending on no man, but on law and fact. The fact of a discount arising, the law operates as a matter of course.

A perfect regulation of the currency, filling the gap when gold and silver go abroad, and retiring on their return. In the event of famine, plague, etc., and we should have all to buy and nothing to sell, as our coin went abroad this paper would take the place of the coin without a jar. We would save the interest on all the paper afloat.

This paper would rest upon the property of the nation, and not upon any supposed gold or silver in the Treasury. A run on the nation would be met by interest-bearing bonds at 2, 3, 4, or 5 per cent., as the case demanded.

7. Maine—Bank.

Suggests that as the Government no longer needs to force a market for its bonds, the section of the currency act requiring banks to hold them be repealed, leaving it optional with the banks to hold bonds and have circulation, or to dispense with both.

If holders of long-time bonds did not feel that the banks must have them, it is possible that they would decline, and the banks or the Government might feel it advisable to purchase them.

Suggests that as State banks were driven out of existence by tax on circulation, it would not be improper to return the tax on circulation paid by national banks since the war, less the actual cost of maintaining the system.

8. District of Columbia—Employé of Treasury Department.

Suggests that inasmuch as the motive for the compulsory provision of law requiring banks to deposit United States bonds before commencing business no longer exists, the law should be modified or changed from a compulsory provision to an optional one, retaining all the other features of the national-bank act not inconsistent with this provision.

Such a change would not alter the present condition of the banks; they would still be the means of providing circulation, and of procuring the greatest elasticity; the scarcity of bonds or high premiums would cease to be an impediment to the successful establishment of banking associations, and it would allay the fears of Congress as to contraction of the currency.

9. Florida.

Thinks that the national bank, like the internal-revenue system, is a war measure, and therefore no longer necessary, as it is doing a work which the Government can do at a less cost to the people. The Government alone should issue currency.

10. Kansas—Bank.

As the need for creating a market for United States bonds has ceased, would amend the law so as to leave it optional with the banks to deposit bonds and issue circulation or not. Banks already organized to have the option of redeeming circulation with lawful money and to withdraw bonds.

PROPOSITION II.

To increase the inducements for the banks to deposit United States bonds as a basis of national-bank circulation.

(*a*) By increasing amount of circulation issued on such bonds—
1. To par of bond.
2. To, or nearly to, their market value.
(*b*) By reducing or taking off the tax on circulation.

1. OHIO—BANK.

Suggests raising circulation to the face value of the bonds deposited, and the reduction of tax on circulation to one-half of 1 per cent. per annum.

2. NEW YORK—BANK.

Thinks plan No. I, proposition No. V, inadmissible, unless the Government, in consideration of the 1 per cent. sinking fund, and the lien on the assets of the banks, guarantees prompt redemption of the notes as now, but doubts the wisdom of this. Thinks that any issue of currency on credit of any kind whatever, which requires the refusal of a bank note because the bank issuing it has failed, ought not to be sanctioned by the Government, for however certain ultimate payment may be, necessity to discredit the note would be fatal to the system.

Can see no better reason to advocate the plan for the deposit of silver as security for national bank issues, as it would introduce too much of the speculative element into banking, and probably lead to grave results with the Treasury in depreciation of silver. It would have a tendency to delay and prevent an international agreement upon a ratio with gold for unlimited free coinage of both metals. Suggests:

(1) That 1 per cent. be taken off the tax on circulation, for the reason that when national banks were authorized the Government needed every resource of taxation, and the banks then bought 6 per cent. bonds at par or under, in currency, with interest payable in gold and salable at 150 to 200, which gave the banks equal to 10 or 12 per cent. on their investment. The current interest rates and the general business of the country enabled the banks to then make large profits. The tax ought now to be removed.

(2) One hundred dollars, instead of $90 on the $100 of United States bonds, should be issued to the banks when $100 will not exceed 90 per cent. of the market value of the bonds deposited.

These two provisions will enable the banks to use United States bonds at some profit for circulation, as they are now outstanding for the term of existence of any bank now organized.

(3) Urges legislation against State taxation of national banks.

Suggests that the issue of currency is not the most useful function of national banks; they are necessary to the country and to the Government as an agency to bring the people in contact with the Government, and to place commerce and the wealth of the country in sympathy and support of the financial plans of the Treasury, and without a substitute system of much the same character, commerce and industry must be turned backward a generation.

Objects to a return to the old State-bank system, and also objects to the engrafting of any such system on the national-bank system.

3. OHIO—BANK.

Is satisfied to see the national-bank notes disappear with the public debt. To reduce the "harm" to a minimum he would have Congress authorize the issue of notes to banks equal to the market value of securities deposited.

See also plans Nos. 3, 5, and 6 under proposition III.

PROPOSITION III.

To provide by new issues of bonds for a continuance of the present or of some modified system of national-bank circulation based on United States bonds.

1. MARYLAND—PRIVATE BANK.

Suggests issuing a large long loan at 2½ per cent. per annum interest, at par, for United States notes, and the retiring of the 4½'s on the best terms. If a larger amount is wanted then retire part of the 4's.

Make this long loan convertible into greenbacks at the option of the holder, and again reconvertible into said loan in sums of $100 and multiples, bearing interest from the date of reissue.

2. KANSAS—MERCHANT.

Is certain of one thing in connection with the national-bank question, and that is that the people are not ready to surrender the national banks and return to the old State-bank system.

Suggests that a United States bond having fifty or a hundred years to run be sold or exchanged for the 4's now held by the banks, and that 95 or 98 per cent. of currency be issued to the banks on these bonds instead of 90 per cent., as now. These new bonds could bear 1 or 1½ per cent. interest. This would be as profitable to the banks as the present system, and much cheaper to the people, and money thus brought into the Treasury could be used in paying off bonds bearing interest at a higher rate. Believes the banks would be eager to take such bonds.

If this plan is impracticable, then suggests the issuing of coin notes or certificates (not gold or silver certificates), the Government to issue all the currency and to supply the banks in this way.

Suggests the continued supervision by the Government of the banks as being a good thing.

3. VIRGINIA.

Suggests that Congress authorize the issue of 2 per cent. non-taxable bonds, not exceeding $600,000,000, of forty years duration, to be good as a basis for national bank circulation, and when originally issued to be passed only to national-banks in exchange, dollar for dollar, for United States 4's of 1907.

These bonds, after the original issue, to stand in all respects as other Government bonds.

The banks to issue circulation to the face value of these bonds, instead of 90 per cent., to which they are limited in case of other classes of bonds. The circulation to be further secured in case of failure by first lien on the assets of the bank.

Circulation based on these bonds to be free of tax.

The charter of any bank depositing these bonds as a basis of circulation, to the extent of not less than 30 per cent. of capital, and keeping the same up to that standard, not to expire until the maturity of the bonds.

The only problem to solve is to so adjust the time of the bonds, rate of interest, per centum of circulation, taxation, franchises, and hinderances to the use of other classes of bonds, so as to make it the interest of the banks to lose the premiums on the 4's to make the exchange.

These bonds might be for fifty or one hundred years instead of forty, redeemable at the pleasure of the Government after forty years.

4. NEW YORK—BANK.

Congress to provide a bond to be called the "bankers' bond," bearing 2½ per cent. interest, and running perpetually, at the option of the holders. These bonds to be issued only to bankers as a basis for circulation, and when deposited with the United States Treasurer, the Comptroller of the Currency to issue to the banks an equal amount of national-bank currency, free from tax to the Government.

Such a bond would never fluctuate, and as the Government would stand ready at all times to redeem them at par in case of a failure of a bank, the holder of the national-bank currency could not possibly sustain any loss.

This bond should read "United States banker's bond, good for deposit with the United States Treasurer as security for circulation of national banks only, and payable in gold, at par, at the option of the holder, with interest at the rate of 2½ per cent. per annum, payable in gold quarterly."

All the 3 per cent. bonds now outstanding, that have not been called, and those now held by the United States Treasurer for the banks, that have been called, but not yet exchanged, to be converted into 2½ per cent. bonds, and supplied to the banks as needed.

If the demand is greater than the remaining 3 per cent. bonds unpaid, then the temporary retirement of greenbacks could be provided for until the 4½ per cent. bonds mature, when the greenbacks could be reissued.

5. NEW YORK—BANK.

Suggests in lieu of plan No. 1, under proposition No. V, the following:

1. Cease further payment of the public debt, or stop at $1,200,000,000.
2. That the Secretary of the Treasury be authorized to fund $1,200,000,000 into a new bond bearing interest sufficient to float it at par, say 2 per cent. to 3 per cent., to be called United States consols, to run at the pleasure of the Government after fifty years, and at the pleasure of the holder after one hundred years.

5. NEW YORK—BANK—Continued.

Make this bond the basis of the national-bank system, and pay old bonds as they become due with them; if refused, pay the holder of the old bonds in cash and sell the new bonds to new purchasers for cash to reimburse the Government for the amount paid on the old bond.

These bonds to be bought by the banks to replace the old ones as they fall due.

Holders of such bonds to use them as collateral, and as such they would be regarded by bankers as better security than human indorsers.

The Secretary of the Treasury should be authorized to receive such bonds at their par value and to issue in lieu thereof an equal amount of United States currency to supply banks, in suitable denominations, and to retain the accruing interest upon said bonds, until the accumulation shall amount to 10 per cent., after which all additional interest shall be paid the bond owner.

This will relieve the present generation of the burden of paying the public debt, and leave a permanent banking bond, and will not disturb the present system further than requiring additional issue to each bank of 10 per cent. more currency than under the present system.

6. NEW JERSEY—BANK.

Thinks the holding of United States bonds by national banks a strong bond of union and would be sorry to have the system abolished.

Is opposed to the Government issuing notes while the country is in a state of profound peace, thus interfering with the legitimate business of banking.

Favors something being done to continue the national banking system, and thinks the only thing that can be done is for the Government to withdraw a part of its circulating notes, and issue bonds of long date, for banking purposes, at a low rate of interest, say 2½ per cent. per annum, the circulation of the banks to be taxed one-half of 1 per cent. per annum, or bonds bearing interest at 2 per cent., the circulation being free from all tax.

7. MASSACHUSETTS—BANK.

Suggests that Congress authorize a loan bearing 2 per cent. interest, payable semi-annually. These bonds to be payable at the option of the Government on ninety or more days' notice, and on six, twelve, or eighteen months' notice by the holders.

Such bonds, with removal of present tax, would induce the banks to take all the needed circulation, and would not stimulate an excess. The banks would be enabled to secure bonds without premium and to dispose of them without loss.

This plan would afford a reasonable elasticity to circulation, either by the Department having control of the calling in of the bonds or the banks in surrendering them.

The Government would be subjected to no loss, because after redeeming the outstanding 2½ (?) per cent. bonds, it can, even at the present high prices, buy the 4s, 4½s, and 6s, at a rate that will net more than 2 per cent. It is assumed that few besides the banks would purchase the 2 per cent. bonds, for the reason that few now purchase for investment the higher rate bonds at prices that net 2¼ to 2½ per cent.

8. COLORADO—BANK.

Suggests the purchase by the Government of the telegraph lines, instruments, right of way, etc., of the country, the perfection and extension of the system by proper legislation, issuing for this purpose bonds running 20 to 25 years and bearing interest at 2 per cent. per annum. To induce national banks to subscribe for these bonds at par, an issue of notes should be authorized to the amount of 98 per cent. of the face of the bonds and the taxation on circulation should be lowered to one-half of 1 per cent. per annum. Banks should be required to carry at least 30 per cent. of their capital in bonds, instead of 25 per cent., which is the minimum now.

PROPOSITION IV.

To substitute some other security for United States bonds deposited in the Treasury as a basis for national-bank circulation.

1. PENNSYLVANIA.

Favors coinage of the silver dollar and the issuing of certificates of all coin and bullion, gold and silver, held by the Government, as the needs of banking may require; the issue of currency to the banks on presentation by them of the certificates, dollar for dollar, the banks to pay 3 per cent. interest on the amount issued, and the interest to go towards paying the national debt. The annual surplus revenue to be invested in bullion only as banking facilities may require.

1. PENNSYLVANIA—Continued.

To prevent these certificates from going into the market and being held at premium, he would issue them only to banks when organized or ready to take the currency.

2. KANSAS—BANK.

Suggests the substitution of school-district bonds for United States bonds, and a provision that no school bonds shall be accepted as security for circulation unless the total amount of bonds issued by the district does not exceed one-fifth of the taxable property of the district.

Would also protect the interest of the nation as to legality of issue, etc.

3. PENNSYLVANIA—BANK.

Suggests the issue of currency based upon a pledge of silver at either its value of one-sixteenth the worth of gold or, better still, its market value. Either security would be better than that of the greenback currency, for which but 30 per cent. in gold is held as security, and this would meet with better favor with the Southern and Western sections.

As banks are now subject to a positive loss on their currency, based upon the present prices of United States bonds, why not remove the requirement, as its repeal would enable the Government to purchase its bonds at a much lower figure than it will be compelled to pay with the banks in competition.

Does not think that the withdrawal of circulation from national banks will cause them to withdraw from the system.

4. MASSACHUSETTS—BANKER.

Is in favor of retention of the present system with some amendments to the law.

The present currency passes freely, because the people have confidence in the security behind every national-bank bill, and in the watchfulness of the Government over all national banks.

Favors specie basis. Business is largely done on the Government's promise, but the time has come for the Government to pay its promises, and he would be glad to have it do so, and to continue the present national-bank system.

Would change the law so that banks, as bonds are called, or as they need to issue new circulation, may deposit gold or silver bullion at its market value, or gold or silver coin at par, with the United States Treasurer, and be allowed 100 per cent. for said deposit, and have the tax on circulation, now collected by the Government, removed.

Would have the local tax the same rate as it is in Massachusetts on savings banks, viz, one-half of 1 per cent.

The great pile of silver dollars could remain in the Treasury vaults until some bank failed, then the holders of the notes of the failed bank would not object to receiving silver dollars in exchange for the bank notes.

5. NEW MEXICO—BANK.

Amend the national-bank act retaining all its restrictions and ramifications, powers, and privileges.

The banks to deposit with the United States Treasurer the amount of their capital stock in gold, receiving in return a charter and national currency to the full amount of its capital deposited.

The charter to carry a certificate in effect as follows:

"This is to certify that (name of bank) has deposited with the Treasurer of the United States $—— in gold, as a guaranty for the redemption of a like amount of its notes, with interest at the rate of 2 per cent. per annum, during the existence of the charter."

The whole expense of examinations, redemptions, issues and reissues, to be borne by the Government.

This would bring into the national banking system a large percentage of State and private banks and thereby protect the public from organizations without bona fide capital.

6. MASSACHUSETTS—BANKER.

Suggests that banks be allowed to deposit gold or silver and be given 100 per cent. circulation for the amount deposited, and that tax on circulation be removed and local taxation adjusted.

That the United States Treasurer be allowed to use 40 per cent. of this deposit to purchase municipal bonds, subject to the approval of a board of directors consisting of three selected men (say the Comptroller of the Currency, Secretary of State, and Secretary of the Interior, or some other good man).

6. MASSACHUSETTS—BANKER—Continued.

The income from the 10 per cent. thus invested would pay the expense of the Government, and if more, the balance to revert to the banks.

Banks having bonds soon to be called, or called, soon to be paid, will receive specie therefor, and new banks can deposit the specie or send to the Treasurer gold or silver certificates.

7. OHIO—BANK EXAMINER.

Suggests as follows:

1. That all distinction between legal tender and national currency be abolished, as the currency is all issued by the Government, and there should be but one and that should be national currency, the same exactly for all the banks.
2. That gold or silver be deposited as a basis for circulation, and that the Government issue therefor a certificate calling for national currency to the full amount of deposits.
3. National banks to be relieved from taxation, 5 per cent. redemption fund, and otherwise, except upon real estate and shares of stock, the taxation not to be in excess of 1 per cent. per annum, and to be a municipal tax so assessed and collected.
4. The reserve held by the banks to be gold or silver coin, the currency to be used for circulation and the coin for reserve; the banks to receive 3 per cent. interest upon the reserve required by law to be held by them; such interest to be payable in coin certificates issued by the Government based upon the coin deposited by the banks for their circulation, upon which the Government should have the right to issue interest-bearing certificates, up to 50 per cent. of said deposits.
5. As an inducement for national banks to come under this plan, if application be made within two years, the Government to sell the bank's coin for the amount of their bonds now held as security for circulation.

The difference between the amount of circulation so charged to them and the full present value of the bonds also to be paid to the banks in currency. This would be the redemption of the bonds now held to secure circulation. The circulation would be increased 15 per cent., as 5 per cent. redemption fund heretofore locked up would be released.

The Government to make good its own notes as they become worn out or mutilated by use.

Under this plan the banks would have to purchase coin of the Government, or elsewhere, for their reserve, and as there would be no discrimination at against silver, this money would become more popular with the banks as is would become more valuable to them, as much so as gold. The circulation and reserve of the banks would be based upon coin—a change to be desired.

Banks would not enter upon this plan except for the franchise and freedom from taxation and a long-settled future which it would afford, and any plan agreed upon should stand for fifty years.

The ratio of interest charged by national banks should not exceed 5 per centum per annum.

All officers connected with national banks should give a good and sufficient bond to the United States as security for deposits entrusted to them.

If a bank operating under this plan desires to close business it would have to furnish to the full satisfaction of the Government evidence that all its obligations to its depositors and others had been paid off, then return an amount of its currency equal to the amount received; and any balance found due to the bank would be paid to its order in coin.

This plan is in the direct interest of the business men of the country, to whom it would be a relief to get money at the lowest rates of interest possible, and to accomplish which the General Government would bear part of the burden, and would be a gainer to the extent of the amount of coin it was allowed to use of that deposited by the banks, of which 50 per cent. would be sufficient to keep in reserve.

Of course the Government could not change the rate of interest for national banks already established, without their consent, but banks established under this plan, charging only 5 per cent. interest, would get all the deposits and business, and this would induce other banks to come into the system.

PROPOSITION V.

To preserve the note-issuing function of the banks, but to substitute credit for security and to provide for Government redemption out of a fund created by deposits by the banks, or by a tax on their circulation:

a. Upon the credit of the individual bank;
b. Upon the credit of certain banks combined;
c. Upon the credit of all the banks.

1. New York—Bank.

Suggests as follows:

1. Amend the national bank law, retaining all restrictions, ramifications, powers, and privileges, so as to legalize the issue of circulating notes to the amount of 50 per cent. of capital without the deposit of bonds as security.
2. In case of failure the currency to be preferred before any other liability.
3. One per cent. per annum of this currency to be deposited in the Treasury as a guaranty fund for the redemption of the notes of any broken bank whose assets may be inadequate to redeem its issue of currency.

By strictly enforcing the requirements of the national-bank laws, and by applying the best civil-service rules to bank examiners, this suggested currency would be sound in principle and as uniform in value in every part of the country as is our present issue of national-bank notes.

The proposed new issue of a circulating medium need in no way interfere with banks now organized and managed.

When the guaranty fund shall amount to more than 5 per cent. on notes outstanding, the excess can, with safety, be covered annually into the Treasury.

Believes the result of twenty-three years of national banking will demonstrate that not over one-tenth of the proposed guarantee fund will ever be required to protect the public against loss, leaving nine-tenths of accumulation to be covered into the Treasury.

As regards "elasticity," thinks it apparent that banks working under the proposed change can retire and reissue their currency with great freedom and facility, as compared with the present system.

Objectors to this proposed change may assert that the "safety fund" system of New York was a failure, and that this is like in character, but contributions to the safety fund were only one-half of 1 per cent. per annum, and ended when 3 per cent. on the capital had been paid, and it was liable for deposits as well as for circulation.

Circulating notes were issued by bank officers without restraining guards or State supervision. The legal limit, however, was two of currency to one of capital.

Several banks made what were called "over-issues" rendering false statements, thus avoiding payment of the assessment to the "safety-fund."

The New York "safety-fund" was a delusion, and should not be named in connection with the national-bank system, under which banks can issue only notes furnished by the Treasury Department.

The writer is of the opinion that the amendment proposed will bring a large percentage of the State and private banks into the national system.

2. Pennsylvania—Bank.

Opposes the retirement of greenbacks in exchange for national-bank notes.

Favors the retention of United States notes so that the present limitation of national-bank circulation might be continued, or perhaps a limit equal to the capital stock of the banks.

Would tax all banks every year and set the tax apart as a general fund for redemption of circulation of failed banks and then reimburse the general fund if the assets of the shareholders were sufficient.

Would make circulation the first lien, and would adjust the tax on circulation so as to encourage the taking out of the full proportion.

Urges additional legislation to perfect governmental supervision of the banks, and opposes the repeal of the 10 per cent. tax of State bank circulation.

3. Pennsylvania.—

Suggests that national banks be entitled to issue circulating notes without deposit of United States bonds as security for such circulation, as follows:

1. Banks with a capital of over $2,000,000, to the amount of 25 per cent. of capital.
2. Banks with a capital of $2,000,000 and less, to the amount of 50 per cent. of capital.

3. PENNSYLVANIA—Continued.

The notes to be issued under the following provisions:

The Treasury Department to print and deliver notes to banks as at present, in denominations of $5, $10, $20, $50, $100.

The banks to keep on hand, in addition to the reserve held for other liabilities, a reserve equal to 25 per cent. of the amount of circulation, in lawful money of the United States.

The banks to keep on deposit in the Treasury, as at present, 5 per cent. redemption fund for mutilated notes.

The banks to pay semi-annually a tax of one-quarter of 1 per cent. on the average amount of circulation outstanding during the previous six months.

The banks to be entitled to withdraw all or any part of their circulating notes on furnishing the Treasury Department a duly certified resolution from their board of directors, and depositing with the Redemption Bureau, in lawful money of the United States, the amount to be withdrawn.

To have the power at any time to increase or decrease the amount of circulation within prescribed limits.

Circulating notes to be the first liability of issuing banks.

4. MISSOURI—BANK.

Thinks plan No. I, Proposition V, has much merit and would approve of it if a further section were added, making it obligatory for the Treasury Department to cancel and redeem a like amount of legal-tender notes as soon as national-bank currency is increased under the amended law, say above $300,000,000, thereby finding an outlet for surplus between the last redemption of 3s and the first redemption of 4½ per cent. bonds.

5. MASSACHUSETTS—BANK.

After a careful study of the subject and an examination of the different plans suggested, is of the opinion that plan No. I, Proposition V, is the most feasible, and would be the most generally satisfactory, and he therefore heartily indorses it.

6. MINNESOTA—ATTORNEY AT LAW.

Favors a law requiring all banks issuing notes to become associated together as one association, and to pay a pro rata assessment from their surplus, and if no surplus, then from their capital, to make good to all note-holders the value of the notes held by them of all failed banks belonging to the association.

Provide for a joint and several inspection by the Government and bank inspectors, with power to close up insolvent institutions when they shall jointly report the particular bank insolvent.

Give the association a first lien for indemnity upon the assets of the bank to the extent of its notes outstanding, and require the deposit of a fund by the associated banks sufficient to pay at once, on presentation, the notes of insolvent banks, and require any bank thus associated to redeem such notes of failed banks as shall be presented, to be reimbursed out of the redemption fund.

Make the Secretary of the Treasury, or the Comptroller of the Currency, a member of a commission to be appointed by the banking association, and give such commission power to investigate and admit applicant banks of not less than $——— paid in.

That circulating notes be provided as now, to be printed at the expense of a fund provided by the association.

There would be no safer guaranty to the people than the consolidation of the capital of the banks, and the privileges thus granted would be compensated by the guarantee of the banks against loss to note-holders. The association thus responsible would closely watch for any irregularities.

7. NEW YORK—BANK.

Suggests that the profits on lost circulation be pledged for redemption of notes issued without pledge of bonds. This will amount to $20,000,000 or more. With a yearly tax of 1 per cent., say $3,000,000, a fund could be collected that would place the security beyond a contingency. This fund would ultimately belong to the Government.

Many bankers think it unjust that the Government should retain the profit on lost circulation, but if the fund could for a time be utilized to benefit the banks they would doubtless cheerfully relinquish any claim they might have upon it.

8. PENNSYLVANIA—BANK.

Suggests two plans, as follows:

1. A circulation based on a bond deposited at par value and the tax removed; or,
2. The Government to guarantee to each bank under these restrictions, circulation limited to one-half its capital (with maximum limit, if desired), the notes to be absolutely a first claim and subjected to 1 per cent. tax, to be used as a sinking fund.

Banks electing the second plan to be examined twice a year by the bank examiner.

9. KENTUCKY—BANKER.

Suggests that national banks be allowed to invest in real-estate mortgages as security.

Also that the basing of circulation on capital alone discourages the building up of surplus, which should be equally with capital a basis for circulation, with the same preventions of reduction or impairment as are required in case of capital.

A circulation might be allowed equal to 75 per cent. of capital and surplus, making the notes a first lien on all assets of the issuing bank, continuing the present tax, but holding it as a fund to pay the notes of broken banks whose assets prove insufficient for that purpose, and beyond that assess the banks pro rata on their circulation.

With the present supervision (which might be improved) the Government could afford to guarantee this circulation, in consideration of its use of the tax fund.

TABLE SHOWING, BY STATES AND TERRITORIES, THE ESTIMATED POPULATION OF EACH, AND THE AGGREGATE CAPITAL, SURPLUS, UNDIVIDED PROFITS, AND INDIVIDUAL DEPOSITS* OF NATIONAL AND STATE BANKS, LOAN AND TRUST COMPANIES, AND SAVINGS AND PRIVATE BANKS IN THE UNITED STATES ON JUNE 1, 1887; THE AVERAGE OF THESE PER CAPITA OF POPULATION, AND THE PER-CAPITA AVERAGES OF SUCH RESOURCES IN EACH CLASS OF BANKS AND IN ALL.

States and Territories.	Estimated population June 1, 1887.	All banks.		National banks.	State banks.	Loan and trust companies.	Savings banks.	Private banks.
		Capital, etc.	Average per capita.	Average per capita.	Average per capita.	Average per capita.	Average per capita.	Average per capita.
Maine	667,400	$63,918,725.80	$95.77	$35.58	....	$1.14	$59.06	....
New Hampshire	371,100	69,721,728.21	187.87	37.26	$0.27	.99	149.30	....
Vermont	333,700	32,824,355.01	98.36	47.05	....	....	50.41	....
Massachusetts	2,036,600	612,581,949.97	297.86	123.45	....	23.92	147.88	$0.61
Rhode Island	326,200	99,438,611.58	304.83	123.39	9.52	....	171.92	....
Connecticut	691,300	172,646,586.14	248.65	85.70	9.07	5.86	117.30	.73
New York	5,670,700	1,449,517,396.11	252.08	88.46	33.10	32.44	100.18	1.42
New Jersey	1,320,000	92,721,678.51	70.24	43.01	3.78	....	22.65	.77
Pennsylvania	4,921,800	432,207,506.45	87.81	55.64	8.05	12.39	9.41	2.28
Delaware	164,700	11,016,126.12	66.88	42.93	5.49	....	18.46	....
Maryland	1,064,300	71,817,972.70	67.47	42.57	5.86	....	18.98	.06
District of Columbia	216,200	11,171,155.07	51.67	47.18	....	....	3.91	.58
Virginia	1,753,900	23,942,066.16	13.65	8.86	4.85	....	....	....
West Virginia	766,600	9,384,564.32	12.24	7.00	5.25	....	....	....
North Carolina	1,675,500	9,131,962.80	5.45	3.93	1.39	....	.01	.10
South Carolina	1,239,000	11,905,378.57	9.61	52.13	4.26	....	....	.13
Georgia	1,842,800	18,848,434.52	10.23	4.67	4.86	....	....	[illegible]
Florida	338,100	4,025,318.01	11.91	6.63	4.42	....	....	.85
Alabama	1,485,400	16,839,156.20	11.34	7.17	1.27	....	....	2.89
Mississippi	1,386,000	4,568,364.47	3.29	1.66	1.41	....	....	.21
Louisiana	1,118,800	24,827,420.16	22.19	11.75	7.35	....	....	.08
Texas	2,240,900	32,339,006.01	14.43	11.84	.87	....	....	1.71
Arkansas	1,069,600	4,487,740.84	4.20	3.35	.85	....	....	....
Kentucky	1,923,800	65,182,408.62	33.88	16.46	16.27	....	....	1.15
Tennessee	1,780,700	30,952,439.48	17.38	12.24	5.14	....	....	....
Ohio	3,645,400	165,483,694.40	45.39	33.14	3.83	....	4.24	4.17
Indiana	2,228,200	58,874,744.88	26.42	18.87	2.33	....	1.13	4.09
Illinois	3,529,500	174,282,553.31	49.38	35.34	2.19	....	5.16	6.08
Michigan	2,017,200	87,809,747.46	43.53	25.59	15.87	....	....	2.06
Wisconsin	1,534,500	56,582,833.77	36.87	15.04	15.92	....	....	5.01
Iowa	1,986,100	67,468,295.62	33.97	16.27	5.05	....	6.34	6.31
Minnesota	1,067,100	77,791,106.66	72.89	42.40	19.54	1.46	3.92	5.51
Missouri	2,543,700	112,650,512.82	44.28	13.87	26.40	.51	....	3.40
Kansas	1,520,500	52,923,593.43	34.66	19.54	11.28	....	....	3.90
Nebraska	729,000	41,434,306.53	56.83	38.96	11.65	2.01	....	4.20
Colorado	324,000	23,926,379.14	73.84	60.90	9.11	....	....	3.83
Nevada	78,900	714,091.30	9.05	6.22	....	....	....	2.83
California	1,120,300	209,482,734.37	186.98	24.44	84.78	....	68.75	9.01
Oregon	245,200	9,719,318.44	39.63	32.23	1.50	....	....	5.90
Arizona	66,300	796,024.00	12.00	3.82	....	....	....	8.18
Dakota	236,800	13,243,993.03	55.92	40.98	....	....	....	14.94
Idaho	47,400	1,316,292.09	27.76	20.63	....	....	....	7.14
Montana	54,700	11,444,616.06	209.22	209.22	....	....	....	....
New Mexico	142,800	3,054,642.31	21.39	18.93	....	....	....	2.46
Utah	192,000	7,456,939.63	38.83	18.31	....	....	....	20.52
Washington	118,100	6,411,341.80	54.28	45.49	....	....	....	8.79
Wyoming	30,600	4,306,892.85	140.74	102.70	....	....	....	37.96
Total	59,893,000	4,563,192,203.50	76.19	34.01	10.69	5.07	22.92	2.58

* Deposits due from and to banks should mutually cancel each other, and therefore they are omitted as misleading.

NOTE.—Mr. E. B. Elliott, Actuary of the Treasury Department, prepared these estimates by special request.

NUMBER OF BANKS ORGANIZED, IN LIQUIDATION, AND IN OPERATION, WITH THEIR CAPITAL, BONDS ON DEPOSIT, AND CIRCULATION ISSUED, REDEEMED, AND OUTSTANDING ON OCTOBER 31, 1887.

States and Territories.	Banks.			Capital stock paid in.	U. S. bonds on deposit.	Circulation.		
	Organized.	In liquidation.	In operation.			Issued.	Redeemed.	Outstanding.*
Maine	83	10	73	$10,335,000	$5,540,930	$34,456,960	$26,726,751	$7,730,209
New Hampshire	54	5	49	6,205,000	4,107,300	21,878,125	17,188,657	3,689,468
Vermont	63	14	49	7,566,000	3,668,400	30,271,420	25,404,487	4,866,933
Massachusetts	266	15	251	95,940,500	34,557,800	292,532,485	240,305,630	52,226,855
Rhode Island	64	3	61	20,340,050	4,596,800	61,579,095	51,181,338	10,397,757
Connecticut	96	13	83	24,644,370	10,245,750	81,079,940	66,652,513	15,427,427
Eastern States	626	60	566	165,030,920	62,717,000	521,798,025	427,459,376	94,338,649
New York	425	101	324	86,339,760	30,387,200	264,357,365	226,185,206	38,172,159
New Jersey	92	11	81	13,025,120	7,013,100	48,182,500	40,059,693	8,122,807
Pennsylvania	354	51	303	66,607,990	19,098,500	184,819,465	148,236,096	36,583,369
Delaware	17	....	17	2,083,985	1,682,700	6,358,825	4,884,648	1,474,177
Maryland	51	3	48	14,509,960	2,062,450	36,598,780	29,974,776	6,624,004
Dist. Columbia	13	5	8	1,827,000	1,010,000	4,903,900	4,102,800	801,100
Middle States	952	171	781	184,393,815	61,853,950	545,220,835	453,443,129	91,777,706
Virginia	39	14	25	3,796,300	1,551,350	11,605,630	9,602,886	2,002,744
West Virginia	27	7	20	2,061,000	628,900	7,140,480	5,922,688	1,217,792
North Carolina	21	3	18	2,426,000	863,500	6,218,760	5,161,590	1,057,170
South Carolina	17	2	15	1,749,200	692,250	5,330,255	4,515,772	814,483
Georgia	27	6	21	3,070,520	888,500	7,763,670	6,324,053	1,439,617
Florida	12	2	10	550,000	217,500	319,450	160,387	159,063
Alabama	23	3	20	3,484,000	851,000	4,803,080	3,654,647	1,148,433
Mississippi	14	2	12	1,055,000	320,000	443,730	183,899	259,831
Louisiana	17	4	13	3,425,000	1,418,800	10,303,910	8,171,649	2,132,261
Texas	97	6	91	10,041,000	2,417,800	5,603,980	3,255,986	2,347,994
Arkansas	10	3	7	950,000	422,500	1,190,120	820,437	369,683
Kentucky	81	13	68	13,200,400	3,925,000	33,132,245	25,918,940	7,213,305
Tennessee	56	16	40	7,485,000	1,594,250	10,618,300	8,567,007	2,051,293
Southern States	441	81	360	53,296,420	15,701,350	104,482,610	82,268,941	22,213,669
Missouri	77	27	50	11,826,000	1,412,050	16,395,665	13,803,212	2,592,453
Ohio	298	82	216	41,058,120	15,219,950	96,277,840	75,411,112	20,866,728
Indiana	152	59	93	11,704,500	5,046,800	49,870,755	42,109,198	7,761,557
Illinois	243	65	178	29,286,500	5,848,500	49,059,165	41,344,028	7,715,137
Michigan	149	41	108	14,546,050	3,114,750	26,919,810	22,276,128	4,643,682
Wisconsin	89	32	57	5,210,000	1,680,500	12,164,100	9,875,260	2,288,840
Iowa	176	47	129	10,132,300	2,856,000	20,965,710	16,993,900	3,971,810
Minnesota	76	18	58	13,753,700	2,112,950	11,372,770	9,157,334	2,215,436
Kansas	162	21	141	10,952,520	2,818,000	6,799,070	4,085,567	2,713,503
Nebraska	110	6	104	8,415,550	1,945,000	5,360,730	3,330,716	2,030,014
Western States	1,532	398	1,134	156,835,240	42,054,500	295,185,615	238,385,455	56,799,160
Nevada	3	1	2	150,000	36,500	200,720	183,693	17,027
Oregon	23	....	23	1,840,000	644,800	1,426,120	755,630	670,490
Colorado	40	9	31	2,755,400	926,500	4,114,260	3,045,846	1,068,414
Utah	10	3	7	850,000	390,000	1,465,910	1,064,885	401,025
Idaho	6	....	6	350,000	92,800	394,670	306,415	88,255
Montana	22	5	17	2,000,000	500,600	1,583,790	1,112,186	471,604
Wyoming	8	....	8	1,075,000	273,750	454,380	283,755	170,625
New Mexico	10	1	9	850,000	270,000	1,384,530	1,023,607	360,923
Dakota	69	7	62	3,775,000	992,500	1,914,190	918,411	995,779
Washington	23	3	20	1,475,000	317,500	1,013,340	447,622	565,718
Arizona	4	3	1	100,000	25,000	88,790	51,230	37,560
California	36	3	33	6,875,000	1,941,250	3,189,690	1,460,965	1,728,725
Pacific States & Territories	254	35	219	22,055,400	6,411,200	17,230,390	10,684,245	6,546,145
Add for mutilated notes	....	....	....	....	....	....	....	125,945
Total currency banks	....	....	....	....	....	1,483,917,475	1,212,242,146	271,675,329
Add gold banks	....	....	....	....	....	3,465,240	3,225,311	239,929
United States	3,805	†715	†3,060	581,611,795	188,828,000	1,487,382,715	1,215,467,457	272,041,203

* Including $102,826,136 for which lawful money has been deposited with the Treasurer of the United States to retire an equal amount of circulation which has not been presented for redemption.

† One bank restored to solvency and resumed business, making total going banks 3,061.

NATIONAL-BANK CURRENCY ISSUED, REDEEMED, AND OUTSTANDING FOR THE YEAR ENDING OCTOBER 31, 1887.

Denomination of notes on each plate.	Amount.	Total.	Ones.	Twos.	Fives.	Tens.	Twenties.	Fifties.	One hundreds.	Five hundreds.	One thousands.
Issued, including those canceled:											
$20—$20—$20—$50	$196,350						$107,100	$89,250			
$20—$20—$20—$20	61,000						61,000				
$10—$10—$20—$50	1,170					$260	260	650			
$50—$50	33,600							33,600			
$100—$100	9,000								$9,000		
$5—$5—$5—$5	14,128,120				$14,128,120						
$10—$10—$10—$10	397,720					397,720					
$10—$10—$10—$20	17,852,750					10,711,650	7,141,100				
$50—$100	5,007,450							1,669,150	3,338,300		
Totals		$37,690,160.00			14,128,120	11,109,630	7,312,460	1,792,650	3,347,300		
Canceled: *											
$5—$5—$5—$5	187,300				187,300						
$10—$10—$10—$20	341,900					205,140	136,760				
$10—$10—$10—$10	236,200					236,200					
$20—$20—$20—$50	119,460						65,160	54,300			
$50—$100	49,200							16,400	32,800		
Totals		934,060.00			187,300	441,340	201,920	70,700	32,800		
Actual issues to banks from October 31, 1886, to November 1, 1887		36,756,100.00			13,940,820	10,668,290	7,110,540	1,721,950	3,314,500		
Total issues to banks prior to November 1, 1886		1,447,161,375.00	$23,167,677	$15,495,038	488,336,800	416,959,700	258,912,360	90,758,700	134,200,100	$11,962,000	$7,369,000
Total issues to banks since organization		1,483,917,475.00	23,167,677	15,495,038	502,277,620	427,627,990	266,022,900	92,480,650	137,514,600	11,962,000	7,369,000
Total redeemed and destroyed		1,212,265,888.00	22,776,403	15,293,440	425,854,095	337,999,280	201,838,820	76,807,150	112,745,200	11,646,500	7,305,000
Total whole notes outstanding		271,651,587.00	391,274	201,598	76,423,525	89,628,710	64,184,080	15,673,560	24,769,400	315,500	64,000
Total fractions outstanding		23,742.60									
Total national-bank currency outstanding †		271,675,329.60									

* National-bank currency canceled is such as has never been issued, but is left on hand in the vaults in this office by banks which extend their corporate existence, fail, or go into voluntary liquidation.

† Exclusive of gold notes, $239,929; amount due banks for mutilated notes, $125,945.

NUMBER AND DENOMINATIONS OF NATIONAL-BANK NOTES ISSUED AND REDEEMED AND THE NUMBER OF EACH DENOMINATION OUTSTANDING, ON OCTOBER 31, IN EACH YEAR FROM 1868 TO 1887.

	Ones.	Twos.	Fives.	Tens.	Twenties.	Fifties.	One hundreds.	Five hundreds.	One thousands.
1868.									
Issued	8, 896, 576	2, 078, 160	23, 106, 728	7, 915, 914	2, 219, 322	355, 181	267, 350	13, 486	4, 743
Redeemed	254, 754	73, 176	482, 132	142, 359	36, 355	17, 256	15, 583	1, 759	1, 846
Outstanding	8, 641, 822	2, 004, 984	22, 624, 596	7, 773, 555	2, 182, 967	337, 925	251, 767	11, 727	2, 900
1869.									
Issued	9, 589, 160	3, 209, 388	23, 676, 760	8, 094, 645	2, 269, 764	363, 523	274, 799	13, 668	4, 769
Redeemed	904, 013	232, 224	985, 940	272, 495	71, 655	22, 859	25, 968	2, 585	2, 415
Outstanding	8, 685, 147	2, 977, 164	22, 690, 820	7, 821, 150	2, 198, 109	334, 664	248, 831	11, 083	2, 354
1870.									
Issued	10, 729, 327	3, 590, 157	24, 636, 720	8, 413, 244	2, 370, 056	378, 482	284, 460	13, 926	4, 779
Redeemed	2, 568, 703	667, 733	1, 737, 983	484, 135	129, 185	47, 845	43, 599	3, 952	3, 263
Outstanding	8, 160, 624	2, 922, 424	22, 898, 737	7, 929, 109	2, 240, 871	330, 637	240, 861	9, 974	1, 516
1871.									
Issued	12, 537, 657	4, 195, 791	28, 174, 940	9, 728, 375	2, 779, 392	433, 426	321, 163	14, 642	4, 843
Redeemed	5, 276, 057	1, 493, 326	6, 276, 374	933, 445	245, 361	82, 972	76, 287	6, 017	4, 005
Outstanding	7, 261, 606	2, 702, 465	21, 898, 566	8, 794, 930	2, 534, 031	350, 454	244, 876	8, 625	838
1872.									
Issued	14, 297, 360	4, 782, 628	31, 033, 348	11, 253, 452	3, 225, 688	497, 190	367, 797	15, 621	4, 933
Redeemed	7, 919, 389	2, 408, 389	5, 960, 667	1, 699, 702	438, 852	126, 180	110, 989	7, 867	4, 315
Outstanding	6, 377, 971	2, 374, 239	25, 072, 681	9, 553, 750	2, 786, 836	371, 010	256, 808	7, 754	618
1873.									
Issued	15, 524, 189	5, 195, 111	34, 894, 456	12, 560, 799	3, 608, 219	559, 722	416, 590	16, 496	5, 148
Redeemed	9, 891, 606	3, 120, 723	9, 141, 963	2, 573, 070	653, 071	168, 976	144, 057	9, 658	4, 530
Outstanding	5, 632, 583	2, 074, 388	25, 752, 493	9, 987, 329	2, 955, 148	390, 746	272, 533	6, 838	618
1874.									
Issued	16, 548, 259	5, 539, 113	39, 243, 136	13, 337, 076	3, 962, 109	666, 950	492, 482	17, 344	5, 240
Redeemed	11, 143, 606	3, 555, 019	13, 041, 605	3, 912, 707	1, 171, 608	231, 556	196, 572	11, 676	4, 683
Outstanding	5, 404, 653	1, 984, 094	26, 201, 531	9, 424, 369	2, 790, 501	435, 394	295, 910	5, 668	557
1875.									
Issued	18, 046, 176	6, 039, 752	47, 055, 184	17, 410, 507	5, 296, 064	884, 165	645, 838	18, 476	5, 530
Redeemed	14, 092, 126	4, 616, 623	24, 926, 771	7, 608, 532	2, 204, 464	381, 037	299, 428	14, 471	5, 048
Outstanding	3, 954, 050	1, 423, 129	22, 128, 413	9, 801, 975	3, 091, 600	503, 128	346, 410	4, 005	482
1876.									
Issued	18, 849, 264	6, 307, 448	51, 783, 528	20, 008, 652	6, 086, 492	985, 615	710, 900	18, 721	5, 539
Redeemed	15, 556, 708	5, 124, 546	32, 382, 056	10, 369, 214	3, 052, 246	515, 784	395, 785	16, 217	5, 272
Outstanding	3, 292, 556	1, 182, 902	19, 401, 472	9, 639, 438	3, 034, 246	469, 831	315, 115	2, 504	267
1877.									
Issued	20, 616, 024	6, 896, 968	56, 816, 848	22, 266, 064	6, 776, 253	1, 079, 781	767, 317	20, 022	5, 668
Redeemed	16, 815, 568	5, 555, 526	38, 115, 868	12, 434, 779	3, 703, 528	634, 679	479, 317	17, 615	5, 411
Outstanding	3, 800, 456	1, 341, 442	18, 700, 980	9, 831, 285	3, 072, 725	445, 102	288, 000	2, 407	257
1878.									
Issued	22, 478, 415	7, 517, 765	61, 191, 288	24, 157, 293	7, 344, 167	1, 147, 578	812, 903	20, 210	6, 204
Redeemed	18, 194, 196	6, 026, 692	42, 683, 433	13, 859, 149	4, 133, 178	728, 222	541, 859	18, 895	5, 900
Outstanding	4, 284, 219	1, 491, 073	18, 507, 855	10, 298, 144	3, 210, 989	419, 356	271, 044	1, 315	304
1879.									
Issued	23, 167, 677	7, 747, 519	65, 578, 440	25, 004, 223	7, 869, 951	1, 211, 701	850, 720	20, 570	6, 340
Redeemed	19, 600, 477	6, 501, 270	45, 996, 076	14, 930, 599	4, 437, 343	785, 263	581, 604	19, 287	6, 057
Outstanding	3, 567, 200	1, 246, 249	19, 582, 364	10, 073, 624	3, 432, 608	426, 408	269, 116	1, 283	283
1880.									
Issued	23, 167, 677	7, 747, 519	60, 131, 976	27, 203, 168	8, 266, 398	1, 253, 866	879, 490	20, 763	6, 363
Redeemed	20, 875, 215	6, 913, 889	49, 149, 824	15, 821, 110	4, 684, 820	825, 499	610, 601	19, 484	6, 124
Outstanding	2, 292, 462	863, 650	19, 982, 152	11, 382, 058	3, 581, 578	428, 366	268, 889	1, 279	239

NUMBER AND DENOMINATIONS OF NATIONAL-BANK NOTES ISSUED AND REDEEMED AND THE NUMBER OF EACH DENOMINATION OUTSTANDING, ETC.—Continued.

	Ones.	Twos.	Fives.	Tens.	Twenties.	Fifties.	One hundreds.	Five hundreds.	One thousands.
1881.									
Issued	23, 167, 677	7, 747, 519	73, 612, 504	29, 477, 519	8, 940, 817	1, 357, 574	959, 712	21, 959	7, 144
Redeemed......	21, 838, 565	7, 286, 434	53, 516, 488	17, 346, 635	5, 084, 992	891, 80[illegible]	660, 202	20, 495	6, 943
Outstanding.	1, 329, 112	461, 085	20, 096, 016	12, 130, 884	3, 855, 825	465, 084	299, 510	1, 464	201
1882.									
Issued	23, 167, 677	7, 747, 519	78, 697, 424	32, 042, 260	9, 751, 784	1, 453, 324	1, 035, 118	22, 787	7, 187
Redeemed......	22, 353, 877	7, 484, 149	59, 313, 238	19, 770, 934	5, 751, 707	980, 182	719, 130	20, 880	6, 990
Outstanding.	813, 800	263, 370	19, 384, 191	12, 271, 326	4, 000, 077	473, 142	315, 988	1, 907	197
1883.									
Issued.........	23, 167, 677	7, 747, 519	83, 447, 208	34, 544, 086	10, 578, 846	1, 556, 000	1, 114, 722	23, 163	7, 277
Redeemed......	22, 593, 909	7, 570, 903	65, 142, 567	22, 712, 355	6, 424, 638	1, 090, 703	789, 125	21, 367	7, 092
Outstanding.	573, 768	176, 616	18, 304, 641	11, 831, 731	4, 154, 208	465, 306	325, 597	1, 796	185
1884.									
Issued.........	23, 167, 677	7, 747, 519	88, 101, 188	37, 182, 102	11, 442, 091	1, 661, 010	1, 199, 750	23, 736	7, 369
Redeemed......	22, 671, 936	7, 603, 285	71, 039, 357	26, 050, 107	7, 481, 762	1, 216, 573	874, 543	21, 981	7, 156
Outstanding.	495, 741	144, 234	17, 061, 831	11, 131, 995	3, 960, 329	444, 437	325, 207	1, 755	213
1885.									
Issued.........	23, 167, 677	7, 747, 519	93, 208, 400	39, 804, 001	12, 318, 173	1, 758, 533	1, 287, 686	23, 924	7, 369
Redeemed......	22, 731, 963	7, 628, 877	76, 817, 066	29, 382, 872	8, 563, 797	1, 345, 762	971, 922	22, 727	7, 238
Outstanding	435, 714	118, 642	16, 391, 334	10, 421, 129	3, 754, 376	412, 771	315, 764	1, 197	131
1886.									
Issued.........	23, 167, 677	7, 747, 519	97, 667, 360	41, 695, 970	12, 945, 618	1,815, 174	1, 342, 001	23, 924	7, 369
Redeemed	22, 757, 987	7, 639, 806	81, 109, 272	31, 767, 278	9, 397, 854	1, 451, 301	1, 055, 330	23, 138	7, 290
Outstanding.	409, 690	107, 713	16, 558, 088	9, 928, 692	3, 547, 764	363, 873	286, 671	786	79
1887.									
Issued..	23, 167, 677	7, 747, 519	100, 455, 524	42, 762, 799	13, 301, 145	1, 849, 618	1, 375, 146	23, 924	7, 369
Redeemed......	22, 776, 403	7, 646, 720	85, 170, 819	33, 799, 928	10, 091, 941	1, 536, 148	1, 127, 452	23, 293	7, 305
Outstanding.	391, 274	100, 799	15, 284, 705	8, 962, 871	3, 209, 204	313, 470	247, 694	631	64

STATEMENT OF MONTHLY INCREASE OR DECREASE OF NATIONAL-BANK CIRCULATION FOR THE YEAR ENDING OCTOBER 31, 1887, PRECEDED BY QUARTERLY IN- OR DECREASE SINCE JANUARY 14, 1875.

	National-bank circulation.		Increase.	Decrease.
	Issued.	Retired.		
From January 14 to 31, 1875	$537,580	$255,000	$281,080	
For quarter ending—				
April 30, 1875	4,409,220	3,336,804	1,072,416	
July 31, 1875	4,124,165	5,423,930		$1,299,765
October 31, 1875	1,915,710	5,553,971		3,638,261
January 31, 1876	2,504,600	3,852,731		1,348,131
April 30, 1875	877,580	5,425,530		4,547,950
July 31, 1876	1,107,110	9,663,984		8,556,874
October 31, 1876	2,604,390	8,564,727		5,960,337
January 31, 1877	3,188,630	4,759,015		1,570,385
April 30, 1877	4,363,010	5,005,596		642,586
July 31, 1877	3,000,230	4,984,339		1,984,109
October 31, 1877	5,754,160	3,516,321	2,237,839	
January 31, 1878	6,725,585	2,701,885	4,023,700	
April 30, 1878	3,036,760	1,906,721	1,130,039	
July 31, 1878	4,252,980	3,455,080	797,900	
October 31, 1878	2,276,360	2,924,430		648,070
January 31, 1879	3,097,060	747,327	2,349,733	
April 30, 1879	7,039,300	1,822,988	5,216,312	
July 31, 1879	3,674,830	2,715,524	959,306	
October 31, 1879	9,122,300	1,754,558	7,367,742	
January 31, 1880	7,289,805	674,129	6,615,676	
April 30, 1880	3,163,820	1,555,766	1,608,054	
July 31, 1880	1,748,660	2,427,398		678,738
October 31, 1880	1,199,930	1,535,760		335,830
January 31, 1881	2,234,780	1,361,534	873,246	
April 30, 1881	12,690,890	4,426,596	8,264,294	
July 31, 1881	9,569,410	4,734,578	4,834,832	
October 31, 1881	6,481,550	3,182,551	3,301,909	
January 31, 1882	5,625,200	3,354,153	2,271,047	
April 30, 1882	2,991,400	4,414,865		1,423,465
July 31, 1882	4,054,740	5,741,450		1,686,710
October 31, 1882	9,792,910	5,611,497	4,181,413	
January 31, 1883	4,588,850	4,927,020		338,170
April 30, 1883	3,638,650	6,510,245		2,871,595
July 31, 1883	3,527,100	6,868,245		3,341,145
October 31, 1883	2,755,600	6,369,273		3,613,673
January 31, 1884	2,748,270	5,172,714		2,424,444
April 30, 1884	2,052,294	8,430,804		6,378,510
July 31, 1884	2,778,960	7,883,997		5,105,037
October 31, 1884	2,792,170	6,833,874		4,041,704
January 31, 1885	1,265,520	7,842,055		6,576,535
April 30, 1885	2,125,260	8,135,112		6,009,852
July 31, 1885	2,160,110	5,731,673		3,571,563
October 31, 1885	5,591,760	6,758,154		1,166,394
January 31, 1886	7,751,794	5,581,261	2,170,533	
April 30, 1886	4,700,384	8,397,163		3,696,779
July 31, 1886	1,469,325	8,425,486		6,956,161
October 31, 1886	1,566,700	6,468,227		4,901,527
	191,970,402	227,724,716	59,560,061	95,314,375
November, 1886	414,905	2,559,454		2,144,549
December, 1886	369,765	2,896,759		2,526,994
January, 1887	431,880	4,094,760		3,662,880
February, 1887	447,500	4,472,480		4,024,980
March, 1887	1,649,890	3,565,077		1,915,187
April, 1887	864,325	2,976,500		2,112,175
May, 1887	674,500	3,315,544		2,641,044
June, 1887	1,657,890	4,765,824		3,107,934
July, 1887	604,280	3,226,350		2,622,070
August, 1887	999,510	3,185,093		2,185,583
September, 1887	1,435,040	2,798,550		1,363,510
October, 1887	1,586,800	2,437,886		851,086
	11,163,345	40,324,277		29,160,932
Total	203,133,747	268,048,993	59,560,061	124,475,307
Surrendered to this office and retired from January 14, 1875, to October 31, 1887		15,477,733		15,477,733
Grand total	203,133,747	283,526,726	59,560,061	139,953,040

TABLE SHOWING, BY STATES, THE AMOUNT OF NATIONAL BANK CIRCULATION ISSUED, THE AMOUNT OF LAWFUL MONEY DEPOSITED IN THE UNITED STATES TREASURY TO RETIRE NATIONAL-BANK CIRCULATION FROM JUNE 20, 1874, TO NOVEMBER 1, 1887, AND THE AMOUNT REMAINING ON DEPOSIT AT THE LATTER DATE.

States and Territories.	Additional circulation issued since June 20, 1874.	Lawful money deposited to retire national-bank circulation since June 20, 1874.				Lawful money on deposit with the United States Treasurer at date.
		For redemption of notes of liquidating banks.	To retire circulation under act of July 12, 1882.	To retire circulation under act of June 20, 1874.	Total deposits.	
Maine	$2,728,480	$786,500	$1,909,615	$2,923,350	$5,079,465	$2,725,664
New Hampshire	1,473,905	465,983	818,650	1,230,750	2,515,383	1,060,976
Vermont	3,244,915	1,050,277	1,293,745	4,112,310	6,465,332	1,867,879
Massachusetts	34,192,920	1,886,185	20,472,888	39,107,424	61,466,496	21,722,568
Rhode Island	4,191,650	222,750	4,738,955	7,706,120	12,667,825	5,711,173
Connecticut	6,872,760	948,381	4,991,742	9,581,142	15,521,265	5,919,887
New York	39,411,595	8,383,393	10,556,800	47,120,535	66,060,728	19,999,976
New Jersey	4,815,185	1,389,908	1,806,722	6,476,843	9,673,473	2,141,560
Pennsylvania	26,242,120	4,349,115	13,913,280	30,959,557	49,221,953	18,973,877
Delaware	604,225	....	159,320	231,750	391,070	126,107
Maryland	2,931,910	166,000	2,994,000	5,209,810	8,371,310	3,333,505
District of Columbia	502,000	455,604	....	665,000	1,120,724	56,712
Virginia	1,599,250	1,028,210	551,280	2,162,630	3,742,120	831,378
West Virginia	474,604	829,200	475,485	776,490	2,081,265	510,400
North Carolina	1,380,550	290,900	....	1,969,135	2,260,035	189,230
South Carolina	246,030	22,500	84,170	1,091,695	1,798,365	261,268
Georgia	851,530	330,925	395,550	1,428,575	2,155,050	551,466
Florida	191,350	19,210	....	7,790	27,000	17,955
Alabama	651,330	135,000	45,000	1,013,320	1,193,320	316,496
Mississippi	326,240	....	....	38,150	38,150	1,301
Louisiana	2,553,490	666,413	789,850	3,109,400	4,565,663	689,999
Texas	2,594,755	135,830	30,290	992,400	1,158,520	180,366
Arkansas	500,750	11,250	....	312,750	324,000	33,919
Kentucky	6,607,500	1,070,417	1,100,840	8,037,953	10,209,210	3,429,974
Tennessee	1,797,320	854,191	151,920	2,160,451	3,166,565	924,883
Missouri	3,363,055	1,230,185	360,170	5,693,100	7,283,455	735,385
Ohio	10,857,755	6,902,758	4,108,391	15,645,212	26,656,361	6,056,896
Indiana	7,661,700	5,088,610	837,000	11,038,361	16,964,880	3,283,751
Illinois	7,094,420	3,074,854	1,251,085	11,561,121	16,487,060	2,546,747
Michigan	4,747,030	2,811,293	280,440	5,324,442	8,416,175	1,493,267
Wisconsin	2,526,200	1,219,990	482,770	2,350,769	4,053,529	610,661
Iowa	4,102,379	1,077,566	393,750	4,555,745	6,027,061	1,181,847
Minnesota	2,228,035	862,079	353,800	2,482,081	3,697,960	462,211
Kansas	2,696,200	848,191	15,750	883,670	1,747,611	239,388
Nebraska	2,215,210	93,670	194,800	1,137,330	1,425,800	377,670
Nevada	47,250	....	....	13,500	13,500	1,583
Oregon	438,610	....	....	83,310	83,310	53,390
Colorado	1,272,140	347,475	186,490	428,310	962,275	198,579
Utah	488,150	161,191	....	379,050	540,241	37,909
Idaho	67,750	....	....	74,250	74,250	15,989
Montana	631,070	189,940	....	272,250	462,190	21,850
Wyoming	157,225	....	....	15,750	15,750	170
New Mexico	247,500	15,500	....	285,200	300,700	164,080
Dakota	1,231,365	100,000	....	295,905	396,565	99,482
Washington	759,740	40,500	....	304,850	345,350	43,578
Arizona	75,590	50,500	....	2,500	53,000	15,690
California	2,411,340	90,000	....	647,650	737,650	179,590
Lawful money deposited prior to June 20, 1874, and remaining at that date	....	....	....	....	3,813,675	....
Total	*207,868,247	50,922,953	75,806,357	242,480,749	373,032,734	102,586,207

* This includes circulation issued under act July 12, 1882.

STATEMENT SHOWING THE AMOUNT OF NATIONAL-BANK NOTES OUTSTANDING ON OCTOBER 31, 1887, THE AMOUNT OF LAWFUL MONEY ON DEPOSIT WITH THE TREASURER OF THE UNITED STATES TO REDEEM NATIONAL-BANK NOTES, AND THE KINDS AND AMOUNTS OF UNITED STATES BONDS ON DEPOSIT TO SECURE CIRCULATION AND PUBLIC DEPOSITS.

NATIONAL-BANK NOTES.		
Total amount outstanding October 1, 1887		$272, 652, 501
Additional circulation issued during the intervening month:		
To new banks	$238, 520	
To banks increasing circulation	1, 348, 280	
Total	1, 586, 800	
Surrendered and destroyed during the intervening month	2, 438, 027	
Decrease in total circulation during the month		851, 227
Total amount outstanding, November 1, 1887 *		271, 801, 274
Decrease in total circulation during the preceding twelve months	29, 432, 546	
Circulation secured by U. S. bonds (as below)		169, 215, 067
Decrease during the preceding month	716, 613	
Decrease during the preceding twelve months	50, 495, 589	
Amount of outstanding circulation represented by lawful money on deposit with the Treasurer of the United States, to redeem notes of—		
Insolvent national banks	958, 902	
Liquidating national banks	7, 792, 493	
National banks reducing circulation under section 4 of the act of June 20, 1874	48, 756, 970	
National banks retiring circulation under section 6, act of July 12, 1882	45, 077, 842	
Total lawful money on deposit		102, 586, 207
Decrease in aggregate deposit during the preceding month	134, 614	
Increase in aggregate deposit during the preceding twelve months	21, 063, 043	

	To secure circulating notes.	To secure public deposits.†
U. S. REGISTERED BONDS ON DEPOSIT.		
Pacific Railroad bonds, 6 per cents	$3, 256, 000	$425, 000
Funded loan of 1891, 4½ per cents	69, 696, 100	9, 965, 500
Funded loan of 1907, 4 per cents	115, 731, 400	22, 684, 000
Funded loan of 1882, 3 per cents	144, 500	550, 000
Totals	188, 828, 000	33, 624, 500

*Circulation of national gold banks not included in the above, $239,020.
†Amounting to $31,767,478.

TABLE, BY STATES, TERRITORIES, AND RESERVE CITIES, EXHIBITING THE NUMBER OF BANKS IN EACH, WITH THEIR CAPITAL, MINIMUM AMOUNT OF BONDS REQUIRED BY LAW, BONDS ACTUALLY HELD AND CIRCULATION OUTSTANDING THEREON ON OCTOBER 5, 1887.

States, Territories, and reserve cities.	No of banks.	Capital.	United States bonds.		Circulation outstanding October 5, 1887.
			Minimum required.	Held October 5, 1887.	
Maine	72	$10,440,700	$2,227,500	$5,483,500	$4,875,561
New Hampshire	49	6,205,000	1,501,250	4,019,500	3,588,015
Vermont	49	7,506,000	1,541,500	8,801,000	3,478,100
Massachusetts	198	41,799,500	8,144,375	24,061,250	21,459,690
Boston	54	50,950,000	2,700,000	9,908,150	8,851,502
Rhode Island	61	20,340,050	2,453,250	5,183,000	4,642,918
Connecticut	83	24,505,410	3,501,085	9,716,100	8,608,693
Division No. 1	566	104,797,660	22,068,960	62,266,400	55,507,474
New York	269	34,724,200	7,682,700	19,468,550	17,406,488
New York City	47	49,150,000	2,337,500	9,695,000	8,295,502
Albany	6	1,750,000	300,000	1,148,000	1,016,400
New Jersey	81	13,024,220	2,608,535	16,874,600	6,060,523
Pennsylvania	237	33,551,140	7,129,042	15,198,800	13,379,865
Philadelphia	43	22,638,000	2,137,500	2,737,500	2,401,149
Pittsburgh	23	10,180,000	1,125,000	1,765,500	1,569,260
Division No. 2	706	165,037,620	23,315,387	56,887,950	50,120,277
Delaware	17	2,084,085	442,700	1,596,700	1,415,860
Maryland	31	2,706,700	680,250	1,517,000	1,332,140
Baltimore	17	11,713,260	850,000	2,050,000	1,822,900
District of Columbia	1	252,000	50,000	250,000	194,180
Washington	7	1,575,000	325,000	680,000	534,805
Virginia	25	3,796,300	760,250	1,352,500	1,204,380
West Virginia	20	1,961,000	501,250	761,250	655,525
Division No. 3	118	24,178,245	3,615,450	8,207,450	7,159,850
North Carolina	18	2,412,280	565,570	928,500	795,710
South Carolina	15	1,698,000	412,000	624,750	559,875
Georgia	21	3,050,520	575,130	988,500	877,650
Florida	8	500,000	125,000	180,500	146,750
Alabama	20	3,485,100	632,625	900,500	782,330
Mississippi	12	1,055,000	263,750	320,000	277,230
Louisiana	5	500,000	125,000	125,000	101,740
New Orleans	8	2,925,000	400,000	1,350,000	1,214,095
Texas	91	9,919,750	2,239,937	2,415,300	2,107,535
Arkansas	7	950,000	225,000	410,000	348,740
Kentucky	59	9,758,000	2,093,475	3,411,000	3,055,890
Louisville	9	3,551,500	450,000	694,000	624,490
Tennessee	40	7,460,000	1,090,000	1,483,750	1,326,895
Division No. 4	313	47,266,050	9,217,387	13,831,800	12,219,830
Ohio	192	22,706,020	5,235,505	10,112,650	9,008,926
Cincinnati	15	10,400,000	750,000	3,612,000	3,226,840
Cleveland	9	6,700,000	450,000	605,000	544,450
Indiana	93	11,804,500	2,616,125	4,723,800	4,217,870
Illinois	160	14,341,500	3,460,375	4,770,500	4,219,305
Chicago	18	15,050,000	900,000	1,050,000	817,150
Michigan	100	10,674,600	2,318,659	3,012,750	2,673,585
Detroit	8	3,883,540	400,000	400,000	328,750
Wisconsin	53	4,442,000	1,098,000	1,373,000	1,225,623
Milwaukee	3	650,000	150,000	300,000	270,000
Division No. 5	651	100,832,160	17,378,653	29,965,700	26,532,490
Iowa	128	10,150,000	2,412,500	3,060,500	2,713,023
Minnesota	58	13,740,000	1,628,750	1,881,050	1,675,725
Missouri	35	2,517,280	620,320	782,750	694,615
Saint Louis	5	3,000,000	250,000	710,000	637,750
Kansas City	8	5,940,000	385,000	400,000	315,000
Saint Joseph	2	300,000	75,000	157,550	119,350
Kansas	139	10,530,800	2,532,700	2,748,250	2,205,210
Nebraska	95	6,006,100	1,476,525	1,504,000	1,345,220
Omaha	8	2,400,000	350,000	350,000	314,500
Division No. 6	478	54,584,180	9,739,795	11,594,100	10,110,993

TABLE, BY STATES, TERRITORIES, AND RESERVE CITIES, EXHIBITING THE NUMBER OF BANKS IN EACH, WITH THEIR CAPITAL, ETC.—Continued.

States, Territories, and reserve cities.	No. of banks.	Capital.	United States bonds.		Circulation outstanding October 5, 1887.
			Minimum required.	Held October 5, 1887.	
Colorado	31	$2,751,850	$662,963	$989,000	$880,330
Nevada	2	150,000	37,500	37,500	33,720
California	30	4,170,000	890,000	1,088,750	939,900
San Francisco	3	2,700,000	150,000	750,000	659,796
Oregon	23	1,795,000	423,750	644,800	506,160
Arizona	1	100,000	25,000	25,000	22,000
Division No. 7	90	11,666,850	2,189,213	3,535,050	3,101,990
Dakota	62	3,720,000	930,000	962,500	801,925
Idaho	6	350,000	87,500	92,800	81,940
Montana	17	1,975,000	406,250	480,000	422,280
New Mexico	9	850,000	212,500	240,000	215,990
Utah	7	850,000	212,500	390,000	202,130
Washington	18	1,280,000	320,000	405,000	356,540
Wyoming	8	1,075,000	218,750	223,750	200,645
Division No. 8	127	10,100,000	2,387,500	2,794,050	2,431,450
United States	3,049	578,462,765	89,912,347	189,083,100	167,283,343

TABLE, BY STATES, TERRITORIES, AND RESERVE CITIES, EXHIBITING THE NUMBER OF BANKS IN EACH WITH CAPITAL OF $150,000 AND UNDER, AND THOSE WITH CAPITAL EXCEEDING $150,000, AND SHOWING THE AMOUNT OF BONDS DEPOSITED TO SECURE CIRCULATION ON OCTOBER 5, 1887.

States, Territories, and reserve cities.	Banks with capital of $150,000 and under.			Banks with capital over $150,000.			Total.		
	No.	Capital.	United States bonds.	No.	Capital.	United States bonds.	No.	Capital.	United States bonds.
Maine	58	$6,110,000	$3,431,500	14	$1,330,700	$2,052,000	72	$10,440,700	$5,483,500
New Hampshire	41	4,405,000	3,069,500	8	1,800,000	950,000	49	6,205,000	4,019,500
Vermont	36	3,566,000	1,896,000	13	4,000,000	1,995,000	49	7,566,000	3,891,000
Massachusetts	86	10,177,500	5,793,850	112	34,613,000	18,270,400	198	44,790,500	24,064,250
Boston	....	......	....	51	50,950,000	9,908,150	51	50,950,000	9,908,150
Rhode Island	26	2,813,000	1,708,900	35	17,527,050	3,475,000	61	20,340,050	5,183,900
Connecticut	29	3,204,340	1,790,500	51	21,301,070	7,925,600	83	24,505,410	9,716,100
Division No. 1	276	30,275,840	17,710,250	290	134,521,820	44,556,150	566	164,797,660	62,266,400
New York	210	18,931,100	11,086,250	59	15,793,100	8,382,800	269	34,724,200	19,468,550
New York City	1	150,000	150,000	46	49,000,000	9,545,000	47	49,150,000	9,695,000
Albany	..	....	.....	6	1,700,000	1,148,000	6	1,700,000	1,148,000
New Jersey	53	4,814,220	2,730,000	28	8,210,000	4,144,000	81	13,024,220	6,874,000
Pennsylvania	178	16,716,170	9,173,800	59	16,834,970	6,025,000	237	33,551,140	15,198,800
Philadelphia	1	150,000	37,500	42	22,508,000	2,700,000	43	22,658,000	2,737,500
Pittsburgh	1	100,000	25,000	22	10,080,000	1,740,500	23	10,180,000	1,765,500
Division No. 2	444	40,861,550	23,203,150	262	124,176,070	33,684,800	706	165,037,620	56,887,950
Delaware	13	970,800	773,500	4	1,113,185	823,200	17	2,083,985	1,596,700
Maryland	28	2,145,000	1,217,000	3	651,700	300,000	31	2,796,700	1,517,000
Baltimore	....	....	....	17	11,713,260	2,050,000	17	11,713,000	2,050,000
District of Columbia	....	....	....	1	252,000	250,000	1	252,000	250,000
Washington	1	100,000	100,000	6	1,475,000	580,000	7	1,575,000	680,000
Virginia	17	1,441,000	452,500	8	2,355,300	900,000	25	3,796,300	1,352,500
West Virginia	18	1,605,000	661,250	2	356,000	100,000	20	1,961,000	761,250
Division No. 3	77	6,261,800	3,204,250	41	17,916,445	5,003,200	118	24,178,245	8,207,450
North Carolina	12	1,062,280	528,500	6	1,350,000	400,000	18	2,412,280	928,500
South Carolina	12	1,048,000	199,750	3	650,000	425,000	15	1,698,000	624,750
Georgia	16	1,300,520	728,500	5	1,750,000	260,000	21	3,050,520	988,500
Florida	8	500,000	180,500	....	....	....	8	500,000	180,500
Alabama	12	1,010,100	330,500	8	2,475,000	530,000	20	3,485,100	860,500
Mississippi	12	1,055,000	320,000	...	....	....	12	1,055,000	320,000
Louisiana	4	300,000	75,000	1	200,000	50,000	5	500,000	125,000
New Orleans	....	....	....	8	2,925,000	1,350,000	8	2,925,000	1,350,000
Texas	79	6,559,750	1,800,300	12	3,360,000	615,000	91	9,919,750	2,415,300
Arkansas	6	700,000	210,000	1	250,000	200,000	7	950,000	410,000
Kentucky	36	3,773,000	1,338,000	23	5,985,000	2,073,000	59	9,758,000	3,411,000
Louisville	....	....	....	9	3,551,500	694,000	9	3,551,500	694,000
Tennessee	29	2,160,000	843,750	11	5,300,000	640,000	40	7,460,000	1,483,750
Division No. 4	226	19,469,550	6,574,800	87	27,796,500	7,257,000	313	47,266,050	13,831,800
Ohio	155	13,542,020	6,387,750	37	9,254,000	3,724,900	192	22,796,020	10,112,650
Cincinnati	....	....	....	15	10,400,000	3,612,000	15	10,400,000	3,612,000
Cleveland	....	....	....	9	6,700,000	605,000	9	6,700,000	605,000
Indiana	72	6,264,500	2,873,800	21	5,630,000	1,850,000	93	11,894,500	4,723,800
Illinois	148	11,441,500	4,026,500	12	2,900,000	750,000	160	14,341,500	4,776,500
Chicago	....	....	....	18	15,050,000	1,050,000	18	15,050,000	1,050,000
Michigan	88	6,874,000	2,407,750	12	3,800,000	605,000	100	10,674,000	3,012,750
Detroit	....	....	....	8	3,883,540	400,000	8	3,883,540	400,000
Wisconsin	49	3,592,000	1,123,000	4	850,000	250,000	53	4,442,000	1,373,000
Milwaukee	....	....	....	3	650,000	300,000	3	650,000	300,000
Division No. 5	512	41,714,020	16,818,800	139	59,117,540	13,146,900	651	100,832,160	29,965,700
Iowa	122	8,450,000	2,760,000	6	1,700,000	300,000	128	10,150,000	3,060,500
Minnesota	39	2,715,000	801,050	19	11,025,000	1,080,000	58	13,740,000	1,881,050
Missouri	34	2,317,280	732,750	1	200,000	50,000	35	2,517,280	782,750
Saint Louis	....	....	....	5	3,000,000	710,000	5	3,000,000	710,000
Kansas City	1	140,000	50,000	7	5,800,000	350,000	8	5,940,000	400,000
Saint Joseph	1	100,000	50,000	1	200,000	107,550	2	300,000	157,550
Kansas	131	8,530,800	2,298,250	8	2,000,000	450,000	139	10,530,800	2,748,250
Nebraska	93	5,506,100	1,404,000	2	500,000	100,000	95	6,006,100	1,504,000
Omaha	2	200,000	50,000	6	2,200,000	300,000	8	2,400,000	350,000
Division No. 6	423	27,959,180	8,146,550	55	26,625,000	3,447,550	478	54,584,180	11,594,100

TABLE, BY STATES, TERRITORIES, AND RESERVE CITIES, EXHIBITING THE NUMBER OF BANKS IN EACH, ETC.—Continued.

States, Territories, and reserve cities.	Banks with capital of $150,000 and under.			Banks with capital over $150,000.			Total.		
	No.	Capital.	United States bonds.	No.	Capital.	United States bonds.	No.	Capital.	United States bonds.
Colorado	26	$1,651,850	$559,000	5	$1,100,000	$430,000	31	$2,751,850	$939,000
Nevada	2	150,000	37,500	...	....	....	2	150,000	37,500
California	21	1,760,000	566,250	9	2,410,000	522,500	30	4,170,000	1,088,750
San Francisco	...	....	....	3	2,700,000	750,000	3	2,700,000	750,000
Oregon	21	1,295,000	344,800	2	500,000	300,000	23	1,795,000	644,800
Arizona	1	100,000	25,000	...	....	....	1	100,000	25,000
Division No. 7	71	4,956,850	1,532,550	19	6,710,000	2,002,500	90	11,666,850	3,535,050
Dakota	62	3,720,000	962,500	...	....	....	62	3,720,000	962,500
Idaho	6	350,000	92,800	...	....	....	6	350,000	92,800
Montana	15	1,225,000	330,600	2	750,000	150,000	17	1,975,000	480,600
New Mexico	9	850,000	240,000	...	....	....	9	850,000	240,000
Utah	5	450,000	140,000	2	400,000	250,000	7	850,000	390,000
Washington	18	1,280,000	405,000	...	....	....	18	1,280,000	405,000
Wyoming	6	475,000	123,750	2	600,000	100,000	8	1,075,000	223,750
Division No. 8	121	8,350,000	2,294,650	6	1,750,000	500,000	127	10,100,000	2,794,650
United States	2,150	170,849,390	70,485,000	899	398,613,375	109,598,100	3,049	578,462,765	180 083,100

TABLE, BY STATES, TERRITORIES, AND RESERVE CITIES, EXHIBITING THE NUMBER OF BANKS IN EACH WITH CAPITAL OF $250,000 AND UNDER, AND SHOWING THE AMOUNT OF BONDS DEPOSITED TO SECURE CIRCULATION ON OCTOBER 5, 1887, AMOUNT OF BONDS REQUIRED BY PROPOSED CODE, AND AMOUNT OF BONDS WHICH MIGHT BE WITHDRAWN UPON ADOPTION OF CODE.

States, Territories, and reserve cities.	No. of banks.	Capital.	United States bonds to secure circulation October 5, 1887.	Amount of bonds required to be held under the proposed code.	Amount of bonds that may be withdrawn upon adoption of the code.
Maine	64	$6,410,000	$4,111,500	$641,000	$3,470,500
New Hampshire	47	5,605,000	3,769,500	566,500	3,203,000
Vermont	41	4,606,000	2,510,000	460,600	2,049,400
Massachusetts	148	23,400,500	12,952,000	2,340,050	10,611,950
Boston	5	1,100,000	250,000	110,000	140,000
Rhode Island	35	4,613,250	2,558,900	461,325	2,094,575
Connecticut	40	7,477,210	4,367,500	747,721	3,619,779
Division No. 1	380	53,301,960	30,555,400	5,330,196	25,225,204
New York	251	27,422,260	14,959,550	2,742,226	12,217,324
New York City	6	1,250,000	940,000	125,000	815,000
Albany	3	650,000	348,000	65,000	283,000
New Jersey	60	8,214,220	4,543,600	821,422	3,722,178
Pennsylvania	200	22,981,170	11,913,800	2,298,117	9,615,683
Philadelphia	12	2,008,000	587,500	200,800	326,700
Pittsburgh	8	1,630,000	810,500	163,000	647,500
Division No. 2	558	64,755,650	34,102,950	6,475,565	27,627,385
Delaware	16	1,583,985	1,226,700	158,398	1,068,302
Maryland	30	2,545,000	1,467,000	254,500	1,212,500
Baltimore	1	230,000	50,000	23,000	27,000
District of Columbia	......	......	......	......	......
Washington	5	975,000	480,000	97,500	382,500
Virginia	22	2,496,300	1,152,500	249,630	902,870
West Virginia	20	1,961,000	761,250	196,100	565,150
Division No. 3	94	9,791,285	5,137,450	979,128	4,158,322
North Carolina	17	2,112,280	828,500	211,228	617,272
South Carolina	15	1,698,000	624,750	169,800	454,950
Georgia	19	2,050,520	878,000	205,052	672,948
Florida	8	500,000	180,500	50,000	130,500
Alabama	16	1,985,100	550,500	198,510	351,990
Mississippi	12	1,055,000	320,000	105,500	214,500
Louisiana	5	500,000	125,000	50,000	75,000
New Orleans	1	200,000	200,000	20,000	180,000
Texas	85	7,704,750	2,115,300	770,475	1,335,825
Arkansas	7	950,000	410,000	95,000	315,000
Kentucky	53	7,408,900	2,541,000	740,890	1,800,110
Louisville	......	......	......	......	......
Tennessee	34	3,260,000	1,183,750	326,000	857,750
Division No. 4	272	29,514,550	9,957,300	2,951,455	7,005,845
Ohio	178	17,986,020	7,976,300	1,798,602	6,177,698
Cincinnati	3	650,000	150,000	65,000	85,000
Cleveland	1	200,000	50,000	20,000	30,000
Indiana	85	9,044,500	4,223,800	904,450	3,319,350
Illinois	150	14,041,500	4,726,500	1,404,150	3,322,350
Chicago	5	1,050,000	400,000	105,000	295,000
Michigan	95	8,274,600	2,762,750	827,460	1,935,290
Detroit	1	200,000	50,000	20,000	30,000
Wisconsin	53	4,442,000	1,373,000	444,200	928,800
Milwaukee	3	650,000	300,000	65,000	235,000
Division No. 5	583	56,538,620	22,012,350	5,653,862	16,358,488
Iowa	126	9,250,000	2,960,500	925,000	2,035,500
Minnesota	46	4,240,000	1,146,050	424,000	722,050
Missouri	35	2,517,280	782,750	251,728	531,022
Saint Louis	......	......	......	......	......
Kansas City	3	590,000	150,000	59,000	91,000
Saint Joseph	2	300,000	157,550	30,000	127,550
Kansas	137	9,930,800	2,648,250	993,080	1,655,170
Nebraska	94	5,706,100	1,454,000	570,610	883,390
Omaha	4	700,000	150,000	70,000	80,000
Division No. 6	447	33,234,180	9,449,100	3,323,418	6,125,682

TABLE, BY STATES, TERRITORIES, AND RESERVE CITIES, EXHIBITING THE NUMBER OF BANKS IN EACH WITH CAPITAL OF $250,000 AND UNDER, ETC.—Continued.

States, Territories, and reserve cities.	No. of banks.	Capital.	United States bonds to secure circulation October 5, 1887.	Amount of bonds required to be held under the proposed code.	Amount of bonds that may be withdrawn upon adoption of the code.
Colorado	30	$2,451,850	$939,000	$245,185	$693,815
Nevada	2	150,000	37,500	15,000	22,500
California	27	2,970,000	888,750	297,000	591,750
San Francisco	1	200,000	50,000	20,000	30,000
Oregon	23	1,795,000	644,800	179,500	465,300
Arizona	1	100,000	25,000	10,000	15,000
Division No. 7	84	7,666,850	2,585,050	766,685	1,818,365
Dakota	62	3,720,000	962,500	372,000	590,500
Idaho	6	350,000	92,800	35,000	57,800
Montana	16	1,475,000	380,600	147,500	233,100
New Mexico	9	850,000	240,000	85,000	155,000
Utah	7	850,000	390,000	85,000	305,000
Washington	18	1,280,000	405,000	128,000	277,000
Wyoming	7	675,000	173,750	67,500	106,250
Division No. 8	125	9,200,000	2,644,650	920,000	1,724,650
United States	2,552	264,003,093	116,444,250	26,400,309	90,043,941

TABLE, BY STATES, TERRITORIES, AND RESERVE CITIES, EXHIBITING THE NUMBER OF BANKS IN EACH WITH CAPITAL OF OVER $250,000, AND SHOWING THE AMOUNT OF BONDS DEPOSITED TO SECURE CIRCULATION ON OCTOBER 5, 1887, AMOUNT OF BONDS REQUIRED BY PROPOSED CODE, AND AMOUNT OF BONDS WHICH MIGHT BE WITHDRAWN UPON ADOPTION OF CODE.

States, Territories, and reserve cities.	No. of banks.	Capital.	United States bonds to secure circulation, October 5, 1887.	Amount of bonds required to be held under the proposed code.	Amount of bonds that may be withdrawn upon adoption of the code.
Maine	8	$4, 036, 700	$1, 372, 000	$200, 000	$1, 172, 000
New Hampshire	2	600, 000	250, 000	50, 000	200, 000
Vermont	8	2, 900, 000	1, 375, 000	200, 000	1, 175, 000
Massachusetts	50	21, 390, 000	11, 112, 250	1, 250, 000	9, 862, 250
Boston	49	49, 850, 000	9, 658, 150	1, 225, 000	8, 433, 150
Rhode Island	26	15, 696, 800	2, 625, 000	650, 000	1, 975, 000
Connecticut	34	17, 028, 200	5, 318, 600	850, 000	4, 468, 600
Division No. 1	177	111, 495, 700	31, 711, 000	4, 425, 000	27, 286, 000
New York	18	7, 302, 000	4, 509, 000	450, 000	4, 059, 000
New York City	41	47, 900, 000	8, 755, 000	1, 025, 000	7, 730, 000
Albany	3	1, 100, 000	800, 000	75, 000	725, 000
New Jersey	12	4, 810, 000	2, 331, 000	300, 000	2, 031, 000
Pennsylvania	28	10, 569, 970	3, 285, 000	700, 000	2, 585, 000
Philadelphia	31	20, 050, 000	2, 150, 000	775, 000	1, 375, 000
Pittsburgh	15	8, 550, 000	955, 000	375, 000	580, 000
Division No. 2	148	100, 281, 970	22, 785, 000	3, 700, 000	19, 085, 000
Delaware	1	500, 000	370, 000	25, 000	345, 000
Maryland	1	251, 700	50, 000	25, 000	25, 000
Baltimore	16	11, 483, 260	2, 000, 000	400, 000	1, 600, 000
District of Columbia	1	252, 000	250, 000	25, 000	225, 000
Washington	2	600, 000	200, 000	50, 000	150, 000
Virginia	3	1, 300, 000	200, 000	75, 000	125, 000
West Virginia	.....	.....	.....	.....	.....
Division No. 3	24	14, 386, 960	3, 070, 000	600, 000	2, 470, 000
North Carolina	1	300, 000	100, 000	25, 000	75, 000
South Carolina	.....	.....	.....	.....	.....
Georgia	2	1, 000, 000	110, 500	50, 000	60, 500
Florida	.....	.....	.....	.....	.....
Alabama	4	1, 500, 000	350, 000	100, 000	250, 000
Mississippi	.....	.....	.....	.....	.....
Louisiana	.....	.....	.....	.....	.....
New Orleans	7	2, 725, 000	1, 150, 000	175, 000	975, 000
Texas	6	2, 125, 000	300, 000	150, 000	150, 000
Arkansas	.....	.....	.....	.....	.....
Kentucky	6	2, 350, 000	870, 000	150, 000	720, 000
Louisville	9	3, 551, 500	694, 000	225, 000	469, 000
Tennessee	6	4, 200, 000	300, 000	150, 000	150, 000
Division No. 4	41	17, 751, 500	3, 874, 500	1, 025, 000	2, 849, 500
Ohio	14	4, 810, 000	2, 136, 350	350, 000	1, 786, 350
Cincinnati	12	9, 750, 000	3, 462, 000	300, 000	3, 162, 000
Cleveland	8	6, 500, 000	555, 000	200, 000	355, 000
Indiana	8	2, 850, 000	500, 000	200, 000	300, 000
Illinois	1	300, 000	50, 000	25, 000	25, 000
Chicago	13	14, 000, 000	650, 000	325, 000	325, 000
Michigan	5	2, 400, 000	250, 000	125, 000	125, 000
Detroit	7	3, 683, 540	350, 000	175, 000	175, 000
Wisconsin	.....	.....	.....	.....	.....
Milwaukee	.....	.....	.....	.....	.....
Division No. 5	68	44, 293, 540	7, 953, 350	1, 700, 000	6, 253, 350
Iowa	2	900, 000	100, 000	50, 000	50, 000
Minnesota	12	9, 500, 000	735, 000	300, 000	435, 000
Missouri	.....	.....	.....	.....	.....
Saint Louis	5	3, 000, 000	710, 000	125, 000	585, 000
Kansas City	5	5, 350, 000	250, 000	125, 000	125, 000
Saint Joseph	.....	.....	.....	.....	.....
Kansas	2	600, 000	100, 000	50, 000	50, 000
Nebraska	1	300, 000	50, 000	25, 000	25, 000
Omaha	4	1, 700, 000	200, 000	100, 000	100, 000
Division No. 6	31	21, 350, 000	2, 145, 000	775, 000	1, 370, 000

TABLE, BY STATES, TERRITORIES, AND RESERVE CITIES, EXHIBITING THE NUMBER OF BANKS IN EACH WITH CAPITAL OF OVER $250,000, ETC.—Continued.

States, Territories, and reserve cities.	No. of banks.	Capital.	United States bonds to secure circulation October 5, 1887.	Amount of bonds required to be held under the proposed code.	Amount of bonds that may be withdrawn upon adoption of the code.
Colorado	1	$300, 000	$50, 000	$25, 000	$25, 000
Nevada					
California	3	1, 200, 000	200, 000	75, 000	125, 000
San Francisco	2	2, 500, 000	700, 000	50, 000	650, 000
Oregon					
Arizona					
Division No. 7	6	4, 000, 000	950, 000	150, 000	800, 000
Dakota					
Idaho					
Montana	1	500, 000	100, 000	25, 000	75, 000
New Mexico					
Utah					
Washington					
Wyoming	1	400, 000	50, 000	25, 000	25, 000
Division No. 8	2	900, 000	150, 000	50, 000	100, 000
United States	497	314, 459, 670	72, 638, 850	12, 425, 000	60, 213, 850

NATIONAL BANKS THAT HAVE GONE INTO VOLUNTARY LIQUIDATION UNDER THE PROVISIONS OF SECTIONS 5220 AND 5221 OF THE REVISED STATUTES OF THE UNITED STATES, WITH THE DATES OF LIQUIDATION, THE AMOUNT OF THEIR CAPITAL, CIRCULATION ISSUED AND RETIRED, AND CIRCULATION OUTSTANDING OCTOBER 31, 1887.

Name and location of bank.	Date of liquidation.	Capital.	Circulation.		
			Issued.	Retired.	Outstanding.
First National Bank, Penn Yan, N. Y.*	Apr. 6, 1864	....	....	....	....
First National Bank, Norwich, Conn*	May 2, 1864	....	....	....	....
Second National Bank, Ottumwa, Iowa†	May 2, 1864	....	....	....	....
Second National Bank, Canton, Ohio†	Oct. 3, 1864	....	....	....	....
First National Bank, Lansing, Mich†	Dec. 5, 1864	....	....	....	....
First National Bank, Columbia, Mo	Sept. 19, 1864	$100,000	$90,000	$89,875	$125
First National Bank, Carondelet, Mo	Mar. 15, 1865	30,000	25,500	25,389	111
First National Bank, Utica, N. Y.*	June 9, 1865	....	....	....	....
Pittston National Bank, Pittston, Pa	Sept. 16, 1865	200,000	....	....	....
Fourth National Bank, Indianapolis, Ind.	Nov. 30, 1865	100,000	100,000	99,180	820
Berkshire National Bank, Adams, Mass.‡	Dec. 8, 1865	100,000	....	....	....
National Union Bank, Rochester, N. Y	Apr. 26, 1866	400,000	192,500	191,283	1,217
First National Bank, Leonardsville, N. Y.	July 11, 1866	50,000	45,000	44,375	625
Farmers' National Bank, Richmond, Va.	Oct. 22, 1866	100,000	85,000	83,108	1,892
Farmers' National Bank, Waukesha, Wis.	Nov. 25, 1866	100,000	90,000	89,495	505
National Bank of Metropolis, Washington, D. C	Nov. 28, 1866	200,000	180,000	176,535	3,465
First National Bank, Providence, Pa	Mar. 1, 1867	100,000	90,000	88,620	1,380
National State Bank, Dubuque, Iowa	Mar. 9, 1867	150,000	127,000	125,556	1,444
First National Bank of Newton, Newtonville, Mass	Mar. 11, 1867	150,000	130,000	128,584	1,416
First National Bank, New Ulm, Minn	Apr. 18, 1867	60,000	54,000	53,125	875
National Bank of Crawford County, Meadville, Pa	Apr. 19, 1867	300,000	....	....	....
Kittanning National Bank, Kittanning, Pa.‡	Apr. 20, 1867	200,000	....	....	....
City National Bank, Savannah, Ga.†	May 28, 1867	100,000	....	....	....
Ohio National Bank, Cincinnati, Ohio	July 3, 1867	500,000	450,000	443,590	6,410
First National Bank, Kingston, N. Y	Sept. 26, 1867	200,000	180,000	177,599	2,401
First National Bank, Bluffton, Ind	Dec. 5, 1867	50,000	45,000	44,561	439
National Exchange Bank, Richmond, Va.	Dec. 5, 1867	200,000	180,000	179,050	950
First National Bank, Skaneateles, N. Y	Dec. 21, 1867	150,000	135,000	133,566	1,434
First National Bank, Jackson, Miss	Dec. 26, 1867	100,000	45,500	45,280	220
First National Bank, Downingtown, Pa	Jan. 14, 1868	100,000	90,000	88,881	1,119
First National Bank, Titusville, Pa	Jan. 15, 1868	100,000	86,750	85,669	1,081
Appleton National Bank, Appleton, Wis.	Jan. 21, 1868	50,000	45,000	44,351	649
National Bank of Whitestown, N. Y	Feb. 14, 1868	120,000	45,500	45,178	322
First National Bank, New Brunswick, N. J	Feb. 26, 1868	100,000	90,000	88,579	1,421
First National Bank, Cuyahoga Falls, Ohio	Mar. 4, 1868	50,000	45,000	44,415	585
First National Bank, Cedarburg, Wis	Mar. 23, 1868	100,000	90,000	89,377	623
Commercial National Bank, Cincinnati, Ohio	Apr. 28, 1868	500,000	345,950	343,115	2,835
Second National Bank, Watertown, N. Y.	July 21, 1868	100,000	90,000	88,580	1,420
First National Bank, South Worcester, N. Y	Aug. 4, 1868	175,500	157,400	155,676	1,724
National Mechanics and Farmers' Bank, Albany, N. Y	Aug. 4, 1868	350,000	314,950	312,565	2,385
Second National Bank, Des Moines, Iowa.	Aug. 5, 1868	50,000	42,500	42,122	378
First National Bank, Steubenville, Ohio.	Aug. 8, 1868	150,000	135,000	132,842	2,158
First National Bank, Plumer, Pa	Aug. 25, 1868	100,000	87,500	85,977	1,523
First National Bank, Danville, Va	Sept. 30, 1868	50,000	45,000	44,595	405
First National Bank, Dorchester, Mass	Nov. 23, 1868	150,000	132,500	130,293	2,207
First National Bank, Oskaloosa, Iowa	Dec. 17, 1868	75,000	67,500	66,950	550
Merchants and Mechanics' National Bank, Troy, N. Y	Dec. 31, 1868	300,000	184,750	182,931	1,819
National Savings Bank, Wheeling, W. Va	Jan. 7, 1869	100,000	90,000	89,245	755
First National Bank, Marion, Ohio	Jan. 12, 1869	125,000	109,850	108,832	1,018
National Insurance Bank, Detroit, Mich.	Feb. 26, 1869	200,000	85,000	84,394	606
National Bank of Lansingburg, N. Y	Mar. 6, 1869	150,000	135,000	133,662	1,338
National Bank of North America, New York, N. Y	Apr. 15, 1869	1,000,000	333,000	330,384	2,616
First National Bank, Hallowell, Me	Apr. 19, 1869	60,000	53,350	52,857	493
First National Bank, Clyde, N. Y	Apr. 23, 1869	50,000	44,000	43,230	770
Pacific National Bank, New York, N. Y.	May 10, 1869	422,700	134,990	133,912	1,078
Grocers' National Bank, New York, N. Y.	June 7, 1869	390,000	85,250	84,736	514
Savannah National Bank, Savannah, Ga.	June 22, 1869	100,000	85,000	84,385	615
First National Bank, Frostburg, Md	July 30, 1869	50,000	45,000	44,723	277
First National Bank, La Salle, Ill	Aug. 30, 1869	50,000	45,000	44,465	535

* New bank with same title. † Never completed organization. ‡ Consolidated with another bank.

NATIONAL BANKS THAT HAVE GONE INTO VOLUNTARY LIQUIDATION UNDER THE PROVISIONS OF SECTIONS 5220 AND 5221 OF THE REVISED STATUTES, ETC.—Continued.

Name and location of bank.	Date of liquidation.	Capital.	Circulation.		
			Issued.	Retired.	Outstanding.
National Bank of Commerce, Georgetown, D. C	Oct. 28, 1869	$100,000	$90,000	$88,980	$1,020
Miner's National Bank, Salt Lake City, Utah	Dec. 2, 1869	150,000	135,000	133,842	1,158
First National Bank, Vinton, Iowa	Dec. 13, 1869	50,000	42,500	42,279	221
National Exchange Bank, Philadelphia, Pa	Jan. 8, 1870	300,000	175,750	173,330	2,420
First National Bank, Decatur, Ill	Jan. 10, 1870	100,000	85,250	84,170	1,080
National Union Bank, Oswego, N. Y	Jan. 11, 1870	100,000	88,250	87,121	1,129
First National Bank, Berlin, Wis	Jan. 25, 1870	500,000	44,000	43,610	390
Central National Bank, Cincinnati, Ohio	Mar. 31, 1870	500,000	425,000	420,615	4,385
First National Bank, Dayton, Ohio	Apr. 9, 1870	150,000	135,000	133,678	1,322
National Bank of Chemung, Elmira, N. Y	June 10, 1870	100,000	90,000	89,443	557
Merchants' National Bank, Milwaukee, Wis	June 14, 1870	100,000	90,000	89,170	830
First National Bank, Saint Louis, Mo	July 16, 1870	200,000	179,990	178,463	1,527
Chemung Canal National Bank, Elmira, N. Y	Aug. 3, 1870	100,000	90,000	89,084	916
Central National Bank, Omaha, Nebr*	Sept. 23, 1870	100,000	....	....	....
First National Bank, Clarksville, Va	Oct. 13, 1870	50,000	27,000	26,860	140
First National Bank, Burlington, Vt	Oct. 15, 1870	300,000	270,000	266,103	3,897
First National Bank, Lebanon, Ohio	Oct. 24, 1870	100,000	85,000	84,239	761
National Exchange Bank, Lansingburg, N. Y	Dec. 27, 1870	100,000	90,000	89,301	699
Muskingum National Bank, Zanesville, Ohio	Jan. 7, 1871	100,000	90,000	89,125	875
United National Bank, Winona, Minn	Feb. 15, 1871	50,000	45,000	44,525	475
First National Bank, Des Moines, Iowa	Mar. 25, 1871	100,000	90,000	89,079	921
Saratoga County National Bank, Waterford, N. Y	Mar. 28, 1871	150,000	135,000	133,858	1,142
State National Bank, Saint Joseph, Mo	Mar. 31, 1871	100,000	90,000	89,439	561
First National Bank, Fenton, Mich	May 2, 1871	100,000	49,500	48,983	517
First National Bank, Wellsburg, W. Va	June 24, 1871	100,000	90,000	89,148	852
Clarke National Bank, Rochester, N. Y	Aug. 11, 1871	200,000	180,000	178,022	1,978
Commercial National Bank, Oshkosh, Wis	Nov. 22, 1871	100,000	90,000	89,168	832
Fort Madison National Bank, Fort Madison, Iowa	Dec. 26, 1871	75,000	67,500	66,920	580
National Bank of Maysville, Ky	Jan. 6, 1872	300,000	270,000	268,241	1,759
Fourth National Bank, Syracuse, N. Y	Jan. 9, 1872	105,500	91,700	90,692	1,008
American National Bank, New York, N. Y	May 10, 1872	500,000	450,000	443,131	6,869
Carroll County National Bank, Sandwich, N. H	May 24, 1872	50,000	45,000	44,288	712
Second National Bank, Portland, Me	June 24, 1872	100,000	81,000	79,619	1,381
Atlantic National Bank, Brooklyn, N. Y	July 15, 1872	200,000	165,000	163,340	1,660
Merchants and Farmers' National Bank, Quincy, Ill	Aug. 8, 1872	150,000	135,000	133,500	1,500
First National Bank, Rochester, N. Y	Aug. 9, 1872	400,000	206,100	203,569	2,531
Lawrenceburg National Bank, Ind	Sept. 10, 1872	200,000	180,000	177,548	2,452
Jewett City National Bank, Jewett City, Conn	Oct. 4, 1872	60,000	48,750	48,092	658
First National Bank, Knoxville, Tenn	Oct. 22, 1872	100,000	80,910	79,874	1,036
First National Bank, Goshen, Ind	Nov. 7, 1872	115,000	103,500	102,071	1,429
Kidder National Gold Bank, Boston, Mass	Nov. 8, 1872	300,000	120,000	120,000	....
Second National Bank, Zanesville, Ohio	Nov. 16, 1872	154,700	138,140	136,168	1,072
Orange County National Bank, Chelsea, Vt	Jan. 14, 1873	200,000	180,000	176,976	3,024
Second National Bank, Syracuse, N. Y	Feb. 18, 1873	100,000	90,000	88,715	1,285
Richmond National Bank, Richmond, Ind*	Feb. 28, 1873	230,000	207,000	207,000	....
First National Bank, Adams, N. Y	Mar. 7, 1873	75,000	66,900	65,870	1,030
Mechanics' National Bank, Syracuse N. Y	Mar. 11, 1873	110,000	93,800	92,695	1,105
Farmers and Mechanics' National Bank, Rochester, N. Y	Apr. 15, 1873	100,000	83,250	82,148	1,102
Montana National Bank, Helena, Mont	Apr. 15, 1873	100,000	31,500	31,365	135
First National Bank, Havana, N. Y	June 3, 1873	50,000	45,000	44,270	730
Merchants and Farmers' National Bank, Ithaca, N. Y	June 30, 1873	50,000	45,000	44,185	815
National Bank of Cazenovia, N. Y	July 18, 1873	150,000	116,770	115,113	1,657
Merchants' National Bank, Memphis, Tenn	Aug. 30, 1873	250,000	225,000	221,873	3,127

* New bank with same title.

NATIONAL BANKS THAT HAVE GONE INTO VOLUNTARY LIQUIDATION UNDER THE PROVISIONS OF SECTIONS 5220 AND 5221 OF THE REVISED STATUTES, ETC.—Continued.

Name and location of bank.	Date of liquidation.	Capital.	Circulation.		
			Issued.	Retired.	Outstanding.
Manufacturers' National Bank, Chicago, Ill	Sept. 25, 1873	$500,000	$150,000	$143,398	$6,602
Second National Bank, Chicago, Ill	Sept. 25, 1873	100,000	97,500	95,756	1,744
Merchants' National Bank, Dubuque, Iowa	Sept. 30, 1873	200,000	180,000	175,265	4,735
Beloit National Bank, Beloit, Wis	Oct. 2, 1873	50,000	45,000	44,216	784
Union National Bank, Saint Louis, Mo	Oct. 22, 1873	500,000	150,300	147,828	2,472
City National Bank, Green Bay, Wis	Nov. 29, 1873	50,000	45,000	43,990	1,010
First National Bank, Shelbina, Mo	Jan. 1, 1874	100,000	90,000	88,828	1,172
Second National Bank, Nashville, Tenn	Jan. 8, 1874	125,000	92,920	91,215	1,705
First National Bank, Oneida, N. Y	Jan. 13, 1874	125,000	110,500	108,589	1,911
Merchants' National Bank, Hastings, Minn	Feb. 7, 1874	100,000	90,000	88,105	1,895
National Bank of Tecumseh, Mich	Mar. 3, 1874	50,000	45,000	44,210	790
Gallatin National Bank, Shawneetown, Ill	Mar. 7, 1874	250,000	225,000	222,528	2,472
First National Bank, Brookville, Pa	Mar. 26, 1874	100,000	90,000	88,445	1,555
Citizens' National Bank, Sioux City, Iowa	Apr. 14, 1874	50,000	45,000	44,705	295
Citizens' National Bank, Charlottesville, Va	Apr. 27, 1874	100,000	90,000	88,709	1,291
Farmers' National Bank, Warren, Ill	Apr. 28, 1874	50,000	45,000	44,181	819
First National Bank, Medina, Ohio	May 6, 1874	75,000	45,000	44,601	399
Croton River National Bank, South East, N. Y	May 25, 1874	200,000	166,550	163,318	3,232
Merchants' National Bank of West Virginia, Wheeling, W. Va	July 7, 1874	500,000	450,000	442,982	7,018
Central National Bank, Baltimore, Md	July 15, 1874	200,000	180,000	178,066	1,934
Second National Bank, Leavenworth Kans	July 22, 1874	100,000	90,000	87,526	2,474
Teutonia National Bank, New Orleans, La	Sept. 2, 1874	300 000	270,000	265,780	4,220
City National Bank, Chattanooga, Tenn	Sept. 10, 1874	170,000	148,001	146,003	1,998
First National Bank, Cairo, Ill	Oct. 10, 1874	100,000	90,000	88,204	1,796
First National Bank, Olathe, Kans	Nov. 9, 1874	50,000	45,000	44,497	503
First National Bank, Beverly, Ohio	Nov. 10, 1874	102,000	90,000	88,102	1,898
Union National Bank, La Fayette, Ind	Dec. 4, 1874	250,000	224,095	219,453	4,642
Ambler National Bank, Jacksonville, Fla*	Dec. 7, 1874	42,500	....	....	....
Mechanics' National Bank, Chicago, Ill	Dec. 30, 1874	250,000	125,900	123,020	2,880
First National Bank, Evansville, Wis	Jan. 9, 1875	55,000	45,000	44,432	568
First National Bank, Baxter Springs, Kans	Jan. 12, 1875	50,000	36,000	35,535	465
People's National Bank, Pueblo, Colo	Jan. 12, 1875	50,000	27,000	26,778	222
National Bank of Commerce, Green Bay, Wis	Jan. 12, 1875	100,000	90,000	88,860	1,140
First National Bank, Millersburg, Ohio	Jan. 12, 1875	100,000	60,400	59,731	669
First National Bank, Staunton, Va	Jan. 23, 1875	100,000	90,000	88,597	1,403
National City Bank, Milwaukee, Wis	Feb. 24, 1875	100,000	60,000	58,675	1,325
Irasburg National Bank of Orleans, Irasburg, Vt	Mar. 17, 1875	75,000	67,500	66,104	1,396
First National Bank, Pekin, Ill	Mar. 25, 1875	100,000	90,000	88,144	1,856
Merchants' and Planters' National Bank, Augusta, Ga	Mar. 30, 1875	200,000	169,000	165,830	3,170
Monticello National Bank, Monticello, Iowa	Mar. 30, 1875	100,000	45,000	44,264	736
Iowa City National Bank, Iowa City, Iowa	Apr. 14, 1875	125,000	104,800	102,671	2,129
First National Bank, Wheeling, W. Va	Apr. 22, 1875	250,000	225,000	219,410	5,590
First National Bank, Mount Clemens, Mich	May 20, 1875	50,000	27,000	26,830	170
First National Bank, Knob Noster, Mo	May 29, 1875	50,000	43,800	43,358	442
First National Bank, Brodhead, Wis	June 24, 1875	50,000	45,000	44,342	658
Auburn City National Bank, Auburn, N. Y	June 26, 1875	200,000	141,300	137,987	3,313
First National Bank, El Dorado, Kans	June 30, 1875	50,000	45,000	44,400	600
First National Bank, Junction City, Kans	July 1, 1875	50,000	45,000	44,565	435
First National Bank, Chetopa, Kans	July 19, 1875	50,000	36,000	35,567	433
First National Bank, Golden, Colo	Aug. 25, 1875	50,200	27,000	26,765	235
National Bank of Jefferson, Wis	Aug. 26, 1875	60,000	54,000	52,707	1,293
Green Lane National Bank, Green Lane, Pa	Sept. 9, 1875	100,000	90,000	89,267	733
State National Bank, Topeka, Kans	Sept. 15, 1875	60,500	30,600	30,407	193
Farmers' National Bank, Marshalltown, Iowa	Sept. 18, 1875	50,000	27,000	26,765	235

* Never completed organization.

NATIONAL BANKS THAT HAVE GONE INTO VOLUNTARY LIQUIDATION UNDER THE PROVISIONS OF SECTIONS 5220 AND 5221 OF THE REVISED STATUTES, ETC.—Continued.

Name and location of bank.	Date of liquidation.	Capital.	Circulation.		
			Issued.	Retired.	Outstanding.
Richland National Bank, Mansfield, Ohio	Sept. 25, 1875	$150,000	$130,300	$126,549	$3,751
Planters' National Bank, Louisville, Ky.	Sept. 30, 1875	350,000	315,000	304,784	10,216
First National Bank, Gallatin, Tenn	Oct. 1, 1875	75,000	45,000	44,430	570
First National Bank, Charleston, W. Va.	Oct. 2, 1875	100,000	90,000	88,790	1,210
People's National Bank, Winchester, Ill	Oct. 4, 1875	75,000	67,500	66,217	1,283
First National Bank, New Lexington, Ohio	Oct. 12, 1875	50,000	45,000	44,475	525
First National Bank, Ishpeming, Mich	Oct. 20, 1875	50,000	45,000	44,006	994
Fayette County National Bank, Washington, Ohio	Oct. 26, 1875	100,000	81,280	80,033	1,247
Merchants' National Bank, Fort Wayne, Ind	Nov. 8, 1875	100,000	46,820	45,955	865
Kansas City National Bank, Kansas City, Mo	Nov. 13, 1875	100,000	65,991	64,574	1,417
First National Bank, Schoolcraft, Mich.	Nov. 17, 1875	50,000	45,000	44,302	698
First National Bank, Curwensville, Pa.	Dec. 17, 1875	100,000	90,000	87,308	2,692
National Marine Bank, Saint Paul, Minn	Dec. 28, 1875	100,000	59,710	57,705	2,005
First National Bank, Rochester, Ind	Jan. 11, 1876	50,000	45,000	42,895	2,105
First National Bank, Lodi, Ohio	Jan. 11, 1876	100,000	90,000	87,407	2,593
Iron National Bank, Portsmouth, Ohio	Jan. 19, 1876	100,000	90,000	88,537	1,463
First National Bank, Ashland, Nebr	Jan. 26, 1876	50,000	45,000	44,464	536
First National Bank, Paxton, Ill	Jan. 28, 1876	50,000	45,000	43,809	1,191
First National Bank, Bloomfield, Iowa	Feb. 5, 1876	55,000	49,500	48,235	1,265
Marietta National Bank, Marietta, Ohio.	Feb. 16, 1876	150,000	90,000	87,321	2,679
Salt Lake City National Bank, Salt Lake City, Utah	Feb. 21, 1876	100,000	45,000	43,871	1,129
First National Bank, La Grange, Mo	Feb. 24, 1876	50,000	45,000	44,221	779
First National Bank, Atlantic, Iowa	Mar. 7, 1876	50,000	45,000	44,235	765
First National Bank, Spencer, Ind	Mar. 11, 1876	70,000	63,000	62,179	821
National Currency Bank, New York, N. Y	Mar. 23, 1876	100,000	45,000	43,500	1,500
Caverna National Bank, Caverna, Ky	May 13, 1876	50,000	45,000	44,415	585
City National Bank, Pittsburgh, Pa	May 25, 1876	200,000	68,929	67,025	1,904
National State Bank, Des Moines, Iowa.	June 21, 1876	100,000	50,795	48,755	2,040
First National Bank, Trenton, Mo	June 22, 1876	50,000	45,000	44,296	704
First National Bank, Bristol, Tenn	July 10, 1876	50,000	45,000	44,460	540
First National Bank, Leon, Iowa	July 11, 1876	60,000	45,000	43,546	1,454
Anderson County National Bank, Lawrenceburgh, Ky	July 29, 1876	100,000	45,000	44,480	520
First National Bank, Newport, Ind	Aug. 7, 1876	60,000	45,000	43,478	1,522
First National Bank, De Pere, Wis	Aug. 17, 1876	50,000	31,500	31,158	342
Second National Bank, Lawrence, Kans.	Aug. 23, 1876	100,000	67,500	66,165	1,335
Commercial National Bank, Versailles, Ky	Aug. 26, 1876	170,000	153,000	148,897	4,103
State National Bank, Atlanta, Ga	Aug. 31, 1876	200,000	73,725	71,160	2,565
Syracuse National Bank, Syracuse, N. Y	Sept. 25, 1876	200,000	117,961	112,363	5,598
First National Bank, Northumberland, Pa	Oct. 6, 1876	100,000	62,106	59,411	2,695
First National Bank, Lancaster, Mo	Nov. 14, 1876	50,000	27,000	26,752	248
First National Bank, Council Grove, Kans	Nov. 28, 1876	50,000	26,500	26,024	476
National Bank Commerce, Chicago, Ill.	Dec. 2, 1876	250,000	71,465	69,311	2,154
First National Bank, Palmyra, Mo	Dec. 12, 1876	100,000	46,140	44,420	1,720
First National Bank, Newton, Iowa	Dec. 16, 1876	50,000	45,000	42,639	2,361
National Southern Kentucky Bank, Bowling Green, Ky	Dec. 23, 1876	50,000	27,000	26,593	407
First National Bank, Monroe, Iowa	Jan. 1, 1877	60,000	35,700	34,934	766
First National Bank, New London, Conn	Jan. 9, 1877	100,000	38,300	35,981	2,319
Winona Deposit National Bank, Winona, Minn	Jan. 28, 1877	100,000	63,285	60,571	2,714
First National Bank, South Charleston, Ohio	Feb. 24, 1877	100,000	90,000	86,975	3,025
Lake Ontario National Bank, Oswego, N. Y	Feb. 24, 1877	275,000	66,405	61,591	4,814
First National Bank, Sidney, Ohio	Feb. 26, 1877	52,000	46,200	44,697	1,503
Chillicothe National Bank, Ohio	Apr. 9, 1877	100,000	53,825	51,185	2,640
First National Bank, Manhattan, Kans	Apr. 13, 1877	52,000	44,200	43,299	901
National Bank, Monticello, Ky	Apr. 23, 1877	60,000	49,500	46,580	2,920
First National Bank, Rockville, Ind	Apr. 25, 1877	200,000	173,090	166,490	6,600
Georgia National Bank, Atlanta, Ga	May 31, 1877	100,000	45,000	43,184	1,816
First National Bank, Adrian, Mich	June 11, 1877	100,000	43,500	42,094	1,406

NATIONAL BANKS THAT HAVE GONE INTO VOLUNTARY LIQUIDATION UNDER THE PROVISIONS OF SECTIONS 5220 AND 5221 OF THE REVISED STATUTES, ETC.—Continued.

Name and location of bank.	Date of liquidation.	Capital.	Circulation.		
			Issued.	Retired.	Outstanding.
First National Bank, Napoleon, Ohio	June 30, 1877	$50,000	$45,000	$43,613	$1,367
First National Bank, Lancaster, Ohio	Aug. 1, 1877	60,000	54,000	51,794	2,206
First National Bank, Minerva, Ohio	Aug. 24, 1877	50,000	45,000	43,924	1,076
Kinney National Bank, Portsmouth, Ohio	Aug. 28, 1877	100,000	90,000	87,835	2,165
First National Bank, Green Bay, Wis	Oct. 19, 1877	50,000	45,000	43,352	1,648
National Exchange Bank, Wakefield, R. I	Oct. 27, 1877	70,000	31,650	32,047	2,003
First National Bank, Union City, Ind	Nov. 10, 1877	50,000	45,000	43,405	1,595
First National Bank, Negaunee, Mich	Nov. 13, 1877	50,000	45,000	43,695	1,305
Tenth National Bank, New York, N. Y	Nov. 23, 1877	500,000	441,000	412,325	28,675
First National Bank, Paola, Kans	Dec. 1, 1877	50,000	44,350	42,983	1,367
National Exchange Bank, Troy, N. Y	Dec. 6, 1877	100,000	90,000	86,166	3,834
Second National Bank, La Fayette, Ind	Dec. 20, 1877	200,000	52,167	47,117	5,050
Stato National Bank, Minneapolis, Minn	Dec. 31, 1877	100,000	82,500	78,403	4,097
Second National Bank, Saint Louis, Mo	Jan. 8, 1878	200,000	53,055	47,163	5,892
First National Bank, Sullivan, Ind	Jan. 8, 1878	50,000	45,000	43,995	1,005
Rockland County National Bank, Nyack, N. Y	Jan. 10, 1878	100,000	89,000	85,231	3,769
First National Bank, Wyandotte, Kans	Jan. 19, 1878	50,000	45,000	43,795	1,205
First National Bank, Boone, Iowa	Jan. 22, 1878	50,000	32,400	31,110	1,290
First National Bank, Pleasant Hill, Mo	Feb. 7, 1878	50,000	45,000	43,632	1,368
National Bank of Gloversville, N. Y	Feb. 28, 1878	100,000	64,750	62,062	2,688
First National Bank, Independence, Mo	Mar. 1, 1878	50,000	27,000	24,651	2,349
National State Bank, Lima, Ind	Mar. 2, 1878	100,000	33,471	31,392	2,079
First National Bank, Tell City, Ind	Mar. 4, 1878	50,000	44,500	43,675	825
First National Bank, Pomeroy, Ohio	Mar. 5, 1878	200,000	75,713	70,481	5,232
Eleventh Ward National Bank, Boston, Mass	Mar. 14, 1878	200,000	89,400	86,355	3,045
First National Bank, Prophetstown, Ill	Mar. 19, 1878	50,000	45,000	44,238	762
First National Bank, Jackson, Mich	Mar. 26, 1878	100,000	88,400	84,215	4,185
First National Bank, Eau Claire, Wis	Mar. 30, 1878	60,000	38,461	37,216	1,245
First National Bank, Washington, Ohio	Apr. 5, 1878	200,000	69,750	65,092	4,658
First National Bank, Middleport, Ohio	Apr. 20, 1878	80,000	31,500	30,825	675
First National Bank, Streator, Ill	Apr. 24, 1878	50,000	40,500	39,775	725
First National Bank, Muir, Mich	Apr. 25, 1878	50,000	44,200	43,109	1,091
Kane County National Bank, Saint Charles, Ill	May 31, 1878	50,000	26,300	25,288	1,012
First National Bank, Carthage, Mo	June 1, 1878	50,000	44,500	43,415	1,085
Security National Bank, Worcester, Mass	June 5, 1878	100,000	49,000	46,890	2,110
First National Bank, Lake City, Colo	June 15, 1878	50,000	29,300	28,909	391
People's National Bank, Norfolk, Va	July 31, 1878	100,000	85,705	79,265	6,440
Topeka National Bank, Topeka, Kans	Aug. 7, 1878	100,000	89,300	82,595	6,705
First National Bank, Saint Joseph, Mo	Aug. 13, 1878	100,000	67,110	61,826	5,284
First National Bank, Winchester, Ind	Aug. 24, 1878	60,000	54,700	49,035	5,665
Muscatine National Bank, Muscatine, Iowa	Sept. 2, 1878	100,000	44,200	39,926	4,274
Traders' National Bank, Chicago, Ill	Sept. 4, 1878	200,000	43,700	38,695	5,005
Union National Bank, Rahway, N. J	Sept. 10, 1878	100,000	89,200	83,499	5,701
First National Bank, Sparta, Wis	Sept. 14, 1878	50,000	45,000	42,797	2,203
Herkimer County National Bank, Little Falls, N. Y	Oct. 11, 1878	200,000	178,300	166,190	12,110
Farmers' National Bank, Bangor, Me	Nov. 22, 1878	100,000	89,100	82,952	6,148
Pacific National Bank, Council Bluffs, Iowa	Nov. 30, 1878	100,000	45,000	43,263	1,737
First National Bank, Anamosa, Iowa	Dec. 14, 1878	50,000	44,500	40,815	3,685
Smithfield National Bank, Pittsburgh, Pa	Dec. 16, 1878	200,000	78,750	70,100	8,650
First National Bank, Buchanan, Mich	Dec. 21, 1878	50,000	27,000	26,185	815
First National Bank, Prairie City, Ill	Dec. 24, 1878	50,000	27,000	23,610	3,390
Corn Exchange National Bank, Chicago, Ill	Jan. 4, 1879	500,000	59,160	51,613	7,547
Franklin National Bank, Columbus, Ohio	Jan. 4, 1879	100,000	93,070	86,423	6,647
Traders' National Bank, Bangor, Me	Jan. 14, 1879	100,000	76,400	68,917	7,483
First National Bank, Gonic, N. H	Jan. 14, 1879	60,000	45,597	42,393	3,204
First National Bank, Salem, N. C	Jan. 14, 1879	150,000	128,200	117,470	10,730
First National Bank, Granville, Ohio	Jan. 14, 1879	50,000	34,365	31,509	2,856
Commercial National Bank, Petersburgh, Va	Jan. 14, 1879	120,000	99,800	89,303	10,497
First National Gold Bank, Stockton, Cal	Jan. 14, 1879	300,000	238,600	212,841	25,759
First National Bank, Sheboygan, Wis	Jan. 14, 1879	50,000	45,000	43,954	1,046
First National Bank, Boscobel, Wis	Jan. 21, 1879	50,000	43,900	42,132	1,768
National Marine Bank, Oswego, N. Y	Jan. 25, 1879	120,000	44,300	41,214	3,086
Central National Bank, Hightstown, N. J	Feb. 15, 1879	100,000	32,400	31,265	1,135

NATIONAL BANKS THAT HAVE GONE INTO VOLUNTARY LIQUIDATION UNDER THE PROVISIONS OF SECTIONS 5220 AND 5221 OF THE REVISED STATUTES, ETC.—Continued.

Name and location of bank.	Date of liquidation.	Capital.	Circulation.		
			Issued.	Retired.	Outstanding.
Brookville National Bank, Brookville, Ind	Feb. 18, 1879	$100,000	$89,000	$81,170	$7,830
Farmers' National Bank, Centreville, Iowa	Feb. 27, 1879	50,000	41,500	40,288	1,212
First National Bank, Clarinda, Iowa	Mar. 1, 1879	50,000	45,000	43,807	1,193
Waterville National Bank, Waterville, Mo	Mar. 3, 1879	125,000	110,300	102,665	7,635
First National Bank, Tremont, Pa	Mar. 4, 1879	75,000	64,600	57,174	7,426
First National Bank, Atlanta, Ill	Apr. 15, 1879	50,000	26,500	24,230	2,270
Union National Bank, Aurora, Ill	Apr. 22, 1879	125,000	82,000	74,077	7,923
National Bank of Menasha, Wis	Apr. 26, 1879	50,000	44,500	42,844	1,656
National Exchange Bank, Jefferson City, Mo	May 8, 1879	50,000	45,000	41,839	3,161
First National Bank, Hannibal, Mo	May 15, 1879	100,000	88,200	79,990	8,210
Merchants' National Bank, Winona, Minn	June 16, 1879	100,000	35,000	33,662	1,338
Farmers' National Bank, Keithsburg, Ill	July 3, 1879	50,000	27,000	24,650	2,350
First National Bank, Franklin, Ky	July 5, 1879	100,000	54,000	49,970	4,030
National Bank of Salem, Salem, Ind	July 8, 1879	50,000	44,400	43,277	1,123
Fourth National Bank, Memphis, Tenn	July 19, 1879	125,000	45,000	40,610	4,390
Bedford National Bank, Bedford, Ind	July 21, 1879	100,000	87,200	84,156	3,044
First National Bank, Afton, Iowa	Aug. 15, 1879	50,000	26,500	24,989	1,511
First National Bank, Deer Lodge, Mont	Aug. 16, 1879	50,000	45,000	43,490	1,510
First National Bank, Batavia, Ill	Aug. 30, 1879	50,000	44,300	41,450	2,850
National Gold Bank and Trust Company, San Francisco, Cal	Sept. 1, 1879	750,000	40,000	27,510	12,490
Gainesville National Bank, Gainesville, Ala	Nov. 25, 1879	100,000	90,000	79,994	10,006
First National Bank, Hackensack, N. J	Dec. 6, 1879	100,000	90,000	83,063	6,937
National Bank of Delavan, Delavan, Wis	Jan. 7, 1880	50,000	27,000	24,410	2,590
Mechanics' National Bank, Nashville, Tenn	Jan. 13, 1880	100,000	90,000	76,950	13,050
Manchester National Bank, Manchester, Ohio	Jan. 13, 1880	50,000	48,303	43,738	4,565
First National Bank, Meyersdale, Pa	Mar. 5, 1880	50,000	30,600	29,540	1,060
First National Bank, Mifflinburg, Pa	Mar. 8, 1880	100,000	90,000	79,775	10,225
National Bank of Michigan, Marshall, Mich	May 14, 1880	120,000	100,800	92,197	8,603
National Exchange Bank, Houston, Tex	Sept. 10, 1880	100,000	31,500	27,613	3,887
Ascutney National Bank, Windsor, Vt	Oct. 19, 1880	100,000	90,000	80,932	9,068
First National Bank, Seneca Falls, N. Y	Nov. 23, 1880	60,000	54,000	51,778	2,222
First National Bank, Baraboo, Wis	Nov. 27, 1880	50,000	27,000	25,260	1,740
Bundy National Bank, New Castle, Ind	Dec. 6, 1880	50,000	45,000	43,834	1,166
Vineland National Bank, Vineland, N. J	Jan. 11, 1881	50,000	45,000	43,568	1,432
Ocean County National Bank, Tom's River, N. J	Jan. 11, 1881	100,000	119,405	105,620	13,785
Hungerford, National Bank, Adams, N. Y	Jan. 27, 1881	50,000	45,000	39,145	5,855
Merchants' National Bank, Minneapolis, Minn	Jan. 31, 1881	150,000	98,268	94,580	3,688
Farmers' National Bank, Mechanicsburg, Ohio	Feb. 18, 1881	100,000	30,140	28,525	1,615
First National Bank, Green Spring, Ohio	Feb. 18, 1881	50,000	45,000	42,841	2,159
First National Bank, Cannon Falls, Minn	Feb. 21, 1881	50,000	45,000	42,615	2,385
First National Bank, Coshocton, Ohio	Feb. 21, 1881	50,000	53,058	50,453	2,605
Manufacturers' National Bank, Three Rivers, Mich	Feb. 25, 1881	50,000	45,000	42,880	2,120
First National Bank, Lansing, Iowa	Feb. 25, 1881	50,000	45,000	42,576	2,424
First National Bank, Watertown, N. Y	May 26, 1881	100,000	75,510	63,145	12,365
First National Bank, Americus, Ga	June 17, 1881	60,000	45,000	42,942	2,058
First National Bank, Saint Joseph, Mich	June 30, 1881	50,000	26,500	24,386	2,114
First National Bank, Logan, Ohio	July 8, 1881	50,000	45,000	42,565	2,435
First National Bank, Rochelle, Ill	Aug. 9, 1881	50,000	45,000	42,283	2,717
First National Bank, Shakopee, Minn	Aug. 10, 1881	50,000	45,000	41,335	3,665
National State Bank, Oskaloosa, Iowa	Aug. 13, 1881	50,000	81,665	72,895	8,770
First National Bank, Hobart, N. Y	Aug. 27, 1881	100,000	90,000	79,830	10,170
Attica National Bank, Attica, N. Y	Aug. 30, 1881	50,000	45,000	41,660	3,340
National Bank of Brighton, Boston, Mass	Oct. 4, 1881	300,000	270,000	242,294	27,706
Clement National Bank, Rutland, Vt*	Aug. 1, 1881	100,000	....	....	....
First National Bank, Lisbon, Iowa	Nov. 1, 1881	50,000	45,000	43,400	2,000
First National Bank, Warsaw, Ind	Dec. 1, 1881	50,000	48,500	45,310	3,190
Brighton National Bank, Brighton, Iowa	Dec. 15, 1881	50,000	45,000	42,044	2,956
Merchants' National Bank, Denver, Colo	Dec. 24, 1881	120,000	72,000	57,140	14,860
Merchants' National Bank, Holly, Mich	Dec. 31, 1881	50,000	45,000	42,525	2,475

* New bank with same title.

NATIONAL BANKS THAT HAVE GONE INTO VOLUNTARY LIQUIDATION UNDER THE PROVISIONS OF SECTIONS 5220 AND 5221 OF THE REVISED STATUTES, ETC.—Continued.

Name and location of bank.	Date of liquidation.	Capital.	Circulation.		
			Issued.	Retired.	Outstanding.
First National Bank, Alliance, Ohio	Jan. 3, 1882	$50,000	$15,000	$10,418	$4,582
National Union Bank, New London, Conn	Jan. 10, 1882	300,000	112,818	95,986	16,832
National Bank of Royalton, Vt	Jan. 10, 1882	100,000	90,000	78,067	11,933
First National Bank, Whitehall, N. Y	Jan. 18, 1882	50,000	45,000	38,519	6,481
National Bank of Pulaski, Tenn	Jan. 23, 1882	70,000	43,700	37,198	6,502
First National Bank, Alton, Ill	Mar. 30, 1882	100,000	90,000	78,957	11,043
Havana National Bank, Havana, N. Y	Apr. 15, 1882	50,000	45,000	41,322	3,678
First National Bank, Brownsville, Pa	May 2, 1882	75,000	67,500	56,040	11,460
Second National Bank, Franklin, Ind	June 20, 1882	100,000	81,060	66,075	14,985
Merchants' National Bank, Georgetown, Colo	June 22, 1882	50,000	45,000	41,988	3,012
Commercial National Bank, Toledo, Ohio	July 6, 1882	100,000	90,000	81,700	8,300
Harmony National Bank, Harmony, Pa	July 7, 1882	50,000	45,000	39,000	6,000
First National Bank, Liberty, Ind	July 22, 1882	60,000	54,000	48,506	5,494
Manufacturers' National Bank, Amsterdam, N. Y	Aug. 1, 1882	80,000	72,000	64,320	7,680
First National Bank, Bay City, Mich	Nov. 8, 1882	400,000	156,100	135,479	20,621
First National Bank, Ripley, Ohio	Nov. 10, 1882	100,000	69,201	56,588	12,613
National Bank of State of New York, New York, N. Y	Dec. 6, 1882	800,000	397,004	354,017	42,987
First National Bank, Wellington, Ohio	Dec. 12, 1882	100,000	90,000	79,011	10,989
Second National Bank, Jefferson, Ohio	Dec. 26, 1882	100,000	90,000	74,668	15,332
First National Bank, Painesville, Ohio	Dec. 30, 1882	200,000	162,800	134,556	28,244
Saint Nicholas National Bank, New York, N. Y	Dec. 30, 1882	500,000	450,000	375,168	74,832
Fifth National Bank, Chicago, Ill	Dec. 30, 1882	500,000	29,700	19,327	10,373
First National Bank, Dowagiac, Mich	Jan. 3, 1883	50,000	45,000	40,058	4,942
First National Bank, Greenville, Ill	Jan. 9, 1883	150,000	59,400	47,053	12,347
Merchants' National Bank, East Saginaw, Mich	Jan. 9, 1883	200,000	101,100	85,703	15,397
Logan County National Bank, Russellville, Ky	Jan. 9, 1883	50,000	40,050	36,370	3,680
National Bank of Vandalia, Ill	Jan. 11, 1883	100,000	90,000	72,840	17,160
Traders' National Bank, Charlotte, N. C	Jan. 16, 1883	50,000	38,800	34,771	4,029
First National Bank, Norfolk, Nebr	Feb. 3, 1883	45,000	11,240	8,930	2,310
First National Bank, Midland City, Mich.*	Feb. 5, 1883	30,000	....	....	....
Citizens' National Bank, New Ulm, Minn	Mar. 1, 1883	50,000	27,000	21,680	5,320
National Bank of Owen, Owenton, Ky	Mar. 5, 1883	56,000	48,900	40,530	8,370
Merchants' National Bank, Nashville, Tenn	June 30, 1883	300,000	141,200	99,830	41,370
Indiana National Bank, Bedford, Ind	Aug. 25, 1883	35,000	11,250	11,250	None.
Stockton National Bank, Stockton, Cal	Oct. 1, 1883	100,000	90,000	71,830	18,170
Wall Street National Bank, New York, N. Y	Oct. 15, 1883	500,000	102,800	82,244	20,556
Commercial National Bank, Reading, Pa	Oct. 23, 1883	150,000	135,000	101,130	33,870
Corn Exchange National Bank, Chicago, Ill.*	Nov. 10, 1883	700,000	....	....	....
Farmers' National Bank, Sullivan, Ind	Dec. 24, 1883	50,000	45,000	32,710	12,290
City National Bank, La Salle, Ill	Jan. 8, 1884	100,000	22,500	12,660	9,840
Hunt County National Bank, Greenville, Tex	Jan. 22, 1884	68,250	17,300	10,070	7,230
Waldoboro' National Bank, Waldoboro', Me	Jan. 31, 1884	50,000	44,000	33,158	10,842
Third National Bank, Nashville, Tenn	Feb. 20, 1884	300,000	167,600	128,765	38,835
Madison County National Bank, Anderson, Ind	Mar. 25, 1884	50,000	45,000	35,040	9,960
First National Bank, Phenix, Ariz	Apr. 7, 1884	50,000	11,240	8,230	3,010
Cobbossee National Bank, Gardiner, Me	Apr. 18, 1884	150,000	90,000	66,092	23,908
Mechanics' and Traders' National Bank, New York, N. Y	Apr. 24, 1884	200,000	85,400	62,400	23,000
Princeton National Bank, Princeton, N. J	May 17, 1884	100,000	72,500	58,300	14,200
Kearsarge National Bank, Warner, N. H	June 30, 1884	50,000	23,586	19,241	4,345
Second National Bank, Lansing, Mich	July 31, 1884	50,000	40,000	26,949	13,051
First National Bank, Ellensburg, Wash	Aug. 9, 1884	50,000	13,500	9,050	4,450
German National Bank, Millerstown, Pa	Aug. 12, 1884	50,000	45,000	27,295	17,705
Exchange National Bank, Cincinnati, Ohio	Aug. 27, 1884	500,000	78,000	46,120	31,880
First National Bank, Rushville, Ill	Sept. 30, 1884	75,000	66,500	38,394	28,106
Mechanics' National Bank, Peoria, Ill	Oct. 4, 1884	100,000	72,000	43,418	28,582
First National Bank, Freeport, Pa	Oct. 10, 1884	50,000	44,200	26,630	17,570
Genesee County National Bank, Batavia, N. Y	Oct. 11, 1884	50,000	45,000	32,640	12,360
Valley National Bank, Red Oak, Iowa	Oct. 20, 1884	50,000	22,150	14,000	8,150
Merchants' National Bank, Bismarck, Dak	Oct. 28, 1884	75,000	22,500	12,990	9,510

NATIONAL BANKS THAT HAVE GONE INTO VOLUNTARY LIQUIDATION UNDER THE PROVISIONS OF SECTIONS 5220 AND 5221 OF THE REVISED STATUTES, ETC.—Continued.

Name and location of bank.	Date of liquidation.	Capital.	Circulation.		
			Issued.	Retired.	Outstanding.
Manufacturers' National Bank, Minneapolis, Minn	Nov. 1, 1884	$300,000	$45,000	$23,700	$21,300
Farmers and Merchants' National Bank, Uhrichsville, Ohio	Nov. 10, 1884	50,000	34,000	20,510	14,090
Metropolitan National Bank, New York, N. Y	Nov. 18, 1884	3,000,000	1,447,000	966,100	480,900
First National Bank, Grand Forks, Dak.	Dec. 2, 1884	50,000	19,250	15,080	4,170
Iron National Bank, Gunnison, Colo	Dec. 8, 1884	50,000	11,250	6,860	4,390
Freehold National Banking Company, Freehold, N. J	Dec. 10, 1884	50,000	93,000	65,360	27,640
Albia National Bank, Albia, Iowa	Dec. 16, 1884	50,000	11,240	7,060	4,180
First National Bank, Carlinville, Ill	Dec. 16, 1884	50,000	22,450	16,301	6,149
Freeman's National Bank, Augusta, Me.	Dec. 26, 1884	100,000	90,000	58,825	31,175
First National Bank, Kokomo, Ind	Jan. 1, 1885	250,000	45,000	28,520	16,480
First National Bank, Sabetha, Kans	Jan. 2, 1885	50,000	10,740	6,610	4,130
First National Bank, Wyoming, Ill	Jan. 13, 1885	50,000	11,200	5,620	5,580
First National Bank, Tarentum, Pa	Jan. 13, 1885	50,000	42,500	24,420	18,080
First National Bank, Walnut, Ill	Jan. 21, 1885	60,000	36,000	19,750	16,250
Farmers' National Bank, Franklin, Tenn.	Jan. 24, 1885	50,000	10,740	6,100	4,640
Citizens' National Bank, Sabetha, Kans.	Jan. 27, 1885	50,000	11,240	6,470	4,770
First National Bank, Tucson, Ariz	Jan. 31, 1885	100,000	28,100	20,670	7,430
Ripon National Bank, Ripon, Wis	Feb. 7, 1885	50,000	16,200	8,115	8,085
Farmers' National Bank, Franklin, Ohio.	Apr. 1, 1885	50,000	27,350	16,540	10,810
First National Bank, Prescott, Ariz	Apr. 9, 1885	50,000	11,250	6,000	5,250
National Union Bank, Swanton, Vt	Apr. 28, 1885	50,000	43,800	25,390	18,410
German National Bank, Memphis, Tenn.	May 6, 1885	175,300	120,100	67,630	52,470
Merchants and Farmers' National Bank, Shakopee, Minn	May 12, 1885	50,000	10,240	5,160	5,080
First National Bank, Superior, Wis	May 16, 1885	60,000	18,900	14,540	4,360
Shetucket National Bank, Norwich, Conn	May 18, 1885	100,000	72,000	42,732	29,268
Cumberland National Bank, Cumberland, R. I	June 5, 1885	125,000	106,200	63,759	42,441
First National Bank, Columbia, Tenn	July 14, 1885	100,000	66,800	32,647	34,153
Union National Bank, New York, N. Y.	July 21, 1885	1,200,000	25,100	9,742	15,358
Manufacturers' National Bank, Appleton, Wis	Oct. 10, 1885	50,000	45,000	20,673	24,327
First National Bank, Plankinton, Dak	Oct. 21, 1885	50,000	11,250	4,560	6,690
First National Bank, Centerville, Ind	Oct. 3, 1885	50,000	27,350	14,250	13,100
Valley National Bank, St. Louis, Mo	Dec. 4, 1885	250,000	44,960	16,740	28,220
First National Bank, Belton, Tex	Jan. 6, 1886	50,000	23,490	8,920	14,570
First National Bank, Granville, Ohio	Feb. 15, 1886	50,000	26,500	10,510	15,990
Concordia National Bank, Concordia, Kans	Mar. 12, 1886	50,000	11,240	4,530	6,710
Citizens' National Bank, Beloit, Wis	Mar. 22, 1886	50,000	11,240	4,750	6,490
First National Bank, Dayton, Wash	Mar. 24, 1886	50,000	13,490	7,820	5,670
First National Bank, Macomb, Ill	Apr. 14, 1886	100,000	89,520	30,113	59,407
First National Bank, Jesup, Iowa	Apr. 20, 1886	50,000	25,760	12,280	13,480
Dallas National Bank, Dallas, Tex	May 8, 1886	150,000	33,750	9,660	24,090
First National Bank, Lewistown, Ill	May 12, 1886	50,000	45,000	13,430	31,570
First National Bank, Cedar Rapids, Iowa	May 28, 1886	100,000	35,490	10,538	24,952
First National Bank, Socorro, N. Mex	July 31, 1886	50,000	15,500	4,320	11,180
Custer County National Bank, Broken Bow, Nebr	Aug. 9, 1886	50,000	11,240	11,240	....
Roanoke National Bank, Roanoke, Va	Sept. 16, 1886	50,000	11,250	3,690	7,560
First National Bank, Brownville, Nebr.	Sept. 16, 1886	50,000	39,680	8,739	30,941
First National Bank, Leslie, Mich	Sept. 25, 1886	50,000	13,410	3,980	9,430
Mount Vernon National Bank, Mount Vernon, Ill	Oct. 11, 1886	51,100	45,000	10,745	34,255
National Bank, Piedmont, W. Va	Oct. 14, 1886	50,000	45,000	11,710	33,290
First National Bank, Saint Clair, Mich	Oct. 20, 1886	50,000	39,310	10,248	29,062
First National Bank, Milford, Mich	Oct. 21, 1886	50,000	45,000	8,710	36,290
National Bank, Kingwood, W. Va	Oct. 21, 1886	125,000	96,140	20,230	75,910
Merchants' National Bank, Lima, Ohio	Oct. 22, 1886	50,000	45,000	9,350	35,650
Hubbard National Bank, Hubbard, Ohio.	Oct. 23, 1886	50,000	45,000	10,599	34,401
Commercial National Bank, Marshalltown, Iowa	Oct. 25, 1886	150,000	22,500	4,200	18,300
First National Bank, Indianapolis, Ind	Nov. 11, 1886	500,000	162,325	30,295	132,030
First National Bank, Concord, Mich	Nov. 27, 1886	50,000	11,250	2,700	8,550
Jamestown National Bank, Jamestown, Dak	Nov. 29, 1886	50,000	11,250	1,500	9,750
First National Bank, Berea, Ohio	Dec. 1, 1886	50,000	45,000	9,909	35,091
First National Bank, Allerton, Iowa	Dec. 6, 1886	50,000	11,250	3,380	7,870
Second National Bank, Hillsdale, Mich.	Dec. 18, 1886	50,000	13,892	3,228	10,664

NATIONAL BANKS THAT HAVE GONE INTO VOLUNTARY LIQUIDATION UNDER THE PROVISIONS OF SECTIONS 5220 AND 5221 OF THE REVISED STATUTES, ETC.—Continued.

Name and location of bank.	Date of liquidation.	Capital.	Circulation.		
			Issued.	Retired.	Outstanding.
Topton National Bank, Topton, Pa	Dec. 28, 1886	$50,000	$18,000	$2,960	$15,040
First National Bank, Warsaw, Ill	Dec. 31, 1886	50,000	38,250	3,470	34,780
First National Bank, Hamburgh, Iowa	Dec. 31, 1886	50,000	13,500	3,425	10,075
Darlington National Bank, Darlington, S. C	Feb. 10, 1887	100,000	22,500	5,910	16,560
Union National Bank, Cincinnati, Ohio	Feb. 14, 1887	500,000	237,230	49,052	188,178
Roberts National Bank, Titusville, Pa	Feb. 28, 1887	100,000	75,610	12,300	63,310
National Bank, Rahway, N. J	Mar. 9, 1887	100,000	42,500	6,184	36,316
Olney National Bank, Olney, Ill	Mar. 11, 1887	60,000	27,000	4,630	22,370
Metropolitan National Bank, Leavenworth, Kans	Mar. 15, 1887	100,000	22,500	2,590	19,910
Ontario County National Bank, Canandaigua, N. Y	Mar. 23, 1887	50,000	11,250	1,100	10,150
Winsted National Bank, Winsted, Conn	Apr. 12, 1887	50,000	11,250	2,120	9,130
Council Bluffs National Bank, Council Bluffs, Iowa	May 5, 1887	100,000	22,500	1,130	21,370
First National Bank, Homer, Ill	June 22, 1887	50,000	11,250	5,130	6,120
First National Bank, Beloit, Wis	June 30, 1887	50,000	11,250	1,350	9,900
Mystic National Bank, Mystic, Conn	July 7, 1887	52,450	47,205	3,166	44,039
Exchange National Bank, Louisiana, Mo	July 12, 1887	50,000	11,250	1,130	10,120
Exchange National Bank, Downs, Kans	Aug. 1, 1887	50,000	11,250	550	10,700
Total		61,208,700	37,589,847	33,585,367	4,004,480

NATIONAL BANKS THAT HAVE GONE INTO VOLUNTARY LIQUIDATION UNDER THE PROVISIONS OF SECTIONS 5220 AND 5221 OF THE REVISED STATUTES OF THE UNITED STATES, FOR THE PURPOSE OF ORGANIZING NEW ASSOCIATIONS WITH THE SAME OR DIFFERENT TITLE, WITH DATE OF LIQUIDATION, AMOUNT OF CAPITAL, CIRCULATION ISSUED, RETIRED, AND OUTSTANDING ON OCTOBER 31, 1887.

Name and location of bank.	Date of liquidation.	Capital.	Circulation.		
			Issued.	Retired.	Outstanding.
First National Bank, Rondout, N. Y.	Oct. 30, 1880	$300,000	$270,000	$240,734	$29,266
First National Bank, Huntington, Ind.	Jan. 31, 1881	100,000	90,000	84,711	5,289
First National Bank, Indianapolis, Ind.	July 5, 1881	300,000	279,248	241,009	38,239
First National Bank, Valparaiso Ind.	Apr. 24, 1882	50,000	45,000	40,947	4,053
First National Bank, Stillwater, Minn.	Apr. 29, 1882	130,000	83,456	77,980	5,476
First National Bank, Chicago, Ill.	Apr. 29, 1882	1,000,000	90,000	78,708	11,292
First National Bank, Woodstock, Ill.	Apr. 30, 1882	50,000	45,000	40,810	4,190
Second National Bank, Cincinnati, Ohio.	Apr. 28, 1882	200,000	180,000	151,690	28,310
Second National Bank, New York, N. Y.	Apr. 28, 1882	300,000	376,890	323,670	53,220
First National Bank, Portsmouth, N. H.	Apr. 29, 1882	300,000	286,000	249,816	36,184
First National Bank, Richmond, Ind.	May 5, 1882	200,000	87,400	72,182	15,218
Second National Bank, Cleveland, Ohio.	May 6, 1882	1,000,000	510,800	425,445	85,355
First National Bank, New Haven, Conn.	May 6, 1882	500,000	355,310	313,760	41,550
First National Bank, Akron, Ohio	May 2, 1882	100,000	114,822	93,733	21,089
First National Bank Worcester, Mass.	May 4, 1882	300,000	252,000	225,083	26,917
First National Bank, Barre, Mass.	May 9, 1882	150,000	135,000	116,215	18,785
First National Bank, Davenport, Iowa.	May 9, 1882	100,000	45,000	36,830	8,170
First National Bank, Kendallville, Ind.	May 12, 1882	150,000	90,000	77,346	12,654
First National Bank, Cleveland, Ohio	May 13, 1882	300,000	266,462	220,875	45,587
First National Bank, Youngstown, Ohio	May 15, 1882	500,000	441,529	388,665	52,864
First National Bank, Evansville, Ind.	May 15, 1882	500,000	442,870	376,040	66,830
First National Bank, Salem, Ohio.	May 15, 1882	50,000	110,540	93,780	16,760
First National Bank, Scranton, Pa.	May 18, 1882	200,000	45,000	35,710	9,290
First National Bank, Centreville, Ind.	May 18, 1882	50,000	64,525	57,271	7,254
First National Bank, Fort Wayne, Ind.	May 22, 1882	300,000	45,000	35,339	9,661
First National Bank, Strasburgh, Pa.	May 22, 1882	100,000	79,200	68,629	10,573
First National Bank, Marietta, Pa.	May 27, 1882	100,000	99,000	83,085	15,915
First National Bank, La Fayette, Ind.	May 31, 1882	150,000	175,060	154,378	20,682
First National Bank, McConnelsville, Ohio	May 31, 1882	50,000	84,640	71,596	13,044
First National Bank, Milwaukee, Wis.	May 31, 1882	200,000	229,170	194,632	34,538
Second National Bank, Akron, Ohio	May 31, 1882	100,000	102,706	86,040	16,666
First National Bank, Ann Arbor, Mich.	June 1, 1882	100,000	85,078	74,092	10,986
First National Bank, Geneva, Ohio	June 1, 1882	100,000	90,000	73,950	16,050
First National Bank, Oberlin, Ohio	June 1, 1882	50,000	58,382	48,690	9,692
First National Bank Philadelphia, Pa.	June 10, 1882	1,000,000	799,800	657,750	142,050
First National Bank, Troy, Ohio.	June 10, 1882	200,000	180,000	153,690	26,310
Third National Bank, Cincinnati, Ohio	June 14, 1882	800,000	609,500	506,720	102,780
First National Bank, Cambridge City, Ind.	June 15, 1882	50,000	45,000	36,638	8,362
First National Bank, Lyons, Iowa	June 15, 1882	100,000	90,000	70,477	19,523
First National Bank, Detroit, Mich.	June 17, 1882	500,000	336,345	295,378	40,967
First National Bank, Wilkes Barre, Pa.	June 20, 1882	375,000	337,500	285,385	52,115
First National Bank, Iowa City, Iowa	June 24, 1882	100,000	88,400	77,390	11,010
First National Bank, Nashua, N. H.	June 24, 1882	100,000	90,000	77,548	12,452
First National Bank, Johnstown, Pa.	June 24, 1882	60,000	54,000	45,345	8,655
First National Bank, Pittsburgh, Pa.	June 29, 1882	750,000	594,000	492,440	101,560
First National Bank, Terre Haute, Ind.	June 29, 1882	200,000	141,575	118,208	23,367
First National Bank, Hollidaysburgh, Pa.	June 30, 1882	50,000	45,000	40,065	4,935
First National Bank, Bath, Me.	June 30, 1882	200,000	180,000	155,232	24,768
First National Bank, Janesville, Wis.	June 30, 1882	125,000	121,050	102,100	18,950
First National Bank, Michigan City, Ind.	June 30, 1882	100,000	45,000	42,838	2,162
First National Bank, Monmouth, Ill.	July 3, 1882	75,000	45,000	41,584	3,416
First National Bank, Marion, Iowa.	July 11, 1882	50,000	45,000	40,834	4,166
First National Bank, Marlborough, Mass	Aug. 3, 1882	200,000	180,000	156,971	23,029
National Bank of Stanford, Ky.	Oct. 3, 1882	150,000	135,000	117,891	17,109
First National Bank, Sandusky, Ohio.	Oct. 6, 1882	150,000	90,000	73,021	16,979
First National Bank, Sandy Hill, N. Y.	Dec. 31, 1882	50,000	45,000	37,888	7,112
First National Bank, Lawrenceburgh, Ind	Feb. 24, 1883	100,000	90,000	77,585	12,415
First National Bank, Cambridge, Ohio.	Feb. 24, 1883	100,000	80,800	65,595	15,205
First National Bank, Oshkosh, Wis.	Feb. 24, 1883	100,000	47,800	42,840	4,960
First National Bank, Grand Rapids, Mich	Feb. 24, 1883	400,000	155,900	141,360	14,540
First National Bank, Delphos, Ohio.	Feb. 24, 1883	50,000	45,000	39,479	5,521
First National Bank, Freeport, Ill	Feb. 24, 1883	100,000	53,500	48,649	4,851
First National Bank, Elyria, Ohio	Feb. 24, 1883	100,000	90,000	75,004	14,996
First National Bank, Troy, N. Y.	Feb. 24, 1883	300,000	229,550	198,400	31,150
Second National Bank, Detroit, Mich	Feb. 24, 1883	1,000,000	363,700	297,262	66,438
Second National Bank, Peoria, Ill.	Feb. 24, 1883	100,000	90,000	65,385	24,615
National Fort Plain Bank, Fort Plain, N. Y	Feb. 24, 1883	200,000	174,300	145,621	28,679

NATIONAL BANKS THAT HAVE GONE INTO VOLUNTARY LIQUIDATION UNDER THE PROVISIONS OF SECTIONS 5220 AND 5221 OF THE REVISED STATUTES, ETC.—Continued.

Name and location of bank.	Date of liquidation.	Capital.	Circulation.		
			Issued.	Retired.	Outstanding.
Logansport National Bank, Logansport, Ind	Dec. 1, 1883	$100,000	$16,850	$12,810	$4,040
National Bank of Birmingham, Ala	May 14, 1884	50,000	45,000	33,932	11,068
First National Bank, Westfield, N. Y	June 1, 1884	50,000	42,800	29,345	13,455
First National Bank, Independence, Iowa	Oct. 31, 1884	100,000	90,000	59,150	30,850
First National Bank, Sturgis, Mich	Dec. 31, 1884	50,000	43,850	29,629	14,221
National Bank of Rutland, Vt	Jan. 13, 1885	500,000	238,700	159,953	78,747
Kent National Bank, Chestertown, Md	Feb. 12, 1885	50,000	29,450	22,430	7,020
National Fulton County Bank, Gloversville, N. Y	Feb. 20, 1885	150,000	135,000	87,171	47,829
First National Bank, Centralia, Ill	Feb. 25, 1885	80,000	70,600	38,900	31,700
National Exchange Bank, Albion, Mich	Feb. 28, 1885	75,000	30,600	17,053	13,547
First National Bank, Paris, Mo	Mar. 31, 1885	100,000	89,155	46,850	42,305
First National Bank, Yakima, Wash	June 20, 1885	50,000	11,650	7,660	6,990
First National Bank, Flint, Mich	June 30, 1885	200,000	122,500	67,049	55,451
Total		17,570,000	12,441,963	10,387,944	2,054,019

NAMES OF BANKS IN LIQUIDATION UNDER SECTION 7, ACT JULY 12, 1882, WITH DATE OF EXPIRATION OF CHARTER, CIRCULATION ISSUED, RETIRED, AND OUTSTANDING OCTOBER 31, 1887.

Name and location of bank.	Date of liquidation.	Capital.	Circulation.		
			Issued.	Retired.	Outstanding.
First National Bank, Pontiac, Mich	Dec. 31, 1881	$50,000	$88,800	$75,225	$13,665
First National Bank, Washington, Iowa	Apr. 11, 1882	100,000	88,565	76,124	12,441
First National Bank, Fremont, Ohio	May 22, 1882	100,000	90,000	75,311	14,689
Second National Bank, Dayton, Ohio	May 26, 1882	300,000	262,941	217,035	45,906
First National Bank, Girard, Pa	June 1, 1882	100,000	90,000	78,205	11,795
First National Bank, Xenia, Ohio	Feb. 24, 1883	120,000	108,000	87,130	20,870
First National Bank, Peru, Ill	Feb. 24, 1883	100,000	45,000	34,744	10,256
First National Bank, Elmira, N. Y	Feb. 24, 1883	100,000	90,000	75,120	14,880
First National Bank, Chittenango, N. Y	Feb. 24, 1883	150,000	135,000	122,125	12,875
First National Bank, Eaton, Ohio	July 4, 1884	50,000	44,300	28,280	16,020
First National Bank, Leominster, Mass	July 5, 1884	300,000	244,400	180,560	63,840
First National Bank, Winona, Minn	July 21, 1884	50,000	44,200	31,744	12,456
American National Bank, Hallowell, Me	Sept. 10, 1884	75,000	67,500	47,745	19,755
First National Bank, Attica, Ind	Oct. 28, 1884	56,000	50,400	36,495	13,905
Citizens' National Bank, Indianapolis, Ind	Nov. 11, 1884	300,000	87,800	54,641	33,159
First National Bank, North East, Pa	Dec. 23, 1884	50,000	24,550	16,117	8,433
First National Bank, Galva, Ill	Jan. 2, 1885	50,000	36,000	22,954	13,046
First National Bank, Thorntown, Ind	Jan. 13, 1885	50,000	43,740	26,470	17,270
Muncie National Bank, Muncie, Ind	Jan. 28, 1885	200,000	161,000	94,472	66,528
Merchants' National Bank, Evansville, Ind	Feb. 6, 1885	250,000	90,800	55,501	35,299
Saybrook National Bank, Essex, Conn	Feb. 20, 1885	100,000	61,200	41,870	19,330
Union National Bank, Albany, N. Y	Mar. 7, 1885	250,000	144,400	102,172	42,228
Battenkill National Bank, Manchester, Vt	Mar. 21, 1885	75,000	57,700	35,898	21,802
First National Bank, Owosso, Mich	Apr. 14, 1885	60,000	47,700	29,129	18,571
Coventry National Bank, Anthony, R. I	Apr. 17, 1885	100,000	89,000	55,555	33,445
State National Bank, Keokuk, Iowa	May 23, 1885	150,000	45,000	21,780	23,220
Tolland County National Bank, Tolland, Conn	June 6, 1885	100,000	44,100	25,281	18,819
City National Bank, Hartford, Conn	June 9, 1885	550,000	90,000	54,367	35,633
West River National Bank, Jamaica, Vt	Aug. 17, 1885	60,000	54,000	29,858	24,142
National Bank, Lebanon, Tenn	Aug. 30, 1886	50,000	24,550	5,820	18,730
Total		4,046,000	2,550,736	1,837,728	713,008

NAMES OF BANKS IN LIQUIDATION UNDER SECTION 7, ACT JULY 12, 1882, WITH DATE OF EXPIRATION OF CHARTER, CIRCULATION ISSUED, RETIRED, AND OUTSTANDING, SUCCEEDED BY ASSOCIATIONS WITH THE SAME OR DIFFERENT TITLE, OCTOBER 31, 1887.

Name and location of bank.	Date of liquidation.	Capital.	Circulation.		
			Issued.	Retired.	Outstanding.
First National Bank, Kittanning, Pa	July 2, 1882	$200,000	$199,500	$167,550	$31,950
National Bank of Beaver County, New Brighton, Pa	Nov. 12, 1884	200,000	97,300	61,253	36,047
National Bank, Beaver Dam, Wis	Dec. 24, 1884	50,000	41,100	27,199	13,901
Merchants' National Bank, Cleveland, Ohio	Dec. 27, 1884	800,000	228,100	144,323	83,777
Union National Bank, Chicago, Ill	Dec. 29, 1884	1,000,000	62,800	32,610	30,190
First National Bank, Le Roy, N. Y	Jan. 2, 1885	150,000	135,000	89,274	45,726
Evansville National Bank, Evansville, Ind	Jan. 3, 1885	600,000	543,050	321,669	221,381
National Albany Exchange Bank, Albany, N. Y	Jan. 10, 1885	300,000	243,000	162,010	80,990
National Bank, Galena, Ill	Jan. 11, 1885	100,000	55,900	31,200	24,700
National State Bank, Lafayette, Ind	Jan. 16, 1885	300,000	615,000	562,455	52,545
First National Bank, Knoxville, Ill	Jan. 16, 1885	60,000	43,600	25,621	17,979
Farmers' National Bank, Ripley, Ohio	Jan. 17, 1885	100,000	87,400	49,920	37,480
City National Bank, Grand Rapids, Mich	Jan. 21, 1885	300,000	45,000	31,670	13,330
Lee County National Bank, Dixon, Ill	Jan. 21, 1885	100,000	41,500	27,671	13,829
Fort Wayne National Bank, Fort Wayne, Ind	Jan. 25, 1885	350,000	257,300	145,346	111,954
National Exchange Bank, Tiffin, Ohio	Mar. 1, 1885	125,000	50,500	28,503	21,997
National Bank, Malone, N. Y	Mar. 9, 1885	200,000	65,900	40,404	25,496
Jefferson National Bank, Steubenville, Ohio	Mar. 21, 1885	150,000	132,600	71,162	61,438
First National Bank, Battle Creek, Mich	Mar. 28, 1885	100,000	89,200	43,690	45,510
Central National Bank, Danville, Ky	Mar. 28, 1885	200,000	180,000	96,032	83,968
Knox County National Bank, Mount Vernon, Ohio	Apr. 1, 1885	75,000	53,200	29,161	24,039
First National Bank, Houghton, Mich	Apr. 18, 1885	100,000	45,000	25,260	19,740
National Bank, Fort Edward, N. Y	Apr. 22, 1885	100,000	88,900	56,705	32,195
National Bank, Salem, N. Y	May 4, 1885	100,000	86,100	51,135	34,965
National Exchange Bank, Seneca Falls, N. Y	May 6, 1885	100,000	88,400	53,352	35,048
Trumbull National Bank, Warren, Ohio	July 5, 1885	150,000	132,400	57,780	74,620
Attleborough National Bank, North Attleborough, Mass	July 17, 1885	100,000	84,300	46,965	37,335
American National Bank, Detroit, Mich	July 24, 1885	400,000	251,500	123,330	128,170
First National Bank, Paris, Ill	Aug. 12, 1885	125,000	111,500	49,070	62,430
First National Bank, Saint John, Mich	Aug. 14, 1885	50,000	21,000	10,490	10,510
Second National Bank, Pontiac, Mich	Sept. 1, 1885	100,000	43,000	23,397	19,603
Raleigh National Bank of North Carolina, Raleigh, N. C	Sept. 5, 1885	400,000	123,900	62,417	61,483
First National Bank, Danville, Ky	Sept. 22, 1885	150,000	130,500	59,089	71,411
Total		7,535,000	4,474,350	2,808,613	1,665,737

NATIONAL BANKS THAT HAVE BEEN PLACED IN THE HANDS OF RECEIVERS, TOGETHER WITH THEIR CAPITAL, CIRCULATION ISSUED, LAWFUL MONEY DEPOSITED WITH THE TREASURER TO REDEEM CIRCULATION, THE AMOUNT REDEEMED, AND THE AMOUNT OUTSTANDING ON OCTOBER 31, 1887.

Name and location of bank.	Capital stock.	Lawful money deposited.	Circulation.		
			Issued.	Redeemed.	Outstanding.
First National Bank, Attica, N. Y	$50,000	$14,000	$44,000	$43,752	$248
Venango National Bank, Franklin, Pa	300,000	85,000	85,000	84,754	246
Merchants' National Bank, Washington, D. C	200,000	180,000	180,000	179,294	706
First National Bank, Medina, N. Y	50,000	40,000	40,000	39,752	248
Tennessee National Bank, Memphis, Tenn	100,000	90,000	90,000	89,679	321
First National Bank, Selma, Ala	100,000	85,000	85,000	84,557	443
First National Bank, New Orleans, La	500,000	180,000	180,000	178,746	1,254
National Unadilla Bank, Unadilla, N. Y	120,000	100,000	100,000	99,770	230
Farmers and Citizens' National Bank, Brooklyn, N. Y	300,000	253,900	253,900	252,530	1,370
Croton National Bank, New York, N. Y	200,000	180,000	180,000	179,616	384
First National Bank, Bethel, Conn	60,000	26,300	26,300	26,095	205
First National Bank, Keokuk, Iowa	100,000	90,000	90,000	89,604	396
National Bank of Vicksburg, Miss	50,000	25,500	25,500	25,429	71
First National Bank, Rockford, Ill	50,000	45,000	45,000	44,688	312
First National Bank of Nevada, Austin, Nev	250,000	129,700	129,700	128,602	1,098
Ocean National Bank, New York, N. Y	1,000,000	800,000	800,000	791,537	8,463
Union Square National Bank, New York, N. Y	200,000	50,000	50,000	49,677	323
Eighth National Bank, New York, N. Y	250,000	243,393	243,393	240,658	2,735
Fourth National Bank, Philadelphia, Pa	200,000	179,000	179,000	177,415	1,585
Waverly National Bank, Waverly, N. Y	106,100	71,000	71,000	70,012	988
First National Bank, Fort Smith, Ark	50,000	45,000	45,000	44,475	525
Scandinavian National Bank, Chicago, Ill	250,000	135,000	135,000	134,471	529
Walkill National Bank, Middletown, N. Y	175,000	118,900	118,900	117,426	1,474
Crescent City National Bank, New Orleans, La	500,000	450,000	450,000	446,540	3,460
Atlantic National Bank, New York, N. Y	300,000	100,000	100,000	98,609	1,391
First National Bank, Washington, D. C	500,000	450,000	450,000	440,569	9,431
National Bank of Commonwealth, New York, N. Y	750,000	234,000	234,000	230,105	3,895
Merchants' National Bank, Petersburg, Va	400,000	360,000	360,000	354,385	5,615
First National Bank, Petersburg, Va	200,000	179,200	179,200	175,830	3,370
First National Bank, Mansfield, Ohio	100,000	90,000	90,000	88,446	1,554
New Orleans National Banking Association, New Orleans, La	600,000	360,000	360,000	354,000	6,000
First National Bank, Carlisle, Pa	50,000	45,000	45,000	44,235	765
First National Bank, Anderson, Ind	50,000	45,000	45,000	44,045	955
First National Bank, Topeka, Kans	100,000	90,000	90,000	88,531	1,469
First National Bank, Norfolk, Va	100,000	95,000	95,000	93,100	1,900
Gibson County National Bank, Princeton, Ind	50,000	43,800	43,800	43,315	485
First National Bank of Utah, Salt Lake City, Utah	150,000	118,191	118,191	116,439	1,752
Cook County National Bank, Chicago, Ill	500,000	285,100	285,100	281,733	3,367
First National Bank, Tiffin, Ohio	100,000	45,000	45,000	43,663	1,337
Charlottesville National Bank, Charlottesville, Va	200,000	140,585	140,585	143,215	3,370
Miners' National Bank, Georgetown, Colo	150,000	45,000	45,000	44,370	630
Fourth National Bank, Chicago, Ill	200,000	85,700	85,700	81,948	3,752
First National Bank, Bedford, Iowa	30,000	27,000	27,000	25,910	1,090
First National Bank, Osceola, Iowa	50,000	45,000	45,000	41,201	709
First National Bank, Duluth, Minn	100,000	45,000	45,000	44,132	868
First National Bank, La Crosse, Wis	50,000	45,000	45,000	43,898	1,102
City National Bank, Chicago, Ill	250,000	137,200	137,200	132,691	4,518
Watkins National Bank, Watkins, N. Y	75,000	67,500	67,500	64,992	2,508
First National Bank, Wichita, Kans	60,000	43,200	43,200	42,344	856
First National Bank, Greenfield, Ohio	50,000	29,062	29,062	28,356	1,306
National Bank of Fishkill, N. Y	200,000	177,200	177,200	171,049	6,151
First National Bank, Franklin, Ind	132,000	92,092	92,092	87,942	4,150
Northumberland County National Bank, Shamokin, Pa	67,000	60,300	60,300	57,930	2,370
First National Bank, Winchester, Ill	50,000	45,000	45,000	43,502	1,498
National Exchange Bank, Minneapolis, Minn	100,000	90,000	90,000	85,175	4,825
National Bank of State of Missouri, Saint Louis, Mo	2,500,000	1,693,660	1,693,660	1,665,171	28,489
First National Bank, Delphi, Ind	50,000	45,000	45,000	43,610	1,390
First National Bank, Georgetown, Colo	75,000	45,000	45,000	43,405	1,595
Lock Haven National Bank, Lock Haven, Pa	120,000	71,200	71,200	66,983	4,217
Third National Bank, Chicago, Ill	750,000	597,840	597,840	549,071	48,769
Central National Bank, Chicago, Ill	200,000	45,000	45,000	43,168	1,832

NATIONAL BANKS THAT HAVE BEEN PLACED IN THE HANDS OF RECEIVERS, ETC.—Continued.

Name and location of bank.	Capital stock.	Lawful money deposited.	Circulation.		
			Issued.	Redeemed.	Outstanding.
First National Bank, Kansas City, Mo	$500,000	$44,940	$44,940	$39,970	$4,970
Commercial National Bank, Kansas City, Mo	100,000	44,500	44,500	41,968	2,532
First National Bank, Ashland, Pa	112,500	75,554	75,554	69,089	6,465
First National Bank, Tarrytown, N. Y	100,000	89,200	89,200	84,234	4,966
First National Bank, Allentown, Pa	250,000	78,641	78,641	72,966	5,675
First National Bank, Waynesburg, Pa	100,000	69,345	69,345	68,285	1,060
Washington County National Bank, Greenwich, N. Y	200,000	114,220	114,220	108,577	5,643
First National Bank, Dallas, Tex	50,000	29,800	29,800	28,895	905
People's National Bank, Helena, Mont	100,000	89,300	89,300	85,681	3,619
First National Bank, Bozeman, Mont	50,000	44,400	44,400	43,205	1,195
Merchants' National Bank, Fort Scott, Kans	50,000	35,328	35,328	34,031	1,297
Farmers' National Bank, Platte City, Mo	50,000	27,000	27,000	26,260	740
First National Bank, Warrensburg, Mo	100,000	45,000	45,000	43,488	1,512
German American National Bank, Washington, D. C	130,000	62,500	62,500	61,470	1,030
German National Bank, Chicago, Ill	500,000	42,795	42,795	35,700	7,095
Commercial National Bank, Saratoga Springs, N. Y	100,000	86,900	86,900	83,334	3,566
Second National Bank, Scranton, Pa	200,000	91,465	91,465	83,513	7,952
National Bank of Poultney, Vt	100,000	90,000	90,000	85,687	4,313
First National Bank, Monticello, Ind	50,000	27,000	27,000	25,910	1,090
First National Bank, Butler, Pa	50,000	71,165	71,165	52,505	18,660
First National Bank, Meadville, Pa	100,000	89,500	89,500	80,667	8,833
First National Bank, Newark, N. J	300,000	326,643	326,643	299,577	27,066
First National Bank, Brattleboro', Vt	300,000	90,000	90,000	77,033	12,967
Mechanics' National Bank, Newark, N. J	500,000	450,000	450,000	391,143	58,857
First National Bank, Buffalo, N. Y	100,000	99,500	99,500	88,265	11,235
Pacific National Bank, Boston, Mass	961,300	450,000	450,000	426,452	23,548
First National Bank, Union Mills, Pa	50,000	43,000	43,000	37,480	5,520
Vermont National Bank, Saint Albans, Vt	200,000	65,200	65,200	52,333	12,867
First National Bank, Leadville, Colo	60,000	53,000	53,000	42,955	10,045
City National Bank, Lawrenceburg, Ind	100,000	77,000	77,000	54,200	22,800
First National Bank, Saint Albans, Vt	100,000	89,980	89,980	66,428	23,552
First National Bank, Monmouth, Ill	75,000	27,000	27,000	15,770	11,230
Marine National Bank, New York, N. Y	400,000	260,100	260,100	207,676	52,424
Hot Springs National Bank, Hot Springs, Ark	50,000	40,850	40,850	21,870	18,980
Richmond National Bank, Richmond, Ind	250,000	158,900	158,900	105,641	53,259
First National Bank, Livingston, Mont	50,000	11,240	11,240	7,345	3,895
First National Bank, Albion, N. Y	100,000	90,000	90,000	62,356	27,644
First National Bank, Jamestown, Dak	50,000	18,650	18,650	14,027	4,623
Logan National Bank, West Liberty, Ohio	50,000	23,400	23,400	13,450	9,950
Middletown National Bank, Middletown, N. Y	200,000	140,000	176,000	123,786	52,214
Farmers' National Bank, Bushnell, Ill	50,000	44,000	44,000	28,211	15,789
Schoharie County National Bank, Schoharie, N. Y	50,000	38,350	38,350	22,430	15,920
Exchange National Bank, Norfolk, Va	300,000	228,200	228,200	137,688	90,512
First National Bank, Lake City, Minn	50,000	44,420	44,420	17,577	26,843
Lancaster National Bank, Clinton, Mass	100,000	72,360	72,360	31,430	41,030
First National Bank, Sioux Falls, Dak	50,000	10,740	11,250	4,815	6,435
First National Bank, Wahpeton, Dak	50,000	8,120	17,120	6,205	10,915
First National Bank, Angelica, N. Y	100,000	89,000	89,000	32,126	56,874
City National Bank, Williamsport, Pa	100,000	43,140	43,140	15,050	28,090
Abington National Bank, Abington, Mass*	150,000	108,870	131,370	47,925	83,445
First National Bank, Blair, Nebr	50,000	26,180	26,180	6,350	19,830
First National Bank, Pine Bluff, Ark	50,000	15,030	26,280	7,305	18,975
Palatka National Bank, Palatka, Fla	50,000	19,210	19,210	1,595	17,615
Fidelity National Bank, Cincinnati, Ohio	1,000,000	10,000	90,000	2,235	87,765
Henrietta National Bank, Henrietta, Tex	50,000	....	11,250	....	11,250
National Bank, Sumter, S. C	50,000	....	11,250	....	11,250
First National Bank, Dansville, N. Y	50,000	4,480	11,250	....	11,250
First National Bank, Corry, Pa	100,000	29,379	44,450	....	44,450
Stafford National Bank, Stafford Springs, Conn	200,000	94,048	94,048	....	94,048
Total	24,058,900	14,023,675	14,818,276	13,392,311	1,425,965

INSOLVENT NATIONAL BANKS, WITH NUMBER OF BANK, DATE OF APPOINTMENT OF RECEIVERS, AMOUNT OF CAPITAL STOCK AND CLAIMS PROVED, AND RATE OF DIVIDENDS PAID TO CREDITORS.

No. of bank.	Name and location of bank.	Receiver appointed.	Capital stock.	Proved claims.	Dividends paid.	Remarks.
					Pr. ct.	
100	First National Bank of Attica, N. Y.	Apr. 14, 1865	$50,000	$122,089	58	Finally closed.
1176	Venango National Bank of Franklin, Pa.	May 1, 1866	500,000	434,531	23.37	Do.
627	Merchants' National Bank of Washington, D. C.	May 8, 1866	200,000	669,513	24.7	Do.
220	First National Bank of Medina, N. Y.	Mar. 13, 1867	50,000	82,338	30.15	Do.
1225	Tennessee National Bank of Memphis, Tenn.	Mar. 21, 1867	100,000	376,932	17½	Do.
1537	First National Bank of Selma, Ala.	Apr. 30, 1867	100,000	289,467	46.6	Do.
162	First National Bank of New Orleans, La.	May 20, 1867	500,000	1,119,313	70	Do.
1463	National Unadilla Bank, Unadilla, N. Y.	Aug. 20, 1867	120,000	127,801	45.9	Do.
1223	Farmers and Citizens' National Bank of Brooklyn, N. Y.	Sept. 6, 1867	300,000	1,191,500	96	Do.
1556	Croton National Bank of New York, N. Y.	Oct. 1, 1867	200,000	170,752	88.5	Do.
1141	First National Bank of Bethel, Conn.	Feb. 28, 1868	60,000	68,986	100	Do.
80	First National Bank of Keokuk, Iowa.	Mar. 3, 1868	100,000	205,256	68⅓	Do.
803	National Bank of Vicksburg, Miss.	Apr. 24, 1868	50,000	33,362	40.2	Do.
429	First National Bank of Rockford, Ill.	Mar. 15, 1869	50,000	69,874	41.9	Do.
1331	First National Bank of Nevada, Austin, Nev.	Oct. 14, 1869	250,000	170,012	92.7	Do.
1232	Ocean National Bank of New York, N. Y.	Dec. 13, 1871	1,000,000	1,28[illegible],254	100	Finally closed; 46 per cent. of interest paid.
1691	Union Square National Bank of New York, N. Y.	Dec. 15, 1871	200,000	157,170	100	Finally closed; 10 per cent. paid to stockholders.
384	Eighth National Bank of New York, N. Y.	Dec. 15, 1871	250,000	378,772	100	Finally closed.
286	Fourth National Bank of Philadelphia, Pa.	Dec. 20, 1871	200,000	645,558	100	Do.
1102	Waverly National Bank of Waverly, N. Y.	Apr. 23, 1872	106,100	79,864	100	Finally closed; 32.5 per cent. paid to stockholders.
1631	First National Bank of Fort Smith, Ark.	May 2, 1872	50,000	15,142	100	Finally closed; 13 per cent. paid to stockholders.
1078	Scandinavian National Bank of Chicago, Ill.	Dec. 12, 1872	250,000	249,174	57.46	Finally closed.
1473	Wallkill National Bank of Middletown, N. Y.	Dec. 31, 1872	175,000	171,468	100	Finally closed; 30 per cent. of interest paid.
1937	Crescent City National Bank of New Orleans, La.	Mar. 18, 1873	500,000	657,020	84.83	Finally closed.
1388	Atlantic National Bank of New York, N. Y.	Apr. 28, 1873	300,000	574,513	100	Finally closed; 50 per cent. of interest paid.
26	First National Bank of Washington, D. C.	Sept. 19, 1873	500,000	1,619,965	100	Finally closed.
1372	National Bank of the Commonwealth, New York, N. Y.	Sept. 22, 1873	750,000	796,995	100	Finally closed; 35.8 per cent. paid to stockholders.
1548	Merchants' National Bank of Petersburgh, Va.	Sept. 25, 1873	400,000	992,636	34	Finally closed.
1378	First National Bank of Petersburgh, Va.	Sept. 25, 1873	200,000	167,285	76	Do.
436	First National Bank of Mansfield, Ohio.	Oct. 18, 1873	100,000	175,068	57.5	Do.
1825	New Orleans National Banking Association, New Orleans, La.	Oct. 23, 1873	600,000	1,429,595	62	Do.
21	First National Bank of Carlisle, Pa.	Oct. 24, 1873	50,000	67,292	73.5	Do.

INSOLVENT NATIONAL BANKS, WITH NUMBER OF BANK, DATE OF APPOINTMENT OF RECEIVERS, ETC.—Continued.

No. of bank.	Name and location of bank.	Receiver appointed.	Capital stock.	Proved claims.	Dividends paid.	Remarks.
					Pr. ct.	
44	First National Bank of Anderson, Ind.	Nov. 23, 1873	$50,000	$143,705	39.5	Finally closed.
1660	First National Bank of Topeka, Kans.	Dec. 16, 1873	100,000	55,372	58.3	Do.
271	First National Bank of Norfolk, Va.	June 3, 1874	100,000	170,330	57.5	Do.
2066	Gibson County National Bank of Princeton, Ind.	Nov. 28, 1874	50,000	62,646	100	Do.
1695	First National Bank of Utah, Salt Lake City, Utah.	Dec. 10, 1874	150,000	93,021	24.301	Do.
1845	Cook County National Bank of Chicago, Ill.	Feb. 1, 1875	500,000	1,795,992	14.941	Do.
900	First National Bank of Tiffin, Ohio.	Oct. 22, 1875	100,000	237,824	66	Do.
1468	Charlottesville National Bank of Charlottesville, Va.	Oct. 28, 1875	200,000	376,756	62.56	Do.
2199	Miners' National Bank of Georgetown, Colo.	Jan. 24, 1876	150,000	177,512	76.5	Do.
276	Fourth National Bank of Chicago, Ill.*	Feb. 1, 1876	200,000	35,801	51	Do.
2298	First National Bank of Bedford, Iowa.	Feb. 1, 1876	30,000	56,457	22.5	Do.
1776	First National Bank of Osceola, Iowa.	Feb. 25, 1876	50,000	34,535	100	Do.
1954	First National Bank of Duluth, Minn.	Mar. 13, 1876	100,000	87,786	100	Finally closed; interest paid in full.
1313	First National Bank of La Crosse, Wis.	Apr. 11, 1876	50,000	135,952	48.4	Finally closed.
818	City National Bank of Chicago, Ill.	May 17, 1876	250,000	703,658	77.512	Do.
456	Watkins National Bank of Watkins, N. Y.	July 12, 1876	75,000	59,226	100	Finally closed; 13 per cent. paid to stockholders.
1913	First National Bank of Wichita, Kans.	Sept. 23, 1876	60,000	97,464	70	Finally closed.
101	First National Bank of Greenfield, Ohio.*	Dec. 12, 1876	50,000	35,023	27	Do.
971	National Bank of Fishkill, N. Y.	Jan. 27, 1877	200,000	352,062	100	Finally closed; 38.5 per cent. of interest paid.
50	First National Bank of Franklin, Ind.	Feb. 13, 1877	132,000	185,760	100	Finally closed; interest paid in full.
689	Northumberland County National Bank of Shamokin, Pa.	Mar. 12, 1877	67,000	175,932	81.59	Finally closed.
1484	First National Bank of Winchester, Ill.	Mar. 16, 1877	50,000	140,735	63.6	Do.
719	National Exchange Bank of Minneapolis, Minn.	May 24, 1877	100,000	227,355	89.179	Do.
1665	National Bank of the State of Missouri, Saint Louis, Mo.	June 23, 1877	2,500,000	1,935,721	100	Interest paid in full.
1949	First National Bank of Delphi, Ind.	July 20, 1877	50,000	133,112	100	Finally closed; interest paid in full.
1991	First National Bank of Georgetown, Colo.	Aug. 18, 1877	75,000	196,356	37.648	Finally closed.
1273	Lock Haven National Bank of Lock Haven, Pa.	Aug. 20, 1877	120,000	254,617	100	Do.
236	Third National Bank of Chicago, Ill.	Nov. 24, 1877	750,000	1,061,598	100	Interest paid in full.
2047	Central National Bank of Chicago, Ill.	Dec. 1, 1877	200,000	298,324	60	
1612	First National Bank of Kansas City, Mo.	Feb. 11, 1878	500,000	392,394	100	Finally closed.
1995	Commercial National Bank of Kansas City, Mo.	Feb. 11, 1878	100,000	75,175	100	Finally closed; 37.165 per cent. paid to stockholders.
403	First National Bank of Ashland, Pa.*	Feb. 28, 1878	112,500	29,204	100	Finally closed.
362	First National Bank of Tarrytown, N. Y.	Mar. 23, 1878	100,000	118,371	90.5	Do.

* Formerly in voluntary liquidation.

INSOLVENT NATIONAL BANKS, WITH NUMBER OF BANK, DATE OF APPOINTMENT OF RECEIVERS, AMOUNT OF CAPITAL STOCK, ETC.—Continued.

No. of bank.	Name and location of bank.	Receiver appointed.	Capital stock.	Proved claims.	Dividends paid.	Remarks.
					Pr. ct.	
161	First National Bank of Allentown, Pa.*	Apr. 15, 1878	$250,000	$90,424	88	Finally closed.
305	First National Bank of Waynesburg, Pa.	May 15, 1878	100,000	36,150	60	Do.
1260	Washington County National Bank of Greenwich, N. Y.	June 8, 1878	200,000	262,887	100	Do.
2157	First National Bank of Dallas, Tex.	June 8, 1878	50,000	77,104	38.1	Do.
2105	People's National Bank of Helena, Mont.	Sept. 13, 1878	100,000	108,048	40	
2027	First National Bank of Bozeman, Mont.	Sept. 14, 1878	50,000	70,191	98.35	Do.
1927	Merchants' National Bank of Fort Scott, Kans.*	Sept. 25, 1878	50,000	27,801	60	Do.
2356	Farmers' National Bank of Platte City, Mo.	Oct. 1, 1878	50,000	32,449	100	Finally closed; 18 per cent. paid to stockholders.
1856	First National Bank of Warrensburg, Mo.	Nov. 1, 1878	100,000	156,260	100	Finally closed; interest paid in full.
2358	German American National Bank of Washington, D. C.	Nov. 1, 1878	130,000	282,370	50	
1734	German National Bank of Chicago, Ill.*	Dec. 20, 1878	500,000	197,353	100	Finally closed; 42.3 per cent. of interest paid.
1227	Commercial National Bank of Saratoga Springs, N. Y.	Feb. 11, 1879	100,000	128,832	100	Finally closed; interest paid in full.
49	Second National Bank of Scranton, Pa.*	Mar. 15, 1879	200,000	132,461	100	Do.
1200	National Bank of Poultney, Vt.	Apr. 7, 1879	100,000	81,801	100	Do.
2208	First National Bank of Monticello, Ind.	July 18, 1879	50,000	21,182	98	Finally closed.
309	First National Bank of Butler, Pa.	July 23, 1879	50,000	108,385	81	Finally closed; 11 per cent. since last report.
115	First National Bank of Meadville, Pa.	June 9, 1880	100,000	93,625	100	Finally closed; interest paid in full.
52	First National Bank of Newark, N. J.	June 14, 1880	300,000	580,592	100	Do.
470	First National Bank of Brattleboro', Vt.	June 19, 1880	300,000	104,749	100	Do.
1251	Mechanics' National Bank of Newark, N. J.	Nov. 2, 1881	500,000	2,730,179	61.25	
235	First National Bank of Buffalo, N. Y.	Apr. 22, 1882	100,000	894,735	38	
2373	Pacific National Bank of Boston, Mass.	May 22, 1882	961,300	2,465,393	50	30 per cent. since last report.
110	First National Bank of Union Mills, Union City, Pa.	Mar. 24, 1883	50,000	186,993	65	
1583	Vermont National Bank of Saint Albans, Vt.	Aug. 9, 1883	200,000	401,492	42.5	
2420	First National Bank of Leadville, Colo.	Jan. 24, 1884	60,000	200,854	40	10 per cent. since last report.
2889	City National Bank of Lawrenceburgh, Ind.*	Mar. 11, 1884	100,000	46,441	81.10	Finally closed.
269	First National Bank of Saint Albans, Vt.	Apr. 22, 1884	100,000	291,010	25	
2751	First National Bank of Monmouth, Ill.	Apr. 22, 1884	75,000	237,524	95	
1215	Marine National Bank of New York, N. Y.	May 13, 1884	400,000	4,474,197	50	
2887	Hot Springs National Bank of Hot Springs, Ark.	June 2, 1884	50,000	36,526	100	
2090	Richmond National Bank of Richmond, Ind.	July 23, 1884	250,000	365,931	50	20 per cent. since last report.
3006	First National Bank of Livingston, Mont.	Aug. 25, 1884	50,000	28,350	75	Since last report.
166	First National Bank of Albion, N. Y.	Aug. 26, 1884	100,000	158,608	....	
2578	First National Bank of Jamestown, Dak.	Sept. 13, 1884	50,000	8,131	100	Finally closed; interest paid in full.

* Formerly in voluntary liquidation.

INSOLVENT NATIONAL BANKS, WITH NUMBER OF BANK, DATE OF APPOINTMENT OF RECEIVERS, AMOUNT OF CAPITAL STOCK, ETC.—Continued.

No. of bank.	Name and location of bank.	Receiver appointed.	Capital stock.	Proved claims.	Dividends paid.	Remarks.
					Pr. ct.	
2942	Logan National Bank of West Liberty, Ohio.	Oct. 18, 1884	$50,000	$80,665	50	10 per cent. since last report.
1276	Middletown National Bank of Middletown, N. Y.	Nov. 29, 1884	200,000	649,863	70	15 per cent. since last report.
1701	Farmers' National Bank of Bushnell, Ill.	Dec. 17, 1884	50,000	86,258	40	
1510	Schoharie County National Bank of Schoharie, N. Y.	Mar. 23, 1885	50,000	140,333	40	10 per cent. since last report.
1137	Exchange National Bank of Norfolk, Va.	Apr. 9, 1885	300,000	2,894,799	40	Do.
1740	First National Bank of Lake City, Minn.	Jan. 4, 1886	50,000	127,524	100	Finally closed; interest paid in full.
583	Lancaster National Bank of Clinton, Mass.	Jan. 20, 1886	100,000	170,384	70	20 per cent. since last report.
2465	First National Bank of Sioux Falls, Dak.	Mar. 11, 1886	50,000	51,041	20	
2624	First National Bank of Wahpeton, Dak.	Apr. 8, 1886	50,000	110,122	10	Since last report.
564	First National Bank of Angelica, N. Y.	Apr. 19, 1886	100,000	63,600	85	10 per cent. since last report.
2139	City National Bank of Williamsport, Pa.	May 4, 1886	100,000	130,772	100	Finally closed; interest paid in full.
1386	Abington National Bank of Abington, Mass.	Aug. 2, 1886	150,000	116,626	100	Do.
2724	First National Bank of Blair, Nebr.	Sept. 8, 1886	50,000	80,452	100	Do.
2776	First National Bank of Pine Bluff, Ark.	Nov. 20, 1886	50,000	64,061	25	
3266	Palatka National Bank of Palatka, Fla.	June 3, 1887	50,000	9,370	100	Finally closed; interest paid in full.
3461	Fidelity National Bank of Cincinnati, Ohio.	June 27, 1887	1,000,000	2,386,569	25	
3022	Henrietta National Bank of Henrietta, Tex.	Aug. 17, 1887	50,000	64,784	50	
3082	National Bank of Sumter, S. C.	Aug. 21, 1887	50,000	....	....	
75	First National Bank of Dansville, N. Y.	Sept. 8, 1887	50,000	....	....	
605	First National Bank of Corry, Pa.	Oct. 11, 1887	100,000	....	....	
686	Stafford National Bank of Stafford Springs, Conn.	Oct. 17, 1887	200,000	....	....	
	Total	....	24,058,900	46,055,215	....	

INSOLVENT NATIONAL BANKS, WITH DATES OF FAILURE, CAUSES OF FAILURE, NOMINAL ASSETS, AMOUNTS COLLECTED, CLAIMS PROVED, DIVIDENDS PAID, AND DATES OF CLOSING.

Title of bank.	Date of organization.	Receiver appointed.	Cause of failure.	Nominal assets.	Amount collected.	Claims proved.	Dividends.	Finally closed.
							Per cent.	
First National Bank, Attica, N. Y.	Jan. 14, 1864	Apr. 14, 1865			$76,373.02	$122,089	58	Jan. 2, 1867
Venango National Bank, Franklin, Pa.	May 20, 1865	May 1, 1866		$986,637.00	122,239.37	434,531	23.37	Feb. 2, 1885
Merchants' National Bank, Washington, D. C.	Dec. 14, 1864	May 8, 1866				669,513	24.7	July 29, 1678
First National Bank, Medina, N. Y.	Feb. 3, 1864	Mar. 13, 1867				82,338	39.15	July 28, 1870
Tennessee National Bank, Memphis, Tenn.	June 5, 1865	Mar. 21, 1867				376,932	17.33	Feb. 4, 1870
First National Bank, Selma, Ala.	Aug. 24, 1865	Apr. 30, 1867				289,467	46.6	Nov. 23, 1882
First National Bank, New Orleans, La.	Dec. 18, 1863	May 20, 1867		1,987,238.90	942,509.63	1,119,313	79	Sept. 28, 1882
National Unadilla Bank, Unadilla, N. Y.	July 17, 1865	Aug. 20, 1867				127,801	45.9	Dec. 19, 1874
Farmers and Citizens' National Bank, Brooklyn, N. Y.	June 5, 1865	Sept. 6, 1867				1,191,500	96	Nov. 18, 1874
Croton National Bank, New York, N. Y.	Sept. 9, 1865	Oct. 1, 1867				170,752	88.5	Aug. 15, 1872
First National Bank, Bethel, Conn.	May 15, 1865	Feb. 28, 1868				68,986	100	Apr. 7, 1881
First National Bank, Keokuk, Iowa	Sept. 9, 1863	Mar. 3, 1868				205,256	68.33	Nov. 30, 1872
National Bank, Vicksburg, Miss.	Feb. 14, 1865	Apr. 24, 1868				33,562	49.2	Nov. 25, 1882
First National Bank, Rockford, Ill.	May 29, 1864	Mar. 15, 1869				69,874	41.9	Dec. 4, 1875
First National Bank of Nevada, Austin, Nev.	June 23, 1865	Oct. 14, 1869				170,012	92.7	May 16, 1884
Ocean National Bank, New York, N. Y.	June 6, 1865	Dec. 13, 1871		2,935,921.00	1,730,845.00	1,282,254	100	Apr. 20, 1882
Union Square National Bank, New York, N. Y.	Mar. 30, 1869	Dec. 15, 1871				157,120	100	Nov. 16, 1874
Eighth National Bank, New York, N. Y.	Apr. 6, 1864	Dec. 15, 1871				378,772	100	Sept. 1, 1875
Fourth National Bank, Philadelphia, Pa.	Feb. 26, 1864	Dec. 20, 1871				645,558	100	Feb. 13, 1872
Waverly National Bank, Waverly, N. Y.	May 29, 1865	Apr. 23, 1872		139,617.00	67,827.00	79,864	100	Oct. 2, 1877
First National Bank, Fort Smith, Ark.	Feb. 6, 1866	May 2, 1872				15,142	100	Jan. 3, 1876
Scandinavian National Bank, Chicago, Ill.	May 7, 1872	Dec. 12, 1872		400,574.00	169,661.00	249,174	57.46	Feb. 15, 1886
Wallkill National Bank, Middletown, N. Y.	July 21, 1865	Dec. 31, 1872		227,871.00	218,204.00	171,468	100	Jan. 8, 1680
Crescent City National Bank, New Orleans, La.	Feb. 15, 1872	Mar. 18, 1873		806,993.00	612,027.00	657,020	84.83	June 1, 1881
Atlantic National Bank, New York, N. Y.	July 1, 1865	Apr. 28, 1873		742,419.00	786,360.00	574,513	100	Apr. 29, 1884
First National Bank, Washington, D. C.	July 16, 1863	Sept. 19, 1873				1,619,965	100	July 24, 1876
National Bank of the Commonwealth, New York, N. Y.	July 1, 1865	Sept. 22, 1873	Injudicious banking and depreciation of securities.	3,509,000.00	2,042,009.00	796,995	100	Mar. 31, 1883
Merchants' National Bank, Petersburg, Va.	Sept. 1, 1865	Sept. 25, 1873	Defalcation by officers; fraudulent management and depreciation of securities.	1,019,841.00	299,358.00	992,636	34	May 1, 1876
First National Bank, Petersburg, Va.	July 1, 1865	Sept. 25, 1873	do	272,634.00	112,321.00	167,285	76	May 15, 1876
First National Bank, Mansfield, Ohio	May 24, 1864	Oct. 18, 1873				175,068	57.5	Nov. 30, 1883

INSOLVENT NATIONAL BANKS, WITH DATES OF FAILURE, CAUSES OF FAILURE, NOMINAL ASSETS, ETC.—Continued

Title of bank.	Date of organization.	Receiver appointed.	Cause of failure.	Nominal assets.	Amount collected.	Claims proved.	Dividends.	Finally closed.
							Per cent.	
New Orleans National Banking Association, New Orleans, La.	May 27, 1871	Oct. 23, 1873	Investments in real estate and mortgages and failure of large debtors.	....	....	$1,429,595	62	Mar. 21, 1887
First National Bank, Carlisle, Pa.	July 7, 1863	Oct. 24, 1873	....	$115,304.00	$56,911.00	67,292	73.5	Dec. 6, 1882
First National Bank, Anderson, Ind.	July 31, 1863	Nov. 23, 1873	Injudicious banking and depreciation of securities.	....	....	143,765	39.5	....
First National Bank, Topeka, Kans.	Aug. 23, 1866	Dec. 16, 1873	Fraudulent management and depreciation of securities.	205,348.00	68,314.00	55,372	58.3	Sept. 11, 1878
First National Bank, Norfolk, Va.	Feb. 23, 1864	June 3, 1874	Excessive loans to officers and directors, and depreciation of securities.	217,913.00	109,769.00	176,330	57.5	June 2, 1883
Gibson County National Bank, Princeton, Ind.	Nov. 30, 1872	Nov. 28, 1874	Investments in real estate and mortgages and depreciation of securities.	124,833.00	67,252.00	62,646	100	Sept. 18, 1876
First National Bank of Utah, Salt Lake City, Utah.	Nov. 15, 1869	Dec. 10, 1874	Injudicious banking and depreciation of securities.	229,433.00	30,332.00	93,021	24.391	May 14, 1879
Cook County National Bank, Chicago, Ill.	July 8, 1871	Feb. 1, 1875	.... do	3,266,323.00	365,274.00	1,795,992	14.911	Nov. 20, 1883
First National Bank, Tiffin, Ohio.	Mar. 16, 1865	Oct. 22, 1875	Depreciation of securities	312,059.00	196,903.00	237,824	66	Mar. 19, 1879
Charlottesville National Bank, Charlottesville, Va.	July 19, 1865	Oct. 28, 1875	Fraudulent management and injudicious banking.	563,083.00	281,754.00	376,756	62.56	Apr. 5, 1886
Miners' National Bank, Georgetown, Colo.	Oct. 30, 1874	Jan. 24, 1876	Injudicious banking and depreciation of securities.	232,357.00	193,775.00	177,512	76.5	June 2, 1884
Fourth National Bank, Chicago, Ill.	Feb. 24, 1864	Feb. 1, 1876	.... do	227,236.00	33,319.00	35,801	51	Mar. 4, 1886
First National Bank, Bedford, Iowa	Sept. 18, 1875	Feb. 1, 1876	Fraudulent management	....	....	56,457	22.5	Mar. 28, 1883
First National Bank, Osceola, Iowa	Jan. 26, 1871	Feb. 25, 1876	Injudicious banking and depreciation of securities.	....	....	34,525	100	Feb. 28, 1876
First National Bank, Duluth, Minn.	Apr. 6, 1872	Mar. 13, 1876	Fraudulent management and depreciation of securities.	231,061.00	575,661.00	87,786	100	Jan. 31, 1881
First National Bank, La Crosse, Wis	June 20, 1865	Apr. 11, 1876	.... do	169,912.00	85,107.00	135,952	48.4	July 20, 1882
City National Bank, Chicago, Ill	Feb. 18, 1865	May 17, 1876	Injudicious banking and depreciation of securities.	1,104,000.00	642,749.00	703,658	77.512	Feb. 28, 1885
Watkins National Bank, Watkins, N. Y.	June 2, 1864	July 12, 1876	Excessive loans to officers and directors, and depreciation of securities.	....	....	59,226	100	....
First National Bank, Wichita, Kans.	Jan. 2, 1872	Sept. 23, 1876	Defalcation by officers and fraudulent management.	208,825.00	79,594.00	97,461	70	July 14, 1880
First National Bank, Greenfield, Ohio	Oct. 7, 1863	Dec. 12, 1876	....	21,522.00	9,175.00	35,023	27	Nov. 25, 1882

INSOLVENT NATIONAL BANKS, DATE OF ORGANIZATION, FAILURE, AND CLOSING, ... SETS, AMOUNTS COLLECTED FROM ALL SOURCES, LOANS AND DISBURSEMENTS, ... PAID, AND REMAINING ASSETS RETURNED TO STOCKHOLDERS.

	Name and location of bank.	Date of organization.
1	National Bank, Fishkill, N. Y ..(b)..	Apr. 1, 1865
2	First National Bank, Franklin, Ind ..(b)..	Aug. 5, 1863
3	Northumberland County National Bank, Shamokin, Pa ..(m)..	Jan. 9, 1865
4	First National Bank, Winchester, Ill ..(w)..	July 25, 1865
5	National Exchange Bank, Minneapolis, Minn ..(m)..	Jan. 16, 1865
6	National Bank of the State of Missouri, Saint Louis, Mo ..(o)..	Oct. 30, 1866
7	First National Bank, Delphi, Ind ..(w)..	Mar. 25, 1872
8	First National Bank, Georgetown, Colo ..(u)..	May 31, 1872
9	Lock Haven National Bank, Lock Haven, Pa ..(v)..	June 14, 1865
10	Third National Bank, Chicago, Ill ..(c)..	Feb. 5, 1864
11	Central National Bank, Chicago, Ill ..(v)..	Sept. 18, 1872
12	First National Bank, Kansas City, Mo ..(x)..	Nov. 23, 1865
13	Commercial National Bank, Kansas City, Mo ..(v)..	June 3, 1872
14	First National Bank, Ashland, Pa ..(v)..	Apr. 27, 1864
15	First National Bank, Tarrytown, N. Y ..(v)..	Apr. 5, 1864
16	First National Bank, Allentown, Pa ..(n)..	Dec. 16, 1863
17	First National Bank, Waynesburgh, Pa ..(v)..	Mar. 5, 1864
18	Washington County National Bank, Greenwich, N. Y ..(p)..	June 30, 1865
19	First National Bank, Dallas, Tex ..(c)..	July 16, 1874
20	People's National Bank, Helena, Mont ..(q)..	May 13, 1873
21	First National Bank, Bozeman, Mont ..(q)..	Aug. 14, 1872
22	Merchants' National Bank, Fort Scott, Kans ..(x)..	Jan. 20, 1872
23	Farmers' National Bank, Platte City, Mo ..(n)..	May 5, 1877
24	First National Bank, Warrensburgh, Mo ..(x)..	July 31, 1871
25	German American National Bank, Washington, D. C ..(p)..	May 14, 1877
26	German National Bank, Chicago, Ill ..(b)..	Nov. 15, 1870
27	Commercial National Bank, Saratoga Springs, N. Y ..(x)..	June 6, 1865
28	Second National Bank, Scranton, Pa ..(x)..	Aug. 5, 1863
29	National Bank, Poultney, Vt ..(x)..	May 31, 1865
30	First National Bank, Monticello, Ind ..(n)..	Dec. 3, 1874
31	First National Bank, Butler, Pa ..(e)..	Mar. 11, 1864
32	First National Bank, Meadville, Pa ..(r)..	Oct. 27, 1863
33	First National Bank, Newark, N. J ..(f)..	Aug. 7, 1863
34	First National Bank, Brattleborough, Vt ..(n)..	June 30, 1864
35	Mechanics' National Bank, Newark, N. J ..(c)..	June 9, 1865
36	First National Bank, Buffalo, N. Y ..(p)..	Feb. 5, 1864
37	Pacific National Bank, Boston, Mass ..(s)..	Nov. 9, 1877
38	First National Bank Union Mills, Union City, Pa ..(s)..	Oct. 23, 1863
39	Vermont National Bank, Saint Albans, Vt ..(r)..	Oct. 11, 1865
40	First National Bank, Leadville, Colo ..(b)..	Mar. 19, 1879
41	City National Bank, Lawrenceburgh, Ind ..(g)..	Feb. 24, 1883
42	First National Bank, Saint Albans, Vt ..(p)..	Feb. 20, 1864
43	First National Bank, Monmouth, Ill ..(b)..	July 7, 1882
44	Marine National Bank, New York, N. Y ..(f)..	June 3, 1865
45	Hot Springs National Bank, Hot Springs, Ark ..(c)..	Feb. 17, 1883
46	Richmond National Bank, Richmond, Ind ..(h)..	Mar. 5, 1873
47	First National Bank, Livingston, Mont ..(x)..	July 16, 1883
48	First National Bank, Albion, N. Y ..(b)..	Dec. 22, 1863
49	First National Bank, Jamestown, Dak ..(c)..	Oct. 25, 1881
50	Logan National Bank, West Liberty, Ohio ..(p)..	May 7, 1883
51	Middletown National Bank, Middletown, N. Y ..(f)..	June 11, 1865
52	Farmers' National Bank, Bushnell, Ill ..(l)..	Feb. 18, 1871
53	Schoharie County National Bank, Schoharie, N. Y ..(b)..	Aug. 9, 1865
54	Exchange National Bank, Norfolk, Va ..(o)..	May 13, 1865
55	First National Bank, Lake City, Minn ..(c)..	Nov. 29, 1870
56	Lancaster National Bank, Clinton, Mass ..(b)..	Nov. 22, 1864
57	First National Bank, Sioux Falls, Dak ..(j)..	Mar. 15, 1880
58	First National Bank, Wahpeton, Dak ..(j)..	Feb 2, 1882
59	First National Bank, Angelica, N. Y ..(a)..	Nov. 3, 1864
60	City National Bank, Williamsport, Pa ..(d)..	Mar. 17, 1874
61	Abington National Bank, Abington, Mass ..(l)..	July 1, 1865
62	First National Bank, Blair, Nebr ..(u)..	June 7, 1882
63	First National Bank, Pine Bluff, Ark ..(v)..	Sept. 18, 1882
64	Palatka National Bank, Palatka, Fla ..(n)..	Nov. 20, 1884
65	Fidelity National Bank, Cincinnati, Ohio ..(b)..	Feb. 27, 1886
66	Henrietta National Bank, Henrietta, Tex ..(k)..	Aug. 8, 1883
67	National Bank, Sumter, S. C ..(a)..	Nov. 26, 1883
68	First National Bank, Dansville, N. Y ..(b)..	Sept. 4, 1863
69	First National Bank, Corry, Pa ..(v)..	Dec. 6, 1864
70	Stafford National Bank, Stafford Springs, Conn ..(b)..	Jan. 7, 1865
	Total	

FOR THE PAST ELEVEN YEARS, WITH AMOUNTS OF NOMINAL AND ADDITIONAL AS-
LOSSES ON ASSETS, EXPENSES OF RECEIVERSHIP, CLAIMS PROVED, DIVIDENDS

Capital stock.	Receiver appointed.	
$200,000	Jan. 27, 1877	1
132,000	Feb. 13, 1877	2
67,000	Mar. 12, 1877	3
50,000	Mar. 16, 1877	4
100,000	May 24, 1877	5
2,500,000	June 23, 1877	6
50,000	July 20, 1877	7
75,000	Aug. 18, 1877	8
120,000	Aug. 20, 1877	9
750,000	Nov. 24, 1877	10
200,000	Dec. 1, 1877	11
500,000	Feb. 11, 1878	12
100,000	Feb. 11, 1878	13
112,500	Feb. 28, 1878	14
100,000	Mar. 23, 1878	15
250,000	Apr. 15, 1878	16
100,000	May 15, 1878	17
200,000	June 8, 1878	18
50,000	June 8, 1878	19
100,000	Sept. 13, 1878	20
50,000	Sept. 14, 1878	21
50,000	Sept. 25, 1878	22
50,000	Oct. 1, 1878	23
100,000	Nov. 1, 1878	24
130,000	Nov. 1, 1878	25
500,000	Dec. 20, 1878	26
100,000	Feb. 11, 1879	27
200,000	Nov. 15, 1879	28
100,000	Apr. 7, 1879	29
50,000	July 18, 1879	30
50,000	July 23, 1879	31
100,000	June 9, 1880	32
300,000	June 14, 1880	33
300,000	June 19, 1880	34
500,000	Nov. 2, 1881	35
100,000	Apr. 22, 1882	36
961,300	May 22, 1882	37
50,000	Mar. 24, 1883	38
200,000	Aug. 9, 1883	39
60,000	Jan. 24, 1884	40
100,000	Mar. 11, 1884	41
100,000	Apr. 22, 1884	42
75,000	Apr. 22, 1884	43
400,000	May 13, 1884	44
50,000	June 2, 1884	45
250,000	July 23, 1884	46
50,000	Aug. 25, 1884	47
100,000	Aug. 26, 1884	48
50,000	Sept. 13, 1884	49
50,000	Oct. 18, 1884	50
200,000	Nov. 29, 1884	51
50,000	Dec. 17, 1884	52
50,000	Mar. 23, 1885	53
300,000	Apr. 9, 1885	54
50,000	Jan. 4, 1886	55
100,000	Jan. 20, 1886	56
50,000	Mar. 11, 1886	57
50,000	Apr. 8, 1886	58
100,000	Apr. 10, 1886	59
100,000	May 4, 1886	60
150,000	Aug. 2, 1886	61
50,000	Sept. 8, 1886	62
50,000	Nov. 20, 1886	63
50,000	June 3, 1887	64
1,000,000	June 27, 1887	65
50,000	Aug. 17, 1887	66
50,000	Aug. 24, 1887	67
50,000	Sept. 8, 1887	68
100,000	Oct. 11, 1887	69
200,000	Oct. 17, 1887	70
13,732,800		

Cause of failure.

a Defalcation of officers.

b Defalcation of officers and fraudulent management.

c Defalcation of officers and excessive loans to others.

d Defalcation of officers and depreciation of securities.

e Depreciation of securities.

f Excessive loans to others, injudicious banking, and depreciation of securities.

g Excessive loans to officers and directors, and depreciation of securities.

h Excessive loans to officers and directors, and investments in real estate and mortgages.

i Excessive loans to others and depreciation of securities.

j Excessive loans to others and investments in real estate and mortgages.

k Excessive loans and failure of large debtors.

l Excessive loans to officers and directors.

m Failure of large debtors.

n Fraudulent management.

o Fraudulent management, excessive loans to officers and directors, and depreciation of securities.

p Fraudulent management and depreciation of securities.

q Fraudulent management and injudicious banking.

r Fraudulent management, defalcation of officers, and depreciation of securities.

s Fraudulent management, injudicious banking, investments in real estate and mortgages, and depreciation of securities.

t Fraudulent management, excessive loans to officers and directors, and excessive loans to others.

u Injudicious banking.

v Injudicious banking and depreciation of securities.

w Injudicious banking and failure of large debtors.

x Investments in real estate and mortgages, and depreciation of securities.

INSOLVENT NATIONAL BANKS, DATE OF ORGANIZATION, FAILURE,

	Nominal assets at date of suspension.			Additional assets received since date of suspension.	Total assets.	Offsets allowed and settled.	Loss on assets compounded or sold by order of court.	Nominal value of assets returned to stockholders.
	Estimated good.	Estimated doubtful.	Estimated worthless.					
1	$104,065	$202,000	$51,403	$40,441	$558,418	$13,192	$223,375	....
2	86,402	58,188	200,000	24,217	369,806	60,311	203,702	....
3	67,240	112,026	25,041	14,770	219,083	8,487	90,588	....
4	67,541	66,025	79,101	14,270	226,937	6,537	117,173	....
5	135,231	90,704	124,371	18,411	368,717	21,498	139,309	....
6	935,090	2,818,906	633,744	433,400	4,822,109	166,831	1,771,099	....
7	175,254	6,250	6,506	13,478	201,578	62,774	1,310	$34,259
8	34,308	52,027	629,113	30,398	746,506	36,508	606,580	....
9	220,481	150,650	24,900	34,350	430,471	41,324	143,664	....
10	1,330,215	631,797	330,704	205,650	2,588,366	310,813	50,322	....
11	157,438	161,441	170,712	16,073	505,664	7,245	70,038	....
12	1,118,118	313,726	405,000	19,817	1,856,661	1,482,725	22,550	....
13	52,349	74,724	51,175	6,723	184,971	22,902	67,306	....
14	107,318	41,584	19,070	8,859	176,831	16,072	....	112,816
15	100,904	....	153,467	20,280	274,750	161,949	....	....
16	19,879	132,445	185,220	2,171	339,715	20,608	208,000	....
17	....	15,869	42,284	1,861	60,014	714	47,239	....
18	311,324	27,894	236,971	13,749	589,938	18,541	6,972	270,987
19	48,140	36,245	67,423	4,303	156,122	30,088	106,292	....
20	32,559	95,251	166,151	67,042	361,003	12,492	32,372	....
21	39,010	76,046	833	21,090	136,479	7,700	20,141	....
22	21,225	15,543	46,588	1,892	85,248	178	65,804	....
23	9,561	18,691	42,206	1,944	72,492	10,947	8,207	....
24	90,933	194,457	11,578	33,375	330,363	55,255	118,507	....
25	250,280	139,514	37,923	61,147	494,870	165,846	42,883	....
26	104,966	101,971	475,052	29,881	711,870	6,170	521,783	....
27	133,169	167,503	28,969	17,085	346,726	17,475	101,810	66,059
28	264,008	101,178	104,858	47,591	518,535	36,737	203,982	72,754
29	68,078	97,257	18,384	19,500	203,279	3,353	25,720	77,592
30	23,646	6,734	4,374	15,017	49,771	8,411	64	....
31	12,647	134,716	34,737	27,503	209,603	11,920	100,502	....
32	115,012	22,515	12,863	19,198	169,618	3,345	26,043	26,430
33	418,951	64,041	55,805	41,173	580,060	154,945	4,000	....
34	51,574	....	302,654	43,895	398,123	4,902	801	302,654
35	1,114,503	185,002	78,286	105,709	1,483,500	73,925	48,113	....
36	488,892	65,526	696,987	34,520	1,285,925	172,063	55,204	....
37	648,710	1,416,793	1,397,334	380,880	3,843,717	161,843	464,691	....
38	161,699	46,829	16,300	23,678	248,515	4,376	14,013	....
39	124,114	520,017	118,618	19,572	783,221	19,141	5,541	....
40	72,107	56,042	102,112	31,922	262,278	7,069	11,380	....
41	13,993	14,500	2,554	1,599	32,646	52	16,017	....
42	217,314	96,873	49,951	66,932	431,070	9,888	18,356	....
43	172,940	96,543	9,688	26,491	305,662	4,416	....	....
44	2,770,636	1,736,166	1,508,609	823,725	6,845,076	442,937	3,010	....
45	31,058	27,774	27,100	6,290	92,321	5,381	29,096	....
46	367,109	72,356	171,319	119,487	730,271	32,233	184,046	....
47	33,513	15,304	22,255	535	71,637	....	6,333	....
48	55,762	44,446	113,329	1,120	214,667	4,146	6,541	....
49	7,519	29,826	29,352	3,312	70,009	5	49,155	....
50	60,006	22,695	....	39,410	122,201	11,099	....	....
51	660,810	53,692	167,075	100,607	931,181	20,007	2,036	....
52	13,170	3,871	62,229	11,775	91,048	638	3,123	....
53	96,891	39,593	28,010	4,715	169,209	508	30,182	....
54	1,273,711	1,441,378	938,816	110,783	3,764,688	150,070	143,150	....
55	57,487	91,996	7,201	57,094	214,768	584	....	65,573
56	144,850	138,707	8,094	56,509	348,160	17,856	4,807	....
57	48,510	137,850	3,821	2,580	192,770	37,157	3,493	....
58	21,410	66,085	44,881	1,854	134,233	1,108	3,007	....
59	59,810	28,450	70,448	7,115	165,842	1,281	....	....
60	154,870	26,825	24,398	35,202	241,304	4,104	816	70,715
61	122,551	168,164	5,462	21,633	317,810	3,721	76,659	38,017
62	235,474	8,000	6,834	5,439	255,747	5,645	2,358	43,097
63	50,793	82,612	4,000	888	139,292	122	....	....
64	15,616	32,092	8,791	1,790	58,319	....	....	44,098
65	2,464,079	915,577	2,491,511	6,877	4,881,044	....	....	....
66	74,171	33,999	12,005	1,370	121,535	3,451	....	....
67	66,081	....	159	....	66,240	....	....	....
68	17,449	8,397	37,572	....	63,418	....	....	....
69	156,586	20,239	66,710	....	243,535	....	....	....
70	208,243	119,800	60,869	....	388,981	....	....	....
	19,034,293	14,156,456	13,178,640	3,591,916	49,961,305	4,190,827	6,424,182	.,239,132

AND CLOSING, FOR THE PAST ELEVEN YEARS, ETC.—Continued.

Nominal value of remaining assets.	Collected from assets.	Collected from assessment upon shareholders.	Total collections from all sources.	Loans paid and other disbursements.	Dividends paid.	Legal expenses.	Receiver's salary and other expenses.	
....	$321,851	$122,127	$143,978	$5,000	$388,856	$25,040	$25,082	1
....	105,703	91,920	197,633	520	173,512	5,146	9,716	2
....	111,908	43,232	155,140	4,797	136,474	966	12,903	3
....	103,227	8,014	111,271	8,995	89,715	2,082	10,660	4
....	207,910	9,540	217,450	753	202,753	1,808	12,016	5
$836,957	2,846,622	245,108	3,091,730	658,784	2,165,288	79,892	151,793	6
....	103,235	....	103,235	4,050	81,911	2,690	10,910	7
....	103,328	....	103,328	....	73,800	11,987	17,251	8
....	245,483	47,940	293,423	7,816	251,617	6,668	21,271	9
893,100	1,325,125	....	1,325,125	145,179	1,071,774	10,923	53,851	10
274,465	144,916	65,132	210,048	....	177,251	12,077	14,129	11
....	351,377	....	351,377	1,701	316,828	5,414	27,314	12
....	94,613	....	94,613	3,048	52,514	576	1,604	13
....	47,941	....	47,941	....	33,195	3,974	6,013	14
....	109,801	16,455	126,256	....	107,575	5,546	13,135	15
....	51,107	54,536	105,643	1,576	79,725	11,006	13,336	16
....	12,061	16,447	28,508	....	21,710	2,315	4,483	17
....	284,438	123,430	407,868	114,220	262,887	10,129	4,930	18
....	19,742	16,500	36,242	....	29,377	825	6,040	19
252,614	64,395	23,622	88,017	9,702	65,368	1,325	11,476	20
30,534	78,134	1,811	79,945	2,125	69,033	634	8,153	21
....	19,266	2,880	22,146	272	16,670	1,488	3,716	22
32,510	20,819	....	20,819	1,633	11,803	860	3,005	23
....	156,601	16,277	172,878	47,315	160,870	3,838	8,176	24
160,448	125,693	52,361	178,054	51,982	87,260	9,804	21,873	25
....	183,917	80,257	264,174	49,466	182,572	....	32,136	26
....	157,782	....	157,782	2,021	137,428	5,785	12,110	27
....	205,062	54,950	260,012	57,745	166,587	10,245	24,551	28
....	96,605	....	96,605	53	88,170	....	7,517	29
11,877	29,419	4,677	34,096	10	20,758	1,792	11,206	30
....	91,121	23,001	114,122	8,420	82,030	7,107	16,475	31
....	113,791	....	113,791	....	66,176	3,225	6,739	32
93,431	327,684	267,311	594,995	7,037	528,305	13,593	10,600	33
....	89,766	64,655	154,421	....	99,847	2,973	10,832	34
127,031	1,234,491	495,550	1,730,041	....	1,627,558	25,982	19,693	35
614,741	443,857	4,450	448,307	1,910	330,990	35,370	26,342	36
2,278,756	935,427	583,811	1,519,238	114,791	1,150,230	58,135	130,108	37
86,039	144,067	8,287	152,354	....	118,740	7,935	14,807	38
553,040	204,899	23,704	228,603	....	160,024	9,550	30,904	39
129,781	114,043	4,348	118,391	3,700	80,842	5,110	15,989	40
....	16,577	23,732	40,309	3,392	26,800	2,223	7,885	41
294,611	108,215	4,898	113,113	17,307	71,887	3,705	12,585	42
56,607	244,639	63,486	308,125	13,190	225,648	6,543	15,779	43
3,563,559	2,835,561	266,024	3,101,585	563,465	2,237,557	46,408	56,951	44
22,064	35,783	13,569	49,352	....	36,526	3,177	9,597	45
208,688	215,304	73,731	289,035	60,710	205,303	3,176	15,593	46
44,160	21,144	16,450	37,594	....	21,262	1,906	10,010	47
146,765	57,215	4,200	61,415	6,359	....	10,052	9,358	48
....	20,849	....	20,849	6,515	8,807	52	5,473	49
79,258	31,844	23,500	55,344	1,748	40,347	2,084	7,083	50
413,166	494,085	....	494,085	5,612	454,807	13,525	12,083	51
45,298	41,980	15,000	56,980	....	34,503	1,825	7,040	52
66,107	72,412	1,400	73,812	....	56,131	1,051	10,861	53
2,222,253	1,249,213	153,509	1,402,722	164,413	1,157,386	21,829	31,026	54
....	148,611	....	148,611	231	131,024	103	2,314	55
145,876	179,531	....	179,531	....	119,209	256	9,248	56
125,494	26,626	....	26,626	1,657	10,208	1,507	6,051	57
111,557	18,501	....	18,501	625	11,011	1,122	4,949	58
98,015	66,543	....	66,543	....	52,928	921	5,115	59
....	165,669	....	165,669	16,177	135,574	1,423	7,321	60
....	198,513	....	198,513	....	117,878	198	5,208	61
....	204,047	....	204,047	106,424	82,946	324	4,279	62
94,804	44,276	....	44,276	....	16,238	....	3,322	63
....	14,251	....	14,251	82	9,402	....	1,348	64
4,081,734	1,199,310	....	1,199,310	....	506,642	893	14,251	65
61,060	60,621	....	60,621	....	32,391	....	1,024	66
66,240	....	....	....	....	....	....	....	67
63,418	....	....	....	....	....	....	....	68
243,535	....	....	....	....	....	....	....	69
388,081	....	....	....	....	....	....	....	70
18,909,208	19,197,956	3,231,901	22,429,857	2,282,543	16,851,406	529,789	1,131,234	

INSOLVENT NATIONAL BANKS, DATE OF ORGANIZATION, FAILURE, AND CLOSING FOR THE PAST ELEVEN YEARS, ETC.—Continued.

	Balance in hands of Comptroller or receiver.	Amount returned to shareholders in cash.	Amount of assessment upon shareholders.	Amount of claims proved.	Dividends, per cent.	Interest dividends, per cent.	Finally closed.	
1			$140,000	$352,062	100	38.50	Aug. 11, 1884	1
2		$8,739	132,000	185,700	100	100	Sept. 14, 1881	2
3			67,000	175,952	81.50		Jan. 18, 1883	3
4			50,000	140,735	63.00		July 23, 1881	4
5			53,000	227,355	89.170		June 10, 1880	5
6	$32,903		510,025	1,935,721	100	100		6
7		3,026		133,112	100	100	Oct. 15, 1881	7
8	200			196,356	37.0483		Oct. 5, 1885	8
9			72,000	254,647	100		Mar. 3, 1882	9
10	43,308			1,061,508	100	100		10
11	6,588		200,000	298,324	60			11
12				302,394	100		July 6, 1881	12
13		36,871		75,175	100	100	Mar. 9, 1882	13
14		5,849		29,204	100	100	Aug. 5, 1879	14
15			50,000	118,871	90.50		June 20, 1882	15
16			125,000	90,424	88		Mar. 9, 1885	16
17			36,000	36,109	60		Sept. 7, 1885	17
18		15,682	100,000	262,887	100		July 5, 1879	18
19			50,000	77,104	38.10		Mar. 24, 1885	19
20	86		100,000	168,048	40			20
21			21,500	70,191	98.35			21
22			17,000	27,801	60		Apr. 8, 1881	22
23	108	3,420		32,449	100	100	Oct. 10, 1879	23
24		12,079	50,000	156,200	100	100	Mar. 15, 1881	24
25	7,135		130,000	282,370	50			25
26			121,750	197,353	100	42.30	Mar. 1, 1884	26
27		820		128,832	100	100	Jan. 17, 1881	27
28		884	100,000	132,461	100	100	Apr. 24, 1880	28
29		850		81,801	100	100	Aug. 1, 1881	29
30	240		10,000	21,182	98		Feb. 6, 1883	30
31			50,000	108,385	81		Aug. 6, 1887	31
32		7,651		93,625	100	100	Feb. 4, 1882	32
33	1,357	23,103	300,000	580,502	100	100	Feb. 18, 1885	33
34		40,700	75,000	104,749	100	100	Oct. 12, 1885	34
35	56,858		500,000	2,730,179	61.25			35
36	44,080		100,000	891,735	38			36
37	65,965		961,300	2,645,393	50			37
38	10,812		50,000	180,993	65			38
39	19,125		200,000	401,492	42.50			39
40	13,241		60,000	200,854	40			40
41			50,000	46,441	81.10		Oct. 25, 1886	41
42	7,620		100,000	291,010	25			42
43	46,965		75,000	237,524	95			43
44	107,204		400,000	4,474,197	50			44
45	52		25,000	36,526	100			45
46	4,262		250,000	365,931	50			46
47	4,320		32,500	28,350	75			47
48	35,046		100,000	158,008				48
49				8,131	100	100	Oct. 29, 1885	49
50	2,882		50,000	80,665	50			50
51	7,308			649,863	70			51
52	13,021		50,000	86,258	40			52
53	5,169		50,000	140,333	40			53
54	27,468		300,000	2,894,709	40			54
55		14,850		127,521	100	100	June 1, 1886	55
56	50,758			170,384	70			56
57	8,143			51,041	20			57
58	704			101,122	10			58
59	7,579			63,669	85			59
60		5,172		130,772	100	100	Aug. 18, 1887	60
61		75,229		110,026	100	100	Feb. 17, 1887	61
62		10,074		80,452	100	100	Apr. 30, 1887	62
63	24,716			64,956	25			63
64		3,329		9,379	100	100	Oct. 17, 1887	64
65	500,524			2,386,569	25			65
66	20,600			64,784	50			66
67								67
68								68
69								69
70								70
	1,303,268	271,615	6,034,075	28,137,949				

LIABILITIES OF THE NATIONAL BANKS, AND THE RESERVE REQUIRED AND HELD AT THREE DATES IN THE YEARS 1884, '85, '86, '87.

STATES AND TERRITORIES EXCLUSIVE OF RESERVE CITIES.

Date.	No. of banks.	Net deposits.	Reserve required.	Reserve held.		Classification of reserve.			
				Amount.	Ratio to deposits.	Specie.	Other lawful money.	Due from agents.	Redemption fund.
		Millions.	*Millions.*	*Millions.*	*Per cent.*	*Millions.*	*Millions.*	*Millions.*	*Millions.*
Apr. 24, 1884	2,340	576.0	86.4	162.5	28.2	36.4	31.5	83.7	10.9
June 20, 1884	2,370	544.7	81.7	146.0	26.8	36.4	32.0	66.8	10.7
Sept. 30, 1884	2,417	535.8	80.4	156.3	29.2	35.2	30.9	79.7	10.5
May 6, 1885	2,432	540.3	81.1	171.0	31.6	40.7	30.2	90.0	10.1
July 1, 1885	2,442	552.2	82.8	170.3	30.8	40.1	28.1	92.1	10.0
Oct. 1, 1885	2,467	570.8	85.6	177.5	31.1	41.5	29.9	95.9	10.2
Mar. 1, 1886	2,518	596.1	89.4	181.6	30.4	45.1	27.7	98.9	9.8
June 3, 1886	2,552	611.7	91.8	181.6	29.7	49.1	29.7	93.5	9.3
Oct. 7, 1886	2,590	637.6	95.6	186.2	29.2	47.8	30.1	99.5	8.7
May 13, 1887	2,676	682.8	102.4	198.9	29.1	51.1	32.9	107.8	6.8
Aug. 1, 1887	2,724	683.0	102.4	189.5	27.7	48.9	31.3	102.6	6.6
Oct. 5, 1887	2,756	690.6	103.6	190.9	27.6	50.8	32.6	100.9	6.6

NEW YORK CITY.

Apr. 24, 1884	47	282.2	70.5	75.2	26.6	49.5	24.9	....	0.8
June 20, 1884	45	231.8	57.9	69.1	29.8	43.5	24.9	....	0.7
Sept. 30, 1884	44	254.9	63.7	90.8	35.6	63.1	27.0	....	0.7
May 6, 1885	44	297.7	74.4	123.5	41.5	96.5	26.4	....	0.6
July 1, 1885	45	312.7	78.2	132.8	42.5	96.5	37.5	....	0.6
Oct. 1, 1885	44	312.9	78.2	115.7	37.0	91.5	23.7	....	0.5
Mar. 1, 1886	45	323.6	80.9	101.2	31.3	77.2	23.5	....	0.5
June 3, 1886	45	296.8	74.2	89.9	30.3	57.9	31.5	....	0.4
Oct. 7, 1886	43	282.8	70.7	77.0	27.2	64.1	12.5	....	0.4
May 13, 1887	46	299.7	74.9	82.8	27.6	63.6	18.8	....	0.4
Aug. 1, 1887	46	294.0	73.5	82.6	28.1	65.0	17.2	....	0.4
Oct. 5, 1887	47	284.3	71.1	80.1	28.2	63.6	16.1	....	0.4

CHICAGO.

May 13, 1887	18	68.0	17.0	20.7	30.4	13.0	7.6	....	0.05
Aug. 1, 1887	18	66.3	16.6	22.0	33.1	14.6	7.2	....	0.05
Oct. 5, 1887	18	64.6	16.2	19.7	30.5	12.9	6.7	....	0.05

SAINT LOUIS.

May 13, 1887	5	9.1	2.2	3.3	36.4	1.5	1.8	....	0.03
Aug. 1, 1887	5	10.8	2.7	3.4	31.9	1.6	1.8	....	0.03
Oct. 5, 188	5	10.3	2.6	2.7	26.4	1.3	1.3	....	0.03

LIABILITIES OF THE NATIONAL BANKS, AND THE RESERVE REQUIRED AND HELD AT THREE DATES, ETC.—Continued.

OTHER RESERVE CITIES.*

Date.	No. of banks.	Net deposits.	Reserve required.	Reserve held.		Classification of reserve.			
				Amount.	Ratio to deposits.	Specie.	Other lawful money.	Due from agents.	Redemption fund.
		Millions.	*Millions.*	*Millions.*	*Per cent.*	*Millions.*	*Millions.*	*Millions.*	*Millions.*
Apr. 24, 1884	202	338.0	84.5	101.1	30.8	28.8	33.3	38.8	3.2
June 20, 1884	204	302.8	75.7	91.1	30.1	29.7	20.9	28.4	3.1
Sept. 30, 1884	203	308.0	77.0	99.0	32.2	30.3	33.3	32.3	3.1
May 6, 1885	202	346.5	86.6	124.0	35.8	40.2	39.9	40.9	3.0
July 1, 1885	202	356.5	89.1	123.4	34.6	41.0	38.8	40.7	2.9
Oct. 1, 1885	203	364.5	91.1	122.2	33.5	41.9	35.0	42.4	2.9
Mar. 1, 1886	205	378.0	94.5	124.0	32.8	49.3	28.2	43.9	2.7
June 3, 1886	212	387.2	96.8	122.8	31.7	50.5	30.2	39.0	2.5
Oct. 7, 1886	217	381.5	95.4	113.9	29.9	44.5	26.0	41.3	2.2
Mar. 4, 1887	210	345.1	86.3	106.1	30.7	38.0	26.4	40.2	1.4
Aug. 1, 1887	231	335.5	83.9	98.4	29.3	34.8	24.2	37.7	1.2
Oct. 5, 1887	223	338.5	84.6	100.7	29.7	36.3	23.2	40.0	1.2

SUMMARY.*

Date.	No. of banks.	Net deposits.	Reserve required.	Amount.	Ratio to deposits.	Specie.	Other lawful money.	Due from agents.	Redemption fund.
Apr. 24, 1884	2,589	1,106.2	241.4	341.8	28.6	114.7	89.7	122.5	14.9
June 20, 1884	2,625	1,079.3	215.3	306.2	28.4	109.6	86.8	95.2	14.5
Sept. 30, 1884	2,661	1,098.7	221.1	346.1	31.6	128.6	91.2	112.0	14.3
May 6, 1885	2,678	1,184.5	242.1	418.5	35.3	177.4	96.5	130.9	13.7
July 1, 1885	2,689	1,221.4	250.1	426.5	34.9	177.6	102.6	132.8	13.5
Oct. 1, 1885	2,714	1,248.2	251.9	415.4	33.3	174.9	88.6	138.3	13.6
Mar. 1, 1886	2,768	1,297.6	264.8	406.8	31.3	171.6	79.4	142.8	12.9
June 3, 1886	2,809	1,295.7	262.8	394.2	30.4	157.5	91.6	133.0	12.2
Oct. 7, 1886	2,852	1,301.8	201.7	377.2	28.9	156.4	68.7	140.8	11.4
May 13, 1887	2,955	1,404.7	282.0	411.9	29.3	167.3	87.6	148.1	8.8
Aug. 1, 1887	3,014	1,389.7	270.1	396.0	28.5	165.1	82.3	140.3	8.3
Oct. 5, 1887	3,049	1,388.4	278.0	394.2	28.4	165.1	79.9	140.9	8.3

* Includes Chicago and Saint Louis up to 1887.

TABLE SHOWING, BY GEOGRAPHICAL DIVISIONS, THE RESERVE CITIES AND CENTRAL RESERVE CITIES, THE NUMBER OF BANKS IN OPERATION AT EVERY DATE ON WHICH REPORTS OF CONDITION HAVE BEEN MADE, FROM MARCH 11, 1882, TO OCTOBER 5, 1887, INCLUSIVE, TOGETHER WITH THE AMOUNT OF RESERVE REQUIRED AND THE AMOUNT HELD AT EACH OF THOSE DATES, AND THE CLASSIFICATION OF THE RESERVE HELD, SHOWING AMOUNTS AND PERCENTAGES IN EACH CASE.

[Division No. 1.—Maine, New Hampshire, Vermont, Massachusetts, Rhode Island, and Connecticut, excluding reserve cities.]

Dates.	No. of banks.	Amount of reserve required, 15 per cent. of net deposits.	Reserve held.		Classification of reserve held.				
			Amount.	Ratio.	Lawful money (6 per cent.). Amount.	Lawful money (6 per cent.). Ratio.	With reserve agents (9 per cent.). Amount.	With reserve agents (9 per cent.). Ratio.	Five per cent. redemption fund.
1882.				Per ct.		Per ct.		Per ct.	
Mar. 11..	502	$14,902,790	$20,478,018	20.55	$7,223,511	7.24	$17,716,653	17.76	$4,538,454
May 19..	503	15,008,704	31,457,478	31.31	7,405,171	7.46	19,488,807	19.40	4,473,500
July 1...	504	15,505,375	29,835,966	28.86	7,583,373	7.34	17,833,751	17.25	4,416,842
Oct. 3...	505	16,296,303	29,332,584	27.00	7,916,022	7.29	16,949,161	15.96	4,467,401
Dec. 30..	507	16,234,969	33,151,031	30.50	8,197,588	7.56	20,509,426	18.93	4,444,017
1883.									
Mar. 13..	507	15,342,235	28,288,504	27.66	7,552,020	7.38	16,299,167	15.94	4,437,377
May 1...	509	15,309,783	27,968,728	27.40	7,495,816	7.34	16,040,290	15.72	4,432,583
June 22.	510	15,369,906	28,844,230	28.15	7,685,718	7.50	16,722,020	16.32	4,436,483
Oct. 2....	511	16,161,030	31,164,435	28.93	7,650,078	7.10	19,099,067	17.73	4,414,690
Dec. 31..	512	16,426,477	34,548,821	31.55	8,144,345	7.44	21,965,101	20.06	4,439,375
1884.									
Mar. 7...	514	15,959,007	32,510,901	30.56	7,875,750	7.40	20,374,517	19.15	4,260,634
Apr. 24..	514	16,081,733	31,236,427	27.15	8,138,314	7.59	18,787,103	17.52	4,331,010
June 20..	514	15,103,083	27,470,063	27.28	8,231,410	8.17	14,972,792	14.87	4,266,461
Sept. 30.	514	15,614,046	32,199,345	30.93	8,199,770	7.88	19,833,278	19.05	4,166,297
Dec. 20..	515	15,216,181	31,576,643	31.13	8,273,291	8.16	19,211,124	18.94	4,092,228
1885.									
Mar. 10..	514	15,553,913	33,563,306	32.37	8,416,680	8.12	21,146,721	20.39	3,999,986
May 6...	511	16,093,617	34,886,766	32.52	8,641,121	8.05	22,184,176	20.68	4,061,469
July 1...	512	16,580,066	34,507,448	31.31	8,951,595	8.10	21,637,813	19.58	4,008,010
Oct. 1...	506	17,218,577	34,416,314	29.98	9,549,345	8.32	20,832,605	18.15	4,034,364
Dec. 24..	506	17,150,864	32,831,670	28.71	9,562,800	8.36	19,311,376	16.89	3,957,494
1886.									
Mar. 1..	507	17,185,207	32,588,870	28.44	9,773,588	8.53	18,969,980	16.56	3,846,302
June 3...	510	16,473,718	32,509,786	27.91	10,304,208	8.85	18,555,748	15.93	3,649,830
Aug. 27.	509	17,388,516	31,345,788	27.04	10,316,250	8.90	17,449,280	15.05	3,580,240
Oct. 7....	510	18,295,909	35,762,441	29.32	10,335,491	8.47	21,995,854	18.03	3,431,096
Dec. 28..	511	17,815,957	33,220,398	27.98	10,888,902	9.17	19,338,260	16.28	3,002,236
1887.									
Mar. 4...	511	17,464,118	34,081,099	29.27	10,261,663	8.81	21,137,117	18.15	2,682,319
May 13..	513	17,918,113	33,354,311	27.92	10,470,249	8.77	20,384,444	17.06	2,499,618
Aug. 1...	512	17,228,499	28,645,014	24.94	10,202,657	8.88	16,106,385	14.02	2,335,972
Oct. 5....	512	17,758,954	32,079,549	27.10	10,081,047	8.51	19,698,402	16.64	2,300,100

TABLE SHOWING, BY GEOGRAPHICAL DIVISIONS, THE RESERVE CITIES AND CENTRAL RESERVE CITIES, THE NUMBER OF BANKS IN OPERATION, ETC.—Continued.

[Division No. 2.—New York, New Jersey, and Pennsylvania, excluding reserve cities.]

Dates.	No. of banks.	Amount of reserve required, 15 per cent. of net deposits.	Reserve held.		Classification of reserve held.				
			Amount.	Ratio.	Lawful money (6 per cent.).		With reserve agents (9 per cent.).		Five per cent. redemption fund.
					Amount.	Ratio.	Amount.	Ratio.	
1882.				*Per ct.*		*Per ct.*		*Per ct.*	
Mar. 11..	507	$24, 513, 895	$47, 919, 202	29. 32	$14, 540, 614	8. 90	$30, 249, 865	18. 51	$3, 122, 723
May 19..	514	24, 825, 609	49, 038, 897	29. 63	15, 827, 208	9. 56	30, 100, 831	18. 19	3, 110, 858
July 1...	515	25, 243, 576	47, 501, 012	28. 23	15, 228, 446	9. 05	29, 217, 784	17. 36	3, 054, 782
Oct. 3...	515	25, 702, 509	47, 834, 868	27. 92	15, 881, 966	9. 27	28, 868, 395	16. 85	3, 084, 507
Dec. 30..	521	26, 500, 579	48, 071, 228	27. 21	16, 667, 008	9. 43	28, 338, 020	16. 04	3, 066, 200
1883.									
Mar. 13..	525	26, 151, 831	48, 307, 519	27. 71	15, 222, 686	8. 74	30, 026, 506	17. 22	3, 048, 327
May 1...	532	26, 557, 410	45, 564, 935	25. 74	16, 633, 462	9. 38	25, 905, 781	14. 63	3, 035, 692
June 22..	537	26, 409, 027	50, 817, 552	28. 86	16, 240, 341	9. 22	31, 528, 884	17. 91	3, 048, 327
Oct. 2...	545	26, 885, 132	48, 979, 043	27. 33	16, 912, 419	9. 44	29, 011, 331	16. 19	3, 055, 293
Dec. 31..	549	26, 992, 446	50, 577, 804	28. 11	17, 734, 066	9. 86	29, 840, 086	16. 58	3, 003, 652
1884.									
Mar. 7...	550	27, 003, 470	53, 829, 445	29. 90	16, 983, 453	9. 43	33, 924, 115	18. 84	2, 921, 877
Apr. 24..	554	27, 240, 954	53, 358, 232	29. 38	18, 854, 083	10. 38	31, 556, 160	17. 38	2, 947, 990
June 20..	561	25, 502, 692	45, 241, 638	26. 61	18, 801, 649	11. 06	23, 558, 015	13. 86	2, 881, 974
Sept. 30..	563	25, 245, 939	49, 189, 650	29. 23	18, 694, 389	11. 11	27, 634, 801	16. 42	2, 860, 460
Dec. 20..	566	24, 531, 549	50, 799, 720	31. 06	18, 036, 445	11. 03	29, 977, 889	18. 33	2, 785, 386
1885.									
Mar. 10..	559	25, 258, 857	55, 463, 538	32. 94	18, 925, 754	11. 24	33, 766, 999	20. 05	2, 770, 785
May 6..	559	25, 204, 559	53, 071, 039	31. 58	20, 044, 604	11. 93	30, 262, 857	18. 01	2, 763, 578
July 1...	561	25, 615, 062	51, 945, 847	30. 42	19, 178, 305	11. 23	30, 033, 212	17. 59	2, 734, 330
Oct. 1...	557	26, 201, 732	56, 170, 958	32. 05	20, 055, 448	11. 44	33, 297, 308	19. 00	2, 818, 202
Dec. 24..	567	26, 813, 401	58, 345, 580	32. 60	18, 913, 441	10. 57	36, 653, 591	20. 48	2, 778, 548
1886.									
Mar. 1...	570	27, 453, 351	56, 026, 945	30. 61	18, 960, 011	10. 36	34, 334, 359	18. 76	2, 732, 575
June 3...	571	27, 533, 873	54, 618, 391	29. 75	20, 795, 357	11. 33	31, 241, 898	17. 02	2, 581, 136
Aug. 27..	572	28, 253, 322	56, 916, 208	30. 21	20, 185, 336	10. 71	34, 176, 300	18. 14	2, 554, 572
Oct. 7...	572	28, 830, 549	54, 836, 089	28. 53	20, 192, 341	10. 51	32, 249, 120	16. 78	2, 394, 628
Dec. 28..	575	28, 702, 675	53, 341, 795	27. 79	20, 360, 434	10. 61	30, 849, 802	16. 07	2, 131, 559
1887.									
Mar. 4...	576	29, 020, 465	54, 867, 707	28. 36	19, 405, 628	10. 03	33, 449, 631	17. 29	2, 012, 508
May 13..	580	29, 685, 015	56, 268, 209	28. 48	20, 193, 151	10. 20	34, 160, 474	17. 26	1, 914, 584
Aug. 1..	586	29, 837, 428	51, 361, 676	25. 82	19, 291, 157	9. 70	30, 226, 408	15. 20	1, 844, 111
Oct. 5...	587	30, 064, 960	52, 090, 784	26. 44	19, 775, 576	9. 87	31, 376, 441	15. 65	1, 844, 767

TABLE SHOWING, BY GEOGRAPHICAL DIVISIONS, THE RESERVE CITIES AND CENTRAL RESERVE CITIES, THE NUMBER OF BANKS IN OPERATION, ETC.—Continued.

[Division No. 3.—Delaware, Maryland, Virginia, West Virginia, and the District of Columbia, excluding reserve cities.]

Dates.	No. of banks.	Amount of reserve required, 15 per cent. of net deposits.	Reserve held.		Classification of reserve held.				
			Amount.	Ratio.	Lawful money (6 per cent.).		With reserve agents (9 per cent.).		Five per cent. redemption fund.
					Amount.	Ratio.	Amount.	Ratio.	
1882.				Per ct.		Per ct.		Per ct.	
Mar. 11.	73	$3,326,580	$6,300,888	28.41	$2,702,126	12.18	$3,212,987	14.49	$1,385,775
May 19..	74	3,229,343	5,846,228	27.16	2,867,270	13.32	2,597,775	12.07	381,183
July 1...	74	3,293,618	6,330,795	28.83	2,951,218	13.44	3,000,277	13.66	379,300
Oct. 3...	76	3,600,294	7,027,363	29.28	2,883,425	12.01	3,752,436	15.63	391,502
Dec. 30..	77	3,559,230	6,432,974	27.11	2,943,333	12.40	3,098,400	13.06	391,241
1883.									
Mar. 13..	77	3,527,516	5,733,788	24.38	2,337,863	9.94	3,008,054	12.79	387,871
May 1...	77	3,528,471	5,790,224	24.61	2,713,896	11.54	2,691,407	11.44	384,861
June 22..	78	3,621,398	6,406,495	26.54	2,774,761	11.49	3,243,785	13.44	387,940
Oct. 2...	82	4,152,516	7,383,800	26.67	3,088,028	11.15	3,901,193	14.09	394,569
Dec. 31..	82	3,998,030	6,620,987	24.82	3,018,536	11.33	3,210,691	12.05	391,760
1884.									
Mar. 7...	83	3,877,353	6,822,590	26.36	2,873,867	11.12	3,582,688	13.86	366,035
Apr. 24..	83	3,812,038	6,440,614	25.37	3,045,651	11.98	3,027,832	11.91	373,331
June 20..	83	3,513,153	5,375,113	22.95	2,975,931	12.71	2,025,960	8.65	373,222
Sept. 30.	88	3,702,825	6,837,101	27.70	3,220,417	13.05	3,246,528	13.15	370,156
Dec. 20...	88	3,365,854	6,407,992	28.82	2,942,926	13.12	3,164,161	14.10	360,905
1885.									
Mar. 10..	88	3,301,044	6,282,532	28.04	3,048,637	13.58	2,895,180	12.93	343,700
May 6...	87	2,834,130	5,624,698	29.56	2,985,242	15.69	2,280,321	12.03	359,135
July 1...	87	2,919,436	5,311,397	27.29	2,758,277	14.17	2,199,965	11.30	353,155
Oct. 1...	88	3,286,340	7,338,927	33.50	3,134,687	14.31	3,850,486	17.57	353,754
Dec. 24..	89	3,162,147	7,070,981	33.54	2,887,700	13.70	3,825,340	18.15	357,881
1886.									
Mar. 1...	89	3,163,328	6,579,113	31.20	3,079,948	14.60	3,153,202	14.95	345,963
June 3...	90	3,259,103	6,761,881	31.12	3,414,420	15.71	3,034,136	13.97	313,325
Aug. 27..	91	3,490,850	7,337,721	31.53	3,313,468	14.24	3,714,380	15.96	309,873
Oct. 7...	89	3,525,434	7,125,856	30.32	3,405,443	14.49	3,414,134	14.53	306,279
Dec. 28..	91	3,459,845	6,826,991	29.60	3,124,102	13.54	3,414,702	14.80	288,187
1887.									
Mar. 4...	91	3,541,988	6,685,225	28.31	3,061,122	12.96	3,370,568	14.27	253,535
May 13..	92	3,434,211	6,233,763	27.16	3,351,755	14.64	2,640,664	11.53	241,344
Aug. 1..	93	3,681,532	6,591,665	26.86	3,397,925	13.84	2,952,617	12.03	241,123
Oct. 5...	94	3,789,907	6,641,421	26.29	3,402,471	13.47	3,004,141	11.89	234,809

TABLE SHOWING, BY GEOGRAPHICAL DIVISIONS, THE RESERVE CITIES AND CENTRAL RESERVE CITIES, THE NUMBER OF BANKS IN OPERATION, ETC.—Continued.

[Division No. 4.—North Carolina, South Carolina, Georgia, Florida, Alabama, Mississippi, Louisiana, Texas, Arkansas, Kentucky, and Tennessee, excluding reserve cities.]

Dates.	No. of banks.	Amount of reserve required, 15 per cent. of net deposits.	Reserve held.		Classification of reserve held.				
					Lawful money (6 per cent.).		With reserve agents (9 per cent.).		Five per cent. redemption fund.
			Amount.	Ratio.	Amount.	Ratio.	Amount.	Ratio.	
1882.				Per ct.		Per ct.		Per ct.	
Mar. 11..	141	$5, 185, 281	$10, 013, 832	28. 97	$5, 466, 058	15. 81	$3, 758, 544	10. 87	$789, 230
May 10..	144	4, 915, 899	10, 118, 504	30. 87	5, 419, 385	16. 54	3, 906, 752	11. 92	792, 367
July 1...	148	5, 115, 956	10, 326, 820	30. 28	5, 227, 153	15. 33	4, 313, 224	12. 65	786, 443
Oct. 3...	154	5, 266, 274	9, 392, 645	26. 75	4, 771, 320	13. 59	3, 827, 425	10. 90	793, 894
Dec. 30..	159	5, 978, 914	12, 718, 655	31. 91	6, 340, 182	15. 91	5, 584, 656	14. 01	793, 817
1883.									
Mar. 13..	164	6, 116, 981	13, 254, 160	32. 50	6, 306, 960	15. 69	6, 086, 190	14. 92	771, 001
May 1...	169	6, 190, 802	12, 890, 743	31. 23	6, 543, 434	15. 85	5, 555, 724	13. 46	791, 585
June 22.	175	6, 143, 331	12, 353, 975	30. 16	6, 475, 724	15. 81	5, 075, 892	12. 39	802, 350
Oct. 2...	191	6, 267, 968	10, 275, 182	24. 59	6, 589, 276	15. 77	3, 887, 690	9. 30	798, 216
Dec. 31..	197	6, 761, 077	12, 940, 873	28. 71	6, 968, 150	15. 46	5, 170, 200	11. 48	802, 505
1884.									
Mar. 7...	201	6, 816, 002	13, 644, 672	30. 08	6, 883, 358	15. 15	5, 979, 687	13. 16	781, 627
Apr. 24..	204	6, 874, 431	12, 348, 517	26. 95	6, 803, 162	14. 84	4, 762, 025	10. 39	783, 330
June 20..	208	6, 449, 163	11, 364, 136	26. 43	6, 826, 409	15. 88	3, 782, 006	8. 80	755, 721
Sept. 30.	216	6, 042, 864	11, 108, 565	27. 72	6, 334, 635	15. 72	4, 087, 448	10. 15	746, 482
Dec. 20..	220	6, 491, 216	14, 500, 732	33. 67	7, 007, 016	16. 19	6, 806, 367	15. 73	747, 349
1885.									
Mar. 10..	226	6, 669, 784	15, 008, 820	33. 96	7, 964, 807	17. 91	6, 385, 184	14. 36	748, 829
May 6...	229	6, 483, 495	13, 065, 477	30. 23	7, 563, 398	17. 50	4, 765, 739	11. 03	736, 340
July 1...	232	6, 442, 590	12, 404, 357	28. 88	7, 159, 393	16. 67	4, 532, 187	10. 55	712, 777
Oct. 1....	232	6, 388, 330	11, 874, 404	27. 88	6, 826, 279	16. 03	4, 322, 638	10. 15	725, 487
Dec. 24..	235	7, 142, 014	15, 834, 011	33. 25	8, 001, 784	16. 80	7, 141, 940	15. 00	690, 287
1886.									
Mar. 1...	240	7, 583, 952	16, 308, 788	32. 26	8, 523, 863	16. 86	7, 114, 169	14. 07	670, 756
June 3..	245	7, 493, 963	15, 598, 452	31. 23	8, 108, 413	16. 23	6, 863, 196	13. 74	626, 843
Aug. 27.	251	7, 301, 409	13, 950, 029	28. 67	7, 650, 300	15. 72	5, 690, 062	11. 71	607, 468
Oct. 7...	251	7, 520, 683	13, 597, 692	27. 12	7, 565, 181	15. 09	5, 474, 973	10. 92	557, 538
Dec. 28..	253	8, 863, 744	21, 096, 851	35. 70	9, 659, 357	16. 35	10, 914, 071	18. 47	523, 423
1887.									
Mar. 4...	265	9, 951, 682	22, 483, 366	33. 89	10, 365, 065	15. 62	11, 607, 039	17. 50	511, 262
May 13..	279	9, 403, 413	18, 093, 369	28. 86	9, 623, 458	15. 35	7, 965, 043	12. 71	504, 868
Aug. 1..	290	9, 227, 123	15, 981, 046	25. 98	8, 924, 833	14. 51	6, 555, 611	10. 66	500, 602
Oct. 5..	296	9, 183, 326	16, 341, 084	26. 69	9, 728, 521	15. 89	6, 100, 154	9. 96	512, 359

TABLE SHOWING, BY GEOGRAPHICAL DIVISIONS, THE RESERVE CITIES AND CENTRAL RESERVE CITIES, THE NUMBER OF BANKS, ETC.—Continued.

[Division No. 5.—Ohio, Indiana, Illinois, Michigan, and Wisconsin, excluding reserve cities.]

Dates.	No. of banks.	Amount of reserve required, 15 per cent. of net deposits.	Reserve held.		Classification of reserve held.				
			Amount.	Ratio.	Lawful money (6 per cent.).		With reserve agents (9 per cent.).		Five per cent. redemption fund.
					Amount.	Ratio.	Amount.	Ratio.	
1882.				Per ct.		Per ct.		Per ct.	
Mar. 11..	503	$19,032,152	$27,800,100	20.78	$17,235,102	13.58	$18,080,973	14.73	$1,903,025
May 19..	512	18,777,697	37,819,405	30.22	17,572,569	14.04	18,358,481	14.67	1,888,355
July 1...	514	18,063,931	37,703,899	29.82	16,982,358	13.43	18,910,824	14.96	1,810,720
Oct. 3...	519	19,272,709	35,969,848	27.99	17,205,670	13.39	16,875,972	13.13	1,888,206
Dec. 30..	523	18,845,485	35,817,290	28.51	17,047,739	13.57	16,905,080	13.46	1,863,871
1883.									
Mar. 13..	530	19,081,900	36,507,835	27.17	16,401,301	12.89	18,281,364	14.38	1,825,170
May 1..	536	18,894,570	34,009,157	27.00	17,003,343	13.50	15,146,612	12.03	1,859,202
June 22	541	18,080,838	32,831,223	25.14	15,616,973	12.54	15,394,648	12.36	1,819,607
Oct. 2...	554	18,503,099	34,705,552	28.04	16,503,659	13.34	16,347,350	13.21	1,854,543
Dec. 31..	534	17,961,597	34,790,630	29.05	16,853,215	14.07	16,142,536	13.48	1,794,879
1884.									
Mar. 7..	538	17,808,933	34,832,320	29.34	16,401,984	13.87	16,636,811	14.01	1,733,525
Apr. 24..	560	17,392,091	32,294,504	27.81	16,913,978	14.59	13,623,182	11.75	1,757,434
June 20.	560	16,640,340	30,968,073	29.15	16,180,847	14.59	13,081,876	11.79	1,699,350
Sept. 30.	574	15,784,480	31,515,494	29.98	16,127,236	15.33	13,764,179	13.08	1,634,079
Dec. 20..	572	15,040,275	33,478,235	33.39	15,563,304	15.52	16,332,719	16.29	1,582,152
1885.									
Mar. 10..	567	15,800,692	36,876,186	35.07	16,882,000	16.03	18,475,898	17.54	1,517,079
May 6...	568	15,954,519	35,963,168	33.81	17,117,106	16.09	17,336,757	16.30	1,509,305
July 1...	567	16,118,869	36,162,987	33.65	15,936,895	14.83	18,738,134	17.43	1,487,958
Oct. 1...	570	16,501,187	37,477,345	34.07	17,019,462	15.47	18,934,890	17.21	1,522,993
Dec. 24..	570	16,497,191	36,226,910	32.93	16,050,608	14.59	18,653,616	16.96	1,522,596
1886.									
Mar. 1..	571	17,184,603	38,467,958	33.57	16,692,494	14.57	20,284,810	17.78	1,490,654
June 3..	575	17,452,850	36,682,622	31.53	17,849,509	15.34	17,426,446	14.98	1,406,667
Aug. 27.	582	18,313,951	41,304,412	33.88	17,118,272	14.02	22,807,315	18.73	1,378,825
Oct. 7...	580	18,438,101	39,891,410	32.45	17,974,624	14.62	20,594,220	16.75	1,322,566
Dec. 28..	576	18,828,474	40,251,058	32.07	18,082,937	14.41	20,974,170	16.71	1,193,951
1887.									
Mar. 4..	582	19,446,236	42,186,629	32.54	18,037,038	13.91	23,012,354	17.75	1,136,637
May 13..	584	20,082,778	41,866,938	31.27	19,111,576	14.27	21,673,404	16.19	1,081,958
Aug. 1..	594	20,814,218	44,475,533	32.05	18,401,230	13.26	25,021,687	18.03	1,052,616
Oct. 5...	598	20,576,959	40,983,916	29.88	19,171,016	13.98	20,771,852	15.14	1,041,048

TABLE SHOWING, BY GEOGRAPHICAL DIVISIONS, THE RESERVE CITIES AND CENTRAL RESERVE CITIES, THE NUMBER OF BANKS IN OPERATION, ETC.—Continued.

[Division No. 6.—Iowa, Minnesota, Missouri, Kansas, and Nebraska (Omaha transferred to division No. 9, October 5, 1887; Kansas City and Saint Joseph transferred to division No. 9, May 13, 1887, excluding reserve cities.]

Dates.	No. of banks.	Amount of reserve required, 15 per cent. of net deposits.	Reserve held.		Classification of reserve held.				
			Amount.	Ratio.	Lawful money (6 per cent.). Amount.	Lawful money (6 per cent.). Ratio.	With reserve agents (9 per cent.). Amount.	With reserve agents (9 per cent.). Ratio.	Five per cent. redemption fund.
1882.				*Per ct.*		*Per ct.*		*Per ct.*	
Mar. 11..	157	$6,541,424	$11,849,067	27.17	$5,719,125	13.11	$5,665,681	12.99	$465,161
May 19..	165	6,707,034	12,348,739	27.62	5,557,107	12.43	6,323,635	14.14	467,997
July 1...	171	6,945,887	12,192,356	26.33	5,865,877	12.67	5,866,168	12.68	460,311
Oct. 3....	184	7,211,774	11,866,093	24.68	5,934,099	12.34	5,440,789	11.32	491,205
Dec. 30..	197	7,314,811	12,985,546	26.63	6,513,480	13.35	5,975,158	12.23	496,908
1883.									
Mar. 13..	207	7,692,300	13,786,065	26.88	6,048,070	11.79	7,237,137	14.11	500,858
May 1...	216	8,607,308	13,928,636	26.09	6,926,476	12.98	6,496,862	12.17	505,298
June 22.	227	8,669,016	16,331,528	28.26	6,739,738	11.66	9,100,816	15.75	490,974
Oct. 2....	237	9,087,854	15,692,927	25.90	7,240,980	11.95	7,922,362	13.08	529,585
Dec. 31..	270	9,269,439	16,068,106	26.00	7,756,806	12.55	7,788,201	12.60	523,099
1884.									
Mar. 7...	287	9,365,609	16,334,768	26.16	7,297,414	11.69	8,526,486	13.66	510,868
Apr. 24..	298	9,712,119	17,385,106	26.85	8,463,096	13.07	8,406,680	12.98	515,330
June 20.	309	9,546,762	16,682,585	26.21	9,366,090	14.72	6,806,014	10.69	510,451
Sept. 30..	320	9,158,231	16,305,178	26.70	8,130,878	13.32	7,677,976	12.58	494,324
Dec. 20..	320	8,643,147	15,874,452	27.55	7,734,917	13.42	7,642,884	13.26	496,651
1885.									
Mar. 10..	336	9,202,146	18,064,151	29.45	8,442,274	13.76	9,131,647	14.89	490,230
May 6...	340	9,613,675	19,112,996	29.73	8,803,813	13.69	9,806,853	15.25	502,330
July 1...	346	10,105,532	20,186,373	29.96	8,868,049	13.16	10,827,681	16.07	490,643
Oct. 1....	359	10,526,279	19,159,727	27.30	8,896,805	12.68	9,768,829	13.92	494,093
Dec. 24..	363	10,511,542	19,128,184	27.30	9,309,286	13.28	9,315,121	13.29	503,777
1886.									
Mar. 1...	377	10,872,988	19,373,302	26.73	8,838,140	12.19	10,043,854	13.86	491,308
June 3..	391	12,203,046	23,020,432	28.30	11,204,906	13.77	11,339,220	13.94	476,306
Aug. 27..	404	12,349,300	24,464,927	29.72	10,229,545	12.43	13,747,424	16.70	487,553
Oct. 7....	406	12,377,733	21,931,867	26.58	11,019,342	13.35	10,422,066	12.63	490,459
Dec. 28..	418	12,811,418	23,053,002	26.99	11,752,951	13.76	10,848,107	12.70	451,944
1887.									
Mar. 4...	427	14,184,873	27,752,343	29.35	11,860,366	12.54	15,441,590	16.33	450,387
May 13..	428	13,368,183	26,723,837	29.99	12,010,369	13.48	14,290,849	16.04	422,619
Aug. 1...	438	12,435,313	25,056,695	30.22	10,458,690	12.62	14,175,769	17.10	422,236
Oct. 5....	455	12,258,402	22,367,310	27.37	10,275,484	12.57	11,660,633	14.27	431,193

TABLE SHOWING, BY GEOGRAPHICAL DIVISIONS, THE RESERVE CITIES AND CENTRAL RESERVE CITIES, THE NUMBER OF BANKS IN OPERATION, ETC.—Continued.

[Division No. 7.—Colorado, Nevada, California, and Oregon, excluding reserve cities.]

Dates.	No. of banks.	Amount of reserves required, 15 per cent. of net deposits.	Reserve held.		Classification of reserve held.				
					Lawful money (6 per cent.).		With reserve agents (9 per cent.).		Five per cent. redemption fund.
			Amount.	Ratio.	Amount.	Ratio.	Amount.	Ratio.	
1882.				Per ct.		Per ct.		Per ct.	
Mar. 11..	30	$2,576,675	$5,408,452	31.53	$2,542,858	14.83	$2,758,864	16.08	$106,730
May 19..	31	2,696,322	5,872,661	32.72	2,637,314	14.69	3,122,481	17.40	112,866
July 1...	32	2,693,926	5,682,235	31.69	2,460,625	13.72	3,109,475	17.34	112,135
Oct. 3...	32	2,868,124	6,241,813	32.69	2,791,278	14.63	3,330,785	17.44	116,750
Dec. 30..	33	2,871,064	6,379,306	33.37	3,166,266	16.56	3,096,131	16.20	116,909
1883.									
Mar. 13.	33	2,866,867	6,081,382	31.86	3,594,598	18.83	2,374,534	12.44	112,250
May 1...	34	2,890,642	5,487,840	28.51	3,133,202	16.28	2,240,755	11.64	113,883
June 22.	38	2,984,656	6,355,648	31.97	3,203,157	16.11	3,033,366	15.26	119,125
Oct. 2...	43	3,206,008	5,839,540	27.33	3,098,370	14.51	2,619,307	12.27	121,863
Dec. 31..	42	3,241,147	6,447,703	29.88	3,558,027	16.50	2,763,101	12.80	126,575
1884.									
Mar. 7..	43	3,009,761	5,626,902	28.08	3,217,309	16.05	2,287,585	11.46	122,008
Apr. 24..	43	3,028,531	5,791,614	28.68	3,207,082	15.88	2,462,898	12.20	121,634
June 20.	45	2,748,621	5,492,659	29.97	3,664,908	20.00	1,717,837	9.37	109,914
Sept. 30.	46	2,660,518	5,798,359	32.69	3,346,017	18.86	2,341,155	13.20	111,187
Dec. 20..	47	2,560,777	5,524,939	32.36	3,180,260	18.63	2,239,427	13.12	105,252
1885.									
Mar. 10..	47	2,663,353	5,078,551	33.07	3,450,529	19.43	2,419,586	13.63	108,436
May 6...	49	2,683,438	5,699,692	31.86	3,336,534	18.65	2,256,198	12.61	106,960
July 1...	50	2,721,004	5,697,478	31.41	2,966,876	16.36	2,626,141	14.48	104,461
Oct. 1...	51	2,920,866	6,635,005	34.07	3,260,554	16.74	3,264,417	16.76	110,034
Dec. 24..	54	3,189,900	7,038,522	33.10	3,732,709	17.55	3,192,688	15.01	113,125
1886.									
Mar. 1...	57	3,329,624	7,529,982	33.92	3,947,515	17.78	3,465,653	15.61	116,814
June 3..	61	3,598,749	7,672,897	31.98	4,034,927	16.82	3,527,877	14.70	110,093
Aug. 27.	67	3,863,2[illegible]6	8,288,012	32.18	4,096,387	15.91	4,075,587	15.82	116,038
Oct. 7...	68	3,971,589	7,896,910	29.83	4,104,213	15.50	3,672,731	13.87	119,966
Dec. 28..	71	4,329,961	9,221,771	31.95	5,276,940	18.28	3,828,979	13.26	115,853
1887.									
Mar. 4..	71	4,674,444	10,289,333	33.02	5,672,302	18.20	4,504,028	14.45	113,003
May 12..	75	5,276,435	11,540,554	32.81	5,990,889	17.03	5,438,612	15.46	111,053
Aug. 1..	83	5,719,220	11,799,916	30.95	6,134,729	16.09	5,548,590	14.55	116,507
Oct. 5...	86	6,330,097	13,784,605	32.66	7,276,703	17.24	6,385,396	15.13	122,506

TABLE SHOWING, BY GEOGRAPHICAL DIVISIONS, THE RESERVE CITIES AND CENTRAL RESERVE CITIES, THE NUMBER OF BANKS IN OPERATION, ETC.—Continued.

[Division No. 8.—Arizona, Dakota, Idaho, Montana, New Mexico, Utah, Washington, and Wyoming.]

Dates.	No. of banks.	Amount of reserve required, 15 per cent. of net deposits.	Reserve held.		Classification of reserve held.				
			Amount.	Ratio.	Lawful money (6 per cent.).		With reserve agents (9 per cent.).		Five per cent. redemption fund.
					Amount.	Ratio.	Amount.	Ratio.	
1882.									
				Per ct.		Per ct.		Per ct.	
Mar. 11	32	$1,144,070	$1,804,032	24.42	$1,234,034	16.17	$547,337	7.17	$82,641
May 19	38	1,340,340	2,242,753	25.10	1,346,771	15.07	803,072	8.99	92,910
July 1	38	1,379,900	2,335,024	25.38	1,265,644	13.76	970,470	10.55	98,920
Oct. 3	41	1,662,285	2,686,299	24.24	1,566,209	14.13	1,019,233	9.20	100,857
Dec. 30	48	1,815,318	3,276,376	27.07	1,893,011	15.64	1,276,446	10.55	106,919
1883.									
Mar. 13	54	1,857,414	3,171,854	25.62	1,944,893	15.71	1,118,433	9.03	108,528
May 1	55	2,072,505	3,196,343	23.13	1,946,749	14.09	1,139,293	8.25	110,301
June 22	60	2,234,510	3,787,433	25.42	1,946,924	13.07	1,726,181	11.59	114,328
Oct. 2	70	2,362,081	3,453,105	21.93	2,000,374	12.70	1,331,438	8.46	121,293
Dec. 31	74	2,280,534	3,746,766	24.64	2,450,974	16.12	1,177,548	7.75	118,244
1884.									
Mar. 7	78	2,206,520	3,406,474	23.16	2,332,136	15.85	955,815	6.50	118,523
Apr. 24	84	2,256,846	3,584,760	23.83	2,421,783	16.10	1,038,881	6.90	124,096
June 20	87	2,194,632	3,402,695	23.26	2,377,061	16.25	899,284	6.15	126,350
Sept. 30	87	2,162,177	3,263,041	22.64	2,077,673	14.41	1,066,754	7.40	118,614
Dec. 20	86	2,193,537	3,581,574	24.49	2,357,403	16.12	1,114,624	7.62	109,547
1885.									
Mar. 10	88	2,132,223	3,703,384	26.05	2,525,590	17.77	1,068,609	7.52	109,185
May 6	89	2,124,719	3,587,997	25.33	2,387,887	16.86	1,089,153	7.69	110,957
July 1	92	2,317,930	3,939,596	25.48	2,354,579	15.24	1,473,460	9.53	111,557
Oct. 1	94	2,492,432	4,420,239	26.60	2,600,691	15.65	1,704,733	10.26	114,815
Dec. 24	107	2,633,014	4,881,391	27.80	3,166,234	18.03	1,594,293	9.08	120,864
1886.									
Mar. 1	107	2,643,604	4,716,817	26.86	3,057,426	17.41	1,535,412	8.74	123,977
June 3	109	2,745,657	4,688,187	25.61	3,091,659	16.89	1,471,191	8.04	125,339
Aug. 27	113	2,615,777	5,173,780	29.67	3,135,269	17.98	1,913,185	10.97	125,335
Oct. 7	114	2,675,213	5,149,624	28.87	3,360,609	18.79	1,669,970	9.36	119,045
Dec. 28	111	2,852,550	5,258,108	27.65	3,560,333	18.70	1,577,946	8.25	119,829
1887.									
Mar. 4	121	3,019,568	4,961,765	24.65	3,418,756	16.98	1,421,601	7.06	121,408
May 13	125	3,258,730	4,782,756	22.02	3,357,718	15.46	1,303,545	6.00	121,493
Aug. 1	128	3,501,233	5,626,017	24.13	3,492,525	14.96	2,010,740	8.57	122,752
Oct. 5	128	3,630,696	5,730,545	23.68	3,715,106	15.35	1,888,860	7.80	126,480

TABLE SHOWING, BY GEOGRAPHICAL DIVISIONS, THE RESERVE CITIES AND CENTRAL RESERVE CITIES, THE NUMBER OF BANKS IN OPERATION, ETC.—Continued.

[Division No. 9.—Reserve cities—Boston, Albany, Philadelphia, Pittsburgh, Baltimore, Washington, New Orleans, Louisville, Cincinnati, Cleveland, Chicago, Detroit, Milwaukee, Saint Louis, and San Francisco.]

Dates.	No. of banks.	Amount of reserve required, 15 per cent. of net deposits.	Reserve held.		Classification of reserve held.				
			Amount.	Ratio.	Lawful money (6 per cent.). Amount.	Lawful money (6 per cent.). Ratio.	With reserve agents (9 per cent.). Amount.	With reserve agents (9 per cent.). Ratio.	Five per cent. redemption fund.
1882.				Per ct.		Per ct.		Per ct.	
Mar. 11	192	$77, 032, 003	$93, 401, 093	30. 31	$54, 818, 246	17. 79	$34, 852, 796	11. 31	$3, 730, 051
May 19	192	80, 294, 028	102, 352, 099	31. 87	59, 318, 593	18. 47	39, 467, 976	12. 29	3, 566, 430
July 1	193	81, 760, 651	95, 874, 953	29. 32	57, 206, 564	17. 49	35, 233, 042	10. 77	3, 435, 347
Oct. 3	193	79, 694, 569	89, 143, 583	27. 96	52, 413, 086	16. 44	33, 213, 032	10. 42	3, 517, 465
Dec. 30	195	77, 095, 866	95, 051, 887	30. 82	54, 211, 536	17. 58	37, 282, 190	12. 09	3, 558, 161
1883.									
Mar. 13	198	77, 419, 867	89, 796, 888	29. 00	49, 661, 801	16. 04	36, 592, 761	11. 82	3, 542, 326
May 1	199	78, 644, 546	91, 787, 852	29. 18	54, 129, 582	17. 21	34, 090, 027	10. 84	3, 568, 243
June 22	200	83, 005, 153	103, 900, 990	31. 29	59, 515, 283	17. 93	40, 821, 353	12. 29	3, 564, 354
Oct. 2	200	80, 961, 109	100, 638, 235	31. 08	56, 425, 407	17. 42	40, 798, 990	12. 60	3, 413, 838
Dec. 31	202	83, 646, 150	105, 535, 835	31. 54	63, 273, 391	18. 91	38, 942, 133	11. 64	3, 320, 311
1884.									
Mar. 7	202	85, 297, 591	111, 255, 631	32. 61	61, 563, 512	18. 04	46, 437, 308	13. 61	3, 254, 811
Apr. 24	202	84, 514, 593	104, 165, 958	30. 81	62, 160, 250	18. 39	38, 827, 197	11. 49	3, 178, 511
June 20	204	75, 708, 561	91, 103, 676	30. 08	59, 623, 045	19. 69	28, 403, 338	9. 38	3, 077, 293
Sept. 30	203	76, 984, 342	99, 022, 475	32. 16	63, 578, 992	20. 65	32, 340, 900	10. 50	3, 102, 583
Dec. 20	203	78, 739, 375	103, 685, 153	32. 92	66, 011, 790	20. 96	34, 672, 781	11. 01	3, 000, 582
1885.									
Mar. 10	202	83, 402, 537	118, 522, 306	35. 50	74, 383, 404	22. 28	41, 172, 443	12. 33	2, 966, 459
May 6	202	86, 028, 706	123, 962, 577	35. 77	80, 109, 098	23. 12	40, 912, 049	11. 81	2, 941, 430
July 1	202	89, 118, 504	123, 423, 045	31. 62	79, 828, 139	22. 39	40, 661, 809	11. 41	2, 933, 097
Oct. 1	203	91, 118, 639	122, 186, 751	33. 52	76, 907, 632	21. 10	42, 402, 600	11. 63	2, 876, 510
Dec. 24	202	91, 151, 185	117, 043, 608	32. 11	74, 674, 927	20. 48	39, 551, 479	10. 88	2, 817, 202
1886.									
Mar. 1	205	94, 506, 304	124, 034, 337	32. 81	77, 446, 733	20. 49	43, 904, 247	11. 61	2, 683, 357
June 3	212	96, 810, 237	122, 784, 157	31. 71	80, 738, 933	20. 85	39, 567, 423	10. 22	2, 477, 801
Aug. 27	215	93, 802, 939	110, 584, 456	29. 42	68, 232, 506	18. 19	40, 072, 689	10. 68	2, 279, 261
Oct. 7	217	95, 303, 710	113, 951, 757	29. 88	70, 489, 135	18. 48	41, 271, 509	10. 82	2, 191, 113
Dec. 28	218	94, 305, 102	112, 821, 235	29. 91	70, 633, 785	18. 72	40, 371, 942	10. 70	1, 815, 508
1887.									
Mar. 4	220	99, 518, 660	124, 447, 510	31. 26	73, 631, 556	18. 50	49, 217, 253	12. 36	1, 598, 701
May 13*	210	86, 270, 809	106, 121, 301	30. 75	64, 496, 954	18. 69	40, 210, 839	11. 65	1, 413, 508
Aug. 1†	221	83, 889, 106	98, 389, 974	29. 32	59, 504, 534	17. 73	37, 672, 340	11. 23	1, 213, 090
Oct. 5	223	84, 021, 164	100, 714, 633	29. 75	59, 524, 848	17. 59	39, 993, 709	11. 82	1, 196, 076

* Kansas City and Saint Joseph included from May 13, 1887, and Chicago and Saint Louis transferred to Division No. 10.

† Omaha included from August 1, 1887.

TABLE SHOWING, BY GEOGRAPHICAL DIVISIONS, THE RESERVE CITIES AND CENTRAL RESERVE CITIES, THE NUMBER OF BANKS IN OPERATION, ETC.—Continued.

[Division No. 10.]

Dates.	New York City.			Chicago.			Saint Louis.		
	No. of banks.	Amount of reserve required = 25 per cent. of net deposits.	Ratio of reserve held.	No. of banks.	Amount of reserve required = 25 per cent. of net deposits.	Ratio of reserve held.	No. of banks.	Amount of reserve required = 25 per cent. of net deposits.	Ratio of reserve held.
1882.			Per ct.			Per ct.			Per ct.
Mar. 11	50	$63, 982, 629	25.16	......	......	......	......	......	......
May 19	50	66, 708, 718	26.14	......	......	......	......	......	......
July 1	50	69, 337, 200	25.99	......	......	......	......	......	......
Oct. 3	50	63, 503, 245	25.36	......	......	......	......	......	......
Dec. 30	48	64, 391, 243	26.14	......	......	......	......	......	......
1883.									
Mar. 13	48	62, 437, 901	23.59	......	......	......	......	......	......
May 1	48	63, 422, 340	25.48	......	......	......	......	......	......
June 22	48	69, 809, 040	28.81	......	......	......	......	......	......
Oct. 2	48	66, 735, 374	26.53	......	......	......	......	......	......
Dec. 31	47	63, 509, 209	27.58	......	......	......	......	......	......
1884.									
Mar. 7	47	75, 373, 069	28.94	......	......	......	......	......	......
Apr. 24	47	70, 540, 863	26.65	......	......	......	......	......	......
June 20	45	57, 918, 702	29.82	......	......	......	......	......	......
Sept. 30	44	63, 787, 684	35.63	......	......	......	......	......	......
Dec. 20	44	68, 335, 552	38.29	......	......	......	......	......	......
1885.									
Mar. 10	44	73, 191, 705	40.12	......	......	......	......	......	......
May 6	44	74, 436, 136	41.48	......	......	......	......	......	......
July 1	45	78, 181, 211	42.47	......	......	......	......	......	......
Oct 1	44	78, 214, 626	36.98	......	......	......	......	......	......
Dec. 24	45	75, 516, 839	32.76	......	......	......	......	......	......
1886.									
Mar. 1	45	80, 887, 727	31.28	......	......	......	......	......	......
June 3	45	74, 187, 977	30.28	......	......	......	......	......	......
Aug. 27	45	70, 386, 879	27.46	......	......	......	......	......	......
Oct. 7	45	70, 697, 561	27.24	......	......	......	......	......	......
Dec. 28	45	73, 607, 025	29.89	......	......	......	......	......	......
1887.									
Mar. 4	45	78, 607, 422	28.70	......	......	......	......	......	......
May 13	46	74, 921, 637	27.04	18	$16, 998, 940	30.41	5	2, 280, 864	36.40
Aug. 1	46	73, 497, 514	28.11	18	16, 579, 934	33.14	5	2, 710, 000	31.89
Oct. 5	47	71, 084, 776	28.18	18	16, 161, 735	30.53	5	2, 574, 207	20.44

AVERAGE WEEKLY DEPOSITS, CIRCULATION, AND RESERVE OF THE NATIONAL BANKS OF NEW YORK CITY, AS REPORTED TO THE NEW YORK CLEARING-HOUSE, FOR THE MONTHS GIVEN, IN THE YEARS 1881, 1882, 1883, 1884, 1885, 1886, 1887.

Week ending—	Liabilities.			Reserve.			
	Circulation.	Net deposits.	Total.	Specie.	Legal tenders.	Total.	Ratio to liabilities.
							Per cent.
Sept. 3, 1881	$19,660,400	$278,241,700	$297,911,100	$57,816,100	$13,226,600	$71,042,700	23.85
Sept. 10, 1881	19,764,500	277,011,700	296,776,200	59,991,600	12,591,300	72,582,900	24.46
Sept. 17, 1881	19,768,100	279,404,900	299,173,000	61,224,100	11,970,000	73,203,100	24.47
Sept. 24, 1881	19,747,500	277,268,600	297,016,100	60,476,000	12,451,300	72,927,300	24.55
Oct. 1, 1881	19,841,400	270,727,400	290,568,800	54,954,600	12,150,400	67,105,000	23.09
Oct. 8, 1881	19,849,400	263,081,600	282,931,000	53,287,900	12,153,800	65,441,700	23.13
Oct. 15, 1881	19,878,400	254,224,700	274,103,100	51,008,300	12,452,700	63,461,000	23.15
Oct. 22, 1881	19,901,400	250,299,000	270,200,400	54,016,200	12,496,500	66,512,700	24.61
Oct. 29, 1881	19,930,400	251,480,300	271,410,700	55,961,200	12,947,900	68,909,100	25.61
Sept. 2, 1882	18,278,400	271,999,400	290,277,800	49,775,400	19,953,100	69,728,500	24.02
Sept. 9, 1882	18,307,000	265,566,900	283,873,900	47,148,500	19,418,800	66,567,300	23.46
Sept. 16, 1882	18,357,500	263,736,700	282,094,200	48,571,500	18,694,500	67,263,000	23.84
Sept. 23, 1882	18,623,700	260,205,800	278,829,500	47,114,000	17,993,700	65,107,700	23.35
Sept. 30, 1882	18,768,100	251,858,100	270,644,200	44,925,500	18,389,000	63,314,500	23.25
Oct. 7, 1882	18,894,800	249,136,800	268,031,600	47,016,000	18,384,500	65,400,500	24.03
Oct. 14, 1882	18,732,000	249,629,700	268,361,700	48,281,000	18,002,700	66,283,700	24.70
Oct. 21, 1882	18,749,400	247,974,400	266,723,800	49,518,200	17,023,900	66,542,100	24.97
Oct. 28, 1882	18,764,500	247,575,400	266,339,900	48,374,200	17,204,700	65,578,900	24.77
Sept. 1, 1883	15,622,600	269,961,900	285,584,500	53,529,000	21,729,000	75,258,000	26.35
Sept. 8, 1883	15,527,000	268,805,500	284,332,500	52,601,400	21,074,500	73,675,900	25.91
Sept. 15, 1883	15,519,700	272,325,100	287,844,800	53,997,400	20,062,700	74,060,100	25.73
Sept. 22, 1883	15,394,600	271,728,200	287,122,800	49,360,600	22,443,300	71,803,900	25.01
Sept. 29, 1883	15,184,800	268,496,600	283,681,400	50,067,900	20,566,800	70,634,700	24.90
Oct. 6, 1883	15,069,100	265,592,500	280,661,600	51,586,700	20,122,500	71,709,200	25.51
Oct. 13, 1883	15,164,200	268,942,000	284,106,200	50,894,000	21,145,800	72,039,800	25.36
Oct. 20, 1883	15,252,900	262,635,700	277,888,600	47,262,900	20,719,700	67,982,600	24.47
Oct. 27, 1883	15,336,200	258,589,600	273,925,800	46,372,800	20,617,600	66,990,400	24.46
Sept. 6, 1884	14,221,000	251,527,200	265,748,200	64,899,900	25,060,800	89,960,700	33.85
Sept. 13, 1884	14,132,300	251,654,700	265,787,000	64,288,200	25,191,800	89,480,000	33.67
Sept. 20, 1884	14,081,400	254,141,200	268,222,600	65,409,500	25,268,000	90,677,500	33.81
Sept. 27, 1884	14,083,300	252,765,500	266,848,800	64,302,000	25,375,700	89,677,700	33.61
Oct. 4, 1884	13,578,400	254,696,800	270,275,200	67,470,600	25,817,300	93,287,900	34.52
Oct. 11, 1884	12,884,700	261,801,600	274,686,300	68,922,500	27,654,100	96,576,600	35.16
Oct. 18, 1884	12,752,700	261,527,700	274,280,400	67,579,400	27,875,500	95,451,900	34.80
Oct. 25, 1884	12,910,900	261,405,400	274,316,300	67,638,000	27,354,200	94,992,200	34.63
Sept. 5, 1885	9,704,700	321,859,000	331,563,700	102,921,100	28,701,900	131,623,000	39.70
Sept. 12, 1885	9,753,300	320,910,000	330,663,300	100,255,300	28,842,300	129,097,600	39.04
Sept. 19, 1885	9,785,800	319,060,800	328,706,600	97,333,200	27,662,800	124,996,000	38.01
Sept. 26, 1885	9,808,600	316,767,000	326,575,000	95,037,900	26,014,800	121,052,000	37.07
Oct. 3, 1885	9,902,900	315,002,600	324,905,500	92,351,600	24,516,600	116,868,200	35.97
Oct. 10, 1885	9,921,200	315,596,200	325,517,400	93,642,500	23,002,000	116,644,500	35.83
Oct. 17, 1885	9,954,000	317,296,700	327,250,700	91,945,300	22,221,100	114,166,400	34.89
Oct. 24, 1885	10,006,000	313,767,200	323,773,200	87,309,100	21,059,800	108,368,900	33.47
Oct. 31, 1885	9,989,800	313,399,700	323,389,500	84,954,600	21,874,900	106,829,500	33.03
Sept. 4, 1886	8,059,200	283,366,700	291,425,900	61,371,600	19,071,400	80,443,000	27.60
Sept. 11, 1886	8,058,000	282,417,800	290,475,800	63,403,700	16,929,300	80,333,000	27.66
Sept. 18, 1886	8,104,800	281,466,500	289,571,300	63,823,900	15,876,700	79,700,600	27.52
Sept. 25, 1886	8,136,100	283,170,900	291,307,000	66,714,600	15,252,200	81,966,800	28.14
Oct. 2, 1886	8,161,800	282,295,800	290,457,600	64,111,700	14,607,700	78,719,400	27.10
Oct. 9, 1886	8,110,700	281,170,758	289,281,458	65,090,900	13,069,500	78,160,400	27.02
Oct. 16, 1886	8,215,900	295,713,900	303,929,800	65,028,600	13,133,100	78,161,700	25.72
Oct. 23, 1886	8,246,400	283,693,500	291,939,900	65,668,400	12,803,800	78,472,200	26.88
Oct. 30, 1886	8,234,900	284,522,500	292,757,400	66,188,100	13,177,200	79,365,300	27.11
Sept. 3, 1887	8,112,000	281,345,100	289,457,100	59,175,700	18,786,100	77,961,800	26.93
Sept. 10, 1887	8,115,600	279,915,600	288,031,200	58,851,300	17,769,000	76,620,300	26.60
Sept. 17, 1887	8,126,000	279,288,500	287,414,500	59,052,900	16,389,600	75,442,500	26.25
Sept. 24, 1887	8,235,300	278,573,000	286,808,300	60,635,900	16,259,600	76,895,500	26.81
Oct. 1, 1887	8,202,500	281,647,300	289,849,800	61,619,200	15,767,500	80,386,700	27.73
Oct. 8, 1887	8,186,800	285,703,700	293,890,500	64,317,500	16,269,700	80,587,200	27.42
Oct. 15, 1887	8,199,100	289,861,500	298,060,600	64,663,100	16,885,400	81,548,500	27.36
Oct. 22, 1887	8,216,200	289,542,800	297,759,000	64,918,700	16,735,800	81,654,500	27.42
Oct. 29, 1887	8,115,100	289,601,900	297,717,000	66,005,800	17,542,400	83,548,200	28.06
Nov. 5, 1887	8,046,100	289,954,700	298,000,800	64,639,800	17,810,700	82,450,500	27.67
Nov. 12, 1887	8,033,700	288,289,700	296,323,400	63,791,600	18,070,800	81,862,400	27.63

STATE OF THE LAWFUL-MONEY RESERVE OF THE NATIONAL BANKS AS

STATES AND

	Dates.	No. of banks.	Net deposits.	Reserve required.
1	Oct. 1, 1881	1,895	$507,247,143	$76,196,945
2	Dec. 31, 1881	1,926	518,701,965	77,809,257
3	Mar. 11, 1882	1,945	515,198,159	77,283,080
4	May 19, 1882	1,981	519,247,650	77,891,110
5	July 1, 1882	1,996	527,588,049	79,142,169
6	Oct. 3, 1882	2,026	545,842,669	81,880,361
7	Dec. 30, 1882	2,065	554,215,520	83,140,390
8	Mar. 13, 1883	2,097	550,892,283	82,637,104
9	May 1, 1883	2,128	556,309,464	83,449,581
10	June 22, 1883	2,169	560,731,879	84,112,683
11	Oct. 2, 1883	2,253	577,880,812	86,695,688
12	Dec. 31, 1883	2,280	579,512,711	86,930,753
13	Mar. 7, 1884	2,314	573,619,524	86,046,715
14	Apr. 24, 1884	2,340	575,995,025	86,399,253
15	June 20, 1884	2,376	544,660,331	81,699,049
16	Sept. 30, 1884	2,417	535,807,406	80,371,110
17	Dec. 20, 1884	2,417	520,283,576	78,042,530
18	Mar. 10, 1885	2,425	537,613,418	80,642,012
19	May 6, 1885	2,432	540,281,214	81,042,182
20	July 1, 1885	2,442	552,196,593	82,829,489
21	Oct. 1, 1885	2,467	570,838,327	85,625,749
22	Dec. 24, 1885	2,485	580,879,155	87,131,873
23	Mar. 1, 1886	2,518	596,051,483	89,407,722
24	June 3, 1886	2,552	611,733,799	91,760,069
25	Aug. 27, 1886	2,580	623,886,736	93,583,010
26	Oct. 7, 1886	2,590	637,564,136	95,634,620
27	Dec. 28, 1886	2,612	651,697,492	97,754,624
28	Mar. 4, 1887	2,644	675,355,824	101,303,374
29	May 13, 1887	2,676	682,845,855	102,426,878
30	Aug. 1, 1887	2,724	682,963,777	102,444,566
31	Oct. 5, 1887	2,756	690,622,007	103,593,301

RESERVE

1	Oct. 1, 1881	237	604,438,599	151,109,650
2	Dec. 31, 1881	238	577,163,351	144,290,838
3	Mar. 11, 1882	242	564,058,531	141,014,632
4	May 19, 1882	242	590,883,075	147,720,769
5	July 1, 1882	243	604,391,647	151,097,911
6	Oct. 3, 1882	243	572,791,257	143,197,814
7	Dec. 30, 1882	243	565,948,445	141,487,111
8	Mar. 13, 1883	246	559,431,070	139,857,768
9	May 1, 1883	247	568,267,546	142,066,886
10	June 22, 1883	248	611,259,171	152,814,793
11	Oct. 2, 1883	248	590,785,930	147,696,483
12	Dec. 31, 1883	249	612,621,435	153,155,359
13	Mar. 7, 1884	249	642,682,644	160,670,660
14	Apr. 24, 1884	249	620,221,832	155,055,456
15	June 20, 1884	249	534,629,056	133,657,263
16	Sept. 30, 1884	247	562,888,105	140,722,026
17	Dec. 20, 1884	247	588,299,710	147,074,927
18	Mar. 10, 1885	246	626,616,971	156,654,242
19	May 6, 1885	246	644,259,607	161,064,902
20	July 1, 1885	247	669,199,214	167,299,805
21	Oct. 1, 1885	247	677,333,060	169,333,265
22	Dec. 24, 1885	247	666,672,097	166,668,024
23	Mar. 1, 1886	250	701,576,125	175,394,031
24	June 3, 1886	257	683,992,858	170,998,214
25	Aug. 27, 1886	260	656,759,355	164,189,838
26	Oct. 7, 1886	262	664,245,121	166,061,280
27	Dec. 28, 1886	263	671,648,508	167,912,127
28	Mar. 4, 1887	265	712,504,329	178,126,082
29	May 13, 1887	270	721,869,242	180,467,310
30	Aug. 1, 1887	290	706,708,847	176,677,212
31	Oct. 5, 1887	293	697,767,889	174,441,972

SHOWN BY THEIR REPORTS FROM OCTOBER 1, 1881, TO OCTOBER 5, 1887.

TERRITORIES.

Reserve held.		Classification of reserve held.					
Amount.	Ratio to liabilities.	Specie.	Legal tenders.	United States certificates of deposit.	Due from reserve agents.	Redemption fund with Treasurer.	
$158, 299, 042	31. 2	$27, 509, 821	$26, 473, 002	$620, 000	$92, 335, 036	$11, 361, 183	1
159, 060, 717	30. 7	30, 283, 767	28, 905, 001	595, 000	87, 745, 656	11, 531, 293	2
150, 725, 091	29. 3	29, 161, 734	26, 897, 694	610, 000	82, 509, 924	11, 455, 739	3
154, 776, 359	29. 8	30, 036, 477	28, 160, 027	535, 000	84, 721, 969	11, 322, 286	4
151, 908, 107	28. 8	30, 089, 064	26, 837, 020	620, 000	83, 221, 970	11, 119, 453	5
150, 351, 513	27. 5	30, 024, 289	28, 318, 646	610, 000	80, 064, 196	11, 334, 382	6
158, 832, 406	28. 7	31, 095, 498	31, 038, 111	635, 000	84, 783, 917	11, 279, 882	7
155, 131, 167	28. 2	30, 072, 360	28, 871, 031	565, 000	84, 431, 394	11, 191, 382	8
148, 836, 606	26. 7	31, 414, 155	30, 367, 252	585, 000	75, 216, 795	11, 253, 404	9
157, 728, 089	28. 1	31, 055, 220	29, 053, 116	575, 000	85, 825, 601	11, 219, 153	10
157, 493, 584	27. 2	31, 253, 194	30, 245, 600	585, 000	84, 119, 738	11, 290, 052	11
167, 741, 690	28. 6	33, 178, 829	32, 695, 299	610, 000	88, 057, 473	11, 200, 089	12
167, 008, 072	29. 1	33, 471, 053	29, 850, 218	595, 000	92, 267, 704	10, 815, 097	13
162, 466, 664	28. 2	36, 352, 684	30, 944, 464	550, 000	83, 664, 701	10, 954, 155	14
145, 997, 562	26. 8	36, 407, 051	31, 448, 254	575, 000	66, 843, 814	10, 723, 443	15
156, 304, 783	29. 2	35, 238, 175	30, 392, 840	500, 000	79, 652, 110	10, 521, 599	16
161, 864, 287	31. 1	34, 587, 231	29, 943, 391	565, 000	86, 489, 195	10, 279, 470	17
175, 030, 558	32. 6	38, 832, 602	30, 134, 197	665, 000	95, 289, 830	10, 088, 839	18
171, 011, 833	31. 6	40, 736, 669	29, 508, 036	635, 000	89, 991, 054	10, 141, 074	19
170, 245, 483	30. 8	40, 065, 640	27, 473, 329	635, 000	92, 068, 593	10, 003, 921	20
177, 470, 804	31. 1	41, 467, 335	29, 375, 936	500, 000	95, 954, 541	10, 172, 992	21
181, 357, 249	31. 2	42, 195, 802	28, 898, 910	530, 000	99, 667, 965	10, 044, 572	22
181, 591, 775	30. 4	45, 138, 994	27, 257, 991	475, 000	98, 901, 439	9, 818, 351	23
181, 552, 648	29. 6	49, 082, 209	29, 236, 191	465, 000	93, 459, 713	9, 289, 535	24
188, 847, 786	30. 2	47, 370, 313	28, 214, 619	460, 000	103, 642, 532	9, 160, 322	25
186, 191, 889	29. 2	47, 824, 967	29, 672, 277	460, 000	99, 493, 068	8, 741, 577	26
192, 278, 074	29. 5	50, 326, 810	31, 879, 137	500, 000	101, 746, 037	7, 826, 981	27
203, 307, 527	30. 1	50, 881, 172	30, 643, 308	555, 000	113, 943, 928	7, 281, 059	28
198, 863, 737	29. 1	51, 145, 531	32, 418, 634	545, 000	107, 857, 035	6, 897, 537	29
189, 537, 502	27. 7	48, 955, 455	30, 878, 291	470, 000	102, 597, 807	6, 636, 009	30
190, 919, 164	27. 6	50, 821, 078	32, 120, 936	475, 000	100, 879, 879	6, 613, 271	31

CITIES.

163, 348, 058	27. 0	85, 102, 735	26, 677, 602	6, 120, 000	40, 693, 147	4, 754, 569	1
161, 410, 332	28. 0	82, 253, 632	31, 188, 403	7, 335, 000	35, 784, 810	4, 848, 397	2
157, 802, 939	28. 0	79, 620, 297	29, 725, 208	8, 835, 000	34, 852, 796	4, 769, 548	3
172, 827, 165	29. 2	81, 177, 310	37, 797, 217	9, 850, 000	39, 467, 976	4, 534, 632	4
167, 963, 478	27. 8	80, 731, 158	37, 153, 139	10, 425, 000	35, 233, 042	4, 461, 139	5
153, 557, 836	26. 8	72, 883, 489	34, 904, 871	8, 035, 000	33, 213, 032	4, 481, 464	6
162, 987, 772	28. 7	75, 331, 063	37, 410, 310	7, 840, 000	37, 282, 190	4, 493, 609	7
148, 706, 922	26. 6	67, 899, 006	31, 977, 037	7, 840, 000	36, 592, 761	4, 407, 118	8
156, 419, 122	27. 5	72, 193, 111	37, 889, 216	7, 835, 000	34, 090, 027	4, 411, 768	9
184, 362, 295	30. 2	84, 299, 176	44, 779, 342	10, 070, 000	40, 821, 353	4, 392, 424	10
171, 448, 006	29. 0	76, 564, 789	40, 437, 307	9, 375, 000	40, 708, 990	4, 271, 832	11
182, 221, 554	29. 7	81, 097, 329	47, 864, 407	10, 230, 000	38, 942, 133	4, 087, 595	12
198, 511, 843	30. 9	88, 609, 073	45, 987, 877	13, 450, 000	46, 437, 308	4, 027, 585	13
179, 371, 793	28. 9	78, 392, 023	46, 768, 164	11, 440, 000	38, 827, 197	3, 944, 410	14
160, 231, 029	30. 0	73, 254, 631	45, 468, 958	9, 295, 000	28, 403, 338	3, 809, 102	15
189, 850, 706	33. 7	93, 371, 299	46, 651, 819	13, 700, 000	32, 340, 900	3, 786, 688	16
208, 349, 105	35. 4	105, 159, 648	46, 420, 164	18, 475, 000	34, 672, 781	3, 615, 312	17
235, 974, 313	37. 7	128, 263, 181	40, 883, 125	22, 095, 000	41, 172, 443	3, 560, 564	18
247, 455, 612	38. 4	136, 078, 750	47, 828, 963	18, 500, 000	40, 612, 049	3, 535, 850	19
256, 228, 121	38. 3	137, 546, 852	52, 228, 023	22, 285, 000	40, 661, 809	3, 501, 437	20
237, 894, 989	35. 1	133, 405, 237	40, 362, 183	18, 300, 000	42, 402, 609	3, 424, 960	21
215, 991, 777	32. 4	123, 158, 550	38, 686, 556	11, 235, 000	39, 551, 479	3, 360, 192	22
225, 227, 964	32. 1	126, 476, 925	39, 756, 893	11, 955, 000	43, 904, 247	3, 134, 897	23
212, 639, 672	31. 0	108, 377, 660	50, 400, 597	11, 385, 000	39, 567, 423	2, 908, 991	24
187, 891, 591	28. 6	101, 630, 179	35, 825, 132	7, 655, 000	40, 072, 689	2, 708, 591	25
190, 985, 722	28. 7	108, 562, 730	33, 140, 045	5, 395, 000	41, 271, 509	2, 616, 438	26
200, 813, 518	29. 9	116, 656, 737	35, 860, 691	5, 695, 000	40, 371, 942	2, 229, 148	27
214, 680, 473	30. 1	120, 794, 734	35, 584, 790	7, 090, 000	49, 217, 253	1, 999, 696	28
212, 050, 477	29. 5	116, 170, 136	47, 176, 454	7, 480, 000	40, 210, 839	1, 913, 048	29
206, 466, 135	29. 2	116, 148, 755	43, 509, 051	7, 340, 000	37, 672, 349	1, 705, 980	30
203, 291, 575	29. 1	114, 264, 376	41, 621, 319	5, 715, 000	39, 993, 709	1, 697, 171	31

LAWFUL-MONEY RESERVE OF THE NATIONAL BANKS AS SHOWN BY THE REPORTS

	Cities, States, and Territories.	No. of banks.	Deposits.	Reserve required (25 per cent.).	Reserve held.	Ratio of reserve.
						Per ct.
1	New York City	47	$284,339,105	$71,084,776	$80,114,690	28.18
2	Chicago	18	64,646,938	16,161,735	19,739,388	30.53
3	Saint Louis	5	10,297,188	2,574,297	2,722,864	26.44
	Totals of central reserve cities	70	359,283,231	89,820,808	102,576,942	28.55
1	Boston	54	92,113,350	23,028,337	25,765,096	27.97
2	Albany	6	9,728,934	2,432,233	3,050,840	31.36
3	Philadelphia	43	81,642,059	20,410,515	25,420,214	31.14
4	Pittsburgh	23	26,797,251	6,699,313	7,406,295	27.36
5	Baltimore	17	18,377,726	4,594,432	5,985,381	32.57
6	Washington	7	6,436,273	1,609,068	2,288,808	35.56
7	New Orleans	8	10,491,129	2,622,783	2,718,929	25.91
8	Louisville	9	7,456,084	1,864,021	1,807,035	24.24
9	Cincinnati	15	25,396,147	6,349,037	7,488,305	29.49
10	Cleveland	9	10,915,115	2,728,779	2,920,125	26.75
11	Detroit	8	12,652,175	3,163,044	3,693,684	29.19
12	Milwaukee	3	5,874,862	1,468,715	1,752,158	29.82
13	Kansas City	8	14,135,898	3,533,974	5,182,163	36.66
14	Saint Joseph	2	2,601,562	650,390	670,507	25.77
15	Omaha	8	10,322,425	2,580,606	3,221,350	31.21
16	San Francisco	3	3,543,668	885,917	1,283,143	36.21
	Totals of reserve cities	223	338,484,658	84,621,164	100,714,633	29.75
	Totals of all the reserve cities	293	697,767,889	174,441,972	203,291,575	29.12
				15 *per cent.*		
1	Maine	72	10,112,332	1,516,850	2,751,043	27.21
2	New Hampshire	49	6,890,484	1,033,573	2,200,846	31.94
3	Vermont	49	6,720,560	1,008,084	1,717,275	25.55
4	Massachusetts	198	54,494,538	8,174,181	14,306,786	26.25
5	Rhode Island	61	15,321,123	2,298,168	3,698,768	24.14
6	Connecticut	83	24,853,986	3,728,098	7,403,931	29.79
7	New York	269	88,772,384	13,315,858	22,203,218	24.94
8	New Jersey	81	39,675,377	5,951,306	10,068,633	25.38
9	Pennsylvania	237	71,985,304	10,797,796	20,718,933	28.78
10	Delaware	17	4,066,472	609,971	1,230,916	30.27
11	Maryland	31	6,705,176	1,005,776	1,819,234	27.13
12	District of Columbia	1	805,844	120,876	366,643	45.74
13	Virginia	25	10,648,550	1,597,282	2,304,498	21.64
14	West Virginia	20	3,040,011	456,002	920,130	30.27
15	North Carolina	18	3,518,049	527,707	937,034	26.63
16	South Carolina	15	3,865,578	579,837	1,073,573	27.77
17	Georgia	21	4,926,282	738,942	1,273,087	25.86
18	Florida	8	1,532,936	229,940	340,250	22.20
19	Alabama	20	5,772,056	865,808	1,355,076	23.49
20	Mississippi	12	1,245,493	186,824	444,159	35.66
21	Louisiana	5	831,412	124,716	222,949	26.81
22	Texas	91	13,368,011	2,005,202	4,562,072	34.13
23	Arkansas	7	2,412,782	361,917	500,520	20.76
24	Kentucky	50	11,257,769	1,688,665	2,967,876	26.33
25	Tennessee	40	12,491,787	1,873,768	2,661,738	21.30
26	Ohio	192	40,805,984	6,120,898	11,512,506	28.21
27	Indiana	93	25,191,133	3,778,670	8,138,062	32.31
28	Illinois	160	35,235,878	5,285,383	12,208,059	34.65
29	Michigan	100	23,095,161	3,464,274	5,580,859	24.18
30	Wisconsin	53	12,851,562	1,927,734	3,537,470	27.53
31	Iowa	128	19,687,484	2,953,122	5,758,104	29.25
32	Minnesota	58	30,165,674	4,524,851	6,972,302	23.10
33	Missouri	35	4,442,271	666,341	1,611,121	36.27
34	Kansas	139	17,483,905	2,622,586	5,515,220	31.54
35	Nebraska	95	9,943,345	1,491,502	2,510,413	25.25
36	Colorado	31	16,165,701	2,424,855	5,681,788	35.15
37	Nevada	2	455,059	68,259	62,189	13.67
38	California	30	19,568,245	2,935,237	6,817,822	34.84
39	Oregon	23	6,011,638	901,746	1,222,866	20.34
40	Arizona	1	194,627	29,194	33,027	16.85
41	Dakota	62	5,935,815	890,372	1,333,444	22.46
42	Idaho	6	570,500	85,575	115,972	20.33
43	Montana	17	8,196,546	1,229,482	1,814,317	22.11
44	New Mexico	9	1,583,249	237,483	382,802	24.12
45	Utah	7	2,423,687	363,553	757,357	31.25
46	Washington	18	3,618,199	542,730	810,190	22.39
47	Wyoming	8	1,682,048	252,307	483,346	28.74
	Totals of country banks	2,756	690,622,907	103,593,391	190,919,164	27.64
	United States	3,049	1,388,390,806	278,035,273	394,210,739	28.39

OF THEIR CONDITION AT THE CLOSE OF BUSINESS ON OCTOBER 5, 1887.

Cash reserve.		Classification of reserve held.					
Required.	Held.	Specie.	Legal tenders.	United States certificates of deposit.	Due from reserve agents.	Redemption fund with Treasurer.	
$70, 662, 876	$79, 692, 790	$63, 622, 929	$14, 464, 861	$1, 605, 000	....	$421, 900	1
16, 114, 485	19, 692, 138	12, 958, 418	6, 623, 720	110, 000	....	47, 250	2
2, 542, 352	2, 690, 919	1, 338, 040	1, 212, 879	140, 000	....	31, 945	3
89, 319, 713	102, 075, 847	77, 919, 387	22, 301, 460	1, 855, 000	....	501, 095	
11, 291, 253	12, 395, 938	9, 996, 676	2, 204, 262	195, 000	$12, 923, 920	445, 832	1
1, 190, 287	1, 234, 042	935, 192	98, 850	200, 000	1, 705, 140	51, 658	2
10, 143, 691	17, 123, 368	11, 558, 936	4, 334, 432	1, 230, 000	8, 173, 712	123, 134	3
3, 309, 946	4, 679, 331	2, 980, 318	1, 699, 013	....	2, 707, 512	79, 422	4
2, 251, 092	3, 817, 282	2, 130, 100	877, 182	810, 000	2, 075, 849	92, 250	5
791, 113	1, 612, 930	945, 334	587, 596	80, 000	649, 037	26, 841	6
1, 281, 016	2, 071, 948	776, 215	1, 295, 733	....	586, 231	60, 750	7
916, 147	1, 034, 501	262, 254	792, 247	....	720, 807	31, 727	8
3, 096, 184	4, 632, 417	663, 168	2, 639, 249	1, 330, 000	2, 699, 218	156, 670	9
1, 351, 027	1, 714, 379	818, 379	881, 000	15, 000	1, 179, 021	26, 725	10
1, 572, 622	1, 896, 083	1, 064, 667	831, 416	....	1, 779, 601	18, 000	11
727, 607	1, 061, 693	532, 678	529, 015	....	676, 965	13, 500	12
1, 759, 112	2, 918, 519	1, 486, 764	1, 426, 755	....	2, 232, 894	15, 750	13
322, 361	367, 094	156, 384	210 710	....	297, 746	5, 667	14
1, 283, 103	1, 853. 139	947, 445	905, 694	....	1, 353, 811	14, 400	15
426, 083	1, 097, 184	1, 090, 479	6, 705	....	152, 209	33, 750	16
41, 712, 544	59, 524, 846	36, 344, 980	19, 319, 859	3, 860, 000	39, 093, 709	1, 196, 076	
131, 032, 257	161, 600, 695	114, 264, 376	41, 621, 319	5, 715, 000	39, 093, 709	1, 697, 171	
511, 289	912, 026	693, 630	219, 296	....	1, 600, 389	238, 028	1
341. 910	516, 827	394, 034	122, 493	....	1, 505, 536	178, 783	2
338, 472	562, 093	387, 694	174, 399	....	993, 278	161, 904	3
2, 838, 288	4, 461, 264	3, 047, 953	1, 221, 311	195, 000	8, 764, 061	1, 078, 461	4
827, 529	1, 185, 839	675, 492	510, 347	....	2, 283, 584	229, 345	5
1, 326, 018	2, 439, 398	1, 748, 295	691, 103	....	4, 551, 554	412, 979	6
4, 070, 152	8, 393, 416	5, 199, 687	2, 953, 729	240, 000	12, 041, 823	867, 979	7
2, 258, 258	3, 670, 113	1, 852, 444	1, 807, 669	10, 000	6, 002, 859	305, 661	8
4, 050, 668	7, 712, 047	4, 774, 820	2, 927, 227	10, 000	12, 335, 759	671, 129	9
215, 280	423, 802	273, 039	140, 253	10, 000	735, 252	71, 772	10
377, 083	818, 488	440, 975	377, 513	....	939, 178	61, 568	11
43, 850	273, 709	168, 630	105, 140	....	81, 594	11, 250	12
615, 015	1, 361, 274	606, 840	754, 434	....	883, 470	50, 745	13
170, 211	525, 018	275, 962	249, 046	....	364, 638	30, 474	14
194, 582	449, 462	195, 240	254, 222	....	446, 321	41, 251	15
2?0, 930	795, 982	325, 301	470, 681	....	250, 078	27, 513	16
277, 784	1, 013, 432	547, 216	466, 116	....	216, 072	44, 483	17
88, 727	223, 202	107, 762	115, 440	....	108, 926	8, 122	18
331, 190	776, 773	365, 449	411, 324	....	541, 371	37, 832	19
69, 885	293, 961	153, 407	140, 554	....	138, 086	12, 112	20
47, 037	161, 446	99, 713	61, 733	....	55, 879	5, 624	21
706, 480	3, 076, 721	1, 256, 595	1, 820, 126	....	1, 382, 250	104, 001	22
137, 612	262, 980	166, 680	96, 300	....	219, 653	17, 887	23
615, 638	1, 089, 635	556, 561	533, 074	....	1, 728, 671	149, 570	24
723, 922	1, 584, 027	863, 549	721, 378	....	1, 012, 847	63, 964	25
2, 276, 635	6, 200, 495	2, 923, 056	3, 277, 439	....	4, 882, 761	429, 310	26
1, 429, 151	4, 479, 101	2, 501, 486	1, 977, 615	....	3, 453, 169	205, 702	27
2, 029, 717	4, 524, 032	2, 692, 576	1, 821, 456	10, 000	7, 473, 837	211, 090	28
1, 331, 950	2, 489, 627	1, 635, 912	853, 715	....	2, 962, 832	134, 400	29
746, 911	1, 477, 761	995, 860	481, 901	....	1, 099, 253	60, 456	30
1, 127, 322	2, 531, 893	1, 540, 458	991, 435	....	3, 091, 454	134, 817	31
1, 778, 613	3, 353, 338	2, 387, 278	966, 060	....	3, 540, 735	78, 319	32
252, 451	626, 166	324, 023	302, 143	....	940, 742	35, 213	33
1, 002, 903	2, 668, 425	1, 460, 158	1, 208, 267	....	2, 731, 616	115, 179	34
560, 535	1, 095, 662	767, 474	328, 188	....	1, 347, 086	67, 665	35
952, 365	2, 313, 611	1, 422, 990	890, 621	....	3, 324, 235	43, 942	36
26, 020	57, 487	57, 487	....	....	3, 015	1, 687	37
1, 154, 948	3, 919, 548	3, 571, 927	347, 621	....	2, 850, 407	47, 867	38
349, 094	986, 057	947, 474	38, 583	....	207, 739	29, 010	39
11, 228	31, 902	19, 352	12, 550	....	....	1, 125	40
338, 826	837, 643	449, 654	387, 989	....	452, 493	43, 308	41
32, 500	88, 563	48, 848	39, 715	....	23, 231	4, 175	42
483, 183	1, 384, 488	760, 193	624, 295	....	408, 200	21, 650	43
90, 673	183, 766	99, 513	84, 223	....	188, 297	10, 709	44
138, 401	377, 740	307, 242	70, 498	....	302, 067	17, 550	45
200, 066	545, 494	494, 374	51, 120	....	246, 883	17, 813	46
96, 893	265, 600	236, 016	29, 584	....	207, 677	10, 069	47
38, 792, 012	83, 426, 014	50, 821, 078	32, 129, 936	475, 000	100, 879, 879	6, 613, 271	
169, 824, 269	245, 026, 709	165, 085, 454	73, 751, 255	6, 190, 000	140, 873, 588	8, 310, 442	

ABSTRACT OF REPORTS OF EARNINGS AND DIVIDENDS OF NATIONAL BANKS

	States, Territories, and reserve cities.	No. of banks.	Capital stock.	Surplus.	Capital and surplus.
1	Maine	71	$10,300,000	$2,373,735.09	$12,733,735.09
2	New Hampshire	49	6,155,000	1,397,072.60	7,552,072.60
3	Vermont	49	7,691,000	1,548,346.50	9,239,346.50
4	Massachusetts	195	45,090,500	13,820,321.58	58,910,821.58
5	Boston	54	50,950,000	11,051,206.03	62,001,206.03
6	Rhode Island	61	20,334,050	4,146,355.82	24,480,405.82
7	Connecticut	84	24,671,820	6,960,034.71	31,631,854.71
	Division No. 1	563	165,252,370	41,888,072.33	207,140,442.33
8	New York	268	35,224,850	9,882,105.57	45,106,955.57
9	New York City	45	45,150,000	27,523,704.21	72,673,704.21
10	Albany	6	1,750,000	1,240,000.00	2,990,000.00
11	New Jersey	74	12,293,350	4,214,680.08	16,508,030.08
12	Pennsylvania	230	32,875,290	10,880,739.38	43,756,029.38
13	Philadelphia	40	20,359,300	10,150,902.97	30,510,202.97
14	Pittsburgh	23	10,180,000	4,072,343.05	14,252,343.05
	Division No. 2	686	157,832,790	67,964,475.26	225,797,265.26
15	Delaware	16	2,033,985	771,250.00	2,805,235.00
16	Maryland	28	2,716,700	880,778.11	3,597,478.11
17	Baltimore	17	11,713,260	3,382,029.57	15,095,289.57
18	District of Columbia	1	252,000	60,000.00	312,000.00
19	Washington	6	1,325,000	386,500.00	1,711,500.00
20	Virginia	25	3,781,300	1,292,015.55	5,073,315.55
21	West Virginia	19	1,861,000	457,840.67	2,318,840.67
	Division No. 3	112	23,683,245	7,230,413.90	30,913,658.90
22	North Carolina	17	2,376,000	532,548.83	2,908,548.83
23	South Carolina	16	1,798,000	787,680.00	2,585,680.00
24	Georgia	17	2,736,300	906,832.99	3,643,132.99
25	Florida	9	550,000	46,000.00	596,000.00
26	Alabama	12	1,935,000	401,150.87	2,336,150.87
27	Mississippi	8	650,000	96,288.57	746,288.57
28	Louisiana	1	100,000	11,000.00	111,000.00
29	New Orleans	8	3,425,000	1,165,000.00	4,590,000.00
30	Texas	73	7,459,100	2,289,983.56	9,749,083.56
31	Arkansas	6	755,000	212,300.00	967,300.00
32	Kentucky	50	9,758,900	2,251,089.75	12,012,989.75
33	Louisville	9	3,551,500	934,003.09	4,485,503.09
34	Tennessee	34	5,476,140	1,076,307.80	6,552,447.80
	Division No. 4	260	40,570,940	10,713,194.46	51,284,134.46
35	Ohio	186	22,249,000	4,905,737.57	27,154,737.57
36	Cincinnati	13	9,600,000	1,444,000.00	11,044,000.00
37	Cleveland	9	6,600,000	800,000.00	7,400,000.00
38	Indiana	92	11,894,500	3,436,825.19	15,331,325.19
39	Illinois	153	14,011,500	4,488,954.76	18,500,454.76
40	Chicago	15	13,950,000	3,715,000.00	17,665,000.00
41	Michigan	97	10,484,600	2,100,215.92	12,584,815.92
42	Detroit	7	3,300,000	424,300.00	3,724,300.00
43	Wisconsin	47	3,985,000	1,069,668.66	5,054,668.66
44	Milwaukee	3	650,000	390,000.00	1,040,000.00
	Division No. 5	622	96,724,600	22,783,702.10	119,508,302.10
45	Iowa	126	10,140,000	2,504,706.08	12,644,706.08
46	Minnesota	52	12,305,000	2,301,052.39	14,606,052.39
47	Missouri	39	5,831,000	873,472.29	6,704,472.29
48	Saint Louis	5	3,000,000	1,065,000.00	4,065,000.00
49	Kansas	103	7,087,100	1,230,209.99	8,317,309.99
50	Nebraska	89	7,198,175	1,322,568.57	8,520,743.57
	Division No. 6	414	45,561,275	9,297,010.22	54,858,285.22
51	Colorado	27	2,435,000	895,500.00	3,330,500.00
52	Nevada	2	150,000	30,000.00	180,000.00
53	California	23	3,080,000	712,063.10	3,792,063.10
54	San Francisco	3	2,600,000	253,891.24	2,853,891.24
55	Oregon	17	1,285,000	100,850.00	1,385,850.00
	Division No. 7	72	9,550,000	1,993,204.34	11,543,204.34

IN THE UNITED STATES FROM SEPTEMBER 1, 1886, TO MARCH 1, 1887.

Dividends.	Net earnings.	Ratios.			Charged off.		
		Dividend to capital.	Dividend to capital and surplus.	Earnings to capital and surplus.	Premiums.	Losses.	
		Per cent.	Per cent.	Per cent.			
$305, 000. 00	$225, 541. 40	3. 52	2. 87	1. 77	$20, 125. 22	$309, 914. 26	1
227, 050. 00	303, 504. 70	3. 00	3. 01	4. 02	32, 803. 79	14, 241. 33	2
263, 930. 00	340, 887. 31	3. 43	2. 86	3. 69	45, 776. 07	42, 110. 10	3
1, 551, 520. 67	1, 718, 388. 16	3. 44	2. 63	2. 92	159, 822. 19	388, 117. 61	4
1, 368, 863. 20	1, 730, 027. 11	2. 69	2. 19	2. 76	203, 746. 74	471, 035. 10	5
642, 914. 00	822, 804. 47	3. 16	2. 63	3. 36	98, 369. 39	90, 961. 15	6
890, 202. 50	1, 034, 473. 73	3. 64	2. 84	3. 27	50, 302. 01	246, 858. 10	7
5, 318, 480. 37	6, 170, 706. 07	3. 22	2. 57	2. 98	611, 036. 11	1, 626, 245. 58	
1, 334, 190. 77	1, 090, 766. 07	3. 78	2. 96	4. 41	97, 423. 51	356, 562. 87	8
2, 042, 562. 45	4, 274, 257. 49	4. 52	2. 81	5. 88	53, 281. 16	867, 495. 91	9
114, 700. 00	162, 653. 45	6. 55	3. 63	5. 44	5, 625. 00	12, 034. 23	10
533, 982. 00	846, 138. 15	4. 50	3. 36	5. 05	40, 340. 89	109, 208. 20	11
1, 615, 240. 10	2, 031, 672. 75	5. 00	3. 76	4. 64	111, 781. 13	200, 871. 25	12
829, 660. 00	1, 196, 054. 48	4. 08	2. 72	3. 02	103, 991. 72	178, 227. 35	13
368, 750. 00	597, 527. 30	3. 62	2. 50	4. 19	11, 864. 09	57, 685. 09	14
6, 889, 094. 32	11, 099, 069. 69	4. 36	3. 05	4. 91	424, 307. 50	1, 842, 084. 90	
88, 920. 07	127, 390. 33	4. 37	3. 17	4. 54	1, 100. 00	9, 013. 72	15
115, 577. 14	147, 984. 76	4. 25	3. 21	4. 11	17, 092. 37	15, 482. 51	16
421, 571. 10	508, 248. 73	3. 60	2. 70	3. 06	6, 438. 57	189, 185. 76	17
10, 080. 00	11, 917. 94	4. 00	3. 23	3. 82	2, 500. 00	2, 431. 80	18
49, 375. 00	87, 807. 91	3. 73	2. 88	5. 13	875. 00	7, 795. 93	19
138, 942. 00	205, 471. 82	3. 67	2. 74	4. 05	13, 227. 63	68, 250. 83	20
72, 330. 00	73, 866. 49	3. 89	3. 12	3. 19	3, 890. 57	10, 549. 07	21
896, 805. 21	1, 252, 689. 98	3. 79	2. 90	4. 05	45, 124. 14	293, 709. 74	
93, 330. 00	121, 437. 30	3. 93	3. 21	4. 18	5, 030. 56	44, 844. 91	22
77, 350. 00	105, 323. 50	4. 30	2. 90	4. 07	28, 650. 00	24, 459. 16	23
101, 875. 00	126, 033. 23	3. 72	2. 82	3. 48	12, 018. 13	15, 041. 30	24
25, 000. 00	36, 210. 08	4. 55	4. 10	6. 08	3, 496. 29	3, 663 19	25
83, 000. 00	103, 170. 83	4. 20	3. 55	6. 98	3, 000. 00	19, 352. 35	26
30, 500. 00	45, 168. 40	5. 62	4. 80	6. 05	235. 35	1, 131. 25	27
4, 000. 00	4, 737. 52	4. 00	3. 64	4. 31	1, 000. 00	....	28
187, 750. 00	200, 119. 60	5. 48	4. 00	4. 36	7, 431. 57	60, 929. 40	29
521, 506. 00	556, 151. 96	6. 99	5. 35	5. 70	8, 043. 33	258, 309. 97	30
41, 000. 00	61, 466. 38	5. 43	4. 24	6. 35	1, 562. 50	4, 288. 02	31
371, 795. 00	439, 458. 30	3. 81	3. 00	3. 66	67, 893 71	63, 493. 05	32
133, 000. 00	132, 991. 40	3. 75	2. 96	2. 96	31, 007. 23	30, 358. 39	33
256, 341. 66	373, 883. 99	4. 68	3. 91	5. 71	2, 999. 32	59, 364. 45	34
1, 932, 597. 66	2, 367, 052. 67	4. 76	3. 77	4. 02	173, 267. 90	586, 130. 94	
835, 724. 57	997, 330. 28	3. 76	3. 08	3. 67	70, 260. 58	218, 326. 74	35
302, 500. 00	455, 546. 23	3. 15	2. 74	4. 12	23, 117. 50	54, 395. 54	36
102, 000. 00	287, 095. 25	2. 91	2. 50	3. 80	11, 657. 56	75, 101. 64	37
578, 180. 00	664, 637. 69	4. 86	3. 77	4. 34	59, 512. 79	86, 487. 32	38
692, 230. 00	977, 487. 60	4. 04	3. 74	5. 28	15, 106. 06	150, 443. 42	39
550, 000. 00	1, 132, 195. 30	3. 99	3. 15	6. 41	7, 845. 86	321, 085. 07	40
537, 261. 86	690, 571. 41	5. 12	4. 27	5. 49	22, 118. 91	56, 185. 20	41
140, 000. 00	185, 737. 67	4. 24	3. 76	4. 99	3, 312. 50	25, 750. 00	42
194, 572. 02	280, 316. 21	4. 88	3. 85	5. 72	13, 502. 03	28, 481. 33	43
26, 000. 00	54, 489. 02	4. 00	2. 50	5. 24	7, 700. 00	4, 010. 58	44
4, 054, 468. 45	5, 735, 306. 66	4. 19	3. 40	4. 80	234, 193. 79	1, 020, 267. 02	
545, 250. 00	641, 110. 20	5. 38	4. 31	5. 07	28, 904. 56	99, 536. 23	45
524, 150. 00	997, 235. 15	4. 26	3. 59	6. 83	4, 752. 49	73, 743. 53	46
216, 994. 33	391, 491. 24	3. 72	3. 24	5. 84	22, 666. 30	20, 179. 45	47
105, 000. 00	145, 039. 03	3. 50	2. 58	3. 57	19, 026. 68	51, 222. 93	48
412, 992. 00	747, 995. 13	5. 83	4. 07	9. 00	14, 198. 55	36, 641. 06	49
385, 389. 15	613, 111. 95	5. 35	4. 52	7. 22	35, 047. 66	52, 170. 68	50
2, 189, 776. 38	3, 535, 985. 70	4. 81	3. 99	6. 45	124, 596. 24	333, 493. 86	
193, 400. 00	303, 911. 43	7. 94	5. 80	9. 13	23, 216. 48	88, 695. 76	51
8, 000. 00	10, 403. 30	5. 33	4. 44	5. 78	....	3, 752. 93	52
144, 625. 36	263, 340. 88	4. 70	3. 81	7. 00	5, 132. 85	41, 394. 16	53
52, 500. 00	77, 872. 88	2. 02	1. 84	2. 73	5, 000. 00	12, 354. 51	54
64, 800. 00	131, 537. 42	5. 04	4. 68	9. 49	28, 528. 34	4, 357. 09	55
463, 325. 36	789, 065. 91	4. 80	3. 97	6. 83	64, 507. 67	150, 555. 35	

ABSTRACT OF REPORTS OF EARNINGS AND DIVIDENDS OF NATIONAL BANKS IN

	States, Territories, and reserve cities.	No. of banks.	Capital stock.	Surplus.	Capital and surplus.
56	Dakota	54	$3,197,000	$585,087.17	$3,782,087.17
57	Idaho	6	350,000	27,129.59	377,129.59
58	Montana	16	1,875,000	368,250.00	2,243,250.00
59	New Mexico	9	825,000	168,208.81	993,208.81
60	Utah	7	850,000	325,250.00	1,175,250.00
61	Washington	18	1,130,000	188,902.02	1,318,902.02
62	Wyoming	7	953,550	190,000.00	1,143,550.00
	Division No. 8	117	9,180,550	1,852,827.59	11,033,377.59
	United States	2,855	548,355,770	163,731,900.20	712,087,670.20

THE UNITED STATES, FROM SEPTEMBER 1, 1886, TO MARCH 1, 1887—Continued.

Dividends.	Net earnings.	Ratios.			Charged off.		
		Dividend to capital.	Dividend to capital and surplus.	Earnings to capital and surplus.	Premiums.	Losses.	
$115,500.00	$226,018.83	3.73	3.17	6.13	$11,472.07	$40,484.50	56
15,000.00	23,166.84	4.29	3.98	6.14	1,423.36	....	57
76,400.00	210,977.82	4.07	3.41	9.41	4,818.41	16,952.40	58
58,500.00	49,869.57	7.00	5.89	5.02	439.40	10,781.43	59
39,500.00	72,163.10	4.65	3.36	6.14	9,695.83	3,606.29	60
37,550.00	95,506.34	3.31	2.85	7.24	1,378.40	31,747.76	61
61,500.00	65,184.75	6.45	5.37	5.70	10,598.07	1,270.16	62
404,040.00	742,917.25	4.45	3.71	6.79	39,845.56	110,935.54	
22,148,587.75	31,698,794.83	4.04	3.11	4.45	1,716,899.00	5,963,431.93	

ABSTRACT OF REPORTS OF EARNINGS AND DIVIDENDS OF NATIONAL BANKS

	States, Territories, and reserve cities.	No. of banks.	Capital stock.	Surplus.	Capital and surplus.
1	Maine	72	$10,385,000	$2,419,208.45	$12,804,208.45
2	New Hampshire	40	6,155,000	1,451,240.21	7,606,240.21
3	Vermont	49	7,516,000	1,571,125.79	9,087,125.79
4	Massachusetts	197	44,815,500	14,148,180.64	58,963,680.64
5	Boston	54	50,950,000	12,377,608.09	63,327,608.09
6	Rhode Island	61	20,334,050	4,218,358.39	24,552,408.39
7	Connecticut	84	24,681,820	6,933,068.94	31,614,888.94
	Division No. 1	566	164,837,370	43,118,790.51	207,956,160.51
8	New York	269	34,790,301	10,058,979.68	44,849,280.68
9	New York City	45	45,150,000	28,825,702.28	73,975,702.28
10	Albany	6	1,750,000	1,243,000.00	2,993,000.00
11	New Jersey	75	11,928,070	4,481,270.18	16,409,340.18
12	Pennsylvania	233	33,350,340	11,464,029.91	44,814,369.91
13	Philadelphia	41	21,558,000	10,500,803.08	32,058,803.08
14	Pittsburgh	23	10,180,000	4,234,877.29	14,414,877.29
	Division No. 2	692	158,706,711	70,808,722.42	229,515,433.42
15	Delaware	17	2,071,985	799,350.00	2,871,335.00
16	Maryland	30	2,766,700	908,392.65	3,675,092.65
17	Baltimore	17	11,263,260	3,516,510.62	14,779,770.62
18	District of Columbia	1	252,000	60,000.00	312,000.00
19	Washington	7	1,575,000	481,203.75	2,056,203.75
20	Virginia	25	3,796,300	1,414,892.31	5,211,192.31
21	West Virginia	20	1,891,000	463,426.19	2,354,426.19
	Division No. 3	117	23,616,245	7,643,775.52	31,260,020.52
22	North Carolina	18	2,412,280	544,490.00	2,956,770.00
23	South Carolina	16	1,748,000	788,800.00	2,536,800.00
24	Georgia	18	2,818,375	951,731.71	3,770,106.71
25	Florida	8	500,000	60,080.00	560,080.00
26	Alabama	19	3,166,710	552,903.66	3,719,613.66
27	Mississippi	10	775,000	124,368.27	899,368.27
28	Louisiana	3	400,000	30,308.44	430,308.44
29	New Orleans	8	3,425,000	1,199,000.00	4,624,000.00
30	Texas	84	9,150,000	2,460,004.69	11,610,004.69
31	Arkansas	7	900,000	111,500.00	1,011,500.00
32	Kentucky	59	9,808,900	2,299,309.43	12,108,209.43
33	Louisville	9	3,551,500	945,111.62	4,496,611.62
34	Tennessee	39	7,172,250	1,300,757.80	8,473,007.80
	Division No. 4	298	45,828,015	11,368,966.28	57,196,981.28
35	Ohio	187	22,164,000	5,164,608.76	27,328,608.66
36	Cincinnati	13	9,800,000	1,720,000.00	11,520,000.00
37	Cleveland	9	6,700,000	892,000.00	7,592,000.00
38	Indiana	92	11,894,500	3,522,593.82	15,417,095.82
39	Illinois	156	14,044,500	4,547,135.69	18,591,635.69
40	Chicago	16	14,310,000	3,987,000.00	18,297,000.00
41	Michigan	97	10,484,600	2,233,096.80	12,717,696.80
42	Detroit	7	3,300,000	451,000.00	3,751,000.00
43	Wisconsin	50	4,195,000	1,133,583.99	5,328,583.99
44	Milwaukee	3	650,000	390,000.00	1,040,000.00
	Division No. 5	630	97,542,600	24,041,020.96	121,583,620.96
45	Iowa	126	10,085,000	2,600,190.52	12,685,190.52
46	Minnesota	56	13,040,000	2,378,452.39	15,418,452.39
47	Missouri	31	2,281,000	553,047.48	2,834,047.48
48	Saint Louis	5	3,000,000	1,070,000.00	4,070,000.00
49	Kansas City	5	3,200,000	397,500.00	3,597,500.00
50	Saint Joseph	2	300,000	106,000.00	406,000.00
51	Kansas	116	8,210,100	1,487,020.17	9,697,120.17
52	Nebraska	89	5,640,000	897,447.84	6,537,447.84
53	Omaha	8	2,200,000	570,500.00	2,770,500.00
	Division No. 6	438	47,956,100	10,061,058.40	58,017,158.40
54	Colorado	28	2,505,000	928,000.00	3,433,000.00
55	Nevada	2	150,000	40,000.00	190,000.00
56	California	24	3,350,000	722,550.05	4,072,550.05
57	San Francisco	3	2,700,000	259,046.02	2,959,046.02
58	Oregon	10	1,605,000	150,850.00	1,755,850.00
	Division No. 7	76	10,310,000	2,100,446.07	12,410,446.07

IN THE UNITED STATES FROM MARCH 1, 1887, TO SEPTEMBER 1, 1887.

Dividends.	Net earnings.	Ratios. Dividend to capital.	Ratios. Dividend to capital and surplus.	Ratios. Earnings to capital and surplus.	Charged off. Premiums.	Charged off. Losses.	
$396,800.00	$496,673.25	3.82	3.10	3.88	$67,082.03	$77,650.87	1
230,550.00	318,527.82	3.75	3.03	4.10	37,087.90	49,397.27	2
262,930.00	316,208.82	3.50	2.89	3.48	11,963.24	40,284.18	3
1,545,340.97	2,234,865.99	3.45	2.62	3.79	268,921.46	725,458.69	4
1,357,200.00	2,084,227.12	2.66	2.14	3.29	106,498.75	626,289.72	5
655,289.00	851,053.91	3.22	2.67	3.47	33,023.07	102,985.53	6
907,668.50	923,224.42	3.68	2.87	2.92	59,867.20	282,140.36	7
5,355,787.47	7,224,781.33	3.25	2.58	3.47	584,444.65	1,904,206.62	
1,466,840.11	1,902,401.04	4.22	3.27	4.24	191,747.83	493,015.42	8
2,076,100.00	4,176,686.48	4.60	2.81	5.65	103,677.99	1,006,329.84	9
66,500.00	130,899.78	3.80	2.22	4.37	2,000.00	7,544.43	10
562,204.00	818,503.19	4.71	3.43	4.99	38,241.22	197,711.99	11
1,243,431.68	1,678,068.88	3.73	2.77	3.74	204,908.49	373,050.31	12
863,500.00	1,181,335.68	4.01	2.69	3.68	30,064.55	261,677.07	13
384,750.00	608,842.55	3.78	2.67	4.63	11,155.63	79,225.25	14
6,663,385.79	10,554,740.60	4.20	2.90	4.60	581,795.71	2,418,554.31	
89,948.85	132,161.84	4.34	3.13	4.60	9,520.99	1,993.00	15
130,418.00	143,835.01	4.71	3.55	3.01	38,918.54	4,520.90	16
414,192.42	418,944.15	3.68	2.80	2.83	21,728.85	213,089.76	17
10,080.00	11,542.05	4.00	3.23	3.70	12,955.78	....	18
49,375.00	99,669.54	3.13	2.40	4.85	....	19,870.49	19
140,772.00	212,083.65	3.71	2.70	4.07	26,708.12	28,208.96	20
65,980.00	78,891.65	3.40	2.80	3.35	10,160.83	10,763.40	21
900,766.27	1,097,127.89	3.81	2.88	3.51	110,093.11	278,446.51	
73,500.00	107,271.10	3.05	2.49	3.63	3,200.00	46,977.76	22
66,870.00	134,734.68	3.83	2.64	5.31	38,109.82	39,340.38	23
102,110.00	207,677.07	5.75	4.30	5.50	1,585.87	34,183.85	24
24,750.00	41,470.25	4.05	4.42	7.73	2,874.42	1,180.50	25
119,500.00	422,578.16	3.77	3.21	11.36	750.00	26,592.14	26
22,000.00	80,984.80	2.84	2.45	9.00	2,593.38	1,214.45	27
12,000.00	34,446.53	3.00	2.79	8.00	781.22	1,263.60	28
121,750.00	221,659.00	3.55	2.63	4.79	17,750.00	108,633.02	29
417,472.22	526,681.06	4.56	3.60	4.54	20,419.08	355,082.74	30
131,250.00	79,684.54	14.58	12.98	7.88	5,343.75	8,935.73	31
390,895.00	435,273.97	3.99	3.23	3.59	60,437.94	58,810.95	32
133,060.00	142,136.63	3.75	2.96	3.16	5,131.25	46,856.14	33
255,419.00	543,400.09	3.56	3.01	6.41	6,784.55	106,735.60	34
1,930,576.22	2,977,907.88	4.21	3.38	5.21	165,851.28	835,788.84	
906,062.83	1,158,200.39	4.09	3.32	4.24	88,618.27	248,133.09	35
310,000.00	747,769.67	3.16	2.69	6.49	12,500.00	46,151.60	36
177,000.00	279,666.11	2.64	2.33	3.68	4,315.00	37,560.86	37
498,000.00	641,259.21	4.19	3.23	4.18	82,327.62	94,742.23	38
689,935.00	837,715.65	4.01	3.71	4.51	44,305.29	150,793.09	39
507,000.00	1,282,847.28	3.54	2.77	7.01	7,337.60	183,049.32	40
480,130.00	676,148.44	4.58	3.78	5.32	35,504.05	76,727.90	41
120,000.00	175,574.05	3.64	3.20	4.68	937.50	44,143.98	42
242,575.00	353,019.89	5.78	4.55	6.63	16,667.73	13,809.09	43
42,000.00	58,970.87	6.46	4.04	5.67	20,458.69	5,531.32	44
3,972,702.83	6,214,171.56	4.07	3.27	5.11	313,001.84	909,643.08	
504,500.00	663,175.22	5.00	3.98	5.23	26,580.59	66,134.98	45
596,100.00	665,575.01	4.57	3.87	4.32	25,371.98	128,223.59	46
107,258.00	144,303.12	4.70	3.78	5.09	7,216.42	9,860.36	47
110,000.00	204,349.70	3.67	2.70	5.02	375.00	23,143.35	48
130,000.00	301,860.94	4.06	3.01	8.39	812.50	76,768.92	49
10,000.00	15,427.23	3.33	2.46	3.80	....	16,336.83	50
439,553.88	650,553.45	5.35	4.53	6.71	31,790.32	137,747.13	51
361,539.71	469,580.91	6.41	5.53	7.18	27,295.42	16,797.07	52
69,000.00	97,482.95	3.14	2.49	3.52	4,047.50	5,116.80	53
2,327,951.59	3,212,308.53	4.85	4.01	5.54	124,398.73	480,169.03	
206,000.00	280,829.86	8.22	6.00	8.44	17,093.12	104,577.19	54
6,000.00	12,768.39	4.00	3.16	6.72	200.00	1,700.00	55
186,500.00	295,467.08	5.57	4.58	7.26	9,962.64	71,085.96	56
52,500.00	96,041.33	1.94	1.77	3.25	2,114.60	21,773.60	57
52,500.00	208,016.17	3.27	2.99	11.65	3,971.87	8,349.05	58
503,500.00	902,122.83	4.88	4.06	7.27	33,342.23	207,485.80	

ABSTRACT OF REPORTS OF EARNINGS AND DIVIDENDS OF NATIONAL BANKS

	States, Territories, and reserve cities.	No. of banks.	Capital stock.	Surplus.	Capital and surplus.
59	Dakota	60	$3,587,500	$663,481.15	$4,250,981.15
60	Idaho	6	350,000	20,845.94	370,845.94
61	Montana	17	1,925,000	412,950.00	2,337,950.00
62	New Mexico	9	850,000	172,671.46	1,022,671.46
63	Utah	7	850,000	368,000.00	1,218,000.00
64	Washington	18	1,130,000	232,456.93	1,362,456.93
65	Wyoming	8	1,055,000	235,307.80	1,290,307.80
	Division No. 8	125	9,747,500	2,111,773.28	11,859,273.28
	United States	2,942	558,544,541	171,254,553.44	729,799,094.44

IN THE UNITED STATES FROM MARCH 1, 1887, TO SEPTEMBER 1, 1887—Continued.

Dividends.	Net earnings.	Ratios.			Charged off.		
		Dividend to capital.	Dividend to capital and surplus.	Earnings to capital and surplus.	Premiums.	Losses.	
$149,000.00	$130,007.57	4.15	3.51	3.21	$10,159.74	$121,215.96	59
....	12,744.20	....	....	3.36	1,200.71	8,529.39	60
28,630.00	186,734.54	1.49	1.23	7.99	2,840.88	12,172.09	61
42,600.00	37,740.31	4.94	4.11	3.69	1,483.41	12,777.11	62
45,500.00	61,641.84	5.35	3.74	5.06	1,773.44	10,808.51	63
50,500.00	112,203.52	4.47	3.71	8.24	2,507.77	1,307.56	64
33,500.00	77,602.23	3.18	2.00	6.01	428.66	1,402.79	65
349,150.00	624,734.21	3.58	2.94	5.27	20,400.61	177,333.41	
22,003,820.17	32,808,074.83	3.94	3.01	4.50	1,943,228.16	7,211,627.60	

EARNINGS AND DIVIDENDS OF THE NATIONAL BANKS, ARRANGED BY GEOGRAPHICAL DIVISIONS, FOR SEMI-ANNUAL PERIODS FROM SEPTEMBER 1, 1878, TO SEPTEMBER 1, 1887.

Geographical divisions.	No. of banks	Capital.	Surplus.	Dividends.	Net earnings.	Ratios.		
						Dividends to capital.	Dividends to capital and surplus.	Earnings to capital and surplus.
						Pr. ct.	Pr. ct.	Pr. ct.
Sept., 1878, to March, 1879:								
New England States...	544	$165,645,820	$38,037,115	$5,295,347	$3,658,989	3.2	2.0	1.8
Middle States..........	630	173,979,076	50,084,782	6,876,398	5,826,602	4.0	3.1	2.6
Southern States........	175	30,882,800	5,240,054	1,077,333	961,734	3.5	3.0	2.7
Western States........	694	93,905,700	23,382,183	4,291,976	4,231,275	4.6	3.6	3.6
Total...............	2,043	464,413,996	116,744,134	17,541,054	14,678,600	3.8	3.0	2.5
March, 1879, to Sept., 1879:								
New England States...	542	164,430,120	37,441,984	5,257,526	4,761,422	3.2	2.6	2.4
Middle States..........	640	169,645,936	49,779,783	6,690,394	7,128,979	3.9	3.0	3.2
Southern States........	175	30,281,800	5,198,481	1,056,594	979,496	3.5	3.0	2.7
Western States........	688	90,754,200	22,729,103	4,397,353	4,003,303	4.8	3.9	3.5
Total...............	2,045	455,132,056	115,149,351	17,401,867	16,873,200	3.8	3.1	3.0
Sept., 1879, to March, 1880:								
New England States...	546	164,820,020	37,869,312	5,409,351	5,610,287	3.3	2.7	2.8
Middle States..........	640	169,399,170	51,306,583	7,151,166	9,220,826	4.2	3.2	4.2
Southern States........	175	30,432,700	5,210,198	1,246,470	1,278,695	4.1	3.5	3.6
Western States........	685	89,428,200	22,840,408	4,314,286	5,042,976	4.8	3.8	4.5
Total...............	2,046	454,080,090	117,226,501	18,121,273	21,152,784	4.0	3.2	3.7
March, 1880, to Sept., 1880:								
New England States...	548	165,380,242	38,450,297	5,858,434	7,413,622	3.5	2.9	3.6
Middle States..........	654	169,343,870	52,762,674	7,120,204	9,805,448	4.2	3.2	4.1
Southern States........	176	30,423,700	5,516,335	1,139,203	1,434,102	3.7	3.2	4.0
Western States........	694	89,067,250	23,416,343	4,172,359	5,380,078	4.7	3.7	4.8
Total...............	2,072	454,215,062	120,145,649	18,290,200	24,033,250	4.0	3.2	4.2
Sept., 1880, to March, 1881:								
New England States...	550	165,623,120	38,044,841	5,900,861	6,757,787	3.6	2.9	3.3
Middle States..........	657	170,739,045	54,536,248	6,974,934	9,162,771	4.1	3.1	4.1
Southern States........	178	30,448,760	5,898,107	1,264,398	1,905,690	4.2	3.5	5.2
Western States........	702	90,034,000	24,102,592	4,737,324	6,625,773	5.3	4.2	5.8
Total...............	2,087	456,844,865	122,481,788	18,877,517	24,452,021	4.1	3.3	4.2
March, 1881, to Sept., 1881:								
New England States...	550	165,373,120	39,878,448	6,005,608	8,166,022	3.6	2.9	4.0
Middle States..........	660	171,560,315	55,747,501	7,558,407	11,925,784	4.4	3.3	5.3
Southern States........	181	30,973,950	6,530,694	1,282,120	2,300,624	4.1	3.4	6.1
Western States........	709	91,027,100	25,081,751	4,653,833	6,778,112	5.1	3.9	5.8
Total...............	2,100	458,934,485	127,238,394	19,499,968	29,170,542	4.3	3.3	5.0
Sept., 1881, to March, 1882:								
New England States...	553	162,650,870	40,703,776	5,952,275	7,123,339	3.7	2.9	3.5
Middle States..........	666	171,488,315	57,470,278	7,367,409	10,210,373	4.3	3.2	4.5
Southern States........	188	31,672,700	6,928,882	1,333,715	1,981,226	4.2	3.5	5.1
Western States........	730	94,542,600	26,188,953	5,261,976	7,768,661	5.6	4.3	6.4
Total...............	2,137	460,354,485	131,291,889	19,915,375	27,083,599	4.3	3.4	4.6
March, 1882, to Sept., 1882:								
New England States...	555	165,515,870	41,033,290	5,729,842	6,732,530	3.5	2.8	3.3
Middle States..........	678	173,270,315	58,491,695	7,194,528	9,704,231	4.1	3.1	4.2
Southern States........	194	32,212,700	7,503,078	1,289,362	2,062,960	4.0	3.2	5.2
Western States........	770	102,948,830	26,542,862	6,662,821	7,737,803	6.5	5.1	6.0
Total...............	2,197	473,947,715	133,570,931	20,896,553	26,237,635	4.4	3.4	4.3
Sept., 1882, to March, 1883:								
New England States...	557	165,652,070	41,341,240	5,819,093	6,200,443	3.5	2.8	3.0
Middle States..........	687	174,375,472	62,118,691	7,542,146	9,990,021	4.3	3.2	4.2
Southern States........	207	33,963,000	8,228,309	1,405,019	2,108,093	4.1	3.3	5.2
Western States........	816	109,099,800	25,881,856	5,518,844	8,133,477	5.1	4.1	6.0
Total...............	2,267	483,091,342	137,570,105	20,285,102	26,432,934	4.2	3.3	4.2

EARNINGS AND DIVIDENDS OF THE NATIONAL BANKS, ETC.—Continued.

Geographical divisions.	No. of banks	Capital.	Surplus.	Dividends.	Net earnings.	Ratios.		
						Dividends to capital.	Dividends to capital and surplus.	Earnings to capital and surplus.
						Pr. ct.	Pr. ct.	Pr. ct.
March, 1883, to Sept., 1883:								
New England States	562	$166,793,070	$41,727,679	$5,861,182	$6,651,505	3.5	2.8	3.2
Middle States	698	173,915,465	63,453,454	7,556,795	9,960,635	4.3	3.2	4.2
Southern States	224	35,685,300	9,084,011	1,415,529	2,433,336	4.0	3.2	5.4
Western States	875	118,246,305	26,967,043	5,560,070	8,528,648	4.7	3.8	5.9
Total	2,359	494,640,140	141,232,187	20,393,576	27,574,214	4.1	3.2	4.3
Sept., 1883, to March, 1884:								
New England States	565	167,478,070	41,863,161	5,726,356	6,095,915	3.4	2.7	2.9
Middle States	715	175,317,315	64,841,178	7,639,670	9,529,978	4.4	3.2	4.0
Southern States	248	38,214,310	9,854,923	1,700,113	2,950,096	4.4	3.5	6.1
Western States	963	126,959,605	29,041,587	6,016,667	9,418,775	4.7	3.9	6.0
Total	2,491	507,969,300	145,600,849	21,082,806	27,991,764	4.1	3.2	4.3
March, 1884, to Sept., 1884:								
New England States	568	167,600,370	41,905,905	5,551,003	5,738,456	3.3	2.6	2.7
Middle States	723	175,767,355	64,580,406	7,080,673	8,198,912	4.0	2.9	3.4
Southern States	264	40,638,300	10,726,209	1,691,520	2,747,018	4.2	3.3	5.3
Western States	1,027	134,599,700	30,508,955	5,838,871	7,683,633	4.3	3.5	4.7
Total	2,582	518,605,725	147,721,475	20,171,667	24,368,019	3.9	3.0	3.7
Sept., 1884, to March, 1885:								
New England States	567	167,400,370	41,413,826	5,661,537	4,388,812	3.4	2.7	2.1
Middle States	732	173,212,145	64,741,009	7,156,680	7,474,752	4.1	3.0	3.1
Southern States	278	42,648,400	11,527,942	1,790,726	2,426,838	4.2	3.3	4.5
Western States	1,073	139,638,800	31,088,344	5,828,707	7,310,780	4.2	3.4	4.3
Total	2,650	522,899,715	148,771,121	20,437,650	21,601,202	3.9	3.0	3.2
March, 1885, to Sept., 1885:								
New England States	562	165,668,370	40,786,007	5,391,401	4,725,395	3.3	2.6	2.3
Middle States	731	172,907,352	64,247,888	6,953,332	7,297,159	4.0	2.9	3.1
Southern States	287	43,500,300	11,505,477	1,655,261	2,282,782	3.8	3.0	4.2
Western States	1,085	142,523,580	30,364,123	6,218,477	7,718,959	4.5	3.6	4.5
Total	2,665	524,599,602	146,903,495	20,218,471	22,024,295	3.9	3.0	3.3
Sept., 1885, to March, 1886:								
New England States	559	165,203,920	41,128,387	5,375,226	5,925,381	3.2	2.6	2.8
Middle States	738	172,435,295	67,583,309	7,044,535	9,484,324	4.0	2.9	3.9
Southern States	294	44,437,400	12,053,524	1,969,190	2,705,274	4.4	3.4	4.7
Western States	1,117	148,879,580	32,767,699	6,946,485	9,412,687	4.6	3.8	5.2
Total	2,708	530,956,195	153,532,919	21,335,436	27,527,666	4.0	3.1	4.0
March, 1886, to Sept., 1886:								
New England States	563	165,352,320	41,581,845	5,338,635	6,736,479	3.2	2.5	3.2
Middle States	744	173,628,875	70,044,187	7,328,798	9,789,135	4.2	3.0	4.0
Southern States	303	45,444,000	11,967,821	1,994,537	2,553,055	4.3	3.4	4.0
Western States	1,174	153,138,453	33,470,925	6,485,172	8,834,050	4.2	3.5	4.7
Total	2,784	537,563,648	157,064,778	21,147,142	27,912,719	3.9	3.0	4.0
Sept., 1886, to March, 1887:								
New England States	563	165,252,370	41,897,072	5,318,480	6,176,707	3.2	2.6	3.0
Middle States	754	175,873,735	73,445,033	7,574,627	12,072,419	4.3	3.0	4.8
Southern States	313	46,213,240	12,463,050	2,143,870	2,646,393	4.6	3.0	4.5
Western States	1,225	161,016,425	35,926,745	7,111,610	10,803,275	4.4	3.6	5.5
Total	2,885	548,355,770	163,731,900	22,148,587	31,698,794	4.0	3.1	4.5
March, 1887, to Sept., 1887:								
New England States	566	164,837,370	43,118,790	5,335,787	7,224,781	3.2	2.6	3.5
Middle States	764	176,635,656	76,574,179	7,357,400	11,360,893	4.2	2.9	4.5
Southern States	343	51,515,315	13,247,285	2,137,328	3,268,973	4.1	3.3	5.0
Western States	1,269	165,556,200	38,314,299	7,153,305	10,953,427	4.3	3.5	5.4
Total	2,942	558,544,541	171,254,553	22,003,820	32,808,074	3.9	3.0	4.5
General average	2,392	494,730,485	138,735,112	19,987,115	25,201,354	4.0	3.2	4.0

TABLE, BY STATES AND RESERVE CITIES, OF THE RATIOS TO CAPITAL, AND TO
FROM MARCH 1, 1883,

	States, Territories, and reserve cities.	Ratio of dividends to capital for six months ending—										Ratio of	
		March 1, 1883.	Sept. 1, 1883.	March 1, 1884.	Sept. 1, 1884.	March 1, 1885.	Sept. 1, 1885.	March 1, 1886.	Sept. 1, 1886.	March 1, 1887.	Sept. 1, 1887.	March 1, 1883.	Sept. 1, 1883.
		P. ct.	P. ct.	P. ct.	P. ct.	P. ct.	P. ct.	P. ct.	P. ct.	P. ct.	P. ct.	P. ct.	P. ct.
1	Maine	4.3	4.2	4.1	4.1	4.1	4.3	4.3	4.1	3.5	3.8	3.4	3.3
2	New Hampshire	3.8	3.9	3.7	3.7	3.7	3.7	3.6	3.8	3.7	3.7	3.2	3.2
3	Vermont	3.8	4.2	3.9	3.8	3.6	3.2	3.5	3.4	3.4	3.5	3.1	3.4
4	Massachusetts	3.7	3.7	3.6	3.3	3.6	3.4	3.4	3.3	3.4	3.4	2.9	2.8
5	Boston	2.9	2.9	2.7	2.8	2.8	2.7	2.5	2.6	2.7	2.7	2.3	2.3
6	Rhode Island	3.4	3.5	3.4	3.3	3.3	3.2	3.1	3.1	3.2	3.2	2.8	2.9
7	Connecticut	4.0	4.0	3.9	3.8	3.7	3.6	3.6	3.7	3.6	3.7	3.1	3.1
8	New York	4.0	4.4	4.2	3.9	3.7	3.7	3.8	3.7	3.8	4.2	3.2	3.5
9	New York City	4.7	4.6	4.7	4.3	4.5	4.3	4.3	5.5	4.5	4.6	3.2	3.1
10	Albany	6.1	4.2	6.2	4.2	6.2	3.3	4.3	4.9	6.6	3.8	3.4	2.4
11	New Jersey	4.7	4.6	4.7	4.4	4.5	4.4	4.4	4.4	4.5	4.7	3.6	3.5
12	Pennsylvania	3.9	3.9	4.0	3.5	3.8	3.7	3.7	3.7	5.0	3.7	3.1	3.1
13	Philadelphia	4.9	4.7	4.7	4.6	4.6	4.6	4.5	4.4	4.1	4.0	3.3	3.1
14	Pittsburgh	3.8	3.7	3.8	3.7	3.8	3.7	3.6	3.6	3.6	3.8	2.9	2.8
15	Delaware	4.5	4.8	4.6	4.8	4.8	4.0	4.4	4.3	4.4	4.3	3.4	3.5
16	Maryland	4.7	4.4	4.4	4.5	4.2	4.1	4.6	4.3	4.3	4.7	3.6	3.4
17	Baltimore	3.6	3.8	3.7	3.8	3.8	3.7	3.7	3.7	3.6	3.7	2.9	3.1
18	District of Columbia	4.0	4.0	4.0	4.0	4.0	4.0	4.0	4.0	4.0	4.0	3.2	3.2
19	Washington	2.4	3.3	3.4	3.4	3.4	3.4	3.4	3.2	3.7	3.1	2.0	2.6
20	Virginia	4.2	4.1	5.7	4.0	4.2	4.0	4.9	3.2	3.7	3.7	3.1	3.1
21	West Virginia	4.3	4.1	4.1	3.7	3.9	3.7	3.9	3.7	3.9	3.5	3.4	3.3
22	North Carolina	3.9	3.4	3.9	3.3	4.5	3.7	4.3	3.8	3.9	3.0	3.3	2.8
23	South Carolina	4.0	4.1	4.3	4.0	4.3	4.3	4.0	7.3	4.3	3.8	2.9	2.9
24	Georgia	3.7	3.4	3.5	3.2	3.7	3.6	3.8	3.3	3.7	5.7	3.0	2.7
25	Florida	7.6	2.5	2.5	2.5	3.0	2.3	1.5	1.4	4.6	4.9	6.8	2.2
26	Alabama	4.0	3.5	3.8	3.6	4.5	4.4	3.9	4.8	4.3	3.8	3.4	2.9
27	Mississippi	8.0	.....	7.4	2.8	5.4	3.1	7.3	3.3	5.6	2.8	7.7	..
28	Louisiana	5.0	5.0	4.0	4.0	4.0	4.0	4.0	4.0	4.0	3.0	5.0	4.9
29	New Orleans	4.1	4.2	6.6	3.6	4.1	3.9	3.7	3.5	5.5	3.5	3.0	3.0
30	Texas	5.3	3.9	5.0	5.7	5.5	3.3	5.9	4.4	7.0	4.6	4.0	2.9
31	Arkansas	5.9	4.0	5.8	4.4	4.4	3.8	4.9	3.9	5.4	14.6	4.9	3.4
32	Kentucky	3.6	3.8	3.6	4.1	3.6	3.8	3.7	3.8	3.8	4.0	3.1	3.2
33	Louisville	3.4	3.9	3.5	3.8	3.3	3.5	3.6	3.6	3.8	3.7	2.8	3.2
34	Tennessee	5.4	5.0	5.0	4.7	5.3	4.4	5.1	8.1	4.7	3.6	4.6	4.2
35	Ohio	4.3	4.1	4.0	4.0	3.8	3.7	3.7	3.7	3.8	4.1	3.6	3.4
36	Cincinnati	3.5	3.8	3.3	3.2	3.1	3.3	3.5	2.8	3.2	3.2	3.1	3.4
37	Cleveland	4.1	4.1	3.8	4.1	2.3	2.8	3.2	3.1	2.9	2.6	3.5	3.5
38	Indiana	5.1	4.6	4.1	3.9	3.7	4.6	4.3	4.4	4.9	4.2	4.0	3.6
39	Illinois	6.0	5.7	5.7	5.0	4.9	4.9	5.0	5.2	4.9	4.9	4.6	4.3
40	Chicago	5.0	3.9	3.7	4.7	4.9	4.3	4.6	3.8	4.0	3.5	3.8	3.1
41	Michigan	5.6	5.3	5.9	4.4	4.8	4.5	4.7	4.2	5.1	4.6	4.4	4.3
42	Detroit	4.2	3.7	4.2	4.2	4.6	4.7	4.7	3.7	4.2	3.6	3.8	3.4
43	Wisconsin	4.3	4.5	7.0	5.3	4.8	4.1	6.1	4.6	4.9	5.8	3.4	3.7
44	Milwaukee	4.3	4.9	4.9	6.5	6.5	4.9	8.0	6.4	4.0	6.5	3.0	3.4
45	Iowa	5.3	4.9	4.9	4.4	4.5	5.0	4.6	4.9	5.4	5.0	4.3	4.0
46	Minnesota	5.3	5.1	5.2	3.1	3.9	4.1	4.3	4.2	4.3	4.6	4.4	4.2
47	Missouri	9.7	4.1	4.2	1.1	3.5	8.7	4.8	3.9	3.7	4.7	8.0	3.4
48	Saint Louis	2.7	3.9	3.6	3.0	3.5	2.8	3.8	3.8	3.5	3.7	2.2	3.2
49	Kansas City	....	....	....	....	....	....	....	....	....	4.1	....	...
50	Saint Joseph	....	....	....	....	....	....	....	....	....	3.3	....	...
51	Kansas	6.1	5.9	7.4	8.8	3.9	5.6	5.2	4.9	5.8	5.3	5.3	4.9
52	Nebraska	4.9	4.9	5.9	4.9	4.9	5.3	5.8	5.2	5.4	6.4	4.1	4.1
53	Omaha	....	....	....	....	....	....	....	....	....	3.1	....	...
54	Colorado	12.0	7.2	7.0	10.0	9.6	7.0	7.7	7.2	7.9	8.2	8.0	4.8
55	Nevada	10.0	10.0	12.0	10.0	10.0	8.0	10.0	8.0	5.3	4.0	8.0	7.9
56	California	5.2	5.6	7.9	3.5	4.5	4.3	8.9	4.9	4.7	5.6	4.3	4.6
57	San Francisco	4.0	4.0	4.0	4.0	4.0	4.0	4.0	3.5	2.0	1.9	3.5	3.5
58	Oregon	14.2	19.3	10.8	6.0	5.8	5.6	4.6	3.8	5.0	3.3	12.0	16.5
59	Arizona	5.0	7.0	7.0	3.3	...	....	...	...	...	...	5.0	6.9
60	Dakota	3.3	1.9	3.0	4.6	4.9	4.0	4.9	3.1	3.7	4.1	2.8	1.6
61	Idaho	20.0	15.0	22.5	....	14.0	...	10.0	....	4.3	..	16.7	2.5
62	Montana	....	10.9	....	4.1	0.8	1.7	2.0	2.2	4.1	1.5	..	0.5
63	New Mexico	12.2	7.3	8.9	7.8	6.1	5.5	8.1	4.8	7.1	4.9	9.8	5.8
64	Utah	4.6	3.6	5.2	4.7	3.9	5.6	4.1	4.1	4.7	5.3	3.2	2.6
65	Washington	9.5	4.2	1.6	3.1	3.9	3.9	4.3	7.1	3.3	4.5	8.2	3.9
66	Wyoming	6.9	3.4	22.5	3.0	3.6	3.7	7.5	3.3	6.5	3.2	5.6	2.7
	Average	4.2	4.1	4.2	3.9	3.9	3.8	4.0	3.9	4.0	3.9	3.3	3.2

NOTE.—Figures printed in bold-face type in column

CAPITAL AND SURPLUS, OF THE EARNINGS AND DIVIDENDS OF NATIONAL BANKS, TO SEPTEMBER 1, 1887.

dividends to capital and surplus for six months ending—								Ratio of earnings to capital and surplus for six months ending—										
March 1, 1884.	Sept. 1, 1884.	March 1, 1885.	Sept. 1, 1885.	March 1, 1886.	Sept. 1, 1886.	March 1, 1887.	Sept. 1, 1887.	March 1, 1883.	Sept. 1, 1883.	March 1, 1884.	Sept. 1, 1884.	March 1, 1885.	Sept. 1, 1885.	March 1, 1886.	Sept. 1, 1886.	March 1, 1887.	Sept. 1, 1887.	
P. ct.	P. ct.	P. ct.	P. ct.	P. ct.	P. ct.	P. ct.	P. ct.	P. ct.	P. ct.	P. ct.	P. ct.	P. ct.	P. ct.	P. ct.	P. ct.	P. ct.	P. ct.	
3.8	3.3	3.3	3.5	3.5	3.2	2.0	3.1	3.5	3.6	2.4	2.3	2.9	3.3	4.1	3.4	1.8	3.0	1
3.1	3.1	3.1	3.1	3.0	3.1	3.0	3.0	2.9	3.9	3.0	2.9	3.7	3.0	3.8	3.7	4.0	4.2	2
3.2	3.2	3.0	2.7	2.9	2.9	2.9	2.9	3.2	3.4	3.3	2.6	2.0	2.3	3.6	3.3	3.7	3.5	3
2.8	2.5	2.8	2.6	2.6	2.5	2.6	2.6	2.9	3.5	2.9	3.0	2.2	2.5	2.5	3.0	2.9	3.8	4
2.2	2.3	2.3	2.2	2.1	2.1	2.2	2.1	2.7	2.7	2.5	2.4	1.4	1.7	2.5	3.0	2.8	3.3	5
2.9	2.7	2.8	2.7	2.6	2.5	2.6	2.7	2.7	3.6	3.3	3.3	2.2	2.5	2.6	3.4	3.4	3.5	6
3.1	3.0	2.9	2.8	2.8	2.8	2.8	2.9	3.7	2.9	3.3	2.7	2.1	2.4	3.2	3.6	3.3	2.9	7
3.3	3.1	3.0	3.0	3.0	2.9	3.0	3.3	4.1	4.3	3.5	4.0	2.9	3.2	4.1	3.9	4.4	4.2	8
3.2	2.9	3.0	2.9	2.8	3.2	2.8	2.8	4.1	4.7	3.0	2.2	2.9	3.0	4.4	4.6	5.9	6.6	9
3.5	2.4	3.5	2.0	2.5	2.4	3.8	2.2	5.1	3.3	4.1	2.4	4.1	1.0	1.6	2.4	5.4	4.4	10
3.6	3.3	3.4	3.4	3.3	3.3	3.4	3.4	4.7	4.4	4.7	4.0	3.3	3.2	4.0	4.9	5.1	5.0	11
3.1	2.7	2.9	2.8	2.8	2.7	3.8	2.8	4.5	3.8	4.5	3.9	3.7	3.1	3.6	3.5	4.6	3.7	12
3.1	3.0	3.0	3.0	2.9	2.8	2.7	2.7	3.9	3.8	4.4	4.1	2.7	3.4	3.4	3.6	3.9	3.7	13
2.9	2.7	2.8	2.7	2.6	2.6	2.6	2.7	3.3	3.7	4.3	3.9	3.3	2.6	3.5	3.7	4.2	4.6	14
3.4	3.6	3.5	3.6	3.3	3.2	3.2	3.1	4.6	5.1	4.9	3.8	5.0	4.4	4.4	3.9	4.5	4.6	15
3.4	3.4	3.2	3.1	3.5	3.2	3.2	3.5	4.2	4.5	4.4	4.4	3.6	3.5	4.0	3.6	4.1	3.9	16
3.0	3.0	3.0	2.9	2.9	2.9	2.8	2.8	3.9	3.5	3.9	3.9	3.8	2.7	3.4	3.0	4.0	2.8	17
3.2	3.2	3.2	3.2	3.2	3.2	3.2	3.3	3.9	4.5	2.8	3.6	3.6	3.6	4.0	3.9	3.8	3.7	18
2.7	2.7	2.7	2.7	2.6	2.5	2.0	2.4	2.5	3.8	4.4	3.7	1.5	4.3	3.1	4.5	5.1	4.8	19
4.3	3.0	3.0	2.9	3.7	2.4	2.7	2.7	4.5	5.1	6.3	5.2	3.8	4.7	3.6	3.2	4.1	4.1	20
3.2	3.0	3.1	2.9	3.1	2.9	3.1	2.8	3.9	3.7	3.9	3.9	3.1	2.5	3.7	3.4	3.2	3.3	21
3.2	2.7	3.6	3.0	3.4	2.5	3.2	2.5	3.3	4.9	4.2	4.6	3.7	2.9	3.6	2.9	4.2	3.6	22
3.1	2.8	3.0	3.0	2.8	5.0	3.0	2.6	5.0	6.4	6.6	6.7	3.3	3.9	4.3	3.6	4.1	5.3	23
2.7	2.4	2.7	2.7	2.9	2.5	2.8	4.3	4.8	4.8	5.5	4.8	3.8	4.3	2.4	5.7	3.5	5.5	24
2.2	2.2	2.7	2.0	1.4	1.3	4.2	4.4	2.0	11.6	6.2	6.9	4.6	7.3	5.2	4.4	6.1	7.7	25
3.9	3.0	3.9	3.8	3.3	3.4	3.6	3.2	2.7	2.8	3.9	3.3	4.9	6.0	6.8	4.7	7.0	11.4	26
7.0	2.6	5.1	2.8	6.6	3.0	4.9	2.4	5.2	8.5	5.8	8.0	5.4	9.2	7.0	8.8	6.1	9.0	27
3.8	3.8	3.7	3.7	3.6	3.6	3.6	2.8	5.8	6.6	6.3	5.0	4.2	5.4	5.0	3.8	4.3	8.0	28
4.8	2.7	3.0	2.8	2.6	2.6	4.1	2.6	5.3	6.3	6.5	5.1	2.9	4.2	3.0	2.1	4.4	4.8	29
3.7	4.3	4.2	2.5	4.5	3.3	5.4	3.6	11.9	10.8	12.3	8.5	8.0	4.3	6.2	6.7	5.7	4.5	30
5.0	3.3	3.2	3.0	3.9	3.1	4.2	13.0	10.1	5.3	8.4	12.0	5.2	4.3	4.9	6.5	6.4	7.9	31
3.0	3.5	3.0	3.2	3.0	3.1	3.1	3.2	4.5	4.5	4.4	4.4	4.1	3.9	5.6	4.1	3.7	3.6	32
2.8	3.1	2.7	2.9	2.9	2.8	3.0	3.0	4.0	4.4	4.4	3.8	2.5	3.1	3.6	4.7	3.0	3.2	33
4.2	4.0	4.3	3.7	4.2	6.9	3.9	3.0	6.7	5.5	7.8	5.4	5.3	4.9	5.0	5.8	5.7	6.4	34
3.3	3.3	3.1	3.0	3.1	3.1	3.1	3.3	5.0	4.7	4.5	3.4	3.5	2.9	3.5	3.5	3.7	4.2	35
3.0	2.9	2.7	2.9	3.1	2.4	2.7	2.7	4.5	3.5	3.7	2.9	3.2	3.4	3.6	3.5	4.1	6.5	36
3.3	3.6	2.0	2.5	2.8	2.7	2.6	2.3	5.8	4.3	5.0	2.4	2.2	4.0	3.7	3.2	3.9	3.7	37
3.2	3.1	2.9	3.6	3.4	3.4	3.8	3.2	4.6	4.7	4.2	3.4	3.3	3.7	5.9	3.8	4.3	4.2	38
4.3	3.8	3.7	3.7	3.8	3.9	3.7	3.7	5.9	5.8	5.1	5.2	5.0	4.4	5.0	4.7	5.3	4.5	39
2.9	3.6	3.9	3.5	3.7	3.1	3.2	2.8	10.8	7.8	6.1	5.7	1.6	5.2	5.9	5.1	6.4	7.0	40
4.8	3.6	3.9	3.8	3.9	3.5	4.3	3.8	6.0	6.2	6.3	4.0	4.3	4.1	4.6	5.2	5.5	5.3	41
3.9	3.9	4.2	4.3	4.2	3.3	3.8	3.2	0.7	7.4	6.7	5.6	5.9	4.0	8.6	4.8	5.0	4.7	42
5.7	4.3	3.8	3.3	4.8	3.6	3.9	4.5	5.7	6.2	6.5	5.0	4.8	4.7	5.6	5.0	5.7	6.6	43
3.2	4.2	4.2	3.2	5.2	4.2	2.5	4.0	9.5	8.9	6.0	5.6	1.3	5.4	7.4	6.6	5.3	5.7	44
4.0	3.6	3.6	4.1	3.7	4.0	4.3	4.0	6.6	6.0	5.9	5.1	4.9	4.7	4.7	4.3	5.1	5.2	45
4.3	2.6	3.3	3.5	3.7	3.6	3.6	3.0	6.9	5.7	7.9	4.3	4.6	4.0	4.9	4.3	6.8	4.3	46
3.5	3.4	2.9	7.4	4.0	3.3	3.2	3.8	5.2	5.5	6.6	5.5	5.5	6.4	5.0	4.8	5.8	5.1	47
2.9	2.4	2.7	2.2	2.9	2.9	2.6	2.7	0.9	5.7	5.0	3.8	3.7	3.6	3.5	4.7	3.6	5.0	48
....	....	....	....	....	....	....	3.6	....	....	....	....	....	....	....	....	....	8.4	49
....	....	....	....	....	....	....	2.5	....	....	....	....	....	....	....	....	....	3.8	50
6.2	7.7	3.4	4.8	4.5	4.2	5.0	4.5	8.6	8.5	10.7	9.2	7.5	8.1	7.6	7.7	9.0	6.7	51
5.0	4.2	4.2	4.5	5.0	4.3	4.5	5.5	8.9	8.0	11.3	7.3	7.5	7.2	6.8	3.1	7.2	7.2	52
....	....	....	....	....	....	....	2.5	....	....	....	....	....	....	....	....	....	3.5	53
4.8	6.5	6.0	4.7	5.3	5.3	5.8	6.0	12.2	9.8	15.4	8.7	8.1	5.1	6.7	6.3	9.1	8.4	54
9.5	7.5	7.5	6.0	7.5	6.1	4.4	3.2	12.9	11.2	12.4	12.6	8.5	8.6	8.0	9.2	5.8	6.7	55
6.6	2.7	3.6	3.5	7.1	3.9	3.8	4.6	6.7	6.8	7.7	6.1	7.6	6.5	6.5	6.3	7.0	7.3	56
3.5	3.5	3.5	3.5	3.4	3.0	1.8	1.8	4.8	5.2	4.6	3.5	2.1	3.3	3.5	3.1	2.7	3.2	57
9.6	5.4	5.3	5.1	4.2	3.5	4.7	3.0	14.4	24.6	10.5	16.6	9.8	11.7	11.5	7.1	9.5	11.8	58
6.8	3.3	....	....	....	....	....	....	5.5	7.7	9.0	1.8	1.4	....	....	....	....	....	59
2.4	3.8	4.1	3.3	4.0	2.6	3.2	3.5	11.2	9.5	7.6	3.2	4.0	4.2	5.1	4.8	6.1	3.2	60
20.4	...	13.0	....	9.2	....	40.0	....	17.0	12.0	22.7	10.4	10.0	6.0	7.0	5.8	6.1	3.4	61
....	3.4	0.7	1.4	2.5	1.0	3.4	1.2	10.3	10.1	9.8	9.2	7.7	5.2	6.4	4.8	9.4	8.0	62
7.0	6.0	5.1	4.5	6.5	3.0	5.9	4.1	8.6	8.6	7.7	7.2	2.6	5.7	7.2	5.5	5.0	3.7	63
3.5	3.4	2.7	3.8	3.1	3.0	3.4	3.7	5.9	7.8	9.1	6.5	7.0	3.5	5.7	8.8	6.1	5.1	64
1.5	2.9	3.6	3.5	3.8	6.2	2.9	3.7	16.5	8.8	11.1	8.4	8.5	10.1	6.1	7.1	7.2	8.2	65
10.4	2.6	2.9	3.2	6.3	2.8	5.4	2.6	8.8	8.3	11.4	7.9	7.5	8.6	7.6	6.2	5.7	6.0	66
3.2	3.0	3.0	3.0	3.1	3.0	3.1	3.0	4.2	4.3	4.3	3.7	3.2	3.3	4.0	4.0	4.5	4.5	

for 1884 and 1886 signify percentage of loss.

CLASSIFICATION OF THE LOANS AND DISCOUNTS OF THE NATIONAL BANKS IN THE RESERVE CITIES AND IN THE STATES AND TERRITORIES ON OCTOBER 5, 1887.

Cities, States, and Territories.	No. of banks.	On single-name paper.	On U.S. bonds.	On other bonds and stocks.	All other loans.	Total.
New York City	47	$17, 585, 496. 27	$1,445,000.00	$95, 075, 844. 27	$143, 906, 910. 58	$258, 014, 181. 12
Chicago	18	15, 498, 985. 93	500. 00	10, 821, 735. 83	34, 754, 971. 62	61, 076, 193. 38
Saint Louis	5	279, 603. 00	....	1, 182, 214. 28	8, 920, 936. 13	10, 382, 753. 41
Boston	54	17, 249, 382. 98	38, 350. 00	19, 689, 465. 11	86, 093, 214. 79	123, 070, 412. 88
Albany	6	494, 236. 31	7, 280. 00	3, 011, 017. 84	5, 267, 397. 27	8, 779, 931. 42
Philadelphia	43	13, 427, 173. 71	11, 175. 00	11, 562, 816. 00	58, 426, 272. 80	83, 427, 437. 51
Pittsburgh	23	1, 293, 066. 32	....	3, 454, 425. 99	27, 198, 002. 81	31, 946, 395. 12
Baltimore	17	5, 401, 897. 60	700. 00	3, 829, 249. 81	16, 927, 506. 79	26, 159, 354. 20
Washington	7	27, 130. 24	52, 230. 00	686, 552. 19	3, 257, 011. 11	4, 022, 923. 54
New Orleans	8	403, 502. 72	7, 500. 00	2, 641, 223. 15	6, 879, 479. 97	9, 933, 705. 84
Louisville	9	276, 651. 11	....	553, 343. 41	8, 504, 829. 32	9, 334, 823. 84
Cincinnati	15	4, 678, 786. 92	40, 700. 00	3, 532, 112. 87	16, 336, 388. 46	24, 587, 988. 25
Cleveland	9	1, 648, 688. 00	....	2, 335, 446. 50	13, 584, 390. 75	17, 568, 525. 25
Detroit	8	893, 288. 33	7, 700. 00	1, 621, 586. 28	10, 254, 461. 41	12, 777, 036. 02
Milwaukee	3	666, 926. 14	....	598, 076. 65	3, 057, 508. 29	4, 322, 511. 08
Kansas City	8	3, 026, 033. 58	....	431, 366. 56	10, 910, 306. 57	14, 367, 706. 71
Saint Joseph	2	433, 028. 16	....	4, 270. 00	1, 504, 717. 54	1, 942, 015. 70
Omaha	8	2, 060, 459. 96	7, 500. 00	130, 486. 11	6, 872, 093. 51	9, 070, 539. 58
San Francisco	3	2, 693, 570. 10	....	551, 320. 50	1, 540, 766. 38	4, 785, 656. 98
Total	203	88, 040, 807. 38	1, 619, 535. 00	161, 712, 553. 35	465, 097, 196. 10	716, 470, 091. 83
Maine	72	1, 241, 747. 20	2, 139. 50	1, 013, 961. 13	16, 867, 808. 06	19, 125, 655. 89
New Hampshire	49	815, 624. 25	1, 550. 00	1, 305, 254. 18	7, 529, 178. 06	9, 651, 606. 49
Vermont	49	969, 662. 81	13, 121. 95	361, 770. 55	11, 487, 754. 03	12, 832, 309. 34
Massachusetts	198	14, 920, 402. 43	514, 013. 55	5, 936, 075. 03	70, 191, 054. 59	91, 561, 545. 60
Rhode Island	61	7, 491, 158. 94	15, 854. 68	928, 731. 16	26, 050, 490. 00	34, 486, 234. 78
Connecticut	83	6, 648, 917. 31	41, 675. 00	3, 618, 867. 49	32, 691, 840. 06	43, 001, 299. 86
New York	269	8, 855, 687. 82	105, 325. 69	7, 500, 324. 06	82, 330, 989. 31	98, 792, 326. 88
New Jersey	81	3, 257, 158. 44	76, 200. 00	6, 023, 184. 73	31, 073, 173. 93	40, 429, 717. 10
Pennsylvania	237	5, 619, 730. 42	30, 550. 00	2, 070, 785. 23	72, 485, 839. 43	80, 206, 911. 08
Delaware	17	72, 736. 05	100. 00	169, 522. 67	4, 759, 404. 38	5, 001, 764. 00
Maryland	31	285, 917. 53	200. 00	165, 268. 56	6, 455, 779. 44	6, 907, 165. 53
District of Columbia	1	....	....	....	346, 726. 45	346, 726. 45
Virginia	25	547, 888. 99	24, 500. 00	706, 771. 97	9, 507, 466. 67	10, 786, 627. 63
West Virginia	20	136, 542. 40	....	17, 705. 00	3, 834, 945. 85	3, 989, 193. 25
North Carolina	18	347, 739. 41	....	82, 578. 21	4, 821, 477. 14	5, 251, 794. 76
South Carolina	15	147, 783. 16	....	289, 750. 27	4, 415, 926. 16	4, 854, 459. 59
Georgia	21	757, 316. 38	....	931, 205. 40	5, 868, 997. 57	7, 557, 519. 35
Florida	8	307, 529. 91	....	23, 230. 62	1, 080, 693. 88	1, 411, 454. 41
Alabama	20	1, 550, 802. 55	300, 478. 00	610, 747. 82	5, 904, 296. 58	8, 366, 324. 95
Mississippi	12	295, 656. 88	....	335, 455. 56	1, 600, 481. 81	2, 233, 594. 25
Louisiana	5	207, 214. 46	....	104, 682. 78	764, 152. 06	1, 076, 049. 30
Texas	91	4, 246, 716. 06	....	658, 077. 01	15, 252, 409. 70	20, 157, 203. 67
Arkansas	7	143, 217. 13	2, 500. 00	222, 636. 20	2, 412, 730. 11	2, 781, 084. 44
Kentucky	59	1, 092, 066. 95	28, 600. 00	624, 530. 86	15, 719, 548. 81	17, 464, 746. 62
Tennessee	40	3, 881, 590. 88	....	2, 377, 126. 61	12, 669, 584. 44	18, 928, 301. 93
Ohio	192	4, 4?9, 667. 51	1, 450. 00	2, 060, 025. 52	44, 353, 187. 21	50, 833, 330. 24
Indiana	93	3, 392, 224. 93	38, 158. 61	691, 577. 24	23, 663, 365. 21	27, 785, 325. 99
Illinois	160	6, 885, 654. 45	70, 521. 35	750, 824. 70	27, 898, 100. 36	35, 605, 100. 86
Michigan	100	4, 703, 482. 57	....	443, 510. 81	24, 271, 603. 31	29, 418, 596. 69
Wisconsin	53	1, 716, 661. 01	....	282, 161. 86	11, 341, 708. 10	13, 340, 531. 00
Iowa	128	4, 949, 026. 12	82, 427. 10	519, 974. 37	18, 227, 513. 05	23, 728, 910. 64
Minnesota	58	13, 638, 004. 86	9, 100. 00	1, 536, 673. 44	22, 673, 267. 19	37, 857, 045. 49
Missouri	35	492, 669. 57	7, 250. 00	52, 069. 41	4, 451, 887. 41	5, 003, 870. 39
Kansas	139	2, 524, 416. 30	2, 101. 24	129, 399. 73	18, 345, 533. 15	21, 001, 450. 42
Nebraska	95	2, 084, 369. 93	43, 201. 83	75, 558. 48	11, 416, 126. 13	13, 619, 256. 37
Colorado	31	3, 927, 214. 55	50. 00	327, 693. 08	7, 973, 901. 37	12, 228, 859. 00
Nevada	2	208, 332. 03	....	38, 501. 16	260, 836. 94	507, 670. 13
California	30	3, 320, 214. 86	11, 150. 00	758, 929. 53	10, 204, 812. 08	14, 295, 106. 47
Oregon	23	1, 893, 706. 27	....	49, 443. 79	3, 742, 473. 79	5, 685, 623. 85
Arizona	1	28, 518. 21	....	....	119, 956. 37	148, 474. 58
Dakota	62	879, 975. 39	41, 700. 00	60, 539. 90	5, 711, 869. 23	6, 691, 084. 52
Idaho	6	182, 133. 70	....	34, 241. 50	314, 904. 47	561, 279. 67
Montana	17	2, 508, 651. 75	....	233, 806. 25	5, 349, 345. 14	8, 091, 803. 14
New Mexico	9	499, 791. 91	....	43, 424. 56	1, 161, 821. 18	1, 705, 037. 65
Utah	7	749, 475. 44	....	33, 932. 47	1, 273, 277. 49	2, 056, 685. 40
Washington	18	546, 912. 11	....	86, 860. 00	3, 102, 036. 96	3, 735, 809. 07
Wyoming	8	651, 512. 11	....	39, 502. 02	1, 779, 035. 87	2, 470, 050. 30
Total	2, 756	124, 035, 462. 67	1, 413, 918. 50	41, 335, 893. 52	60?, 790, 280. 62	863, 575, 555. 31
United States	3, 019	212, 076, 270. 05	3, 033, 453. 50	206, 048, 446. 87	1, 158, 887, 476. 72	1, 580, 045, 647. 14

CLEARINGS AND BALANCES OF THE BANKS OF NEW YORK CITY FOR THE WEEKS ENDING AT THE DATES GIVEN.

Week ending—	Clearings.	Balances.
Sept. 2, 1882	$787,790,346.10	$27,396,024.64
Sept. 9, 1882	806,162,117.62	29,780,380.41
Sept. 16, 1882	1,010,034,295.97	30,418,411.78
Sept. 23, 1882	950,962,831.49	27,978,458.28
Sept. 30, 1882	1,011,393,332.57	34,393,848.91
Oct. 7, 1882	1,124,300,247.43	30,742,717.31
Oct. 14, 1882	990,817,864.93	35,772,217.86
Oct. 21, 1882	1,044,396,226.21	33,023,283.86
Oct. 28, 1882	857,810,086.35	26,633,506.70
Nov. 4, 1882	991,296,926.46	37,122,701.71
Nov. 11, 1882	950,409,956.50	26,909,785.92
Nov. 18, 1882	1,054,584,665.67	33,238,877.77
Nov. 25, 1882	1,246,998,567.95	28,657,750.01
Sept. 1, 1883	645,021,546.86	26,472,986.85
Sept. 8, 1883	739,732,907.18	31,195,740.55
Sept. 15, 1883	732,316,071.00	30,914,820.30
Sept. 22, 1883	700,082,400.54	30,061,000.19
Sept. 29, 1883	763,567,336.28	30,200,285.71
Oct. 6, 1883	759,872,865.58	32,814,144.42
Oct. 13, 1883	833,963,918.88	31,303,439.92
Oct. 20, 1883	919,608,026.44	31,917,817.51
Oct. 27, 1883	906,319,847.51	31,844,418.48
Nov. 3, 1883	817,096,284.43	29,708,441.71
Nov. 10, 1883	622,487,073.40	28,478,107.32
Nov. 17, 1883	783,094,622.25	33,519,486.15
Nov. 24, 1883	682,451,400.44	28,333,268.64
Sept. 6, 1884	463,912,628.57	21,278,921.75
Sept. 13, 1884	422,613,919.74	22,703,210.60
Sept. 20, 1884	492,069,873.06	21,412,397.53
Sept. 27, 1884	491,357,661.20	22,028,008.11
Oct. 4, 1884	554,662,098.69	22,658,517.10
Oct. 11, 1884	496,582,476.56	26,358,572.40
Oct. 18, 1884	518,575,214.80	28,696,794.93
Oct. 25, 1884	605,195,931.55	27,673,214.95
Nov. 1, 1884	458,532,568.11	23,225,190.59
Nov. 8, 1884	477,210,695.35	28,209,591.59
Nov. 15, 1884	527,541,755.74	26,823,201.26
Nov. 22, 1884	555,711,509.01	26,496,903.13
Nov. 29, 1884	459,294,007.66	21,392,407.63
Sept. 5, 1885	476,800,526.79	22,990,787.52
Sept. 12, 1885	484,537,657.96	23,969,367.46
Sept. 19, 1885	480,733,380.21	24,410,808.93
Sept. 26, 1885	471,652,648.41	22,978,989.63
Oct. 3, 1885	572,076,277.97	30,158,232.32
Oct. 10, 1885	639,566,549.70	28,462,678.38
Oct. 17, 1885	702,000,829.74	29,632,037.42
Oct. 24, 1885	828,373,048.53	30,475,583.77
Oct. 31, 1885	695,214,389.87	29,590,574.77
Nov. 7, 1885	775,416,616.98	30,751,563.50
Nov. 14, 1885	770,244,286.01	27,323,721.40
Sept. 4, 1886	485,535,545.80	28,387,297.77
Sept. 11, 1886	520,437,476.86	21,865,163.40
Sept. 18, 1886	590,366,637.81	28,050,351.78
Sept. 25, 1886	691,723,656.66	25,603,758.94
Oct. 2, 1886	744,533,107.30	31,285,172.38
Oct. 9, 1886	830,726,858.70	29,904,285.79
Oct. 16, 1886	774,127,054.20	30,952,375.09
Oct. 23, 1886	734,586,656.19	27,767,549.06
Oct. 30, 1886	625,698,664.48	26,667,923.82
Nov. 6, 1886	735,609,027.93	31,825,400.11
Nov. 13, 1886	704,572,284.86	28,065,256.87
Sept. 3, 1887	629,926,782.37	29,322,367.47
Sept. 10, 1887	502,627,925.28	22,329,268.73
Sept. 17, 1887	628,634,786.18	31,404,534.44
Sept. 24, 1887	659,648,314.43	30,974,662.90
Oct. 1, 1887	573,717,723.42	31,069,309.36
Oct. 8, 1887	676,201,491.67	29,825,323.74
Oct. 15, 1887	718,896,811.83	31,170,113.34
Oct. 22, 1887	742,551,452.00	33,350,889.58
Oct. 29, 1887	647,590,728.82	29,809,361.75
Nov. 5, 1887	706,280,839.34	31,289,781.13
Nov. 12, 1887	602,240,351.60	23,758,351.99

ABSTRACT OF REPORTS OF CONDITION

OF

State Banks, Loan and Trust Companies, Savings and Private Banks,

1886-'87,

ARRANGED BY STATES AND TERRITORIES.

NOTE.—Under the heading "official" are placed reports from State officers, and under heading "unofficial" reports from additional banks to this office.

STATE BANKS—OFFICIAL.

NEW HAMPSHIRE.

March 31, 1887.] [1 bank.

Resources.		Liabilities.	
Loans on real estate	$36, 607	Capital stock paid in	$50, 000
Loans on personal and collateral security	30, 421	Surplus fund	15, 210
Other loans and discounts	....	Other undivided profits	....
Overdrafts	....		
U. S. bonds	....	State-bank notes outstanding	1, 130
State bonds	5, 000		
R. R. bonds and stocks	2, 500	Dividends unpaid	950
Bank stocks	2, 400		
Other stocks, bonds, and mortgages	....	Individual deposits	35, 342
Due from other banks and bankers	....	State, county, and municipal deposits	....
Real estate, furniture, and fixtures	1, 851		
Current expenses and taxes paid	....	Deposits of State, county, and municipal disbursing officers	....
Gold coins			
Gold certificates			
Silver coins	7, 009	Due to other banks and bankers	3, 153
Silver certificates		Other liabilities	....
Legal tenders and national-bank notes			
Other resources	....		
Total	105, 791	Total	105, 791

RHODE ISLAND.

November 16, 1886.] [10 banks.

Resources.		Liabilities.	
Loans on real estate	....	Capital stock paid in	$1, 766, 685
Loans on personal and collateral security	$75, 312	Surplus fund	....
Other loans and discounts	2, 609, 864	Other undivided profits	160, 775
Overdrafts	....		
U. S. bonds	3, 800	State-bank notes outstanding	3, 148
State bonds	....		
R. R. bonds and stocks	....	Dividends unpaid	8, 723
Bank stocks	....		
Other stocks, bonds, and mortgages	127, 750	Individual deposits	1, 177, 883
Due from other banks and bankers	139, 968	State, county, and municipal deposits	....
Real estate, furniture, and fixtures	225, 005		
Current expenses and taxes paid	3, 233	Deposits of State, county, and municipal disbursing officers	....
Gold coins			
Gold certificates			
Silver coins	142, 778	Due to other banks and bankers	105, 905
Silver certificates		Other liabilities	14, 000
Legal tenders and national-bank notes			
Other resources	....		
Total	3, 327, 719	Total	3, 327, 719

CONNECTICUT.

October 1, 1886.] [8 banks.

Resources.		Liabilities.	
Loans on real estate	$4, 546, 407	Capital stock paid in	$2, 390, 000
Loans on personal and collateral security	....	Surplus fund	497, 598
Other loans and discounts	....	Other undivided profits	....
Overdrafts	....		
U. S. bonds	....	State-bank notes outstanding	19, 286
State bonds	206, 864		
R. R. bonds and stocks	320, 972	Dividends unpaid	....
Bank stocks	3, 800		
Other stocks, bonds, and mortgages	....	Individual deposits	3, 407, 182
Due from other banks and bankers	937, 685	State, county, and municipal deposits	....
Real estate, furniture, and fixtures	232, 127		
Current expenses and taxes paid	....	Deposits of State, county, and municipal disbursing officers	....
Gold coins			
Gold certificates			
Silver coins	552, 445	Due to other banks and bankers	486, 294
Silver certificates		Other liabilities	....
Legal tenders and national-bank notes			
Other resources	....		
Total	6, 800, 360	Total	6, 800, 360

STATE BANKS—OFFICIAL.

NEW YORK.

June 4, 1887.] [71 banks.

Resources.		Liabilities.	
Loans on real estate	....	Capital stock paid in	$8,428,000
Loans on personal and collateral security	....	Surplus fund	2,077,764
Other loans and discounts	$44,049,244	Other undivided profits	3,157,311
Overdrafts	80,227		
U. S. bonds	....	State-bank notes outstanding	5,470
State bonds	....		
R. R. bonds and stocks	....	Dividends unpaid	....
Bank stocks	....		
Other stocks, bonds, and mortgages	2,438,777	Individual deposits	37,688,748
Due from other banks and bankers	5,510,298	State, county, and municipal deposits	....
Real estate, furniture, and fixtures	794,695		
Current expenses and taxes paid	180,941	Deposits of State, county, and municipal disbursing officers	2,000
Checks and other cash items	876,449		
Gold coins			
Gold certificates	660,943	Due to other banks and bankers	3,061,954
Silver coins		Other liabilities	1,906,324
Silver certificates			
Legal tenders and national-bank notes	1,605,740		
Other resources	130,257		
Total	56,327,571	Total	56,327,571

NEW YORK CITY.

June 4, 1887.] [31 banks.

Resources.		Liabilities.	
Loans on real estate	....	Capital stock paid in	$14,712,700
Loans on personal and collateral security	....	Surplus fund	5,141,937
Other loans and discounts	$80,698,086	Other undivided profits	3,795,694
Overdrafts	22,094		
U. S. bonds	....	State-bank notes outstanding	2,605
State bonds	....		
R. R. bonds and stocks	....	Dividends unpaid	....
Bank stocks	....		
Other stocks, bonds, and mortgages	1,867,915	Individual deposits	112,699,172
Due from other banks and bankers	6,389,106	State, county, and municipal deposits	....
Real estate, furniture, and fixtures	2,214,526		
Current expenses and taxes paid	381,881	Deposits of State, county, and municipal disbursing officers	86,193
Checks and other cash items	37,484,131		
Gold coins			
Gold certificates	11,508,025	Due to other banks and bankers	8,045,360
Silver coins		Other liabilities	816,937
Silver certificates			
Legal tenders and national-bank notes	4,624,403		
Other resources	110,401		
Total	145,300,598	Total	145,300,598

NEW JERSEY.

December 31, 1886.] [8 banks.

Resources.		Liabilities.	
Loans on real estate	....	Capital stock paid in	$1,209,350
Loans on personal and collateral security	....	Surplus fund	332,333
Other loans and discounts	$3,340,181	Other undivided profits	159,785
Overdrafts	216		
U. S. bonds	88,700	State-bank notes outstanding	....
State bonds	....		
R. R. bonds and stocks	....	Dividends unpaid	14,435
Bank stocks	21,700		
Other stocks, bonds, and mortgages	408,795	Individual deposits	3,284,201
Due from other banks and bankers	526,576	State, county, and municipal deposits	....
Real estate, furniture, and fixtures	123,719		
Current expenses and taxes paid	12,532	Deposits of State, county, and municipal disbursing officers	....
Gold coins			
Gold certificates			
Silver coins	295,849	Due to other banks and bankers	103,247
Silver certificates		Other liabilities	30,479
Legal tenders and national-bank notes			
Other resources	321,564		
Total	5,139,832	Total	5,139,832

STATE BANKS—OFFICIAL.

PENNSYLVANIA.

November —, 1886.] [80 banks.

Resources.		Liabilities.	
Loans on real estate	$24,079,175	Capital stock paid in	$7,888,473
Loans on personal and collateral security	....	Surplus fund	1,857,204
Other loans and discounts	....	Other undivided profits	805,336
Overdrafts	....		
U. S. bonds	738,007	State-bank notes outstanding	71,066
State bonds	....		
R. R. bonds and stocks	....	Dividends unpaid	....
Bank stocks	....		
Other stocks, bonds, and mortgages	5,073,996	Individual deposits	29,117,308
Due from other banks and bankers	4,517,022	State, county, and municipal deposits	....
Real estate, furniture, and fixtures	2,929,561		
Current expenses and taxes paid	196,660	Deposits of State, county, and municipal disbursing officers	....
Gold coin Gold certificates Silver coin Silver certificates	943,123	Due to other banks and bankers Other liabilities	572,629 456,928
Legal tenders and national-bank notes	1,840,675		
Other resources	450,785		
Total	40,769,004	Total	40,769,004

MARYLAND.

July and September, 1887.] [8 banks.

Loans on real estate	....	Capital stock paid in	$1,979,390
Loans on personal and collateral security	$1,331,302	Surplus fund	335,000
Other loans and discounts	3,170,772	Other undivided profits	125,072
Overdrafts	2,057		
U. S. bonds	55,000	State-bank notes outstanding	69
State bonds	204,487		
R. R. bonds and stocks	....	Dividends unpaid	43,016
Bank stocks	29,010		
Other stocks, bonds, and mortgages	317,372	Individual deposits	3,799,136
Due from other banks and bankers	357,695	State, county, and municipal deposits	....
Real estate, furniture, and fixtures	434,168		
Current expenses and taxes paid	12,105	Deposits of State, county, and municipal disbursing officers	....
Gold coins Gold certificates Silver coins Silver certificates Legal tenders and national-bank notes	522,450	Due to other banks and bankers Other liabilities	106,629 48,510
Other resources	305		
Total	6,436,822	Total	6,436,822

NORTH CAROLINA.

June 30, 1887.] [11 banks.

Loans on real estate	$160,636	Capital stock paid in	$691,410
Loans on personal and collateral security	....	Surplus fund	173,503
Other loans and discounts	1,511,825	Other undivided profits	55,203
Overdrafts	48,750		
U. S. bonds	....	State-bank notes outstanding	....
State bonds	31,000		
R. R. bonds and stocks	....	Dividends unpaid	4,080
Bank stocks	....		
Other stocks, bonds, and mortgages	70,450	Individual deposits	1,424,785
Due from other banks and bankers	106,383	State, county, and municipal deposits	....
Real estate, furniture, and fixtures	119,321		
Current expenses and taxes paid	14,456	Deposits of State, county, and municipal disbursing officers	....
Gold coins	47,245		
Gold certificates	....		
Silver coins	37,164	Due to other banks and bankers	61,273
Silver certificates	....	Other liabilities	64,626
Legal tenders and national-bank notes	183,428		
Other resources	54,222		
Total	2,474,880	Total	2,474,880

STATE BANKS—OFFICIAL.

GEORGIA.*

June 30, 1887.] [25 banks.

Resources.		Liabilities.	
Loans on real estate	$11,550	Capital stock paid in	$10,295,840
Loans on personal and collateral security	380,702	Surplus fund	1,334,268
Other loans and discounts	9,460,083	Other undivided profits	229,404
Overdrafts	12,649		
U. S. bonds	....	State-bank notes outstanding	....
State bonds	....		
R. R. bonds and stocks	....	Dividends unpaid	43,271
Bank stocks	....		
Other stocks, bonds, and mortgages	6,971,614	Individual deposits	6,393,906
Due from other banks and bankers	1,020,958	State, county, and municipal deposits	21,146
Real estate, furniture, and fixtures	575,973		
Current expenses and taxes paid	72,129	Deposits of State, county, and municipal disbursing officers	21,891
Gold coins, Gold certificates, Silver coins, Silver certificates, Legal tenders and national-bank notes	1,458,058	Due to other banks and bankers	1,564,872
		Other liabilities	1,218,135
Other resources	1,159,160		
Add for cents	71	Add for cents	34
Total	21,122,947	Total	21,122,947

* This report is not included in any summary, having been received after the other statistics were in type. Much of the information, however, is duplicated in unofficial reports and tables.

KENTUCKY.

June 30, 1887.] [71 banks.

Resources.		Liabilities.	
Loans on real estate	$146,571	Capital stock paid in	$11,555,686
Loans on personal and collateral security	1,921,309	Surplus fund	2,073,500
Other loans and discounts	18,781,392	Other undivided profits	817,827
Overdrafts	46,635		
U. S. bonds	....	State-bank notes outstanding	35,976
State bonds	52,850		
R. R. bonds and stocks	28,000	Dividends unpaid	281,740
Bank stocks	....		
Other stocks, bonds, and mortgages	1,119,556	Individual deposits	16,852,350
Due from other banks and bankers	3,108,133	State, county, and municipal deposits	....
Real estate, furniture, and fixtures	805,540		
Current expenses and taxes paid	26,930	Deposits of State, county, and municipal disbursing officers	....
Gold coins, Gold certificates, Silver coins, Silver certificates, Legal tenders and national-bank notes	2,641,821	Due to other banks and bankers	1,106,945
		Other liabilities	484,310
Other resources	4,529,597		
Total	33,208,334	Total	33,208,334

OHIO.

April 7, 1887.] [46 banks.

Resources.		Liabilities.	
Loans on real estate	$2,063,993	Capital stock paid in	$3,079,605
Loans on personal and collateral security	....	Surplus fund	385,500
Other loans and discounts	7,587,217	Other undivided profits	200,353
Overdrafts	44,915		
U. S. bonds	230,769	State-bank notes outstanding	....
State bonds	....		
R. R. bonds and stocks	....	Dividends unpaid	1,411
Bank stocks	....		
Other stocks, bonds, and mortgages	913,291	Individual deposits	10,314,788
Due from other banks and bankers	1,538,795	State, county, and municipal deposits	....
Real estate, furniture, and fixtures	608,160		
Current expenses and taxes paid	68,592	Deposits of State, county, and municipal disbursing officers	....
Checks and other cash items	391,646		
Gold coins, Gold certificates, Silver coins, Silver certificates	159,012	Due to other banks and bankers	218,200
		Other liabilities	249,688
Legal tenders and national-bank notes	706,003		
Other resources	107,218		
Total	14,449,641	Total	14,449,641

STATE BANKS—OFFICIAL.

INDIANA.

October 31, 1886.] [32 banks.

Resources.		Liabilities.	
Loans on real estate	....	Capital stock paid in	$1,676,000
Loans on personal and collateral security	....	Surplus fund	235,874
Other loans and discounts	$3,434,568	Other undivided profits	143,636
Overdrafts	50,696	State-bank notes outstanding	....
U.S. bonds	....	Dividends unpaid	....
State bonds	....	Individual deposits	3,126,849
R. R. bonds and stocks	....	State, county, and municipal deposits	....
Bank stocks	....	Deposits of State, county, and municipal disbursing officers	....
Other stocks, bonds, and mortgages	101,242	Due to other banks and bankers	23,124
Due from other banks and bankers	801,675	Other liabilities	14,548
Real estate, furniture, and fixtures	224,330		
Current expenses and taxes paid	35,357		
Gold coins; Gold certificates; Silver coins; Silver certificates; Legal tenders and national-bank notes	569,914		
Other resources	2,849		
Total	5,220,631	Total	5,220,631

MICHIGAN.

July 4, 1887.] [62 banks.

Resources.		Liabilities.	
Loans on real estate	$508,591	Capital stock paid in	$4,556,150
Loans on personal and collateral security	27,606	Surplus fund	746,235
Other loans and discounts	23,436,616	Other undivided profits	642,866
Overdrafts	41,837	State-bank notes outstanding	....
U. S. bonds	214,600	Dividends unpaid	29,756
State bonds	528,483	Individual deposits	26,069,050
R. R. bonds and stocks	....	State, county, and municipal deposits	....
Bank stocks	....	Deposits of State, county, and municipal disbursing officers	....
Other stocks, bonds, and mortgages	1,160,985	Due to other banks and bankers	458,281
Due from other banks and bankers	3,669,402	Other liabilities	625,096
Real estate, furniture, and fixtures	499,710		
Current expenses and taxes paid	112,327		
Gold coins; Gold certificates; Silver coins; Silver certificates; Legal tenders and national-bank notes	2,664,713		
Other resources	262,565		
Total	33,127,434	Total	33,127,434

WISCONSIN.

July 4, 1887.] [56 banks.

Resources.		Liabilities.	
Loans on real estate	....	Capital stock paid in	$3,350,340
Loans on personal and collateral security	....	Surplus fund	1,111,523
Other loans and discounts	$16,314,038	Other undivided profits	10,311
Overdrafts	132,256	State-bank notes outstanding	223
U. S. bonds	181,516	Dividends unpaid	1,333
State bonds	1,000	Individual deposits	19,960,417
R. R. bonds and stocks	....	State, county, and municipal deposits	....
Bank stocks	....	Deposits of State, county, and municipal disbursing officers	....
Other stocks, bonds, and mortgages	1,716,468	Due to other banks and bankers	1,282,354
Due from other banks and bankers	4,210,455	Other liabilities	22,257
Real estate, furniture, and fixtures	496,414		
Current expenses and taxes paid	25,428		
Gold coins; Gold certificates; Silver coins; Silver certificates; Legal tenders and national-bank notes	2,656,852		
Other resources	4,331		
Total	25,738,758	Total	25,738,758

STATE BANKS—OFFICIAL.

IOWA.

June 30, 1887.] [65 banks.

Resources.		Liabilities.	
Loans on real estate	....	Capital stock paid in	$3,579,843
Loans on personal and collateral security	....	Surplus fund	441,982
Other loans and discounts	$7,444,217	Other undivided profits	252,817
Overdrafts	186,166		
U. S. bonds	....	State-bank notes outstanding	....
State bonds	....		
R. R. bonds and stocks	....	Dividends unpaid	....
Bank stocks	....		
Other stocks, bonds, and mortgages	....	Individual deposits	5,747,286
Due from other banks and bankers	1,413,227	State, county, and municipal deposits	....
Real estate, furniture, and fixtures	545,905		
Current expenses and taxes paid	....	Deposits of State, county, and municipal disbursing officers	....
Gold coins	}		
Gold certificates	}		
Silver coins	} 674,036	Due to other banks and bankers	254,378
Silver certificates	}	Other liabilities	....
Legal tenders and national-bank notes.	}		
Other resources	12,755		
Total	10,276,306	Total	10,276,306

MINNESOTA.

July 23, 1887.] [54 banks.

Loans on real estate	....	Capital stock paid in	$5,228,000
Loans on personal and collateral security	....	Surplus fund	691,587
Other loans and discounts	$15,439,215	Other undivided profits	501,538
Overdrafts	99,161		
U. S. bonds	21,550	State-bank notes outstanding	....
State bonds	....		
R. R. bonds and stocks	....	Dividends unpaid	12,544
Bank stocks	....		
Other stocks, bonds, and mortgages	948,445	Individual deposits	14,429,516
Due from other banks and bankers	2,434,323	State, county, and municipal deposits	....
Real estate, furniture, and fixtures	835,374		
Current expenses and taxes paid	69,848	Deposits of State, county, and municipal disbursing officers	....
Gold coins	213,657		
Gold certificates	....		
Silver coins	119,672	Due to other banks and bankers	778,670
Silver certificates	....	Other liabilities	367,657
Legal tenders and national-bank notes.	1,539,572		
Other resources	288,605		
Total	22,009,512	Total	22,009,512

MISSOURI.

May 14, 1887.] [212 banks.

Loans on real estate	$2,602,527	Capital stock paid in	$11,626,403
Loans on personal and collateral security	41,101,608	Surplus fund	6,596,349
Other loans and discounts	5,603	Other undivided profits	....
Overdrafts	593,573		
U. S. bonds	758,971	State-bank notes outstanding	....
State bonds	....		
R. R. bonds and stocks	....	Dividends unpaid	75,428
Bank stocks	....		
Other stocks, bonds, and mortgages	4,008,958	Individual deposits	49,173,704
Due from other banks and bankers	8,068,591	State, county, and municipal deposits	....
Real estate, furniture, and fixtures	2,086,539		
Current expenses and taxes paid	734	Deposits of State, county, and municipal disbursing officers	....
Checks and other cash items	2,121,911		
Gold coins	1,158,329		
Gold certificates	....	Due to other banks and bankers	6,310,267
Silver coins	270,883	Other liabilities	288,860
Silver certificates	....		
Legal tenders and national-bank notes.	7,383,676		
Other resources	3,958,117		
Total	74,180,011	Total	74,180,011

STATE BANKS—OFFICIAL.

CALIFORNIA.

July 1, 1887.] [28 banks.

Resources.		Liabilities.	
Loans on real estate	$13, 508, 018	Capital stock paid in	$31, 061, 935
Loans on personal and collateral security	34, 653, 984	Surplus fund	11, 402, 287
Other loans and discounts	17, 905, 633	Other undivided profits	....
Overdrafts	....		
U. S. bonds	....	State-bank notes outstanding	....
State bonds	....		
R. R. bonds and stocks	....	Dividends unpaid	....
Bank stocks	....		
Other stocks, bonds, and mortgages	2, 378, 217	Individual deposits	52, 513, 971
Due from other banks and bankers	10, 335, 401	State, county, and municipal deposits	....
Real estate, furniture, and fixtures	3, 188, 231		
Current expenses and taxes paid	....	Deposits of State, county, and municipal disbursing officers	....
Gold coins			
Gold certificates	} 15, 579, 208		
Silver coins		Due to other banks and bankers	5, 872, 134
Silver certificates		Other liabilities	514, 343
Legal tenders and national-bank notes	....		
Other resources	3, 725, 798		
Total	101, 364, 670	Total	101, 364, 670

AGGREGATE RESOURCES AND LIABILITIES OF 914 STATE BANKS IN THE UNITED STATES

Loans on real estate	$23, 653, 410	Capital stock paid in	$114,830,660
Loans on personal and collateral security	70, 141, 632	Surplus fund	34, 115, 460
Other loans and discounts	269, 897, 676	Other undivided profits	10, 828, 524
Overdrafts	1, 348, 583		
U. S. bonds	2, 202, 913	State-bank notes outstanding	138, 973
State bonds	1, 029, 683		
R. R. bonds and stocks	351, 472	Dividends unpaid	473, 416
Bank stocks	56, 910		
Other stocks, bonds, and mortgages	22, 052, 256	Individual deposits	390, 821, 088
Due from other banks and bankers	54, 184, 825	State, county, and municipal deposits	....
Real estate, furniture, and fixtures	16, 365, 170		
Current expenses and taxes paid	1, 141, 024	Deposits of State, county, and municipal disbursing officers	88, 193
Gold coins			
Gold certificates			
Silver coins	} 100,182,861	Due to other banks and bankers	28, 949, 795
Silver certificates		Other liabilities	6, 011, 165
Legal tenders and national-bank notes			
Other resources	13, 950, 459		
Total	586, 257, 874	Total	586, 257, 874

STATE BANKS—UNOFFICIAL.

DELAWARE.

June 30, 1887.] [2 banks.

Resources.		Liabilities.	
Loans on real estate	$124,550	Capital stock paid in	$356,000
Loans on personal and collateral security	....	Surplus fund	41,558
Other loans and discounts	721,337	Other undivided profits	9,585
Overdrafts	....		
U. S. bonds	....	State-bank notes outstanding	....
State bonds	....		
R. R. bonds and stocks	....	Dividends unpaid	....
Bank stocks	2,506		
Other stocks, bonds, and mortgages	....	Individual deposits	407,427
Due from other banks and bankers	91,847	State, county, and municipal deposits	....
Real estate, furniture, and fixtures	25,828		
Current expenses and taxes paid	448	Deposits of State, county, and municipal disbursing officers	....
Gold coins			
Gold certificates			
Silver coins	39,104	Due to other banks and bankers	73,924
Silver certificates		Other liabilities	38,530
Legal tenders and national-bank notes			
Other resources	11,314		
Total	1,017,024	Total	1,017,024

VIRGINIA.

June 30, 1887.] [39 banks.

Resources.		Liabilities.	
Loans on real estate	$633,446	Capital stock paid in	$1,000,255
Loans on personal and collateral security	3,548,348	Surplus fund	451,588
Other loans and discounts	1,669,296	Other undivided profits	199,125
Overdrafts	94,903		
U. S. bonds	20,000	State-bank notes outstanding	....
State bonds	189,409		
R. R. bonds and stocks	276,810	Dividends unpaid	14,187
Bank stocks	83,821		
Other stocks, bonds, and mortgages	485,236	Individual deposits	5,056,769
Due from other banks and bankers	894,581	State, county, and municipal deposits	17,787
Real estate, furniture, and fixtures	149,460		
Current expenses and taxes paid	52,670	Deposits of State, county, and municipal disbursing officers	28,832
Gold coins			
Gold certificates			
Silver coins	582,058	Due to other banks and bankers	117,005
Silver certificates		Other liabilities	38,748
Legal tenders and national-bank notes			
Other resources	44,258		
Total	8,724,296	Total	8,724,296

WEST VIRGINIA.

June 30, 1887.] [14 banks.

Resources.		Liabilities.	
Loans on real estate	$59,220	Capital stock paid in	$810,855
Loans on personal and collateral security	3,092,776	Surplus fund	246,739
Other loans and discounts	96,654	Other undivided profits	57,430
Overdrafts	5,112		
U. S. bonds	800	State-bank notes outstanding	13,791
State bonds	....		
R. R. bonds and stocks	101,900	Dividends unpaid	30,190
Bank stocks	....		
Other stocks, bonds, and mortgages	115,935	Individual deposits	2,807,123
Due from other banks and bankers	368,681	State, county, and municipal deposits	....
Real estate, furniture, and fixtures	156,888		
Current expenses and taxes paid	9,957	Deposits of State, county, and municipal disbursing officers	7,188
Gold coins			
Gold certificates			
Silver coins	291,786	Due to other banks and bankers	215,540
Silver certificates		Other liabilities	35,114
Legal tenders and national-bank notes			
Other resources	23,261		
Total	4,322,970	Total	4,322,970

STATE BANKS—UNOFFICIAL.

SOUTH CAROLINA.

June 30, 1887.] [10 banks.

Resources.		Liabilities.	
Loans on real estate	$618,003	Capital stock paid in	$788,704
Loans on personal and collateral security	1,566,594	Surplus fund	137,412
Other loans and discounts	624,530	Other undivided profits	228,355
Overdrafts	10,490		
U. S. bonds	50,000	State-bank notes outstanding	....
State bonds	....		
R. R. bonds and stocks	....	Dividends unpaid	153
Bank stocks	....		
Other stocks, bonds, and mortgages	1,872,307	Individual deposits	4,121,254
Due from other banks and bankers	242,410	State, county, and municipal deposits	....
Real estate, furniture, and fixtures	123,055		
Current expenses and taxes paid	16,515	Deposits of State, county, and municipal disbursing officers	4,751
Gold coins			
Gold certificates			
Silver coins	279,212	Due to other banks and bankers	112,656
Silver certificates		Other liabilities	10,005
Legal tenders and national-bank notes			
Other resources	18		
Total	5,403,200	Total	5,403,200

GEORGIA.

June 30, 1887.] [16 banks.

Loans on real estate	$114,402	Capital stock paid in	$2,738,850
Loans on personal and collateral security	3,969,921	Surplus fund	946,011
Other loans and discounts	3,825,806	Other undivided profits	310,901
Overdrafts	118,177		
U. S. bonds	....	State-bank notes outstanding	....
State bonds	7,570		
R. R. bonds and stocks	12,000	Dividends unpaid	28,024
Bank stocks	19,600		
Other stocks, bonds, and mortgages	722,002	Individual deposits	4,958,305
Due from other banks and bankers	496,308	State, county, and municipal deposits	70,119
Real estate, furniture, and fixtures	307,352		
Current expenses and taxes paid	31,113	Deposits of State, county, and municipal disbursing officers	....
Gold coins			
Gold certificates			
Silver coins	1,045,316	Due to other banks and bankers	1,280,681
Silver certificates		Other liabilities	512,337
Legal tenders and national-bank notes			
Other resources	124,721		
Total	10,854,378	Total	10,854,378

FLORIDA.

June 30, 1887.] [6 banks.

Loans on real estate	$48,030	Capital stock paid in	$290,100
Loans on personal and collateral security	744,832	Surplus fund	230,578
Other loans and discounts	28,672	Other undivided profits	137,012
Overdrafts	20,921		
U. S. bonds	....	State-bank notes outstanding	....
State bonds	15,000		
R. R. bonds and stocks	150	Dividends unpaid	250
Bank stocks	....		
Other stocks, bonds, and mortgages	32,800	Individual deposits	830,108
Due from other banks and bankers	149,701	State, county, and municipal deposits	....
Real estate, furniture, and fixtures	395,902		
Current expenses and taxes paid	6,512	Deposits of State, county, and municipal disbursing officers	005
Gold coin			
Gold certificates			
Silver coins	134,307	Due to other banks and bankers	39,134
Silver certificates		Other liabilities	70,005
Legal tenders and national-bank notes			
Other resources	30,085		
Total	1,613,032	Total	1,613,032

STATE BANKS—UNOFFICIAL.

ALABAMA.

June 30, 1887.] [7 banks.

Resources.		Liabilities.	
Loans on real estate	....	Capital stock paid in	$735,000
Loans on personal and collateral security	$524,918	Surplus fund	158,840
Other loans and discounts	1,150,098	Other undivided profits	69,302
Overdrafts	48,824		
U. S. bonds	....	State-bank notes outstanding	....
State bonds	1,030		
R. R. bonds and stocks	13,953	Dividends unpaid	491
Bank stocks	....		
Other stocks, bonds, and mortgages	44,527	Individual deposits	934,206
Due from other banks and bankers	225,661	State, county, and municipal deposits	....
Real estate, furniture, and fixtures	131,880		
Current expenses and taxes paid	24,695	Deposits of State, county, and municipal disbursing officers	1,852
Gold coins			
Gold certificates			
Silver coins	221,900	Due to other banks and bankers	35,107
Silver certificates		Other liabilities	406,471
Legal tenders and national-bank notes			
Other resources	13,958		
Total	2,401,389	Total	2,401,369

MISSISSIPPI.

June 30, 1887.] [9 banks.

Resources.		Liabilities.	
Loans on real estate	$59,500	Capital stock paid in	$759,050
Loans on personal and collateral security	423,473	Surplus fund	29,044
Other loans and discounts	704,147	Other undivided profits	68,490
Overdrafts	41,358		
U. S. bonds	....	State-bank notes outstanding	....
State bonds	31,290		
R. R. bonds and stocks	1,200	Dividends unpaid	50
Bank stocks	....		
Other stocks, bonds, and mortgages	84,062	Individual deposits	1,102,906
Due from other banks and bankers	308,688	State, county, and municipal deposits	10,186
Real estate, furniture, and fixtures	68,508		
Current expenses and taxes paid	16,421	Deposits of State, county, and municipal disbursing officers	....
Gold coins			
Gold certificates			
Silver coins	157,025	Due to other banks and bankers	176,407
Silver certificates		Other liabilities	10,145
Legal tenders and national-bank notes			
Other resources	213,116		
Total	2,168,878	Total	2,168,878

LOUISIANA.

June 30, 1887.] [5 banks.

Resources.		Liabilities.	
Loans on real estate	$473,858	Capital stock paid in	$2,017,300
Loans on personal and collateral security	1,989,590	Surplus fund	200,000
Other loans and discounts	2,705,028	Other undivided profits	288,603
Overdrafts	....		
U. S. bonds	....	State-bank notes outstanding	8,507
State bonds	263,848		
R. R. bonds and stocks	4,770	Dividends unpaid	39,476
Bank stocks	....		
Other stocks, bonds, and mortgages	546,701	Individual deposits	5,660,873
Due from other banks and bankers	81,601	State, county, and municipal deposits	....
Real estate, furniture, and fixtures	228,642		
Current expenses and taxes paid	11,617	Deposits of State, county, and municipal disbursing officers	....
Gold coins			
Gold certificates			
Silver coins	1,914,995	Due to other banks and bankers	266,361
Silver certificates		Other liabilities	5
Legal tenders and national-bank notes			
Other resources	230,055		
Total	8,541,305	Total	8,541,305

STATE BANKS—UNOFFICIAL.

TEXAS.

Jnne 30, 1887.] [9 banks.

Resources.		Liabilities.	
Loans on real estate	$2,656	Capital stock paid in	$761,098
Loans on personal and collateral security	876,087	Surplus fund	88,353
Other loans and discounts	540,584	Other undivided profits	124,408
Overdrafts	25,385		
U. S. bonds	....	State-bank notes outstanding	....
State bonds	....		
R. R. bonds and stocks	....	Dividends unpaid	....
Bank stocks	21,400		
Other stocks, bonds, and mortgages	14,560	Individual deposits	976,851
Due from other banks and bankers	230,904	State, county, and municipal deposits	13,400
Real estate, furniture, and fixtures	132,230		
Current expenses and taxes paid	14,670	Deposits of State, county, and municipal disbursing officers	1,863
Gold coins, Gold certificates, Silver coins, Silver certificates, Legal tenders and national-bank notes	380,791	Due to other banks and bankers	74,110
		Other liabilities	220,203
Other resources	21,208		
Total	2,260,475	Total	2,260,475

ARKANSAS.

Jnne 30, 1887.] [6 banks.

Loans on real estate	$75,276	Capital stock paid in	$265,000
Loans on personal and collateral security	407,772	Surplus fund	44,244
Other loans and discounts	13,000	Other undivided profits	7,180
Overdrafts	14,342		
U. S. bonds	9,000	State-bank notes outstanding	....
State bonds	53,551		
R. R. bonds and stocks	....	Dividends unpaid	....
Bank stocks	4,000		
Other stocks, bonds, and mortgages	28,281	Individual deposits	593,264
Due from other banks and bankers	203,153	State, county, and municipal deposits	....
Real estate, furniture, and fixtures	28,023		
Current expenses and taxes paid	2,138	Deposits of State, county, and municipal disbursing officers	52,391
Gold coins, Gold certificates, Silver coins, Silver certificates, Legal tenders and national-bank notes	128,168	Due to other banks and bankers	3,650
		Other liabilities	1,000
Other resources	34		
Total	966,738	Total	966,738

TENNESSEE.

June 30, 1887.] [27 banks.

Loans on real estate	$98,141	Capital stock paid in	$2,924,254
Loans on personal and collateral security	4,754,492	Surplus fund	153,087
Other loans and discounts	1,439,055	Other undivided profits	479,701
Overdrafts	232,951		
U. S. bonds	4,793	State-bank notes outstanding	....
State bonds	679		
R. R. bonds and stocks	47,374	Dividends unpaid	17,498
Bank stocks	49,053		
Other stocks, bonds, and mortgages	418,708	Individual deposits	5,590,552
Due from other banks and bankers	1,095,163	State, county, and municipal deposits	3,922
Real estate, furniture, and fixtures	221,612		
Current expenses and taxes paid	51,392	Deposits of State, county, and municipal disbursing officers	12,960
Gold coins, Gold certificates, Silver coins, Silver certificates, Legal tenders and national-bank notes	1,050,786	Due to other banks and bankers	302,561
		Other liabilities	126,916
Other resources	140,352		
Total	9,612,351	Total	9,612,351

STATE BANKS—UNOFFICIAL.

ILLINOIS.

June 30, 1887.] [48 banks.

Resources.		Liabilities.	
Loans on real estate	$594,014	Capital stock paid in	$1,055,500
Loans on personal and collateral security	4,165,881	Surplus fund	676,927
Other loans and discounts	833,465	Other undivided profits	213,568
Overdrafts	105,211		
U. S. bonds	138,285	State-bank notes outstanding	....
State bonds	7,100		
R. R. bonds and stocks	1,000	Dividends unpaid	116,277
Bank stocks	74,975		
Other stocks, bonds, and mortgages	223,234	Individual deposits	5,178,069
Due from other banks and bankers	1,420,245	State, county, and municipal deposits	660,640
Real estate, furniture, and fixtures	430,744	Deposits of State, county, and municipal disbursing officers	85,805
Current expenses and taxes paid	20,470		
Gold coins; Gold certificates; Silver coins; Silver certificates; Legal tenders and national-bank notes	921,557	Due to other banks and bankers	228,096
		Other liabilities	172,624
Other resources	51,325		
Total	8,906,506	Total	8,906,506

KANSAS.

June 30, 1887.] [149 banks.

Resources.		Liabilities.	
Loans on real estate	$1,442,835	Capital stock paid in	$6,618,545
Loans on personal and collateral security	8,338,434	Surplus fund	490,117
Other loans and discounts	1,613,426	Other undivided profits	880,004
Overdrafts	184,098		
U. S. bonds	14,365	State-bank notes outstanding	20,005
State bonds	7,457		
R. R. bonds and stocks	....	Dividends unpaid	18,121
Bank stocks	43,800		
Other stocks, bonds, and mortgages	401,358	Individual deposits	9,151,026
Due from other banks and bankers	2,603,194	State, county, and municipal deposits	165,117
Real estate, furniture, and fixtures	904,562	Deposits of State, county, and municipal disbursing officers	210,054
Current expenses and taxes paid	570,135		
Gold coins; Gold certificates; Silver coins; Silver certificates; Legal tenders and national-bank notes	2,383,193	Due to other banks and bankers	345,834
		Other liabilities	878,915
Other resources	274,571		
Total	18,787,428	Total	18,787,428

NEBRASKA.

June 30, 1887.] [140 banks.

Resources.		Liabilities.	
Loans on real estate	$1,007,453	Capital stock paid in	$2,864,000
Loans on personal and collateral security	4,937,864	Surplus fund	340,922
Other loans and discounts	360,082	Other undivided profits	455,075
Overdrafts	112,021		
U. S. bonds	....	State-bank notes outstanding	38,500
State bonds	25,376		
R. R. bonds and stocks	100	Dividends unpaid	11,230
Bank stocks	24,600		
Other stocks, bonds, and mortgages	67,860	Individual deposits	4,830,206
Due from other banks and bankers	1,326,092	State, county, and municipal deposits	147,581
Real estate, furniture, and fixtures	672,056	Deposits of State, county, and municipal disbursing officers	....
Current expenses and taxes paid	118,848		
Gold coins; Gold certificates; Silver coins; Silver certificates; Legal tenders and national-bank notes	601,867	Due to other banks and bankers	173,315
		Other liabilities	465,938
Other resources	76,323		
Total	9,333,443	Total	9,333,442

STATE BANKS—UNOFFICIAL.

COLORADO.

June 30, 1887.] [8 banks.

Resources.		Liabilities.	
Loans on real estate	$214, 693	Capital stock paid in	$505, 000
Loans on personal and collateral security	1, 532, 677	Surplus fund	83, 778
Other loans and discounts	4, 875	Other undivided profits	84, 777
Overdrafts	30, 717	State-bank notes outstanding	....
U. S. bonds	....		
State bonds	10, 410	Dividends unpaid	....
R. R. bonds and stocks	....		
Bank stocks	....	Individual deposits	2, 270, 135
Other stocks, bonds, and mortgages	153	State, county, and municipal deposits	28, 258
Due from other banks and bankers	808, 987	Deposits of State, county, and municipal disbursing officers	1, 887
Real estate, furniture, and fixtures	50, 057	Due to other banks and bankers	42, 178
Current expenses and taxes paid	18, 604	Other liabilities	115, 000
Gold coins			
Gold certificates			
Silver coins	461, 273		
Silver certificates			
Legal tenders and national-bank notes			
Other resources	7, 565		
Total	3, 140, 013	Total	3, 140, 013

OREGON.

June 30, 1887.] [4 banks.

Loans on real estate	$47, 736	Capital stock paid in	$170, 000
Loans on personal and collateral security	179, 541	Surplus fund	15, 162
Other loans and discounts	12, 333	Other undivided profits	10, 261
Overdrafts	1, 611	State-bank notes outstanding	....
U. S. bonds	....		
State bonds	....	Dividends unpaid	377
R. R. bonds and stocks	....		
Bank stocks	....	Individual deposits	173, 390
Other stocks, bonds, and mortgages	....	State, county, and municipal deposits	....
Due from other banks and bankers	42, 210	Deposits of State, county, and municipal disbursing officers	....
Real estate, furniture, and fixtures	22, 193	Due to other banks and bankers	....
Current expenses and taxes paid	1, 443	Other liabilities	2, 266
Gold coins			
Gold certificates			
Silver coins	60, 309		
Silver certificates			
Legal tenders and national-bank notes			
Other resources	4, 020		
Total	371, 456	Total	371, 456

AGGREGATE RESOURCES AND LIABILITIES OF 499 STATE BANKS IN THE UNITED STATES.

Loans on real estate	$5, 613, 963	Capital stock paid in	$26, 169, 717
Loans on personal and collateral security	41, 053, 200	Surplus fund	4, 404, 260
Other loans and discounts	16, 494, 483	Other undivided profits	3, 023, 966
Overdrafts	1, 047, 027		
U. S. bonds	237, 243	State-bank notes outstanding	89, 983
State bonds	612, 720		
R. R. bonds and stocks	459, 257	Dividends unpaid	276, 333
Bank stocks	324, 555		
Other stocks, bonds and mortgages	5, 057, 846	Individual deposits	55, 738, 334
Due from other banks and bankers	10, 590, 056	State, county, and municipal deposits	1, 132, 109
Real estate, furniture, and fixtures	4, 109, 932		
Current expenses and taxes paid	982, 648	Deposits of State, county, and municipal disbursing officers	408, 278
Gold coins			
Gold certificates			
Silver coins	10, 662, 857	Due to other banks and bankers	3, 495, 619
Silver certificates		Other liabilities	3, 185, 372
Legal tenders and national-bank notes			
Other resources	1, 278, 184		
Total	98, 523, 971	Total	98, 523, 971

STATE BANKS—OFFICIAL AND UNOFFICIAL.*

AGGREGATE RESOURCES AND LIABILITIES OF STATE BANKS FROM 1882 TO 1887.

Resources and liabilities.	1882–'83.	1883–'84.	1884–'85.	1885–'86.	1886–'87.
	754 banks.	817 banks.	975 banks.	849 banks.	1,413 banks.
Resources.					
Loans on real estate					$29,207,373
Loans on pers'l and collat'l security	$322,358,227	$331,049,510	$347,880,520	$331,183,626	120,194,832
Other loans and discounts					286,302,150
Overdrafts	1,392,061	1,262,725	1,349,998	1,169,388	2,305,610
U. S. bonds	5,287,606	2,337,705	2,904,806	4,302,421	2,530,150
State, county, and municipal bonds					1,642,403
R. R. bonds and stocks	22,083,304	31,452,019	32,644,859	27,194,093	810,729
Bank stocks					381,465
Other stocks, bonds, and mortgages					27,710,102
Due from other banks and bankers	58,709,516	48,836,089	50,002,405	49,747,429	64,774,881
Real estate, furniture, and fixtures	13,593,791	15,058,411	15,873,312	14,605,853	20,475,102
Current expenses and taxes paid	918,403	1,025,237	1,130,883	1,047,782	2,123,672
Gold coins					
Gold certificates	17,429,817	25,376,565	29,867,724	24,734,684	
Silver coins					
Silver certificates					110,845,718
Legal tenders and nat'l-bank notes	25,302,316	28,787,615	30,904,221	14,726,940	
Checks and other cash items	35,118,379	28,219,414	25,072,022	51,668,218	
Other resources	9,943,706	7,671,876	5,701,111	8,224,886	15,237,643
Total	512,137,026	521,077,766	553,562,701	528,695,920	684,781,845
Liabilities.					
Capital stock paid in	102,454,801	110,020,351	125,278,240	109,611,596	141,000,377
Surplus fund	23,762,738	31,483,942	30,669,575	27,813,508	38,519,720
Other undivided profits	11,287,623	12,718,894	11,574,736	10,095,760	14,452,490
State-bank notes outstanding	187,978	177,554	98,120	103,430	228,956
Dividends unpaid	442,652	473,785	403,026	430,690	749,749
Individual deposits	334,995,702	325,365,060	344,307,996	342,882,767	446,560,022
State, county, and municipal deposits	....	....	....	....	1,132,109
Deposits of State, county and municipal officers	....	....	....	....	496,471
Due to other banks and bankers	20,651,930	27,125,108	20,950,453	27,800,280	32,445,414
Other liabilities	16,353,542	13,712,513	11,200,706	9,957,880	9,196,537
Total	512,137,026	521,077,766	553,562,701	528,695,920	684,781,845

* Official only, prior to 1886–'87.

LOAN AND TRUST COMPANIES—OFFICIAL.

MAINE.

September 25 and October 5, 1886.] [2 companies.

Resources.		Liabilities.	
Loans on real estate	$107,141	Capital stock paid in	$190,297
Loans on personal and collateral security	15,907	Surplus fund	16,440
Other loans and discounts	398,438	Other undivided profits	17,225
Overdrafts	....		
U. S. bonds	3,516	State-bank notes outstanding	....
State bonds	43,025		
R. R. bonds and stocks	75,931	Dividends unpaid	822
Bank stocks	12,801		
Other stocks, bonds, and mortgages	32,863	Individual deposits	539,161
Due from other banks and bankers	*69,221	State, county, and municipal deposits	....
Real estate, furniture, and fixtures	3,904		
Current expenses and taxes paid	1,108	Deposits of State, county, and municipal disbursing officers	....
Gold coins	....		
Gold certificates	....		
Silver coins	....	Due to other banks and bankers	....
Silver certificates	....	Other liabilities	....
Legal tenders and national-bank notes	....		
Other resources	....		
Total	763,945	Total	763,945

*Includes cash on hand.

NEW HAMPSHIRE.

March 31, 1887.] [1 company.

Loans on real estate	$543,205	Capital stock paid in	$200,000
Loans on personal and collateral security	227,710	Surplus fund	27,350
Other loans and discounts	....	Other undivided profits	23,200
Overdrafts	....		
U. S. bonds	....	State-bank notes outstanding	....
State bonds	2,582		
R. R. bonds and stocks	....	Dividends unpaid	....
Bank stocks	500		
Other stocks, bonds, and mortgages	15,000	Individual deposits	110,084
Due from other banks and bankers	9,058	State, county, and municipal deposits	....
Real estate, furniture, and fixtures	1,929		
Current expenses and taxes paid	....	Deposits of State, county, and municipal disbursing officers	....
Gold coins			
Gold certificates			
Silver coins	} 4,305	Due to other banks and bankers	....
Silver certificates		Other liabilities	400,000
Legal tenders and national-bank notes			
Other resources	30,214		
Total	834,503	Total	834,503

MASSACHUSETTS.

October, November, and December, 1886.] [9 companies.

Loans on real estate	$9,128,260	Capital stock paid in	$4,150,000
Loans on personal and collateral security	....	Surplus fund	415,202
Other loans and discounts	25,172,919	Other undivided profits	659,075
Overdrafts	....		
U. S. bonds	2,438,506	State-bank notes outstanding	....
State bonds	....		
R. R. bonds and stocks	....	Dividends unpaid	194,518
Bank stocks	....		
Other stocks, bonds, and mortgages	7,046,290	Individual deposits	43,972,419
Due from other banks and bankers	805,100	State, county, and municipal deposits	....
Real estate, furniture, and fixtures	830,041		
Current expenses and taxes paid	90,348	Deposits of State, county, and municipal disbursing officers	....
Gold coins			
Gold certificates			
Silver coins	} 4,167,516	Due to other banks and bankers	30,320
Silver certificates		Other liabilities	1,536,917
Legal tenders and national-bank notes			
Other resources	370,471		
Total	50,958,400	Total	50,958,400

LOAN AND TRUST COMPANIES—OFFICIAL.

CONNECTICUT.

October 1, 1886.] [7 companies.

Resources.		Liabilities.	
Loans on real estate	$380,282	Capital stock paid in	$980,600
Loans on personal and collateral security	....	Surplus fund	251,990
Other loans and discounts	2,095,417	Other undivided profits	....
Overdrafts	....		
U. S. bonds	....	State-bank notes outstanding	....
State bonds	....		
R. R. bonds and stocks	....	Dividends unpaid	3,457
Bank stocks	....		
Other stocks, bonds, and mortgages	696,609	Individual deposits	2,820,975
Due from other banks and bankers	674,436	State, county, and municipal deposits	....
Real estate, furniture, and fixtures	294,027		
Current expenses and taxes paid	13,489	Deposits of State, county, and municipal disbursing officers	....
Gold coins			
Gold certificates			
Silver coins	142,307	Due to other banks and bankers	224,545
Silver certificates		Other liabilities	....
Legal tenders and national-bank notes			
Other resources	....		
Total	4,296,567	Total	4,296,567

NEW YORK CITY.

October 1, 1886.] [15 companies.

Resources.		Liabilities.	
Loans on real estate	....	Capital stock paid in	$13,900,000
Loans on personal and collateral security	....	Surplus fund	8,659,852
Other loans and discounts	$104,719,444	Other undivided profits	7,268,965
Overdrafts	1,055		
U. S. bonds	24,454,821	State-bank notes outstanding	....
State bonds	....		
R. R. bonds and stocks	....	Dividends unpaid	278,757
Bank stocks	....		
Other stocks, bonds, and mortgages	19,470,876	Individual deposits	139,348,535
Due from other banks and bankers	11,562,193	State, county, and municipal deposits	....
Real estate, furniture, and fixtures	5,097,550		
Current expenses and taxes paid	8,579	Deposits of State, county, and municipal disbursing officers	....
Gold coins			
Gold certificates			
Silver coins	6,752,751	Due to other banks and bankers	846,149
Silver certificates		Other liabilities	4,379,233
Legal tenders and national-bank notes			
Other resources	1,714,216		
Total	174,681,491	Total	174,681,491

NEW YORK STATE.

October 1, 1886.] [5 companies.

Resources.		Liabilities.	
Loans on real estate	....	Capital stock paid in	$1,431,900
Loans on personal and collateral security	....	Surplus fund	173,358
Other loans and discounts	$9,220,882	Other undivided profits	669,738
Overdrafts	263		
U. S. bonds	1,506,993	State-bank notes outstanding	....
State bonds	....		
R. R. bonds and stocks	....	Dividends unpaid	48,425
Bank stocks	....		
Other stocks, bonds, and mortgages	2,483,617	Individual deposits	12,558,214
Due from other banks and bankers	1,315,317	State, county, and municipal deposits	....
Real estate, furniture, and fixtures	195,134		
Current expenses and taxes paid	....	Deposits of State, county, and municipal disbursing officers	....
Gold coins			
Gold certificates			
Silver coins	149,408	Due to other banks and bankers	35,000
Silver certificates		Other liabilities	26,157
Legal tenders and national-bank notes			
Other resources	71,183		
Total	14,942,792	Total	14,942,792

LOAN AND TRUST COMPANIES—OFFICIAL.

MINNESOTA.

July 23, 1887.] [3 companies.

Resources.		Liabilities.	
Loans on real estate	$908,427	Capital stock paid in	$1,000,000
Loans on personal and collateral security	51,130	Surplus fund	50,000
Other loans and discounts	....	Other undivided profits	75,800
Overdrafts	....		
U. S. bonds	....	State-bank notes outstanding	....
State bonds	....		
R. R. bonds and stocks	....	Dividends unpaid	....
Bank stocks	....		
Other stocks, bonds, and mortgages	2,930	Individual deposits	434,083
Due from other banks and bankers	80,908	State, county, and municipal deposits	....
Real estate, furniture, and fixtures	317,217		
Current expenses and taxes paid	19,104	Deposits of State, county, and municipal disbursing officers	....
Gold coins			
Gold certificates			
Silver coins	2,543	Due to other banks and bankers	....
Silver certificates		Other liabilities	20,000
Legal tenders and national-bank notes			
Other resources	107,505		
Total	1,579,943	Total	1,579,943

AGGREGATE RESOURCES AND LIABILITIES OF 42 LOAN AND TRUST COMPANIES IN THE UNITED STATES.

Resources.		Liabilities.	
Loans on real estate	$11,067,315	Capital stock paid in	$21,858,797
Loans on personal and collateral security	294,756	Surplus fund	9,594,192
Other loans and discounts	141,607,100	Other undivided profits	8,714,132
Overdrafts	1,318		
U. S. bonds	28,403,836	State-bank notes outstanding	....
State bonds	45,607		
R. R. bonds and stocks	75,931	Dividends unpaid	525,970
Bank stocks	13,201		
Other stocks, bonds, and mortgages	30,648,205	Individual deposits	190,799,370
Due from other banks and bankers	14,516,239	State, county, and municipal deposits	....
Real estate, furniture, and fixtures	7,648,811		
Current expenses and taxes paid	132,778	Deposits of State, county, and municipal disbursing officers	....
Gold coins			
Gold certificates			
Silver coins	11,218,823	Due to other banks and bankers	1,136,023
Silver certificates		Other liabilities	6,429,208
Legal tenders and national-bank notes			
Other resources	2,383,681		
Total	248,057,701	Total	248,057,701

LOAN AND TRUST COMPANIES—UNOFFICIAL.

PHILADELPHIA, PA.

June 30, 1887.] [10 companies.

Resources.		Liabilities.	
Loans on real estate	$2,178,174	Capital stock paid in	$12,241,072
Loans on personal and collateral security	30,216,480	Surplus fund	5,988,438
Other loans and discounts	36,728	Other undivided profits	2,536,009
Overdrafts	11,402		
U. S. bonds	383,881	State-bank notes outstanding	....
State bonds	132,541		
R. R. bonds and stocks	7,324,417	Dividends unpaid	35,086
Bank stocks	117,350		
Other stocks, bonds, and mortgages	5,650,108	Individual deposits	40,244,503
Due from other banks and bankers	3,801,031		
Real estate, furniture, and fixtures	3,379,770	State, county, and municipal deposits	38,034
Current expenses and taxes paid	100,098		
Gold coins	860,011	Deposits of State, county, and municipal disbursing officers	....
Gold certificates	....		
Silver coins	....	Due to other banks and bankers	4,308,872
Silver certificates	10,881	Other liabilities	....
Legal tenders and national-bank notes	1,516,281		
Checks and other cash items	3,111,084		
Other resources	469,752		
Total	65,388,054	Total	65,388,054

MISSOURI.

June 30, 1887.] [2 companies.

Resources.		Liabilities.	
Loans on real estate	$881,263	Capital stock paid in	$1,200,000
Loans on personal and collateral security	32,773	Surplus fund	....
Other loans and discounts	1,324,382	Other undivided profits	50,850
Overdrafts	....		
U. S. bonds	....	State-bank notes outstanding	....
State bonds	....		
R. R. bonds and stocks	....	Dividends unpaid	20,100
Bank stocks	....		
Other stocks, bonds, and mortgages	15,188	Individual deposits	42,536
Due from other banks and bankers	316,056		
Real estate, furniture, and fixtures	17,494	State, county, and municipal deposits	....
Current expenses and taxes paid	1,828		
Gold coins		Deposits of State, county, and municipal disbursing officers	....
Gold certificates			
Silver coins	52,465	Due to other banks and bankers	....
Silver certificates		Other liabilities	1,330,520
Legal tenders and national-bank notes			
Other resources	1,747		
Total	2,044,096	Total	2,044,096

NEBRASKA.

June 30, 1887.] [4 companies.

Resources.		Liabilities.	
Loans on real estate	$2,143,241	Capital stock paid in	$1,055,000
Loans on personal and collateral security	....	Surplus fund	250,163
Other loans and discounts	314,609	Other undivided profits	50,535
Overdrafts	....		
U. S. bonds	....	State-bank notes outstanding	....
State bonds	....		
R. R. bonds and stocks	....	Dividends unpaid	....
Bank stocks	2,000		
Other stocks, bonds, and mortgages	115,317	Individual deposits	104,213
Due from other banks and bankers	160,377		
Real estate, furniture, and fixtures	41,101	State, county, and municipal deposits	....
Current expenses and taxes paid	120,805		
Gold coins		Deposits of State, county, and municipal disbursing officers	....
Gold certificates			
Silver coins	34,679	Due to other banks and bankers	107,002
Silver certificates		Other liabilities	1,390,894
Legal tenders and national-bank notes			
Other resources	94,587		
Total	3,035,806	Total	3,035,806

LOAN AND TRUST COMPANIES—UNOFFICIAL.

AGGREGATE RESOURCES AND LIABILITIES OF 16 LOAN AND TRUST COMPANIES IN THE UNITED STATES.

Resources.		Liabilities.	
Loans on real estate	$5,202,078	Capital stock paid in	$14,496,072
Loans on personal and collateral security	36,249,262	Surplus fund	6,247,601
Other loans and discounts	1,675,719	Other undivided profits	2,637,394
Overdrafts	11,492		
U. S. bonds	383,881	State-bank notes outstanding	....
State bonds	132,541		
R. R. bonds and stocks	7,324,417	Dividends unpaid	55,276
Bank stocks	110,350		
Other stocks, bonds, and mortgages	5,780,673	Individual deposits	40,391,311
Due from other banks and bankers	4,270,264	State, county, and municipal deposits	38,084
Real estate, furniture, and fixtures	3,438,461		
Current expenses and taxes paid	800,731	Deposits of State, county, and municipal disbursing officers	....
Gold coins			
Gold certificates			
Silver coins	5,603,401	Due to other banks and bankers	4,470,874
Silver certificates		Other liabilities	2,730,414
Legal tenders and national-bank notes			
Other resources	506,086		
Total	71,067,936	Total	71,067,956

LOAN AND TRUST COMPANIES—OFFICIAL AND UNOFFICIAL.

AGGREGATE RESOURCES AND LIABILITIES OF LOAN AND TRUST COMPANIES FROM 1882 TO 1887.

Resources and liabilities.	1882-'83.	1883-'84.	1884-'85.	1885-'86.	1886-'87.
	34 banks.	35 banks.	40 banks.	42 banks.	58 banks.
Resources.					
Loans on real estate					$16, 269, 993
Loans on pers'l and collat'l security	$140, 022, 358	$158, 018, 000	$141, 542, 049	$156, 828, 458	86, 544, 018
Other loans and discounts					143, 282, 819
Overdrafts	100, 075	367, 749	135, 919	419	12, 810
U. S. bonds	17, 437, 990	23, 371, 084	25, 376, 400	27, 985, 658	28, 787, 717
State, county, and municipal bonds					178, 148
R. R. bonds and stocks	30, 322, 420	27, 879, 858	29, 750, 200	43, 816, 716	7, 400, 348
Bank stocks					132, 651
Other stocks, bonds, and mortgages					36, 428, 878
Due from other banks and bankers	9, 561, 148	16, 517, 457	23, 458, 985	16, 160, 112	18, 795, 503
Real estate, furniture, and fixtures	6, 567, 756	6, 152, 771	8, 759, 201	9, 774, 575	11, 087, 272
Current expenses and taxes paid	213, 183	209, 842	302, 052	664, 407	433, 509
Gold coins					
Gold certificates	825, 483	552, 102	1, 386, 005		
Silver coins					
Silver certificates				19, 644, 510	16, 822, 224
Legal tenders and nat'l-bank notes	2, 956, 753	3, 871, 090	8, 557, 796		
Checks and other cash items	88, 483	88, 802	94, 672		
Other resources	4, 246, 338	2, 841, 937	9, 023, 654	3, 439, 646	2, 049, 767
Total	212, 342, 587	239, 871, 001	248, 380, 683	278, 314, 591	310, 125, 657
Liabilities.					
Capital stock paid in	22, 778, 175	23, 938, 600	26, 428, 600	27, 644, 150	36, 365, 769
Surplus fund	8, 812, 723	10, 101, 544	10, 695, 984	21, 071, 152	15, 841. 791
Other undivided profits	6, 788, 967	9, 619, 067	8, 508, 000	2, 849, 549	11, 351, 526
State-bank notes outstanding	*				
Dividends unpaid	22, 350	25, 283	19, 251	38, 000	581, 255
Individual deposits	165, 378, 515	188, 745, 022	188, 417, 293	214, 063, 415	240, 190, 711
State, county, and municipal deposits					38, 084
Deposits of State, county, and municipal disbursing officers					
Due to other banks and bankers	267, 006	761, 888	197, 803	192, 243	5, 606, 897
Other liabilities	8, 294, 822	6, 580, 388	14, 122, 602	11, 855, 182	9, 159, 622
Total	212, 342, 587	239, 871, 691	248, 380, 683	278, 314, 501	310, 125, 657

SAVINGS BANKS—OFFICIAL.

MAINE.

November 1, 1886.] [54 banks.

Resources.		Liabilities.	
Loans on real estate	$6,113,414	Capital stock paid in	....
Loans on personal and collateral security	....	Surplus fund	$1,429,363
Other loans and discounts	4,760,801	Other undivided profits	770,499
Overdrafts	....		
U. S. bonds	3,207,929	State-bank notes outstanding	....
State bonds	....		
R. R. bonds and stocks	8,215,531	Dividends unpaid	60,204
Bank stocks	1,900,238		
Other stocks, bonds, and mortgages	12,520,728	Individual deposits	37,215,072
Due from other banks and bankers	....	State, county, and municipal deposits	....
Real estate, furniture, and fixtures	1,102,727		
Current expenses and taxes paid	....	Deposits of State, county, and municipal disbursing officers	....
Gold coins			
Gold certificates			
Silver coins	1,063,740	Due to other banks and bankers	....
Silver certificates		Other liabilities	....
Legal tenders and national-bank notes			
Other resources	584,018		
Total	39,475,138	Total	39,475,138

NEW HAMPSHIRE.

March 31, 1887.] [66 banks.

Resources.		Liabilities.	
Loans on real estate	$25,320,509	Capital stock paid in	....
Loans on personal and collateral security	7,382,850	Surplus fund	$4,004,680
Other loans and discounts	....	Other undivided profits	....
Overdrafts	....		
U. S. bonds	463,050	State-bank notes outstanding	....
State bonds	7,063,047		
R. R. bonds and stocks	8,007,584	Dividends unpaid	....
Bank stocks	1,906,815		
Other stocks, bonds, and mortgages	3,707,881	Individual deposits	50,822,702
Due from other banks and bankers	663,062	State, county, and municipal deposits	....
Real estate, furniture, and fixtures	708,724		
Current expenses and taxes paid	....	Deposits of State, county, and municipal disbursing officers	....
Gold coins			
Gold certificates			
Silver coins	220,545	Due to other banks and bankers	....
Silver certificates		Other liabilities	16,604
Legal tenders and national-bank notes			
Other resources	....		
Total	55,444,136	Total	55,444,136

VERMONT.

June 30, 1887.] [28 banks.

Resources.		Liabilities.	
Loans on real estate	$9,714,717	Capital stock paid in	$460,000
Loans on personal and collateral security	1,981,732	Surplus fund	340,900
Other loans and discounts	203,102	Other undivided profits	420,212
Overdrafts	....		
U. S. bonds	201,400	State-bank notes outstanding	....
State bonds	3,151,781		
R. R. bonds and stocks	....	Dividends unpaid	....
Bank stocks	368,208		
Other stocks, bonds, and mortgages	....	Individual deposits	15,587,050
Due from other banks and bankers	625,706	State, county, and municipal deposits	....
Real estate, furniture, and fixtures	218,474		
Current expenses and taxes paid	....	Deposits of State, county, and municipal disbursing officers	....
Gold coins			
Gold certificates			
Silver coins	135,259	Due to other banks and bankers	....
Silver certificates		Other liabilities	50,676
Legal tenders and national-bank notes			
Other resources	213,300		
Total	16,873,838	Total	16,873,838

SAVINGS BANKS—OFFICIAL.

MASSACHUSETTS.

October 30, 1886.] [172 banks.

Resources.		Liabilities.	
Loans on real estate	$112, 208, 878	Capital stock paid in	....
Loans on personal and collateral security	82, 300, 472	Surplus fund	$12, 928, 350
Other loans and discounts	....	Other undivided profits	....
Overdrafts	....	State-bank notes outstanding	....
U. S. bonds	10, 393, 028	Dividends unpaid	....
State bonds	32, 021, 245	Individual deposits	291, 107, 900
R. R. bonds and stocks	17, 224, 908	State, county, and municipal deposits	....
Bank stocks	26, 723, 512	Deposits of State, county, and municipal disbursing officers	....
Other stocks, bonds, and mortgages	....	Due to other banks and bankers	....
Due from other banks and bankers	12, 101, 701	Other liabilities	276, 827
Real estate, furniture, and fixtures	5, 300, 447		
Current expenses and taxes paid	....		
Gold coins, Gold certificates, Silver coins, Silver certificates, Legal tenders and national-bank notes	850, 426		
Other resources	4, 301, 338		
Total	304, 403, 077	Total	304, 403, 077

RHODE ISLAND.

November 6, 1886.] [37 banks.

Resources.		Liabilities.	
Loans on real estate	$22, 030, 587	Capital stock paid in	....
Loans on personal and collateral security	9, 356, 151	Surplus fund	$44, 500
Other loans and discounts	....	Other undivided profits	2, 752, 748
Overdrafts	....	State-bank notes outstanding	....
U. S. bonds	800, 000	Dividends unpaid	....
State bonds	9, 241, 792	Individual deposits	53, 284, 821
R. R. bonds and stocks	7, 362, 844	State, county, and municipal deposits	....
Bank stocks	2, 700, 908	Deposits of State, county, and municipal disbursing officers	....
Other stocks, bonds, and mortgages	93, 200	Due to other banks and bankers	....
Due from other banks and bankers	....	Other liabilities	29, 046
Real estate, furniture, and fixtures	2, 707, 849		
Current expenses and taxes paid	....		
Gold coins, Gold certificates, Silver coins, Silver certificates, Legal tenders and national-bank notes	1, 187, 335		
Other resources	630, 389		
Total	56, 111, 115	Total	56, 111, 115

CONNECTICUT.

October 1, 1886.] [85 banks.

Resources.		Liabilities.	
Loans on real estate	$40, 538, 284	Capital stock paid in	....
Loans on personal and collateral security	3, 481, 725	Surplus fund	$3, 395, 780
Other loans and discounts	6, 489, 075	Other undivided profits	1, 449, 901
Overdrafts	....	State-bank notes outstanding	....
U. S. bonds	3, 116, 542	Dividends unpaid	....
State bonds	16, 082, 995	Individual deposits	97, 424, 820
R. R. bonds and stocks	18, 154, 126	State, county, and municipal deposits	....
Bank stocks	6, 171, 539	Deposits of State, county, and municipal disbursing officers	....
Other stocks, bonds, and mortgages	....	Due to other banks and bankers	....
Due from other banks and bankers	*3, 355, 874	Other liabilities	421, 377
Real estate, furniture, and fixtures	4, 738, 928		
Current expenses and taxes paid	....		
Gold coins	....		
Gold certificates	....		
Silver coins	....		
Silver certificates	....		
Legal tenders and national-bank notes	....		
Other resources	562, 140		
Total	102, 691, 828	Total	102, 691, 828

* Includes cash on hand.

SAVINGS BANKS—OFFICIAL.

NEW YORK.

January 1, 1887.] [115 banks.

Resources.		Liabilities.	
Loans on real estate	$160,072,875	Capital stock paid in	....
Loans on personal and collateral security	14,530,030	Surplus fund	$85,633,320
Other loans and discounts	....	Other undivided profits	....
Overdrafts	....		
U. S. bonds	131,984,410	State-bank notes outstanding	....
State bonds	140,044,704		
R. R. bonds and stocks	....	Dividends unpaid	....
Bank stocks	....		
Other stocks, bonds, and mortgages	....	Individual deposits	482,486,730
Due from other banks and bankers	30,795,122	State, county, and municipal deposits	....
Real estate, furniture, and fixtures	8,034,653		
Current expenses and taxes paid	1,590,967	Deposits of State, county, and municipal disbursing officers	....
Gold coins			
Gold certificates			
Silver coins	5,830,998	Due to other banks and bankers	....
Silver certificates		Other liabilities	160,808
Legal tenders and national-bank notes			
Other resources	92,407,108		
Total	568,280,807	Total	568,280,807

NEW JERSEY.

December 31, 1886.] [25 banks.

Resources.		Liabilities.	
Loans on real estate	$9,570,425	Capital stock paid in	....
Loans on personal and collateral security	1,586,137	Surplus fund	$2,412,877
Other loans and discounts	....	Other undivided profits	....
Overdrafts	....		
U. S. bonds	10,305,382	State-bank notes outstanding	....
State bonds	....		
R. R. bonds and stocks	....	Dividends unpaid	....
Bank stocks	....		
Other stocks, bonds, and mortgages	5,283,653	Individual deposits	27,482,135
Due from other banks and bankers	837,936	State, county, and municipal deposits	....
Real estate, furniture, and fixtures	1,135,531		
Current expenses and taxes paid	....	Deposits of State, county, and municipal disbursing officers	....
Gold coins			
Gold certificates			
Silver coins	371,713	Due to other banks and bankers	....
Silver certificates		Other liabilities	181,214
Legal tenders and national-bank notes			
Other resources	886,449		
Total	30,076,220	Total	30,076,220

MARYLAND.

March 1 and September 30, 1887.] [2 banks.

Resources.		Liabilities.	
Loans on real estate	$100,737	Capital stock paid in	$30,105
Loans on personal and collateral security	....	Surplus fund	....
Other loans and discounts	121,616	Other undivided profits	14,879
Overdrafts	....		
U. S. bonds	....	State-bank notes outstanding	....
State bonds	200		
R. R. bonds and stocks	6,000	Dividends unpaid	9,252
Bank stocks	7,928		
Other stocks, bonds, and mortgages	1,000	Individual deposits	204,125
Due from other banks and bankers	4,800	State, county, and municipal deposits	....
Real estate, furniture, and fixtures	5,496		
Current expenses and taxes paid	....	Deposits of State, county, and municipal disbursing officers	....
Gold coins			
Gold certificates			
Silver coins	1,155	Due to other banks and bankers	6,582
Silver certificates		Other liabilities	6,295
Legal tenders and national-bank notes			
Other resources	13,207		
Total	271,238	Total	271,238

SAVINGS BANKS—OFFICIAL.

WASHINGTON, D. C.

June 30, 1887.] [1 bank.

Resources.		Liabilities.	
Loans on real estate	$112,563	Capital stock paid in	....
Loans on personal and collateral security	234,268	Surplus fund	....
Other loans and discounts	....	Other undivided profits	$11,464
Overdrafts	....		
U. S. bonds	160,000	State-bank notes outstanding	....
State bonds	30,000		
R. R. bonds and stocks	21,000	Dividends unpaid	....
Bank stocks	....		
Other stocks, bonds, and mortgages	227,500	Individual deposits	834,524
Due from other banks and bankers	4,546	State, county, and municipal deposits	....
Real estate, furniture, and fixtures	....		
Current expenses and taxes paid	7,272	Deposits of State, county, and municipal disbursing officers	....
Gold coins	400		
Gold certificates	....		
Silver coins	1,287	Due to other banks and bankers	....
Silver certificates	7,500	Other liabilities	....
Legal tenders and national-bank notes	10,650		
Other resources	29,002		
Total	845,988	Total	845,988

NORTH CAROLINA.

June 30, 1887.] [1 bank.

Resources.		Liabilities.	
Loans on real estate	$1,000	Capital stock paid in	$5,991
Loans on personal and collateral security	....	Surplus fund	....
Other loans and discounts	8,606	Other undivided profits	374
Overdrafts	....		
U. S. bonds	....	State-bank notes outstanding	....
State bonds	3,100		
R. R. bonds and stocks	....	Dividends unpaid	....
Bank stocks	....		
Other stocks, bonds, and mortgages	1,500	Individual deposits	11,307
Due from other banks and bankers	1,021	State, county, and municipal deposits	....
Real estate, furniture, and fixtures	957		
Current expenses and taxes paid	....	Deposits of State, county, and municipal disbursing officers	....
Gold coins	17		
Gold certificates	....		
Silver coins	100	Due to other banks and bankers	....
Silver certificates	....	Other liabilities	....
Legal tenders and national-bank notes	1,360		
Other resources	2		
Total	17,672	Total	17,672

OHIO.

April 7, 1887.] [4 banks.

Resources.		Liabilities.	
Loans on real estate	$4,394,655	Capital stock paid in	....
Loans on personal and collateral security	....	Surplus fund	$70,000
Other loans and discounts	1,131,103	Other undivided profits	318,326
Overdrafts	....		
U. S. bonds	2,255,000	State-bank notes outstanding	....
State bonds	500,000		
R. R. bonds and stocks	....	Dividends unpaid	....
Bank stocks	....		
Other stocks, bonds, and mortgages	6,693,881	Individual deposits	15,065,630
Due from other banks and bankers	967,451	State, county, and municipal deposits	....
Real estate, furniture, and fixtures	247,406		
Current expenses and taxes paid	16,330	Deposits of State, county, and municipal disbursing officers	....
Gold coins }			
Gold certificates }			
Silver coins }	4,334	Due to other banks and bankers	....
Silver certificates }		Other liabilities	1,000,000
Legal tenders and national-bank notes	221,366		
Other resources	22,366		
Total	16,453,985	Total	16,453,985

SAVINGS BANKS—OFFICIAL.

INDIANA.

October 30, 1886.] [6 banks.

Resources.		Liabilities.	
Loans on real estate	$1,645,330	Capital stock paid in	....
Loans on personal and collateral security	....	Surplus fund	$168,853
Other loans and discounts	....	Other undivided profits	43,697
Overdrafts	....		
U.S. bonds	127,397	State-bank notes outstanding	....
State bonds	....		
R.R. bonds and stocks	....	Dividends unpaid	....
Bank stocks	....		
Other stocks, bonds, and mortgages	91,830	Individual deposits	2,312,013
Due from other banks and bankers	....	State, county, and municipal deposits	....
Real estate, furniture, and fixtures	133,870		
Current expenses and taxes paid	8,503	Deposits of State, county, and municipal disbursing officers	....
Gold coins	} 354,832		
Gold certificates			
Silver coins		Due to other banks and bankers	....
Silver certificates		Other liabilities	43,854
Legal tenders and national-bank notes			
Other resources	200,655		
Total	2,568,417	Total	2,568,417

IOWA.

June 30, 1887.] [37 banks.

Resources.		Liabilities.	
Loans on real estate	....	Capital stock paid in	$2,128,603
Loans on personal and collateral security	....	Surplus fund	218,891
Other loans and discounts	$10,326,774	Other undivided profits	273,403
Overdrafts	67,081		
U.S. bonds	....	State-bank notes outstanding	....
State bonds	....		
R.R. bonds and stocks	....	Dividends unpaid	....
Bank stocks	....		
Other stocks, bonds, and mortgages	....	Individual deposits	9,969,019
Due from other banks and bankers	1,461,610	State, county, and municipal deposits	....
Real estate, furniture, and fixtures	339,843		
Current expenses and taxes paid	....	Deposits of State, county, and municipal disbursing officers	....
Gold coins	} 471,039		
Gold certificates			
Silver coins		Due to other banks and bankers	76,431
Silver certificates		Other liabilities	....
Legal tenders and national-bank notes			
Other resources	....		
Total	12,666,347	Total	12,666,347

MINNESOTA.

July 23, 1887.] [7 banks.

Resources.		Liabilities.	
Loans on real estate	$1,918,298	Capital stock paid in	*$150,000
Loans on personal and collateral security	768,237	Surplus fund	103,985
Other loans and discounts	....	Other undivided profits	34,923
Overdrafts	10,276		
U.S. bonds	55,000	State-bank notes outstanding	....
State bonds	....		
R.R. bonds and stocks	....	Dividends unpaid	52,852
Bank stocks	....		
Other stocks, bonds, and mortgages	662,712	Individual deposits	3,891,650
Due from other banks and bankers	659,883	State, county, and municipal deposits	....
Real estate, furniture, and fixtures	68,514		
Current expenses and taxes paid	10,241	Deposits of State, county, and municipal disbursing officers	....
Gold coins	4,639		
Gold certificates	....		
Silver coins	3,387	Due to other banks and bankers	4,986
Silver certificates	....	Other liabilities	4,405
Legal tenders and national-bank notes	70,558		
Other resources	11,140		
Total	4,242,801	Total	4,242,801

* Of two banks only.

SAVINGS BANKS—OFFICIAL.

CALIFORNIA.

June 30, 1887.] [24 banks.

Resources.		Liabilities.	
Loans on real estate	$42,963,926	Capital stock paid in	$4,216,377
Loans on personal and collateral security	1,000,815	Surplus fund	2,731,080
Other loans and discounts	8,571,063	Other undivided profits	....
Overdrafts	....		
U. S. bonds }		State-bank notes outstanding	....
State bonds }			
R. R. bonds and stocks }	17,860,209	Dividends unpaid	....
Bank stocks }			
Other stocks, bonds, and mortgages }		Individual deposits	70,077,898
Due from other banks and bankers	1,609,286	State, county, and municipal deposits	....
Real estate, furniture, and fixtures	3,104,876		
Current expenses and taxes paid	....	Deposits of State, county, and municipal disbursing officers	....
Gold coins }			
Gold certificates }			
Silver coins }	1,994,883	Due to other banks and bankers	591
Silver certificates }		Other liabilities	558,652
Legal tenders and national-bank notes	....		
Other resources	479,544		
Total	77,584,602	Total	77,584,602

AGGREGATE RESOURCES AND LIABILITIES OF 664 SAVINGS BANKS IN THE UNITED STATES, 1886–'87.

Loans on real estate	$446,024,258	Capital stock paid in	*$6,991,166
Loans on personal and collateral security	122,631,426	Surplus fund	114,091,457
Other loans and discounts	31,612,743	Other undivided profits	6,096,426
Overdrafts	77,357		
U. S. bonds	106,219,198	State-bank notes outstanding	....
State bonds	209,038,864		
R. R. bonds and stocks	58,992,053	Dividends unpaid	122,308
Bank stocks	39,778,238		
Other stocks, bonds, and mortgages	47,150,157	Individual deposits	1,157,867,483
Due from other banks and bankers	53,139,067	State, county, and municipal deposits	....
Real estate, furniture, and fixtures	27,848,385		
Current expenses and taxes paid	1,633,313	Deposits of State, county, and municipal disbursing officers	....
Gold coins }			
Gold certificates }			
Silver coins }	12,842,682	Due to other banks and bankers	88,588
Silver certificates }		Other liabilities	2,755,937
Legal tenders and national-bank notes }			
Other resources	70,425,624		
Total	1,288,013,365	Total	1,288,013,365

* Of 84 banks.

SAVINGS BANKS—UNOFFICIAL.

PHILADELPHIA, PA.

June 30, 1887.] [5 banks.

Resources.		Liabilities.	
Loans on real estate	$6,880,383	Capital stock paid in	$444,700
Loans on personal and collateral security	9,120,310	Surplus fund	2,053,782
Other loans and discounts	4,538,502	Other undivided profits	857,442
Overdrafts	....		
U. S. bonds	5,251,086	State-bank notes outstanding	....
State bonds	3,110,778		
R. R. bonds and stocks	13,723,201	Dividends unpaid	6,250
Bank stocks	....		
Other stocks, bonds, and mortgages	459,080	Individual deposits	42,210,099
Due from other banks and bankers	55,680	State, county, and municipal deposits	....
Real estate, furniture, and fixtures	1,018,040		
Current expenses and taxes paid	106,000	Deposits of State, county, and municipal disbursing officers	....
Gold coins	1,100,817		
Gold certificates	....		
Silver coins	1,318	Due to other banks and bankers	....
Silver certificates	....	Other liabilities	50,002
Legal tenders and national-bank notes	122,397		
Other resources	1,013,933		
Total	46,531,275	Total	46,531,275

DELAWARE.

June 30, 1887.] [2 banks.

Loans on real estate	....	Capital stock paid in	....
Loans on personal and collateral security	$385,500	Surplus fund	$260,740
Other loans and discounts	....	Other undivided profits	....
Overdrafts	....		
U. S. bonds	....	State-bank notes outstanding	....
State bonds	....		
R. R. bonds and stocks	81,670	Dividends unpaid	....
Bank stocks	52,601		
Other stocks, bonds, and mortgages	2,053,407	Individual deposits	2,771,392
Due from other banks and bankers	....	State, county, and municipal deposits	....
Real estate, furniture, and fixtures	107,785		
Current expenses and taxes paid	....	Deposits of State, county, and municipal disbursing officers	....
Gold coins }			
Gold certificates }			
Silver coins }	35,822	Due to other banks and bankers	....
Silver certificates }		Other liabilities	....
Legal tenders and national-bank notes }			
Other resources	264,287		
Total	3,041,132	Total	3,041,132

MARYLAND.

June 30, 1887.] [8 banks.

Loans on real estate	$2,451,457	Capital stock paid in	....
Loans on personal and collateral security	2,729,974	Surplus fund	$1,110,870
Other loans and discounts	451,362	Other undivided profits	22,827
Overdrafts	....		
U. S. bonds	8,197,000	State-bank notes outstanding	....
State bonds	3,603,531		
R. R. bonds and stocks	1,487,728	Dividends unpaid	2,284
Bank stocks	222,666		
Other stocks, bonds, and mortgages	321,679	Individual deposits	18,816,837
Due from other banks and bankers	186,838	State, county, and municipal deposits	....
Real estate, furniture, and fixtures	442,461		
Current expenses and taxes paid	19,504	Deposits of State, county, and municipal disbursing officers	....
Gold coins }			
Gold certificates }			
Silver coins }	198,110	Due to other banks and bankers	2,200
Silver certificates }		Other liabilities	580,517
Legal tenders and national-bank notes }			
Other resources	232,225		
Total	20,544,535	Total	20,544,535

SAVINGS BANKS—UNOFFICIAL.

CHICAGO, ILL.

June 30, 1887.] [5 banks.

Resources.		Liabilities.	
Loans on real estate	$1,476,568	Capital stock paid in	$2,655,000
Loans on personal and collateral security	10,685,865	Surplus fund	1,260,461
Other loans and discounts	1,282,150	Other undivided profits	228,238
Overdrafts	12,768		
U. S bonds	581,470	State-bank notes outstanding	....
State bonds	11,642		
R. R. bonds and stocks	124,219	Dividends unpaid	62,544
Bank stocks	14,175		
Other stocks, bonds, and mortgages	609,304	Individual deposits	14,061,258
Due from other banks and bankers	1,728,142	State, county, and municipal deposits	....
Real estate, furniture, and fixtures	163,079		
Current expenses and taxes paid	2,633	Deposits of State, county, and municipal disbursing officers	....
Gold coins; Gold certificates; Silver coins; Silver certificates; Legal tenders and national-bank notes	2,600,126	Due to other banks and bankers	....
		Other liabilities	1,262,916
Other resources	58,276		
Total	19,530,417	Total	19,530,417

AGGREGATE RESOURCES AND LIABILITIES OF 20 SAVINGS BANKS IN THE UNITED STATES.

Loans on real estate	$10,817,408	Capital stock paid in	$3,000,700
Loans on personal and collateral security	22,921,709	Surplus fund	5,603,853
Other loans and discounts	6,292,074	Other undivided profits	1,108,507
Overdrafts	12,768		
U. S. bonds	14,029,556	State-bank notes outstanding	....
State bonds	6,725,951		
R. R. bonds and stocks	15,416,878	Dividends unpaid	71,078
Bank stocks	289,442		
Other stocks, bonds, and mortgages	3,534,070	Individual deposits	77,868,586
Due from other banks and bankers	1,970,669	State, county, and municipal deposits	....
Real estate, furniture, and fixtures	1,791,365		
Current expenses and taxes paid	128,137	Deposits of State, county, and municipal disbursing officers	....
Gold coins; Gold certificates; Silver coins; Silver certificates; Legal tenders and national-bank notes	5,162,553	Due to other banks and bankers	2,200
		Other liabilities	1,893,435
Other resources	551,788		
Total	89,647,359	Total	89,647,359

SAVINGS BANKS—OFFICIAL AND UNOFFICIAL.*

AGGREGATE RESOURCES AND LIABILITIES OF SAVINGS BANKS FROM 1882 TO 1887.

Resources and liabilities.	1882-'83.	1883-'84.	1884-'85.	1885-'86.	1886-'87.
	630 banks.	636 banks.	646 banks.	638 banks.	684 banks.
Resources.					
Loans on real estate	$328, 197, 856	$358, 686, 040	$380, 953, 028	$418, 372, 642	$457, 441, 666
Loans on pers'l and collat'l security	155, 874, 522	141, 457, 111	133, 716, 902	127, 677, 702	145, 553, 135
Other loans and discounts	....	....	....	....	37, 904, 817
Overdrafts	....	....	....	....	90, 125
U. S. bonds	210, 017, 313	193, 226, 202	191, 980, 698	197, 171, 307	180, 218, 754
State, county, and municipal bonds.	190, 629, 915	222, 218, 006	228, 993, 250	241, 051, 536	215, 764, 815
R. R. bonds and stocks	41, 695, 701	50, 991, 570	59, 585, 489	63, 511, 735	74, 408, 931
Bank stocks	36, 587, 817	37, 929, 754	38, 469, 693	39, 029, 813	40, 097, 680
Other stocks, bonds, and mortgages	....	....	....	....	50, 684, 227
Due from other banks and bankers.	43, 181, 029	52, 358, 971	46, 125, 014	43, 689, 103	55, 109, 727
Real estate, furniture, and fixtures	37, 224, 601	34, 467, 276	32, 174, 810	30, 984, 883	29, 639, 750
Current expenses and taxes paid	144, 223	156, 944	166, 636	142, 717	1, 761, 450
Gold coins					
Gold certificates					
Silver coins	12, 998, 594	14, 079, 452	13, 423, 064	19, 757, 941	18, 005, 235
Silver certificates					
Legal tenders and nat'l-bank notes.					
Checks and other cash items					
Other resources	53, 235, 771	69, 166, 584	68, 445, 304	79, 451, 562	70, 980, 412
Total	1, 118, 790, 944	1, 177, 740, 919	1, 203, 025, 698	1, 260, 840, 941	1, 377, 660, 724
Liabilities.					
Capital stock paid in	....	....	....	....	10, 090, 866
Surplus fund	72, 784, 155	82, 395, 717	88, 047, 315	96, 924, 117	119, 695, 310
Other undivided profits	15, 738, 223	16, 904, 753	13, 106, 359	15, 326, 391	7, 204, 033
State bank notes outstanding	....	....	....	....	....
Dividends unpaid	....	....	....	....	193, 386
Individual deposits	1, 024, 856, 787	1, 073, 294, 955	1, 095, 172, 147	1, 141, 530, 578	1, 235, 736, 069
State, county, and municipal deposits	....	....	....	....	....
Deposits of State, county, and municipal disbursing officers	....	....	....	....	....
Due to other banks and bankers	....	....	....	....	90, 788
Other liabilities	5, 411, 779	5, 145, 494	6, 099, 877	7, 050, 855	4, 649, 372
Total	1, 118, 790, 944	1, 177, 740, 919	1, 203, 025, 698	1, 260, 840, 941	1, 377, 660, 724

* Official only, prior to 1886-'87.

TABLE, BY STATES, OF THE AGGREGATE DEPOSITS OF SAVINGS BANKS, WITH THE NUMBER OF THEIR DEPOSITORS AND THE AVERAGE AMOUNT DUE TO EACH, IN 1885-'86 AND 1886-'87.

States.	1885-'86.			1886-'87.		
	Number of depositors.	Amount of deposits.	Average to each depositor.	Number of depositors.	Amount of deposits.	Average to each depositor.
Maine	109, 398	$35, 111, 600	$320. 95	114, 691	$37, 215, 071	$324. 47
New Hampshire	121, 216	47, 231, 919	389. 65	132, 714	50, 822, 762	382. 94
Vermont	49, 453	11, 723, 675	237. 07	53, 810	15, 587, 050	289. 67
Massachusetts	848, 787	274, 998, 413	323. 99	906, 039	291, 197, 900	321. 40
Rhode Island	116, 381	51, 816, 390	445. 23	119, 150	53, 284, 821	447. 18
Connecticut	256, 097	92, 481, 425	361. 12	266, 888	97, 424, 820	365. 04
New York	1, 208, 072	457, 030, 250	378. 33	1, 264, 535	482, 486, 730	381. 55
New Jersey	91, 681	25, 335, 780	276. 35	98, 137	27, 482, 135	280. 04
Pennsylvania	143, 645	37, 530, 370	261. 27	156, 722	42, 219, 099	269. 39
Delaware	....	....	....	12, 744	2, 771, 302	217. 46
Maryland	*77, 212	30, 542, 992	395. 57	59, 565	19, 020, 962	319. 33
District of Columbia	7, 605	793, 943	104. 40	8, 245	834, 524	101. 22
North Carolina	....	....	....	*377	11, 307	30. 00
Ohio	*34, 553	12, 823, 374	371. 12	*41, 050	15, 065, 650	366. 93
Indiana	....	....	....	9, 933	2, 312, 013	232. 75
Illinois	....	....	....	*28, 038	14, 061, 258	501. 51
Iowa	....	....	....	*39, 638	9, 969, 019	251. 50
Minnesota	14, 361	3, 654, 528	254. 48	15, 474	3, 402, 950	219. 91
California	*80, 489	60, 435, 919	750. 86	*90, 245	70, 077, 899	776. 52
Total	3, 158, 950	1, 141, 530, 578	361. 36	3, 418, 013	1, 235, 247, 371	361. 39

* Estimated.

PRIVATE BANKS—OFFICIAL.

WISCONSIN.

July 4, 1887.] [68 banks.

Resources.		Liabilities.	
Loans on real estate	....	Capital stock paid in	$986,435
Loans on personal and collateral security	....	Surplus fund	470,036
Other loans and discounts	$5,256,468	Other undivided profits	....
Overdrafts	108,056		
U. S. bonds	....	State-bank notes outstanding	....
State bonds	....		
R. R. bonds and stocks	....	Dividends unpaid	....
Bank stocks	....		
Other stocks, bonds, and mortgages	416,740	Individual deposits	6,220,610
Due from other banks and bankers	1,788,491	State, county, and municipal deposits	....
Real estate, furniture, and fixtures	320,28[illegible]		
Current expenses and taxes paid	26,182	Deposits of State, county, and municipal disbursing officers	....
Gold coins }			
Gold certificates }	280,607		
Silver coins }		Due to other banks and bankers	....
Silver certificates }		Other liabilities	1,3[illegible],306
Legal tenders and national-bank notes	584,017		
Other resources	213,343		
Total	9,031,387	Total	9,031,387

MISSOURI.

May 4, 1887.] [85 banks.

Loans on real estate	$552,770	Capital stock paid in	$1,331,241
Loans on personal and collateral security	5,087,416	Surplus fund	801,010
Other loans and discounts	....	Other undivided profits	38,609
Overdrafts	243,737		
U. S. bonds	89,600	State-bank notes outstanding	....
State bonds	....		
R. R. bonds and stocks	....	Dividends unpaid	....
Bank stocks	....		
Other stocks, bonds, and mortgages	176,541	Individual deposits	6,495,824
Due from other banks and bankers	1,557,420	State, county, and municipal deposits	....
Real estate, furniture, and fixtures	436,865		
Current expenses and taxes paid	....	Deposits of State, county, and municipal disbursing officers	....
Gold coins	167,084		
Gold certificates	....		
Silver coins	63,174	Due to other banks and bankers	531,366
Silver certificates	....	Other liabilities	125,728
Legal tenders and national-bank notes	736,374		
Other resources	213,757		
Total	9,324,738	Total	9,324,733

CALIFORNIA.

June 30, 1887.] [29 banks.

Loans on real estate	$1,536,604	Capital stock paid in	$3,578,468
Loans on personal and collateral security	4,681,098	Surplus fund	400,577
Other loans and discounts	520,885	Other undivided profits	....
Overdrafts	....		
U. S. bonds }		State-bank notes outstanding	....
State bonds }			
R. R. bonds and stocks }	478,077	Dividends unpaid	....
Bank stocks }			
Other stocks, bonds, and mortgages }		Individual deposits	6,118,496
Due from other banks and bankers	813,903	State, county, and municipal deposits	....
Real estate, furniture, and fixtures	693,691		
Current expenses and taxes paid	....	Deposits of State, county, and municipal disbursing officers	....
Gold coins }			
Gold certificates }	1,548,508		
Silver coins }		Due to other banks and bankers	340,531
Silver certificates }		Other liabilities	158,826
Legal tenders and national-bank notes	....		
Other resources	321,142		
Total	10,5[illegible]6,808	Total	10,596,808

PRIVATE BANKS—OFFICIAL.

AGGREGATE RESOURCES AND LIABILITIES OF 182 PRIVATE BANKS IN THE UNITED STATES.

Resources.		Liabilities.	
Loans on real estate	$2,089,374	Capital stock paid in	$5,806,144
Loans on personal and collateral security	9,771,504	Surplus fund	1,081,523
Other loans and discounts	5,777,353	Other undivided profits	38,000
Overdrafts	352,393		
U. S. bonds	89,600	State-bank notes outstanding	....
State bonds	....		
R. R. bonds and stocks	....	Dividends unpaid	....
Bank stocks	....		
Other stocks, bonds, and mortgages	1,101,358	Individual deposits	18,843,930
Due from other banks and bankers	4,159,814	State, county, and municipal deposits	....
Real estate, furniture, and fixtures	1,450,849		
Current expenses and taxes paid	26,182	Deposits of State, county, and municipal disbursing officers	....
Gold coins; Gold certificates; Silver coins; Silver certificates; Legal tenders and national-bank notes	3,767,071	Due to other banks and bankers	871,807
		Other liabilities	1,020,800
Other resources	367,535		
Total	28,953,023	Total	28,053,023

PRIVATE BANKS—UNOFFICIAL.

MASSACHUSETTS.

June 30, 1887.] [5 banks.

Resources.		Liabilities.	
Loans on real estate	$309,837	Capital stock paid in	$231,000
Loans on personal and collateral security	685,712	Surplus fund	65,566
Other loans and discounts	88,404	Other undivided profits	134,502
Overdrafts	....		
U. S. bonds	500	State-bank notes outstanding	....
State bonds	....		
R. R. bonds and stocks	1,800	Dividends unpaid	87
Bank stocks	11,495		
Other stocks, bonds, and mortgages	203,478	Individual deposits	627,880
Due from other banks, and bankers	32,772	State, county, and municipal deposits	....
Real estate, furniture, and fixtures	1,713		
Current expenses and taxes paid	903	Deposits of State, county, and municipal disbursing officers	....
Gold coins			
Gold certificates			
Silver coins	69,003	Due to other banks and bankers	....
Silver certificates		Other liabilities	174,186
Legal tenders and national-bank notes			
Other resources	7,604		
Total	1,433,221	Total	1,433,221

CONNECTICUT.

June 30, 1887.] [4 banks.

Resources.		Liabilities.	
Loans on real estate	$34,200	Capital stock paid in	$78,000
Loans on personal and collateral security	103,180	Surplus fund	28,241
Other loans and discounts	278,333	Other undivided profits	15,580
Overdrafts	934		
U. S. bonds	8,380	State-bank notes outstanding	....
State bonds	....		
R. R. bonds and stocks	....	Dividends unpaid	....
Bank stocks	2,550		
Other stocks, bonds, and mortgages	18,846	Individual deposits	387,378
Due from other banks, and bankers	80,115	State, county, and municipal deposits	....
Real estate, furniture, and fixtures	1,692		
Current expenses and taxes paid	4,858	Deposits of State, county, and municipal disbursing officers	....
Gold coins			
Gold certificates			
Silver coins	51,037	Due to other banks and bankers	75,916
Silver certificates		Other liabilities	43
Legal tenders and national-bank notes			
Other resources	1,033		
Total	585,158	Total	585,158

NEW YORK.

June 30, 1887.] [41 banks.

Resources.		Liabilities.	
Loans on real estate	$474,706	Capital stock paid in	$1,218,272
Loans on personal and collateral security	1,040,362	Surplus fund	638,161
Other loans and discounts	4,007,934	Other undivided profits	185,650
Overdrafts	35,571		
U. S. bonds	2,523,061	State-bank notes outstanding	....
State bonds	23,880		
R. R. bonds and stocks	1,043,547	Dividends unpaid	30,000
Bank stocks	32,950		
Other stocks, bonds, and mortgages	518,681	Individual deposits	6,013,485
Due from other banks and bankers	876,802	State, county, and municipal deposits	76,903
Real estate, furniture, and fixtures	219,625		
Current expenses and taxes paid	19,459	Deposits of State, county, and municipal disbursing officers	67,100
Gold coins			
Gold certificates			
Silver coins	365,644	Due to other banks and bankers	2,178,481
Silver certificates		Other liabilities	1,772,232
Legal tenders and national-bank notes			
Other resources	112,053		
Total	12,200,284	Total	12,200,284

PRIVATE BANKS—UNOFFICIAL.

NEW JERSEY.

June 30, 1887.] [3 banks.

Resources.		Liabilities.	
Loans on real estate	$24,150	Capital stock paid in	$160,325
Loans on personal and collateral security	471,816	Surplus fund	93,000
Other loans and discounts	208,735	Other undivided profits	9,125
Overdrafts	....		
U. S. bonds	....	State-bank notes outstanding	....
State bonds	....		
R. R. bonds and stocks	77,265	Dividends unpaid	365
Bank stocks	....		
Other stocks, bonds, and mortgages	43,497	Individual deposits	754,489
Due from other banks and bankers	161,204	State, county, and municipal deposits	10,049
Real estate, furniture, and fixtures	28,892		
Current expenses and taxes paid	5,826	Deposits of State, county, and municipal disbursing officers	10,000
Gold coins			
Gold certificates			
Silver coins	92,782	Due to other banks and bankers	34,298
Silver certificates		Other liabilities	40,012
Legal tenders and national-bank notes			
Other resources	6,487		
Total	1,120,654	Total	1,120,654

PENNSYLVANIA.

June 30, 1887.] [46 banks.

Resources.		Liabilities.	
Loans on real estate	$658,871	Capital stock paid in	$1,571,351
Loans on personal and collateral security	3,204,940	Surplus fund	518,859
Other loans and discounts	3,592,657	Other undivided profits	171,150
Overdrafts	64,522		
U. S. bonds	92,600	*State-bank notes outstanding	....
State bonds	4,050		
R. R. bonds and stocks	357,561	Dividends unpaid	13,648
Bank stocks	68,500		
Other stocks, bonds, and mortgages	380,070	Individual deposits	8,990,050
Due from other banks and bankers	1,802,352	State, county, and municipal deposits	....
Real estate, furniture, and fixtures	329,781		
Current expenses and taxes paid	50,056	Deposits of State, county, and municipal disbursing officers	7,504
Gold coins			
Gold certificates			
Silver coins	852,104	Due to other banks and bankers	196,367
Silver certificates		Other liabilities	74,207
Legal tenders and national-bank notes			
Other resources	75,400		
Total	11,543,130	Total	11,543,130

MARYLAND.

June 30, 1887.] [3 banks.

Resources.		Liabilities.	
Loans on real estate	$11,400	Capital stock paid in	$16,000
Loans on personal and collateral security	51,225	Surplus fund	102
Other loans and discounts	77,221	Other undivided profits	1,152
Overdrafts	73		
U. S. bonds	....	State-bank notes outstanding	....
State bonds	....		
R. R. bonds and stocks	1,000	Dividends unpaid	....
Bank stocks	....		
Other stocks, bonds, and mortgages	22,000	Individual deposits	47,859
Due from other banks and bankers	11,195	State, county, and municipal deposits	....
Real estate, furniture, and fixtures	25,519		
Current expenses and taxes paid	333	Deposits of State, county, and municipal disbursing officers	827
Gold coins			
Gold certificates			
Silver coins	7,912	Due to other banks and bankers	19,242
Silver certificates		Other liabilities	122,862
Legal tenders and national-bank notes			
Other resources	166		
Total	208,044	Total	208,044

PRIVATE BANKS—UNOFFICIAL.

WASHINGTON, D. C.

June 30, 1887.] [1 bank.

Resources.		Liabilities.	
Loans on real estate	....	Capital stock paid in	$33,000
Loans on personal and collateral security	....	Surplus fund	3,088
Other loans and discounts	$102,085	Other undivided profits	10,030
Overdrafts	....		
U. S. bonds	....	State-bank notes outstanding	....
State bonds	....		
R. R. bonds and stocks	....	Dividends unpaid	....
Bank stocks	....		
Other stocks, bonds, and mortgages	....	Individual deposits	79,490
Due from other banks and bankers	3,000	State, county, and municipal deposits	....
Real estate, furniture, and fixtures	....		
Current expenses and taxes paid	104	Deposits of State, county, and municipal disbursing officers	....
Gold coins; Gold certificates; Silver coins; Silver certificates; Legal tenders and national-bank notes	20,466	Due to other banks and bankers	47
		Other liabilities	....
Other resources	....		
Total	125,655	Total	125,655

NORTH CAROLINA.

June 30, 1887.] [2 banks.

Loans on real estate	....	Capital stock paid in	$40,000
Loans on personal and collateral security	$160,506	Surplus fund	11,585
Other loans and discounts	....	Other undivided profits	11,405
Overdrafts	2,462		
U. S. bonds	....	State-bank notes outstanding	....
State bonds	....		
R. R. bonds and stocks	....	Dividends unpaid	....
Bank stocks	....		
Other stocks, bonds, and mortgages	1,049	Individual deposits	112,535
Due from other banks and bankers	21,816	State, county, and municipal deposits	....
Real estate, furniture, and fixtures	2,507		
Current expenses and taxes paid	2,384	Deposits of State, county, and municipal disbursing officers	819
Gold coins; Gold certificates; Silver coins; Silver certificates; Legal tenders and national-bank notes	14,040	Due to other banks and bankers	7,814
		Other liabilities	20,706
Other resources	4		
Total	204,864	Total	204,864

SOUTH CAROLINA.

June 30, 1887.] [3 banks.

Loans on real estate	$32,991	Capital stock paid in	$87,850
Loans on personal and collateral security	41,230	Surplus fund	31,330
Other loans and discounts	11,418	Other undivided profits	....
Overdrafts	3,157		
U. S. bonds	....	State-bank notes outstanding	....
State bonds	....		
R. R. bonds and stocks	....	Dividends unpaid	....
Bank stocks	....		
Other stocks, bonds, and mortgages	4,702	Individual deposits	51,161
Due from other banks and bankers	26,459	State, county, and municipal deposits	....
Real estate, furniture, and fixtures	14,601		
Current expenses and taxes paid	745	Deposits of State, county, and municipal disbursing officers	6,143
Gold coins; Gold certificates; Silver coins; Silver certificates; Legal tenders and national-bank notes	16,343	Due to other banks and bankers	6,000
		Other liabilities	....
Other resources	30,796		
Total	182,484	Total	182,484

PRIVATE BANKS—UNOFFICIAL.

GEORGIA.

June 30, 1887.] [12 banks.

Resources.		Liabilities.	
Loans on real estate	$90,282	Capital stock paid in	$740,770
Loans on personal and collateral security	504,301	Surplus fund	155,378
Other loans and discounts	265,120	Other undivided profits	23,672
Overdrafts	18,168		
U. S. bonds	....	State-bank notes outstanding	....
State bonds	4,500		
R. R. bonds and stocks	107,077	Dividends unpaid	2,000
Bank stocks	2,000		
Other stocks, bonds, and mortgages	51,044	Individual deposits	372,785
Due from other banks and bankers	103,574	State, county, and municipal deposits	6,904
Real estate, furniture, and fixtures	226,408		
Current expenses and taxes paid	9,548	Deposits of State, county, and municipal disbursing officers	500
Gold coins			
Gold certificates			
Silver coins	70,120	Due to other banks and bankers	43,844
Silver certificates		Other liabilities	162,520
Legal tenders and national-bank notes			
Other resources	25,048		
Total	1,508,379	Total	1,508,379

FLORIDA.

June 30, 1887.] [2 banks.

Resources.		Liabilities.	
Loans on real estate	$5,050	Capital stock paid in	$53,000
Loans on personal and collateral security	129,693	Surplus fund	....
Other loans and discounts	....	Other undivided profits	5,381
Overdrafts	9,414		
U. S. bonds	....	State-bank notes outstanding	....
State bonds	....		
R. R. bonds and stocks	....	Dividends unpaid	667
Bank stocks	41,000		
Other stocks, bonds, and mortgages	1,670	Individual deposits	228,120
Due from other banks and bankers	67,197	State, county, and municipal deposits	....
Real estate, furniture, and fixtures	4,548		
Current expenses and taxes paid	2,339	Deposits of State, county, and municipal disbursing officers	....
Gold coins			
Gold certificates			
Silver coins	44,007	Due to other banks and bankers	15,496
Silver certificates		Other liabilities	3,499
Legal tenders and national-bank notes			
Other resources	204		
Total	306,172	Total	306,172

ALABAMA.

June 30, 1887.] [5 banks.

Resources.		Liabilities.	
Loans on real estate	$212,905	Capital stock paid in	$312,000
Loans on personal and collateral security	961,367	Surplus fund	335,793
Other loans and discounts	237,507	Other undivided profits	2,178,839
Overdrafts	5,250		
U. S. bonds	3,500	State-bank notes outstanding	....
State bonds	63,033		
R. R. bonds and stocks	35,000	Dividends unpaid	....
Bank stocks	12,992		
Other stocks, bonds, and mortgages	2,201,051	Individual deposits	1,471,209
Due from other banks and bankers	257,990	State, county, and municipal deposits	....
Real estate, furniture, and fixtures	136,046		
Current expenses and taxes paid	17,373	Deposits of State, county, and municipal disbursing officers	21,657
Gold coins			
Gold certificates			
Silver coins	294,300	Due to other banks and bankers	24,391
Silver certificates		Other liabilities	105,172
Legal tenders and national-bank notes			
Other resources	9,347		
Total	4,449,061	Total	4,449,061

PRIVATE BANKS—UNOFFICIAL.

MISSISSIPPI.

June 30, 1887.] [2 banks.

Resources.		Liabilities.	
Loans on real estate	$18,000	Capital stock paid in	$120,000
Loans on personal and collateral security	10,200	Surplus fund	30,400
Other loans and discounts	122,837	Other undivided profits	14,576
Overdrafts	7,732		
U. S. bonds	....	State-bank notes outstanding	....
State bonds	....		
R. R. bonds and stocks	13,021	Dividends unpaid	....
Bank stocks	....		
Other stocks, bonds, and mortgages	17,987	Individual deposits	120,937
Due from other banks and bankers	35,363	State, county, and municipal deposits	....
Real estate, furniture, and fixtures	51,550		
Current expenses and taxes paid	8,460	Deposits of State, county, and municipal disbursing officers	3,510
Gold coins			
Gold certificates			
Silver coins	39,809	Due to other banks and bankers	18,587
Silver certificates		Other liabilities	10,998
Legal tenders and national-bank notes			
Other resources	22,948		
Total	342,978	Total	342,978

LOUISIANA.

June 30, 1887.] [2 banks.

Resources.		Liabilities.	
Loans on real estate	$1,400	Capital stock paid in	$33,000
Loans on personal and collateral security	27,529	Surplus fund	....
Other loans and discounts	....	Other undivided profits	8,925
Overdrafts	13,780		
U. S. bonds	....	State-bank notes outstanding	....
State bonds	....		
R. R. bonds and stocks	....	Dividends unpaid	....
Banks stocks	....		
Other stocks, bonds, and mortgages	....	Individual deposits	52,285
Due from other banks and bankers	7,035	State, county, and municipal deposits	....
Real estate, furniture, and fixtures	2,964		
Current expenses and taxes paid	450	Deposits of State, county, and municipal disbursing officers	....
Gold coins			
Gold certificates			
Silver coins	34,306	Due to other banks and bankers	....
Silver certificates		Other liabilities	....
Legal tenders and national-bank notes			
Other resources	6,737		
Total	94,210	Total	94,210

TEXAS.

June 30, 1887.] [18 banks.

Resources.		Liabilities.	
Loans on real estate	$896,484	Capital stock paid in	$1,700,800
Loans on personal and collateral security	1,141,907	Surplus fund	91,273
Other loans and discounts	533,172	Other undivided profits	129,185
Overdrafts	106,948		
U. S. bonds	....	State-bank notes outstanding	....
State bonds	37,500		
R. R. bonds and stocks	37,917	Dividends unpaid	....
Bank stocks	6,250		
Other stocks, bonds, and mortgages	225,405	Individual deposits	1,910,563
Due from other banks and bankers	611,349	State, county, and municipal deposits	15,000
Real estate, furniture, and fixtures	323,124		
Current expenses and taxes paid	26,235	Deposits of State, county, and municipal disbursing officers	6,000
Gold coins			
Gold certificates			
Silver coins	417,880	Due to other banks and bankers	58,812
Silver certificates		Other liabilities	460,262
Legal tenders and national-bank notes			
Other resources	22,793		
Total	4,386,964	Total	4,386,964

PRIVATE BANKS—UNOFFICIAL.

KENTUCKY.

June 30, 1887.] [15 banks.

Resources.		Liabilities.	
Loans on real estate	$4,317	Capital stock paid in	$631,700
Loans on personal and collateral security	847,797	Surplus fund	128,511
Other loans and discounts	702,677	Other undivided profits	41,552
Overdrafts	12,406		
U. S. bonds	600	State-bank notes outstanding	....
State bonds	23,000		
R. R. bonds and stocks	33,004	Dividends unpaid	2,422
Bank stocks	15,580		
Other stocks, bonds, and mortgages	42,329	Individual deposits	1,406,540
Due from other banks and bankers	396,723	State, county, and municipal deposits	20,000
Real estate, furniture, and fixtures	46,416	Deposits of State, county, and municipal disbursing officers	....
Current expenses and taxes paid	14,811		
Gold coins }			
Gold certificates }			
Silver coins }	94,331	Due to other banks and bankers	58,124
Silver certificates }		Other liabilities	44,784
Legal tenders and national-bank notes }			
Other resources	102,612		
Total	2,336,633	Total	2,336,633

OHIO.

June 30, 1887.] [77 banks.

Resources.		Liabilities.	
Loans on real estate	$966,560	Capital stock paid in	$2,949,975
Loans on personal and collateral security	7,724,039	Surplus fund	826,018
Other loans and discounts	2,079,427	Other undivided profits	387,561
Overdrafts	103,264		
U. S. bonds	312,067	State-bank notes outstanding	....
State bonds	15,130		
R. R. bonds and stocks	158,888	Dividends unpaid	6,656
Bank stocks	75,100		
Other stocks, bonds, and mortgages	425,396	Individual deposits	11,059,045
Due from other banks and bankers	1,718,453	State, county, and municipal deposits	12,160
Real estate, furniture, and fixtures	663,703		
Current expenses and taxes paid	98,966	Deposits of State, county, and municipal disbursing officers	52,220
Gold coins	203,045		
Gold certificates	9,570		
Silver coins	67,419	Due to other banks and bankers	456,442
Silver certificates	41,393	Other liabilities	256,521
Legal tenders and national-bank notes	994,567		
Other resources	349,512		
Total	16,006,598	Total	16,006,598

INDIANA.

June 30, 1887.] [44 banks.

Resources.		Liabilities.	
Loans on real estate	$202,634	Capital stock paid in	$2,371,142
Loans on personal and collateral security	4,089,506	Surplus fund	214,761
Other loans and discounts	747,935	Other undivided profits	204,682
Overdrafts	80,085		
U. S. bonds	819,320	State-bank notes outstanding	....
State bonds	21,500		
R. R. bonds and stocks	....	Dividends unpaid	5,796
Bank stocks	14,750		
Other stocks, bonds, and mortgages	340,122	Individual deposits	6,319,457
Due from other banks and bankers	1,782,405	State, county, and municipal deposits	84,182
Real estate, furniture, and fixtures	515,140		
Current expenses and taxes paid	26,205	Deposits of State, county, and municipal disbursing officers	90,143
Gold coins }			
Gold certificates }			
Silver coins }	1,938,760	Due to other banks and bankers	302,471
Silver certificates }		Other liabilities	203,192
Legal tenders and national-bank notes }			
Other resources	122,444		
Total	9,797,826	Total	9,797,826

PRIVATE BANKS—UNOFFICIAL.

ILLINOIS.

June 30, 1887.] [99 banks.

Resources.		Liabilities.	
Loans on real estate	$1,804,555	Capital stock paid in	$4,246,028
Loans on personal and collateral security	12,281,915	Surplus fund	3,785,552
Other loans and discounts	1,512,569	Other undivided profits	448,140
Overdrafts	215,743		
U. S. bonds	376,398	State-bank notes outstanding	....
State bonds	104,337		
R. R. bonds and stocks	1,028,832	Dividends unpaid	28,111
Bank stocks	91,000		
Other stocks, bonds, and mortgages	415,300	Individual deposits	15,128,207
Due from other banks and bankers	3,702,410	State, county, and municipal deposits	200,313
Real estate, furniture, and fixtures	1,630,503		
Current expenses and taxes paid	110,809	Deposits of State, county, and municipal disbursing officers	208,937
Gold coins			
Gold certificates			
Silver coins	2,094,687	Due to other banks and bankers	989,645
Silver certificates		Other liabilities	794,710
Legal tenders and national-bank notes			
Other resources	560,004		
Total	25,928,652	Total	25,928,652

MICHIGAN.

June 30, 1887.] [55 banks.

Loans on real estate	$517,230	Capital stock paid in	$994,077
Loans on personal and collateral security	1,257,774	Surplus fund	170,196
Other loans and discounts	855,671	Other undivided profits	87,270
Overdrafts	35,328		
U. S. bonds	37,630	State-bank notes outstanding	1,000
State bonds	35,317		
R. R. bonds and stocks	2,500	Dividends unpaid	5,008
Bank stocks	1,500		
Other stocks, bonds, and mortgages	12,013	Individual deposits	2,914,008
Due from other banks and bankers	790,820	State, county, and municipal deposits	11,062
Real estate, furniture, and fixtures	244,287		
Current expenses and taxes paid	22,277	Deposits of State, county, and municipal disbursing officers	15,056
Gold coins			
Gold certificates			
Silver coins	415,965	Due to other banks and bankers	56,971
Silver certificates		Other liabilities	55,300
Legal tenders and national-bank notes			
Other resources	81,675		
Total	4,309,987	Total	4,309,987

IOWA.

June 30, 1887.] [139 banks.

Loans on real estate	$5,158,542	Capital stock paid in	$5,130,606
Loans on personal and collateral security	5,574,653	Surplus fund	867,596
Other loans and discounts	1,145,956	Other undivided profits	397,610
Overdrafts	303,523		
U. S. bonds	20,000	State-bank notes outstanding	....
State bonds	6,961		
R. R. bonds and stocks	6,000	Dividends unpaid	27,377
Bank stocks	84,020		
Other stocks, bonds, and mortgages	111,698	Individual deposits	6,143,252
Due from other banks and bankers	1,597,347	State, county, and municipal deposits	97,453
Real estate, furniture, and fixtures	1,288,553		
Current expenses and taxes paid	81,989	Deposits of State, county, and municipal disbursing officers	153,668
Gold coins			
Gold certificates			
Silver coins	970,391	Due to other banks and bankers	53,870
Silver certificates		Other liabilities	3,707,976
Legal tenders and national-bank notes			
Other resources	229,775		
Total	16,579,408	Total	16,579,408

PRIVATE BANKS—UNOFFICIAL.

MINNESOTA.

June 30, 1887.] [40 banks.

Resources.		Liabilities.	
Loans on real estate	$919,081	Capital stock paid in	$2,895,015
Loans on personal and collateral security	2,647,014	Surplus fund	180,000
Other loans and discounts	764,703	Other undivided profits	162,452
Overdrafts	44,938	State-bank notes outstanding	....
U. S. bonds	....	Dividends unpaid	....
State bonds	256	Individual deposits	2,042,758
R. R. bonds and stocks	....	State, county, and municipal deposits	130,085
Bank stocks	2,500	Deposits of State, county, and municipal disbursing officers	56,804
Other stocks, bonds, and mortgages	68,401	Due to other banks and bankers	70,061
Due from other banks and bankers	1,111,229	Other liabilities	571,778
Real estate, furniture, and fixtures	539,036		
Current expenses and taxes paid	35,183		
Gold coins; Gold certificates; Silver coins; Silver certificates; Legal tenders and national-bank notes	358,085		
Other resources	231,204		
Total	6,724,652	Total	6,724,652

KANSAS.

June 30, 1887.] [55 banks.

Loans on real estate	$1,304,235	Capital stock paid in	$2,852,934
Loans on personal and collateral security	2,611,048	Surplus fund	505,744
Other loans and discounts	309,832	Other undivided profits	170,357
Overdrafts	38,887	State-bank notes outstanding	1,155
U. S. bonds	....	Dividends unpaid	13,807
State bonds	....	Individual deposits	2,426,720
R. R. bonds and stocks	....	State, county, and municipal deposits	141,125
Bank stocks	90,274	Deposits of State, county, and municipal disbursing officers	310,264
Other stocks, bonds, and mortgages	63,884	Due to other banks and bankers	40,706
Due from other banks and bankers	760,555	Other liabilities	794,892
Real estate, furniture, and fixtures	592,120		
Current expenses and taxes paid	50,020		
Gold coins; Gold certificates; Silver coins; Silver certificates; Legal tenders and national-bank notes	1,340,484		
Other resources	61,431		
Total	7,257,770	Total	7,257,770

NEBRASKA.

June 30, 1887.] [34 banks.

Loans on real estate	$241,539	Capital stock paid in	$1,256,262
Loans on personal and collateral security	1,474,343	Surplus fund	127,810
Other loans and discounts	276,506	Other undivided profits	139,833
Overdrafts	32,814	State-bank notes outstanding	....
U. S. bonds	....	Dividends unpaid	1,639
State bonds	5,806	Individual deposits	1,538,131
R. R. bonds and stocks	....	State, county, and municipal deposits	64,785
Bank stocks	10,300	Deposits of State, county, and municipal disbursing officers	....
Other stocks, bonds, and mortgages	95,040	Due to other banks and bankers	100,490
Due from other banks and bankers	375,683	Other liabilities	355,624
Real estate, furniture, and fixtures	520,016		
Current expenses and taxes paid	40,180		
Gold coins; Gold certificates; Silver coins; Silver certificates; Legal tenders and national-bank notes	229,737		
Other resources	281,817		
Total	3,584,583	Total	3,584,583

PRIVATE BANKS—UNOFFICIAL.

OREGON.

June 30, 1887.] [3 banks.

Resources.		Liabilities.	
Loans on real estate	$190,227	Capital stock paid in	$180,282
Loans on personal and collateral security	855,283	Surplus fund	5,000
Other loans and discounts	....	Other undivided profits	438,409
Overdrafts	77,365		
U. S. bonds	26,000	State-bank notes outstanding	....
State bonds	....		
R. R. bonds and stocks	....	Dividends unpaid	2,603
Bank stocks	4,000		
Other stocks, bonds, and mortgages	32,836	Individual deposits	818,181
Due from other banks and bankers	51,845	State, county, and municipal deposits	6,707
Real estate, furniture, and fixtures	108,663		
Current expenses and taxes paid	4,991	Deposits of State, county, and municipal disbursing officers	....
Gold coins			
Gold certificates			
Silver coins	110,478	Due to other banks and bankers	5,609
Silver certificates		Other liabilities	1,858
Legal tenders and national-bank notes			
Other resources	2,961		
Total	1,404,649	Total	1,404,649

COLORADO.

June 30, 1887.] [8 banks.

Resources.		Liabilities.	
Loans on real estate	$12,310	Capital stock paid in	$221,300
Loans on personal and collateral security	588,564	Surplus fund	....
Other loans and discounts	50,402	Other undivided profits	29,095
Overdrafts	4,687		
U. S. bonds	....	State-bank notes outstanding	....
State bonds	9,279		
R. R. bonds and stocks	....	Dividends unpaid	....
Bank stocks	....		
Other stocks, bonds, and mortgages	3,815	Individual deposits	993,961
Due from other banks and bankers	419,218	State, county, and municipal deposits	....
Real estate, furniture, and fixtures	43,497		
Current expenses and taxes paid	2,174	Deposits of State, county, and municipal disbursing officers	51,607
Gold coins			
Gold certificates			
Silver coins	167,402	Due to other banks and bankers	6,264
Silver certificates		Other liabilities	....
Legal tenders and national-bank notes			
Other resources	870		
Total	1,302,227	Total	1,302,227

NEVADA.

June 30, 1887.] [2 banks.

Resources.		Liabilities.	
Loans on real estate	$30,000	Capital stock paid in	$108,150
Loans on personal and collateral security	74,109	Surplus fund	10,093
Other loans and discounts	....	Other undivided profits	3,122
Overdrafts	38,561		
U. S. bonds	....	State-bank notes outstanding	....
State bonds	....		
R. R. bonds and stocks	....	Dividends unpaid	....
Bank stocks	....		
Other stocks, bonds, and mortgages	1,686	Individual deposits	93,247
Due from other banks and bankers	30,684	State, county, and municipal deposits	....
Real estate, furniture, and fixtures	21,917		
Current expenses and taxes paid	2,039	Deposits of State, county, and municipal disbursing officers	....
Gold coins			
Gold certificates			
Silver coins	24,616	Due to other banks and bankers	....
Silver certificates		Other liabilities	....
Legal tenders and national-bank notes			
Other resources	....		
Total	223,612	Total	222 612

PRIVATE BANKS—UNOFFICIAL.

UTAH.

June 30, 1887.] [7 banks.

Resources.		Liabilities.	
Loans on real estate	$844,365	Capital stock paid in	$995,907
Loans on personal and collateral security	1,400,570	Surplus fund	1,061,667
Other loans and discounts	20,055	Other undivided profits	63,724
Overdrafts	106,674	State-bank notes outstanding	....
U. S. bonds	....	Dividends unpaid	219
State bonds	....	Individual deposits	1,818,718
R. R. bonds and stocks	930	State, county, and municipal deposits	233
Bank stocks	....	Deposits of State, county, and municipal disbursing officers	....
Other stocks, bonds, and mortgages	31,945	Due to other banks and bankers	12,108
Due from other banks and bankers	287,709	Other liabilities	25,900
Real estate, furniture, and fixtures	59,633		
Current expenses and taxes paid	4,098		
Gold coins; Gold certificates; Silver coins; Silver certificates; Legal tenders and national-bank notes	336,446		
Other resources	883,031		
Total	3,978,476	Total	3,978,476

IDAHO.

June 30, 1887.] [2 banks.

Resources.		Liabilities.	
Loans on real estate	$18,450	Capital stock paid in	$127,660
Loans on personal and collateral security	48,250	Surplus fund	25,000
Other loans and discounts	....	Other undivided profits	131,751
Overdrafts	6,918	State-bank notes outstanding	....
U. S. bonds	....	Dividends unpaid	....
State bonds	....	Individual deposits	54,016
R. R. bonds and stocks	....	State, county, and municipal deposits	....
Bank stocks	15,000	Deposits of State, county, and municipal disbursing officers	....
Other stocks, bonds, and mortgages	132,549	Due to other banks and bankers	....
Due from other banks and bankers	7,556	Other liabilities	5,900
Real estate, furniture, and fixtures	45,416		
Current expenses and taxes paid	....		
Gold coins; Gold certificates; Silver coins; Silver certificates; Legal tenders and national-bank notes	15,188		
Other resources	55,000		
Total	344,327	Total	344,327

WYOMING.

June 30, 1887.] [7 banks.

Resources.		Liabilities.	
Loans on real estate	$85,251	Capital stock paid in	$338,000
Loans on personal and collateral security	402,855	Surplus fund	53,905
Other loans and discounts	209,200	Other undivided profits	39,011
Overdrafts	22,337	State-bank notes outstanding	....
U. S. bonds	....	Dividends unpaid	....
State bonds	676	Individual deposits	730,874
R. R. bonds and stocks	....	State, county, and municipal deposits	....
Bank stocks	....	Deposits of State, county, and municipal disbursing officers	....
Other stocks, bonds, and mortgages	16,074	Due to other banks and bankers	3,914
Due from other banks and bankers	198,989	Other liabilities	47,847
Real estate, furniture, and fixtures	157,393		
Current expenses and taxes paid	8,270		
Gold coins; Gold certificates; Silver coins; Silver certificates; Legal tenders and national-bank notes	96,107		
Other resources	16,321		
Total	1,213,581	Total	1,213,581

PRIVATE BANKS—UNOFFICIAL.

NEW MEXICO.

June 30, 1887.] [3 banks.

Resources.		Liabilities.	
Loans on real estate	$20,000	Capital stock paid in	$130,000
Loans on personal and collateral security	176,999	Surplus fund	7,443
Other loans and discounts	2,000	Other undivided profits	10,493
Overdrafts	4,046	State-bank notes outstanding	....
U. S. bonds	....	Dividends unpaid	....
State bonds	....	Individual deposits	104,019
R. R. bonds and stocks	....	State, county, and municipal deposits	....
Bank stocks	....	Deposits of State, county, and municipal disbursing officers	....
Other stocks, bonds, and mortgages	16,584	Due to other banks and bankers	450
Due from other banks and bankers	46,245	Other liabilities	2,520
Real estate, furniture, and fixtures	34,758		
Current expenses and taxes paid	865		
Gold coins			
Gold certificates			
Silver coins	53,334		
Silver certificates			
Legal tenders and national-bank notes			
Other resources	....		
Total	351,831	Total	354,831

DAKOTA.

June 30, 1887.] [77 banks.

Resources.		Liabilities.	
Loans on real estate	$385,055	Capital stock paid in	$2,019,180
Loans on personal and collateral security	1,811,189	Surplus fund	168,323
Other loans and discounts	150,344	Other undivided profits	196,603
Overdrafts	55,172	State-bank notes outstanding	....
U. S. bonds	....	Dividends unpaid	20,650
State bonds	100	Individual deposits	1,155,003
R. R. bonds and stocks	1,000	State, county, and municipal deposits	21,210
Bank stocks	11,230	Deposits of State, county, and municipal disbursing officers	....
Other stocks, bonds, and mortgages	32,101	Due to other banks and bankers	56,084
Due from other banks and bankers	417,079	Other liabilities	116,533
Real estate, furniture, and fixtures	351,740		
Current expenses and taxes paid	53,378		
Gold coins			
Gold certificates			
Silver coins	395,159		
Silver certificates			
Legal tenders and national-bank notes			
Other resources	80,838		
Total	3,793,285	Total	3,793,285

WASHINGTON.

June 30, 1887.] [2 banks.

Resources.		Liabilities.	
Loans on real estate	$10,000	Capital stock paid in	$225,000
Loans on personal and collateral security	500,810	Surplus fund	205,030
Other loans and discounts	45,133	Other undivided profits	5,000
Overdrafts	10,000	State-bank notes outstanding	....
U. S. bonds	....	Dividends unpaid	....
State bonds	....	Individual deposits	513,310
R. R. bonds and stocks	....	State, county, and municipal deposits	....
Bank stocks	....	Deposits of State, county, and municipal disbursing officers	....
Other stocks, bonds, and mortgages	41,000	Due to other banks and bankers	21,388
Due from other banks and bankers	186,347	Other liabilities	100
Real estate, furniture, and fixtures	58,444		
Current expenses and taxes paid	5,120		
Gold coins			
Gold certificates			
Silver coins	96,541		
Silver certificates			
Legal tenders and national-bank notes			
Other resources	4,499		
Total	1,059,897	Total	1,050,807

PRIVATE BANKS—UNOFFICIAL.

ARIZONA.

June 30, 1887.] [2 banks.

Resources.		Liabilities.	
Loans on real estate	$14,500	Capital stock paid in	$90,000
Loans on personal and collateral security	106,489	Surplus fund	80,000
Other loans and discounts	161,028	Other undivided profits	28,329
Overdrafts	25,617		
U. S. bonds	45,000	State-bank notes outstanding	....
State bonds	....		
R. R. bonds and stocks	....	Dividends unpaid	....
Bank stocks	....		
Other stocks, bonds, and mortgages	56,833	Individual deposits	341,229
Due from other banks and bankers	41,927	State, county, and municipal deposits	....
Real estate, furniture, and fixtures	15,640		
Current expenses and taxes paid	7,897	Deposits of State, county, and municipal disbursing officers	3,146
Gold coins			
Gold certificates			
Silver coins	89,507	Due to other banks and bankers	27,324
Silver certificates		Other liabilities	....
Legal tenders and national-bank notes			
Other resources	2,500		
Total	573,028	Total	573,028

AGGREGATE RESOURCES AND LIABILITIES OF 819 PRIVATE BANKS IN THE UNITED STATES.

Loans on real estate	$15,490,166	Capital stock paid in	$34,183,294
Loans on personal and collateral security	54,003,430	Surplus fund	10,556,542
Other loans and discounts	18,587,909	Other undivided profits	5,887,100
Overdrafts	1,506,385		
U. S. bonds	4,265,056	State-bank notes outstanding	2,155
State bonds	356,234		
R. R. bonds and stocks	2,904,872	Dividends unpaid	170,055
Bank stocks	592,991		
Other stocks, bonds, and mortgages	5,641,692	Individual deposits	77,736,527
Due from other banks and bankers	18,066,251	State, county, and municipal deposits	916,192
Real estate, furniture, and fixtures	8,306,977		
Current expenses and taxes paid	725,365	Deposits of State, county, and municipal disbursing officers	1,158,905
Gold coins			
Gold certificates			
Silver coins	11,898,653	Due to other banks and bankers	4,911,254
Silver certificates		Other liabilities	9,943,226
Legal tenders and national-bank notes			
Other resources	3,172,335		
Total	145,525,316	Total	145,525,316

PRIVATE BANKS—OFFICIAL AND UNOFFICIAL.

AGGREGATE RESOURCES AND LIABILITIES OF 1,001 PRIVATE BANKS IN THE UNITED STATES, 1887.

Resources.		Liabilities.	
Loans on real estate	$17,588,540	Capital stock paid in	$40,079,438
Loans on personal and collateral security	63,774,934	Surplus fund	12,238,065
Other loans and discounts	24,365,262	Other undivided profits	5,925,835
Overdrafts	1,858,778		
U. S. bonds	4,351,656	State-bank notes outstanding	2,155
State bonds	356,234		
R. R. bonds and stocks	2,904,872	Dividends unpaid	170,055
Bank stocks	592,991		
Other stocks, bonds, and mortgages	6,743,050	Individual deposits	96,580,437
Due from other banks and bankers	22,226,065	State, county, and municipal deposits	946,192
Real estate, furniture, and fixtures	9,757,816		
Current expenses and taxes paid	751,547	Deposits of State, county, and municipal disbursing officers	1,158,905
Gold coins } Gold certificates } Silver coins } Silver certificates } Legal tenders and national-bank notes }	15,663,724	Due to other banks and bankers	5,813,151
		Other liabilities	11,564,086
Other resources	3,539,870		
Total	174,478,339	Total	174,478,339

REPORT OF THE CONDITION OF THE NATIONAL SAVINGS BANK OF THE DISTRICT OF COLUMBIA, AT WASHINGTON, D. C., AT THE CLOSE OF BUSINESS ON THE 5TH DAY OF OCTOBER, 1887.

DR. RESOURCES.			LIABILITIES.		CR.
Loans and discounts (see schedule)		$358,841.66	Undivided profits		$12,017.23
United States bonds on hand (par value), 4 per cents		160,000.00	Individual deposits subject to check	$818,506.58	
Other stocks, bonds, and mortgages (par; see schedule)		247,500.00	Time certificates of deposit	1,000.00	
Due from State and private banks and bankers (see schedule)		15,480.91			819,506.58
Current expenses and taxes paid		3,645.74			
Premium (market value) on bonds		24,735.00			
Checks and other cash items (see schedule)		4,225.50			
Bills of other banks		250.00			
Fractional paper currency, nickels, and cents		25.97			
Specie, viz:					
Gold coin	$525.00				
Silver coin	225.00				
Silver Treasury certificates (act Feb. 28, 1878)	5,000.00				
		5,750.00			
Legal-tender notes		11,100.00			
Total		831,553.81	Total		831,555.81

SCHEDULES.

Loans and discounts.

On mortgages and other real-estate security	$120,550.00
On United States bonds (demand loans)	3,050.00
On other stocks, bonds, etc. (demand loans)	235,241.66
	358,841.66

Other stocks, bonds, and mortgages.

50,000 District of Columbia 5s	$50,000.00
50,000 District of Columbia 6s	50,000.00
50,000 District of Columbia 3.65s	50,000.00
15,000 Washington Market Company 6s	15,000.00
20,000 Washington and Georgetown Railroad 6s	20,000.00
30,000 State of Georgia 7s	30,000.00
32,500 National Safe Deposit Company stock	32,500.00
Total	247,500.00

I, Benjamin P. Snyder, president of the National Savings Bank of the District of Columbia, do solemnly swear that the above statement is true, to the best of my knowledge and belief.

BENJAMIN P. SNYDER,
President.

DISTRICT OF COLUMBIA,
City of Washington:

Sworn to and subscribed before me this 7th day of October, 1887.
[SEAL.]

D. RITTENHOUSE,
Notary Public.

Correct. Attest:

BENJAMIN P. SNYDER,
ANDREW WYLIE,
Z. C. ROBBINS,
M. G. EMERY,
Directors.

The highest rate of interest paid by the bank is 2 per cent.
Number depositors September 30, 1887, 8,488.

DISTRIBUTION BY STATES, TERRITORIES, AND GEOGRAPHICAL DIVISIONS, NUMBER, ... AND LOAN AND TRUST

States and Territories.	Number of banks reporting distribution of shares of stock.	Number of banks reporting condition.	Number of shares held by—		Same, in detail, held by—				
			State residents.	Non-State residents.	Natural persons.	Religious, charitable, and educational institutions.	Municipal corporations.	Savings banks, loan and trust and insurance companies.	All other corporations.
Maine	2	56	1,813	187	1,834	....	.....	136	30
New Hampshire	2	68	1,989	511	1,882	....	.....	618	....
Vermont	5	28	3,457	43	3,350	....	.....	150	....
Massachusetts	10	181	43,411	2,599	44,247	753	.....	910	100
Rhode Island	5	47	18,846	1,643	17,010	943	34	373	1,529
Connecticut	12	100	30,819	4,581	24,496	521	.....	9,793	590
Division No. 1	36	480	100,335	9,564	93,419	2,217	34	11,980	2,249
New York	96	237	250,275	41,339	281,774	659	735	8,002	444
New Jersey	10	33	16,954⅓	2,106	18,520⅓	198	220	80	42
Pennsylvania	85	95	204,880⅔	11,953	298,595	267	.....	6,014⅔	1,957
Division No. 2	191	365	562,110	55,398	598,889⅓	1,124	955	14,096⅔	2,443
Delaware	1	2	2,351	49	973	514	45	49	819
Maryland	8	20	67,872	2,817	63,648	1,086	.....	4,004	1,951
District of Columbia	1	1	1,015	365	1,055	....	.....	325	....
Virginia	30	39	22,389	2,899	24,706	234	.....	16	242
West Virginia	12	14	9,867	1,580	11,427	.....	.....	20	......
Division No. 3	52	76	103,494	7,710	101,899	1,834	45	4,414	3,012
North Carolina	4	12	2,273	....	2,273	....	.....	....	....
South Carolina	6	10	4,125	835	4,810	25	.....	118	7
Georgia	14	16	59,170	17,419	71,575	1,320	591	1,916	1,187
Florida	1	6	500	....	500	....	.....	....	....
Alabama	3	7	4,380	120	4,117	6	.....	377	....
Mississippi	6	9	7,176½	945½	7,507	....	.....	615	....
Louisiana	4	5	20,118	2,055	20,487	214	.....	53	1,419
Texas	5	9	5,935	362	6,297	....	.....	....	....
Arkansas	3	6	4,650	....	4,650	....	.....	....	....
Kentucky	41	71	56,253⅓	7,245	61,279⅓	1,794	.....	394	31
Tennessee	19	27	32,796⅓	2,604	34,783⅓	25	.....	102	490
Division No. 4	106	178	197,377⅓	31,585½	218,279	3,384	591	3,575	3,134
Ohio	48	50	38,379¼	1,542¼	39,156⅓	10	.....	570	185
Indiana	30	38	20,069	506	20,575	....	.....	....	....
Illinois	12	53	23,337	7,118	30,300	50	.....	105	....
Michigan	33	62	25,606¼	1,583¾	27,145	....	.....	....	45
Wisconsin	33	56	86,985	2,552	89,492	....	.....	....	45
Division No. 5	156	259	194,376⅓	13,302	206,668⅓	60	.....	675	275
Iowa	90	102	59,221	14,968	72,826	3	.....	1,060	300
Minnesota	59	64	60,541	7,859	66,712	80	.....	1,239	369
Missouri	158	214	93,708$\frac{3}{10}$	29,574$\frac{6}{10}$	121,314$\frac{9}{10}$	500	.....	1,102	186
Kansas	111	149	63,272⅓	23,238$\frac{1}{10}$	85,021⅔	....	.....	1,005	481
Nebraska	70	144	25,607⅓	12,213	37,316⅓	....	.....	404	100
Division No. 6	488	673	302,350$\frac{3}{10}$	87,852$\frac{7}{10}$	383,191	673	.....	4,900	1,439
Colorado	5	8	2,475	375	2,850	....	.....	....	....
Nevada	1	...	2,000	1,000	3,000	....	.....	....	....
California	58	112	193,078⅓	25,704⅓	215,645	180	.....	1,740	1,209
Oregon	2	4	917	83	1,000	....	.....	....	....
Division No. 7	66	124	198,470⅓	27,162⅓	222,495	180	.....	1,749	1,209
Dakota	22	......	6,029⅓	4,015⅓	10,045	....	.....	....	....
Idaho	.....	......	....	....	....	....	.....	....	....
Montana	.....	......	....	....	....	....	.....	....	....
New Mexico	.....	......	....	....	....	....	.....	....	....
Utah	1	......	4,000	....	4,000	....	.....	....	....
Washington	1	......	277	223	500	....	.....	....	....
Arizona	1	......	250	250	500	....	.....	....	....
Division No. 8	25	......	10,556⅓	4,488⅓	15,045	....	.....	....	....
United States	1,120	2,155	[illegible]	[illegible]	[illegible]	9,472	1,625	41,380⅓	13,761

AND AVERAGE PAR VALUE OF SHARES OF STOCK OF STATE AND SAVINGS BANKS, COMPANIES, JUNE 30, 1887.

Total shares issued.		Number of shareholders.					Number of shareholders owning specific amounts.				
Number.	Average par value.	Natural persons.	Corporations.	Resident.	Non-resident.	Total.	Owning shares to the par value of $1,000 and less.	Over $1,000 and less than $5,000.	Over $5,000 and less than $30,000.	Over $30,000.	Total.
2,000	100.00	128	5	124	9	133	94	30	9	......	133
2,500	100.00	181	14	159	36	195	147	33	15	......	195
3,500	100.00	184	1	158	27	185	123	51	11	......	185
46,010	98.04	1,020	14	961	73	1,034	313	334	373	14	1,034
20,489	48.67	792	41	705	128	833	617	183	32	1	833
35,400	90.82	1,334	126	1,243	217	1,460	867	435	146	12	1,460
109,899	86.65	3,639	201	3,350	490	3,840	2,161	1,066	586	27	3,840
201,614	81.37	7,103	117	5,685	1,535	7,220	3,203	2,558	1,386	73	7,220
19,060¼	64.39	724	14	661	77	738	442	240	56	......	738
396,833½	65.46	6,771	109	6,205	675	6,880	3,809	2,007	985	79	6,880
617,508	73.94	14,598	240	12,551	2,287	14,838	7,454	4,805	2,427	152	14,838
2,400	50.00	65	10	67	8	75	54	18	2	1	75
70,689	28.71	1,231	55	1,240	46	1,286	810	398	71	7	1,286
1,380	100.00	20	1	18	3	21	3	10	6	2	21
25,288	63.55	1,208	9	1,111	106	1,217	877	270	60	.....	1,217
11,447	68.38	444	1	385	60	445	288	126	30	2	445
111,204	42.06	2,968	76	2,821	223	3,044	2,032	831	169	12	3,044
2,273	100.00	83	......	83	....	83	52	21	10	......	83
4,900	100.00	223	4	208	19	227	137	64	26	......	227
76,589	88.25	2,017	65	1,731	351	2,082	1,012	751	287	32	2,082
500	100.00	12	......	12	....	12	7	2	3	......	12
4,500	100.00	89	3	88	4	92	33	31	28	......	92
8,122	100.00	131	1	115	17	132	38	43	46	5	132
22,173	86.47	641	12	564	89	653	268	290	90	5	653
6,297	100.00	108	......	98	10	108	35	34	36	3	108
4,650	25.00	37	......	37	....	37	15	10	11	1	37
63,498½	89.83	2,498	45	2,202	341	2,543	1,312	938	285	8	2,543
35,460½	86.44	864	12	781	95	876	404	312	155	5	876
228,963	87.45	6,703	142	5,919	926	6,845	3,313	2,496	977	59	6,845
39,921½	90.70	1,148	7	1,064	91	1,155	553	373	214	15	1,155
20,575	88.26	527	......	505	22	527	268	164	89	6	527
30,455	100.00	405	3	323	85	408	147	104	130	27	408
27,190	90.08	857	2	765	94	859	478	248	125	8	859
89,537	10.71	468	3	405	66	471	223	151	92	5	471
207,678½	57.77	3,405	15	3,062	358	3,420	1,669	1,040	650	61	3,420
74,180	78.24	2,528	16	1,900	644	2,544	1,473	751	306	14	2,544
68,400	96.90	1,974	33	1,737	270	2,007	1,000	594	398	15	2,007
123,282⅗	100.37	4,386	23	3,516	893	4,409	2,476	1,308	581	44	4,409
86,510⅓	90.24	2,145	35	1,368	812	2,180	1,132	621	383	44	2,180
37,820½	96.15	887	13	529	371	900	376	277	239	8	900
390,203	92.85	11,920	120	9,050	2,990	12,040	6,457	3,551	1,907	125	12,040
2,850	100.00	112	......	77	35	112	65	26	21	......	112
3,000	100.00	35	......	29	6	35	1	14	17	3	35
218,783	100.65	2,682	30	2,455	257	2,712	1,178	824	593	118	2,712
1,000	100.00	28	......	24	4	28	11	11	6	......	28
225,633	100.63	2,857	30	2,585	302	2,887	1,255	875	636	121	2,887
10,045	88.94	419	......	115	304	419	249	137	32	1	419
....	....	....	......	....	....	....	....	....	....	......	....
....	....	....	......	....	....	....	....	....	....	......	....
....	....	....	......	....	....	....	....	....	....	......	....
4,000	50.00	13	......	13	....	13	5	4	3	1	13
500	100.00	22	......	5	17	22	12	2	8	......	22
500	100.00	9	......	6	3	9	2	5	2	......	
15,045	77.66	463	......	139	324	463	268	148	45	2	463
1,906,133⅓	79.53	46,553	821	39,477	7,900	47,377	24,600	14,812	7,597	559	47,377

AGGREGATE RESOURCES AND LIABILITIES

OF

THE NATIONAL BANKS

FROM

OCTOBER, 1863, TO OCTOBER, 1887.

AGGREGATE RESOURCES AND LIABILITIES OF THE NATIONAL

1863.

Resources.	JANUARY.	APRIL.	JULY.	OCTOBER 5.
				66 banks.
Loans and discounts				$5, 460, 088. 33
U. S. bonds and securities				5, 662, 600. 00
Other items				106, 009. 12
Due from nat'l and other b'ks				2, 625, 597. 05
Real estate, furniture, etc				177, 565. 69
Current expenses				53, 808. 92
Premiums paid				2, 503. 60
Checks and other cash items				492, 138. 58
Bills of nat'l and other banks				764, 725. 00
Specie and other lawful mon'y				1, 446, 607. 62
Total				16, 797, 644. 00

1864.

	JANUARY 4.	APRIL 4	JULY 4.	OCTOBER 3.
	139 banks.	307 banks.	467 banks.	508 banks.
Loans and discounts	$10, 666, 095. 60	$31, 593, 943. 43	$70, 746, 513. 33	$93, 238, 657. 92
U. S. bonds and securities	15, 112, 250. 00	41, 175, 150. 00	92, 530, 500. 00	108, 064, 400. 00
Other items	74, 571. 48	432, 059. 95	842, 017. 73	1, 434, 739. 76
Due from national banks		4, 699, 479. 56	15, 935, 730. 13	19, 965, 720. 47
Due from other b'ks and b'krs	*4, 786, 124. 58	8, 537, 908. 94	17, 337, 558. 66	14, 051, 396 31
Real estate, furniture, etc	381, 144. 00	755, 696. 41	1, 694, 049. 46	2, 202, 318. 20
Current expenses	118, 854. 43	352, 720. 77	502, 341. 31	1, 021, 569. 02
Checks and other cash items	577, 507. 92	2, 651, 916. 96	5, 057, 122. 00	7, 640, 169. 14
Bills of nat'l and other banks	895, 521. 00	1, 660, 000. 00	5, 344, 172. 00	4, 687, 727. 00
Specie and other lawful mon'y	5, 018, 622. 57	22, 961, 411. 64	42, 283, 798. 23	44, 801, 497. 48
Total	37, 630, 091. 58	114, 820, 287. 66	252, 273, 803. 75	297, 108, 195. 90

1865.

	JANUARY 2.	APRIL 3.	JULY 3.	OCTOBER 2.
	638 banks.	907 banks.	1,294 banks.	1,513 banks.
Loans and discounts	$166, 448, 718. 00	$252, 404, 208. 07	$362, 442, 743. 08	$487, 170, 136. 29
U. S. bonds and securities	176, 578, 750. 00	277, 619, 900. 00	391, 744, 850. 00	427, 731, 300. 00
Other items	3, 294, 883. 27	4, 275, 769. 51	12, 569, 120. 38	19, 048, 513. 15
Due from national banks	30, 820, 175. 44	40, 963, 243. 47	76, 977, 539. 59	89, 978, 980. 55
Due from other b'ks and b'krs	19, 836, 072. 83	22, 554, 636. 57	26, 078, 028. 01	17, 393, 232. 25
Real estate, furniture, etc	4, 083, 226. 12	6, 525, 118. 80	11, 231, 257. 28	14, 703, 281. 77
Current expenses	1, 053, 725. 34	2, 298, 025. 65	2, 338, 775. 56	4, 539, 525. 11
Premiums paid	1, 323, 023. 56	1, 823, 291. 84	2, 243, 210. 31	2, 585, 501. 06
Checks and other cash items	17, 837, 496. 77	29, 681, 394. 13	41, 314, 904. 50	72, 309, 854. 44
Bills of nat'l and other banks	14, 275, 153. 00	13, 710, 370. 00	21, 651, 826. 00	16, 247, 241. 00
Specie	4, 481, 937. 68	6, 659, 660. 47	9, 437, 060. 40	18, 072, 012. 59
Legal tenders and frac'l cur'y	72, 535, 504. 67	112, 999, 320. 59	168, 426, [illegible]. 55	189, 988, 496. 28
Total	512, 568, 666. 68	771, 514, 939. 10	1, 126, 455, 481. 66	1, 359, 768, 074. 49

* Including amount due from national banks.

1863.

BANKS FROM OCTOBER, 1863, TO OCTOBER, 1887.

Liabilities.	JANUARY.	APRIL.	JULY.	OCTOBER 5.
				66 banks.
Capital stock	....	....	....	$7,188,393.00
Undivided profits	....	....	....	128,030.06
Individual and other deposits	....	....	....	8,497,681.84
Due to nat'l and other banks*	....	....	....	981,178.59
Other items	....	....	....	2,360.51
Total	....	....	....	16,797,644.00

1864.

	JANUARY 4.	APRIL 4.	JULY 4.	OCTOBER 3.
	139 banks.	307 banks.	467 banks.	508 banks.
Capital stock	$14,740,522.00	$42,204,474.00	$75,213,945.00	$86,782,802.00
Surplus fund	....	....	1,129,910.22	2,010,286.10
Undivided profits	432,827.81	1,625,656.87	3,094,330.11	5,982,392.22
National b'k notes outstanding	30,155.00	9,797,975.00	25,825,665.00	45,260,504.00
Individual and other deposits	19,450,492.53	51,274,914.01	119,414,239.03	122,166,536.40
Due to nat'l and other banks*	2,153,779.38	6,814,930.40	27,382,006.37	34,862,384.81
Other items	822,914.86	3,102,337.38	213,708.02	43,289.77
Total	37,630,691.58	114,820,287.66	252,273,803.75	297,108,195.30

1865.

	JANUARY 2.	APRIL 3.	JULY 3.	OCTOBER 2.
	638 banks.	907 banks.	1,294 banks.	1,513 banks.
Capital stock	$135,618,874.00	$215,326,023.00	$325,834,558.00	$393,157,206.00
Surplus fund	8,663,311.22	17,318,942.65	31,303,565.64	38,713,380.72
Undivided profits	12,283,812.65	17,809,307.14	23,159,408.17	32,350,278.19
National b'k notes outstanding	66,769,375.00	98,896,488.00	131,452,158.00	171,321,903.00
Individual and other deposits	183,479,636.98	262,961,473.13	398,357,559.59	500,910,873.22
United States deposits	37,764,729.77	57,630,141.01	58,032,720.67	48,170,381.31
Due to national banks	30,619,175.57	41,301,031.16	78,261,045.64	90,044,837.08
Due to other b'ks and bankers*	37,104,130.62	50,692,581.64	79,591,594.93	84,155,161.27
Other items	265,020.87	578,051.37	462,871.02	944,053.70
Total	512,568,650.68	771,514,939.10	1,126,455,481.66	1,359,768,074.49

* Including State bank circulation outstanding.

AGGREGATE RESOURCES AND LIABILITIES OF THE NATIONAL

1866.

Resources.	JANUARY 1.	APRIL 2.	JULY 2.	OCTOBER 1.
	1,582 banks.	1,612 banks.	1,634 banks.	1,644 banks.
Loans and discounts	$500,650,109.19	$528,080,526.70	$550,353,094.17	$603,314,704.83
U.S. b'ds dep'd to secure circ'n	298,376,850.00	315,850,300.00	326,483,350.00	331,843,200.00
Other U.S. b'ds and securities	142,003,500.00	125,625,750.00	121,152,950.00	94,974,650.00
Oth'r stocks, b'ds, and mortg's	17,483,753.18	17,379,738.92	17,565,911.46	15,887,490.06
Due from national banks	93,254,551.02	87,564,329.71	96,696,482.66	107,650,174.18
Due from other b'ks and b'k'rs	14,658,229.87	13,682,345.12	13,982,613.23	15,211,117.16
Real estate, furniture, etc	15,436,296.16	15,895,564.46	16,730,923.62	17,134,002.58
Current expenses	3,193,717.78	4,927,599.79	3,032,716.27	5,311,253.35
Premiums paid	2,423,918.02	2,233,516.31	2,398,872.26	2,493,773.47
Checks and other cash items	89,837,684.50	105,490,619.26	96,077,134.53	103,684,249.21
Bills of national and other b'ks	20,406,442.00	18,279,816.00	17,866,742.00	17,437,779.00
Specie	19,205,018.75	17,529,778.42	12,629,376.30	9,226,831.82
Legal tenders and fract'l cur'y	187,846,548.82	189,867,852.52	201,425,041.63	205,793,578.76
Total	1,404,776,619.29	1,442,407,737.31	1,476,395,208.13	1,526,962,804.42

1867.

	JANUARY 7.	APRIL 1.	JULY 1.	OCTOBER 7.
	1,648 banks.	1,642 banks.	1,636 banks.	1,642 banks.
Loans and discounts	$608,771,799.61	$597,648,286.53	$588,450,396.12	$609,675,214.61
U.S. b'ds dep'd to secure circ'n	339,570,700.00	338,863,650.00	337,684,250.00	338,640,150.00
U.S. b'ds dep'd to sec're dep'ts	36,185,950.00	38,465,800.00	38,368,950.00	37,862,100.00
U.S. b'ds and sec'ties on hand	52,949,300.00	46,639,400.00	45,633,700.00	42,460,800.00
Oth'r stocks, b'ds, and mortg's	15,073,737.45	20,194,675.21	21,452,615.43	21,507,881.42
Due from national banks	92,552,206.29	94,121,186.21	92,308,911.87	95,217,610.14
Due from other b'ks and b'k'rs	12,996,157.49	10,737,392.90	9,663,322.82	8,389,226.47
Real estate, furniture, etc	18,925,315.51	19,625,893.81	19,800,905.86	20,639,708.23
Current expenses	2,822,675.18	5,693,784.17	3,249,153.31	5,297,494.13
Premiums paid	2,860,398.85	3,411,325.56	3,338,600.37	2,764,186.35
Checks and other cash items	101,430,220.18	87,951,405.13	128,312,177.79	134,603,231.51
Bills of national banks	19,263,718.00	12,873,785.00	16,138,769.00	11,841,104.00
Bills of other banks	1,176,142.00	825,748.00	531,267.00	333,209.00
Specie	19,726,043.29	11,444,529.15	11,128,672.98	12,798,044.40
Legal tenders and fract'l cu'y	104,872,371.64	93,861,254.17	102,534,613.46	100,550,849.01
Compound-interest notes	82,047,250.00	84,065,790.00	75,488,220.00	56,888,250.00
Total	1,511,222,085.40	1,465,451,105.84	1,494,084,526.01	1,499,469,060.17

1868.

	JANUARY 6.	APRIL 6.	JULY 6.	OCTOBER 5.
	1,642 banks.	1,643 banks.	1,640 banks.	1,643 banks.
Loans and discounts	$616,603,479.89	$628,029,347.65	$655,729,546.42	$657,668,847.81
U.S. b'ds dep'd to secure circ'n	339,064,200.00	339,686,650.00	339,569,100.00	340,487,050.00
U.S. b'ds dep'd to sec're dept's	37,315,750.00	37,446,000.00	37,853,150.00	37,360,150.00
U.S. b'ds and sec'ties on hand	44,164,500.00	45,958,550.00	43,068,350.00	36,817,600.00
Oth'r stocks, b'ds, and mortg's	19,365,864.77	19,874,384.33	20,007,327.42	20,693,406.40
Due from national banks	99,311,416.60	95,900,606.35	114,434,097.93	102,278,547.77
Due from other b'ks and b'k'rs	8,460,199.74	7,074,297.44	8,612,456.72	7,848,822.24
Real estate, furniture, etc	21,125,665.08	22,082,570.25	22,699,829.70	22,747,875.18
Current expenses	2,986,893.86	5,428,460.25	2,938,519.04	5,278,911.22
Premiums paid	2,464,536.96	2,660,106.09	2,432,074.37	1,819,815.50
Checks and other cash items	109,390,266.37	114,993,036.23	124,076,097.71	143,241,394.99
Bills of national banks	16,655,572.00	12,573,514.00	13,210,179.00	11,842,974.00
Bills of other banks	261,269.00	196,106.00	342,550.00	222,668.00
Fractional currency	1,927,876.78	1,825,640.16	1,863,358.91	2,262,791.97
Specie	20,981,601.45	18,373,943.22	20,755,919.04	13,003,713.69
Legal-tender notes	114,306,491.00	84,390,219.00	100,166,100.00	92,453,475.00
Compound-interest notes	39,997,030.00	38,917,490.00	19,473,420.00	4,513,730.00
Three per cent. certificates	8,215,000.00	24,255,000.00	44,905,000.00	59,080,000.00
Total	1,502,017,611.16	1,499,668,920.97	1,572,167,076.26	1,559,621,773.40

BANKS FROM OCTOBER, 1863, TO OCTOBER, 1867—Continued.

1866.

Liabilities.	JANUARY 1. 1,582 banks.	APRIL 2. 1,612 banks.	JULY 2. 1,634 banks.	OCTOBER 1. 1,644 banks.
Capital stock	$403,357,346.00	$409,273,534.00	$414,270,493.00	$415,472,369.00
Surplus fund	43,000,370.78	44,687,810.54	50,151,991.77	53,359,277.64
Undivided profits	28,972,493.70	30,964,422.73	29,286,175.45	32,593,486.69
National b'k notes outstand'g	213,239,530.00	248,886,282.00	267,798,678.00	280,253,818.00
State bank notes outstanding	45,449,155.00	33,800,865.00	19,996,163.00	9,748,025.00
Individual deposits	522,507,829.27	534,734,950.33	533,338,174.25	564,616,777.64
U. S. deposits	29,747,236.15	29,150,729.82	36,038,185.03	30,420,819.80
Dep'ts of U.S. disb'sing officers	....	....	3,066,892.22	2,979,955.77
Due to national banks	94,709,074.15	89,067,501.54	96,496,726.42	110,531,957.31
Due to other b'ks and bankers	23,793,584.24	22,841,641.35	25,951,728.99	26,986,317.57
Total	1,404,776,619.29	1,442,407,737.31	1,476,395,208.13	1,526,962,801.42

1867.

	JANUARY 7. 1,648 banks.	APRIL 1. 1,642 banks.	JULY 1. 1,636 banks.	OCTOBER 7. 1,642 banks.
Capital stock	$420,229,739.00	$419,399,484.00	$418,558,148.00	$420,073,415.00
Surplus fund	59,992,871.57	60,206,013.58	63,232,811.12	66,695,587.01
Undivided profits	26,961,382.60	31,131,034.39	30,656,222.84	33,751,446.21
National b'k notes outstand'g	291,436,749.00	292,788,572.00	291,769,553.00	293,887,941.00
State bank notes outstanding	6,961,499.00	5,460,312.00	4,484,112.00	4,092,153.00
Individual deposits	558,699,768.06	512,046,182.47	539,599,076.10	540,797,837.51
U. S. deposits	27,284,876.93	27,473,005.66	29,838,391.53	23,062,119.92
Dep's of U.S. disb'sing officers	2,477,509.48	2,650,981.39	3,474,192.74	4,352,379.43
Due to national banks	92,761,998.43	91,156,890.89	89,821,751.60	93,111,240.89
Due to other b'ks and bankers	24,416,588.33	23,138,629.46	22,659,267.08	19,644,940.20
Total	1,511,222,985.40	1,465,451,105.84	1,494,084,526.01	1,499,469,060.17

1868.

	JANUARY 6. 1,642 banks.	APRIL 6. 1,643 banks.	JULY 6. 1,640 banks.	OCTOBER 5. 1,643 banks.
Capital stock	$420,260,790.00	$420,676,210.00	$420,105,011.00	$420,634,511.00
Surplus fund	70,586,125.70	72,349,119.60	75,840,118.94	77,995,761.40
Undivided profits	31,399,877.57	32,861,597.08	33,543,223.35	36,095,883.98
National b'k notes outstand'g	294,377,390.00	295,336,044.00	294,908,264.00	295,769,489.00
State bank notes outstanding	3,792,013.00	3,310,177.00	3,163,771.00	2,906,352.00
Individual deposits	534,704,709.00	532,011,480.36	575,842,070.12	580,940,820.85
U. S. deposits	24,305,638.02	22,750,342.77	24,603,676.96	17,573,250.61
Dep'ts of U.S. disb'si'g officers	3,208,783.03	4,976,682.31	3,499,389.99	4,570,478.16
Due to national banks	98,144,669.61	94,073,631.25	113,306,346.34	99,414,397.28
Due to other b'ks and bankers	21,867,648.17	21,323,636.60	27,355,204.56	23,720,829.18
Total	1,502,647,644.10	1,499,669,920.97	1,572,167,076.26	1,559,621,773.49

AGGREGATE RESOURCES AND LIABILITIES OF THE NATIONAL

1869.

Resources.	JANUARY 4.	APRIL 17.	JUNE 12.	OCTOBER 9.
	1,628 banks.	1,620 banks.	1,619 banks.	1,617 banks.
Loans and discounts	$644,945,039.53	$662,084,813.47	$686,347,755.81	$682,883,106.97
U. S. bonds to secure circ'lat'n	338,539,950.00	338,379,250.00	338,699,750.00	339,480,100.00
U. S. bonds to secure deposits.	34,538,350.00	20,721,350.00	27,625,350.00	18,704,000.00
U. S. b'ds and sec'ties on hand.	35,010,600.00	30,226,550.00	27,476,650.00	25,903,950.00
Oth'r stocks, b'ds, and mortg's	20,127,732.96	20,074,435.69	20,777,560.53	22,250,607.14
Due from redeeming agents	65,727,070.80	57,554,382.55	62,912,636.82	56,669,562.84
Due from other national b'nks	36,067,316.84	30,520,527.80	35,536,504.53	35,393,563.47
Due from State b'ks and b'k'rs	7,715,719.34	8,075,595.60	9,140,919.24	8,790,418.57
Real estate, furniture, etc ...	24,280,848.28	24,708,188.13	23,870,271.17	25,160,188.95
Current expenses	3,265,999.81	5,641,195.01	5,820,577.87	5,646,382.96
Premiums paid	1,654,352.70	1,716,210.13	1,809,070.01	2,092,364.85
Checks and other cash items.	142,605,984.92	154,137,191.23	161,614,852.66	108,809,817.37
Bills of other national banks.	14,684,799.00	11,725,239.00	11,524,447.00	10,776,023.00
Fractional currency........	2,280,471.06	2,088,545.18	1,804,855.53	2,090,727.28
Specie......................	29,626,750.26	9,944,532.15	18,455,090.48	23,002,405.83
Legal-tender notes	88,239,300.00	80,875,161.00	80,934,119.00	83,719,295.00
Three per cent. certificates..	52,075,000.00	51,190,000.00	49,815,000.00	45,845,000.00
Total..................	1,640,394,266.50	1,517,753,167.03	1,564,174,410.65	1,497,226,604.33

1870.

	JANUARY 22.	MARCH 24.	JUNE 9.	OCTOBER 8.	DECEMBER 28.
	1,615 banks.	1,615 banks.	1,612 banks.	1,615 banks.	1,648 banks.
Loans and discounts	$688,875,203.70	$710,848,609.39	$719,341,186.06	$715,928,079.81	$725,515,538.49
Bonds for circulation	339,350,750.00	339,251,350.00	338,845,200.00	340,857,450.00	344,104,200.00
Bonds for deposits ..	17,592,000.00	16,102,000.00	15,704,000.00	15,381,500.00	15,189,500.00
U. S. bonds on hand	24,677,100.00	27,292,150.00	28,276,600.00	22,323,800.00	23,893,300.00
Other stocks and b'ds	21,082,412.00	20,524,294.55	23,300,681.87	23,614,721.25	22,686,358.50
Due from red'g ag'nts	71,641,486.05	73,435,117.98	74,635,405.61	66,275,668.92	64,805,062.88
Due from nat'l banks.	31,994,609.26	29,510,688.11	36,128,750.66	33,918,805.65	37,478,166.49
Due from State banks	9,319,560.54	10,238,219.85	10,430,781.32	9,202,496.71	9,824,144.18
Real estate, etc. ..	26,002,713.01	26,330,701.24	26,593,357.00	27,470,746.07	28,021,637.44
Current expenses...	3,469,588.00	6,683,189.54	6,324,955.47	5,871,750.02	6,905,073.32
Premiums paid ..	2,439,591.41	2,680,882.39	3,076,456.74	2,491,222.11	3,251,648.72
Cash items....... ...	111,624,822.00	11,267,703.12	11,497,534.13	12,536,613.57	13,229,403.24
Cl'r'g-house exch'gs.	....	75,317,992.22	84,936,515.64	79,089,688.39	76,208,707.00
National bank notes.	15,840,669.00	14,226,817.00	16,342,582.00	12,512,927.00	17,001,816.00
Fractional currency	2,476,966.75	2,285,499.04	2,184,714.39	2,078,178.05	2,150,522.89
Specie	48,345,383.72	37,096,543.44	31,099,437.78	18,460,011.47	26,307,251.59
Legal-tender notes	87,708,502.00	84,485,078.00	94,573,751.00	79,324,577.00	80,580,745.00
Three per cent. cert'fs	43,820,000.00	43,570,000.00	43,465,000.00	43,345,000.00	41,845,000.00
Total	1,546,261,357.44	1,529,147,735.85	1,565,756,909.67	1,510,713,236.92	1,538,908,105.93

1871.

	MARCH 18.	APRIL 29.	JUNE 10.	OCTOBER 2.	DECEMBER 16.
	1,688 banks.	1,707 banks.	1,723 banks.	1,767 banks.	1,790 banks.
Loans and discounts	$767,858,490.59	$779,321,828.11	$789,416,568.13	$831,552,210.00	$818,996,311.74
Bonds for circulation	351,556,700.00	351,427,200.00	357,388,950.00	364,475,800.00	366,840,200.00
Bonds for deposits	15,231,500.00	15,236,500.00	15,250,500.00	28,087,500.00	23,155,150.00
U. S. bonds on hand	23,911,350.00	22,487,950.00	24,200,300.00	17,753,650.00	17,675,500.00
Other stocks and b'ds	22,763,869.20	22,414,659.05	23,132,871.05	24,517,059.35	23,061,184.20
Due from red'g ag'nts	83,809,188.92	85,032,016.31	92,369,246.71	86,878,608.84	77,985,600.53
Due from nat'l banks	30,201,119.99	38,332,679.74	39,676,579.35	43,525,362.05	43,313,344.78
Due from State banks	10,271,605.34	11,478,174.71	11,853,308.60	12,772,669.81	13,069,301.46
Real estate, etc.....	28,805,814.79	29,242,702.79	29,637,999.30	30,089,783.85	30,070,330.57
Current expenses ..	6,694,011.17	6,704,159.73	6,295,099.46	6,153,370.29	7,330,424.12
Premiums paid ..	3,939,995.20	4,414,755.40	5,026,385.97	5,500,890.17	5,956,073.74
Cash items....... ..	11,642,644.71	12,719,289.81	13,101,497.05	14,058,208.86	13,781,421.76
Cl'r'g-house exch'gs	100,603,917.51	130,855,698.15	102,091,311.75	101,165,854.52	114,538,539.93
National bank notes	13,137,006.00	16,632,323.00	19,101,389.00	14,197,653.00	13,085,904.00
Fractional currency.	2,103,298.16	2,135,763.09	2,160,713.22	2,095,485.79	2,061,600.89
Specie	25,769,166.64	22,732,027.02	19,924,955.16	13,252,998.17	29,595,299.56
Legal tender notes..	91,072,349.00	106,219,176.00	122,137,660.00	109,414,735.00	93,942,707.00
Three per cent. cert'fs	37,570,000.00	33,915,000.00	30,690,000.00	25,075,000.00	21,400,000.00
Total	1,627,032,039.28	1,694,110,913.91	1,703,415,335.65	1,730,566,899.72	1,715,861,807.22

BANKS FROM OCTOBER, 1863, TO OCTOBER, 1887—Continued.

1869.

Liabilities.	JANUARY 4.	APRIL 17.	JUNE 12.	OCTOBER 9.
	1,628 banks.	1,620 banks.	1,619 banks.	1,617 banks.
Capital stock	$419, 040, 931. 00	$420, 818, 721. 00	$422, 659, 260. 00	$426, 399, 151. 00
Surplus fund	81, 169, 936. 52	82, 653, 989. 19	82, 218, 576. 47	86, 165, 334. 32
Undivided profits	35, 318, 273. 71	37, 489, 311. 82	43, 812, 898. 70	40, 687, 300. 92
Nat'l bank notes outstanding	294, 476, 702. 00	292, 457, 098. 00	292, 753, 286. 00	293, 593, 645. 00
State bank notes outstanding	2, 734, 669. 00	2, 615, 387. 00	2, 558, 874. 00	2, 154, 697. 00
Individual deposits	568, 530, 934. 11	547, 922, 174. 91	574, 307, 382. 77	511, 400, 196. 63
U. S. deposits	13, 211, 850. 19	10, 114, 328. 32	10, 301, 907. 71	7, 112, 646. 67
Dep'ts U.S. disburs'g officers	3, 472, 884. 00	3, 665, 131. 61	2, 454, 048. 99	4, 516, 648. 12
Due to national banks	95, 453, 139. 33	92, 662, 648. 49	100, 933, 910. 03	95, 067, 892. 83
Due to State banks and b'k'rs.	26, 984, 945. 74	23, 018, 610. 62	28, 046, 771. 50	23, 849, 371. 62
Notes and bills re-discounted	....	2, 461, 849. 81	2, 392, 205. 61	3, 839, 357. 10
Bills payable	....	1, 870, 913. 26	1, 735, 289. 07	2, 140, 363. 12
Total	1, 540, 394, 266. 50	1, 517, 753, 167. 03	1, 564, 174, 410. 65	1, 497, 226, 604. 33

1870.

	JANUARY 22.	MARCH 24.	JUNE 9.	OCTOBER 8.	DECEMBER 28.
	1,615 banks.	1,615 banks.	1,612 banks.	1,615 banks.	1,648 banks.
Capital stock	$426, 074, 954. 00	$427, 504, 247. 00	$427, 235, 701. 00	$430, 399, 301. 00	$435, 356, 004. 00
Surplus fund	90, 174, 281. 14	90, 229, 954. 59	91, 689, 834. 12	94, 061, 438. 95	94, 705, 740. 34
Undivided profits	34, 300, 430. 80	43, 109, 471. 62	42, 861, 712. 59	38, 608, 618. 91	46, 056, 428. 55
Nat'l bank circulat'n.	292, 838, 935. 00	292, 509, 149. 00	291, 183, 614. 00	291, 798, 640. 00	296, 205, 446. 00
State bank circulat'n	2, 351, 993. 00	2, 279, 469. 00	2, 222, 793. 00	2, 138, 548. 00	2, 091, 799. 00
Dividends unpaid	2, 299, 296. 27	1, 483, 416. 15	1, 517, 595. 18	2, 462, 591. 31	2, 242, 556. 49
Individual deposits.	546, 236, 881. 57	516, 058, 085. 26	542, 261, 563. 18	501, 407, 586. 90	507, 368, 618. 67
U. S. deposits	6, 750, 139. 19	6, 424, 421. 25	10, 677, 873. 92	6, 807, 978. 49	6, 074, 407. 00
Dep'ts U.S. dis. offic's	2, 592, 001. 21	4, 778, 225. 93	2, 592, 967. 54	4, 550, 142. 68	4, 155, 304. 25
Due to national banks	108, 351, 300. 33	109, 667, 715. 95	115, 456, 491. 84	109, 348, 292. 45	106, 090, 414. 53
Due to State banks	28, 904, 849. 14	29, 767, 575. 21	33, 012, 162. 78	29, 693, 910. 89	29, 200, 587. 29
Notes re-discounted	3, 842, 542. 30	2, 462, 647. 49	2, 741, 843. 53	3, 843, 577. 67	4, 612, 131. 08
Bills payable	1, 513, 753. 49	2, 873, 357. 40	2, 302, 756. 90	4, 502, 609. 76	4, 838, 667. 83
Total	1,546,261,357. 44	1,529,147,735. 83	1,565,756,909. 67	1,510,713,236. 92	1,538,998,105. 93

1871.

	MARCH 18.	APRIL 29.	JUNE 10.	OCTOBER 2.	DECEMBER 16.
	1,688 banks.	1,707 banks.	1,723 banks.	1,767 banks.	1,790 banks.
Capital stock	$444, 232, 771. 00	$446, 925, 493. 00	$450, 330, 841. 00	$458, 255, 696. 00	$460, 225, 866. 00
Surplus funds	96, 862, 081. 66	97, 620, 099. 28	98, 322, 203. 80	101, 112, 671. 91	101, 573, 153. 62
Undivided profits	43, 883, 857. 64	44, 776, 030. 71	45, 535, 227. 79	42, 008, 714. 38	48, 630, 925. 81
Nat'l bank circulat'n	301, 713, 460. 00	306, 131, 393. 00	307, 793, 880. 00	315, 519, 117. 00	318, 265, 481. 00
State bank circulat'n.	2, 035, 800. 00	1, 982, 580. 00	1, 968, 058. 00	1, 921, 056. 00	1, 886, 538. 00
Dividends unpaid	1, 263, 767. 70	2, 235, 248. 46	1, 408, 628. 25	4, 540, 194. 61	1, 393, 427. 08
Individual deposits.	561, 190, 830. 41	611, 025, 174. 10	602, 110, 758. 16	600, 868, 486. 55	596, 586, 487. 54
U. S. deposits	6, 314, 957. 81	6, 521, 572. 92	6, 265, 167. 91	20, 511, 935. 98	14, 829, 525. 65
Dep'ts U.S. dis. offic's	4, 813, 016. 66	3, 757, 873. 84	4, 893, 907. 25	5, 393, 598. 89	5, 399, 108. 34
Due to national b'nks	118, 904, 865. 84	128, 037, 469. 17	135, 167, 847. 60	131, 730, 713. 04	118, 657, 614. 16
Due to State banks	37, 311, 519. 13	36, 113, 290. 67	41, 219, 802. 96	40, 211, 971. 67	38, 116, 950. 67
Notes re-discounted.	3, 256, 806. 42	3, 573, 723. 02	3, 120, 079. 09	3, 964, 532. 57	4, 922, 455. 78
Bills payable	5, 248, 266. 01	5, 740, 964. 77	5, 278, 973. 72	4, 528, 191. 12	5, 374, 362. 67
Total	1,627,032,039. 28	1,694,440,912. 94	1,703,415,335. 65	1,730,566,899. 72	1, 715, 861, 807. 22

AGGREGATE RESOURCES AND LIABILITIES OF THE NATIONAL

1872.

Resources.	FEBRUARY 27.	APRIL 19.	JUNE 10.	OCTOBER 3.	DECEMBER 27.
	1,814 banks.	1,843 banks	1,853 banks.	1,919 banks.	1,940 banks.
Loans and discounts	$819 665, 077. 91	$814, 902, 253. 49	$871, 531, 448. 67	$877, 107, 023. 47	$885, 653, 449. 02
Bonds for circulation	370 921, 700 00	374, 428, 450 00	377, 029, 700. 00	382, 046, 400 00	381, 458, 500. 00
Bonds for deposits	15, 870, 000 00	15, 169 000 00	15, 409, 950 00	15, 479, 750 00	16, 104, 750 00
U. S. bonds on hand	21, 323, 150 00	19, 292, 100 00	16, 458, 250 00	12, 142, 550 00	10, 306, 100. 00
Other stocks and b'ds	22, 6 8, 388 80	21, 5 8, 914 06	22, 270 610. 47	23, 533, 151. 73	23, 160, 557. 29
Due from red'g ag'ts	80, 518 329 93	82, 120, 017. 24	91, 564 269. 53	80, 717, 071. 30	86, 401, 459. 44
Due from nat'l banks	38 282, 005 86	36, 607, 592. 61	39, 468, 323. 29	34, 486, 593. 87	42, 707, 613. 54
Due from State banks	12, 269, 822 68	12, 209, 716 01	13, 014, 265. 20	12, 976, 878 01	12, 008, 843. 54
Real estate, etc	30, 637, 676. 75	30, 809, 274. 98	31 123, 843. 21	32, 276, 408. 17	33, 014, 796. 83
Current expenses	6, 265, 655. 13	7, 026, 041. 23	6, 710, 794 00	6, 310, 428 79	8, 454, 803. 97
Premiums paid	6, 308 821. 86	6, 544, 279. 29	6, 616 174. 75	6, 546, 848. 52	7, 097, 847. 86
Cash items	12, 143, 403. 12	12, 461, 171. 40	13, 458, 753. 80	14, 916, 784. 34	13, 696, 723. 85
Clear'g-house exch'gs	93, 154, 319 74	114, 195, 966. 36	88, 592, 800. 16	110, 086, 315. 37	90 145, 482. 72
National-bank notes	15, 552, 087 00	18, 492, 842 00	16, 253, 560. 00	15, 787, 296. 00	19, 070, 322. 00
Fractional currency	2, 278, 142. 24	2, 143, 249 29	2, 069 464. 12	2, 151, 747. 88	2, 270, 576. 32
Specie	25, 507, 825. 32	24, 433, 890. 46	24 256, 644. 14	10, 229, 756 79	19, 047, 336. 45
Legal-tender notes	97, 865, 400. 00	105, 732, 455. 00	122, 994, 417. 00	105, 121, 104 00	102, 922, 369. 00
U. S. cer'fs of deposit	.....	.....	.....	6, 710 000. 00	12, 650, 000 00
Three per cent. cert'fs	18, 980, 000. 00	15, 365, 000. 00	12, 005, 000. 00	7, 140, 000. 00	4, 185, 000. 00
Total	1,719,415,037. 34	1,743,652,213. 55	1,770,837,269. 40	1,755,857,098. 24	1,773,556,532. 43

1873.

	FEBRUARY 28.	APRIL 25.	JUNE 13.	SEPTEMBER 12.	DECEMBER 26.
	1,947 banks.	1,962 banks.	1,968 banks.	1,976 banks.	1,976 banks.
Loans and discounts	$913, 265, 189 67	$912, 064, 267. 31	$925, 557, 682. 42	$944, 220, 116. 34	$856, 816, 555. 05
Bonds for circulation	384, 675, 050 00	386, 763, 800 00	388, 080, 300 00	388, 330, 400 00	389, 384, 400 00
Bonds for deposits	15, 035, 000. 00	16, 235 000 00	15, 035, 000 00	14 805, 000 00	14, 815, 200 00
U. S. bonds on hand	10, 476, 950. 00	9, 613, 550 00	9, 780, 400 00	8, 824, 850 00	8, 620, 850 00
Other stocks and b'ds	22 063, 306 20	22, 449, 146 04	22, 012, 415. 63	23, 709 034. 53	24, 358, 125. 06
Due from red'g ag'nts	95 773, 077. 10	88, 815, 557. 80	97, 143, 326 94	96, 134, 120 66	73, 032, 046. 67
Due from nat'l banks	39 184, 700 09	38, 671, 088 63	43, 328, 792. 29	41, 413, 680 06	40, 404, 757. 97
Due from State banks	13, 595, 679. 17	12, 884, 353. 37	14 073, 287. 77	12, 022, 873. 41	11, 185, 253. 08
Real estate, etc	34, 025, 057. 77	34, 216, 878 07	34, 820, 562. 77	34 661, 823. 21	35, 556, 746. 48
Current expenses	6, 977, 831. 35	7, 450, 015 87	7, 154, 211. 69	6, 985, 436. 99	8, 678, 270. 30
Premiums paid	7, 205, 259 67	7, 550, 967 67	7, 890, 962. 14	7, 752, 843. 87	7, 987, 107. 14
Cash items	11, 761, 714. 50	11, 425, 249 00	13, 0 6, 482. 58	11, 433, 913. 22	12, 321, 972. 80
Clear'g house exch'gs	131, 294, 840. 95	94, 132, 125 24	91, 918, 526. 59	86, 026, 004. 53	62, 881, 342. 16
National-bank notes	15, 908 770 00	19, 310, 202 00	20, 394, 772 00	16, 103, 842. 00	21, 403, 179. 00
Fractional currency	2, 280, 680. 21	2, 198, 973. 37	2, 197, 559. 84	2, 302, 775. 26	2, 287, 454 03
Specie	17, 777, 673. 53	16, 868, 808. 74	27, 950, 086 72	19, 868, 469. 45	26, 907, 037. 58
Legal-tender notes	97, 141, 103 00	100, 605, 187 00	106, 381, 491. 00	92, 522, 062. 00	108, 719, 506. 00
U. S. cert'fs of deposit	18, 460, 000. 00	18, 370, 000. 00	22, 365, 000. 00	20, 610, 000. 00	24, 010, 000. 00
Three per cent. cert'fs	1, 805, 000. 00	710, 000. 00	305, 000. 00	.....	.....
Total	1,839,152,715. 21	1,800,203,280. 11	1,851,234,860. 36	1,830,627,845. 53	1,729,380,303. 61

1874.

	FEBRUARY 27.	MAY 1.	JUNE 26.	OCTOBER 2.	DECEMBER 31.
	1,975 banks.	1,978 banks.	1,983 banks.	2,004 banks.	2,027 banks.
Loans and discounts	$897, 859, 600. 46	$923, 347 030. 79	$926, 195, 671. 70	$954, 394, 791. 59	$955, 862, 580. 51
Bonds for circulation	380, 614, 700 00	380, 249 100 00	390, 281, 700 00	383, 254, 800. 00	382, 976, 200 00
Bonds for deposits	14, 600, 200. 00	14, 890, 200. 00	14, 890, 200. 00	14, 691, 700 00	14, 714, 000 00
U. S. bonds on hand	11, 043, 400 00	10, 152, 000. 00	10, 456, 900. 00	13, 313, 550. 00	15, 290, 300. 00
Other stocks and b'ds	25 305, 776. 24	25, 460, 460. 20	27, 010, 727. 48	27, 807, 826 92	28, 313, 473. 12
Due from res've ag'ts	101, 502, 861. 58	94, 017, 603. 31	97, 871, 517. 06	83, 885, 126 94	80, 488, 831. 45
Due from nat'l banks	36, 621 001. 59	41, 291, 015. 24	45, 770, 715. 59	39, 695, 309. 47	48, 100, 842. 62
Due from State banks	11, 496, 711. 47	12, 374, 394. 28	12, 469, 592. 33	11, 196, 611. 73	11, 655, 573. 07
Real estate, etc	36, 043, 741. 50	36, 708, 066. 79	37, 270, 870. 51	38, 112, 920. 52	39, 190, 683. 04
Current expenses	6, 998, 875. 75	7, 547, 403. 05	7, 550, 125. 20	7, 658, 738. 82	5, 510, 566. 47
Premiums paid	8, 741, 028. 77	8, 480 370 84	8, 563, 262. 27	8, 376, 659. 07	8, 626, 112. 16
Cash items	10, 269, 955. 50	11, 019, 020. 71	10, 496, 257. 00	12, 296, 416. 77	14, 005, 517. 33
Clear'g house exch'gs	62, 768, 110. 19	94. 87., 706. 52	63, 896, 271. 31	97, 383, 687. 11	112, 995, 317. 55
National-bank notes	20, 904, 251. 00	20, 673, 452. 00	23, 527, 991. 00	18, 450, 013. 00	22, 532, 336. 00
Fractional currency	2, 309, 919. 73	2, 487, 186. 09	2, 283, 898. 92	2, 221, 913. 42	2, 302, 668. 74
Specie	33, 365, 863. 58	32, 569, 169. 26	22, 326, 207. 27	21, 240, 945. 23	22, 436, 761. 04
Legal-tender notes	102, 717, 563. 60	101, 692, 930. 00	103, 108, 350. 00	80, 021, 946. 00	82, 604, 791. 00
U. S. cert'fs of deposit	37, 235, 000. 00	40, 135, 000. 00	47, 780, 000. 00	42, 825, 000. 00	33, 670, 000. 00
Dep. with U. S. Treas	.....	.....	91, 250. 00	20, 349, 950. 15	21, 043, 084. 36
Total	1,808,500,529. 16	1,867,802,796. 28	1,851,840,913. 64	1,877,180,942. 44	1,902,409,638. 46

BANKS FROM OCTOBER, 1863, TO OCTOBER, 1887—Continued.

1872.

Liabilities.	FEBRUARY 27.	APRIL 19.	JUNE 10.	OCTOBER 3.	DECEMBER 27.
	1,814 banks.	1,843 banks.	1,853 banks.	1,919 banks.	1,940 banks.
Capital stock	$464,081,744.00	$467,924,318.00	$470,543,301.00	$479,629,174.00	$482,606,252.00
Surplus fund	103,787,082.62	104,312,525.81	105,181,943.28	110,257,516.45	111,410,248.98
Undivided profits	43,310,344.46	46,428,590.90	50,234,298.32	46,623,784.50	56,702,411.89
Nat'l bank circulation	321,634,675.00	325,305,752.00	327,092,752.00	333,495,027.00	336,289,285.00
State bank circulation	1,830,563.00	1,763,885.00	1,700,935.00	1,567,143.00	1,511,596.00
Dividends unpaid	1,451,746.29	1,561,914.45	1,454,044.06	3,149,749.61	1,356,934.48
Individual deposits	593,645,666.16	620,775,265.78	618,801,619.49	613,290,671.45	598,114,679.26
U. S. deposits	7,114,893.47	6,355,722.95	6,993,014.77	7,853,772.41	7,863,894.93
Dep'ts U.S. dis. officers	5,024,699.44	3,410,371.16	5,463,953.48	4,563,833.79	5,136,597.74
Due to national banks	128,627,494.41	120,755,565.86	132,804,924.02	110,047,347.67	124,218,392.83
Due to State banks	39,025,165.44	35,005,127.84	39,878,826.42	33,789,083.82	34,794,963.37
Notes rediscounted	3,818,686.91	4,225,622.04	4,745,178.22	5,549,431.88	6,545,059.78
Bills payable	6,062,896.91	5,821,551.76	5,042,479.34	6,040,562.66	6,946,416.17
Total	1,719,415,657.34	1,743,652,213.55	1,770,837,269.40	1,755,857,098.24	1,773,556,532.43

1873.

	FEBRUARY 28.	APRIL 25.	JUNE 13.	SEPTEMBER 12.	DECEMBER 26.
	1,947 banks.	1,962 banks.	1,968 banks.	1,976 banks.	1,976 banks.
Capital stock	$484,551,811.00	$487,891,251.00	$490,109,801.00	$491,072,616.00	$490,266,611.00
Surplus fund	114,681,048.73	115,805,574.57	116,847,454.62	120,314,499.20	120,961,267.91
Undivided profits	48,578,045.28	52,415,348.46	55,306,154.69	54,515,131.76	58,375,169.43
Nat'l bank circulation	336,292,459.00	338,163,864.00	338,788,504.00	339,081,799.00	341,320,256.00
State bank circulation	1,368,271.00	1,280,208.00	1,224,470.00	1,188,853.00	1,130,585.00
Dividends unpaid	1,465,993.60	1,462,336.77	1,400,491.90	1,402,547.89	1,269,474.74
Individual deposits	656,187,551.61	616,848,358.25	641,121,775.27	622,685,563.29	540,510,602.78
U. S. deposits	7,044,848.34	7,880,057.73	8,691,001.95	7,829,327.73	7,680,375.26
Dep'ts U.S. dis. officers	5,835,696.60	4,425,750.14	6,416,275.10	8,098,560.13	4,705,593.36
Due to national banks	131,231,842.95	126,631,926.24	137,856,085.67	133,672,732.94	114,996,666.54
Due to State banks	38,124,803.85	35,036,433.18	40,741,788.47	39,298,148.14	36,598,076.29
Notes rediscounted	5,117,810.50	5,403,043.38	5,515,900.07	5,987,512.30	3,811,487.89
Bills payable	5,072,532.75	7,050,128.39	7,215,157.04	5,480,554.09	7,754,137.41
Total	1,839,152,715.21	1,800,303,280.11	1,851,234,800.38	1,830,627,845.53	1,720,380,303.61

1874.

	FEBRUARY 27.	MAY 1.	JUNE 26.	OCTOBER 2.	DECEMBER 31.
	1,975 banks.	1,978 banks.	1,983 banks.	2,004 banks.	2,027 banks.
Capital stock	$490,859,101.00	$490,077,001.00	$491,003,711.00	$493,765,121.00	$495,802,481.00
Surplus fund	123,497,347.20	125,561,081.23	126,239,308.41	128,958,106.84	130,485,641.37
Undivided profits	50,236,919.88	54,331,713.13	58,332,965.71	51,484,437.32	51,477,629.33
Nat'l bank circulation	339,602,955.00	340,267,649.00	338,538,743.00	333,225,298.00	331,193,159.00
State bank circulation	1,078,988.00	1,019,286.00	1,009,021.00	964,567.00	860,417.00
Dividends unpaid	1,291,055.63	2,259,129.91	1,242,474.81	3,516,276.99	6,088,845.01
Individual deposits	595,350,334.90	649,286,298.95	622,863,154.44	669,068,995.88	682,846,607.45
U. S. deposits	7,276,959.87	7,994,422.27	7,322,840.85	7,302,153.58	7,492,307.78
Dep'ts U.S. dis. officers	5,034,024.46	3,297,689.24	3,238,639.20	3,927,828.27	3,579,722.94
Due to national banks	138,435,388.39	135,640,418.24	143,033,822.23	125,102,049.93	129,188,671.42
Due to State banks	48,112,223.40	48,683,924.34	50,227,426.18	50,718,007.87	51,629,602.36
Notes rediscounted	3,448,828.92	4,581,420.38	4,436,256.22	4,197,372.25	6,365,652.97
Bills payable	4,275,602.51	4,772,662.59	4,352,500.57	4,950,727.51	5,398,900.83
Total	1,808,500,529.16	1,867,802,796.28	1,851,840,913.64	1,877,180,942.44	1,902,409,638.40

AGGREGATE RESOURCES AND LIABILITIES OF THE NATIONAL

1875.

Resources.	MARCH 1.	MAY 1.	JUNE 30.	OCTOBER 1.	DECEMBER 17.
	2,029 banks.	2,046 banks.	2,076 banks.	2,088 banks.	2,086 banks.
Loans and discounts	$956,485,939.35	$971,835,298.74	$972,926,532.14	$984,691,434.40	$962,571,807.70
Bonds for circulation	380,682,650.00	378,026,900.00	375,127,900.00	370,321,700.00	363,618,100.00
Bonds for deposits	14,492,200.00	14,372,200.00	14,147,200.00	14,097,200.00	13,981,500.00
U. S. bonds on hand	18,062,150.00	14,207,650.00	12,753,900.00	13,989,950.00	16,009,550.00
Other stocks and b'ds	28,268,841.69	29,102,197.10	32,010,316.18	33,505,045.15	31,657,960.52
Due from res've ag'ts	80,991,175.34	80,620,878.75	89,788,903.73	85,701,259.82	81,462,682.27
Due from nat'l banks	44,720,304.11	46,039,507.57	48,513,388.86	47,028,769.18	44,831,891.48
Due from State banks	12,724,243.07	12,094,086.39	11,025,047.15	11,963,768.90	11,805,551.08
Real estate, etc.	39,430,952.12	40,312,285.09	40,969,020.49	42,366,647.65	41,583,311.94
Current expenses	7,790,581.80	7,706,700.42	4,992,044.34	7,841,213.05	6,218,455.47
Premiums paid	9,006,880.92	8,434,453.14	8,742,393.83	8,670,091.18	9,412,801.54
Cash items	11,734,702.42	13,122,145.88	12,433,100.43	12,758,872.03	11,298,725.72
Clear'g-house exch'gs	81,127,796.39	116,970,819.05	88,924,025.93	75,142,863.45	67,886,907.04
Bills of other banks	18,909,307.00	19,504,610.00	24,261,901.00	18,528,837.00	17,166,190.00
Fractional currency	3,008,592.12	2,702,326.44	2,620,504.26	2,505,631.78	2,901,023.10
Specie	16,667,106.17	10,620,361.64	18,959,582.30	8,050,329.73	17,070,905.90
Legal-tender notes	78,508,170.00	84,015,928.00	87,492,895.00	76,458,734.00	70,725,077.00
U. S. cert's of deposit	37,290,000.00	38,615,000.00	47,310,000.00	48,810,000.00	31,005,000.00
Due from U. S. Treas	21,097,919.76	21,454,422.29	19,640,785.52	19,686,960.30	19,202,256.08
Total	1,869,819,753.22	1,909,847,891.40	1,913,239,201.16	1,882,209,307.02	1,823,469,752.44

1876.

	MARCH 10.	MAY 12.	JUNE 30.	OCTOBER 2.	DECEMBER 22.
	2,091 banks.	2,089 banks.	2,091 banks.	2,089 banks.	2,082 banks.
Loans and discounts	$950,205,556.62	$939,895,085.34	$933,686,530.45	$931,304,714.06	$929,066,408.42
Bonds for circulation	354,547,750.00	344,537,350.00	339,141,750.00	337,170,400.00	336,705,300.00
Bonds for deposits	14,216,500.00	14,128,000.00	14,328,000.00	14,698,000.00	14,757,000.00
U. S. bonds on hand	25,910,650.00	26,577,000.00	30,842,300.00	33,142,150.00	31,937,950.00
Other stocks and b'ds	30,425,430.43	30,905,195.82	32,482,805.75	34,445,157.16	31,565,914.50
Due from res've ag'ts	99,068,360.35	86,769,083.97	87,989,900.90	87,326,950.48	83,789,174.65
Due from nat'l banks	42,341,542.67	44,328,609.46	47,417,029.03	47,525,089.98	44,011,664.07
Due from State banks	11,180,502.15	11,262,193.96	10,989,507.95	12,061,283.08	12,415,841.97
Real estate, etc.	41,937,617.25	42,183,958.78	42,722,415.27	43,121,942.01	43,408,445.49
Current expenses	8,296,207.85	6,820,573.35	5,025,549.38	6,987,644.46	9,818,422.88
Premiums paid	10,916,713.15	10,414,347.28	10,621,634.03	10,715,251.16	10,811,300.66
Cash items	9,517,868.86	9,693,186.37	11,724,502.67	12,043,139.08	10,658,709.26
Clear'g-house exch'gs	58,863,182.43	56,806,632.63	75,328,878.84	87,870,817.06	68,027,016.40
Bills of other banks	18,536,502.00	20,347,964.00	20,398,422.00	15,910,315.00	17,521,663.00
Fractional currency	3,215,594.30	2,771,886.26	1,987,897.44	1,417,203.66	1,146,741.04
Specie	29,077,345.85	21,714,594.36	25,218,469.92	21,360,767.42	32,999,647.89
Legal-tender notes	76,708,440.00	79,858,661.00	90,836,876.00	84,250,847.00	66,221,400.00
U. S. cert's of deposit	30,845,000.00	27,380,000.00	27,955,000.00	29,170,000.00	26,095,000.00
Due from U. S. Treas	18,479,112.79	16,011,680.26	17,063,407.65	16,743,695.40	16,359,491.73
Total	1,834,309,941.70	1,793,396,902.78	1,825,760,967.28	1,827,265,307.61	1,787,407,693.76

1877.

	JANUARY 20.	APRIL 14.	JUNE 22.	OCTOBER 1.	DECEMBER 28.
	2,083 banks.	2,073 banks.	2,078 banks.	2,080 banks.	2,074 banks.
Loans and discounts	$920,561,018.65	$911,946,833.88	$901,731,416.03	$891,920,593.54	$881,856,744.87
Bonds for circulation	337,590,700.00	339,658,100.00	337,754,100.00	336,810,950.00	343,899,550.00
Bonds for deposits	14,782,000.00	15,084,000.00	14,971,000.00	14,903,000.00	13,538,000.00
U. S. bonds on hand	31,988,650.00	32,964,250.00	33,344,050.00	30,088,700.00	28,479,800.00
Other stocks and b'ds	31,819,930.20	32,554,594.44	35,053,755.29	34,435,905.21	32,169,491.03
Due from res've ag'ts	88,098,308.85	84,942,718.41	82,132,999.96	73,284,133.12	75,960,087.27
Due from nat'l banks	44,814,610.88	42,027,778.81	44,567,303.63	45,217,246.82	44,123,924.07
Due from State banks	13,080,990.81	11,911,437.36	11,246,349.70	11,415,761.60	11,479,945.65
Real estate, etc.	43,704,335.47	44,736,549.09	44,818,722.07	45,220,083.25	46,511,932.25
Current expenses	4,131,516.48	7,842,296.86	7,910,864.81	9,015,792.60	8,058,903.60
Premiums paid	10,991,714.50	10,494,505.12	10,320,674.34	9,219,174.62	8,841,939.00
Cash items	10,295,404.19	10,410,623.87	10,009,988.46	11,674,587.50	10,265,959.49
Clear'g-house exch'gs	81,117,889.04	85,159,422.74	57,861,481.13	74,525,215.89	64,664,415.01
Bills of other banks	18,418,727.00	17,042,693.00	20,182,948.00	15,531,467.00	20,312,692.00
Fractional currency	1,238,228.08	1,114,820.00	1,055,123.61	900,805.47	778,084.78
Specie	49,709,267.55	27,070,037.78	21,335,996.06	22,658,820.31	32,907,760.70
Legal-tender notes	72,689,710.00	72,351,573.00	78,904,386.00	66,920,681.00	70,568,248.00
U. S. cert's of deposit	25,470,000.00	33,100,000.00	41,470,000.00	32,410,000.00	26,515,000.00
Due from U. S. Treas	16,411,509.08	16,291,640.81	17,932,571.60	16,021,753.91	16,193,577.08
Total	1,818,171,517.68	[illegible]	1,771,352,833.81	[illegible]	1,737,296,145.79

BANKS FROM OCTOBER, 1863, TO OCTOBER, 1887—Continued.

1875.

Liabilities.	MARCH 1.	MAY 1.	JUNE 30.	OCTOBER 1.	DECEMBER 17.
	2,029 banks.	2,046 banks.	2,076 banks.	2,088 banks.	2,086 banks.
Capital stock	$496,272,901.00	$493,717,143.00	$501,568,563.50	$504,820,760.00	$505,485,865.00
Surplus fund	131,249,079.47	131,604,608.66	133,169,094.79	134,356,076.41	133,085,422.30
Undivided profits	51,650,243.62	55,907,619.95	52,160,101.08	52,964,953.50	50,201,957.81
Nat'l bank circulation	324,525,349.00	323,321,230.00	318,148,406.00	318,350,379.00	314,979,451.00
State bank circulation	824,876.00	815,220.00	786,844.00	772,348.00	752,722.00
Dividends unpaid	1,601,255.48	2,501,742.30	6,105,519.34	4,003,534.90	1,353,396.80
Individual deposits	647,735,879.69	695,347,677.70	686,478,630.48	664,579,619.39	618,517,245.74
U. S. deposits	7,971,932.75	6,797,072.00	6,714,328.70	6,507,531.50	6,652,556.67
Dep'ts U. S. dis. officers	5,330,414.16	2,766,387.41	3,459,061.80	4,271,195.19	4,232,550.87
Due to national banks	137,735,121.44	127,280,034.02	138,914,828.39	129,810,681.60	119,843,665.44
Due to State banks	55,294,663.84	53,037,582.89	55,714,055.18	49,918,530.95	47,048,174.56
Notes re-discounted	4,841,600.20	5,671,031.44	4,261,464.45	5,254,453.66	5,257,160.61
Bills payable	4,786,436.57	6,079,632.94	5,758,299.85	6,500,234.43	7,056,583.64
Total	1,869,819,753.22	1,909,847,801.40	1,913,239,201.16	1,882,209,307.62	1,823,469,752.44

1876.

Liabilities	MARCH 10.	MAY 12.	JUNE 30.	OCTOBER 2.	DECEMBER 22.
	2,091 banks.	2,089 banks.	2,091 banks.	2,089 banks.	2,082 banks.
Capital stock	$504,818,666.00	$500,982,006.00	$500,393,796.00	$499,802,232.00	$497,482,016.00
Surplus fund	133,091,739.50	131,795,199.94	131,897,197.21	132,202,282.00	131,390,664.67
Undivided profits	51,177,031.26	49,039,278.75	46,609,341.51	46,445,215.59	52,327,715.08
Nat'l bank circulation	307,476,155.00	300,252,085.00	294,444,678.00	291,544,020.00	292,011,575.00
State bank circulation	714,539.00	667,060.00	658,938.00	628,847.00	608,548.00
Dividends unpaid	1,405,829.06	2,325,523.51	6,116,679.30	3,848,705.64	1,286,540.28
Individual deposits	629,074,211.05	612,355,096.50	641,432,886.08	651,385,210.10	619,350,223.06
U. S. deposits	6,606,394.90	8,493,878.18	7,667,722.97	7,256,801.42	6,727,155.14
Dep'ts U. S. dis. officers	4,313,015.45	2,505,273.30	3,392,939.48	3,746,781.58	4,749,615.39
Due to national banks	139,407,880.06	127,880,045.04	131,702,164.87	131,535,969.04	122,351,818.09
Due to State banks	54,002,131.54	46,706,969.52	51,403,995.50	48,250,111.63	48,685,302.14
Notes re-discounted	4,631,882.57	4,653,460.08	3,867,622.24	4,464,407.31	4,553,158.76
Bills payable	6,049,566.31	5,650,126.87	6,173,006.03	6,154,784.21	5,882,672.15
Total	1,834,369,941.70	1,793,306,002.78	1,825,760,967.28	1,827,265,367.61	1,787,407,093.76

1877.

Liabilities	JANUARY 20.	APRIL 14.	JUNE 22.	OCTOBER 1.	DECEMBER 28.
	2,083 banks.	2,073 banks.	2,078 banks.	2,080 banks.	2,074 banks.
Capital stock	$493,634,611.00	$489,684,645.00	$481,044,771.00	$479,467,771.00	$477,128,771.00
Surplus fund	130,224,169.02	127,793,320.52	124,714,072.93	122,776,121.24	121,618,455.32
Undivided profits	37,456,530.32	45,609,418.27	50,508,351.70	44,572,678.72	51,530,910.18
Nat'l bank circulation	292,851,351.00	294,710,313.00	290,002,057.00	291,874,236.00	299,240,475.00
State bank circulation	581,242.00	535,963.00	521,611.00	481,738.00	470,540.00
Dividends unpaid	2,448,909.70	1,853,974.79	1,398,101.52	3,623,703.43	1,404,178.34
Individual deposits	659,891,009.76	641,772,528.08	636,267,529.20	616,403,987.12	604,512,514.52
U. S. deposits	7,234,696.96	7,584,267.72	7,187,431.67	7,972,714.75	6,529,031.09
Dep'ts U. S. dis. officers	3,108,316.55	3,076,878.70	3,710,167.20	2,376,983.02	3,780,759.43
Due to national banks	130,293,566.36	125,422,444.43	121,443,601.23	115,028,954.38	115,773,660.58
Due to State banks	49,965,770.27	48,604,820.09	48,352,583.90	46,577,439.68	44,807,958.79
Notes re-discounted	4,000,063.82	3,985,459.75	2,953,128.58	3,791,219.47	4,654,784.51
Bills payable	6,483,320.92	5,969,241.04	6,240,426.88	6,137,116.83	5,843,107.03
Total	1,818,174,517.68	1,796,603,275.29	1,774,352,833.81	1,741,084,663.84	1,737,295,145.79

AGGREGATE RESOURCES AND LIABILITIES OF THE NATIONAL

1878.

Resources.	MARCH 15.	MAY 1.	JUNE 29.	OCTOBER 1.	DECEMBER 6.
	2,063 banks.	2,059 banks.	2,056 banks.	2,053 banks.	2,055 banks.
Loans and discounts.	$854,750,708.87	$817,020,392.40	$835,078,133.13	$833,988,450.59	$826,017,451.87
Bonds for circulation	343,871,350.00	345,256,350.00	347,332,100.00	347,556,650.00	347,812,300.00
Bonds for deposits ..	13,329,000.00	19,536,000.00	28,371,000.00	47,936,850.00	49,110,800.00
U. S. bonds on hand.	34,881,600.00	33,615,700.00	40,479,000.00	40,785,600.00	44,255,850.00
Other stocks and b'ds	34,674,307.21	34,697,320.53	36,094,996.24	36,859,534.82	35,810,810.47
Due from res've agt's	86,016,990.78	71,331,219.27	78,875,055.92	85,083,418.51	81,733,137.00
Due from nat'l banks	39,092,105.87	40,545,522.72	41,897,858.89	41,492,918.75	43,144,220.68
Due from State banks	11,683,050.17	12,413,579.10	12,232,316.30	12,314,698.11	12,259,856.09
Real estate, etc	45,702,303.73	45,901,536.93	46,153,409.35	46,702,470.26	46,728,147.36
Current expenses ...	7,786,572.42	7,239,305.78	4,718,018.66	6,272,560.73	7,608,128.83
Premiums paid......	7,806,252.00	7,574,255.95	7,335,454.49	7,134,735.68	6,978,708.71
Cash items	10,107,583.76	10,989,440.78	11,525,376.07	10,982,432.89	9,985,004.21
Clear'g-house exch'gs	66,498,965.23	95,525,164.28	87,498,287.82	82,372,537.88	61,998,286.11
Bills of other banks.	16,250,569.00	18,363,335.00	17,063,576.00	16,929,721.00	19,392,281.00
Fractional currency.	697,398.86	661,044.69	610,084.25	515,661.04	496,864.34
Specie...............	54,729,558.02	46,023,756.06	29,251,469.77	30,688,606.50	34,355,250.36
Legal-tender notes ..	61,034,972.00	67,245,975.00	71,643,402.00	64,428,600.00	64,672,702.00
U.S. cert'fs of deposit	29,005,000.00	20,095,000.00	36,905,000.00	32,690,000.00	32,520,000.00
Due from U. S. Treas.	16,257,608.98	16,364,030.47	16,798,007.62	16,543,074.36	17,940,918.34
Total..........	1,729,465,956.90	1,741,898,959.05	1,750,464,706.51	1,767,279,133.21	1,742,826,837.37

1879.

	JANUARY 1.	APRIL 4.	JUNE 14.	OCTOBER 2.	DECEMBER 12.
	2,051 banks.	2,048 banks.	2,048 banks.	2,048 banks.	2,052 banks.
Loans and discounts	$823,906,765.68	$814,653,422.69	$835,875,012.36	$878,503,097.45	$933,543,661.93
Bonds for circulation	347,118,300.00	348,487,700.00	352,208,000.00	357,313,300.00	364,272,700.00
Bonds for deposits...	66,507,350.00	309,348,450.00	257,038,200.00	18,204,650.00	14,788,800.00
U. S. bonds on hand .	44,257,250.00	54,601,750.00	62,189,300.00	52,942,100.00	40,677,500.00
Other stocks and b'ds	35,509,400.93	36,747,129.40	37,617,015.13	39,671,916.50	38,836,369.80
Due from res've agt's	77,925,068.68	74,003,830.40	93,413,463.95	107,023,546.81	102,742,452.54
Due from nat'l banks	44,101,948.46	39,143,388.90	48,192,531.93	46,692,994.78	55,352,459.82
Due from State banks	11,892,540.26	10,535,252.99	11,258,520.45	13,630,772.63	14,425,072.00
Real estate, etc......	47,091,904.70	47,461,614.51	47,706,108.26	47,817,169.36	47,902,332.09
Current expenses ...	4,033,021.67	6,693,668.43	6,913,430.46	6,111,256.56	7,474,082.10
Premiums paid......	6,366,048.85	6,609,390.80	5,674,497.80	4,332,419.63	4,150,836.17
Cash items...........	13,564,550.25	10,011,294.64	10,209,082.43	11,306,132.48	10,377,272.77
Clear'g-house exch'gs	100,035,237.82	63,712,445.55	83,152,359.49	112,964,964.25	112,172,677.05
Bills of other banks.	19,535,588.00	17,068,505.00	16,083,481.00	16,707,550.00	16,406,218.00
Fractional currency.	475,538.50	407,177.47	446,217.26	396,065.06	374,227.02
Specie...............	41,499,757.32	41,148,503.41	42,333,287.44	42,173,731.23	79,013,041.59
Legal-tender notes ..	70,601,233.00	64,461,231.00	67,059,152.00	69,196,696.00	54,715,096.00
U. S. cert'fs of deposit	28,915,000.00	21,885,000.00	25,180,000.00	26,770,000.00	10,860,000.00
Due from U. S. Treas.	17,175,435.13	17,029,121.31	16,620,986.20	17,029,065.45	17,054,816.40
Total..........	1,800,592,002.25	1,984,068,030.53	2,019,884,549.16	1,868,787,428.19	1,925,229,617.08

1880.

	FEBRUARY 21.	APRIL 23.	JUNE 11.	OCTOBER 1.	DECEMBER 31.
	2,061 banks.	2,075 banks.	2,076 banks.	2,090 banks.	2,095 banks.
Loans and discounts.	$974,295,360.70	$992,970,823.10	$994,712,616.41	$1,040,977,267.53	$1,071,356,141.79
Bonds for circulation	361,901,700.00	361,274,650.00	359,512,050.00	357,789,350.00	358,042,550.00
Bonds for deposits...	14,917,000.00	14,722,000.00	14,727,000.00	14,827,000.00	14,726,500.00
U. S. bonds on hand.	36,798,600.00	29,509,600.00	28,605,800.00	28,703,400.00	25,016,400.00
Other stocks and b'ds	41,223,583.33	42,491,927.73	41,947,345.75	48,863,150.22	48,628,372.77
Due from res've agt's	117,791,380.81	103,064,229.81	115,935,668.27	134,562,778.76	126,155,014.40
Due from nat'l banks	53,220,034.63	51,403,465.19	56,578,444.69	63,023,736.84	69,079,326.15
Due from State banks	14,501,152.51	13,293,775.91	13,861,582.77	15,881,197.71	17,111,211.03
Real estate, etc......	47,845,915.77	47,808,207.09	47,979,241.53	48,045,832.51	47,784,461.47
Current expenses ...	6,401,743.51	7,007,404.10	6,778,829.19	6,386,182.01	4,442,440.02
Premiums paid......	3,908,050.27	3,701,703.33	3,702,354.60	3,488,470.11	3,288,602.03
Cash items..........	10,320,274.51	9,857,645.31	9,980,170.32	12,729,002.19	14,713,929.02
Clear'g-house exch'gs	166,736,402.64	99,357,056.41	122,390,419.45	121,095,249.72	229,733,991.59
Bills of other banks.	15,369,257.00	21,064,501.00	21,908,193.00	18,210,943.00	21,549,367.00
Fractional currency.	397,187.23	395,747.67	387,226.13	367,171.73	389,921.75
Specie	80,442,051.75	86,420,732.21	99,506,505.26	109,346,509.49	107,172,900.92
Legal-tender notes ..	55,229,408.00	61,048,911.00	64,470,717.00	56,649,458.00	59,216,934.00
U. S. cert'fs of deposit	10,760,000.00	7,890,000.00	12,510,000.00	7,655,000.00	6,150,000.00
Due from U. S. Treas.	16,391,381.37	17,226,060.01	16,950,083.78	17,163,806.00	17,125,822.37
Total..........	2,038,066,498.46	1,974,600,472.95	2,035,493,280.15	2,105,786,625.82	2,241,683,829.01

BANKS FROM OCTOBER, 1863, TO OCTOBER, 1887—Continued.

1878.

Liabilities.	MARCH 15.	MAY 1.	JUNE 29.	OCTOBER 1.	DECEMBER 6.
	2,063 banks.	2,059 banks.	2,056 banks.	2,053 banks.	2,055 banks.
Capital stock	$473,952,541.00	$471,971,627.00	$470,393,366.00	$466,147,436.00	$464,874,996.00
Surplus fund	120,870,290.10	119,231,126.13	118,178,530.75	116,897,779.98	116,402,118.84
Undivided profits	45,040,851.85	43,938,961.98	40,482,522.61	40,936,213.58	44,040,171.84
Nat'l bank circulat'n	300,926,284.00	301,884,704.00	299,621,059.00	301,888,092.00	303,324,733.00
State bank circulat'n	430,339.00	426,504.00	417,808.00	413,913.00	400,715.00
Dividends unpaid	1,207,472.68	1,930,669.58	5,466,350.52	3,118,389.91	1,473,784.86
Individual deposits	602,882,585.17	625,479,771.12	621,632,160.06	620,236,176.82	598,805,775.56
U.S. deposits	7,243,253.29	13,811,474.14	22,686,619.67	41,654,812.08	40,269,825.72
Dep's U.S. dis. officers	3,004,064.90	2,392,281.61	2,903,531.99	3,342,794.73	3,431,436.56
Due to national banks	123,239,448.50	109,720,396.70	117,845,495.88	122,496,513.92	120,261,774.54
Due to State banks	43,970,229.39	44,006,551.05	43,360,527.60	42,636,703.42	41,767,755.07
Notes re-discounted	2,465,390.79	2,834,012.00	2,453,839.77	3,007,324.85	3,228,132.03
Bills payable	4,215,196.23	4,270,819.74	5,022,894.37	4,502,982.02	4,525,617.45
Total	1,729,465,056.90	1,741,898,050.05	1,750,464,706.51	1,767,279,133.21	1,742,826,837.37

1879.

	JANUARY 1.	APRIL 4.	JUNE 14.	OCTOBER 2.	DECEMBER 12.
	2,051 banks.	2,048 banks.	2,048 banks.	2,048 banks.	2,052 banks.
Capital stock	$462,031,396.00	$455,011,302.00	$455,244,415.00	$454,067,365.00	$454,498,515.00
Surplus fund	116,200,863.52	114,823,316.49	114,321,375.87	114,786,528.10	115,429,031.93
Undivided profits	36,836,269.21	40,812,777.59	45,802,845.82	41,300,941.40	47,573,820.73
Nat'l bank circulat'n	303,506,470.00	304,467,139.00	307,328,695.00	313,786,342.00	321,949,154.00
State bank circulat'n	388,368.00	352,452.00	339,927.00	325,954.00	322,502.00
Dividends unpaid	5,816,348.82	2,158,516.79	1,309,059.13	2,658,337.46	1,305,480.45
Individual deposits	643,337,745.26	598,822,694.02	648,934,141.42	719,737,568.89	755,459,966.01
U.S. deposits	59,701,222.80	303,463,505.69	248,421,340.25	11,018,862.74	6,923,323.97
Dep's U.S. dis. officers	3,556,801.25	2,689,189.44	3,682,320.67	3,469,600.02	3,893,217.43
Due to national banks	118,311,635.60	110,481,176.98	137,360,091.60	149,200,257.16	152,484,079.44
Due to State banks	44,035,787.56	43,709,770.14	50,403,064.54	52,022,453.69	50,232,301.93
Notes re-discounted	2,976,434.05	2,224,491.91	2,226,396.39	2,205,015.54	2,116,484.47
Bills payable	3,042,659.18	4,432,544.48	4,510,876.47	4,208,201.89	4,041,640.70
Total	1,800,592,002.25	1,984,068,936.53	2,019,884,549.10	1,868,787,428.19	1,925,229,617.08

1880.

	FEBRUARY 21.	APRIL 23.	JUNE 11.	OCTOBER 1.	DECEMBER 31.
	2,061 banks.	2,075 banks.	2,076 banks.	2,090 banks.	2,095 banks.
Capital stock	$454,548,585.00	$456,097,935.00	$455,909,565.00	$457,553,985.00	$458,540,085.00
Surplus fund	117,044,043.03	117,299,350.00	118,102,014.11	120,518,583.43	121,824,629.03
Undivided profits	42,863,804.05	48,226,087.61	50,443,645.45	46,139,690.24	47,946,741.64
Nat'l bank circulat'n	320,303,874.00	320,759,472.00	318,088,562.00	317,350,036.00	317,484,496.00
State bank circulat'n	303,452.00	299,790.00	290,738.00	271,045.00	258,499.00
Dividends unpaid	1,365,001.01	1,542,447.98	1,330,179.85	3,452,504.17	6,198,238.38
Individual deposits	848,926,599.86	791,555,059.63	833,701,034.20	873,537,637.07	1,006,452,852.82
U.S. deposits	7,850,701.07	7,925,988.37	7,680,905.47	7,548,538.67	7,898,100.94
Dep's U.S. dis. officers	3,069,860.74	3,220,096.64	3,026,757.34	3,344,386.62	3,489,501.01
Due to national banks	170,245,061.08	157,209,759.14	171,462,131.23	192,124,705.10	192,413,295.78
Due to State banks	65,439,334.51	63,317,107.96	67,938,795.35	75,735,677.06	71,185,817.08
Notes re-discounted	1,918,788.88	2,616,900.55	2,258,544.72	3,178,232.50	3,354,697.18
Bills payable	4,181,280.53	4,529,967.98	5,260,417.43	5,031,604.86	4,090,870.05
Total	2,038,060,498.40	1,974,600,472.95	2,035,493,280.15	2,105,786,625.82	2,241,663,829.91

AGGREGATE RESOURCES AND LIABILITIES OF THE NATIONAL

1881.

Resources.	MARCH 11. 2,094 banks.	MAY 6. 2,102 banks.	JUNE 30. 2,115 banks.	OCTOBER 1. 2,132 banks.	DECEMBER 31. 2,164 banks.
Loans and discounts.	$1,073,786,740.70	$1,093,649,282.18	$1,144,988,919.45	$1,173,796,083.09	$1,169,177,557.16
Bonds for circulation	339,811,050.00	352,653,500.00	358,287,500.00	363,335,500.00	368,735,700.00
Bonds for deposits	14,851,500.00	15,240,000.00	15,265,000.00	15,540,000.00	15,715,000.00
U. S. bonds on hand	46,626,150.00	44,116,500.00	48,584,950.00	40,866,750.00	31,884,000.00
Other stocks and b'ds	49,545,154.92	52,908,123.98	58,019,202.61	61,952,402.95	62,663,218.93
Due from res've ag'ts	120,820,601.09	128,017,627.03	156,258,637.05	132,968,183.12	123,530,465.75
Due from nat'l banks	62,295,517.34	64,176,225.67	75,703,509.78	78,505,446.17	77,633,402.77
Due from State banks	17,032,201.61	16,938,734.56	18,850,775.34	19,206,826.62	17,644,704.62
Real estate, etc	47,525,790.02	47,791,318.36	47,831,060.20	47,320,111.16	47,445,050.46
Current expenses	7,810,930.83	6,096,109.78	4,235,911.19	6,731,936.48	4,647,101.04
Premiums paid	3,510,516.71	4,024,763.60	4,115,980.01	4,138,485.71	3,801,728.72
Cash items	10,144,682.87	11,826,603.16	13,534,227.31	14,831,879.50	17,337,964.78
Clear'g-house exch'gs	147,761,541.96	196,633,528.01	143,990,236.84	189,222,255.65	217,214,627.10
Bills of other banks	17,733,032.00	25,120,033.00	21,631,932.00	17,732,712.00	24,190,534.00
Fractional currency	386,560.63	386,950.21	372,110.23	373,915.96	366,361.52
Specie	105,156,195.24	122,628,562.08	128,678,927.50	114,334,736.12	113,680,679.60
Legal-tender notes	52,156,430.00	62,516,296.00	58,728,713.00	53,158,441.00	60,104,387.00
U. S. cert's of deposit	6,120,000.00	8,045,000.00	9,540,000.00	6,740,000.00	7,090,000.00
Due from U. S. Treas	17,015,260.84	18,456,600.14	17,251,868.22	17,472,595.96	18,007,923.40
Total	2,140,110,944.78	2,270,226,817.70	2,325,832,700.75	2,358,387,391.50	2,381,890,866.85

1882.

	MARCH 11. 2,187 banks.	MAY 19. 2,224 banks.	JULY 1. 2,239 banks.	OCTOBER 3. 2,269 banks.	DECEMBER 30. 2,308 banks.
Loans and discounts	$1,182,661,600.53	$1,189,094,830.35	$1,208,932,655.92	$1,243,203,210.08	$1,230,456,213.97
Bonds for circulation	367,333,700.00	360,153,800.00	355,789,550.00	357,631,750.00	357,047,650.00
Bonds for deposits	16,003,000.00	15,920,000.00	15,920,000.00	16,111,000.00	16,344,000.00
U. S. bonds on hand	28,523,450.00	29,662,700.00	27,242,550.00	21,314,750.00	15,492,150.00
Other stocks and b'ds	64,450,086.18	65,274,999.32	66,691,399.56	66,168,916.64	66,648,600.36
Due from res've ag't's	117,452,719.75	124,189,945.23	118,435,012.38	113,277,227.87	122,066,106.75
Due from nat'l banks	68,301,645.12	66,884,512.75	75,366,970.74	68,516,841.06	76,073,227.76
Due from State banks	15,021,432.07	16,860,174.92	16,344,088.66	17,105,468.44	18,405,748.40
Real estate, etc	47,073,247.45	46,956,574.28	46,425,351.40	46,537,066.41	46,903,408.41
Current expenses	8,404,036.21	6,774,571.86	3,020,461.69	7,228,270.17	5,130,505.53
Premiums paid	3,762,382.50	5,062,314.52	5,494,221.35	6,515,155.03	6,472,585.82
Cash items	13,208,120.70	12,205,256.06	20,166,927.35	14,784,025.21	16,281,315.67
Clear'g-house exch'gs	162,088,077.94	107,270,094.71	150,114,220.08	208,366,540.08	155,051,194.81
Bills of other banks	10,440,089.00	25,226,186.00	21,405,758.00	20,680,425.00	23,344,775.00
Fractional currency	389,508.07	390,236.36	373,725.83	396,367.04	401,314.70
Specie	109,084,111.04	112,415,806.73	111,694,202.54	102,857,778.27	106,427,130.40
Legal-tender notes	56,633,572.00	65,060,522.00	64,019,518.00	63,313,517.00	68,478,421.00
U.S. cert's of deposit	9,445,000.00	10,395,000.00	11,045,000.00	8,645,000.00	8,475,000.00
Due from U. S. Treas	17,720,701.07	17,099,385.14	16,850,407.40	17,161,367.04	17,954,069.42
Total	2,309,057,088.72	2,277,024,911.13	2,344,342,086.90	2,399,833,676.84	2,360,793,467.09

1883.

	MARCH 13. 2,343 banks.	MAY 1. 2,375 banks.	JUNE 22. 2,417 banks.	OCTOBER 2. 2,501 banks.	DECEMBER 31. 2,529 banks.
Loans and discounts	$1,249,114,879.43	$1,262,339,081.87	$1,285,591,902.19	$1,309,244,781.01	$1,307,401,250.34
Bonds for circulation	354,746,500.00	354,480,250.00	351,002,900.00	351,412,850.00	345,505,800.00
Bonds for deposits	16,799,000.00	16,949,000.00	17,116,000.00	17,081,000.00	16,846,000.00
U. S. bonds on hand	17,850,100.00	15,870,600.00	16,078,150.00	13,593,050.00	13,151,250.00
Other stocks and b'ds	68,428,685.67	68,340,580.79	68,552,073.03	71,114,031.11	71,609,421.62
Due from res've ag'ts	121,024,151.60	109,306,843.23	126,646,954.62	124,918,728.71	126,999,606.02
Due from nat'l banks	67,264,503.86	68,477,918.02	66,364,638.21	65,714,229.44	77,902,785.07
Due from State banks	16,993,341.72	19,382,120.33	19,451,498.16	18,266,275.05	19,402,047.12
Real estate, etc	47,063,305.68	47,155,609.80	47,502,163.52	48,337,665.02	49,540,760.35
Current expenses	8,049,615.28	7,754,958.86	8,840,278.26	6,808,327.30	4,878,318.44
Premiums paid	7,140,930.81	7,798,445.04	8,079,726.01	8,064,073.60	8,647,252.08
Cash items	11,360,731.07	15,461,050.16	11,409,701.18	13,581,049.94	17,401,804.43
Clear'g-house exch'gs	107,710,465.17	145,990,918.18	90,792,075.08	96,359,211.76	134,545,273.08
Bills of other banks	19,739,526.00	22,655,863.00	26,279,850.00	22,675,447.00	28,809,699.00
Fractional currency	431,931.15	416,318.94	456,447.36	443,051.12	427,754.35
Specie	97,962,266.31	103,607,266.32	115,354,394.02	107,817,183.53	114,276,158.04
Legal-tender notes	68,878,098.00	68,238,198.00	73,832,158.00	70,672,907.00	80,550,796.00
U. S. cert's of deposit	8,465,000.00	8,420,000.00	10,685,000.00	9,070,000.00	10,840,000.00
Due from U. S. Treas	16,728,451.30	17,497,694.31	17,407,906.20	16,586,712.60	16,865,038.85
Total	2,228,018,165.11	2,360,192,235.85	2,364,833,122.44	2,372,656,364.82	2,445,880,017.49

BANKS FROM OCTOBER, 1863, TO OCTOBER, 1887—Continued.

1881.

Liabilities.	MARCH 11.	MAY 6.	JUNE 30.	OCTOBER 1.	DECEMBER 31.
	2,094 banks.	2,102 banks.	2,115 banks.	2,132 banks.	2,164 banks.
Capital stock........	$458, 254, 935. 00	$459, 039, 205. 00	$460, 227, 835. 00	$463, 821, 985. 00	$465, 859, 835. 00
Surplus fund	122, 470, 996. 73	124, 405, 926. 91	126, 679, 517. 67	128, 140, 617. 75	129, 867, 493. 02
Undivided profits...	54, 072, 225. 49	54, 906, 609. 47	54, 684, 137. 16	56, 372, 190. 92	54, 221, 816. 10
Nat'l bank circulation	298, 590, 802. 00	309, 737, 193. 00	312, 223, 352. 00	320, 200, 069. 00	325, 018, 161. 00
State bank circulat'n	252, 765. 00	252, 647. 00	242, 967. 00	244, 399. 00	241, 701. 00
Dividends unpaid...	1, 402, 118. 43	2, 647, 134. 37	5, 871, 595. 59	3, 836, 445. 84	6, 372, 737. 13
Individual deposits.	933, 392, 430. 75	1, 027, 040, 514. 10	1, 031, 731, 043. 42	1, 070, 997, 431. 71	1, 102, 679, 163. 71
U. S. deposits	7, 381, 149. 25	9, 504, 081. 25	8, 971, 826. 73	8, 476, 689. 74	8, 796, 678. 73
Dep's U.S.dis.officers	3, 839, 324. 77	3, 371, 512. 48	3, 272, 610. 45	3, 631, 803. 41	3, 595, 726. 83
Due to national banks	181, 677, 285. 37	191, 250, 091. 60	223, 503, 034. 10	205, 862, 945. 80	197, 252, 326. 01
Due to State banks..	71, 570, 477. 47	80, 700, 506. 06	91, 035, 560. 65	89, 047, 471. 06	79, 380, 429. 38
Notes re-discounted.	2, 616, 203. 05	2, 008, 370. 45	2, 220, 053. 02	3, 001, 105. 30	4, 122, 472. 79
Bills payable.......	4, 584, 231. 47	4, 493, 544. 77	5, 160, 128. 57	4, 664, 077. 12	4. 482, 325. 25
Total..........	2, 140, 110, 044. 78	2, 270, 226, 817. 70	2, 325, 832, 700. 75	2, 358, 387, 391. 59	2, 381, 890, 866. 85

1882.

	MARCH 11.	MAY 10.	JULY 1.	OCTOBER 3.	DECEMBER 30.
	2, 187 banks.	2,224 banks.	2,239 banks.	2,269 banks.	2,308 banks.
Capital stock........	$460, 390, 232. 00	$473, 819, 124. 00	$477, 184, 390. 00	$483, 104, 213. 00	$484, 883, 492. 00
Surplus fund........	130, 924, 139. 66	129, 233, 358. 24	131, 079, 251. 16	131, 977, 450. 77	135, 930, 609. 31
Undivided profits...	60, 475, 764. 98	62, 345, 199. 19	52, 128, 817. 73	61, 180, 310. 53	55, 343, 816. 04
Nat'l bank circulation	323, 651, 577. 00	315, 671, 226. 00	308, 921, 808. 00	314, 721, 215. 00	315, 230, 925. 00
State bank circulat'n	241, 527. 00	241, 319. 00	235, 173. 00	221, 177. 00	207, 273. 00
Dividends unpaid...	1, 418, 110. 12	1, 050, 554. 88	6, 634, 372. 20	3, 153, 836. 36	6, 805, 057. 82
Individual deposits..	1, 036, 505, 098. 20	1, 001, 687, 693. 74	1, 066, 707, 218. 75	1, 122, 472, 682. 46	1, 066, 901, 719. 85
U. S. deposits.......	8, 853, 242. 16	9, 741, 133. 36	9, 817, 224. 44	8, 817, 411. 21	9, 622, 303. 56
Dep's U.S.dis.officers	3, 372, 363. 96	3, 493, 252. 88	2, 867, 385. 63	3, 627, 846. 72	3, 780, 262. 10
Due to national banks	187, 433, 824. 90	192, 067, 865. 26	194, 868, 025. 46	180 075, 740. 77	194, 491, 260. 60
Due to State banks..	78, 350, 675. 85	78, 911, 787. 20	84, 063, 023. 66	79, 885, 652. 22	77, 031, 165. 82
Notes re-discounted.	3, 012, 092. 38	3. 754, 044. 38	4. 165, 210. 99	5, 747, 614. 68	6. 703, 164. 45
Bills payable.......	4, 428, 531. 51	5, 008, 343. 00	5, 657, 665. 88	4, 818, 517. 18	3, 856, 036. 54
Total..........	2, 399, 057, 088. 72	2, 277, 024, 011. 13	2, 344, 342, 686. 90	2, 399, 833, 676. 84	2, 360, 793, 407. 00

1883.

	MARCH 13.	MAY 1.	JUNE 22.	OCTOBER 2.	DECEMBER 31.
	2,343 banks.	2, 375 banks.	2,417 banks.	2,501 banks.	2.529 banks.
Capital stock........	$490 456, 932. 00	$493, 963, 069. 00	$500, 298, 312. 00	$509, 699, 787. 00	$514, 837, 575. 00
Surplus fund	136, 922. 884. 41	137. 775. 004. 39	128. 331. 002 06	141, 991. 789. 18	144. 800, 252. 13
Undivided profits ..	50, 340, 913. 64	60, 739, 878. 85	68, 354, 157. 15	61, 590, 652. 01	58, 787, 045 01
Nat'l bank circulation	312, 778, 053. 00	313, 549, 993. 00	311, 963, 302 00	310, 517, 857 00	304, 044, 131. 00
State bank circulat'n	206, 770. 00	198, 162. 00	189, 253. 00	184, 357. 00	181, 121. 00
Dividends unpaid...	1, 380, 002. 00	2, 840, 029. 87	1, 454, 232. 01	3, 229, 226. 31	7, 082, 682. 28
Individual deposits..	1, 004, 111, 400. 55	1, 067, 062, 238. 35	1, 043, 137, 703. 11	1, 049, 437, 700. 57	1, 106, 453, 008 23
U. S. deposits.......	9, 613, 873. 33	11. 624. 804. 57	10, 190, 757. 58	10. 183, 196 95	10. 026, 777. 79
Dep's U.S.dis.officers	3, 787, 225, 31	3, 618. 114. 79	3, 743, 326. 56	3, 980, 259. 28	3, 768, 862. 04
Due to national banks	191, 296, 850. 14	180. 445. 876. 92	194, 150, 076. 43	183. 828. 076. 27	200, 867, 280. 06
Due to State banks..	80, 251. 068. 26	78, 544, 128. 82	84, 744, 666. 55	84, 602, 073. 01	84, 776, 421. 60
Notes re-discounted.	5, 101, 458. 60	5. 537, 189. 60	5. 107, 514. 12	7, 387, 537. 40	8, 218, 562. 67
bills payable	3, 060, 724. 70	3, 364. 061. 60	3, 137, 250. 77	4, 053, 252. 81	4, 106, 207. 78
Total..........	2. 298, 918, 165. 11	2, 260, 192, 235. 85	2, 364, 833, 122. 44	2, 372, 656, 364. 82	2, 445, 880, 917. 40

AGGREGATE RESOURCES AND LIABILITIES OF THE NATIONAL

1884.

Resources.	MARCH 7. 2,563 banks.	APRIL 24. 2,580 banks.	JUNE 20. 2,625 banks.	SEPTEMBER 30. 2,664 banks.	DECEMBER 20. 2,664 banks.
Loans and discounts	$1,321,548,280.62	$1,333,433,230.51	$1,260,802,035.06	$1,245,294,003.37	$1,234,202,226.44
Bonds for circulation	330,816,150.00	337,342,900.00	334,316,350.00	327,435,000.00	317,586,050.00
Bonds for deposits	16,850,000.00	17,135,000.00	17,060,000.00	16,840,000.00	16,740,000.00
U. S. bonds on hand.	18,672,250.00	15,560,400.00	14,143,000.00	13,579,000.00	12,305,600.00
Other stocks and b'ds	73,155,084.60	73,424,815.97	72,572,306.93	71,363,477.40	73,440,352.07
Due from res've ag'ts	138,705,012.74	122,491,057.08	95,247,152.62	111,093,019.65	121,161,076.80
Due from nat'l banks	64,628,322.58	68,031,209.90	64,891,670.13	66,335,544.67	69,450,881.45
Due from State banks	17,937,976.35	18,145,827.61	16,306,500.01	15,833,982.58	18,320,012.01
Real estate, etc.	49,418,805.02	49,667,126.87	50,149,083.60	49,990,886.01	49,860,936.06
Current expenses	7,813,880.56	8,054,260.82	8,866,558.09	6,913,508.85	9,670,906.14
Premiums paid	9,742,601.42	9,826,386.76	10,605,343.49	11,632,631.68	11,023,447.15
Cash items	11,383,792.57	11,237,075.71	11,382,292.69	13,103,908.55	11,924,152.89
Cl'g-house loan cert's	....	....	10,335,000.00	1,690,000.00	1,870,000.00
Clear'g-house exc'gs	68,403,373.30	83,531,472.58	69,498,913.13	66,257,118.15	75,195,955.95
Bills of other banks	23,485,124.00	26,525,120.00	23,386,695.00	23,258,851.00	22,377,965.00
Fractional currency	491,067.70	480,802.51	473,046.66	469,023.80	456,778.20
Specie	122,080,127.33	114,744,707.09	109,061,682.11	128,609,474.73	139,747,079.53
Legal-tender notes	75,817,695.00	77,712,028.00	76,917,212.00	77,044,659.00	76,369,555.00
U.S. cert's of deposit.	14,045,000.00	11,900,000.00	9,870,000.00	14,200,000.00	19,040,000.00
Due from U.S. Treas.	16,465,785.66	17,468,970.58	17,022,999.34	17,739,606.28	15,442,306.52
Total	2,390,500,628.51	2,396,813,834.02	2,282,508,742.06	2,279,493,860.07	2,297,143,474.27

1885.

	MARCH 10. 2,671 banks.	MAY 6. 2,678 banks.	JULY 1. 2,689 banks.	OCTOBER 1. 2,714 banks.	DECEMBER 24. 2,732 banks.
Loans and discounts	$1,232,327,453.69	$1,241,450,649.79	$1,257,655,547.92	$1,306,143,990.46	$1,343,517,559.06
Bonds for circulation	313,106,200.00	312,168,500.00	310,102,200.00	307,657,050.00	304,770,750.00
Bonds for deposits	16,815,000.00	16,740,000.00	17,607,000.00	17,457,000.00	18,012,000.00
U. S. bonds on hand	14,607,650.00	14,700,250.00	14,588,800.00	14,329,400.00	12,605,750.00
Other stocks and b'ds	75,152,919.35	75,019,208.69	77,249,159.42	77,495,230.25	77,533,841.38
Due from res've ag'ts	130,462,273.26	130,903,103.77	132,733,004.34	138,378,515.15	139,239,444.80
Due from nat'l banks	66,442,051.87	67,856,650.57	77,220,972.20	78,967,097.86	79,452,309.67
Due from State banks	17,572,822.65	17,348,038.11	17,180,008.46	17,087,891.44	18,553,940.46
Real estate, etc	49,699,501.42	49,886,378.87	50,729,896.08	51,293,801.16	51,063,062.01
Current expenses	7,877,320.27	7,096,268.06	3,533,750.49	6,853,302.72	9,416,071.01
Premiums paid	12,330,437.60	12,358,082.70	12,690,063.41	12,511,333.41	11,802,199.86
Cash items	11,228,856.82	11,270,626.48	17,214,373.52	14,347,570.53	12,810,187.64
Cl'g-house loan cert's	1,530,000.00	1,430,000.00	1,380,000.00	1,110,000.00	670,000.00
Clear'g-house exc'gs	59,085,781.09	72,250,129.39	113,158,675.32	84,926,730.76	92,351,206.77
Bills of other banks	22,013,314.00	26,217,171.00	23,465,388.00	23,062,765.00	23,178,052.00
Fractional currency	519,529.96	513,200.12	480,027.18	477,055.17	415,082.64
Trade dollars	....	....	....	1,005,763.69	1,070,961.77
Specie	167,115,873.67	177,433,110.30	177,612,492.02	174,872,572.54	165,354,352.37
Legal-tender notes	71,017,322.00	77,336,999.00	79,701,352.00	69,738,119.00	67,585,466.00
U.S. cert's of deposit	22,760,000.00	19,135,000.00	22,020,000.00	18,800,000.00	11,765,000.00
Due from U.S. Treas.	15,079,935.80	15,473,270.84	14,617,897.02	14,897,114.24	14,981,021.79
Total	2,312,744,247.35	2,340,082,452.09	2,421,852,010.47	2,432,013,002.38	2,457,075,256.13

1886.

	MARCH 1. 2,768 banks.	JUNE 3. 2,809 banks.	AUGUST 27. 2,849 banks.	OCTOBER 7. 2,852 banks.	DECEMBER 28. 2,875 banks.
Loans and discounts	$1,367,705,252.80	$1,398,552,090.71	$1,421,547,199.22	$1,450,957,054.03	$1,470,157,681.13
Bonds for circulation	296,661,400.00	279,414,400.00	270,315,850.00	258,498,050.00	228,384,350.00
Bonds for deposits	18,637,000.00	18,810,000.00	19,084,000.00	20,105,000.00	21,040,000.00
U. S. bonds on hand	16,589,050.00	12,535,550.00	14,368,950.00	12,320,500.00	10,570,200.00
Other stocks and b'ds	80,227,388.98	83,347,119.03	82,439,901.64	81,825,206.40	81,431,000.66
Due from res've ag'ts	142,805,686.91	133,027,136.63	143,715,221.45	140,761,579.01	142,117,979.28
Due from nat'l banks	76,933,579.67	77,632,198.47	78,091,411.58	80,526,615.77	88,271,097.90
Due from State banks	18,834,235.88	17,720,924.26	18,387,215.70	20,140,250.27	21,405,427.08
Real estate, etc	52,262,718.07	53,117,561.42	53,834,583.58	54,090,070.94	54,703,630.37
Current expenses	7,705,850.57	8,684,672.33	5,837,175.21	7,438,741.12	10,283,007.70
Premiums paid	12,237,689.15	13,298,269.23	13,041,463.72	14,303,529.55	15,160,621.67
Cash items	15,135,528.48	12,181,455.80	10,408,081.58	13,277,160.64	13,218,973.44
Cl'g-house loan cert's	565,000.00	205,000.00	85,000.00	....	....
Clear'g-house exc'gs	99,923,636.81	76,140,330.60	62,474,605.00	95,536,911.15	70,525,126.92
Bills of other banks	20,503,303.00	25,129,938.00	21,602,661.00	22,731,085.00	20,132,330.00
Fractional currency	470,175.18	452,361.34	451,308.89	434,220.93	417,833.00
Trade dollars	1,081,570.65	1,713,381.35	1,857,011.56	1,880,794.55	1,827,261.20
Specie	171,615,910.39	157,459,870.49	149,000,492.10	156,387,696.00	166,983,556.01
Legal-tender notes	67,014,880.00	79,650,788.00	64,039,751.00	62,812,322.00	67,739,828.00
U. S. cert's of deposit	12,430,000.00	11,850,000.00	8,115,000.00	5,855,000.00	6,195,000.00
5% fund with Treas	12,953,218.20	12,198,526.43	11,868,912.52	11,358,014.97	10,056,178.39
Due from U. S. Treas	1,513,019.67	1,416,892.00	1,699,303.36	2,502,042.04	975,370.00
Total	2,404,337,120.41	2,474,514,481.80	2,453,666,930.07	2,513,854,751.17	2,507,753,012.95

BANKS FROM OCTOBER, 1863, TO OCTOBER, 1887—Continued.

1884.

Liabilities.	MARCH 7.	APRIL 24.	JUNE 20.	SEPTEMBER 30.	DECEMBER 20.
	2,563 banks.	2,589 banks.	2,625 banks.	2,661 banks.	2,664 banks.
Capital stock	$515,725,005.00	$518,471,841.00	$522,515,996.00	$524,271,345.00	$524,080,005.00
Surplus fund	145,741,679.90	146,017,958.07	145,763,416.17	147,055,037.85	146,867,119.06
Undivided profits	63,614,861.56	67,450,459.00	70,597,487.21	63,231,237.62	70,711,369.05
Nat'l bank circulati'n	298,791,610.00	297,506,243.00	295,175,334.00	289,775,123.00	280,107,013.00
State bank circulati'n	180,589.00	180,576.00	179,600.00	170,653.00	174,645.00
Dividends unpaid	1,422,901.91	1,415,889.58	1,384,686.71	3,686,160.33	1,331,421.54
Individual deposits	1,046,030,167.90	1,060,778,388.06	979,020,349.03	975,243,705.14	987,649,055.68
U. S. deposits	9,956,875.24	11,233,495.77	10,520,759.44	10,367,909.92	10,655,803.72
Dep's U. S. dis. offic'rs	3,836,401,66	3,588,980.50	3,661,320.13	3,703,804.34	3,749,969.85
Due to national banks	207,461,179.63	192,808,042.31	155,785,351.41	173,979,149.89	187,296,348.30
Due to State banks	68,406,363.89	86,778,138.85	70,480,617.11	72,406,206.83	72,572,384.43
Notes re-discounted	6,234,202.32	7,299,284.58	11,343,505.55	11,008,595.07	8,433,724.67
Bills payable	2,968,740.50	3,193,655.20	4,262,244.57	4,560,802.15	3,415,524.07
Cl'g-house loan cert's	....	....	11,895,000.00	....	....
Total	2,390,500,638.51	2,396,813,834.92	2,282,598,742.96	2,279,493,880.07	2,297,143,474.27

1885.

	MARCH 10	MAY 6.	JULY 1.	OCTOBER 1.	DECEMBER 24.
	2,671 banks.	2,678 banks.	2,689 banks.	2,714 banks.	2,732 banks.
Capital stock	$524,255,151.00	$525,195,577.00	$526,273,602.00	$527,524,410.00	$529,360,725.00
Surplus fund	145,907,800.02	145,103,776.01	146,523,790.91	146,624,642.06	150,155,549.52
Undivided profits	60,296,452.56	60,184,358.12	52,229,946.61	59,335,519.11	69,229,645.82
Nat'l bank circulati'n	274,054,157.00	273,703,047.00	269,147,020.00	268,869,597.00	267,430,837.00
State bank circulati'n	162,581.00	144,498.00	144,489.00	136,898.00	133,932.00
Dividends unpaid	1,301,937.73	2,577,236.08	6,414,203.98	3,508,325.38	1,360,977.27
Individual deposits	996,501,617.40	1,035,802,188.56	1,106,376,516.80	1,102,372,450.35	1,111,429,914.08
U. S. deposits	11,006,919.47	11,690,707.52	10,995,974.06	11,552,621.98	12,058,768.36
Dep's U.S. dis. offic'rs	3,039,646.40	3,330,522.70	3,027,218.02	2,714,399.37	3,005,783.11
Due to national banks	205,877,203.09	199,081,104.40	203,932,800.05	213,534,905.08	216,564,533.96
Due to State banks	82,190,567.43	81,966,092.25	88,847,454.78	86,115,061.25	85,060,162.27
Notes re-discounted	6,299,722.15	5,736,012.02	5,864,000.85	8,432,792.61	9,932,828.24
Bills payable	1,850,462.10	2,167,333.33	2,074,259.76	2,191,380.16	1,954,598.60
Total	2,312,744,247.35	2,346,082,452.99	2,421,852,016.47	2,432,913,002.38	2,457,675,256.13

1886.

	MARCH 1.	JUNE 3.	AUGUST 27.	OCTOBER 7.	DECEMBER 28.
	2,768 banks.	2,809 banks.	2,849 banks.	2,852 banks.	2,875 banks.
Capital stock	$533,360,615.00	$539,109,291.72	$545,522,508.00	$548,240,730.00	$550,698,675.00
Surplus fund	152,872,349.01	153,642,034.86	157,003,875.60	157,249,190.87	159,573,479.21
Undivided profits	59,376,381.80	67,662,886.02	62,211,505.63	66,503,404.72	79,208,286.13
Nat'l bank circulati'n	256,972,158.00	244,803,097.00	238,273,085.00	228,672,610.00	202,078,287.00
State bank circulati'n	133,931.00	132,470.00	128,336.00	125,002.00	115,352.00
Dividends unpaid	1,534,905.58	1,526,776.06	1,863,303.62	2,227,810.59	1,500,345.06
Individual deposits	1,152,660,492.06	1,146,246,911.43	1,113,459,187.35	1,172,968,308.64	1,169,716,413.13
U. S. deposits	12,414,566.52	13,670,721.76	14,295,927.74	13,842,023.69	13,705,709.73
Dep's U.S. dis. offic'rs	3,019,018.72	2,708,864.55	2,884,865.62	2,721,276.77	4,276,257.85
Due to national ba'ks	219,778,171.80	204,405,273.11	218,327,437.33	218,305,950.54	223,812,279.46
Due to State banks	92,663,570.46	90,501,102.81	90,306,354.00	99,246,483.31	91,254,533.23
Notes re-discounted	8,376,035.20	8,718,911.71	7,948,698.27	10,594,176.56	9,150,345.79
Bills payable	1,174,874.29	1,145,240.26	1,381,095.01	2,067,693.48	2,444,953.36
Total	2,494,337,129.44	2,474,544,481.89	2,453,666,930.67	2,513,831,751.17	2,507,753,012.95

AGGREGATE RESOURCES AND LIABILITIES OF THE NATIONAL

1887.

Resources.	March 4.	May 13.	August 1.	October 5.
	2,900 banks.	2,955 banks.	3,014 banks.	3,049 banks.
Loans and discounts	$1, 515, 504, 074. 67	$1, 560, 291, 810. 73	$1, 560, 371, 741. 05	$1, 587, 549, 133. 76
U. S. bonds to secure circ'lat'n	211, 537, 150. 00	200, 452, 300. 00	189, 032, 050. 00	189, 083, 100. 00
U. S. bonds to secure deposits	22, 070, 000. 00	24, 090, 500. 00	26, 402, 000. 00	27, 757, 000. 00
U. S. bonds on hand	9, 721, 450. 00	8, 157, 250. 00	7, 808, 000. 00	6, 914, 350. 00
Oth'r stocks, b'ds, and mortg's	87, 441, 034. 86	88, 031, 124. 15	88, 374, 837. 69	88, 831, 009. 96
Due from ap'r'd reserve ag'ts	163, 161, 181. 37	148, 067, 874. 43	140, 270, 155. 75	140, 873, 587. 98
Due from national banks	86, 460, 829. 09	105, 576, 841. 90	99, 487, 707. 80	93, 302, 413. 94
Due from State b'ks and b'k'rs	21, 725, 805. 99	22, 746, 190. 43	20, 952, 187. 80	23, 103, 077. 18
Real estate, furniture, etc	55, 128, 600. 78	55, 729, 098. 76	56, 954, 622. 58	57, 968, 150. 71
Current exp's and taxes paid	8, 064, 292. 40	7, 781, 151. 97	5, 158, 940. 86	8, 253, 890. 72
Premiums paid	15, 537, 721. 22	16, 806, 431. 83	17, 353, 130. 17	17, 288, 771. 35
Checks and other cash items	13, 308, 520. 04	13, 055, 663. 79	16, 914, 070. 02	14, 691, 373. 38
Exchanges for cl'ng-house	89, 230, 104. 59	86, 829, 363. 73	128, 211, 628. 48	88, 775, 457. 90
Bills for other banks	22, 235, 206. 00	25, 188, 137. 00	22, 962, 737. 00	21, 937, 884. 00
Uncurrent and minor coins	577, 878. 03	556, 186. 75	561, 266. 72	540, 594. 50
Trade dollars	1, 803, 661. 40	184, 203. 08	63, 071. 97	509. 25
Specie	171, 678, 006. 15	167, 315, 665. 62	165, 104, 210. 28	165, 085, 454. 78
Legal-tender notes	66, 228, 158. 00	79, 595, 088. 00	74, 477, 342. 00	73, 751, 255. 00
U. S. certificates of deposit	7, 045, 000. 00	8, 025, 000. 00	7, 810, 000. 00	6, 100, 000. 00
5% fund with Treasurer	9, 280, 755. 33	8, 810, 585. 35	8, 341, 088. 77	8, 310, 442. 35
Due from U. S. Treasurer	1, 856, 105. 13	1, 113, 554. 81	690, 818. 42	985, 410. 14
Total	2, 581, 143, 115. 05	2, 620, 314, 022. 42	2, 637, 276, 167. 72	2, 620, 103, 475. 59

BANKS FROM OCTOBER, 1863, TO OCTOBER, 1887—Continued.

1887.

Liabilities.	MARCH 4.	MAY 13.	AUGUST 1.	OCTOBER 5.
	2,900 banks.	2,955 banks.	3,014 banks.	3,049 banks.
Capital stock paid in	$555,351,765.00	$565,629,068.45	$571,648,811.00	$578,462,765.00
Surplus fund	164,337,132.72	167,411,521.03	172,348,398.09	173,913,440.97
Undivided profits	67,248,949.16	70,153,308.11	62,204,634.02	71,451,167.02
Nat'l bank-notes outstanding	186,231,498.00	176,771,529.00	166,625,658.00	167,283,343.00
State bank notes outstanding	100,100.00	98,716.00	98,607.00	98,699.00
Dividends unpaid	1,441,628.17	1,977,314.40	2,230,929.46	2,495,127.83
Individual deposits	1,224,925,698.26	1,266,570,537.67	1,285,076,978.58	1,249,477,126.95
U. S. deposits	15,263,900.94	17,536,485.93	19,186,712.77	20,392,284.04
Deposits U. S. disb'ng offic'rs	4,277,187.61	3,779,735.14	4,074,903.62	4,831,006.14
Due to national banks	249,337,482.40	244,575,545.12	235,966,022.46	227,491,984.15
Due to State banks	103,012,552.48	102,089,438.63	103,603,598.14	102,094,025.68
Notes and bills rediscounted	7,556,837.10	10,132,709.64	11,125,236.08	17,312,806.39
Bills payable	2,082,374.21	2,567,953.30	2,985,987.60	4,888,429.43
Total	2,581,143,115.05	2,629,314,022.42	2,637,276,107.72	2,620,193,475.50

A SUMMARY

OF THE

STATE AND CONDITION

OF

THE NATIONAL BANKS

ON

DECEMBER 28, 1886, MARCH 4, MAY 13, AUGUST 1, AND OCTOBER 5, 1887.

Arranged by States, Territories, and Reserve Cities.

NOTE.—The abstract of each State is exclusive of any reserve city therein.

Abstract of reports since October 7, 1886,

MAINE.

Resources.	DECEMBER 28.	MARCH 4.	MAY 13.	AUGUST 1.	OCTOBER 5.
	71 banks.	71 banks.	72 banks.	72 banks.	72 banks.
Loans and discounts	$18,231,448.55	$17,976,050.75	$18,309,263.20	$18,502,167.80	$19,174,026.59
Bonds for circulation	7,351,000.00	6,501,000.00	5,878,500.00	5,558,500.00	5,483,500.00
Bonds for deposits	170,000.00	170,000.00	170,000.00	170,000.00	170,000.00
U. S. bonds on hand	10,600.00	11,750.00	10,400.00	10,400.00	10,400.00
Other stocks and b'ds	779,273.04	816,977.09	805,954.35	803,014.62	828,932.83
Due from res've ag'ts	1,984,959.25	1,624,733.48	1,615,264.45	1,586,391.92	1,600,388.87
Due from nat'l banks	710,767.10	546,101.59	461,201.54	464,190.00	587,018.27
Due from State banks	21,425.66	14,765.13	15,473.48	12,283.50	15,510.39
Real estate, etc	513,966.04	513,783.91	513,240.91	496,940.63	492,729.57
Current expenses	77,043.58	49,784.34	62,535.58	32,205.45	54,473.76
Premiums paid	207,244.59	260,237.48	274,191.13	272,280.76	266,404.10
Cash items	204,370.30	236,655.61	213,013.69	199,073.81	207,454.64
Clear'g-house exch'gs	85,615.61	79,372.16	60,795.98	72,573.37	66,580.98
Bills of other banks	440,930.00	276,029.00	299,949.00	330,446.00	321,995.00
Uncur't & minor coins	2,796.53	3,707.61	3,114.42	3,416.74	3,063.09
Trade dollars	1,963.00	488.00	231.00	22.00	....
Specie	763,114.86	793,975.17	687,780.19	676,408.61	693,029.93
Legal-tender notes	239,808.00	184,548.00	185,377.00	197,099.00	219,206.00
U. S. cert's of deposit	....	....	....	....	....
5% fund with Treas.	321,255.00	281,865.00	254,750.00	245,482.50	238,627.50
Due from U. S. Treas.	4,788.55	10,780.00	7,532.00	9,670.00	5,950.00
Total	32,251,449.71	30,372,543.91	29,828,574.02	29,641,656.63	30,439,981.46

NEW HAMPSHIRE.

	49 banks.	49 banks.	49 banks.	49 banks.	49 banks.
Loans and discounts	$9,101,003.20	$8,993,811.58	$9,020,[illegible].42	$9,357,589.87	$9,695,037.37
Bonds for circulation	4,440,500.00	4,364,500.00	4,289,500.00	4,019,500.00	4,019,500.00
Bonds for deposits	350,000.00	350,000.00	350,000.00	350,000.00	350,000.00
U. S. bonds on hand	300.00	650.00	4,250.00	5,000.00	1,600.00
Other stocks and b'ds	1,674,904.94	1,769,412.03	1,716,862.58	1,703,589.97	1,753,393.98
Due from res've ag'ts	1,371,739.93	1,272,851.45	1,580,289.69	1,151,839.56	1,505,535.95
Due from nat'l banks	107,564.73	144,021.35	106,459.01	147,305.04	178,512.12
Due from State banks	56,798.28	48,402.05	65,458.14	46,167.36	43,524.55
Real estate, etc	198,493.69	195,941.62	207,077.52	207,682.46	210,474.15
Current expenses	68,149.75	48,934.93	41,001.17	35,140.88	44,478.10
Premiums paid	209,341.88	245,060.46	268,422.96	291,171.00	292,540.02
Cash items	120,399.39	109,091.29	140,403.66	190,032.31	228,541.75
Clear'g-house exch'gs	....	....	....	....	....
Bills of other banks	328,978.00	239,014.00	276,141.00	252,485.00	225,149.00
Uncur't & minor coins	4,789.42	4,848.03	5,823.21	4,984.54	5,138.06
Trade dollars	132.25	407.25	407.00	27.00	....
Specie	387,070.41	372,756.87	379,240.15	385,159.54	394,034.15
Legal-tender notes	141,730.00	124,706.00	132,141.00	138,235.00	122,493.00
U. S. cert's of deposit	....	....	....	....	....
5% fund with Treas.	199,609.67	194,677.50	192,302.50	180,162.50	178,782.50
Due from U. S. Treas.	6,818.34	4,451.20	1,481.20	1,960.00	1,432.16
Total	18,837,323.97	18,484,517.61	18,870,573.23	18,469,032.63	19,250,196.95

VERMONT.

	49 banks.	49 banks.	49 banks.	49 banks.	49 banks.
Loans and discounts	$12,080,011.46	$11,938,056.79	$12,265,214.54	$12,511,864.26	$12,879,765.21
Bonds for circulation	4,076,500.00	4,571,000.00	3,954,500.00	3,898,500.00	3,891,000.00
Bonds for deposits	100,000.00	100,000.00	100,000.00	150,000.00	150,000.00
U. S. bonds on hand	129,600.00	160,950.00	160,150.00	122,850.00	128,600.00
Other stocks and b'ds	824,621.17	806,551.66	768,135.28	772,242.94	820,911.86
Due from res've ag'ts	1,062,360.56	1,016,916.61	1,240,382.13	998,880.01	993,278.39
Due from nat'l banks	191,347.68	174,526.69	213,134.92	169,096.91	213,415.46
Due from State banks	24,805.77	42,0[illegible].02	62,672.30	39,020.22	24,898.43
Real estate, etc	221,128.60	224,183.08	223,319.80	215,856.61	217,659.78
Current expenses	56,675.96	27,926.54	51,168.44	15,414.70	41,232.90
Premiums paid	140,102.92	125,159.50	133,561.46	152,169.00	151,086.10
Cash items	90,768.68	83,605.23	63,303.90	67,850.10	60,006.88
Clear'g-house exch'gs	....	....	....	....	....
Bills of other banks	165,407.00	120,900.00	122,360.00	121,810.00	123,579.00
Uncur't & minor coins	3,684.15	4,534.76	4,270.61	3,815.27	4,349.05
Trade dollars	4,731.01	1,781.85	2,518.00	507.00	4.00
Specie	400,682.78	400,092.49	384,824.26	395,767.91	387,693.58
Legal-tender notes	197,701.00	111,438.00	172,719.00	161,276.00	171,399.00
U. S. cert's of deposit	....	....	....	....	....
5% fund with Treas.	206,348.29	201,065.00	173,872.50	172,060.00	161,903.50
Due from U. S. Treas.	360.00	685.00	10.00	310.00	1,310.00
Total	20,577,225.03	20,116,206.21	20,095,417.11	19,999,389.96	20,434,803.14

by States and reserve cities.

MAINE.

Liabilities.	DECEMBER 28.	MARCH 4.	MAY 13.	AUGUST 1.	OCTOBER 5.
	71 banks.	71 banks.	72 banks.	72 banks.	72 banks.
Capital stock	$10,360,000.00	$10,360,000.00	$10,385,000.00	$10,410,000.00	$10,440,700.00
Surplus fund	2,346,128.02	2,374,735.09	2,396,222.03	2,414,708.45	2,401,401.86
Undivided profits	1,370,360.34	1,100,447.50	1,349,712.12	1,191,330.69	1,343,946.34
Nat'l-bank circulation	6,538,651.00	5,756,770.00	5,231,564.00	4,944,497.00	4,875,561.00
State-bank circulation	....	....	....	....	....
Dividends unpaid	48,058.25	49,254.50	48,984.67	74,163.01	73,158.70
Individual deposits	10,618,758.52	9,730,874.18	9,506,709.64	9,724,620.75	10,116,282.26
U. S. deposits	73,532.53	70,650.72	91,691.23	76,410.50	64,277.60
Dep'ts U.S.dis.officers	63,786.26	64,867.58	61,702.84	72,971.07	101,859.81
Due to national banks	647,422.77	492,577.73	546,623.17	491,014.18	551,540.42
Due to State banks	62,072.02	172,330.50	79,557.00	97,429.73	196,317.72
Notes re-discounted	92,677.00	140,036.11	130,807.12	140,410.45	267,180.55
Bills payable	....	....	....	4,052.20	7,752.20
Total	32,251,449.71	30,372,543.91	29,828,574.02	29,641,656.63	30,439,981.46

NEW HAMPSHIRE.

	49 banks.	49 banks.	49 banks.	49 banks.	49 banks.
Capital stock	$6,155,000.00	$6,155,000.00	$6,205,000.00	$6,205,000.00	$6 205,000.00
Surplus fund	1,331,176.61	1,397,072.00	1,434,547.60	1,451,274.77	1,453,624.77
Undivided profits	747,884.54	576,163.83	595,190.63	537,726.39	639,058.42
Nat'l-bank circulation	3,966,905.00	3,892,185.00	3,792,830.00	3,588,310.00	3,588,015.00
State-bank circulation	6,834.00	6,833.00	6,833.00	6,833.00	6,829.00
Dividends unpaid	34,610.36	20,629.46	30,609.80	40,497.26	34,580.12
Individual deposits	5,576,309.26	5,378,933.01	5,511,929.27	5,632,125.05	6,123,423.51
U. S. deposits	246,377.40	251,507.53	252,883.33	265,029.29	223,031.17
Dep'ts U.S.dis.officers	60,174.15	54,286.57	61,817.95	66,992.22	114,561.02
Due to national banks	466,180.61	405,450.46	578,110.26	406,830.61	500,895.52
Due to State banks	222,703.36	317,074.01	346,831.68	245,771.19	341,208.42
Notes re-discounted	22,019.68	25,782.20	24,171.31	17,112.00	15,000.00
Bills payable	450.00	....	9,810.00	5,530.85	4,970.00
Total	18,837,323.97	18,484,517.61	18,850,573.23	18,469,032.63	19,250,196.95

VERMONT.

	49 banks.	49 banks.	49 banks.	49 banks.	49 banks.
Capital stock	$7,641,000.00	$7,591,000.00	$7,516,000.00	$7,516,000.00	$7,566,000.00
Surplus fund	1,514,978.05	1,551,346.50	1,552,479.33	1,568,887.23	1,571,863.75
Undivided profits	740,355.38	532,669.71	688,410.95	499,867.30	668,328.88
Nat'l-bank circulation	4,175,065.00	4,076,725.00	3,531,505.00	3,464,035.00	3,478,100.00
State-bank circulation	3,500.00	3,500.00	3,500.00	3,500.00	3,500.00
Dividends unpaid	36,012.83	14,249.93	9,962.55	24,012.75	9,095.60
Individual deposits	6,121,700.31	5,939,058.06	6,239,636.44	6,416,438.48	6,627,080.66
U. S. deposits	47,315.32	60,505.72	69,508.48	115,021.43	134,515.47
Dep'ts U.S.dis.officers	5,840.68	4,333.23	4,997.80	7,463.15	8,924.22
Due to national banks	170,995.52	216,667.70	275,731.26	225,381.43	216,530.40
Due to State banks	71,483.59	70,973.90	90,238.79	82,057.50	86,297.70
Notes re-discounted	45,933.52	84,247.12	113,118.20	75,757.36	44,528.12
Bills payable	14.63	29.25	29.25	29.25	20,029.25
Total	20,577,225.03	20,140,200.21	20,095,417.14	19,999,380.96	20,434,803.14

Abstract of reports since October 7, 1886, arranged

MASSACHUSETTS.

Resources.	DECEMBER 28.	MARCH 4.	MAY 13.	AUGUST 1.	OCTOBER 5.
	197 banks.	197 banks.	196 banks.	198 banks.	198 banks.
Loans and discounts.	$89, 403, 330. 25	$89, 862, 784. 01	$91, 900, 537. 80	$91, 379, 755. 60	$91, 685, 952. 03
Bonds for circulation.	30, 541, 750. 00	27, 317, 250. 00	25, 899, 250. 00	24, 404, 250. 00	24, 064, 250. 00
Bonds for deposits...	320, 000. 00	320, 000. 00	320, 000. 00	300, 000. 00	300, 000. 00
U. S. bonds on hand..	230, 150. 00	221, 050. 00	188, 950. 00	136, 100. 00	130, 450. 00
Other stocks and b'ds	4, 606, 697. 09	4, 081, 393. 28	4, 394, 989. 05	4, 373, 494. 71	4, 405, 420. 40
Due from res've ag'ts.	7, 640, 536. 61	9, 186, 017. 18	8, 009, 322. 16	6, 611, 982. 37	8, 704, 060. 86
Due from nat'l banks	1, 196, 325. 81	1, 094, 910. 87	941, 434. 30	1, 201, 728. 52	952, 151. 53
Due from State banks	182, 993. 01	174, 954. 53	230, 452. 00	169, 113. 53	208, 443. 13
Real estate, etc......	2, 170, 188. 71	2, 173, 304. 04	2, 180, 762. 45	2, 233, 010. 87	2, 235, 153. 65
Current expenses....	571, 577. 37	577, 029. 09	236, 848. 83	356, 581. 52	260, 108. 31
Premiums paid......	1, 052, 865. 80	1, 066, 824. 62	1, 094, 957. 30	1, 007, 891. 86	1, 037, 096. 11
Cash items..........	709, 396. 00	705, 500. 36	763, 574. 49	672, 668. 33	804, 714. 29
Clear'g-house exch'gs	66, 969. 58	59, 304. 32	66, 445. 76	72, 593. 19	70, 652. 56
Bills of other banks..	1, 486, 320. 00	1, 160, 920. 00	1, 339, 270. 00	1, 000, 893. 00	1, 215, 864. 00
Uncur't & minor coins	35, 419. 55	50, 481. 97	46, 736. 37	43, 539. 33	41, 616. 11
Trade dollars........	16, 825. 44	16, 298. 14	6, 061. 40	1, 507. 00	....
Specie...............	3, 185, 693. 34	3, 063, 894. 64	3, 120, 546. 60	3, 022, 090. 84	3, 047, 952. 85
Legal-tender notes..	1, 370, 831. 00	1, 197, 636. 00	1, 301, 263. 00	1, 201, 142. 00	1, 221, 311. 00
U. S. cert's of deposit.	180, 000. 00	175, 000. 00	185, 000. 00	190, 000. 00	195, 000. 00
5 % fund with Treas.	1, 360, 773. 50	1, 223, 066. 00	1, 163, 136. 00	1, 092, 531. 00	1, 078, 461. 45
Due from U. S. Treas	39, 810. 41	57, 528. 80	34, 525. 00	12, 590. 00	68, 201. 99
Total...........	146, 464, 463. 14	144, 386, 197. 75	143, 352, 112. 09	139, 489, 478. 67	141, 882, 956. 27

CITY OF BOSTON.

	54 banks.	54 banks.	54 banks.	54 banks.	54 banks.
Loans and discounts	$125, 688, 037. 76	$129, 723, 753. 35	$127, 804, 391. 26	$123, 316, 945. 24	$124, 033, 033. 53
Bonds for circulation	14, 826, 650. 00	12, 751, 650. 00	11, 314, 650. 00	9, 958, 150. 00	9, 908, 150. 00
Bonds for deposits..	275, 000. 00	530, 000. 00	730, 000. 00	1, 235, 000. 00	1, 535, 000. 00
U. S. bonds on hand..	24, 400. 00	76, 700. 00	57, 800. 00	86, 900. 00	38, 250. 00
Other stocks and b'ds	3, 039, 101. 47	3, 365, 534. 44	3, 159, 000. 62	3, 012, 805. 62	2, 657, 201. 50
Due from res've ag'ts	11, 319, 756. 32	12, 171, 284. 20	14, 398, 329. 56	10, 534, 835. 56	12, 923, 926. 40
Due from nat'l banks	10, 775, 408. 57	8, 861, 981. 28	11, 315 440. 22	10, 208, 044. 44	10, 164, 009. 35
Due from State banks	541, 566. 24	129, 105. 62	715, 060. 73	464, 494. 83	500, 171. 67
Real estate, etc......	2, 807, 686. 20	2, 875, 396. 40	2, 914, 482. 81	2, 922, 555. 01	2, 924, 685. 92
Current expenses....	706, 623. 04	1, 138, 941. 97	207, 600. 65	664, 845. 88	42, 568. 85
Premiums paid......	295, 702. 83	410, 136. 89	428, 367. 79	693, 347. 93	681, 945. 60
Cash items..........	448, 070. 60	381, 713. 89	511, 381. 67	485, 490. 23	398, 267. 72
Clear'g-house exch'gs	7, 340, 877. 11	9, 055, 781. 22	12, 206, 292. 15	10, 742, 667. 69	8, 039, 147. 87
Bills of other banks..	1, 947, 015. 00	1, 168, 818. 00	1, 402, 937. 00	971, 806. 00	1, 387, 176. 00
Uncur't & minor coins	11, 378. 32	16, 278. 04	13, 515. 19	13, 318. 78	14, 927. 12
Trade dollars........	405. 00	498. 00	....	....	....
Specie...............	9, 869, 367. 39	10, 594. 800. 62	11, 891, 720. 79	9, 300, 409. 27	9, 996, 076. 28
Legal-tender notes..	3, 026, 330. 00	2, 015, 842. 00	2, 637, 947. 00	2, 019, 027. 00	2, 204, 262. 00
U. S. cert's of deposit	365, 000. 00	475, 000. 00	25, 000. 00	175, 000. 00	195, 000. 00
5 % fund with Treas	653, 953. 15	532, 201. 75	505, 307. 25	439, 405. 75	415, 831. 75
Due from U. S. Treas	74, 359. 22	104, 660. 00	50, 887. 50	37, 601. 00	48, 780. 00
Total...........	194, 036, 719. 21	196, 430, 307. 77	202, 350, 202. 19	187, 332, 800. 13	188, 159, 071. 56

RHODE ISLAND.

	61 banks.	61 banks.	61 banks.	61 banks.	61 banks.
Loans and discounts.	$33, 149, 417. 06	$33, 561, 439. 37	$35, 307, 344. 04	$34, 633, 821. 36	$34, 521, 408. 47
Bonds for circulation.	8, 515, 150. 00	6, 675, 400. 00	5, 818, 400. 00	5, 183, 000. 00	5, 183, 900. 00
Bonds for deposits...	150, 000. 00	150, 000. 00	150, 000. 00	150, 000. 00	150, 000. 00
U. S. bonds on hand..	236, 200. 00	150, 800. 00	138, 650. 00	84, 250. 00	136, 700. 00
Other stocks and b'ds	1, 288, 308. 10	1, 320, 946. 39	1, 331, 100. 70	1, 371, 004. 01	1, 380, 601. 01
Due from res've ag'ts	1, 987, 622. 52	2, 411, 839. 86	2, 303, 312. 27	2, 017, 140. 04	2, 283, 583. 01
Due from nat'l banks	509, 885. 67	857, 368. 53	737, 749. 81	1, 012, 102. 64	807, 982. 40
Due from State banks	95, 624. 96	30, 715. 72	76, 507. 76	50, 247. 25	51, 639. 94
Real estate, etc......	660, 660. 62	625, 205. 26	624, 049. 96	624, 436. 38	635, 976. 51
Current expenses....	127, 642. 57	98, 426. 58	105, 391. 67	76, 509. 17	100, 159. 80
Premiums paid......	365, 062. 02	389, 841. 74	417, 486. 54	409, 090. 65	417, 933. 89
Cash items..........	208, 882. 09	185, 659. 85	174, 131. 88	229, 351. 58	190, 403. 78
Clear'g-house exch'gs	287, 074. 13	450, 850. 21	331, 523. 91	312, 120. 33	357, 005. 86
Bills of other banks..	401, 621. 00	323, 117. 00	345, 211. 00	290, 131. 00	270, 421. 00
Uncur't & minor coins	10, 845. 90	14, 320. 38	13, 915. 48	12, 466. 54	9, 932. 47
Trade dollars........	708. 00	302. 00	516. 00	210. 00	1. 00
Specie...............	661, 627. 57	682, 503. 17	687, 863. 23	687, 708. 15	673, 401. 52
Legal-tender notes..	579, 400. 00	478, 170. 00	558, 958. 00	583, 563. 00	510, 347. 00
U. S. cert's of deposit.	....	....	....	....	....
5% fund with Treas.	361, 317. 38	290, 013. 00	262, 363. 00	228, 165. 50	220, 345. 50
Due from U. S. Treas.	17, 155. 00	28, 186. 25	7, 257. 50	21, 132. 50	10, 352. 50
Total...........	49, 803, 343. 49	48, 731, 114. 31	49, 391, 732. 75	47, 983, 512. 97	47, 923, 276. 44

by States and reserve cities—Continued.

MASSACHUSETTS.

Liabilities.	DECEMBER 28.	MARCH 4.	MAY 13.	AUGUST 1.	OCTOBER 5.
	197 banks.	107 banks.	198 banks.	198 banks.	198 banks.
Capital stock	$45, 240, 500. 00	$45, 110, 500. 00	$45, 065, 500. 00	$44, 690, 500. 00	$44, 790, 500. 00
Surplus fund	13, 757, 100. 43	13, 906, 065. 43	14, 156, 123. 09	14, 187, 383. 48	14, 226, 514. 11
Undivided profits	5, 022, 750. 88	5, 296, 731. 41	4, 348, 837. 67	4, 911, 521. 96	4, 170, 526. 94
Nat'l-bank circulation	27, 179, 800. 00	24, 288, 906. 00	23, 123, 966. 00	21, 785, 851. 00	21, 450, 692. 00
State-bank circulation	....	....	....	....	....
Dividends unpaid....	107, 723. 18	90, 599. 73	181, 347. 13	180, 025. 05	533, 701. 53
Individual deposits...	52, 409, 610. 95	52, 896, 301. 86	53, 413, 309. 88	51, 074, 748. 47	53, 872, 217. 39
U. S. deposits........	268, 467. 43	259, 537. 20	258, 080. 21	250, 702. 89	270, 216. 52
Dep'ts U.S.dis.officers	19, 069. 65	31, 576. 57	38, 900. 79	21, 893. 23	2, 615. 73
Due to national banks	1, 848, 039. 86	1, 980, 638. 02	2, 334, 730. 16	1, 384, 743. 14	2, 031, 262. 84
Due to State banks ..	222, 030. 70	232, 486. 01	199, 312. 71	252, 191. 54	231, 545. 03
Notes re-discounted ..	379, 369. 97	185, 855. 43	221, 386. 05	139, 911. 91	258, 610. 23
Bills payable.........	10, 000. 00	10, 000. 00	10, 000. 00	10, 000. 00	35, 403. 95
Total	146, 464, 403. 14	144, 388, 197. 75	143, 352, 112. 09	139, 489, 478. 67	141, 882, 950. 27

CITY OF BOSTON.

	54 banks.	54 banks.	54 banks.	54 banks.	54 banks.
Capital stock	$50, 950, 000. 00	$50, 950, 000. 00	$50, 950, 000. 00	$50, 950, 000. 00	$50, 950, 000. 00
Surplus fund	11, 816, 205. 23	11, 820, 705. 23	12, 377, 607. 29	12, 377, 607. 29	12, 502, 035. 50
Undivided profits....	4, 075, 846. 15	5, 974, 277. 42	3, 868, 704. 45	5, 503, 708. 18	3, 549, 120. 00
Nat'l-bank circulation	13, 252, 945. 00	11, 347, 210. 00	10, 078, 910. 00	8, 923, 375. 00	8, 854, 500. 00
State-bank circulation	....	....	....	....	....
Dividends unpaid....	44, 580. 29	31, 628. 29	63, 726. 67	43, 428. 87	364, 048. 70
Individual deposits...	75, 845, 177. 79	77, 551, 860. 06	88, 391, 171. 34	73, 204, 580. 59	74, 255, 437. 80
U. S. deposits........	100, 479. 71	283, 447. 51	580, 570. 29	1, 024, 948. 75	1, 410, 208. 00
Dep'ts U.S.dis.officers	36, 840. 79	54, 596. 58	30, 444. 02	49, 936. 01	45, 044. 28
Due to national banks	29, 064, 889. 50	30, 103, 652. 92	27, 391, 769. 59	26, 237, 461. 62	28, 087, 958. 10
Due to State banks...	8, 159, 754. 75	8, 312, 929. 76	8, 498, 707. 04	8, 312, 447. 19	8, 010, 527. 98
Notes re-discounted..	....	....	....	....	....
Bills payable.........	90, 000. 00	....	140, 500. 00	205, 300. 00	9, 500. 00
Total	194, 036, 710. 21	196, 430, 307. 77	202, 350, 202. 19	187, 332, 800. 13	188, 150, 071. 56

RHODE ISLAND.

	61 banks.	61 banks.	61 banks.	61 banks.	61 banks.
Capital stock	$20, 340, 050. 00	$20, 340, 050. 00	$20, 340, 050. 00	$20, 340, 050. 00	$20, 340, 050. 00
Surplus fund	4, 119, 905. 71	4, 146, 705. 24	4, 188, 265. 19	4, 221, 736. 00	4, 243, 887. 72
Undivided profits....	1, 904, 033. 89	1, 735, 430. 86	1, 858, 773. 90	1, 740, 720. 46	1, 887, 273. 13
Nat'l-bank circulation	7, 012, 193. 00	5, 946, 398. 00	5, 278, 728. 00	4, 041, 043. 00	4, 042, 913. 00
State-bank circulation	884. 00	884. 00	884. 00	884. 00	800. 00
Dividends unpaid....	73, 812. 34	99, 057. 01	99, 609. 49	126, 400. 51	145, 021. 11
Individual deposits ..	13, 100, 614. 06	13, 542, 204. 46	14, 547, 315. 78	13, 939, 086. 52	13, 918, 046. 52
U. S. deposits........	62, 089. 66	49, 150. 26	96, 610. 52	63, 054. 89	70, 265. 35
Dep'ts U.S.dis.officers	55, 119. 72	74, 224. 59	24, 379. 02	42, 847. 41	52, 053. 74
Due to national banks	1, 583, 638. 95	1, 679, 137. 21	1, 690, 243. 20	1, 500, 415. 06	1, 582, 004. 28
Due to State banks...	891, 008. 16	1, 117, 206. 68	1, 260, 873. 45	1, 357, 097. 60	1, 040, 271. 59
Notes re-discounted..	....	....	....	....	....
Bills payable.........	....	....	....	....	....
Total	49, 803, 343. 49	48, 731, 114. 31	49, 391, 732. 75	47, 983, 542. 97	47, 923, 276. 44

Abstract of reports since October 7, 1886, arranged

CONNECTICUT.

Resources.	DECEMBER 28. 84 banks.	MARCH 4. 84 banks.	MAY 13. 84 banks.	AUGUST 1. 83 banks.	OCTOBER 5. 83 banks.
Loans and discounts	$43, 042, 062. 02	$43, 689, 838. 64	$44, 213, 692. 14	$44, 067, 483. 83	$43, 114, 000. 64
Bonds for circulation	12, 417, 100. 00	11, 224, 100. 00	10, 583, 600. 00	9, 831, 100. 00	9, 716, 100. 00
Bonds for deposits	300, 000. 00	386, 000. 00	546, 000. 00	611, 000. 00	636, 000. 00
U. S. bonds on hand	264, 350. 00	225, 150. 00	174, 650. 00	150, 750. 00	105, 750. 00
Other stocks and b'ds	3, 439, 169. 84	3, 337, 257. 52	3, 328, 957. 33	3, 405, 016. 54	3, 297, 401. 05
Due from res've ag'ts	5, 201, 039. 74	5, 624, 758. 80	5, 635, 873. 68	3, 740, 145. 45	4, 551, 553. 96
Due from nat'l banks	2, 511, 025. 07	1, 902, 529. 87	2, 688, 171. 82	2, 829, 832. 66	1, 985, 439. 01
Due from State banks	203, 242. 88	231, 161. 23	297, 625. 03	251, 167. 21	254, 436. 65
Real estate, etc	1, 456, 850. 62	1, 464, 096. 60	1, 476, 113. 34	1, 479, 040. 21	1, 461, 700. 01
Current expenses	292, 348. 90	167, 081. 32	240, 811. 20	117, 665. 88	209, 508. 47
Premiums paid	814, 717. 55	814, 624. 83	827, 351. 41	777, 854. 49	763, 630. 69
Cash items	355, 015. 25	381, 205. 23	362, 810. 51	463, 306. 78	441, 280. 88
Clear'g-house exch'gs	247, 565. 50	240, 435. 54	282, 481. 77	308, 198. 41	268, 299. 64
Bills of other banks	813, 106. 00	643, 416. 00	873, 169. 00	737, 309. 00	603, 100. 00
Uncur't & minor coins	13, 884. 08	20, 139. 22	10, 492. 80	18, 280. 78	17, 045. 97
Trade dollars	33, 605. 51	31, 275. 57	8, 774. 27	5, 130. 00	161. 00
Specie	1, 888, 290. 87	1, 857, 703. 00	1, 793, 147. 03	1, 793, 935. 57	1, 748, 294. 62
Legal-tender notes	892, 841. 00	788, 381. 00	881, 390. 00	770, 081. 00	691, 103. 00
U. S. cert's of deposit					
5 % fund with Treas	552, 932. 25	484, 732. 25	453, 194. 75	417, 568. 55	412, 979. 16
Due from U. S. Treas.	30, 299, 80	24, 246. 00	25, 893. 37	14, 120. 50	18, 040. 55
Total	75, 610, 141. 68	73, 538, 132. 62	74, 707, 599. 44	71, 878, 086. 36	70, 295, 835. 20

NEW YORK.

	268 banks.	268 banks.	270 banks.	270 banks.	269 banks.
Loans and discounts	$95, 505, 736. 85	$96, 117, 424. 20	$98, 198, 422. 69	$98, 031, 328. 24	$99, 198, 788. 59
Bonds for circulation	21, 913, 700. 00	21, 258, 700. 00	20, 529, 950. 00	19, 481, 050. 00	19, 468, 550. 00
Bonds for deposits	952, 000. 00	992, 000. 00	1, 048, 000. 00	1, 127, 000. 00	1, 127, 000, 00
U. S. bonds on hand	1, 121, 050. 00	1, 114, 450, 00	999, 700. 00	900, 450. 00	880, 650. 00
Other stocks and b'ds	8, 368, 766. 40	8, 358, 253. 89	8, 371, 880. 20	8, 462, 031. 68	8, 599, 195. 12
Due from res've ag'ts.	13, 195, 193. 23	13, 885, 566. 30	13, 855, 395. 89	11, 731, 896. 94	12, 941, 822. 68
Due from nat'l banks.	2, 650, 931. 23	2, 025, 109. 31	2, 859, 614. 21	2, 658, 424. 20	2, 408, 729. 26
Due from State banks	711, 259. 02	858, 543. 57	736, 252. 01	596, 893. 60	680, 157. 53
Real estate, etc	3, 385, 805. 69	3, 376, 276. 85	3, 368, 812. 71	3, 372, 209. 87	3, 370, 287. 19
Current expenses	712, 683. 61	442, 449. 16	561, 011. 53	233, 629. 86	509, 266. 63
Premiums paid	1, 410, 378. 78	1, 362, 626. 06	1, 406, 445. 50	1, 310, 383. 60	1, 313, 610. 24
Cash items	1, 727, 303. 98	1, 392, 256. 27	1, 618, 484. 24	3, 318, 414. 78	1, 728, 077. 40
Clear'g-house exch'gs	31, 104. 53	37, 654. 57	45, 361. 05	57, 764. 31	47, 829. 99
Bills of other banks	1, 443, 100. 00	1, 310, 695. 00	1, 517, 564. 00	1, 081, 779. 00	1, 237, 440. 00
Uncur't & minor coins	33, 434. 64	42, 121. 40	41, 565. 13	35, 053. 16	34, 406. 84
Trade dollars	252, 170. 63	245, 203. 75	31, 814. 19	14, 323. 02	45. 40
Specie	5, 431, 071. 44	5, 594, 368. 21	5, 320, 827. 11	5, 225, 481. 70	5, 199, 687. 15
Legal-tender notes	3, 041, 742. 00	2, 721, 186. 00	3, 040, 865. 00	2, 822, 606. 00	2, 953, 729. 00
U. S. cert's of deposit	280, 000. 00	340, 000. 00	320, 000. 00	240, 000. 00	240, 000. 00
5 % fund with Treas.	972, 779. 81	911, 368. 20	911, 658. 07	864, 402. 39	867, 970. 09
Due from U. S. Treas.	32, 963. 38	25, 453. 66	20, 056. 88	18, 931. 40	29, 210. 24
Total	163, 182, 963. 22	162, 436, 705. 40	164, 823, 680. 44	161, 614, 052. 75	162, 837, 368. 35

NEW YORK CITY.

	45 banks.	45 banks.	46 banks.	46 banks.	47 banks.
Loans and discounts	$254, 206, 170. 91	$272, 874, 508. 38	$267, 105, 520. 07	$261, 465, 671. 03	$258, 074, 593. 47
Bonds for circulation	9, 492, 000. 00	9, 211, 000. 00	9, 751, 000. 00	9, 545, 000. 00	9, 695, 000. 00
Bonds for deposits	1, 370, 000. 00	1, 405, 000. 00	2, 110, 000. 00	2, 470, 000. 00	2, 820, 000. 00
U. S. bonds on hand	2, 619, 050. 00	1, 767, 750. 00	1, 368, 050. 00	1, 182, 000. 00	525, 300. 00
Other stocks and b'ds	14, 305, 331. 05	16, 703, 783. 63	17, 907, 229. 53	17, 848, 579. 70	16, 492, 593. 25
Due from res've ag'ts					
Due from nat'l banks	21, 519, 091. 12	19, 631, 291. 08	25, 573, 968. 33	23, 426, 700. 70	22, 300, 733. 46
Due from State banks	2, 777, 845. 54	2, 221, 748. 14	2, 346, 726. 77	1, 995, 570. 65	2, 011, 215. 76
Real estate, etc	10, 374, 168. 90	10, 145, 921. 91	10, 157, 565. 28	10, 348, 935. 64	10, 484, 810. 03
Current expenses	1, 300, 861. 27	612, 933. 97	984, 623. 89	365, 849. 91	1, 139, 962. 04
Premiums paid	1, 143, 850. 28	999, 411. 68	1, 425, 050, 23	1, 405, 932. 35	1, 124, 837. 54
Cash items	1, 780, 500. 06	1, 676, 745. 49	1, 840, 357. 07	2, 303, 620. 25	1, 702, 795. 14
Clear'g-house exch'gs	41, 769, 918. 56	58, 822, 085. 28	55, 991, 869. 11	92, 869, 103. 28	60, 514, 349. 13
Bills of other banks	2, 186, 488. 00	1, 379, 982. 00	1, 776, 316. 00	1, 018, 576. 00	1, 408, 873. 00
Uncur't & minor coins	30, 857. 16	41, 213. 62	44, 751. 65	39, 033. 36	40, 613. 48
Trade dollars	213, 054. 05	265, 771. 05	3, 188. 00		
Specie	73, 475, 913. 67	74, 878, 034. 65	63, 638, 191. 17	63, 996, 456. 59	63, 622, 928. 91
Legal-tender notes	12, 437, 729. 00	12, 970, 931. 00	17, 243, 850. 00	15, 845, 149. 00	14, 464, 861. 00
U. S. cert's of deposit	1, 665, 000. 00	1, 080, 000. 00	1, 530, 000. 00	1, 385, 000. 00	1, 605, 000. 00
5 % fund with Treas.	413, 610. 00	400, 995. 00	423, 045. 00	413, 695. 00	421, 900. 00
Due from U. S. Treas.	341, 153. 83	1, 093, 215. 43	386, 273. 01	149, 284. 95	280, 598. 09
Total	456, 393, 622. 40	489, 024, 301. 44	481, 638, 809. 11	510, 005, 058. 44	469, 420, 073. 33

by States and reserve cities—Continued.

CONNECTICUT.

Liabilities.	DECEMBER 28. 84 banks.	MARCH 4. 84 banks.	MAY 13. 84 banks.	AUGUST 1. 83 banks.	OCTOBER 5. 83 banks.
Capital stock	$24,671,820.00	$24,671,820.00	$24,681,820.00	$24,619,370.00	$24,505,410.00
Surplus fund	6,859,108.60	6,971,024.71	6,932,150.71	6,926,004.80	6,908,034.74
Undivided profits	2,572,060.46	1,883,985.59	2,193,444.90	1,655,627.15	1,937,107.33
Nat'l-bank circulation	11,042,491.00	9,967,078.00	9,432,566.00	8,788,130.00	8,698,003.00
State-bank circulation	9,047.00	4,785.00	4,785.00	4,785.00	4,785.00
Dividends unpaid	57,375.46	65,488.70	58,762.83	88,214.79	67,148.01
Individual deposits	25,542,888.26	26,470,056.44	26,062,276.06	26,272,580.19	24,478,665.09
U. S. deposits	300,446.28	296,814.58	407,463.91	536,388.91	526,964.12
Dep'ts U.S. dis. officers	8,113.99	4,495.65	4,537.22	11,390.86	78,160.18
Due to national banks	3,580,347.41	2,589,063.17	4,008,336.21	2,262,331.55	2,310,853.23
Due to State banks	715,317.32	476,945.12	790,298.42	493,540.17	503,462.15
Notes re-discounted	101,122.90	61,575.66	21,158.09	115,601.94	200,703.35
Bills payable	150,000.00	75,000.00	50,000.00	75,000.00	75,750.00
Total	75,610,141.68	73,538,132.62	74,707,599.44	71,878,986.36	70,295,835.20

NEW YORK.

	268 banks.	268 banks.	270 banks.	270 banks.	269 banks.
Capital stock	$34,884,870.00	$34,884,870.00	$34,780,716.45	$34,703,956.00	$34,724,260.00
Surplus fund	9,628,018.99	9,751,980.53	9,880,680.97	10,048,314.14	10,121,879.68
Undivided profits	7,161,614.83	6,031,812.56	6,710,477.07	5,641,658.73	6,499,409.40
Nat'l-bank circulation	19,577,736.00	18,925,556.00	18,271,525.00	17,384,168.00	17,406,488.00
State-bank circulation	29,181.00	24,193.00	24,191.00	24,191.00	24,191.00
Dividends unpaid	87,002.51	76,109.86	70,576.78	141,861.83	78,541.57
Individual deposits	85,236,407.17	87,102,368.18	87,002,834.98	87,590,131.47	87,209,212.02
U. S. deposits	671,925.40	770,234.11	851,807.06	809,437.85	903,172.96
Dep'ts U.S. dis. officers	110,268.91	79,935.06	75,117.74	189,573.98	130,968.65
Due to national banks	4,109,490.42	3,072,336.32	5,050,868.73	3,331,100.39	3,613,100.74
Due to State banks	1,259,611.10	1,269,951.61	1,395,702.44	1,037,175.04	1,151,446.08
Notes re-discounted	360,393.64	336,141.71	639,101.00	572,030.25	738,146.21
Bills payable	66,383.22	50,207.46	64,075.22	80,143.07	176,453.04
Total	163,182,963.22	162,436,705.40	164,823,680.44	161,614,032.75	162,837,368.35

NEW YORK CITY.

	45 banks.	45 banks.	46 banks.	46 banks.	47 banks.
Capital stock	$45,150,000.00	$45,150,000.00	$48,650,000.00	$48,850,000.00	$49,150,000.00
Surplus fund	26,779,409.69	27,523,704.21	28,050,704.21	29,585,762.28	30,585,762.28
Undivided profits	12,210,064.76	10,605,438.77	11,210,860.02	9,163,573.97	10,091,067.65
Nat'l-bank circulation	7,949,812.00	7,678,532.00	8,327,412.00	8,151,352.00	8,295,502.00
State-bank circulation	31,172.00	31,171.00	24,365.00	24,365.00	24,365.00
Dividends unpaid	291,206.30	228,883.70	172,852.06	255,576.50	196,005.44
Individual deposits	226,820,901.92	237,112,207.86	236,554,285.73	264,693,380.91	228,221,855.09
U. S. deposits	758,150.54	930,009.55	1,292,604.45	1,786,256.96	2,344,591.20
Dept's U.S. dis. officers	261,551.03	181,538.17	199,532.43	218,322.26	240,096.59
Due to national banks	101,609,066.59	120,693,404.49	110,302,328.22	110,217,532.49	103,538,530.81
Due to State banks	34,532,285.57	39,486,411.69	36,943,855.99	37,058,935.98	36,633,197.27
Notes re-discounted	....	....	....	....	100,000.00
Bills payable	....	....	....	....	....
Total	456,393,622.40	480,024,301.44	481,638,809.11	510,005,058.44	469,420,973.33

Abstract of reports since October 7, 1886, arranged

CITY OF ALBANY.

Resources.	DECEMBER 28.	MARCH 4.	MAY 13.	AUGUST 1.	OCTOBER 5.
	6 banks.	6 banks.	6 banks.	6 banks.	6 banks.
Loans and discounts	$7,943,044.00	$8,179,455.29	$8,568,676.93	$8,455,604.43	$8,781,559.14
Bonds for circulation	1,218,000.00	1,216,000.00	1,218,000.00	1,148,000.00	1,148,000.00
Bonds for deposits	100,000.00	150,000.00	150,000.00	150,000.00	150,000.00
U. S. bonds on hand	400.00	500.00	....	....	....
Other stocks and b'ds	551,133.37	426,622.12	380,561.20	315,284.72	310,204.22
Due from res've ag'ts	1,285,581.04	1,290,385.78	1,471,881.90	2,080,541.69	1,765,140.10
Due from nat'l banks	668,867.85	747,135.03	821,105.62	889,397.32	857,183.80
Due from State banks	133,136.90	66,809.20	77,187.53	51,275.15	60,473.74
Real estate, etc	276,500.00	276,500.00	279,651.34	307,675.08	307,675.08
Current expenses	....	....	....	....	....
Premiums paid	157,047.25	158,114.75	168,200.00	165,690.00	165,120.00
Cash items	63,402.09	112,348.49	72,466.93	73,648.78	74,541.06
Clear'g-house exch'gs	114,293.02	162,075.20	131,801.84	214,672.70	101,834.83
Bills of other banks	132,828.00	91,533.00	126,645.00	67,957.00	92,068.00
Uncur't & minor coins	1,153.47	1,491.99	1,076.00	1,114.43	822.07
Trade dollars	600.00	600.00	480.00	577.00	....
Specie	892,015.75	920,777.50	1,017,920.50	957,430.70	935,191.50
Legal-tender notes	185,207.00	158,700.00	157,300.00	81,296.00	98,830.00
U. S. cert's of deposit	200,000.00	200,000.00	150,000.00	150,000.00	200,000.00
5 % fund with Treas.	54,807.50	54,807.50	54,807.50	50,807.50	51,657.50
Due from U. S. Treas	7,025.43	410.00	8,874.00	3,238.00	9,522.00
Total	13,985,042.67	14,225,285.85	14,836,697.09	15,164,300.50	15,200,443.04

NEW JERSEY.

	75 banks.	76 banks.	76 banks.	80 banks.	81 banks.
Loans and discounts	$35,602,063.00	$36,342,255.60	$37,587,912.94	$38,503,595.65	$40,467,838.08
Bonds for circulation	7,630,850.00	7,165,850.00	6,750,350.00	6,849,600.00	6,874,000.00
Bonds for deposits	250,000.00	350,000.00	350,000.00	450,000.00	500,000.00
U. S. bonds on hand	647,600.00	465,200.00	275,100.00	177,800.00	182,050.00
Other stocks and b'ds	4,013,271.25	3,952,505.00	4,117,488.24	4,383,321.30	4,328,180.96
Due from res've ag'ts	6,126,063.49	6,500,493.21	6,864,086.19	6,214,489.43	6,092,858.93
Due from nat'l banks	1,512,654.46	1,568,559.81	1,682,395.14	1,420,247.39	1,404,541.62
Due from State banks	183,939.54	266,831.97	318,612.63	237,852.90	216,652.31
Real estate, etc	1,606,401.32	1,613,845.82	1,583,831.08	1,646,179.35	1,669,565.60
Current expenses	292,198.00	163,313.33	210,267.20	123,115.75	170,271.78
Premiums paid	430,589.95	443,582.84	437,410.70	546,038.15	549,985.73
Cash items	779,248.10	717,262.26	688,891.79	1,237,072.72	761,439.36
Clear'g-house exch'gs	....	....	....	....	....
Bills of other banks	566,756.00	434,208.00	471,251.00	409,088.00	497,674.00
Uncur't & minor coins	20,403.39	22,758.20	20,348.79	21,543.94	17,091.38
Trade dollars	82,193.98	82,979.53	11,652.00	5,615.00	4.00
Specie	2,062,785.49	1,870,431.96	1,816,549.02	1,762,777.37	1,852,443.09
Legal-tender notes	1,744,480.00	1,712,592.00	1,908,368.00	1,678,504.00	1,807,669.00
U. S. cert's of deposit	10,000.00	10,000.00	10,000.00	10,000.00	10,000.00
5 % fund with Treas.	337,683.00	319,595.00	298,485.00	303,665.00	305,660.95
Due from U. S. Treas	19,617.00	9,827.00	20,202.00	12,212.00	6,062.00
Total	63,939,666.97	63,821,094.53	65,453,232.62	66,083,617.35	67,714,580.78

PENNSYLVANIA.

	232 banks.	232 banks.	234 banks.	236 banks.	237 banks.
Loans and discounts	$74,187,601.11	$74,702,183.80	$77,481,596.21	$77,984,278.04	$80,471,568.05
Bonds for circulation	18,726,300.00	16,931,050.00	16,242,300.00	15,452,800.00	15,198,800.00
Bonds for deposits	480,000.00	480,000.00	480,000.00	480,000.00	480,000.00
U. S. bonds on hand	560,800.00	633,650.00	655,800.00	405,950.00	490,250.00
Other stocks and b'ds	9,422,205.78	9,433,336.82	9,674,135.29	9,792,622.99	9,829,900.88
Due from res've ag'ts	11,528,604.84	13,051,572.30	13,440,992.25	12,280,021.93	12,335,758.74
Due from nat'l banks	2,896,034.01	2,241,405.34	3,307,405.83	3,132,009.29	2,358,841.61
Due from State banks	1,282,686.77	1,092,749.81	1,387,351.69	1,312,927.60	962,961.74
Real estate, etc	3,608,527.30	3,670,693.53	3,698,928.23	3,739,525.26	3,768,380.17
Current expenses	390,734.92	515,826.73	378,286.33	283,777.86	531,454.56
Premiums paid	1,376,058.20	1,368,287.89	1,425,121.76	1,416,948.71	1,383,779.37
Cash items	791,541.84	810,142.34	794,089.61	709,418.86	905,835.73
Clear'g-house exch'gs	....	....	....	....	....
Bills of other banks	1,217,976.00	1,005,343.00	1,106,587.00	1,030,202.00	1,160,988.00
Uncur't & minor coins	38,042.27	53,487.79	49,188.11	46,269.98	45,783.38
Trade dollars	653,676.16	672,316.81	66,376.15	20,080.13	5.00
Specie	5,011,818.11	4,613,350.54	4,846,736.87	4,722,217.43	4,774,820.34
Legal-tender notes	2,767,928.00	2,533,699.00	2,889,804.00	2,819,571.00	2,927,227.00
U. S. cert's of deposit	10,000.00	10,000.00	10,000.00	10,000.00	10,000.00
5 % fund with Treas.	821,096.38	751,515.40	704,441.50	676,044.12	671,127.40
Due from U. S. Treas	45,098.68	43,415.26	38,559.27	28,501.36	51,071.09
Total	135,817,723.37	134,650,086.36	138,677,700.09	136,552,966.56	138,364,562.66

by States and reserve cities—Continued.

CITY OF ALBANY.

Liabilities.	DECEMBER 28.	MARCH 4.	MAY 13.	AUGUST 1.	OCTOBER 5.
	6 banks.	6 banks.	6 banks.	6 banks.	6 banks.
Capital stock	$1,730,000.00	$1,750,000.00	$1,750,000.00	$1,750,000.00	$1,750,000.00
Surplus fund	1,237,000.00	1,240,000.00	1,240,000.00	1,243,000.00	1,243,000.00
Undivided profits	258,706.29	206,507.75	227,876.68	228,092.02	250,858.02
Nat'l-bank circulation	1,077,330.00	1,083,120.00	1,084,180.00	1,021,380.00	1,016,490.00
State-bank circulation	....	....	....	....	....
Dividends unpaid	18,047.20	12,056.85	2,210.60	21,887.54	14,934.04
Individual deposits	6,677,294.33	6,458,056.85	7,496,793.18	8,110,810.60	7,062,421.67
U. S. deposits	88,357.38	181,427.40	130,000.00	141,544.66	139,284.28
Dep'ts U.S.dis.officers	1,642.62	412.56	510.53	483.74	1,868.78
Due to national banks	2,332,461.06	2,759,711.15	2,310,370.49	2,303,230.59	2,365,219.13
Due to State banks	543,603.79	583,993.29	605,717.12	342,070.36	447,360.52
Notes re-discounted	....	....	....	....	....
Bills payable	....	....	....	....	....
Total	13,985,042.67	14,225,285.85	14,856,697.60	15,164,300.50	15,200,443.04

NEW JERSEY.

	75 banks.	76 banks.	76 banks.	80 banks.	81 banks.
Capital stock	$12,373,350.00	$12,444,500.00	$12,478,070.00	$12,865,890.00	$13,024,220.00
Surplus fund	4,117,352.47	4,248,580.08	4,312,080.08	4,441,767.99	4,501,207.99
Undivided profits	2,402,204.79	1,907,580.49	2,215,506.93	1,908,370.89	2,137,149.36
Nat'l-bank circulation	6,777,047.00	6,311,160.00	5,925,830.00	6,033,648.00	6,060,523.00
State-bank circulation	8,357.00	8,357.00	8,357.00	8,358.00	8,358.00
Dividends unpaid	41,261.40	76,045.63	48,030.28	121,540.05	106,025.06
Individual deposits	34,619,886.82	35,407,669.20	36,540,919.68	37,509,018.63	38,644,239.13
U. S. deposits	212,331.42	280,397.94	300,116.82	363,467.98	437,968.02
Dep'ts U.S.dis.officers	14,826.62	30,885.45	8,744.47	13,816.30	11,717.34
Due to national banks	2,995,405.20	2,668,420.75	3,118,308.93	2,232,245.46	2,253,927.29
Due to State banks	327,806.17	387,470.99	401,020.46	392,470.05	340,368.47
Notes re-discounted	15,078.08	....	72,200.97	....	48,826.12
Bills payable	34,700.00	40,000.00	20,000.00	100,000.00	140,000.00
Total	63,939,666.97	63,821,094.53	65,453,232.62	66,083,617.35	67,714,589.78

PENNSYLVANIA.

	232 banks.	232 banks.	234 banks.	236 banks.	237 banks.
Capital stock	$33,082,840.00	$33,103,840.00	$33,414,630.00	$33,650,340.00	$33,551,140.00
Surplus fund	10,714,276.73	10,931,808.97	11,107,285.10	11,418,204.91	11,480,946.46
Undivided profits	3,740,409.40	3,544,416.23	3,256,540.32	2,076,141.25	3,037,379.87
Nat'l-bank circulation	16,582,015.00	14,922,719.00	14,284,635.00	13,573,645.00	13,370,865.00
State-bank circulation	4,745.00	4,745.00	4,745.00	4,745.00	4,745.00
Dividends unpaid	180,306.70	158,363.60	408,577.38	231,106.18	153,356.31
Individual deposits	66,854,270.61	68,947,226.15	70,914,701.79	71,993,295.74	72,564,898.01
U. S. deposits	396,340.04	419,843.68	436,649.03	434,758.50	421,082.05
Dep'ts U.S.dis.officers	30,743.90	13,449.82	9,646.17	14,116.79	12,355.67
Due to national banks	3,621,379.09	2,150,696.74	4,180,014.98	1,749,648.23	2,366,498.25
Due to State banks	450,378.76	326,936.73	456,356.38	233,432.00	273,082.08
Notes re-discounted	189,347.77	101,550.07	189,332.71	248,041.78	160,123.08
Bills payable	490.28	15,490.28	14,490.28	25,490.28	38,490.28
Total	135,847,723.37	134,650,086.36	138,677,700.09	136,552,966.56	138,364,562.06

Abstract of reports since October 7, 1886, arranged

CITY OF PHILADELPHIA.

Resources.	DECEMBER 28.	MARCH 4.	MAY 13.	AUGUST 1.	OCTOBER 5.
	40 banks.	41 banks.	41 banks.	43 banks.	43 banks.
Loans and discounts	$79,457,036.82	$81,313,540.35	$83,188,161.55	$85,574,872.54	$83,440,471.17
Bonds for circulation	4,664,300.00	4,094,300.00	4,094,300.00	2,737,500.00	2,737,500.00
Bonds for deposits	250,000.00	250,000.00	250,000.00	250,000.00	250,000.00
U. S. bonds on hand	71,100.00	1,100.90	1,160.00	1,100.00	1,100.00
Other stocks and b'ds	3,716,254.75	3,861,774.14	3,552,968.30	2,544,406.50	3,216,808.64
Due from res've ag'ts	5,618,646.98	7,922,438.69	7,594,519.82	7,185,654.77	8,173,712.07
Due from nat'l banks	5,580,547.46	4,013,637.87	6,783,252.06	5,596,180.30	5,733,655.73
Due from State banks	821,890.27	1,013,963.54	1,160,242.33	854,820.19	1,003,812.54
Real estate, etc	3,252,669.81	3,291,485.64	3,356,325.05	3,389,507.09	3,369,096.30
Current expenses	272,187.73	542,385.00	116,167.66	300,406.88	644,352.84
Premiums paid	336,404.24	333,836.44	322,833.05	428,267.03	407,767.83
Cash items	712,052.81	543,534.68	429,226.77	728,118.69	609,925.31
Clear'g-house exch'gs	8,333,354.22	9,401,233.79	7,339,378.82	10,800,589.06	8,095,823.22
Bills of other banks	792,238.00	863,575.00	600,037.00	495,882.00	477,872.00
Uncur't & minor coins	34,434.75	34,156.96	35,883.25	47,809.88	45,092.23
Trade dollars	293,124.00	278,943.00	4,760.00	2,505.00	....
Specie	10,580,134.11	10,003,054.27	9,886,897.75	9,969,082.69	11,558,935.47
Legal-tender notes	4,232,939.00	3,625,923.00	4,395,642.00	3,659,154.00	4,334,432.00
U. S. cert's of deposit	1,330,000.00	1,820,000.00	3,270,000.00	2,900,000.00	1,230,000.00
5 % fund with Treas.	209,737.50	183,883.74	184,183.74	160,158.74	123,133.74
Due from U. S. Treas.	87,310.00	20,940.00	35,680.00	42,071.00	38,800.00
Total	130,649,362.45	133,813,706.11	136,601,559.21	137,719,275.45	135,512,351.09

CITY OF PITTSBURGH.

	23 banks.	23 banks.	23 banks.	23 banks.	23 banks.
Loans and discounts	$28,625,290.39	$28,971,811.37	$31,720,419.35	$31,910,013.63	$31,989,826.00
Bonds for circulation	5,060,500.00	4,106,500.00	3,092,500.00	1,765,500.00	1,765,500.00
Bonds for deposits	250,000.00	300,000.00	400,000.00	400,000.00	400,000.00
U. S. bonds on hand	500.00	2,200.00	3,400.00	1,000.00	5,400.00
Other stocks and b'ds	421,655.76	288,160.52	377,571.47	330,286.47	347,740.59
Due from res've ag'ts	2,502,143.74	3,254,598.30	2,298,223.50	2,599,525.59	2,707,541.98
Due from nat'l banks	976,304.49	1,441,115.69	1,126,506.24	1,499,451.67	1,094,835.46
Due from State banks	250,243.64	168,868.69	172,392.63	219,288.49	200,014.26
Real estate, etc	1,551,526.19	1,553,755.78	1,537,061.38	1,547,395.92	1,549,822.63
Current expenses	137,047.81	134,617.89	124,314.05	84,239.24	151,701.98
Premiums paid	99,236.75	112,637.97	128,949.71	126,390.86	126,101.97
Cash items	200,522.91	220,906.40	283,028.31	243,129.43	306,071.05
Clear'g-house exch'gs	1,328,079.45	1,089,094.55	1,008,291.86	1,116,365.30	1,302,340.52
Bills of other banks	472,043.00	437,057.00	473,680.00	488,233.00	448,975.00
Uncur't & minor coins	9,749.66	10,966.72	14,215.12	15,515.22	14,183.43
Trade dollars	12,790.00	14,008.00	3,034.00	385.00	21.00
Specie	2,497,486.67	2,731,315.64	2,952,005.97	3,070,903.22	2,080,31[illegible].21
Legal-tender notes	1,684,073.00	1,643,794.00	2,129,355.00	2,044,227.00	1,699,013.00
U. S. cert's of deposit	....	....	....	....	....
5 % fund with Treas.	226,902.50	184,162.50	139,137.50	79,422.50	79,422.50
Due from U. S. Treas.	18,790.70	34,846.26	4,038.26	16,412.16	25,241.20
Total	46,385,895.56	46,791,167.37	48,049,002.35	47,557,704.70	47,193,071.38

DELAWARE.

	16 banks.	16 banks.	16 banks.	17 banks.	17 banks.
Loans and discounts	$4,741,463.44	$4,685,929.24	$4,677,166.93	$4,913,719.86	$5,003,555.37
Bonds for circulation	1,585,200.00	1,585,200.00	1,585,200.00	1,5[illegible]6,700.00	1,596,700.00
Bonds for deposits	50,000.00	50,000.00	50,000.00	50,000.00	50,000.00
U. S. bonds on hand	....	....	....	....	....
Other stocks and b'ds	325,104.87	305,660.34	370,084.03	260,037.75	260,502.75
Due from res've ag'ts	903,405.38	1,[illegible]32,955.00	765,275.92	636,088.08	735,252.29
Due from nat'l banks	221,950.09	131,238.67	201,206.32	240,752.11	143,543.88
Due from State banks	71,686.81	47,719.48	76,143.15	39,758.43	45,157.28
Real estate, etc	254,390.06	251,388.06	255,585.10	258,421.61	261,917.52
Current expenses	35,848.09	17,278.36	26,201.60	14,158.88	28,114.12
Premiums paid	139,711.37	137,713.87	137,792.37	137,340.74	134,841.74
Cash items	70,010.22	84,651.18	74,071.11	71,575.19	33,835.75
Clear'g-house exch'gs	....	....	....	....	32,802.39
Bills of other banks	103,268.00	85,603.00	90,610.00	127,740.00	82,322.00
Uncur't & minor coins	1,659.97	2,721.19	2,560.07	2,846.28	2,080.78
Trade dollars	22,959.75	23,036.75	6,209.00	2,036.00	....
Specie	295,687.56	286,189.88	246,306.60	287,566.09	273,639.21
Legal-tender notes	123,593.00	117,570.00	113,260.00	125,468.00	140,253.00
U. S. cert's of deposit	10,000.00	10,000.00	10,000.00	10,000.00	10,000.00
5 % fund with Treas.	70,392.50	68,642.50	69,142.50	71,799.50	71,771.[illegible]
Due from U. S. Treas.	9,170.23	5,750.00	1,530.00	7,260.00	8,150.00
Total	9,038,610.21	8,962,247.61	8,764,491.70	8,863,197.52	8,914,440.02

by States and reserve cities—Continued.

CITY OF PHILADELPHIA.

Liabilities.	DECEMBER 28.	MARCH 4.	MAY 13.	AUGUST 1.	OCTOBER 5.
	40 banks.	41 banks.	41 banks.	43 banks.	43 banks.
Capital stock	$21, 607, 110. 00	$21, 558, 000. 00	$21, 558, 000. 00	$22, 438, 930. 00	$22, 658, 000. 00
Surplus fund	9, 988, 803. 08	10, 260, 803. 08	10, 547, 803. 08	10, 550, 803. 08	10, 550, 803. 08
Undivided profits	2, 031, 159. 54	2, 339, 665. 28	1, 553, 852. 07	2, 050, 074. 66	2, 704, 033. 20
Nat'l-bank circulation	4 106, 179. 00	3, 594, 729. 00	3, 576, 500. 00	2, 300, 830. 00	2, 401, 140. 00
State-bank circulation	....	....	....	....	....
Dividends unpaid	61, 958. 71	42, 223. 66	176, 151. 71	60, 240. 86	42, 783. 12
Individual deposits	75, 650, 444. 24	75, 961, 365. 96	79, 232, 345. 53	78, 555, 361. 78	78, 105, 378. 08
U. S. deposits	213, 349. 85	210, 795. 79	216, 405. 09	218, 008. 22	212, 911. 90
Dep'ts U.S.dis.officers	....	....	....	....	....
Due to national banks	14, 230, 534. 97	16, 304, 743. 79	15, 720, 396. 35	17, 514, 264. 01	14, 685, 297. 86
Due to State banks	3, 189, 755. 35	3, 527, 379. 55	4, 006, 096. 38	3, 920, 752. 94	3, 816, 850. 08
Notes re-discounted	87, 067. 71	....	....	....	35, 144. 17
Bills payable	14, 000. 00	14, 000. 00	14, 000. 00	20. 000. 00	150, 000. 00
Total	130, 649, 362. 45	133, 813, 706. 11	136, 601, 550. 21	137, 719, 275. 45	135, 512, 351. 09

CITY OF PITTSBURGH.

	23 banks.	23 banks.	23 banks.	23 banks.	23 banks.
Capital stock	$10, 180, 000. 00	$10, 180, 000. 00	$10, 180, 000. 00	$10, 180, 000. 00	$10, 180, 000. 00
Surplus fund	3. 911, 508. 20	4, 066, 476. 32	4, 108, 885. 14	4, 334, 877. 29	4, 334, 877. 29
Undivided profits	1, 117, 544. 39	988, 090. 92	1, 008, 737. 26	912, 532. 18	1, 209, 617. 87
Nat'l-bank circulation	4, 517, 805. 00	3, 636, 405. 00	2, 757, 300. 00	1, 572, 440. 00	1, 569, 260. 00
State-bank circulation	....	....	....	....	....
Dividends unpaid	81, 160. 00	81, 910. 50	125, 874. 75	103, 100. 00	88, 969. 00
Individual deposits	21, 826, 772. 48	22, 586, 517. 52	24, 588, 561. 56	24, 741, 110. 56	24, 478, 664. 65
U. S. deposits	206, 700. 93	184, 235. 63	320, 991. 02	217, 770. 59	154, 037. 35
Dep'ts U.S.dis.officers	40, 169. 10	109, 847. 43	63, 084. 35	176, 891. 69	233, 079. 45
Due to national banks	2, 928, 205. 74	3, 152, 233. 75	3, 035, 833. 76	3, 175, 834. 35	3, 030, 922. 06
Due to State banks	1, 526, 9?0. 72	1, 780, 217. 40	1, 817, 793. 27	2, 133, 073. 04	1, 857, 243. 71
Notes re-discounted	30, 000. 00	15, 232. 90	22, 941. 24	....	52, 000. 00
Bills payable	10, 000. 00	10, 000. 00	10, 000. 00	10, 000. 00	5, 000. 00
Total	46, 385, 885. 56	46, 791, 167. 37	48, 019, 002. 35	47, 557, 704. 70	47, 193, 671. 38

DELAWARE.

	16 banks.	16 banks.	16 banks.	17 banks.	17 banks.
Capital stock	$2, 033, 985. 00	$2, 033, 985. 00	$2, 033, 985. 00	$2, 071, 985. 00	$2, 083, 985. 00
Surplus fund	753, 500. 00	771, 250. 00	771, 250. 00	798, 350. 00	799, 350. 00
Undivided profits	207, 800. 52	192, 066. 28	228, 025. 51	166, 012. 35	237, 853. 97
Nat'l-bank circulation	1, 402, 390. 00	1. 412, 490. 00	1, 408, 150 00	1, 424, 500. 00	1 415, 860. 00
State-bank circulation	604. 00	604. 00	594. 00	594. 00	594. 00
Dividends unpaid	6, 083. 04	10, 155. 14	7, 378. 11	13, 056. 26	7, 938. 59
Individual deposits	4, 068, 872. 45	4, 168, 488. 72	3, 774, 735. 58	4, 033, 176. 77	4, 050, 362. 24
U. S. deposits	48, 881. 60	29, 095. 78	39, 728. 90	39, 062. 04	37, 854. 91
Dep'ts U.S.dis.officers	3, 925. 74	3, 845. 83	3, 239. 47	3, 025. 47	4, 171. 90
Due to national banks	426, 754. 28	293, 095. 90	413, 243. 46	266, 588. 47	258, 310. 61
Due to State banks	15, 403. 92	2, 456. 05	21, 815. 50	3, 537. 88	11, 058. 80
Notes re-discounted	9, 800. 00	44, 114. 91	62, 349. 08	42, 319. 28	6, 500. 00
Bills payable	....	....	....	....	....
Total	9, 038, 610. 24	8, 962, 247. 61	8, 761, 494. 70	8, 863, 197. 52	8, 914, 440. 02

Abstract of reports since October 7, 1886, arranged

MARYLAND.

Resources.	DECEMBER 28.	MARCH 4.	MAY 13.	AUGUST 1.	OCTOBER 5.
	30 banks.	30 banks.	30 banks.	30 banks.	31 banks.
Loans and discounts	$6,234,001.31	$6,180,741.68	$6,599,783.25	$6,767,370.99	$6,960,912.90
Bonds for circulation	1,966,500.00	1,826,500.00	1,733,500.00	1,504,500.00	1,517,000.00
Bonds for deposits	....	....	....	80,000.00	80,000.00
U.S. bonds on hand	83,500.00	130,500.00	73,600.00	42,100.00	118,600.00
Other stocks and b'ds	504,502.78	685,913.17	774,792.83	825,750.65	820,570.70
Due from res've ag'ts	939,243.91	859,616.03	674,717.06	908,917.32	939,177.90
Due from nat'l banks	673,054.94	593,929.97	538,503.20	452,956.06	455,436.25
Due from State banks	74,232.28	88,864.42	78,107.38	34,335.75	39,730.65
Real estate, etc	316,768.12	323,453.17	325,572.08	334,768.82	344,816.68
Current expenses	59,779.23	42,002.37	60,972.60	20,087.96	59,846.01
Premiums paid	140,026.42	132,549.13	119,622.56	117,150.56	131,430.32
Cash items	34,066.14	38,890.79	37,228.12	42,217.35	60,561.00
Clear'g-house exch'gs	....	....	....	....	....
Bills of other banks	57,929.00	59,583.00	69,329.00	62,841.00	54,032.00
Uncurr't & minor coins	3,341.82	3,724.89	4,177.73	2,901.68	3,474.75
Trade dollars	15,677.69	16,349.49	4,358.74	1,296.92	....
Specie	380,214.17	422,963.44	444,301.01	420,618.15	440,974.73
Legal-tender notes	310,096.00	307,448.00	392,793.00	358,525.00	377,513.00
U.S. cert's of deposit	....	....	....	....	....
5 % fund with Treas	81,045.31	79,460.50	73,644.50	65,259.50	61,567.50
Due from U.S. Treas	5,862.50	11,200.00	3,660.00	2,646.00	5,262.93
Total	11,978,431.62	11,803,690.05	12,008,063.06	12,053,243.71	12,470,907.50

CITY OF BALTIMORE.

Resources.	DECEMBER 28.	MARCH 4.	MAY 13.	AUGUST 1.	OCTOBER 5.
	17 banks.	17 banks.	17 banks.	17 banks.	17 banks.
Loans and discounts	$26,271,701.05	$27,319,734.73	$27,442,848.67	$26,928,990.88	$26,190,608.13
Bonds for circulation	3,460,000.00	2,960,000.00	2,050,000.00	2,050,000.00	2,050,000.00
Bonds for deposits	300,000.00	400,000.00	400,000.00	400,000.00	400,000.00
U.S. bonds on hand	....	....	....	....	....
Other stocks and b'ds	292,890.87	739,628.75	913,092.69	946,459.57	940,745.80
Due from res've ag'ts	1,919,831.60	1,652,214.63	2,024,822.04	1,437,144.74	2,075,849.23
Due from nat'l banks	1,861,301.37	1,317,459.73	1,251,258.33	1,295,743.34	1,848,175.95
Due from State banks	247,530.99	161,477.78	215,898.37	177,846.68	295,563.83
Real estate, etc	774,062.15	790,558.25	790,472.08	773,903.39	784,393.99
Current expenses	159,106.95	98,428.70	110,491.03	87,474.55	150,577.86
Premiums paid	51,366.31	58,109.62	59,093.37	63,478.13	63,240.63
Cash items	70,870.89	35,313.36	41,397.45	36,258.95	56,510.08
Clear'g-house exch'gs	1,129,228.77	2,012,680.77	1,166,431.97	1,520,960.75	1,192,567.42
Bills of other banks	402,911.00	253,160.00	240,614.00	235,369.00	248,111.00
Uncurr't & minor coins	8,033.03	7,573.24	6,081.30	9,803.81	6,755.26
Trade dollars	86,361.00	85,413.00	60.00	9.00	....
Specie	2,402,432.12	2,598,627.07	2,370,017.73	2,174,109.13	2,130,100.33
Legal-tender notes	1,288,540.00	1,155,273.00	1,451,735.00	1,093,125.00	877,182.00
U.S. cert's of deposit	930,000.00	1,460,000.00	1,030,000.00	1,235,000.00	810,000.00
5 % fund with Treas	155,700.00	133,200.00	92,250.00	93,250.00	92,250.00
Due from U.S. Treas	5,240.00	200.00	30,000.00	2,200.00	4,030.00
Total	41,907,314.10	43,219,142.63	41,706,070.03	40,560,126.92	40,216,621.51

DISTRICT OF COLUMBIA.

Resources.	DECEMBER 28.	MARCH 4.	MAY 13.	AUGUST 1.	OCTOBER 5.
	1 bank.	1 bank.	1 bank.	1 bank.	1 bank.
Loans and discounts	$331,988.32	$311,712.06	$337,113.46	$323,531.04	$347,202.43
Bonds for circulation	250,000.00	250,000.00	250,000.00	250,000.00	250,000.00
Bonds for deposits	....	....	....	....	....
U.S. bonds on hand	151,200.00	151,200.00	151,200.00	151,200.00	151,200.00
Other stocks and b'ds	188,930.00	188,930.00	197,930.00	197,930.00	192,930.00
Due from res've ag'ts	90,204.49	102,523.32	123,856.57	98,078.59	81,594.63
Due from nat'l banks	4,649.80	12,817.01	12,218.70	6,151.72	11,373.35
Due from State banks	10.00	....	1,106.53	244.03	404.69
Real estate, etc	20,000.00	20,000.00	20,000.00	20,000.00	20,000.00
Current expenses	7.50	2,430.31	4,517.49	244.73	3,578.76
Premiums paid	31,444.68	31,444.68	32,357.18	32,357.18	32,357.18
Cash items	6,494.60	18,518.50	5,237.34	10,980.00	6,736.00
Clear'g-house exch'gs	....	....	....	....	....
Bills of other banks	5,308.00	4,450.00	1,560.00	5,292.00	3,046.00
Uncurr't & minor coins	89.22	53.75	23.98	33.63	25.14
Trade dollars	....	....	70.00	....	....
Specie	156,773.00	163,752.00	170,040.00	167,120.50	168,058.75
Legal-tender notes	56,300.00	82,530.00	90,378.00	81,050.00	105,140.00
U.S. cert's of deposit	....	....	....	....	....
5 % fund with Treas	11,250.00	11,250.00	11,250.00	11,250.00	11,250.00
Due from U.S. Treas	....	....	....	....	....
Total	1,304,739.61	1,351,641.36	1,408,889.25	1,356,364.32	1,385,491.93

by States and reserve cities—Continued.

MARYLAND.

Liabilities	DECEMBER 28.	MARCH 4.	MAY 13.	AUGUST 1.	OCTOBER 5.
	30 banks.	30 banks.	30 banks.	30 banks.	31 banks.
Capital stock	$2,771,700.00	$2,746,700.00	$2,706,700.00	$2,760,700.00	$2,706,700.00
Surplus fund	871,147.05	871,078.11	871,183.59	901,580.48	901,580.48
Undivided profits	329,120.41	282,785.92	360,555.80	241,324.04	312,757.99
Nat'l bank circulation	1,710,110.00	1,593,961.00	1,529,016.00	1,329,200.00	1,332,140.00
State-bank circulation	....	....	....	....	....
Dividends unpaid	31,118.44	17,004.65	17,880.12	36,086.74	28,613.61
Individual deposits	5,837,032.13	5,985,393.98	6,048,239.87	6,360,871.17	6,660,594.56
U. S. deposits	....	....	....	58,771.40	80,000.00
Dep'ts U.S.dis.officers	....	....	....	....	....
Due to national banks	319,915.11	185,396.10	284,837.14	108,836.03	257,957.57
Due to State banks	38,795.46	42,403.64	43,305.68	35,400.08	51,563.29
Notes re-discounted	39,487.02	53,966.56	56,324.86	94,407.77	19,000.00
Bills payable	20,000.00	25,000.00	30,000.00	60,000.00	40,000.00
Total	11,978,431.62	11,803,690.05	12,008,063.06	12,053,243.71	12,470,907.50

CITY OF BALTIMORE.

	17 banks.	17 banks.	17 banks.	17 banks.	17 banks.
Capital stock	$11,713,260.00	$11,713,260.00	$11,713,260.00	$11,713,260.00	$11,713,260.00
Surplus fund	3,178,500.00	3,399,000.00	3,410,000.00	3,544,400.00	3,544,400.00
Undivided profits	1,664,569.29	1,197,014.27	1,289,557.45	897,124.39	1,157,434.87
Nat'l-bank circulation	3,062,360.00	2,601,190.00	1,796,540.00	1,818,580.00	1,822,900.00
State-bank circulation	16,663.00	16,663.00	16,563.00	16,543.00	16,543.00
Dividends unpaid	46,830.13	54,509.87	84,216.43	80,377.82	62,907.62
Individual deposits	18,432,968.33	19,004,641.05	19,282,554.90	18,880,358.71	18,188,101.39
U. S. deposits	109,014.96	290,861.73	330,724.43	310,950.17	317,607.88
Dep'ts U.S.dis.officers	45,504.58	63,136.74	29,181.25	57,521.01	38,238.59
Due to national banks	3,119,005.44	3,642,754.13	3,263,309.86	2,702,019.99	2,827,268.32
Due to State banks	518,548.37	516,110.94	482,062.71	448,090.93	527,869.84
Notes re-discounted	....	....	....	....	....
Bills payable	....	....	....	....	....
Total	41,907,314.10	43,219,142.63	41,706,970.03	40,560,126.92	40,216,621.51

DISTRICT OF COLUMBIA.

	1 bank.	1 bank.	1 bank.	1 bank.	1 bank.
Capital stock	$252,000.00	$252,000.00	$252,000.00	$252,000.00	$252,000.00
Surplus fund	60,000.00	60,000.00	60,000.00	60,000.00	60,000.00
Undivided profits	47,395.17	56,190.63	64,141.03	53,100.91	63,238.97
Nat'l-bank circulation	207,600.00	212,020.00	208,800.00	199,630.00	194,130.00
State-bank circulation	....	....	....	....	....
Dividends unpaid	13,980.00	4,268.00	4,236.00	3,388.00	3,080.00
Individual deposits	708,228.60	757,114.98	811,190.95	776,275.47	805,809.96
U. S. deposits	....	....	....	....	....
Dep'ts U.S.dis.officers	....	....	....	....	....
Due to national banks	15,315.98	9,401.91	8,237.44	9,502.06	6,867.99
Due to State banks	219.86	556.14	203.93	407.88	365.01
Notes re-discounted	....	....	....	....	....
Bills payable	....	....	....	....	....
Total	1,304,739.61	1,351,641.66	1,408,889.25	1,356,364.32	1,385,491.93

Abstract of reports since October 7, 1886, arranged

CITY OF WASHINGTON.

Resources.	DECEMBER 28. 6 banks.	MARCH 4. 7 banks.	MAY 13. 7 banks.	AUGUST 1. 7 banks.	OCTOBER 5. 7 banks.
Loans and discounts	$3,507,240.13	$3,570,023.98	$3,937,926.51	$4,013,181.35	$4,028,111.36
Bonds for circulation	630,000.00	680,000.00	680,000.00	680,000.00	680,000.00
Bonds for deposits	100,000.00	100,000.00	100,000.00	100,000.00	100,000.00
U.S. bonds on hand	864,750.00	847,050.00	861,450.00	866,000.00	844,400.00
Other stocks and b'ds	312,219.18	312,800.43	314,238.58	345,781.82	356,133.62
Due from res've ag'ts	417,424.72	898,356.76	912,391.72	740,621.39	649,036.53
Due from nat'l banks	265,901.01	451,766.69	450,943.27	434,645.41	265,775.35
Due from State banks	15,866.09	23,536.35	20,454.27	15,231.56	7,785.21
Real estate, etc	420,532.42	454,653.72	454,891.13	572,842.86	587,592.50
Current expenses	55,808.52	23,850.60	47,932.52	11,379.77	34,788.51
Premiums paid	179,058.01	183,772.48	186,230.40	182,500.85	187,350.60
Cash items	258,316.16	230,902.28	235,457.59	82,051.66	81,132.23
Clear'g-house exch'gs	....	....	....	89,166.60	59,212.95
Bills of other banks	39,170.00	31,783.00	41,506.00	26,963.00	27,162.00
Uncur't & minor coins	8,144.14	8,048.28	8,132.06	7,320.39	7,072.45
Trade dollars	8,039.00	8,039.00	712.00	....	....
Specie	810,203.00	891,706.25	1,015,150.75	909,504.00	945,334.00
Legal-tender notes	622,537.00	695,053.00	720,874.00	718,955.00	587,596.00
U.S. cert's of deposit	200,000.00	30,000.00	10,000.00	100,000.00	80,000.00
5 % fund with Treas	24,734.50	24,703.50	24,970.00	26,866.00	26,841.00
Due from U.S. Treas	2,015.50	46.50	1,360.00	34.00	59.00
Total	8,750,968.38	9,456,782.82	10,024,626.80	9,923,045.66	9,550,283.31

VIRGINIA.

	25 banks.	25 banks.	25 banks.	25 banks.	25 banks.
Loans and discounts	$10,566,880.33	$10,086,250.12	$10,475,483.93	$10,420,144.58	$10,825,495.50
Bonds for circulation	2,115,850.00	1,465,000.00	1,390,000.00	1,352,500.00	1,352,500.00
Bonds for deposits	650,000.00	800,000.00	975,000.00	1,250,000.00	1,250,000.00
U.S. bonds on hand	58,400.00	63,400.00	18,400.00	108,700.00	9,200.00
Other stocks and b'ds	567,240.62	750,748.04	818,454.04	835,276.90	916,769.38
Due from res've ag'ts	1,107,850.32	990,157.72	811,802.10	1,024,452.23	883,478.96
Due from nat'l banks	467,850.22	605,165.61	565,087.96	615,061.89	710,047.65
Due from State banks	280,037.81	230,319.91	210,170.88	268,082.98	260,915.38
Real estate, etc	395,087.85	394,552.52	394,541.75	393,375.36	395,288.58
Current expenses	139,469.59	52,709.87	103,221.70	29,736.09	76,650.48
Premiums paid	257,074.35	320,721.62	306,332.91	320,146.18	320,271.18
Cash items	143,662.71	317,025.50	212,786.34	201,068.80	228,455.53
Clear'g-house exch'gs	15,531.14	....	....	....	....
Bills of other banks	289,837.00	167,983.00	245,797.00	277,866.00	236,836.00
Uncur't & minor coins	4,690.03	5,966.07	5,545.61	4,196.65	2,913.32
Trade dollars	8,521.00	8,877.35	1,463.85	350.00	1.20
Specie	524,893.89	538,749.02	607,867.51	623,325.56	606,840.38
Legal-tender notes	761,154.00	645,264.00	750,935.00	771,221.00	754,434.00
U.S. cert's of deposit	....	....	....	....	....
5 % fund with Treas	88,862.50	60,424.66	55,502.16	58,882.50	59,745.00
Due from U.S. Treas	20.00	647.50	747.50	939.66	1,960.57
Total	18,443,831.36	18,103,962.51	17,967,140.24	18,647,926.37	18,891,803.11

WEST VIRGINIA.

	19 banks.	19 banks.	20 banks.	20 banks.	20 banks.
Loans and discounts	$3,457,531.75	$3,593,057.47	$3,774,317.33	$3,851,439.42	$4,018,987.40
Bonds for circulation	821,250.00	771,250.00	786,250.00	786,250.00	761,250.00
Bonds for deposits	....	....	....	....	50,000.00
U.S. bonds on hand	89,500.00	89,500.00	44,500.00	44,500.00	44,500.00
Other stocks and b'ds	63,736.20	61,636.20	74,636.20	81,064.23	81,064.23
Due from res've ag'ts	373,990.16	355,315.61	265,012.02	284,181.20	304,638.18
Due from nat'l banks	254,264.08	221,556.47	236,841.75	228,963.84	242,815.17
Due from State banks	58,416.49	57,438.38	57,473.55	32,468.93	71,465.57
Real estate, etc	228,320.35	231,004.50	231,059.44	238,265.89	230,782.01
Current expenses	56,089.83	20,780.14	34,904.57	10,924.07	24,421.12
Premiums paid	73,325.32	73,792.00	69,082.80	62,893.75	63,795.03
Cash items	18,977.68	22,172.17	20,595.65	20,657.36	27,198.28
Clear'g-house exch'gs	....	....	....	....	....
Bills of other banks	93,028.00	78,465.00	85,897.00	87,201.00	60,196.00
Uncur't & minor coins	1,463.00	1,739.44	1,719.55	1,082.53	1,829.64
Trade dollars	7,540.73	5,373.28	3,892.75	995.80	16.00
Specie	254,520.46	265,762.93	278,439.99	279,495.12	275,962.36
Legal-tender notes	241,870.00	220,892.00	238,431.00	273,535.00	249,056.00
U.S. cert's of deposit	....	....	....	....	....
5 % fund with Treas	36,636.25	33,756.25	31,806.25	33,931.25	30,473.75
Due from U.S. Treas	696.32	1,716.07	456.07	304.82	2,736.13
Total	6,132,057.52	6,105,207.91	6,238,318.92	6,318,754.81	6,601,186.87

by States and reserve cities—Continued.

CITY OF WASHINGTON.

Liabilities.	DECEMBER 28.	MARCH 4.	MAY 13.	AUGUST 1.	OCTOBER 5.
	6 banks.	7 banks.	7 banks.	7 banks.	7 banks.
Capital stock	$1,325,000.00	$1,450,000.00	$1,532,300.00	$1,575,000.00	$1,575,000.00
Surplus fund	383,000.00	401,500.00	401,500.00	479,703.75	481,203.75
Undivided profits	268,995.28	186,546.65	240,934.12	132,118.75	183,328.17
Nat'l-bank circulation	490,080.00	489,510.00	533,720.00	534,980.00	534,805.00
State-bank circulation	....	....	....	....	....
Dividends unpaid	994.50	2,040.50	1,188.00	3,566.50	2,848.00
Individual deposits	6,029,634.90	6,674,368.65	7,000,313.68	6,869,360.79	6,465,834.37
U. S. deposits	46,746.96	52,014.91	91,075.01	54,865.75	53,965.95
Dep'ts U.S.dis.officers	....	....	....	....	....
Due to national banks	151,542.98	133,520.63	157,931.67	183,493.48	160,432.17
Due to State banks	550,003.76	42,281.48	31,664.32	27,456.64	39,275.90
Notes re-discounted	....	....	....	....	....
Bills payable	....	25,000.00	25,000.00	62,500.00	62,500.00
Total	8,750,068.38	9,456,782.82	10,024,026.80	9,923,045.66	9,559,283.31

VIRGINIA.

	25 banks.	25 banks.	25 banks.	25 banks.	25 banks.
Capital stock	$3,776,300.00	$3,791,300.00	$3,796,300.00	$3,796,300.00	$3,796,300.00
Surplus fund	1,237,779.75	1,352,300.73	1,352,300.73	1,414,502.45	1,414,892.31
Undivided profits	703,661.85	445,945.60	586,776.39	386,646.95	487,530.50
Nat'l-bank circulation	1,862,860.00	1,311,950.00	1,245,410.00	1,210,550.00	1,204,380.00
State-bank circulation	....	....	....	....	....
Dividends unpaid	1,758.65	3,705.65	1,544.65	8,125.65	3,781.65
Individual deposits	9,630,986.07	9,615,368.06	8,959,617.31	9,836,870.76	9,786,470.26
U. S. deposits	327,653.93	403,194.62	604,757.52	895,109.55	1,002,263.10
Dep'ts U.S.dis.officers	110,695.27	97,763.80	79,867.61	103,814.42	92,871.19
Due to national banks	404,519.94	401,090.14	463,522.27	326,345.17	402,355.00
Due to State banks	291,745.72	353,027.75	434,424.39	487,905.03	410,631.28
Notes re-discounted	80,870.18	80,378.66	246,681.87	130,629.89	120,418.82
Bills payable	15,000.00	217,937.50	195,937.50	44,937.50	110,000.00
Total	18,443,831.36	18,103,962.51	17,967,140.24	18,647,926.37	18,891,803.11

WEST VIRGINIA.

	19 banks.	19 banks.	20 banks.	20 banks.	20 banks.
Capital stock	$1,861,000.00	$1,861,000.00	$1,911,000.00	$1,911,000.00	$1,961,000.00
Surplus fund	453,214.54	458,243.75	457,003.75	466,120.98	469,120.98
Undivided profits	163,327.53	84,153.25	135,766.73	77,110.01	121,819.65
Nat'l-bank circulation	719,690.00	676,540.00	688,005.00	687,325.00	655,525.00
State-bank circulation	....	....	....	....	....
Dividends unpaid	12,729.00	20,197.00	14,572.00	23,992.00	15,713.00
Individual deposits	2,635,099.78	2,776,556.77	2,749,544.41	2,909,186.33	3,079,587.22
U. S. deposits	....	....	....	....	4,907.25
Dep'ts U.S.dis.officers	....	....	....	....	....
Due to national banks	147,274.30	117,368.14	144,625.92	149,562.37	153,745.80
Due to State banks	89,733.65	57,235.50	7,839.61	42,307.12	73,238.97
Notes re-discounted	38,088.50	52,541.50	61,900.50	51,122.00	61,000.00
Bills payable	11,000.00	1,372.00	7,371.00	1,029.00	5,529.00
Total	6,132,057.52	6,105,207.91	6,238,318.92	6,318,754.81	6,601,186.87

Abstract of reports since October 7, 1886, arranged

NORTH CAROLINA.

Resources.	DECEMBER 28.	MARCH 4.	MAY 13.	AUGUST 1.	OCTOBER 5.
	17 banks.	17 banks.	18 banks.	18 banks.	18 banks.
Loans and discounts	$4, 576, 557. 14	$4, 828, 540. 02	$5, 157, 010. 33	$5, 254, 464. 62	$5, 323, 203. 27
Bonds for circulation	972, 000. 00	929, 500. 00	928, 500. 00	928, 500. 00	928, 500. 00
Bonds for deposits ..	100, 000. 00	100, 000. 00	100, 000. 00	100, 000. 00	100, 000. 00
U. S. bonds on hand ..	5, 000. 00				
Other stocks and b'ds	215, 797. 72	2[illegible]3, 674. 55	292, 563. 87	290, 935. 81	313, 207. 84
Due from res've ag'ts.	703, 308. 24	599, 778. 02	374, 014. 37	351, 891. 18	446, 320. 97
Due from nat'l banks	355, 116. 87	356, 463. 36	252, 306. 54	157, 072. 28	210, 268. 80
Due from State banks	132, 782. 06	123, 637. 90	34, 791. 32	53, 743. 70	102, 633. 42
Real estate, etc......	277, 125. 83	296, 102. 39	297, 477. 11	307, 406. 50	299, 496. 90
Current expenses....	60, 948. 40	22, 528. 86	47, 419. 03	18, 260. 20	42, 924. 21
Premiums paid......	82, 040. 96	76, 924. 34	78, 877. 47	80, 407. 47	83, 657. 47
Cash items..........	61, 245. 94	48, 922. 96	32, 922. 99	15, 838. 81	51, 426. 12
Clear'g-house exch'gs					
Bills of other banks..	134, 465. 00	133, 833. 00	125, 111. 00	63, 252. 00	100, 344. 00
Uncur't & minor coins	2, 060. 34	2, 210. 48	2, 745. 26	3, 017. 93	2, 900. 38
Trade dollars........	330. 10	214. 50	40. 00	99. 35	93. 65
Specie..............	274, 027. 26	325, 106. 78	365, 428. 80	267, 423. 67	195, 240. 38
Legal-tender notes ..	287, 199. 00	296, 680. 00	279, 216. 00	192, 236. 00	254, 222. 00
U. S. cert's of deposit.					
5 % fund with Treas	39, 099. 50	39, 038. 00	38, 803. 00	40, 816. 31	41, 251. 25
Due from U. S. Treas	662. 99	1, 081. 79	3, 262. 99	2, 162. 99	2, 300. 70
Total..........	8, 280, 367. 35	8, 459, 237. 55	8, 410, 490. 08	8, 127, 618. 85	8, 507, 090. 36

SOUTH CAROLINA.

	16 banks.	16 banks.	16 banks.	16 banks.	15 banks.
Loans and discounts.	$3, 898, 516. 68	$4, 260, 546. 78	$4, 890, 264. 58	$5, 068, 203. 54	$4, 914, 297. 69
Bonds for circulation.	836, 350. 00	773, 850. 00	712, 350. 00	662, 250. 00	624, 750. 00
Bonds for deposits ..	300, 000. 00	300, 000. 00	300, 000. 00	350, 000. 00	375, 000. 00
U. S. bonds on hand..	23, 200. 00	173, 100. 00	23, 100. 00	23, 100. 00	23, 100. 00
Other stocks and b'ds	596, 311. 13	815, 530. 40	601, 699. 50	650, 702. 22	754, 170. 94
Due from res've ag'ts.	1, 579, 543. 38	701, 152. 03	420, 154. 25	148, 709. 50	250, 077. 80
Due from nat'l banks.	667, 172. 27	733, 749. 44	327, 666. 95	144, 378. 40	202, 614. 75
Due from State banks	180, 427. 08	156, 690. 35	110, 456. 92	45, 536. 72	194, 559. 84
Real estate, etc......	188, 180. 18	192, 897. 52	192, 855. 02	186, 016. 01	188, 580. 29
Current expenses....	87, 926. 31	39, 850. 04	83, 189. 93	14, 907. 40	40, 838. 74
Premiums paid......	56, 206. 70	66, 590. 45	71, 569. 51	35, 244. 69	34, 072. 82
Cash items..........	57, 405. 95	52, 309. 84	28, 397. 57	23, 079. 43	66, 169. 37
Clear'g-house exch'gs					
Bills of other banks..	281, 703. 00	142, 401. 00	88, 379. 00	62, 521. 00	106, 570. 00
Uncur't & minor coins	1, 172. 96	2, 911. 20	3, 546. 33	2, 336. 25	2, 034. 45
Trade dollars........	25. 00		10. 00	10. 00	
Specie..............	337, 763. 71	321, 004. 70	208, 536. 20	326, 245. 60	325, 300. 95
Legal-tender notes ..	551, 747. 00	341, 556. 00	313, 308. 00	221, 426. 00	470, 681. 00
U. S. cert's of deposit.					
5 % fund with Treas	36, 385. 75	34, 322. 75	30, 905. 25	28, 915. 25	27, 513. 25
Due from U. S. Treas.	254. 00	12, 200. 00	22, 923. 00	10, 700. 00	2, 500. 00
Total..........	9, 090, 381. 10	9, 210, 731. 50	8, 618, 372. 11	8, 004, 432. 91	8, 632, 840. 89

GEORGIA.

	17 banks.	17 banks.	18 banks.	19 banks.	21 banks.
Loans and discounts	$5, 871, 065. 96	$6, 230, 697. 73	$6, 491, 128. 22	$7, 166, 861. 20	$7, 789, 358. 14
Bonds for circulation	888, 500. 00	888, 500. 00	913, 500. 00	938, 500. 00	988, 500. 00
Bonds for deposits...	110, 000. 00	150, 000. 00	150, 000. 00	150, 000. 00	150, 000. 00
U. S. bonds on hand..	25, 000. 00	25, 000. 00			
Other stocks and b'ds	329, 487. 51	305, 233. 37	290, 321. 32	245, 818. 17	256, 933. 61
Due from res've ag'ts	1, 022, 810. 19	807, 721. 45	510, 479. 67	256, 492. 83	216, 072. 40
Due from nat'l banks	220, 041. 28	228, 889. 52	220, 734. 71	129, 371. 34	330, 816. 03
Due from State banks	191, 324. 43	184, 461. 70	152, 687. 18	100, 571. 15	321, 190. 84
Real estate, etc......	464, 565. 66	456, 022. 72	441, 835. 12	464, 498. 55	465, 889. 61
Current expenses	119, 589. 12	36, 927. 47	74, 894. 37	21, 508. 09	65, 645. 75
Premiums paid......	56, 391. 53	71, 407. 78	72, 254. 65	77, 706. 65	80, 863. 86
Cash items..........	123, 065. 21	171, 396. 12	80, 335. 95	116, 458. 51	189, 705. 00
Clear'g-house exch'gs					
Bills of other banks..	243, 163. 00	231, 611. 00	241, 966. 00	176, 814. 00	226, 809. 00
Uncur't & minor coins	2, 924. 56	4, 128. 70	4, 041. 85	3, 179. 40	4, 081. 24
Trade dollars........					
Specie..............	461, 729. 86	617, 098. 05	539, 133. 83	506, 387. 58	517, 310. 35
Legal-tender notes ..	406, 925. 00	314, 326. 00	305, 626. 00	278, 143. 00	463, 116. 00
U. S. cert's of deposit					
5 % fund with Treas	39, 532. 50	38, 092. 50	39, 239. 04	40, 094. 01	41, 482. 50
Due from U. S. Treas	3, 010. 00	5, 327. 60	10, 889. 40	4, 951. 60	12, 350. 20
Total..........	10, 582, 105. 71	10, 830, 474. 80	10, 512, 067. 31	10, 677, 950. 11	12, 158, 131. 16

by States and reserve cities—Continued.

NORTH CAROLINA.

Liabilities.	DECEMBER 28.	MARCH 4.	MAY 13.	AUGUST 1.	OCTOBER 5.
	17 banks.	17 banks.	18 banks.	18 banks.	18 banks.
Capital stock	$2,370,000.00	$2,376,000.00	$2,401,650.00	$2,412,260.00	$2,412,280.00
Surplus fund	505,805.40	532,548.83	532,548.83	542,490.66	541,490.66
Undivided profits	344,382.69	226,268.89	296,836.63	207,420.05	271,059.35
Nat'l-bank circulation	834,340.00	794,850.00	780,300.00	788,510.00	795,710.00
State-bank circulation	....	....	....	....	....
Dividends unpaid	3,121.00	4,091.00	3,042.00	6,908.50	6,150.50
Individual deposits	3,704,842.42	4,101,380.14	3,875,648.15	3,431,074.18	3,537,066.46
U. S. deposits	53,244.37	37,715.39	46,063.59	57,765.52	48,684.31
Dep'ts U.S.dis.officers	41,588.22	30,641.68	23,653.06	16,870.47	26,492.16
Due to national banks	101,725.71	175,173.76	150,147.39	106,076.47	196,640.62
Due to State banks	45,073.43	40,570.78	60,483.42	50,096.39	27,513.61
Notes re-discounted	180,244.11	130,997.08	240,176.99	463,117.61	541,002.60
Bills payable	....	....	....	45,000.00	100,000.00
Total	8,280,367.35	8,450,237.55	8,410,490.08	8,127,618.85	8,507,090.36

SOUTH CAROLINA.

	16 banks.	16 banks.	16 banks.	16 banks.	15 banks.
Capital stock	$1,798,000.00	$1,729,640.00	$1,748,000.00	$1,748,000.00	$1,608,000.00
Surplus fund	785,000.00	770,000.00	770,000.00	788,800.00	778,800.00
Undivided profits	741,014.42	659,070.21	770,939.29	627,117.94	709,151.07
Nat'l-bank circulation	728,890.00	670,325.00	617,900.00	573,705.00	559,875.00
State-bank circulation	....	....	....	....	....
Dividends unpaid	8,437.50	10,840.50	8,967.50	14,879.00	9,748.50
Individual deposits	4,932,725.27	4,527,916.32	4,004,362.32	3,295,394.63	3,545,114.11
U. S. deposits	202,936.09	218,347.18	228,476.37	283,661.92	323,540.14
Dep'ts U.S.dis.officers	43,221.98	57,285.19	43,974.72	53,064.45	43,387.57
Due to national banks	174,287.29	297,861.68	173,709.97	122,807.34	174,049.61
Due to State banks	273,218.55	250,519.87	161,460.18	204,042.72	273,483.11
Notes re-discounted	300.00	18,925.55	70,491.76	219,003.41	137,720.38
Bills payable	2,350.00	....	....	71,956.50	379,962.40
Total	9,690,381.10	9,210,731.50	8,618,372.11	8,004,432.91	8,632,840.89

GEORGIA.

	17 banks.	17 banks.	18 banks.	19 banks.	21 banks.
Capital stock	$2,736,000.00	$2,736,000.00	$2,823,375.00	$2,903,780.00	$3,050,520.00
Surplus fund	892,651.88	921,832.09	921,832.99	951,731.71	951,731.71
Undivided profits	576,076.04	441,738.65	574,761.96	422,614.09	513,005.18
Nat'l-bank circulation	799,050.00	783,890.00	785,370.00	801,395.00	877,650.00
State-bank circulation	....	....	....	....	....
Dividends unpaid	1,721.50	2,712.00	1,851.00	4,606.50	3,525.00
Individual deposits	4,937,831.26	5,066,051.28	4,637,184.07	4,323,486.72	5,003,216.43
U. S. deposits	57,988.69	91,268.13	108,669.67	108,364.68	111,147.49
Dep'ts U.S.dis.officers	37,742.64	35,445.12	21,138.44	25,182.26	35,202.27
Due to national banks	179,391.09	258,282.30	228,372.87	181,964.64	351,586.97
Due to State banks	315,088.91	463,206.16	223,781.15	239,989.49	292,982.55
Notes re-discounted	48,653.70	19,778.17	215,730.16	687,841.02	910,563.56
Bills payable	....	10,180.00	....	27,000.00	55,000.00
Total	10,582,195.71	10,830,474.80	10,542,067.31	10,677,956.11	12,156,131.16

Abstract of reports since October 7, arranged

FLORIDA.

Resources.	DECEMBER 28.	MARCH 4.	MAY 13.	AUGUST 1.	OCTOBER 5.
	9 banks.	9 banks.	9 banks.	8 banks.	8 banks.
Loans and discounts.	$1,379,795.65	$1,365,414.66	$1,333,838.30	$1,393,026.25	$1,441,829.15
Bonds for circulation.	200,500.00	200,500.00	200,500.00	180,500.00	180,500.00
Bonds for deposits ..	100,000.00	100,000.00	100,000.00	100,000.00	100,000.00
U. S. bonds on hand..	300.00	....	....	1,000.00	1,000.00
Other stocks and b'ds	116,162.44	76,258.83	60,496.69	67,566.70	73,085.09
Due from res've ag'ts	218,310.19	323,070.29	364,513.33	189,568.97	108,026.01
Due from nat'l banks	77,741.60	125,291.18	251,352.07	103,915.77	86,154.14
Due from State banks	97,211.66	91,003.61	93,409.16	64,095.56	63,998.57
Real estate, etc	95,990.78	99,581.80	101,773.33	89,807.35	93,386.14
Current expenses...	29,585.68	24,662.97	22,331.48	15,408.68	12,276.63
Premiums paid	32,725.52	32,255.43	30,759.01	29,064.01	29,334.01
Cash items	28,522.29	27,832.02	39,425.73	16,583.00	10,134.58
Clear'g-house exch'gs	....	....	....	....	....
Bills of other banks..	89,491.00	123,669.00	116,229.00	93,653.00	74,060.00
Uncur't & minor coins	597.47	896.52	1,019.89	1,405.28	948.84
Trade dollars........	33.00	113.00	....	....	....
Specie	46,227.00	66,478.41	91,638.30	75,326.25	107,762.30
Legal-tender notes ..	132,776.00	177,030.00	163,108.00	150,701.00	115,440.00
U. S. cert's of deposit	....	....	....	....	....
5 % fund with Treas.	9,022.00	9,022.00	9,022.00	8,102.57	8,122.00
Due from U. S. Treas.	2,011.07	2,870.77	1,080.77	....	1,250.57
Total..........	2,657,012.35	2,845,949.49	2,989,407.06	2,580,324.39	2,508,208.03

ALABAMA.

Resources.	13 banks.	15 banks.	17 banks.	20 banks.	20 banks.
Loans and discounts	$5,088,235.90	[illegible]	$6,979,674.35	$8,009,124.05	$8,502,536.84
Bonds for circulation	1,018,000.00	1,088,000.00	825,500.00	900,500.00	900,500.00
Bonds for deposits ..	100,000.00	....	....	....	....
U. S. bonds on hand..	50.00	50,000.00	50,000.00	50,000.00	50,000.00
Other stocks and b'ds	638,011.47	803,714.97	771,028.97	803,714.00	834,001.51
Due from res've ag'ts	970,421.15	1,423,008.37	1,170,337.49	574,532.41	541,370.63
Due from nat'l banks	543,838.33	876,834.85	685,172.24	602,688.45	386,820.22
Due from State banks	263,845.86	260,578.73	119,093.47	262,515.91	182,911.27
Real estate, etc	204,405.05	311,830.26	332,094.60	319,063.79	372,648.77
Current expenses....	70,362.98	47,623.34	90,316.19	32,021.15	67,214.06
Premiums paid	81,071.66	89,786.66	96,729.78	118,448.53	115,554.78
Cash items	61,788.54	98,924.86	50,813.85	85,264.10	81,170.79
Clear'g-house exch'gs	....	....	....	....	....
Bills of other banks..	241,621.00	389,550.00	260,202.00	140,029.00	101,393.00
Uncur't & minor coins	1,403.39	2,510.49	3,079.91	2,730.23	2,565.17
Trade dollars........	104.00	104.00	195.00	48.30	1.60
Specie	403,690.30	456,724.35	444,127.00	346,026.00	365,448.65
Legal-tender notes ..	356,831.00	478,983.00	396,363.00	375,110.00	411,324.00
U. S. cert's of deposit	....	....	....	....	....
5 % fund with Treas	40,700.83	47,050.00	35,460.00	36,772.50	37,831.67
Due from U. S. Treas	452.75	1,388.58	8,519.18	2,381.75	2,532.89
Total..........	10,207,014.81	12,564,997.59	12,318,737.03	12,691,570.80	13,015,828.85

MISSISSIPPI.

Resources.	8 banks.	8 banks.	9 banks.	11 banks.	12 banks.
Loans and discounts	$1,609,932.26	$1,552,745.99	$1,649,932.28	$1,914,588.80	$2,292,652.99
Bonds for circulation	225,000.00	225,000.00	250,000.00	287,500.00	320,000.00
Bonds for deposits ..	....	....	....	....	....
U. S. bonds on hand..	....	....	....	....	....
Other stocks and b'ds	65,938.12	50,786.32	54,518.31	63,616.34	70,231.20
Due from res've ag'ts	224,725.33	263,417.07	149,055.19	75,002.70	138,086.35
Due from nat'l banks	189,502.14	130,829.37	123,227.11	73,990.37	72,894.46
Due from State banks	36,376.49	41,383.08	24,560.25	41,701.18	40,270.88
Real estate, etc	43,782.89	43,917.47	43,562.02	46,594.56	46,676.41
Current expenses....	30,533.54	14,689.47	21,696.00	10,297.63	23,596.94
Premiums paid	22,288.41	21,381.18	26,996.31	30,022.53	33,788.15
Cash items	11,966.19	12,295.38	22,072.14	7,160.67	28,331.26
Clear'g-house exch'gs	....	....	....	....	....
Bills of other banks..	16,403.00	16,833.00	10,776.00	11,036.00	18,535.00
Uncur't & minor coins	256.01	519.06	1,281.30	982.91	614.20
Trade dollars........	1.00	1.00	1.00	1.00	....
Specie	108,716.30	109,121.30	116,099.55	132,863.55	153,407.13
Legal-tender notes ..	181,149.00	168,899.00	177,696.00	115,312.00	140,554.00
U. S. cert's of deposit	....	....	....	....	....
5 % fund with Treas.	10,667.55	9,377.06	9,975.00	12,037.00	12,112.00
Due from U. S. Treas	....	6,000.00	4,000.00	5,000.00	....
Total..........	2,780,328.23	2,710,289.65	2,717,361.55	2,828,730.27	3,391,750.97

by States, and reserve cities—Continued.

FLORIDA.

Liabilities.	DECEMBER 28	MARCH 4.	MAY 13.	AUGUST 1.	OCTOBER 5.
	9 banks.	9 banks.	9 banks.	8 banks.	8 banks.
Capital stock	$550,000.00	$550,000.00	$550,000.00	$500,000.00	$500,000.00
Surplus fund	33,500.00	46,500.00	50,000.00	60,080.00	66,180.00
Undivided profits	84,975.55	55,449.63	63,513.18	46,823.36	51,574.17
Nat'l-bank circulation	163,660.00	156,830.00	153,900.00	142,090.00	146,750.00
State-bank circulation	....	....	....	....	....
Dividends unpaid	2.00	26.00	6.00	1,847.50	151.00
Individual deposits	1,612,612.45	1,838,737.91	1,968,280.04	1,634,417.55	1,516,761.27
U. S. deposits	72,533.47	85,020.79	87,934.58	84,718.01	88,500.08
Dep'ts U.S.dis.officers	17,802.35	5,187.32	3,866.04	5,597.71	2,575.15
Due to national banks	76,473.85	58,713.46	62,621.54	76,061.45	84,901.58
Due to State banks	16,535.24	41,692.74	48,027.46	26,587.91	21,142.10
Notes re-discounted	28,917.44	7,791.64	1,339.20	....	20,663.68
Bills payable	....	....	....	....	10,000.00
Total	2,657,012.35	2,815,949.49	2,989,497.06	2,580,324.39	2,508,208.03

ALABAMA.

	13 banks.	15 banks.	17 banks.	20 banks.	20 banks.
Capital stock	$2,435,000.00	$2,720,250.00	$2,855,200.00	$3,306,430.00	$3,485,100.00
Surplus fund	356,500.00	469,500.00	499,500.00	552,780.84	639,903.66
Undivided profits	458,734.80	460,323.69	577,379.09	476,413.99	451,393.71
Nat'l-bank circulation	866,140.00	878,360.00	661,490.00	725,350.00	782,330.00
State-bank circulation	....	....	....	....	....
Dividends unpaid	2,491.00	6,777.60	2,164.00	7,709.00	8,131.60
Individual deposits	5,561,407.70	7,550,769.11	7,111,870.49	6,308,282.46	5,925,317.72
U. S. deposits	83,837.26	....	....	....	....
Dep'ts U.S.dis.officers	6,332.03	....	....	....	....
Due to national banks	271,705.18	290,799.99	254,400.46	415,750.85	232,610.15
Due to State banks	93,253.68	158,194.94	139,278.53	80,682.04	117,295.54
Notes re-discounted	72,513.17	21,022.26	217,454.46	818,072.62	1,173,746.47
Bills payable	....	....	....	....	200,000.00
Total	10,207,914.81	12,564,997.59	12,318,737.03	12,691,570.80	13,015,828.85

MISSISSIPPI.

	8 banks.	8 banks.	9 banks.	11 banks.	12 banks.
Capital stock	$650,000.00	$675,000.00	$775,000.00	$915,000.00	$1,055,000.00
Surplus fund	68,878.14	96,288.57	100,288.57	127,308.27	127,308.27
Undivided profits	102,699.69	62,044.81	98,508.80	65,007.81	102,496.10
Nat'l-bank circulation	108,065.00	194,965.00	206,645.00	229,595.00	277,220.00
State-bank circulation	....	....	....	....	....
Dividends unpaid	50.00	470.00	200.00	720.00	20.00
Individual deposits	1,601,194.13	1,624,534.15	1,472,793.53	1,199,875.30	1,264,007.76
U. S. deposits	....	....	....	....	....
Dep'ts U.S.dis.officers	....	....	....	....	....
Due to national banks	27,058.32	15,107.23	19,018.71	91,510.20	42,665.21
Due to State banks	11,181.83	19,886.94	9,883.01	7,632.46	7,655.98
Notes re-discounted	101,201.12	11,912.92	34,933.93	156,937.14	409,708.25
Bills payable	20,000.00	10,000.00	....	35,000.00	105,509.40
Total	2,780,328.23	2,710,280.65	2,717,361.55	2,828,736.27	3,391,750.97

Abstract of reports since October 7, 1886, arranged

LOUISIANA.

Resources.	DECEMBER 28.	MARCH 4.	MAY 13.	AUGUST 1.	OCTOBER 5.
	1 bank.	3 banks.	4 banks.	5 banks.	5 banks.
Loans and discounts.	$161, 155. 65	$474, 180. 87	$566, 142. 94	$844, 692. 29	$1, 181, 429. 97
Bonds for circulation	50, 000. 00	115, 000. 00	112, 500. 00	125, 000. 00	125, 000. 00
Bonds for deposits ..	....	....	....	....	....
U. S. bonds on hand .	....	....	75, 000. 00	75, 000. 00	75, 000. 00
Other stock and b'ds	32, 805. 50	13, 021. 57	72, 752. 46	43, 352. 34	41, 267. 93
Due from res've ag'ts	10, 777. 30	342, 170. 61	177, 364. 90	40, 287. 92	55, 878. 61
Due from nat'l banks	31, 101. 09	188, 458. 13	87, 688. 87	44, 541. 07	14, 664. 61
Due from State banks	725. 04	13, 064. 31	23, 814. 27	22, 912. 90	4, 146. 16
Real estate, etc......	1, 100. 00	2, 777. 79	3, 787. 89	6, 954. 79	8, 559. 57
Current expenses....	3, 770. 31	5, 723. 82	10, 503. 68	4, 213. 62	8, 479. 82
Premiums paid......	1, 500. 00	8, 412. 50	33, 263. 13	33, 606. 88	33, 109. 38
Cash items.........	....	2, 384. 59	7, 084. 64	11, 647. 09	8, 585. 79
Clear'g-house exch'gs	....	....	....	....	....
Bills of other banks .	1, 355. 00	57, 465. 00	61, 595. 00	30, 075. 00	22, 542. 00
Uncur't & minor coins	65. 30	173. 20	357. 54	266. 45	471. 75
Trade dollars........	....	....	....	....	....
Specie	23, 090. 00	78, 736. 75	102, 300. 40	117, 205. 50	99, 713. 44
Legal-tender notes ..	5, 317. 00	111, 933. 00	54, 148. 00	71, 248. 00	61, 733. 00
U. S. cert's of deposit	....	....	....	....	....
5 % fund with Treas.	2, 250. 00	5, 175. 00	4, 500. 00	5, 624. 00	5, 624. 00
Due from U. S. Treas	....	....	....	....	....
Total.........	325, 018. 28	1, 418, 677. 23	1, 392, 803. 72	1, 476, 627. 85	1, 740, 206. 03

CITY OF NEW ORLEANS.

	8 banks.	8 banks.	8 banks.	8 banks.	8 banks.
Loans and discounts	$10, 864, 887. 73	$8, 703, 752. 40	$10, 194, 226. 65	$9, 525, 434. 09	$9, 951, 461. 45
Bonds for circulation	1, 265, 000. 00	1, 325, 000. 00	1, 375, 000. 00	1, 175, 000. 00	1, 350, 000. 00
Bonds for deposits ..	....	....	200, 000. 00	200, 000. 00	200, 000. 00
U. S. bonds on hand..	207, 550. 00	208, 100. 00	41, 350. 00	4, 350. 00	7, 850. 00
Other stocks and b'ds	1, 069, 632. 45	1, 584, 683. 05	1, 538, 720. 45	1, 536, 026. 52	1, 541, 508. 42
Due from res've ag'ts	919, 493. 33	1, 628, 582. 37	869, 436. 81	503, 177. 03	586, 230. 50
Due from nat'l banks	315, 053. 69	419, 997. 18	367, 699. 80	253, 013. 50	204, 275. 44
Due from State banks	629, 358. 53	954, 969. 00	416, 127. 22	208, 776. 23	329, 208. 51
Real estate, etc......	439, 915. 23	430, 110. 56	473, 330. 66	474, 173. 24	476, 533. 08
Current expenses....	132, 460. 02	64, 590. 03	122, 430. 09	35, 776. 98	106, 704. 97
Premiums paid......	135, 294. 57	138, 575. 85	202, 789. 47	185, 064. 63	201, 673. 80
Cash items.........	1, 619. 51	6, 080. 49	5, 272. 54	3, 931. 30	5, 241. 86
Clear'g-house exch'gs	1, 180, 679. 10	1, 066, 863. 51	794, 389. 28	937, 493. 13	973, 835. 23
Bills of other banks..	124, 683. 00	180, 942. 00	155, 340. 00	164, 504. 00	82, 838. 00
Uncur't & minor coins	4, 627. 09	3, 986. 65	4, 050. 39	4, 019. 65	3, 770. 37
Trade dollars........	....	....	....	....	....
Specie	1, 091, 340. 45	1, 241, 518. 85	1, 297, 874. 20	1, 017, 299. 15	776, 215. 25
Legal-tender notes ..	1, 779, 121. 00	1, 876, 023. 00	1, 791, 720. 00	1, 600, 627. 00	1, 295, 733. 00
U. S. cert's of deposit.	....	....	....	....	....
5 % fund with Treas.	56, 285. 00	56, 425. 00	61, 375. 00	50, 925. 00	60, 750. 00
Due from U. S. Treas.	....	9, 000. 00	5, 000. 00	....	130. 00
Total.........	20, 217, 030. 70	20, 097, 208. 94	19, 916, 141. 59	17, 881, 421. 45	18, 154, 049. 88

TEXAS.

	74 banks.	79 banks.	84 banks.	87 banks.	91 banks.
Loans and discounts	$16, 225, 725. 59	$17, 201, 313. 91	$18, 906, 498. 37	$19, 399, 393. 80	$20, 762, 342. 30
Bonds for circulation	1, 915, 750. 00	2, 105, 250. 00	2, 250, 250. 00	2, 341, 500. 00	2, 415, 300. 00
Bonds for deposits...	325, 000. 00	325, 000. 00	250, 000. 00	350, 000. 00	350, 000. 00
U. S. bonds on hand .	150, 000. 00	....	....	....	....
Other stocks and b'ds	288, 741. 20	291, 318. 79	295, 091. 46	332, 237. 74	345, 606. 25
Due from res've ag'ts	2, 286, 341. 74	1, 481, 488. 48	1, 460, 133. 25	1, 746, 422. 20	1, 382, 249. 96
Due from nat'l banks	1, 216, 808. 38	1, 261, 015. 00	1, 261, 392. 82	1, 143, 885. 06	1, 249, 440. 37
Due from State banks	692, 267. 00	735, 549. 89	681, 265. 48	773, 708. 16	731, 851. 35
Real estate, etc......	892, 007. 00	967, 859. 72	1, 030, 851. 82	1, 048, 044. 78	1, 104, 166. 76
Current expenses....	268, 427. 47	149, 244. 50	237, 210. 18	101, 370. 88	207, 996. 51
Premiums paid......	229, 904. 81	260, 830. 11	311, 516. 03	346, 100. 54	356, 327. 28
Cash items.........	135, 699. 07	183, 065. 27	121, 545. 46	193, 987. 00	180, 075. 15
Clear'g-house exch'gs	....	....	....	....	....
Bills of other banks..	541, 201. 00	715, 280. 00	498, 591. 00	458, 290. 00	687, 003. 00
Uncur't & minor coins	5, 877. 64	7, 957. 02	9, 733. 94	14, 052. 37	8, 524. 15
Trade dollars.......	....	1. 00	9. 00	10. 00	10. 00
Specie	1, 167, 090. 01	1, 370, 249. 65	1, 177, 230. 03	1, 092, 312. 80	1, 256, 591. 67
Legal-tender notes	1, 793, 062. 00	1, 837, 430. 00	1, 398, 243. 00	1, 604, 684. 00	1, 820, 126. 00
U. S. cert's of deposit	....	....	....	....	....
5 % fund with Treas.	85, 871. 35	86, 768. 25	98, 293. 75	101, 925. 25	104, 001. 30
Due from U. S. Treas	3, 482. 83	17, 234. 38	9, 616. 65	5, 856. 10	6, 342. 17
Total.........	28, 251, 157. 09	29, 003, 815. 97	29, 997, 505. 24	31, 056, 880. 46	32, 968, 569. 22

by States and reserve cities—Continued.

LOUISIANA.

Liabilities.	DECEMBER 28. 1 bank.	MARCH 4. 3 banks.	MAY 13. 4 banks.	AUGUST 1. 5 banks.	OCTOBER 5. 5 banks.
Capital stock	$100,000.00	$400,000.00	$420,250.00	$490,800.00	$500,000.00
Surplus fund	10,500.00	11,000.00	11,000.00	30,308.44	30,308.44
Undivided profits	10,398.63	19,295.13	42,174.32	13,880.67	33,418.75
Nat'l bank circulation	45,000.00	82,500.00	69,000.00	73,240.00	101,740.00
State bank circulation					
Dividends unpaid		100.00	56.00	152.00	144.00
Individual deposits	159,119.65	895,113.07	820,847.78	783,777.26	703,496.72
U. S. deposits					
Dep'ts U. S. dis. officers					
Due to national banks		150.30	679.30	59,233.58	167,792.96
Due to State banks		10,518.13	10,796.32	235.90	1,360.74
Notes re-discounted				25,000.00	208,004.42
Bills payable					
Total	325,018.28	1,418,077.23	1,392,803.72	1,476,627.85	1,746,266.03

CITY OF NEW ORLEANS.

Liabilities.	8 banks.	8 banks.	8 banks.	8 banks.	8 banks.
Capital stock	$3,425,000.00	$3,425,000.00	$3,425,000.00	$2,925,000.00	$2,925,000.00
Surplus fund	1,145,000.00	1,165,000.00	1,165,000.00	1,199,000.00	1,199,000.00
Undivided profits	573,264.90	443,850.07	627,184.50	437,012.82	501,923.32
Nat'l bank circulation	1,120,895.00	1,084,355.00	1,214,235.00	1,054,395.00	1,214,995.00
State bank circulation					
Dividends unpaid	21,082.82	13,919.16	9,849.16	35,226.83	14,217.83
Individual deposits	11,450,352.15	11,827,270.83	11,651,370.85	10,626,564.97	9,698,952.77
U. S. deposits			153,262.15	182,844.08	200,000.00
Dep'ts U. S. dis. officers					
Due to national banks	1,106,344.50	1,230,729.79	791,359.42	650,661.45	1,108,449.82
Due to State banks	1,314,256.04	907,103.40	878,860.42	770,716.30	1,050,665.83
Notes re-discounted	51,835.29				171,845.31
Bills payable					
Total	20,217,030.70	20,097,208.94	19,916,141.50	17,881,424.45	18,154,049.88

TEXAS.

Liabilities.	74 banks.	79 banks.	84 banks.	87 banks.	91 banks.
Capital stock	$7,630,000.00	$8,421,000.00	$9,032,902.00	$9,682,350.00	$9,919,750.00
Surplus fund	2,124,081.90	2,290,403.55	2,304,064.55	2,450,811.93	2,431,284.69
Undivided profits	1,652,019.20	814,715.43	1,126,056.68	778,498.38	1,118,964.09
Nat'l bank circulation	1,702,040.00	1,722,800.00	1,926,235.00	1,975,335.00	2,107,535.00
State bank circulation					
Dividends unpaid	4,633.00	6,843.25	3,514.00	19,871.96	12,426.06
Individual deposits	13,066,387.67	13,719,982.95	13,285,209.36	13,629,715.70	13,710,426.47
U. S. deposits	71,203.24	123,848.17	94,716.70	175,567.00	170,572.07
Dep'ts U. S. dis. officers	224,969.98	166,482.39	130,327.58	131,250.78	102,187.12
Due to national banks	866,099.82	871,023.00	784,372.64	744,151.46	953,400.23
Due to State banks	526,963.11	542,363.97	402,399.90	551,137.24	651,024.55
Notes re-discounted	447,759.98	379,302.36	842,837.36	881,251.01	1,513,497.00
Bills payable	38,000.00	34,000.00	64,749.47	37,000.00	217,500.00
Total	28,254,157.99	29,093,815.07	29,997,505.24	31,056,880.46	32,968,569.22

Abstract of reports since October 7, 1886, arranged

ARKANSAS.

Resources.	DECEMBER 28.	MARCH 4.	MAY 13.	AUGUST 1.	OCTOBER 5.
	5 banks.	6 banks.	7 banks.	7 banks.	7 banks.
Loans and discounts	$2,147,813.84	$1,950,924.06	$2,293,210.36	$2,528,030.04	$2,704,460.84
Bonds for circulation	320,000.00	355,000.00	367,500.00	367,500.00	410,000.00
Bonds for deposits	100,000.00	150,000.00	150,000.00	150,000.00	150,000.00
U. S. bonds on hand	90,800.00	80,800.00	70,800.00	80,800.00	50,800.00
Other stocks and b'ds	50,613.77	55,931.56	60,085.14	26,133.60	29,151.96
Due from res've ag'ts	460,087.84	720,192.71	694,841.00	314,826.26	219,653.00
Due from nat'l banks	115,071.16	202,582.53	113,037.63	97,510.00	60,068.64
Due from State banks	101,181.23	77,026.38	93,077.05	70,828.07	111,104.38
Real estate, etc	19,700.27	22,841.21	33,763.40	33,763.00	33,765.20
Current expenses	4,862.91	2,900.65	6,583.35	5,451.05	4,000.53
Premiums paid	72,750.00	85,071.25	85,871.25	98,783.75	96,096.25
Cash items	7,439.31	20,456.45	9,060.27	14,015.28	8,619.96
Clear'g-house exch'gs	....	....	....	....	....
Bills of other banks	45,280.00	74,673.00	64,206.00	48,032.00	59,090.00
Uncur't & minor coins	140.62	478.58	340.59	538.25	1,202.93
Trade dollars	187.00	183.00	6.00	17.00	....
Specie	197,833.85	206,761.35	186,574.95	168,990.45	166,679.60
Legal-tender notes	183,879.00	163,479.00	144,777.00	131,574.00	96,300.00
U. S. cert's of deposit	....	....	....	....	....
5 % fund with Treas.	14,400.00	14,850.00	15,975.00	16,537.00	17,887.00
Due from U. S. Treas.	1,808.15	2,634.25	3,002.20	3,448.20	2.20
Total	3,935,406.95	4,195,790.98	4,303,611.19	4,157,380.65	4,300,581.40

KENTUCKY.

	50 banks.	50 banks.	50 banks.	50 banks.	50 banks.
Loans and discounts	$16,662,298.33	$16,976,361.81	$17,563,028.89	$17,574,316.50	$17,680,028.58
Bonds for circulation	4,263,100.00	3,850,500.00	3,766,000.00	3,411,000.00	3,411,000.00
Bonds for deposits	710,000.00	810,000.00	810,000.00	1,020,000.00	1,020,000.00
U. S. bonds on hand	48,350.00	6,400.00	102,650.00	117,200.00	118,050.00
Other stocks and b'ds	647,721.07	692,397.98	691,572.72	689,562.91	692,002.87
Due from res've ag'ts	1,946,153.67	1,756,031.93	1,244,514.82	1,775,102.32	1,728,670.79
Due from nat'l banks	996,760.51	853,828.23	673,732.76	873,331.70	934,928.48
Due from State banks	287,946.56	245,533.51	256,740.34	222,489.26	244,668.21
Real estate, etc	480,840.67	506,078.93	510,777.08	509,000.85	511,890.50
Current expenses	149,814.04	87,579.39	105,826.17	90,700.66	116,781.39
Premiums paid	341,483.25	339,118.10	337,771.51	323,114.81	326,218.85
Cash items	61,468.71	47,006.52	97,815.26	128,332.55	105,439.18
Clear'g-house exch'gs	....	....	....	....	....
Bills of other banks	332,392.00	277,315.00	260,475.00	237,445.00	259,056.00
Uncur't & minor coins	2,853.48	3,134.90	3,110.19	3,476.87	3,875.12
Trade dollars	9,649.42	7,693.75	2,238.00	20.00	4.00
Specie	575,356.81	535,624.31	505,367.12	538,780.38	556,561.01
Legal-tender notes	506,659.00	492,917.00	509,957.00	518,090.00	533,074.00
U. S. cert's of deposit	....	....	....	....	....
5 % fund with Treas.	182,601.23	166,657.03	162,954.53	146,589.53	149,569.53
Due from U. S. Treas.	2,097.06	1,900.00	1,950.00	....	1,600.00
Total	28,210,545.81	27,656,078.39	27,606,521.02	28,178,553.34	28,395,821.10

CITY OF LOUISVILLE.

	9 banks.	9 banks.	9 banks.	9 banks.	9 banks.
Loans and discounts	$9,020,427.94	$9,050,697.31	$9,400,737.42	$9,290,262.68	$9,455,073.88
Bonds for circulation	914,000.00	744,000.00	694,000.00	694,000.00	691,000.00
Bonds for deposits	1,000,000.00	1,000,000.00	900,000.00	900,000.00	900,000.00
U. S. bonds on hand	1,350.00	1,350.00	....	....	....
Other stocks and b'ds	239,442.35	226,770.12	245,795.08	234,760.67	226,710.22
Due from res've ag'ts	774,684.41	1,052,855.48	643,059.56	998,960.88	720,807.28
Due from nat'l banks	412,530.22	377,003.37	342,618.85	318,122.93	383,546.59
Due from State banks	223,308.41	201,112.92	185,031.67	129,843.35	157,171.31
Real estate, etc	152,341.72	151,373.34	150,839.25	152,697.10	157,243.52
Current expenses	42,440.61	59,756.34	30,330.06	42,757.31	88,735.51
Premiums paid	113,508.24	113,008.24	107,876.99	98,376.99	98,376.99
Cash items	45,684.62	34,511.45	38,798.81	35,388.87	19,972.31
Clear'g-house exch'gs	97,116.50	44,615.31	24,588.27	15,744.78	35,090.81
Bills of other banks	59,441.00	48,642.00	73,680.00	66,742.00	53,644.00
Uncur't & minor coins	258.18	765.83	715.20	1,105.83	596.50
Trade dollars	1,570.00	1,170.00	205.00	....	61.00
Specie	371,371.85	457,273.31	506,626.35	239,199.25	262,251.08
Legal-tender notes	495,400.00	504,218.00	668,576.00	883,780.00	792,247.00
U. S. cert's of deposit	....	....	....	....	....
5 % fund with Treas.	42,477.50	33,477.50	31,227.50	31,227.50	31,727.50
Due from U. S. Treas.	2,160.00	3,560.00	1,000.00	1,000.00	4,078.02
Total	14,069,516.55	14,109,130.55	14,045,706.01	14,133,976.47	14,081,336.58

by States and reserve cities—Continued.

ARKANSAS.

Liabilities.	DECEMBER 28.	MARCH 4.	MAY 13.	AUGUST 1.	OCTOBER 5.
	5 banks.	6 banks.	7 banks.	7 banks.	7 banks.
Capital stock	$705, 000. 00	$800, 000. 00	$850, 000. 00	$900, 000. 00	$950, 000. 00
Surplus fund	188, 000. 00	102, 300. 00	102, 300. 00	111, 500. 00	111, 500. 00
Undivided profits	70, 976. 31	48, 919. 47	86, 484. 15	75, 483. 44	101, 561. 85
Nat'l bank circulation	287, 520. 00	296, 100. 00	308, 040. 00	315, 840. 00	348, 740. 00
State bank circulation	....	....	....	....	....
Dividends unpaid	12, 134. 00	2, 388. 00	1, 332. 00	2, 302. 00	2, 182. 00
Individual deposits	2, 476, 921. 02	2, 711, 130. 09	2, 780, 643. 43	2, 401, 060. 40	2, 313, 140. 08
U. S. deposits	56, 099. 19	45, 309. 17	76, 528. 09	91, 526. 48	100, 409. 87
Dep'ts U.S.dis.officers	22, 975. 06	66, 874. 05	69, 547. 24	56, 706. 38	47, 079. 84
Due to national banks	41, 275. 50	9, 702. 19	12, 956. 78	21, 002. 62	17, 866. 28
Due to State banks	63, 026. 42	113, 068. 01	84, 779. 50	71, 408. 33	40, 801. 03
Notes re-discounted	10, 850. 45	....	....	20, 500. 00	252, 240. 54
Bills payable	....	....	....	....	15, 000. 00
Total	3, 935, 406. 95	4, 195, 790. 98	4, 393, 611. 19	4, 157, 380. 65	4, 200, 581. 49

KENTUCKY.

	50 banks.	50 banks.	50 banks.	59 banks.	59 banks.
Capital stock	$9, 758, 900. 00	$9, 758, 900. 00	$9, 758, 900. 00	$9, 758, 900. 00	$9, 758, 900. 00
Surplus fund	2, 181, 581. 12	2, 254, 089. 75	2, 224, 132. 56	2, 203, 485. 12	2, 290, 885. 12
Undivided profits	967, 860. 18	632, 215. 16	811, 541. 37	504, 517. 38	705, 459. 48
Nat'l bank circulation	3, 809, 080. 00	3, 415, 550. 00	3, 376, 370. 00	3, 052, 100. 00	3, 055, 800. 00
State bank circulation	....	....	....	....	....
Dividends unpaid	19, 001. 00	24, 472. 00	25, 452. 50	58, 598. 50	42, 290. 50
Individual deposits	9, 473, 170. 46	9, 841, 686. 60	9, 384, 302. 24	10, 352, 088. 08	10, 476, 083. 07
U. S. deposits	628, 905. 58	702, 941. 93	679, 144. 77	873, 596. 79	926, 623. 50
Dep'ts U.S.dis.officers	13, 511. 76	24, 785. 12	46, 970. 58	79, 973. 60	71, 828. 00
Due to national banks	676, 500. 23	461, 400. 55	608, 778. 12	485, 205. 94	426, 544. 89
Due to State banks	453, 523. 81	320, 296. 89	356, 318. 02	388, 735. 20	305, 473. 12
Notes re-discounted	219, 202. 11	180, 740. 37	332, 990. 86	331, 292. 64	224, 843. 42
Bills payable	8, 010. 56	....	1, 000. 00	....	15, 000. 00
Total	28, 210, 545. 81	27, 656, 078. 39	27, 606, 521. 02	28, 178, 553. 34	28, 305, 821. 10

CITY OF LOUISVILLE.

	9 banks.	9 banks.	9 banks.	9 banks.	9 banks.
Capital stock	$3, 551, 500. 00	$3, 551, 500. 00	$3, 551, 500. 00	$3, 551, 500. 00	$3, 551, 500. 00
Surplus fund	930, 503. 09	934, 003. 09	935, 111. 62	945, 111. 62	945, 111. 62
Undivided profits	234, 551. 09	251, 963. 48	200, 315. 76	194, 420. 91	304, 691. 03
Nat'l bank circulation	849, 490. 00	669, 400. 00	624, 490. 00	624, 490. 00	624, 490. 00
State bank circulation	....	....	....	....	....
Dividends unpaid	7, 088. 00	5, 918. 50	24, 604. 50	8, 898. 50	6, 684. 00
Individual deposits	3, 773, 744. 28	3, 018, 926. 16	4, 193, 430. 95	4, 071, 809. 51	4, 033, 281. 51
U. S deposits	759, 515. 86	694, 058. 15	754, 508. 03	621, 246. 89	482, 189. 70
Dep'ts U.S.dis.officers	182, 183. 19	248, 596. 66	117, 796. 64	233, 017. 51	364, 504. 85
Due to national banks	1, 681, 102. 58	2, 105, 670. 63	1, 858, 492. 08	1, 782, 353. 06	1, 634, 433. 80
Due to State banks	1, 507, 596. 79	1, 464, 744. 57	1, 606, 112. 94	1, 735, 425. 95	1, 564, 383. 30
Notes re-discounted	558, 181. 67	264, 250. 31	154, 334. 52	345, 702. 32	530, 006. 68
Bills payable	40, 000. 00	....	25, 000. 00	20, 000. 00	40, 000. 00
Total	14, 069, 516. 55	14, 109, 130. 55	14, 045, 706. 04	14, 133, 076. 17	14, 081, 336. 58

Abstract of reports since October 7, 1886, arranged

TENNESSEE.

Resources.	DECEMBER 28. 34 banks.	MARCH 4. 36 banks.	MAY 13. 38 banks.	AUGUST 1. 40 banks.	OCTOBER 5. 40 banks.
Loans and discounts.	$14,016,819.58	$14,951,641.80	$16,956,006.18	$17,848,881.08	$19,232,849.06
Bonds for circulation.	1,387,400.00	1,392,400.00	1,414,400.00	1,486,000.00	1,483,750.00
Bonds for deposits	450,000.00	449,900.00	450,000.00	450,000.00	450,000.00
U.S. bonds on hand	17,400.00	19,400.00	455,400.00	13,700.00	6,750.00
Other stocks and b'ds	541,410.88	586,953.58	447,017.46	450,849.72	445,425.07
Due from res've ag'ts	1,490,962.67	3,049,972.68	1,399,636.10	1,082,710.45	1,012,846.65
Due from nat'l banks	838,393.51	1,253,629.72	1,340,646.15	1,160,050.37	977,706.05
Due from State banks	200,783.34	406,415.08	300,921.92	164,652.30	204,567.32
Real estate, etc	450,730.16	450,820.35	455,491.84	485,569.50	487,821.79
Current expenses	100,704.25	153,931.54	107,769.53	67,372.30	90,921.17
Premiums paid	181,363.12	197,293.79	247,030.34	244,211.42	236,274.92
Cash items	153,350.96	355,892.26	204,629.88	202,534.40	278,657.20
Clear'g-house exch'gs	104,586.59	89,452.55	104,191.87	90,079.73	153,642.30
Bills of other banks	438,204.00	628,463.00	546,607.00	410,618.00	366,234.00
Uncurr't & minor coins	3,830.70	6,231.01	4,500.84	9,436.05	6,004.26
Trade dollars	2,469.25	2,337.25	....	100.00	....
Specie	818,712.94	957,481.39	1,051,284.84	921,660.70	863,549.15
Legal-tender notes	832,075.00	877,444.00	973,326.00	773,085.00	721,378.00
U.S. cert's of deposit	....	....	....	....	....
5% fund with Treas	62,232.40	60,307.50	59,735.00	62,589.50	63,061.12
Due from U.S. Treas	6,308.84	30,817.84	44,992.24	20,148.09	21,613.87
Total	22,161,307.18	25,846,194.42	26,141,096.19	26,041,155.84	27,103,955.55

OHIO.

	186 banks.	187 banks.	188 banks.	191 banks.	192 banks.
Loans and discounts	$46,001,784.58	$47,743,277.38	$49,955,597.64	$50,509,758.55	$51,173,331.06
Bonds for circulation	11,702,650.00	11,316,400.00	10,452,950.00	10,216,650.00	10,112,650.00
Bonds for deposits	790,000.00	865,000.00	965,000.00	995,000.00	905,000.00
U.S. bonds on hand	308,100.00	417,550.00	269,600.00	275,700.00	292,050.00
Other stocks and b'ds	2,172,071.98	2,187,154.72	1,982,421.98	2,265,290.64	2,444,000.85
Due from res've ag'ts	5,534,116.60	5,325,235.55	5,810,420.90	6,604,235.65	4,882,761.35
Due from nat'l banks	1,768,386.88	1,753,635.90	1,595,241.24	2,130,940.74	1,941,433.52
Due from State banks	506,674.39	499,938.18	417,134.63	441,842.61	430,768.56
Real estate, etc	1,847,698.65	1,833,124.43	1,832,174.70	1,877,419.74	1,893,677.74
Current expenses	88,095.27	360,271.59	290,972.36	256,145.68	433,374.08
Premiums paid	554,692.44	634,542.39	672,746.40	700,347.43	720,732.77
Cash items	447,916.30	529,642.66	496,968.75	464,960.49	484,772.03
Clear'g-house exch'gs	78,101.92	35,689.74	54,479.35	79,625.58	56,061.02
Bills of other banks	1,228,274.00	1,418,591.00	1,468,750.00	1,298,078.00	1,381,875.00
Uncurr't & minor coins	27,207.61	26,059.84	24,956.08	22,458.93	28,943.26
Trade dollars	37,211.10	37,272.05	11,201.80	4,866.85	13.00
Specie	2,912,048.34	2,856,559.62	2,875,412.09	2,783,950.31	2,923,055.91
Legal-tender notes	2,518,372.00	2,660,409.00	3,207,551.00	2,084,985.00	3,277,439.00
U.S. cert's of deposit	....	....	....	....	....
5% fund with Treas	493,616.91	456,482.24	446,871.05	438,953.75	429,310.24
Due from U.S. Treas	32,172.09	46,285.52	47,196.41	36,501.24	35,289.96
Total	80,248,250.58	81,438,124.71	82,737,637.23	84,357,738.19	83,931,561.35

CITY OF CINCINNATI.

	14 banks.	13 banks.	15 banks.	15 banks.	15 banks.
Loans and discounts	$24,895,512.93	$26,406,071.40	$28,355,732.22	$24,030,865.86	$24,007,014.49
Bonds for circulation	4,016,000.00	4,650,000.00	4,750,000.00	3,612,000.00	3,612,000.00
Bonds for deposits	1,519,000.00	2,374,000.00	2,876,500.00	2,084,000.00	2,119,000.00
U.S. bonds on hand	478,050.00	556,550.00	403,650.00	411,250.00	807,200.00
Other stocks and b'ds	1,391,938.40	2,801,146.16	2,656,118.43	2,479,722.50	2,567,573.16
Due from res've ag'ts	3,428,202.19	4,275,641.82	2,710,271.91	3,127,526.05	2,699,217.63
Due from nat'l banks	2,087,650.55	1,823,983.75	1,863,820.00	1,765,570.50	1,498,989.47
Due from State banks	801,817.66	891,477.11	882,021.97	835,810.38	722,988.31
Real estate, etc	324,383.07	333,350.37	380,073.58	300,688.38	308,146.16
Current expenses	230,651.66	186,598.03	141,102.41	158,663.71	251,007.62
Premiums paid	622,528.11	809,753.30	910,607.16	824,354.31	784,062.90
Cash items	113,404.30	96,828.30	76,612.57	41,854.58	118,474.14
Clear'g-house exch'gs	310,634.96	468,834.01	323,250.04	263,806.10	323,753.29
Bills of other banks	536,646.00	563,604.00	435,195.00	331,316.00	459,267.00
Uncurr't & minor coins	3,035.55	4,132.33	3,250.16	2,787.90	3,302.42
Trade dollars	18,019.00	20,186.00	2,023.00	....	....
Specie	1,155,171.34	1,231,383.85	1,124,480.80	593,930.00	663,168.33
Legal-tender notes	2,270,925.00	2,539,234.00	2,913,273.00	2,282,023.00	2,630,240.00
U.S. cert's of deposit	850,000.00	860,000.00	1,200,000.00	1,130,000.00	1,330,000.00
5% fund with Treas.	221,040.00	209,080.00	213,750.00	162,540.00	156,070.00
Due from U.S. Treas.	5,000.00	22,545.00	25,510.00	3,040.00	3,000.00
Total	46,170,610.95	51,125,390.36	52,277,851.27	44,631,848.27	45,354,893.01

by States and reserve cities—Continued.

TENNESSEE.

Liabilities.	DECEMBER 28. 34 banks.	MARCH 4. 36 banks.	MAY 13. 38 banks.	AUGUST 1. 40 banks.	OCTOBER 5. 40 banks.
Capital stock	$5,476,140.00	$5,042,500.00	$6,928,980.00	$7,324,690.00	$7,460,000.00
Surplus fund	1,036,043.15	1,121,307.80	1,380,307.80	1,455,757.80	1,461,057.80
Undivided profits	730,062.33	519,044.85	588,909.84	499,540.46	610,713.51
Nat'l-bank circulation	1,244,040.00	1,196,670.00	1,172,560.00	1,308,710.00	1,326,895.00
State-bank circulation	....	....	....	....	....
Dividends unpaid	1,508.00	1,702.00	2,568.00	8,008.50	3,492.00
Individual deposits	10,444,634.82	14,205,474.95	12,891,676.69	12,523,957.22	11,750,221.25
U. S. deposits	239,213.14	258,165.30	332,057.50	325,318.88	326,600.46
Dep'ts U.S.dis.officers	137,470.33	104,307.64	88,164.31	112,000.97	101,714.11
Due to national banks	1,540,129.85	1,274,088.80	1,401,087.50	1,177,386.57	1,533,763.47
Due to State banks	825,565.84	998,335.64	845,685.77	574,368.91	469,139.71
Notes re-discounted	425,599.72	134,507.44	458,080.94	680,566.53	1,901,052.21
Bills payable	60,000.00	....	50,117.84	50,850.00	150,300.00
Total	22,161,307.18	25,846,194.42	26,141,096.19	26,041,155.84	27,103,955.55

OHIO.

	186 banks.	187 banks.	188 banks.	191 banks.	192 banks.
Capital stock	$22,020,000.00	$22,112,000.00	$22,217,200.00	$22,564,370.00	$22,796,020.00
Surplus fund	4,867,527.57	5,006,364.23	5,099,024.10	5,189,691.66	5,206,305.51
Undivided profits	1,090,000.64	1,861,222.81	1,527,633.53	1,557,197.51	2,173,504.23
Nat'l-bank circulation	10,453,559.00	10,081,429.00	9,317,964.00	9,060,179.00	9,008,926.00
State-bank circulation	4,365.00	4,365.00	3,899.00	3,890.00	3,809.00
Dividends unpaid	38,089.40	23,001.12	79,320.73	50,352.80	43,295.80
Individual deposits	37,809,925.72	39,621,347.20	41,428,890.15	42,640,077.41	41,268,742.33
U. S. deposits	492,686.32	455,578.04	657,872.15	750,969.74	757,208.40
Dep'ts U.S.dis.officers	176,438.67	268,062.92	207,222.27	171,247.43	174,583.16
Due to national banks	1,467,286.84	1,081,391.65	1,212,061.71	1,223,879.74	1,487,434.80
Due to State banks	644,292.65	673,379.97	596,866.41	680,963.79	636,342.56
Notes re-discounted	249,478.77	221,482.77	349,683.09	308,193.11	336,963.31
Bills payable	34,000.00	28,500.00	40,000.00	70,717.00	38,156.25
Total	80,248,250.58	81,438,124.71	82,737,687.23	84,357,738.19	83,931,561.85

CITY OF CINCINNATI.

	14 banks.	13 banks.	15 banks.	15 banks.	15 banks.
Capital stock	$10,100,000.00	$10,100,000.00	$11,010,000.00	$10,225,000.00	$10,400,000.00
Surplus fund	1,350,000.00	1,420,000.00	1,595,000.00	1,820,000.00	1,820,000.00
Undivided profits	1,012,408.29	765,771.61	795,310.54	752,409.16	970,568.67
Nat'l-bank circulation	4,353,590.00	4,178,440.00	4,237,990.00	3,228,410.00	3,226,840.00
State-bank circulation	....	....	....	....	....
Dividends unpaid	4,664.00	8,357.00	27,529.50	19,054.00	7,017.50
Individual deposits	18,003,167.62	20,098,969.80	20,367,817.60	17,178,961.32	18,380,460.13
U. S. deposits	1,304,936.61	2,009,881.69	2,509,936.61	2,034,520.52	2,075,184.19
Dep'ts U.S.dis.officers	....	....	....	....	....
Due to national banks	6,812,547.97	8,497,070.67	7,755,675.18	5,800,039.80	5,273,030.40
Due to State banks	2,887,996.46	3,575,058.59	3,439,291.84	2,731,372.53	2,665,453.14
Notes re-discounted	....	....	....	40,771.94	45,079.88
Bills payable	332,300.00	561,850.00	539,300.00	611,300.00	491,200.00
Total	46,170,610.95	51,125,399.36	52,277,851.27	44,531,848.27	45,354,833.91

Abstract of reports since October 7, 1886, arranged

CITY OF CLEVELAND.

Resources.	DECEMBER 28.	MARCH 4.	MAY 13.	AUGUST 1.	OCTOBER 5.
	9 banks.	9 banks.	9 banks.	9 banks.	9 banks.
Loans and discounts	$15, 723, 735. 25	$16, 018, 341. 73	$16, 086, 496. 91	$16, 438, 621. 32	$17, 607, 759. 64
Bonds for circulation.	655, 000. 00	655, 000. 00	505, 000. 00	605, 000. 00	605, 000. 00
Bonds for deposits..	600, 000. 00	605, 000. 00	340, 000. 00	340, 000. 00	340, 000. 00
U. S. bonds on hand..	....	....	....	....	....
Other stocks and b'ds	491, 073. 50	265, 161. 17	214, 518. 50	214, 493. 50	207, 093. 50
Due from res've ag'ts	1, 551, 382. 89	1, 598, 256. 55	1, 413, 773. 52	1, 593, 660. 42	1, 179, 021. 08
Due from nat'l banks	1, 377, 518. 40	1, 233, 121. 19	1, 239, 281. 54	1, 102, 530. 40	1, 033, 033. 94
Due from State banks	447, 225. 03	495, 478. 57	547, 988. 36	412, 817. 83	410, 348. 63
Real estate, etc......	672, 589. 64	675, 424. 27	627, 886. 96	630, 220. 44	644, 081. 58
Current expenses....	77, 227. 06	144, 145. 30	4, 365. 79	106, 011. 77	159, 837. 99
Premiums paid......	22, 000. 00	22, 000. 00	34, 687. 50	34, 687. 50	34, 687. 50
Cash items..........	32, 870. 89	54, 002. 97	26, 469. 20	67, 065. 76	118, 187. 10
Clear'g-house exch'gs	92, 866. 88	123, 875. 00	151, 024. 35	108, 575. 86	180, 789. 52
Bills of other banks..	230, 984. 00	230, 282. 00	195, 772. 00	158, 326. 00	177, 238. 00
Uncur't & minor coins	8, 260. 21	4, 323. 06	2, 128. 20	6, 208. 47	3, 168. 90
Trade dollars	1, 150. 00	1, 100. 00	....	400. 00	....
Specie	1, 084, 037. 93	1, 100, 167. 90	1, 084, 380. 70	837, 026. 29	818, 379. 43
Legal-tender notes ..	877, 700. 00	745, 000. 00	900, 000. 00	686, 000. 00	881, 000. 00
U. S. cert's of deposit.	15, 000. 00	15, 000. 00	15, 000. 00	15, 000. 00	16, 000. 00
5 % fund with Treas.	29, 475. 00	27, 435. 00	21, 675. 00	22, 725. 00	26, 725. 00
Due from U. S. Treas.	1, 040. 00	2, 140. 00	3, 990. 00	1, 040. 00	3, 040. 00
Total..........	23, 991, 136. 68	24, 015, 254. 86	23, 414, 388. 53	23, 443, 019. 56	24, 445, 891. 81

INDIANA.

	92 banks.	92 banks.	92 banks.	93 banks.	93 banks.
Loans and discounts .	$26, 137, 210. 36	$25, 679, 282. 24	$26, 911, 858. 52	$27, 135, 054. 07	$28, 030, 386. 10
Bonds for circulation.	5, 517, 800. 00	5, 355, 300. 00	4, 956, 300. 00	4, 748, 800. 00	4, 723, 800. 00
Bonds for deposits ..	1, 230, 000. 00	1, 230, 000. 00	1, 130, 000. 00	1, 130, 000. 00	1, 200, 000. 00
U. S. bonds on hand..	638, 150. 00	715, 650. 00	633, 150. 00	774, 750. 00	865, 450. 00
Other stocks and b'ds	1, 109, 431. 13	1, 135, 125. 36	1, 151, 476. 83	1, 190, 364. 07	1, 112, 291. 78
Due from res've ag'ts.	3, 971, 198. 22	4, 687, 054. 83	4, 165, 995. 74	4, 359, 523. 28	3, 453, 168. 93
Due from nat'l banks.	2, 040, 126. 19	2, 051, 234. 66	2, 409, 043. 71	2, 455, 700. 36	2, 222, 702. 16
Due from State banks	375, 115. 54	322, 438. 08	436, 537. 01	384, 756. 01	337, 010. 05
Real estate, etc......	1, 164, 263. 74	1, 177, 836. 67	1, 198, 186. 07	1, 215, 540. 75	1, 228, 100. 41
Current expenses....	253, 068. 36	127, 700. 29	230, 694. 78	84, 175. 10	189, 176. 33
Premiums paid......	497, 426. 92	492, 061. 72	531, 893. 31	527, 309. 00	561, 105. 02
Cash items..........	203, 758. 25	241, 612. 78	232, 263. 74	271, 917. 70	272, 670. 68
Clear'g-house exch'gs	57, 650. 60	80, 771. 22	43, 247. 42	101, 712. 43	157, 043. 26
Bills of other banks..	1, 047, 427. 00	745, 109. 00	1, 044, 525. 00	1, 071, 209. 00	906, 951. 00
Uncur't & minor coins	13, 940. 58	17, 982. 19	15, 801. 98	15, 297. 80	14, 519. 14
Trade dollars	20, 961. 45	19, 636. 25	6, 574. 75	172. 85	....
Specie	2, 603, 112. 21	2, 587, 588. 36	2, 701, 483. 68	2, 412, 665. 72	2, 501, 486. 46
Legal-tender notes ..	1, 735, 474. 00	1, 741, 470. 00	1, 867, 942. 00	1, 805, 835. 00	1, 977, 615. 00
U. S. cert's of deposit.	....	....	....	....	....
5 % fund with Treas.	239, 471. 14	225, 110. 99	215, 875. 12	209, 209. 42	205, 701. 92
Due from U. S. Treas.	7, 052. 86	12, 905. 97	12, 239. 32	18, 561. 37	30, 053. 16
Total	48, 043, 538. 55	48, 045, 879. 61	49, 895, 089. 88	49, 912, 834. 13	50, 089, 921. 40

ILLINOIS.

	154 banks.	156 banks.	156 banks.	158 banks.	160 banks.
Loans and discounts.	$32, 003, 573. 01	$33, 725, 843. 62	$35, 544, 864. 06	$35, 162, 556. 98	$36, 048, 215. 84
Bonds for circulation.	5, 331, 650. 00	5, 158, 650. 00	4, 790, 250. 00	4, 740, 500. 00	4, 770, 500. 00
Bonds for deposits ..	905, 000. 00	905, 000. 00	1, 095, 000. 00	1, 195, 000. 00	1, 205, 000. 00
U. S. bonds on hand..	241, 450. 00	274, 650. 00	313, 100. 00	368, 200. 00	368, 800. 00
Other stocks and b'ds	2, 257, 963. 97	2, 273, 600. 14	2, 206, 830. 11	2, 184, 122. 86	2, 460, 694. 37
Due from res've ag'ts	5, 877, 309. 00	7, 186, 858. 12	6, 884, 399. 71	8, 627, 099. 18	7, 473, 836. 61
Due from nat'l banks.	1, 110, 497. 14	1, 580, 701. 53	1, 385, 504. 21	1, 844, 800. 03	1, 817, 133. 08
Due from State banks	211, 393. 45	262, 870. 20	257, 016. 42	292, 214. 65	252, 102. 28
Real estate, etc......	1, 375, 555. 16	1, 303, 213. 34	1, 387, 436. 41	1, 441, 005. 28	1, 473, 420. 00
Current expenses....	275, 342. 71	185, 596. 45	316, 211. 17	126, 380. 74	213, 150. 25
Premiums paid	524, 278. 72	521, 262. 86	532, 599. 30	552, 940. 70	582, 573. 31
Cash items..........	376, 643. 47	385, 342. 23	423, 130. 91	338, 664. 11	426, 550. 67
Clear'g-house exch'gs	61, 587. 20	59, 215. 12	50, 935. 96	95, 608. 00	91, 683. 47
Bills of other banks..	988, 230. 00	916, 426. 00	890, 527. 00	912, 665. 00	906, 942. 00
Uncur't & minor coins	14, 747. 42	20, 045. 17	19, 709. 00	18, 543. 42	20, 531. 44
Trade dollars	3, 214. 05	3, 244. 15	532. 00	708. 00	15. 00
Specie	2, 514, 447. 50	2, 570, 253. 48	2, 604, 391. 09	2, 613, 251. 27	2, 692, 576. 26
Legal-tender notes ..	1, 799, 727. 00	1, 866, 452. 00	1, 812, 004. 00	1, 801, 289. 00	1, 821, 456. 00
U. S. cert's of deposit	10, 000. 00	10, 000. 00	10, 000. 00	10, 000. 00	10, 000. 00
5 % fund with Treas.	235, 772. 43	225, 625. 98	215, 101. 55	208, 550. 40	211, 000. 48
Due from U. S. Treas.	15, 473. 47	20, 614. 09	14, 048. 67	11, 944. 22	18, 335. 97
Total..........	56, 013, 804. 70	59, 635, 461. 48	60, 771, 688. 17	62, 553, 033. 90	63, 023, 698. 58

by States and reserve cities—Continued.

CITY OF CLEVELAND.

Liabilities.	DECEMBER 28. 9 banks.	MARCH 4. 9 banks.	MAY 13. 9 banks.	AUGUST 1. 9 banks.	OCTOBER 5. 9 banks.
Capital stock	$6,650,000.00	$6,700,000.00	$6,700,000.00	$6,700,000.00	$6,700,000.00
Surplus fund	800,000.00	809,000.00	892,000.00	892,000.00	892,000.00
Undivided profits	282,066.86	451,053.02	190,417.14	406,098.25	585,642.60
Nat'l-bank circulation	580,410.00	580,450.00	454,470.00	453,950.00	544,450.00
State-bank circulation	....	....	....	....	....
Dividends unpaid	750.00	327.00	9,053.00	3,314.00	918.00
Individual deposits	12,126,703.15	12,101,415.91	11,216,065.40	10,891,963.09	10,309,915.45
U. S. deposits	532,063.39	525,862.25	289,117.24	286,998.01	284,793.59
Dep'ts U.S.dis.officers	6,653.13	5,000.91	15,731.66	16,809.32	21,185.87
Due to national banks	1,062,263.05	1,158,772.10	1,378,006.49	1,467,772.51	1,202,093.38
Due to State banks	755,107.57	815,343.67	774,857.48	844,183.35	807,669.43
Notes re-discounted	....	....	440,800.03	335,926.00	1,113,274.09
Bills payable	1,177,098.63	750,000.00	1,032,000.00	1,144,000.00	1,894,000.00
Total	23,991,136.68	24,015,254.86	23,414,388.53	23,443,010.56	24,445,891.81

INDIANA.

	92 banks.	92 banks.	92 banks	93 banks.	93 banks.
Capital stock	$11,894,500.00	$11,894,500.00	$11,844,500.00	$11,894,500.00	$11,894,500.00
Surplus fund	3,400,238.72	3,437,825.10	3,467,210.22	3,535,463.22	3,531,613.22
Undivided profits	1,677,803.27	1,112,185.93	1,422,302.04	1,152,072.20	1,505,052.20
Nat'l-bank circulation	4,889,540.00	4,731,790.00	4,410,600.00	4,215,820.00	4,217,870.00
State-bank circulation	....	....	....	....	....
Dividends unpaid	8,210.50	12,805.05	9,442.90	23,981.27	22,035.21
Individual deposits	23,330,772.83	24,002,648.14	25,317,961.37	25,474,245.46	25,254,102.80
U. S. deposits	747,350.63	793,800.10	608,281.63	724,255.97	754,224.57
Dep'ts U.S.dis.officers	324,990.53	305,654.53	321,032.66	220,732.00	262,700.52
Due to national banks	1,421,937.74	1,280,914.17	1,370,942.81	1,342,294.78	1,431,547.15
Due to State banks	1,037,312.00	1,036,008.87	1,098,296.21	1,286,052.21	1,183,850.18
Notes re-discounted	10,705.00	37,500.00	15,420.14	32,515.93	24,446.55
Bills payable	157.63	157.63	....	....	5,000.00
Total	48,943,538.55	48,645,879.61	49,895,080.88	49,912,834.13	50,083,921.40

ILLINOIS.

	154 banks.	156 banks.	156 banks.	154 banks.	160 banks.
Capital stock	$14,036,300.00	$14,018,970.00	$14,038,900.00	$14,161,500.00	$14,341,500.00
Surplus fund	4,284,155.23	4,433,133.92	4,462,440.17	4,528,791.75	4,533,968.58
Undivided profits	2,346,907.60	1,829,535.01	2,077,733.61	1,697,767.15	2,081,019.42
Nat'l-bank circulation	4,754,435.00	4,577,445.00	4,258,770.00	4,170,150.00	4,210,305.00
State-bank circulation	....	....	....	....	....
Dividends unpaid	10,213.00	22,874.50	28,050.00	35,563.25	22,323.75
Individual deposits	29,300,706.06	32,705,614.55	33,537,435.09	35,376,370.64	35,161,306.04
U. S. deposits	848,318.30	869,146.98	911,552.23	1,010,964.55	1,073,068.51
Dep'ts U.S.dis.officers	77,344.89	28,503.27	45,157.53	25,508.45	30,007.07
Due to national banks	491,742.05	455,848.73	532,504.08	662,036.06	574,002.12
Due to State banks	456,761.29	654,088.34	760,771.39	855,481.15	851,907.72
Notes re-discounted	96,781.28	30,724.16	108,303.44	10,000.00	110,590.57
Bills payable	21,000.00	....	10,000.00	....	4,000.00
Total	56,913,864.70	59,635,464.48	60,771,688.17	62,553,033.90	63,023,698.58

Abstract of reports since October 7, 1886, arranged

CITY OF CHICAGO.

Resources.	DECEMBER 28. 15 banks.	MARCH 4. 15 banks.	MAY 13. 18 banks.	AUGUST 1. 18 banks.	OCTOBER 5. 18 banks.
Loans and discounts	$53, 100, 248. 57	$57, 337, 718. 81	$62, 972, 279. 76	$60, 042, 503. 52	$61, 156, 286. 09
Bonds for circulation	900, 000. 00	900, 000. 00	1, 050, 000. 00	1, 050, 000. 00	1, 050, 000. 00
Bonds for deposits	200, 000. 00	340, 000. 00	340, 000. 00	310, 000. 00	340, 000. 00
U. S. bonds on hand	536, 850. 00	557, 150. 00	401, 700. 00	622, 150. 00	421, 750. 00
Other stocks and b'ds	1, 871, 985. 05	2, 109, 920. 74	2, 115, 134. 41	2, 485, 413. 03	2, 518, 569. 40
Due from res've ag'ts	7, 319, 837. 73	8, 870, 074. 16	....	....	....
Due from nat'l banks	4, 327, 939. 12	5, 022, 261. 69	10, 568, 867. 52	10, 182, 857. 01	9, 510, 021. 74
Due from State banks	2, 531, 311. 30	2, 561, 589. 43	2, 961, 030. 54	3, 072, 374. 30	2, 702, 214. 58
Real estate, etc	710, 888. 44	706, 125. 11	707, 036. 01	715, 072. 08	715, 474. 46
Current expenses	134, 051. 06	60, 710. 14	91, 203. 01	48, 069. 33	83, 222. 30
Premiums paid	63, 426. 34	62, 290. 79	94, 142. 01	127, 158. 75	120, 015. 03
Cash items	28, 168. 83	27, 375. 20	31, 608. 62	35, 190. 40	33, 944. 76
Clear'g-house exch'gs	2, 897, 087. 11	3, 700, 656. 95	3, 970, 099. 03	5, 802, 207. 62	4, 426, 304. 00
Bills of other banks	1, 168, 104. 00	1, 139, 283. 00	1, 474, 485. 00	1, 651, 814. 00	969, 093. 00
Uncur't & minor coins	12, 091. 26	19, 935. 10	19, 071. 33	18, 307. 26	21, 081. 82
Trade dollars	....	....	....	....	....
Specie	8, 578, 587. 00	10, 199, 129. 17	13, 003, 485. 40	14, 649, 384. 72	12, 958, 417. 74
Legal-tender notes	4, 686, 676. 00	5, 328, 505. 00	7, 516, 216. 00	7, 171, 452. 00	6, 623, 720. 00
U. S. cert's of deposit	110, 000. 00	110, 000. 00	110, 000. 00	110, 000. 00	110, 000. 00
5 % fund with Treas	40, 500. 00	40, 500. 00	42, 750. 00	47, 250. 00	47, 250. 00
Due from U. S. Treas	42, 620. 00	39, 100. 00	69, 450. 00	39, 250. 00	56, 500. 00
Total	89, 260, 971. 81	99, 132, 325. 29	107, 563, 558. 67	108, 210, 454. 05	103, 864, 765. 52

MICHIGAN.

	97 banks.	97 banks.	97 banks.	99 banks.	100 banks.
Loans and discounts	$25, 973, 076. 39	$26, 922, 743. 71	$27, 964, 986. 55	$28, 649, 456. 19	$29, 076, 187. 23
Bonds for circulation	3, 446, 500. 00	3, 304, 000. 00	3, 221, 500. 00	3, 046, 500. 00	3, 012, 750. 00
Bonds for deposits	50, 000. 00	50, 000. 00	50, 000. 00	50, 000. 00	50, 000. 00
U. S. bonds on hand	74, 850. 00	91, 550. 00	105, 650. 00	100, 150. 00	45, 050. 00
Other stocks and b'ds	627, 319. 29	584, 800. 66	631, 267. 25	647, 968. 83	645, 040. 56
Due from res've ag'ts	3, 452, 909. 71	3, 374, 304. 64	3, 073, 074. 47	3, 122, 597. 57	2, 962, 832. 01
Due from nat'l banks	723, 780. 82	842, 938. 58	772, 134. 50	600, 734. 56	607, 924. 21
Due from State banks	120, 012. 91	117, 806. 65	111, 270. 62	1[illegible], 052. 80	109, 435. 89
Real estate, etc	1, 069, 707. 59	1, 072, 655. 69	1, 033, 647. 78	1, 063, 656. 44	1, 092, 294. 82
Current expenses	244, 850. 51	110, 513. 75	189, 199. 89	70, 110. 10	150, 241. 79
Premiums paid	246, 283. 48	236, 545. 10	245, 801. 78	248, 419. 12	258, 991. 57
Cash items	220, 296. 09	247, 720. 36	186, 658. 58	222, 662. 88	306, 505. 87
Clear'g-house exch'gs	....	....	....	....	....
Bills of other banks	576, 917. 00	368, 405. 00	515, 248. 00	471, 424. 00	406, 022. 00
Uncur't & minor coins	11, 540. 40	15, 863. 73	13, 686. 43	13, 039. 98	14, 388. 39
Trade dollars	3, 775. 45	3, 825. 20	607. 85	287. 75	35. 00
Specie	1, 685, 976. 22	1, 612, 170. 83	1, 607, 034. 61	1, 619, 699. 04	1, 635, 911. 67
Legal-tender notes	912, 108. 00	711, 437. 00	997, 908. 00	957, 568. 00	853, 715. 00
U. S. cert's of deposit	....	....	....	....	....
5 % fund with Treas	155, 067. 00	147, 940. 15	143, 972. 50	135, 444. 50	134, 400. 50
Due from U. S. Treas	33, 763. 97	19, 618. 99	31, 005. 90	17, 588. 25	31, 427. 43
Total	39, 628, 734. 83	39, 834, 849. 04	40, 915, 254. 80	41, 173, 200. 01	42, 002, 243. 91

CITY OF DETROIT.

	7 banks.	7 banks.	7 banks.	8 banks.	8 banks.
Loans and discounts	$10, 926, 840. 25	$10, 750, 271. 63	$11, 312, 877. 41	$12, 525, 686. 25	$12, 805, 817. 39
Bonds for circulation	400, 000. 00	400, 000. 00	400, 000. 00	400, 000. 00	400, 000. 00
Bonds for deposits	500, 000. 00	500, 000. 00	500, 000. 00	500, 000. 00	500, 000. 00
U. S. bonds on hand	....	....	....	200. 00	....
Other stocks and b'ds	3, 000. 00	18, 402. 41	18, 402. 41	11, 629. 84	11, 273. 49
Due from res've ag'ts	1, 207, 170. 01	1, 925, 281. 69	1, 466, 038. 26	1, 856, 872. 22	1, 779, 600. 78
Due from nat'l banks	984, 278. 69	1, 153, 577. 82	1, 025, 383. 07	774, 716. 37	908, 063. 58
Due from State banks	233, 322. 18	210, 025. 51	155, 853. 86	150, 368. 16	209, 848. 81
Real estate, etc	99, 190. 33	99, 170. 23	120, 407. 48	124, 071. 13	122, 071. 13
Current expenses	60, 164. 50	23, 115. 92	38, 125. 78	11, 463. 76	29, 708. 68
Premiums paid	165, 674. 54	165, 362. 04	165, 362. 01	101, 937. 47	101, 875. 97
Cash items	37, 469. 68	35, 565. 13	39, 832. 74	46, 156. 51	20, 945. 58
Clear'g-house exch'gs	251, 417. 22	229, 301. 80	305, 104. 96	370, 646. 98	285, 868. 14
Bills of other banks	189, 141. 00	163, 636. 00	201, 169. 00	232, 163. 00	151, 129. 00
Uncur't & minor coins	6, 188. 42	10, 591. 86	3, 838. 53	4, 311. 95	5, 481. 60
Trade dollars	....	....	....	....	....
Specie	1, 080, 231. 05	1, 106, 227. 55	1, 123, 894. 75	1, 185, 926. 76	1, 061, 667. 01
Legal-tender notes	813, 977. 00	696, 708. 00	910, 538. 00	985, 347. 00	831, 416. 00
U. S. cert's of deposit	....	....	....	....	....
5 % fund with Treas	18, 000. 00	18, 000. 00	18, 000. 00	15, 750. 00	18, 000. 00
Due from U. S. Treas	1, 263. 38	15, 493. 38	6, 333. 33	5, 933. 38	21, 709. 26
Total	16, 077, 331. 25	17, 526, 730. 07	17, 811, 251. 67	19, 393, 180. 78	19, 367, 077. 32

by States and reserve cities—Continued.

CITY OF CHICAGO.

Liabilities.	DECEMBER 28.	MARCH 4.	MAY 13.	AUGUST 1	OCTOBER 5.
	15 banks.	15 banks.	18 banks.	18 banks.	18 banks.
Capital stock	$13, 950, 000. 00	$13, 950, 000. 00	$14, 640, 000. 00	$14, 990, 000. 00	$15, 050, 000. 00
Surplus fund	3, 308, 000. 00	3, 715, 000. 00	3, 885, 000. 00	3, 987, 000. 00	3, 987, 000. 00
Undivided profits	1, 688, 202. 68	1, 066, 554. 13	1, 413, 781. 21	1, 421, 079. 00	1, 755, 143. 79
Nat'l-bank circulation	680, 240. 00	677, 750. 00	671, 535. 00	782, 485. 00	817, 150. 00
State-bank circulation	....	....	....	....	....
Dividends unpaid	2, 000. 00	3, 132. 00	4, 352. 50	7, 338. 00	25, 774. 00
Individual deposits	40, 792, 595. 05	44, 420, 413. 14	51, 401, 893. 56	48, 582, 195. 87	46, 737, 360. 76
U. S. deposits	147, 242. 45	206, 696. 00	299, 483. 44	296, 211. 42	207, 045. 85
Dep'ts U.S. dis. officers	....	....	....	....	....
Due to national banks	16, 817, 773. 66	20, 707, 179. 41	21, 380, 155. 70	22, 466, 992. 14	20, 529, 118. 90
Due to State banks	11, 874, 017. 07	14, 295, 600. 61	13, 861, 357. 26	15, 676, 251. 72	14, 666, 172. 22
Notes re-discounted	....	....	....	....	....
Bills payable	....	....	....	....	....
Total	89, 260, 971. 81	90, 132, 325. 29	107, 563, 558. 67	108, 210, 454. 05	103, 864, 765. 52

MICHIGAN.

	97 banks.	97 banks.	97 banks.	99 banks.	100 banks.
Capital stock	$10, 529, 200. 00	$10 534, 600. 00	$10, 534, 600. 00	$10, 644, 600. 00	$10, 674, 000. 00
Surplus fund	2, 033, 253. 69	2, 106, 715. 92	2, 109, 715. 92	2, 230, 596. 80	2, 190, 396. 80
Undivided profits	1, 690, 528. 79	1, 204, 144. 57	1, 529, 579. 91	1, 131, 031. 47	1, 473, 786. 47
Nat'l-bank circulation	3, 073, 670. 00	2, 934, 915. 00	2, 861, 870. 00	2, 685, 885. 00	2, 673, 585. 00
State-bank circulation	....	....	....	....	....
Dividends unpaid	13, 704. 46	13, 628. 69	8, 359. 31	32, 295. 17	104, 627. 72
Individual deposits	21, 379, 564. 88	22, 040, 440. 95	22, 349, 872. 41	23, 241, 568. 96	23, 315, 420. 44
U. S. deposits	39, 108. 39	43, 533. 28	41, 551. 19	42, 760. 51	38, 410. 48
Dep'ts U.S. dis. officers	7, 263. 18	953. 62	3, 091. 90	2, 916. 17	5, 720. 17
Due to national banks	334, 857. 88	242, 936. 90	286, 482. 60	168, 241. 82	346, 928. 63
Due to State banks	384, 773. 87	307, 461. 07	358, 393. 47	320, 959. 04	407, 435. 95
Notes re-discounted	142, 749. 69	305, 498. 44	831, 738. 09	662, 405. 07	731, 332. 28
Bills payable	....	10, 000. 00	....	10, 000. 00	40, 000. 00
Total	39, 628, 734. 83	39, 834, 849. 04	40, 915, 254. 80	41, 173, 260. 01	42, 002, 243. 04

CITY OF DETROIT.

	7 banks.	7 banks.	7 banks.	8 banks.	8 banks.
Capital stock	$3, 300, 000. 00	$3, 300, 000. 00	$3, 300, 000. 00	$3, 775, 030. 00	$3, 883, 540. 00
Surplus fund	399, 000. 00	424, 300. 00	427, 400. 00	451, 000. 00	454, 000. 00
Undivided profits	454, 614. 98	311, 019. 52	395, 710. 83	301, 001. 66	374, 008. 84
Nat'l-bank circulation	342, 930. 00	336, 080. 00	334, 310. 00	285, 890. 00	328, 750. 00
State-bank circulation	....	....	....	....	....
Dividends unpaid	....	551. 80	412. 50	630. 00	5, 735. 00
Individual deposits	8, 030, 295. 68	8, 571, 329. 41	8, 905, 965. 04	9, 855, 066. 57	9, 084, 103. 73
U. S. deposits	346, 094. 96	237, 419. 10	290, 758. 69	204, 524. 64	193, 543. 84
Dep'ts U.S. dis. officers	96, 712. 97	226, 608. 50	168, 215. 01	192, 713. 42	241, 009. 18
Due to national banks	1, 587, 938. 86	1, 518, 482. 59	1, 426, 943. 13	1, 780, 160. 35	1, 612, 876. 95
Due to State banks	2, 399, 493. 02	2, 600, 940. 05	2, 504, 963. 72	2, 394, 606. 95	2, 470, 323. 15
Notes re-discounted	20, 256. 58	....	29, 536. 75	83, 540. 10	110, 090. 63
Bills payable	....	....	....	....	....
Total	16, 977, 331. 25	17, 526, 730. 97	17, 844, 251. 07	19, 303, 180. 78	19, 367, 077. 32

Abstract of reports since October 7, 1886, arranged

WISCONSIN.

Resources.	DECEMBER 28.	MARCH 4.	MAY 13.	AUGUST 1.	OCTOBER 5.
	47 banks.	50 banks.	51 banks.	53 banks.	53 banks.
Loans and discounts	$11,557,080.56	$12,262,818.54	$13,158,894.39	$13,140,060.37	$13,444,023.36
Bonds for circulation	1,462,500.00	1,444,000.00	1,363,000.00	1,406,750.00	1,373,000.00
Bonds for deposits	100,000.00	100,000.00	150,000.00	150,000.00	150,000.00
U.S. bonds on hand	108,000.00	5,300.00	6,500.00	5,850.00	11,950.00
Other stocks and b'ds	609,449.47	696,188.11	644,301.17	604,277.88	615,572.88
Due from res'veag'ts	2,138,636.33	2,038,900.17	1,738,912.65	2,307,331.13	1,999,253.46
Due from nat'l banks	377,221.30	434,205.13	446,574.72	400,631.58	385,933.15
Due from State banks	125,080.46	111,243.96	67,050.90	145,758.57	115,381.91
Real estate, etc	372,907.01	371,470.64	385,644.36	393,746.00	400,730.50
Current expenses	91,343.25	47,940.91	78,243.61	23,624.41	65,971.82
Premiums paid	122,196.33	115,408.00	123,370.16	129,118.33	131,160.27
Cash items	77,253.03	101,044.03	83,151.47	86,998.49	88,514.95
Clear'g-house exch'gs	....	....	....	....	....
Bills of other banks	261,267.00	215,432.00	260,217.00	253,461.00	246,622.00
Uncur't & minor coins	6,206.37	8,373.97	8,200.45	9,606.47	8,393.04
Trade dollars	319.20	320.00	17.00	....	....
Specie	912,018.14	984,365.23	908,197.77	913,634.41	995,859.66
Legal-tender notes	448,754.00	407,923.00	519,047.00	528,344.00	481,901.00
U.S. cert's of deposit	....	....	....	....	....
5% fund with Treas	65,024.36	61,478.40	60,132.80	60,458.50	60,455.96
Due from U.S. Treas	5,580.54	5,029.70	5,629.70	100.00	2,771.00
Total	18,871,738.25	19,411,441.79	20,007,604.15	20,649,752.04	20,586,515.05

CITY OF MILWAUKEE.

	3 banks.	3 banks.	3 banks.	3 banks.	3 banks.
Loans and discounts	$4,150,235.87	$4,142,446.11	$4,175,758.07	$3,849,261.79	$4,332,906.20
Bonds for circulation	360,000.00	360,000.00	310,000.00	300,000.00	300,000.00
Bonds for deposits	550,000.00	550,000.00	500,000.00	580,000.00	580,000.00
U.S. bonds on hand	2,350.00	1,800.00	....	5,050.00	4,500.00
Other stocks and b'ds	314,659.14	329,629.27	314,104.40	339,873.18	360,500.61
Due from res've ag'ts	587,555.20	750,459.96	938,620.76	739,176.45	676,965.14
Due from nat'l banks	422,053.08	769,560.98	286,764.21	208,883.46	95,678.30
Due from State banks	41,212.20	41,450.05	41,001.40	31,772.33	45,562.89
Real estate, etc	120,000.00	120,000.00	120,000.00	120,000.00	90,000.00
Current expenses	12,782.26	4,749.80	12,576.57	2,308.01	6,500.14
Premiums paid	16,835.85	13,186.60	22,934.60	30,763.35	26,695.46
Cash items	1,895.94	625.03	663.80	529.27	1,850.69
Clear'g-house exch'gs	156,591.41	184,882.09	200,669.80	130,410.07	142,221.41
Bills of other banks	13,852.00	13,616.00	17,081.00	21,447.00	14,001.00
Uncur't & minor coins	3,306.44	3,561.40	4,025.13	2,163.14	3,302.50
Trade dollars	....	....	....	....	....
Specie	708,834.00	718,843.00	813,502.79	726,520.00	532,678.00
Legal-tender notes	467,876.00	499,834.00	504,507.00	597,556.00	520,015.00
U.S. cert's of deposit	....	....	....	....	....
5% fund with Treas	16,200.00	16,200.00	13,950.00	13,500.00	13,500.00
Due from U.S. Treas	5,000.00	11,300.00	2,000.00	5,000.00	....
Total	7,051,299.30	8,532,146.18	8,280,049.53	7,764,214.05	7,765,117.34

IOWA.

	126 banks.	126 banks.	126 banks.	127 banks.	128 banks.
Loans and discounts	$22,464,066.83	$22,976,818.33	$23,501,243.66	$22,847,872.05	$24,154,685.11
Bonds for circulation	3,315,000.00	3,173,000.00	3,080,500.00	3,063,500.00	3,000,500.00
Bonds for deposits	350,000.00	350,000.00	250,000.00	150,000.00	150,000.00
U.S. bonds on hand	109,600.00	130,000.00	107,050.00	100,450.00	950.00
Other stocks and b'ds	902,917.67	937,778.48	923,698.74	898,360.13	934,445.40
Due from res've ag'ts	2,811,092.92	3,208,506.02	3,035,323.43	3,079,001.63	3,091,454.14
Due from nat'l banks	1,306,032.95	1,012,340.05	1,814,064.04	1,753,397.50	1,502,207.28
Due from State banks	271,301.76	268,490.51	218,311.42	264,714.58	263,185.07
Real estate, etc	1,576,211.39	1,582,210.61	1,580,420.09	1,610,524.77	1,607,433.19
Current expenses	315,467.24	152,023.62	272,167.07	90,506.35	252,283.21
Premiums paid	234,478.00	250,666.32	271,036.31	258,716.42	253,000.54
Cash items	272,091.25	237,727.70	264,537.93	258,734.64	322,288.59
Clear'g-house exch'gs	....	....	....	....	....
Bills of other banks	651,880.00	559,479.00	558,232.00	601,207.00	540,162.00
Uncur't & minor coins	10,007.52	14,486.00	13,151.75	14,510.12	13,018.65
Trade dollars	1,227.08	1,368.83	1,110.33	50.00	8.00
Specie	1,474,516.67	1,470,743.65	1,551,472.47	1,370,033.43	1,540,458.28
Legal-tender notes	1,172,231.00	1,095,481.00	1,012,910.00	1,044,661.00	991,435.00
U.S. cert's of deposit	....	....	....	....	....
5% fund with Treas	145,892.81	141,707.00	134,740.20	134,241.54	134,817.08
Due from U.S. Treas	19,026.86	16,697.53	16,405.77	14,001.17	11,300.25
Total	37,401,551.85	38,503,424.65	38,637,285.20	38,103,561.23	38,890,540.79

by States and reserve cities—Continued.

WISCONSIN.

Liabilities.	DECEMBER 28.	MARCH 4.	MAY 13.	AUGUST 1.	OCTOBER 5.
	47 banks.	50 banks.	51 banks.	53 banks.	53 banks.
Capital stock	$3,985,000.00	$4,150,000.00	$4,230,000.00	$4,420,000.00	$4,442,000.00
Surplus fund	1,028,684.36	1,101,668.66	1,097,910.34	1,139,304.13	1,143,677.72
Undivided profits	615,244.37	379,950.29	517,786.58	327,440.37	485,052.27
Nat'l bank circulation	1,300,318.00	1,275,828.00	1,215,648.00	1,247,638.00	1,225,623.00
State bank circulation	....	....	....	....	....
Dividends unpaid	4,019.90	2,221.90	1,751.90	12,222.90	1,550.00
Individual deposits	11,706,652.58	12,229,548.01	12,558,566.69	13,070,073.96	12,970,029.95
U. S. deposits	83,333.37	86,372.41	100,297.26	112,623.22	118,637.40
Dep'ts U.S. dis. officers	7,446.60	5,302.05	6,424.85	7,996.04	7,306.29
Due to national banks	33,660.25	44,537.32	58,364.50	88,373.80	49,810.14
Due to State banks	70,350.38	84,574.25	114,714.57	103,578.76	91,617.03
Notes re-discounted	36,428.44	51,378.90	106,220.37	93,900.86	50,551.25
Bills payable	....	....	....	20,000.00	....
Total	18,871,738.25	19,411,441.79	20,007,694.15	20,649,752.04	20,586,513.05

CITY OF MILWAUKEE.

	3 banks.	3 banks.	3 banks.	3 banks.	3 banks.
Capital stock	$650,000.00	$650,000.00	$650,000.00	$650,000.00	$650,000.00
Surplus fund	390,000.00	390,000.00	390,000.00	390,000.00	390,000.00
Undivided profits	206,112.46	170,621.11	194,451.90	151,951.49	174,734.97
Nat'l bank circulation	309,000.00	324,000.00	279,000.00	270,000.00	270,000.00
State bank circulation	....	....	....	....	....
Dividends unpaid	....	....	....	....	....
Individual deposits	4,675,473.98	5,109,469.49	4,884,938.08	4,299,791.82	4,292,772.96
U. S. deposits	375,514.13	213,027.95	288,537.75	272,759.46	206,094.64
Dep'ts U.S. dis. officers	132,271.58	273,346.79	156,443.70	179,552.53	219,090.71
Due to national banks	893,974.12	1,040,235.50	1,105,902.20	1,106,463.85	962,366.36
Due to State banks	260,392.55	355,445.34	330,775.90	335,637.40	401,490.20
Notes re-discounted	53,520.57	....	....	108,057.50	108,057.50
Bills payable	....	....	....	....	....
Total	7,931,209.39	8,532,146.18	8,280,049.53	7,764,214.05	7,765,117.34

IOWA.

	126 banks.	126 banks.	126 banks.	127 banks.	128 banks.
Capital stock	$10,140,000.00	$10,075,000.00	$10,080,000.00	$10,155,000.00	$10,150,000.00
Surplus fund	2,441,311.35	2,525,004.50	2,532,100.63	2,591,220.15	2,572,730.15
Undivided profits	1,493,824.02	1,017,410.49	1,245,158.98	870,752.09	1,186,045.74
Nat'l bank circulation	2,950,503.00	2,811,233.00	2,736,033.00	2,699,103.00	2,713,023.00
State bank circulation	....	....	....	....	....
Dividends unpaid	26,061.20	27,267.82	21,716.17	34,550.84	19,773.50
Individual deposits	17,518,945.06	18,793,310.70	18,877,423.46	18,700,415.38	19,284,097.83
U. S. deposits	216,710.91	242,105.29	170,511.22	86,037.24	53,961.47
Dep'ts U.S. dis. officers	92,303.10	68,563.21	59,036.33	50,215.25	78,553.48
Due to national banks	876,709.52	1,056,285.33	1,068,278.40	1,010,449.54	940,102.08
Due to State banks	1,397,756.39	1,635,048.00	1,571,690.36	1,590,030.48	1,624,951.05
Notes re-discounted	292,427.27	206,566.31	249,706.65	385,727.26	259,112.49
Bills payable	18,000.00	15,000.00	5,000.00	20,000.00	10,000.00
Total	37,464,551.83	38,503,424.05	38,637,285.20	38,193,561.23	38,899,549.79

Abstract of reports since October 7, 1886, arranged

MINNESOTA.

Resources.	DECEMBER 28.	MARCH 4.	MAY 13.	AUGUST 1.	OCTOBER 5.
	54 banks.	55 banks.	57 banks.	57 banks.	58 banks.
Loans and discounts	$33,264,155.27	$33,546,255.76	$35,802,793.43	$36,803,944.27	$38,056,769.79
Bonds for circulation	1,827,750.00	1,877,750.00	1,849,750.00	1,832,250.00	1,881,050.00
Bonds for deposits	525,000.00	600,000.00	650,000.00	750,000.00	750,000.00
U.S. bonds on hand	5,400.00	400.00	500.00	500.00	500.00
Other stocks and b'ds	633,093.55	632,122.95	645,567.84	580,213.83	681,908.44
Due from res've ag'ts	2,657,901.51	4,105,465.47	3,721,661.98	4,039,307.83	3,540,734.92
Due from nat'l banks	1,441,313.80	1,567,968.70	1,283,388.09	2,113,796.70	1,718,185.54
Due from State banks	518,652.65	501,912.54	483,840.70	419,193.73	790,057.83
Real estate, etc	1,462,391.48	1,444,937.37	1,461,708.64	1,558,772.77	1,661,461.81
Current expenses	215,340.84	191,112.69	201,626.20	89,112.06	175,696.76
Premiums paid	211,205.53	220,591.48	245,922.05	242,785.23	280,785.68
Cash items	342,118.24	638,682.44	683,227.40	1,000,226.67	905,904.12
Clear'g-house exch'gs	242,915.00	....	....	....	....
Bills of other banks	510,280.00	302,184.00	327,327.00	821,870.00	491,407.00
Uncur't & minor coins	4,898.19	7,082.93	8,823.58	11,804.73	10,419.74
Trade dollars	250.00	253.00	71.00	59.00	4.00
Specie	1,870,645.47	2,033,279.58	2,355,319.53	2,564,974.71	2,367,277.50
Legal-tender notes	1,004,884.00	798,547.00	798,409.00	1,151,945.00	966,060.00
U.S. cert's of deposit	....	....	....	....	....
5% fund with Treas.	82,143.93	80,926.18	79,692.87	82,418.68	78,318.68
Due from U.S. Treas.	24,651.53	28,531.69	18,155.90	6,813.74	15,670.65
Total	46,844,999.99	48,608,003.78	50,707,794.21	54,129,988.95	54,395,302.55

MISSOURI.

	39 banks.	40 banks.	32 banks.	34 banks.	35 banks.
Loans and discounts	$14,088,985.30	$15,677,341.03	$4,950,318.67	$4,771,433.53	$5,055,708.34
Bonds for circulation	1,194,600.00	1,229,600.00	787,750.00	770,250.00	782,750.00
Bonds for deposits	250,000.00	300,000.00	....	....	....
U.S. bonds on hand	5,900.00	8,800.00	5,100.00	5,100.00	5,300.00
Other stocks and b'ds	601,611.45	593,966.54	463,487.86	471,794.98	408,320.34
Due from res've ag'ts	2,122,852.80	2,960,726.05	782,039.57	1,160,306.53	940,742.18
Due from nat'l banks	439,016.66	964,607.40	108,052.68	176,223.32	125,372.51
Due from State banks	695,775.07	1,203,007.97	135,107.13	123,022.55	111,098.78
Real estate, etc	380,264.08	385,067.29	247,822.47	267,079.21	282,900.34
Current expenses	134,310.43	72,561.81	68,865.48	22,126.94	45,401.51
Premiums paid	146,276.02	175,135.68	66,765.28	69,359.49	72,270.09
Cash items	90,591.30	125,030.58	46,524.51	40,254.19	54,203.73
Clear'g-house exch'gs	330,668.28	503,924.22	....	....	....
Bills of other banks	565,845.00	830,116.00	187,416.00	227,935.00	186,515.00
Uncur't & minor coins	1,617.87	6,654.12	1,686.83	1,321.56	1,980.14
Trade dollars	782.00	759.00	90.00	....	....
Specie	1,180,846.50	1,240,333.01	307,586.58	314,084.18	324,023.18
Legal-tender notes	749,128.00	1,004,999.00	270,341.00	288,034.00	302,143.00
U.S. cert's of deposit	....	....	....	....	....
5% fund with Treas.	53,050.75	53,071.25	34,918.75	34,571.25	35,213.25
Due from U.S. Treas.	250.00	1,910.00	....	550.00	4,365.09
Total	23,056,366.51	27,397,611.55	8,473,472.81	8,753,048.73	8,832,315.28

CITY OF SAINT LOUIS.

	5 banks.	5 banks.	5 banks.	5 banks.	5 banks.
Loans and discounts	$9,378,484.34	$9,230,319.09	$8,616,511.09	$9,793,360.79	$10,400,404.07
Bonds for circulation	810,000.00	760,000.00	750,000.00	710,000.00	710,000.00
Bonds for deposits	500,000.00	450,000.00	450,000.00	450,000.00	450,000.00
U.S. bonds on hand	89,750.00	5,100.00	1,500.00	2,000.00	2,100.00
Other stocks and b'ds	553,118.50	515,408.50	546,031.18	955,903.00	939,758.00
Due from res've ag'ts	1,321,473.25	1,784,147.06	....	....	....
Due from nat'l banks	701,461.86	918,920.27	2,888,976.01	2,521,358.18	1,406,815.78
Due from State banks	256,183.10	303,862.24	198,384.30	180,084.80	143,407.58
Real estate, etc	274,053.63	283,487.25	283,595.96	285,456.34	285,404.29
Current expenses	76,190.52	67,005.47	75,058.55	45,702.08	112,108.18
Premiums paid	50,372.68	41,581.00	110,051.88	114,083.13	111,211.09
Cash items	30,552.47	42,526.15	62,933.88	40,690.53	33,666.64
Clear'g-house exch'gs	381,378.02	644,075.80	916,623.41	596,775.59	535,892.30
Bills of other banks	93,415.00	136,009.00	304,407.00	111,164.00	78,644.00
Uncur't & minor coins	2,665.45	1,618.29	4,617.15	2,896.22	2,023.30
Trade dollars	....	....	....	....	....
Specie	970,837.97	1,122,722.27	1,409,188.12	1,655,550.57	1,338,010.44
Legal-tender notes	985,334.00	1,088,483.00	1,648,402.00	1,630,279.00	1,212,879.00
U.S. cert's of deposit	30,000.00	140,000.00	110,000.00	140,000.00	140,000.00
5% fund with Treas.	36,445.00	33,065.00	33,715.00	31,945.00	31,915.00
Due from U.S. Treas.	1,000.00	4,000.00	3,000.00	7,000.00	6,000.00
Total	16,617,715.79	17,581,331.29	18,533,146.55	19,283,249.23	17,910,415.66

by States and reserve cities—Continued.

MINNESOTA.

Liabilities.	DECEMBER 28. 54 banks.	MARCH 4. 55 banks.	MAY 13. 57 banks.	AUGUST 1. 57 banks.	OCTOBER 5. 58 banks.
Capital stock	$12,413,000.00	$12,716,200.00	$13,377,080.00	$13,535,000.00	$13,740,000.00
Surplus fund	2,192,278.87	2,209,052.39	2,300,052.39	2,378,052.30	2,380,452.39
Undivided profits	1,854,403.80	1,278,451.00	1,692,853.03	1,307,383.93	1,756,325.17
Nat'l bank circulation	1,622,136.00	1,623,020.00	1,602,995.00	1,631,135.00	1,675,725.00
State-bank circulation	....	....	....	....	....
Dividends unpaid	8,415.14	16,332.50	5,565.34	52,971.34	16,150.31
Individual deposits	22,342,363.17	23,950,403.31	25,242,702.46	28,002,001.34	27,037,970.02
U. S. deposits	106,370.04	209,701.40	338,666.42	341,359.53	249,258.86
Dep'ts U.S.dis.officers	307,949.22	244,179.09	235,032.48	236,294.60	387,217.06
Due to national banks	2,403,844.74	2,508,987.95	2,226,416.99	2,788,682.69	2,691,672.93
Due to State banks	2,217,346.64	2,618,114.61	2,193,748.04	2,868,933.71	2,783,034.72
Notes re-discounted	1,236,832.37	1,054,561.44	1,431,022.06	833,574.39	1,621,975.46
Bills payable	20,000.00	20,000.00	63,000.00	64,000.00	55,500.00
Total	46,844,999.99	48,608,003.78	50,707,794.21	54,120,966.95	54,395,302.55

MISSOURI.

	39 banks.	40 banks.	32 banks.	34 banks.	35 banks.
Capital stock	$5,831,000.00	$6,131,000.00	$2,331,000.00	$2,431,200.00	$2,517,280.00
Surplus fund	754,731.97	855,462.79	538,762.79	556,007.48	534,447.48
Undivided profits	660,466.89	423,250.55	298,792.06	198,118.03	276,484.19
Nat'l-bank circulation	1,074,325.00	1,058,025.00	707,215.00	690,085.00	604,615.00
State-bank circulation	....	....	....	....	....
Dividends unpaid	50,554.00	2,476.00	342.00	2,389.00	544.00
Individual deposits	10,686,373.82	13,535,527.12	4,434,581.26	4,720,147.16	4,028,242.37
U. S. deposits	204,142.10	201,623.16	....	....	....
Dep'ts U.S.dis.officers	25,651.56	10,946.80	....	....	....
Due to national banks	1,343,006.93	1,872,664.97	14,434.85	19,186.37	36,783.48
Due to State banks	2,272,547.91	3,123,842.21	41,447.97	58,344.39	62,098.88
Notes re-discounted	228,566.33	157,784.93	106,896.86	63,480.70	44,819.88
Bills payable	25,000.00	5,000.00	....	5,000.00	15,000.00
Total	23,056,366.51	27,397,611.55	8,473,472.81	8,753,048.73	8,832,315.28

CITY OF SAINT LOUIS.

	5 banks.	5 banks.	5 banks.	5 banks.	5 banks.
Capital stock	$3,000,000.00	$3,000,000.00	$3,000,000.00	$3,000,000.00	$3,000,000.00
Surplus fund	1,052,530.46	1,065,000.00	1,065,000.00	1,070,000.00	1,070,000.00
Undivided profits	362,967.42	280,316.29	365,340.15	318,328.35	462,306.67
Nat'l-bank circulation	726,900.00	684,000.00	670,800.00	631,140.00	637,730.00
State-bank circulation	....	....	....	....	....
Dividends unpaid	19,036.18	19,911.18	23,050.18	25,902.43	11,858.93
Individual deposits	6,056,703.50	6,851,016.58	7,403,782.02	7,372,523.08	6,564,108.34
U. S. deposits	387,625.29	375,684.91	388,589.90	375,749.15	375,749.15
Dep'ts U.S.dis.officers	....	....	....	....	....
Due to national banks	2,626,461.95	2,940,974.79	3,035,079.52	3,272,036.43	2,667,151.10
Due to State banks	2,122,116.80	2,224,005.33	2,520,835.78	3,214,569.79	2,843,140.00
Notes re-discounted	293,284.19	131,422.21	....	....	308,201,38
Bills payable	....	....	....	....	....
Total	16,647,715.79	17,581,331.29	18,533,116.55	19,283,240.23	17,940,445.66

Abstract of reports since October 7, 1880, arranged

KANSAS CITY.

Resources.	DECEMBER 28.	MARCH 4.	MAY 13.	AUGUST 1.	OCTOBER 5.
	— banks.	— banks.	6 banks.	6 banks.	8 banks.
Loans and discounts	....	....	$10, 834, 113. 16	$11, 830, 515. 09	$14, 403, 375. 15
Bonds for circulation	....	....	300, 000. 00	300, 000. 00	400, 000. 00
Bonds for deposits	....	....	150, 000. 00	200, 000. 00	200, 000. 00
U. S. bonds on hand	....	....	57, 500. 00	11, 750. 00	900. 00
Other stocks and b'ds	....	....	138, 476. 58	174, 046. 58	272, 550. 35
Due from res've ag'ts	....	....	3, 109, 235. 63	2, 067, 741. 09	2, 252, 893. 90
Due from nat'l banks	....	....	651, 832. 11	273, 755. 14	500, 309. 51
Due from State banks	....	....	709, 600. 22	579, 972. 16	680, 702. 95
Real estate, etc	....	....	114, 870. 42	205, 854. 55	359, 252. 86
Current expenses	....	....	38, 489. 59	43, 287. 74	31, 291. 09
Premiums paid	....	....	87, 742. 42	100, 763. 17	122, 480. 05
Cash items	....	....	23, 820. 24	28, 342. 79	25, 869. 34
Clear'g-house exch'gs	....	....	473, 409. 84	524, 971. 19	514, 094. 80
Bills of other banks	....	....	908, 315. 00	302, 611. 00	409, 459. 60
Uncur't & minor coins	....	....	2, 439. 77	3, 491. 97	3, 919. 80
Trade dollars	....	....	320. 00	....	5. 00
Specie	....	....	1, 393, 645. 19	1, 452, 610. 67	1, 480, 764. 10
Legal-tender notes	....	....	1, 362, 844. 00	1, 181, 500. 00	1, 426, 753. 00
U. S. cert's of deposit	....	....	....	....	....
5 % fund with Treas	....	....	13, 500. 00	13, 500. 00	15, 750. 00
Due from U. S. Treas	....	....	....	850. 00	3, 220. 00
Total	....	....	20, 460, 103. 17	19, 385, 566. 14	23, 582, 053. 56

CITY OF SAINT JOSEPH.

Resources.	— banks.	— banks.	2 banks.	2 banks.	2 banks.
Loans and discounts	....	....	$1, 932, 801. 58	$1, 791, 412. 05	$1, 949, 081. 06
Bonds for circulation	....	....	123, 050. 00	124, 050. 00	157, 550. 00
Bonds for deposits	....	....	150, 000. 00	150, 000. 00	300, 000. 00
U. S. bonds on hand	....	....	....	....	....
Other stocks and b'ds	....	....	654. 88	654. 88	654. 88
Due from res've ag'ts	....	....	294, 656. 57	443, 306. 22	207, 740. 14
Due from nat'l banks	....	....	73, 711. 16	124, 376. 34	86, 380. 87
Due from State banks	....	....	85, 420. 94	29, 353. 19	28, 603. 22
Real estate, etc	....	....	26, 929. 20	26, 929. 20	26, 929. 20
Current expenses	....	....	12, 073. 64	2, 925. 84	7, 631. 04
Premiums paid	....	....	25, 588. 75	82, 775. 62	40, 633. 12
Cash items	....	....	19, 240. 51	24, 855. 70	17, 000. 32
Clear'g-house exch'gs	....	....	12, 399. 21	33, 605. 22	27, 929. 51
Bills of other banks	....	....	10, 250. 00	14, 384. 00	6, 808. 00
Uncur't & minor coins	....	....	816. 75	813. 77	881. 98
Trade dollars	....	....	....	....	....
Specie	....	....	122, 022. 95	127, 617. 75	156, 384. 15
Legal-tender notes	....	....	157, 622. 00	185, 500. 00	210, 710. 00
U. S. cert's of deposit	....	....	....	....	....
5 % fund with Treas	....	....	5, 535. 00	5, 622. 50	5, 667. 50
Due from U. S. Treas	....	....	....	....	....
Total	....	....	3, 052, 873. 14	3, 119, 082. 28	3, 321, 511. 59

KANSAS.

Resources.	107 banks.	110 banks.	115 banks.	126 banks.	139 banks.
Loans and discounts	$16, 263, 359. 30	$17, 402, 505. 23	$18, 615, 091. 30	$19, 951, 213. 81	$21, 300, 633. 63
Bonds for circulation	2, 067, 000. 00	2, 092, 000. 00	2, 205, 250. 00	2, 452, 000. 00	2, 748, 250. 00
Bonds for deposits	470, 000. 00	450, 000. 00	450, 000. 00	475, 000. 00	525, 000. 00
U. S. bonds on hand	21, 350. 00	9, 050. 00	35, 350. 00	10, 350. 00	11, 950. 00
Other stocks and b'ds	183, 490. 83	184, 562. 61	255, 050. 05	301, 480. 79	308, 978. 70
Due from res've ag'ts	1, 531, 485. 90	2, 211, 632. 15	3, 951, 578. 89	3, 347, 448. 58	2, 731, 615. 85
Due from nat'l banks	1, 459, 569. 93	1, 961, 004. 92	1, 225, 879. 96	951, 204. 42	1, 168, 060. 84
Due from State banks	515, 653. 67	605, 425. 90	735, 905. 94	653, 448. 61	330, 689. 77
Real estate, etc	1, 003, 317. 12	1, 093, 558. 82	1, 165, 746. 74	1, 248, 333. 54	1, 372, 214. 77
Current expenses	252, 920. 17	143, 203. 91	215, 419. 92	130, 492. 84	187, 409. 17
Premiums paid	249, 687. 25	272, 912. 95	300, 205. 39	330, 346. 87	394, 411. 00
Cash items	179, 681. 16	227, 618. 45	251, 795. 42	295, 946. 60	291, 205. 91
Clear'g-house exch'gs	....	....	....	....	....
Bills of other banks	728, 300. 00	807, 879. 00	925, 705. 00	715, 430. 00	763, 347. 00
Uncur't & minor coins	6, 928. 45	7, 092. 61	8, 916. 99	8, 015. 21	9, 426. 42
Trade dollars	6. 00	161. 00	67. 00	6. 00	....
Specie	1, 360, 810. 53	1, 203, 050. 20	1, 444, 219. 08	1, 403, 250. 43	1, 460, 157. 51
Legal-tender notes	878, 981. 00	1, 010, 981. 00	1, 262, 180. 00	1, 207, 416. 00	1, 208, 267. 00
U. S. cert's of deposit	....	....	....	....	....
5 % fund with Treas	89, 447. 41	91, 415. 31	92, 302. 99	104, 237. 73	115, 178. 50
Due from U. S. Treas	7, 750. 80	10, 289. 73	3, 882. 39	7, 311. 51	12, 301. 34
Total	27, 269, 781. 52	20, 794, 243. 70	33, 150, 636. 06	33, 611, 893. 04	34, 948, 098. 10

by States and reserve cities—Continued.

KANSAS CITY.

Liabilities.	DECEMBER 28.	MARCH 4.	MAY 13.	AUGUST 1.	OCTOBER 5.
	— banks.	— banks.	6 banks.	6 banks.	8 banks.
Capital stock	....	....	$2,800,000.00	$5,800,000.00	$5,910,000.00
Surplus fund	....	....	222,500.00	397,560.00	437,000.00
Undivided profits	....	....	352,593.70	250,490.82	267,120.10
Nat'l bank circulation	....	....	269,420.00	270,000.00	315,000.00
State bank circulation	....	....	....	....	....
Dividends unpaid	....	....	40.00	50.00	....
Individual deposits	....	....	9,172,014.62	9,018,827.80	10,364,315.64
U. S. deposits	....	....	121,889.81	168,228.44	174,292.00
Dep'ts U.S.dis.officers	....	....	3,481.41	12,098.91	3,150.96
Due to national banks	....	....	3,004,514.05	2,450,808.22	2,734,209.58
Due to State banks	....	....	3,443,610.49	3,010,552.05	3,347,489.63
Notes re-discounted	....	....	....	....	....
Bills payable	....	....	....	....	....
Total	....	....	20,469,103.17	19,385,566.14	23,582,633.56

CITY OF SAINT JOSEPH.

	— banks.	— banks.	2 banks.	2 banks.	2 banks.
Capital stock	....	....	$300,000.00	$300,000.00	$300,000.00
Surplus fund	....	....	100,000.00	106,000.00	106,000.00
Undivided profits	....	....	31,565.70	9,363.97	34,877.98
Nat'l bank circulation	....	....	110,700.00	112,450.00	119,350.00
State bank circulation	....	....	....	....	....
Dividends unpaid	....	....	....	....	....
Individual deposits	....	....	1,847,167.00	1,748,420.53	1,905,825.06
U. S. deposits	....	....	121,181.54	118,515.48	219,488.59
Dep'ts U.S.dis.officers	....	....	14,522.07	9,475.50	14,235.90
Due to national banks	....	....	143,838.83	183,046.99	197,300.32
Due to State banks	....	....	371,045.00	521,779.81	414,433.14
Notes re-discounted	....	....	13,000.00	10,000.00	10,000.00
Bills payable	....	....	....	....	....
Total	....	....	3,052,873.14	3,119,082.23	3,321,511.50

KANSAS.

	107 banks.	110 banks.	115 banks.	126 banks.	139 banks.
Capital stock	$7,237,100.00	$7,757,400.00	$8,070,100.00	$9,150,900.00	$10,530,800.00
Surplus fund	1,097,937.43	1,255,195.00	1,259,980.99	1,467,436.95	1,434,520.06
Undivided profits	1,143,880.13	684,290.62	997,107.39	672,751.64	970,042.52
Nat'l bank circulation	1,753,630.00	1,784,040.00	1,860,765.00	2,080,445.00	2,293,210.00
State bank circulation	....	....	....	....	....
Dividends unpaid	6,520.79	4,157.35	6,323.37	15,354.87	28,042.12
Individual deposits	14,033,814.55	16,216,452.47	18,910,116.25	18,530,431.84	17,741,267.63
U. S. deposits	177,156.41	185,473.67	163,516.57	223,793.64	228,833.28
Dep'ts U.S.dis.officers	241,722.00	194,436.47	227,488.51	209,703.61	249,108.71
Due to national banks	286,987.38	363,765.19	514,916.85	252,484.50	276,210.16
Due to State banks	237,020.85	203,605.14	482,222.24	455,167.25	490,132.97
Notes re-discounted	934,968.57	1,035,138.82	620,992.48	516,051.64	635,804.83
Bills payable	119,046.41	50,288.07	37,046.41	25,350.00	48,035.02
Total	27,269,784.52	29,791,243.79	33,150,636.06	33,611,802.94	34,948,098.10

Abstract of reports since October 7, 1886, arranged

NEBRASKA.

Resources.	DECEMBER 28. 02 banks.	MARCH 4. 96 banks.	MAY 13. 08 banks.	AUGUST 1. 04 banks.	OCTOBER 5. 05 banks.
Loans and discounts	$10, 660, 930. 47	$20, 234, 700. 50	$21, 305, 500. 88	$13, 060, 580. 82	$13, 808, 300. 25
Bonds for circulation.	1, 868, 500. 00	1, 839, 500. 00	1, 824, 000. 00	1, 500, 000. 00	1, 504, 000. 00
Bonds for deposits ..	550, 000. 00	550, 000. 00	550, 000. 00	....	....
U. S. bonds on hand..	....	10, 000. 00	....	....	....
Other stocks and b'ds	277, 027. 32	247, 734. 30	210, 270. 18	136, 115. 14	181, 432. 72
Due from res'veag'ts	1, 724, 773. 45	2, 865, 250. 08	2, 800, 241. 89	1, 040, 703. 14	1, 347, 086. 41
Due from nat'l banks	1, 098, 864. 15	1, 636, 360. 24	2, 167, 600. 00	705, 700. 84	533, 082. 36
Due from State banks	533, 396. 82	617, 413. 03	922, 701. 51	122, 502. 84	103, 650. 61
Real estate, etc......	1, 230, 883. 25	1, 255, 866. 31	1, 271, 567. 76	002, 110. 08	968, 100. 06
Current expenses....	241, 890. 31	225, 703. 69	245, 553. 84	06, 680. 86	147, 190. 44
Premiums paid......	211, 022. 53	228, 191. 78	245, 320. 20	163, 068. 95	167, 727. 05
Cash items..........	416, 531. 72	433, 170. 73	356, 447. 65	210, 350. 38	241, 125. 72
Clear'g-house exch'gs	131, 846. 21	153, 245. 60	106, 363. 53	....	....
Bills of other banks..	377, 965. 00	282, 420. 00	404, 525. 00	160, 333. 00	125, 188. 00
Uncur't&minor coins	6, 948. 08	9, 081. 79	8, 518. 37	6, 066. 43	6, 853. 02
Trade dollars........	1, 021. 00	2, 067. 60	1, 285. 00	128. 00	....
Specie	1, 200, 041. 18	1, 252, 586. 55	1, 028, 833. 56	770, 526. 95	707, 474. 22
Legal-tender notes ..	851, 834. 00	741, 364. 00	1, 049, 098. 00	334, 765. 00	328, 188. 00
U.S. cert's of deposit	....	....	....	....	....
5 % fund with Treas.	81, 408. 75	80, 267. 75	80, 805. 25	66, 706. 25	67, 665. 25
Due from U.S. Treas.	1, 802. 45	5, 389. 35	6, 775. 00	2, 360. 60	2, 330. 17
Total..........	30, 475, 605. 60	32, 670, 351. 28	35, 665, 480. 52	20, 265, 876. 08	20, 300, 190. 28

CITY OF OMAHA.

	— banks.	— banks.	— banks.	8 banks.	8 banks.
Loans and discounts	....	....	....	$8, 736, 720. 46	$9, 133, 479. 76
Bonds for circulation	....	....	....	350, 000. 00	350, 000. 00
Bonds for deposits...	....	....	....	550, 000. 00	550, 000. 00
U. S. bonds on hand..	....	....	....	....	....
Other stocks and b'ds	....	....	....	133, 128. 61	174, 474. 62
Due from res've ag'ts	....	....	....	1, 407, 340. 87	1, 353, 811. 45
Due from nat'l banks	....	....	....	504, 483. 88	534, 547. 08
Due from State banks	....	....	....	918, 359. 57	576, 540. 09
Real estate, etc......	....	....	....	382, 940. 25	405, 840. 45
Current expenses....	....	....	....	35, 427. 06	35, 711. 41
Premiums paid......	....	....	....	82, 686. 76	79, 555. 51
Cash items..........	....	....	....	151, 352. 64	100, 946. 75
Clear'g-house exch'gs	....	....	....	219, 657. 41	102, 127. 04
Bills of other banks..	....	....	....	336, 702. 00	150, 770. 00
Uncur't&minor coins	....	....	....	3, 482. 71	2, 954. 47
Trade dollars.......	....	....	....	....	....
Specie	....	....	....	1, 332, 505. 84	947, 444. 01
Legal-tender notes ..	....	....	....	601, 101. 00	905, 604. 00
U.S. cert's of deposit.	....	....	....	....	....
5 % fund with Treas.	....	....	....	14, 550. 00	14, 400. 00
Due from U. S. Treas	....	....	....	20. 00	....
Total..........	....	....	....	16, 210, 630. 06	15, 478, 208. 44

COLORADO.

	27 banks.	27 banks.	28 banks.	31 banks.	31 banks.
Loans and discounts	$10, 272, 123. 19	$10, 384, 625. 54	$11, 493, 330. 86	$11, 883, 269. 13	$12, 401, 000. 06
Bonds for circulation.	1, 004, 700. 00	984, 700. 00	926, 500. 00	960, 000. 00	989, 000. 00
Bonds for deposits ..	700, 000. 00	700, 000. 00	800, 000. 00	800, 000. 00	900, 000. 00
U. S. bonds on hand..	51, 000. 00	28, 000. 00	16, 000. 00	16, 000. 00	16, 000. 00
Other stocks and b'ds	736, 321. 65	755, 119. 04	741, 392. 48	700, 224. 41	825, 000. 03
Due from res've ag'ts	2, 076, 001. 66	2, 408, 013. 42	2, 701, 756. 94	3, 105, 383. 09	3, 324, 235. 10
Due from nat'l banks	1, 537, 261. 09	1, 618, 756. 12	2, 050, 562. 81	1, 764, 729. 73	1, 805, 264. 30
Due from State banks	426, 502. 40	548, 313. 07	632, 351. 32	655, 522. 40	673, 863. 77
Real estate, etc......	379, 743. 10	386, 804. 15	360, 807. 84	305, 830. 89	377, 221. 63
Current expenses...	117, 001. 70	79, 735. 31	80, 300. 31	57, 753. 21	74, 068. 84
Premiums paid	164, 083. 55	170, 880. 43	191, 870. 65	106, 152. 40	102, 028. 90
Cash items	99, 730. 03	45, 658. 32	74, 817. 82	82, 753. 48	68, 362. 55
Clear'g-house exch'gs	190, 870. 00	274, 880. 10	252, 060. 02	230, 263. 01	261, 786. 07
Bills of other banks..	314, 730. 00	327, 573. 00	355, 350. 00	557, 732. 00	423, 495. 00
Uncur't&minor coins	1, 078. 72	1, 788. 38	2, 002. 07	4, 750. 93	4, 079. 33
Trade dollars........	....	....	....	....	....
Specie.............	1, 047, 255. 67	1, 274, 630. 50	1, 257, 611. 11	1, 345, 250. 48	1, 422, 080. 47
Legal-tender notes ..	849, 230. 00	796, 627. 00	874, 722. 00	915, 570. 00	890, 621. 60
U. S. cert's of deposit	....	....	....	....	....
5 % fund with Treas.	45, 110. 50	43, 828. 70	40, 067. 00	42, 817. 00	43, 012. 00
Due from U. S. Treas.	10, 052. 54	6, 221. 17	10, 266. 17	14, 803. 30	18, 263. 03
Total..........	20, 016, 394. 70	20, 956, 078. 75	22, 801, 950. 86	23, 025, 384. 36	24, 712, 831. 60

by States and reserve cities—Continued.

NEBRASKA.

Liabilities.	DECEMBER 28.	MARCH 4.	MAY 13.	AUGUST 1.	OCTOBER 5
	92 banks.	96 banks.	98 banks.	94 banks.	95 banks.
Capital stock	$7,535,000.00	$7,750,000.00	$8,160,000.00	$5,933,200.00	$6,006,100.00
Surplus fund	1,220,413.66	1,391,029.67	1,395,340.43	802,880.79	912,407.70
Undivided profits	1,013,811.58	506,945.22	735,660.05	351,082.88	514,330.88
Nat'l-bank circulation	1,658,815.00	1,610,330.00	1,635,380.00	1,332,980.00	1,345,220.00
State-bank circulation					
Dividends unpaid	263.00	1,618.50	5,705.00	9,868.60	9,091.50
Individual deposits	13,513,210.10	15,476,653.31	17,877,700.54	10,292,750.53	9,964,472.02
U. S. deposits	184,208.44	213,894.64	275,263.86		
Dep'ts U.S.dis.officers	320,682.44	257,950.52	211,060.41		
Due to national banks	1,969,838.08	2,210,433.11	2,385,721.97	463,160.18	351,222.96
Due to State banks	1,374,975.52	1,709,163.84	2,174,012.32	473,280.88	381,068.29
Notes re-discounted	1,594,677.87	1,432,294.07	706,735.94	511,663.82	791,677.93
Bills payable	89,800.00	20,029.40	12,900.00	5,000.00	24,500.00
Total	30,475,695.69	32,670,351.28	35,665,480.52	20,265,876.68	20,300,190.28

CITY OF OMAHA.

	— banks.	— banks.	— banks.	8 banks.	8 banks.
Capital stock				$2,400,000.00	$2,400,000.00
Surplus fund				570,500.00	571,500.00
Undivided profits				147,631.02	160,207.60
Nat'l-bank circulation				315,000.00	314,500.00
State-bank circulation					
Dividends unpaid				610.00	1,474.00
Individual deposits				7,818,437.31	7,893,212.85
U. S. deposits				281,696.52	306,850.03
Dep'ts U.S.dis.officers				215,780.98	266,677.84
Due to national banks				2,523,043.56	1,856,665.13
Due to State banks				1,937,930.67	1,421,529.70
Notes re-discounted					283,501.71
Bills payable					
Total				16,210,639.06	15,478,298.44

COLORADO.

	27 banks.	27 banks.	28 banks.	31 banks.	31 banks.
Capital stock	$2,435,000.00	$2,435,000.00	$2,495,000.00	$2,690,000.00	$2,751,830.00
Surplus fund	850,800.00	900,500.00	902,500.00	928,000.00	929,000.00
Undivided profits	769,454.00	604,051.16	694,840.58	684,000.49	812,166.55
Nat'l-bank circulation	894,120.00	878,140.00	803,720.00	829,230.00	880,330.00
State-bank circulation					
Dividends unpaid	30,505.00	991.00	6,961.00	3,061.00	2,953.00
Individual deposits	12,564,859.37	13,372,180.48	14,812,105.50	15,430,272.65	15,819,553.77
U. S. deposits	501,268.85	402,738.82	532,546.07	607,703.12	636,582.51
Dep'ts U.S.dis.officers	122,119.70	117,210.82	110,872.16	93,783.04	116,076.93
Due to national banks	880,080.57	981,649.15	1,306,631.54	1,564,064.10	1,416,804.70
Due to State banks	963,187.30	1,143,459.23	1,090,231.01	1,071,680.30	1,338,139.80
Notes re-discounted	5,000.00	30,158.00	46,543.00	24,529.57	9,271.48
Bills payable					102.05
Total	20,016,394.79	20,956,078.75	22,801,950.86	23,925,384.36	24,712,831.69

Abstract of reports since October 7, 1880, arranged*

NEVADA.

Resources.	DECEMBER 28.	MARCH 4.	MAY 13.	AUGUST 1.	OCTOBER 5.
	2 banks.	2 banks.	2 banks.	2 banks.	2 banks.
Loans and discounts	$425, 788. 13	$438, 204. 44	$404, 273. 96	$479, 134. 75	$513, 821. 33
Bonds for circulation	37, 500. 00	37, 500. 00	37, 500. 00	37, 500. 00	37, 500. 00
Bonds for deposits	....	....	....	....	....
U. S. bonds on hand	....	....	....	....	....
Other stocks and b'ds	21, 813. 76	27, 103. 10	28, 001. 15	25, 349. 08	30, 735. 84
Due from res've ag'ts	7, 096. 95	2, 470. 85	7, 381. 48	1, 963. 06	3, 015. 27
Due from nat'l banks	250. 00	27. 25	838. 11	898. 06	530. 57
Due from State banks	2, 209. 54	5, 114. 20	3, 040. 00	3, 650. 46	7, 446. 93
Real estate, etc	9, 109. 01	20, 109. 01	29, 109. 01	28, 349. 01	30, 340. 01
Current expenses	4, 987. 03	3, 712. 01	6, 484. 17	1, 387. 92	4, 457. 18
Premiums paid	5, 665. 62	5, 667. 62	5, 667. 62	5, 467. 62	5, 467. 62
Cash items	788. 30	793. 78	876. 03	712. 83	719. 93
Clear'g-house exch'gs	....	....	....	....	....
Bills of other banks	5, 077. 00	4, 220. 00	2, 420. 00	500. 00	305. 00
Uncur't & minor coins	35. 36	34. 89	36. 48	16. 85	3. 93
Trade dollars	....	....	....	....	....
Specie	53, 399. 35	60, 233. 10	76, 789. 90	57, 572. 15	57, 486. 42
Legal-tender notes	242. 00	4, 118. 00	2, 650. 00	1, 661. 00	....
U. S. cert's of deposit	....	....	....	....	....
5% fund with Treas.	1, 687. 00	1, 687. 00	1, 687. 50	1, 687. 50	1, 687. 50
Due from U. S. Treas	....	....	10. 00	....	....
Total	575, 649. 05	629, 087. 25	607, 378. 61	645, 861. 39	690, 508. 53

CALIFORNIA.

	DECEMBER 28.	MARCH 4.	MAY 13.	AUGUST 1.	OCTOBER 5.
	24 banks.	24 banks.	25 banks.	28 banks.	3# banks.
Loans and discounts	$9, 756, 723. 21	$10, 109, 081. 55	$11, 140, 004. 85	$12, 907, 788. 27	$14, 445, 417. 19
Bonds for circulation	933, 000. 00	907, 500. 00	920, 000. 00	1, 007, 500. 00	1, 088, 750. 00
Bonds for deposits	50, 000. 00	100, 000. 00	150, 000. 00	150, 000. 00	150, 000. 00
U. S. bonds on hand	24, 500. 00	101, 700. 00	101, 550. 00	154, 300. 00	219, 900. 00
Other stocks and b'ds	413, 828. 42	430, 549. 03	432, 136. 17	461, 330. 28	560, 161. 71
Due from res've ag'ts	1, 564, 008. 12	1, 784, 124. 72	2, 578, 087. 45	2, 145, 530. 73	2, 850, 407. 36
Due from nat'l banks	678, 118. 21	556, 201. 47	807, 830. 25	844, 020. 57	885, 615. 25
Due from State banks	352, 086. 26	377, 607. 71	510, 771. 08	779, 733. 78	1, 020, 441. 17
Real estate, etc	508, 189. 39	518, 172. 42	618, 190. 90	634, 982. 32	670, 994. 69
Current expenses	102, 844. 64	75, 815. 57	101, 584. 04	64, 339. 32	97, 015. 06
Premiums paid	115, 172. 07	141, 982. 91	169, 779. 54	200, 749. 76	242, 392. 93
Cash items	170, 558. 30	157, 170. 18	194, 635. 17	235, 804. 12	256, 175. 74
Clear'g-house exch'gs	....	....	....	....	....
Bills of other banks	98, 332. 00	70, 501. 00	104, 851. 00	145, 543. 00	149, 639. 00
Uncur't & minor coins	965. 75	1, 194. 26	957. 54	3, 357. 72	796. 68
Trade dollars	....	....	....	....	....
Specie	2, 143, 454. 07	2, 188, 149. 15	2, 591, 411. 55	2, 728, 039. 47	3, 571, 927. 42
Legal-tender notes	183, 911. 00	232, 912. 00	257, 393. 00	215, 003. 00	347, 021. 00
U. S. cert's of deposit	....	....	....	....	....
5% fund with Treas.	41, 672. 00	40, 005. 00	41, 400. 00	42, 525. 00	47, 807. 00
Due from U. S. Treas	4, 905. 50	7, 525. 00	3, 505. 00	8, 253. 00	2, 820. 25
Total	17, 151, 269. 54	17, 899, 281. 97	20, 814, 099. 14	22, 727, 711. 34	26, 616, 918. 45

SAN FRANCISCO.

	DECEMBER 28.	MARCH 4.	MAY 13.	AUGUST 1.	OCTOBER 5.
	2 banks.	3 banks.	3 banks.	3 banks.	3 banks.
Loans and discounts	$3, 577, 685. 78	$3, 910, 802. 42	$4, 096, 479. 24	$4, 501, 870. 66	$4, 854, 873. 26
Bonds for circulation	650, 000. 00	700, 000. 00	750, 000. 00	750, 000. 00	750, 000. 00
Bonds for deposits	....	....	....	....	....
U. S. bonds on hand	....	....	50, 000. 00	....	....
Other stocks and b'ds	375, 000. 00	375, 000. 00	375, 000. 00	375, 000. 00	375, 000. 00
Due from res've ag'ts	138, 669. 15	133, 675. 61	65, 575. 44	204, 254. 86	152, 208. 57
Due from nat'l banks	50, 097. 72	96, 769. 05	63, 937. 95	74, 767. 91	107, 447. 70
Due from State banks	276, 865. 46	264, 069. 64	129, 761. 80	82, 696. 31	287, 157. 41
Real estate, etc	79, 193. 57	78, 723. 34	78, 673. 34	78, 673. 34	75, 356. 28
Current expenses	2, 574. 32	9, 450. 28	13, 122. 01	6, 284. 61	6, 928. 63
Premiums paid	11, 314. 60	11, 472. 60	21, 897. 60	72, 958. 00	65, 708. 00
Cash items	1, 008. 78	7, 902. 01	17, 855. 13	4, 321. 72	2, 171. 63
Clear'g-house exch'gs	250, 892. 40	98, 333. 10	235, 741. 24	274, 559. 83	175, 856. 87
Bills of other banks	1, 330. 00	7, 252. 00	7, 428. 00	5, 498. 00	5, 109. 00
Uncur't & minor coins	8. 34	167. 41	499. 62	126. 11	120. 72
Trade dollars	....	....	....	....	....
Specie	983, 772. 50	909, 092. 25	1, 427, 320. 20	961, 070. 75	1, 090, 478. 40
Legal-tender notes	3, 321. 00	2, 266. 00	6, 073. 00	2, 857. 00	6, 705. 00
U. S. cert's of deposit	....	....	....	....	....
5% fund with Treas	29, 250. 00	31, 500. 00	33, 750. 00	33, 750. 00	33, 750. 00
Due from U. S. Treas	....	....	....	4, 666. 67	2, 250. 00
Total	6, 418, 083. 62	6, 720, 536. 04	7, 370, 117. 57	7, 583, 064. 77	7, 991, 811. 50

by States and reserve cities—Continued.

NEVADA.

Liabilities.	DECEMBER 28.	MARCH 4.	MAY 13.	AUGUST 1.	OCTOBER 5.
	2 banks.	2 banks.	2 banks.	2 banks.	2 banks.
Capital stock	$150,000.00	$150,000.00	$150,000.00	150,000.00	$150,000.00
Surplus fund	30,000.00	30,000.00	30,000.00	40,000.00	40,000.00
Undivided profits	15,217.94	12,287.75	20,278.65	8,300.12	12,467.90
Nat'l-bank circulation	31,420.00	33,720.00	33,720.00	33,720.00	33,720.00
State-bank circulation					
Dividends unpaid				1,900.00	
Individual deposits	262,306.08	339,410.05	297,762.81	292,176.18	350,914.62
U. S. deposits					
Dep'ts U.S.dis.officers					
Due to national banks	43,806.08	30,669.54	44,266.65	71,076.50	59,887.80
Due to State banks	42,808.95	23,999.91	31,410.30	45,622.59	52,608.15
Notes re-discounted					
Bills payable					
Total	575,649.05	629,087.25	607,378.61	645,861.39	699,598.53

CALIFORNIA.

Liabilities.	DECEMBER 28.	MARCH 4.	MAY 13.	AUGUST 1.	OCTOBER 5.
	24 banks.	24 banks.	25 banks.	28 banks.	30 banks.
Capital stock	$3,160,000.00	$3,350,000.00	$3,500,000.00	$3,795,000.00	$4,170,000.00
Surplus fund	640,401.13	638,171.47	657,171.47	742,158.42	767,570.05
Undivided profits	577,893.76	417,392.62	549,944.83	454,958.64	610,809.30
Nat'l-bank circulation	797,070.00	777,340.00	781,570.00	814,040.00	939,990.00
State-bank circulation					
Dividends unpaid	1,719.00	4,740.61	2,434.25	9,556.50	14,716.25
Individual deposits	11,653,076.38	12,344,840.78	14,683,703.26	16,500,125.79	19,545,186.09
U. S. deposits	40,872.03	41,998.52	8,682.92	16,062.10	42,552.30
Dep'ts U.S.dis.officers	1,725.00	63,765.36	141,150.04	103,766.93	115,429.50
Due to national banks	126,749.15	97,863.39	250,557.20	83,187.84	149,285.71
Due to State banks	146,263.09	157,609.22	224,385.08	203,355.12	255,839.36
Notes re-discounted					
Bills payable	5,500.00	5,500.00	5,500.00	5,500.00	5,500.00
Total	17,151,269.54	17,890,281.97	20,814,009.14	22,727,711.34	26,616,946.45

SAN FRANCISCO.

Liabilities.	DECEMBER 28.	MARCH 4.	MAY 13.	AUGUST 1.	OCTOBER 5.
	2 banks.	3 banks.	3 banks.	3 banks.	3 banks.
Capital stock	$2,500,000.00	$2,660,000.00	$2,700,000.00	$2,700,000.00	$2,700,000.00
Surplus fund	250,470.35	253,801.24	256,801.24	259,046.02	259,046.02
Undivided profits	119,537.52	135,333.90	131,217.90	211,398.47	253,040.00
Nat'l-bank circulation	494,100.00	623,350.00	662,070.00	646,700.00	659,790.00
State-bank circulation					
Dividends unpaid	2,814.75	2,351.00	2,904.00	3,863.00	2,841.00
Individual deposits	2,211,072.65	2,033,377.48	2,455,171.87	2,718,954.03	2,591,218.61
U. S. deposits					
Dep'ts U.S.dis.officers					
Due to national banks	597,359.81	712,954.39	709,237.00	680,355.95	954,597.82
Due to State banks	273,628.54	305,278.63	458,624.96	363,647.30	571,272.05
Notes re-discounted					
Bills payable					
Total	6,448,983.62	6,720,536.64	7,370,117.57	7,583,064.77	7,991,811.50

Abstract of reports since October 7, 1886, arranged

OREGON.

Resources.	DECEMBER 28.	MARCH 4.	MAY 13.	AUGUST 1.	OCTOBER 5.
	18 banks.	18 banks.	20 banks.	22 banks.	23 banks.
Loans and discounts	$3, 660, 523. 71	$3, 800, 060. 03	$4, 031, 649. 30	$5, 212, 333. 05	$5, 785, 630. 07
Bonds for circulation	612, 100. 00	612, 100. 00	632, 600. 00	657, 300. 00	644, 800. 00
Bonds for deposits	600, 000. 00	600, 000. 00	600, 000. 00	600, 000. 00	600, 000. 00
U. S. bonds on hand	8, 100. 00	9, 600. 00	4, 000. 00	....	....
Other stocks and b'ds	800, 988. 77	983, 148. 84	950, 727. 94	861, 542. 51	765, 147. 78
Due from res've ag'ts	180, 972. 05	218, 519. 97	151, 386. 24	205, 711. 70	207, 738. 58
Due from nat'l banks	223, 555. 48	214, 634. 88	207, 681. 58	356, 7.9. 76	323, 429. 02
Due from State banks	109, 230. 31	242, 101. 28	184, 227. 65	309, 629. 13	103, 331. 04
Real estate, etc	234, 952. 03	247, 644. 72	254, 337. 50	262, 870. 80	272, 120. 62
Current expenses	53, 473. 53	29, 113. 45	54, 202. 40	26, 530. 46	46, 447. 91
Premiums paid	102, 704. 26	79, 771. 21	91, 530. 45	72, 391. 62	89, 788. 46
Cash items	43, 704. 41	29, 781. 73	31, 145. 95	49, 735. 88	69, 118. 39
Clear'g-house exch'gs	....	....	....	....	....
Bills of other banks	19, 365. 00	26, 602. 00	18, 047. 00	22, 140. 00	19, 875. 00
Uncur't & minor coins	860. 47	1, 439. 51	1, 114. 12	926. 22	2, 002. 31
Trade dollars	....	....	....	....	....
Specie	977, 136. 00	1, 082, 132. 80	880, 240. 80	806, 946. 00	947, 473. 88
Legal-tender notes	22, 312. 00	24, 401. 00	50, 038. 00	64, 070. 00	38, 583. 00
U. S. cert's of deposit	....	....	....	....	....
5 % fund with Treas.	27, 383. 00	27, 487. 39	27, 808. 50	29, 568. 00	29, 010. 00
Due from U. S. Treas.	3, 465. 00	550. 00	2, 650. 00	2, 903. 00	1, 600. 00
Total	7, 770, 826. 02	8, 298, 779. 71	8, 773, 477. 43	9, 542, 035. 19	10, 036, 186. 96

ARIZONA.

	— bank.	— bank.	— bank.	1 bank.	1 bank.
Loans and discounts	....	....	....	$160, 547. 98	$173, 584. 15
Bonds for circulation	....	....	....	25, 000. 00	25, 000. 00
Bonds for deposits	....	....	....	....	....
U. S. bonds on hand	....	....	....	....	....
Other stocks and b'ds	....	....	....	54, 117. 45	72, 721. 28
Due from res've ag'ts	....	....	....	....	....
Due from nat'l banks	....	....	....	....	....
Due from State banks	....	....	....	....	1, 320. 48
Real estate, etc	....	....	....	12, 954. 50	12, 954. 50
Current expenses	....	....	....	249. 57	1, 934. 40
Premiums paid	....	....	....	2, 500. 00	2, 500. 00
Cash items	....	....	....	517. 30	1, 170. 26
Clear'g-house exch'gs	....	....	....	....	....
Bills of other banks	....	....	....	4, 937. 00	470. 00
Uncur't & minor coins	....	....	....	....	....
Trade dollars	....	....	....	....	....
Specie	....	....	....	31, 149. 20	19, 351. 95
Legal-tender notes	....	....	....	11, 000. 00	12, 550. 00
U. S. cert's of deposit	....	....	....	....	....
5 % fund with Treas.	....	....	....	....	1, 125. 00
Due from U. S. Treas.	....	....	....	....	....
Total	....	....	....	303, 003. 00	324, 688. 02

DAKOTA.

	54 banks.	56 banks.	60 banks.	62 banks.	62 banks.
Loans and discounts	$5, 227, 140. 48	$5, 418, 118. 91	$6, 244, 244. 25	$6, 700, 629. 48	$6, 833, 776. 08
Bonds for circulation	889, 750. 00	920, 750. 00	931, 000. 00	962, 500. 00	962, 500. 00
Bonds for deposits	200, 000. 00	200, 000. 00	250, 000. 00	275, 000. 00	275, 000. 00
U. S. bonds on hand	....	....	....	....	....
Other stocks and b'ds	338, 453. 78	356, 032. 74	416, 630. 71	430, 965. 44	473, 140. 06
Due from res've ag'ts	495, 771. 81	425, 405. 44	370, 097. 60	410, 467. 39	452, 493. 49
Due from nat'l banks	683, 204. 86	749, 066. 03	600, 230. 04	630, 943. 14	1, 106, 521. 06
Due from State banks	103, 134. 30	126, 673. 48	167, 285. 68	78, 503. 86	135, 278. 36
Real estate, etc	618, 902. 82	662, 849. 07	729, 832. 01	751, 029. 53	770, 358. 42
Current expenses	130, 423. 48	84, 579. 09	134, 725. 95	58, 474. 17	112, 803. 01
Premiums paid	94, 343. 22	101, 243. 84	122, 020. 09	140, 608. 71	138, 924. 04
Cash items	133, 510. 56	89, 009. 02	101, 584. 38	101, 234. 35	163, 518. 57
Clear'g-house exch'gs	....	....	....	....	....
Bills of other banks	187, 612. 00	130, 880. 00	105, 706. 00	106, 342. 00	161, 087. 00
Uncur't & minor coins	2, 360. 27	2, 612. 15	3, 352. 28	4, 473. 71	3, 100. 96
Trade dollars	....	....	....	....	....
Specie	347, 962. 20	302, 748. 60	355, 456. 76	338, 798. 00	449, 654. 35
Legal-tender notes	327, 086. 00	286, 914. 00	287, 424. 00	334, 403. 00	387, 080. 00
U. S. cert's of deposit	....	....	....	....	....
5 % fund with Treas.	38, 824. 25	39, 874. 25	40, 286. 90	42, 576. 75	43, 308. 25
Due from U. S. Treas.	1, 531. 72	2, 469. 72	61. 02	2, 710. 00	2, 510. 00
Total	0, 820, 101. 75	0, 990, 156. 24	10, 880, 806. 55	11, 430, 619. 53	12, 472, 033. 75

by States and reserve cities—Continued.

OREGON.

Liabilities.	DECEMBER 28. 18 banks.	MARCH 4. 18 banks.	MAY 13. 20 banks.	AUGUST 1. 22 banks.	OCTOBER 5. 23 banks.
Capital stock	$1,335,000.00	$1,355,000.00	$1,505,000.00	$1,740,000.00	$1,705,000.00
Surplus fund	96,536.07	103,850.00	107,350.00	150,850.00	152,850.00
Undivided profits	709,339.54	806,900.03	909,960.92	884,075.69	958,658.32
Nat'l bank circulation	534,810.00	531,850.00	526,310.00	580,110.00	566,160.00
State bank circulation	....	....	....	....	....
Dividends unpaid	....	5,606.00	5,600.00	8,840.00	2,497.50
Individual deposits	3,802,134.24	4,461,929.96	4,445,945.80	5,127,707.75	5,325,301.22
U. S. deposits	207,820.97	227,875.78	217,904.38	251,240.50	126,810.64
Dep'ts U.S.dis.officers	355,228.13	303,036.07	327,840.33	317,437.37	382,607.30
Due to national banks	346,497.24	165,219.38	389,015.50	304,354.66	312,603.85
Due to State banks	293,450.83	312,344.37	247,131.79	177,108.18	398,212.38
Notes re-discounted	....	4,273.50	....	....	....
Bills payable	....	832.62	1,322.71	301.95	15,245.69
Total	7,770,826.02	8,298,779.71	8,773,477.43	9,542,035.19	10,036,186.96

ARIZONA.

	— bank.	— bank.	— bank.	1 bank.	1 bank.
Capital stock	....	....	....	$100,000.00	$100,000.00
Surplus fund	....	....	....	....	....
Undivided profits	....	....	....	336.77	6,270.28
Nat'l bank circulation	....	....	....	....	22,000.00
State bank circulation	....	....	....	....	....
Dividends unpaid	....	....	....	....	....
Individual deposits	....	....	....	153,129.23	133,103.00
U. S. deposits	....	....	....	....	....
Dep'ts U.S.dis.officers	....	....	....	....	....
Due to national banks	....	....	....	....	....
Due to State banks	....	....	....	49,537.00	63,314.74
Notes re-discounted	....	....	....	....	....
Bills payable	....	....	....	....	....
Total	....	....	....	303,003.00	324,688.02

DAKOTA.

	54 banks.	56 banks.	60 banks.	62 banks.	62 banks.
Capital stock	$3,080,000.00	$3,260,000.00	$3,575,000.00	$3,692,500.00	$3,720,000.00
Surplus fund	497,216.85	584,867.17	674,387.17	663,481.15	663,831.15
Undivided profits	513,462.40	235,241.84	380,791.84	235,366.31	383,175.99
Nat'l bank circulation	760,085.00	821,065.00	818,300.00	848,780.00	861,925.00
State bank circulation	....	....	....	....	....
Dividends unpaid	192.00	9,765.70	8,036.79	15,918.84	2,390.00
Individual deposits	4,369,168.51	4,538,299.22	4,725,959.54	5,112,837.57	5,818,810.67
U. S. deposits	153,116.61	147,237.95	162,924.26	190,675.96	226,386.50
Dep'ts U.S.dis.officers	19,720.83	26,691.23	35,342.02	12,486.23	19,305.27
Due to national banks	65,383.84	58,363.65	64,892.39	106,448.31	150,723.58
Due to State banks	168,094.65	142,795.13	172,559.03	157,539.76	270,582.15
Notes re-discounted	144,595.56	151,809.26	222,468.09	354,585.40	282,894.35
Bills payable	12,057.00	23,000.00	40,203.62	49,000.00	42,000.00
Total	9,829,101.75	9,909,156.24	10,880,866.55	11,439,619.53	12,472,033.75

Abstract of reports since October 7, 1886, arranged

IDAHO.

	6 banks.	6 banks.	6 banks.	6 banks.	6 banks.
Loans and discounts	$511, 192. 25	$513, 088. 79	$564, 028. 84	$560, 299. 16	$577, 769. 75
Bonds for circulation	105, 300. 00	105, 300. 00	92, 800. 00	92, 800. 00	92, 800. 00
Bonds for deposits	50, 000. 00	50, 000. 00	50, 000. 00	50, 000. 00	50, 000. 00
U. S. bonds on hand	....	....	....	....	....
Other stocks and b'ds	138, 701. 72	126, 885. 11	158, 155. 38	176, 013. 11	190, 186. 17
Due from res've ag'ts	17, 896. 19	20, 999. 70	15, 413. 90	7, 038. 53	23, 234. 45
Due from nat'l banks	28, 921. 38	42, 089. 97	43, 670. 72	22, 449. 29	26, 879. 70
Due from State banks	65, 520. 20	18, 371. 71	33, 680. 42	80, 616. 12	48, 980. 54
Real estate, etc	27, 858. 08	35, 068. 63	35, 236. 43	35, 513. 03	41, 443. 48
Current expenses	19, 158. 97	8, 979. 58	7, 263. 53	11, 052. 62	17, 834. 45
Premiums paid	21, 072. 74	21, 381. 42	16, 474. 56	15, 485. 76	15, 104. 19
Cash items	18, 956. 64	4, 067. 93	5, 197. 01	21, 852. 88	5, 305. 40
Clear'g-house exch'gs	....	....	....	....	....
Bills of other banks	34, 861. 00	54, 611. 00	30, 517. 00	53, 023. 00	51, 385. 00
Uncur't & minor coins	48. 36	38. 66	65. 64	18. 00	23. 72
Trade dollars	10. 00	10. 00	10. 00	....	....
Specie	65, 463. 97	65, 974. 79	51, 988. 70	45, 368. 00	48, 847. 40
Legal-tender notes	49, 907. 00	43, 652. 00	42, 630. 00	41, 048. 00	39, 715. 00
U. S. cert's of deposit	....	....	....	....	....
5 % fund with Treas	4, 727. 50	4, 737. 50	4, 175. 00	4, 175. 00	4, 175. 00
Due from U. S. Treas	100. 00	....	100. 00	....	....
Total	1, 155, 356. 00	1, 115, 856. 88	1, 151, 407. 13	1, 166, 751. 91	1, 233, 684. 31

MONTANA.

Resources.	DECEMBER 28.	MARCH 4.	MAY 13.	AUGUST 1.	OCTOBER 5.
	16 banks.	17 banks.	17 banks.	17 banks.	17 banks.
Loans and discounts	$7, 266, 278. 53	$7, 388, 050. 91	$7, 912, 142. 19	$8, 329, 723. 91	$8, 236, 786. 34
Bonds for circulation	455, 600. 00	468, 100. 00	468, 100. 00	468, 100. 00	480, 000. 00
Bonds for deposits	200, 000. 00	200, 000. 00	200, 000. 00	200, 000. 00	200, 000. 00
U. S. bonds on hand	....	....	....	10, 150. 00	10, 150. 00
Other stocks and b'ds	432, 149. 31	423, 383. 78	428, 593. 78	468, 170. 61	519, 027. 05
Due from res've ag'ts	315, 534. 55	288, 9 9. 97	270, 303. 23	479, 060. 33	408, 208. 50
Due from nat'l banks	480, 569. 36	400, 020. 22	570, 694. 48	636, 092. 07	632, 881. 08
Due from State banks	403, 317. 00	375, 287. 95	606, 817. 13	433, 165. 57	563, 748. 37
Real estate, etc	356, 231. 88	371, 460. 66	360, 837. 41	355, 701. 28	421, 795. 37
Current expenses	100, 721. 56	39, 283. 33	56, 125. 52	25, 765. 57	46, 074. 03
Premiums paid	67, 973. 52	68, 834. 55	68, 029. 02	67, 920. 50	65, 783. 21
Cash items	151, 048. 14	118, 019. 18	57, 825. 77	131, 021. 93	46, 403. 13
Clear'g-house exch'gs	....	....	....	....	....
Bills of other banks	139, 241. 00	72, 601. 00	79, 925. 00	90, 695. 00	82, 535. 00
Uncur't & minor coins	908. 42	1, 109. 73	882. 64	1, 068. 87	960. 89
Trade dollars	....	....	....	....	....
Specie	811, 666. 55	784, 813. 90	757, 975. 10	701, 379. 80	700, 193. 20
Legal-tender notes	445, 493. 00	436, 093. 00	470, 440. 00	558, 610. 00	624, 105. 00
U. S. cert's of deposit	....	....	....	....	....
5 % fund with Treas	20, 499. 50	20, 941. 50	21, 061. 50	21, 061. 50	21, 649. 50
Due from U. S. Treas	4, 782. 17	10, 288. 15	13, 675. 10	14, 462. 49	17, 668. 49
Total	11, 664, 105. 30	11, 527, 237. 83	12, 349, 427. 96	12, 992, 152. 43	13, 138, 821. 35

NEW MEXICO.

	9 banks.	9 banks.	9 banks.	9 banks.	9 banks.
Loans and discounts	$1, 692, 659. 39	$1, 721, 783. 80	$1, 744, 362. 63	$1, 719, 012. 88	$1, 751, 005. 18
Bonds for circulation	202, 500. 00	240, 000. 00	240, 000. 00	240, 000. 00	210, 000. 00
Bonds for deposits	210, 000. 00	100, 000. 00	125, 000. 00	125, 000. 00	125, 000. 00
U. S. bonds on hand	....	....	....	....	....
Other stocks and bd's	25, 804. 18	34, 561. 52	32, 818. 99	34, 403. 71	30, 035. 71
Due from res've ag'ts	240, 886. 30	222, 136. 41	162, 439. 15	202, 327. 88	188, 297. 05
Due from nat'l banks	269, 277. 44	283, 559. 69	507, 342. 88	561, 132. 66	287, 318. 45
Due from State banks	67, 379. 50	67, 449. 74	58, 787. 27	76, 085. 85	50, 162. 21
Real estate, etc	179, 650. 43	185, 483. 08	185, 563. 02	180, 813. 51	179, 647. 85
Current expenses	51, 817. 19	23, 148. 13	25, 912. 26	8, 917. 74	15, 513. 73
Premiums paid	20, 468. 59	29, 121. 03	31, 950. 34	23, 459. 26	22, 130. 06
Cash items	13, 433. 42	17, 011. 18	11, 455. 70	13, 014. 50	11, 521. 86
Clear'g-house exch'gs	....	....	....	....	....
Bills of other banks	29, 366. 00	25, 755. 00	25, 530. 00	18, 745. 00	28, 007. 00
Uncur't & minor coins	937. 27	791. 75	791. 27	674. 06	780. 86
Trade dollars	....	....	....	....	....
Specie	161, 210. 95	137, 516. 90	117, 268. 20	112, 613. 00	99, 543. 40
Legal-tender notes	105, 272. 00	85, 051. 00	87, 477. 00	102, 081. 00	81, 223. 00
U. S. cert's of deposit	....	....	....	....	....
5 % fund with Treas	11, 482. 05	10, 799. 50	10, 700. 50	10, 799. 50	10, 799. 50
Due from U. S. Treas	2, 000. 00	4, 480. 00	1, 030. 00	1, 007. 00	2, 017. 12
Total	3, 341, 304. 80	3, 188, 717. 82	3, 371, 502. 11	3, 434, 138. 18	3, 135, 138. 01

by States and reserve cities—Continued.

IDAHO.

	6 banks.	6 banks.	6 banks.	6 banks.	6 banks.
Capital stock	$350,000.00	$350,000.00	$350,000.00	$350,000.00	$350,000.00
Surplus fund	22,000.00	27,120.59	27,120.59	28,981.13	28,981.13
Undivided profits	96,614.92	65,659.09	69,488.78	77,981.46	89,289.00
Nat'l bank circulation	89,815.00	93,115.00	81,880.00	80,700.00	81,940.00
State bank circulation	....	....	....	....	....
Dividends unpaid	....	....	....	....	....
Individual deposits	501,554.80	437,307.00	533,816.63	520,902.50	576,821.10
U. S. deposits	2,118.73	7,627.35	30,511.43	44,148.04	44,886.61
Dep'ts U.S. dis. officers	22,395.73	42,288.13	14,638.40	120.10	177.02
Due to national banks	4,097.23	706.68	2,082.35	7,183.60	8,755.02
Due to State banks	66,720.59	71,963.44	41,850.86	56,735.08	52,833.53
Notes re-discounted	....	....	....	....	....
Bills payable	....	....	....	....	....
Total	1,155,350.00	1,115,856.88	1,151,407.13	1,166,751.91	1,233,684.31

MONTANA.

Liabilities.	DECEMBER 28.	MARCH 4.	MAY 13.	AUGUST 1.	OCTOBER 5.
	16 banks.	17 banks.	17 banks.	17 banks.	17 banks.
Capital stock	$1,867,500.00	$1,925,000.00	$1,925,000.00	$1,925,000.00	$1,975,000.00
Surplus fund	333,125.00	369,250.00	400,250.00	413,950.00	420,450.00
Undivided profits	1,030,802.27	896,226.66	948,264.13	993,563.53	1,090,974.72
Nat'l bank circulation	397,530.00	414,680.00	413,500.00	409,830.00	422,280.00
State bank circulation	....	....	....	....	....
Dividends unpaid	....	6,400.00	5,040.60	7,880.00	4,860.00
Individual deposits	7,131,484.54	6,978,977.10	7,651,808.54	8,112,102.53	8,120,148.06
U. S. deposits	67,428.73	67,212.22	68,037.10	81,053.50	81,533.52
Dep'ts U.S. dis. officers	109,937.08	107,806.70	90,821.52	90,295.33	72,519.00
Due to national banks	508,828.02	472,537.50	576,906.26	662,421.64	574,834.55
Due to State banks	125,501.02	102,960.50	63,174.12	168,714.36	207,979.97
Notes re-discounted	91,967.83	179,097.00	167,446.20	122,341.54	78,221.53
Bills payable	....	5,000.00	10,000.00	5,000.00	....
Total	11,664,105.39	11,527,237.83	12,340,427.96	12,992,152.43	13,138,821.35

NEW MEXICO.

	9 banks.	9 banks.	9 banks.	9 banks.	9 banks.
Capital stock	$825,000.00	$825,000.00	$850,000.00	$850,000.00	$850,000.00
Surplus fund	164,408.81	168,208.81	169,571.46	172,735.86	176,635.86
Undivided profits	95,058.98	37,164.76	51,084.53	21,807.20	40,683.95
Nat'l bank circulation	236,240.00	215,900.00	215,090.00	215,900.00	215,900.00
State bank circulation	....	....	....	....	....
Dividends unpaid	555.00	575.00	45.00	5,102.00	208.00
Individual deposits	1,620,437.79	1,583,258.17	1,518,828.48	1,058,154.25	1,406,752.20
U. S. deposits	130,171.89	2,100.97	19,680.19	16,100.80	33,570.23
Dep'ts U.S. dis. officers	83,094.20	72,151.11	111,327.27	84,300.73	80,770.53
Due to national banks	113,123.38	152,384.10	300,090.79	271,249.50	133,987.53
Due to State banks	68,274.06	106,939.65	81,538.14	90,987.81	83,607.71
Notes re-discounted	7,000.00	24,986.25	23,436.25	47,401.00	22,917.00
Bills payable	....	....	....	....	....
Total	3,344,304.80	3,188,717.82	3,371,502.11	3,434,138.18	3,135,138.01

Abstract of reports since October 7, 1886, arranged

UTAH.

	7 banks.	7 banks.	7 banks.	7 banks.	7 banks.
Loans and discounts	$2,065,541.03	$2,061,379.79	$2,127,577.07	$1,971,064.65	$2,119,364.03
Bonds for circulation	400,000.00	400,000.00	400,000.00	390,000.00	390,000.00
Bonds for deposits	100,000.00	100,000.00	100,000.00	150,000.00	200,000.00
U.S. bonds on hand	....	....	40,000.00	1,000.00	101,000.00
Other stocks and bd's	194,538.07	194,538.07	181,321.07	189,240.07	164,084.07
Due from res've ag'ts	90,000.13	75,519.25	117,282.33	500,921.72	302,007.14
Due from nat'l banks	248,390.01	180,348.35	264,964.81	140,908.96	134,247.14
Due from State banks	78,724.56	73,210.25	78,409.96	100,514.84	92,155.30
Real estate, etc	124,099.63	123,299.13	123,321.48	127,081.32	125,743.28
Current expenses	34,540.85	17,774.16	15,076.30	12,586.29	22,216.91
Premiums paid	51,885.57	51,385.57	51,885.57	54,155.57	89,832.12
Cash items	10,401.38	9,502.21	7,932.10	14,474.54	13,299.57
Clear'g house exch'gs	....	....	....	....	....
Bills of other banks	29,286.00	12,980.00	12,846.00	29,120.00	52,712.00
Uncur't & minor coins	261.86	1,027.25	1,012.41	503.06	322.01
Trade dollars	19.00	15.00	16.00	16.00	....
Specie	344,302.85	265,317.60	230,786.68	262,146.14	307,242.20
Legal-tender notes	36,023.00	31,571.00	40,150.00	49,148.00	70,408.00
U.S. cert's of deposit	....	....	....	....	....
5 % fund with Treas	17,409.50	17,999.50	18,000.00	17,550.00	17,550.00
Due from U.S. Treas	....	....	....	1,000.00	....
Total	3,826,491.44	3,635,927.13	3,822,590.87	4,012,430.16	4,202,333.86

WASHINGTON.

Resources.	DECEMBER 28.	MARCH 4.	MAY 13.	AUGUST 1.	OCTOBER 5.
	18 banks.	18 banks.	18 banks.	18 banks.	16 banks.
Loans and discounts	$2,551,302.75	$2,775,775.61	$3,070,816.96	$3,454,330.47	$3,831,631.97
Bonds for circulation	402,500.00	402,500.00	380,000.00	392,500.00	405,000.00
Bonds for deposits	....	....	....	....	....
U.S. bonds on hand	50,000.00	....	....	....	1,000.00
Other stocks and b'ds	206,646.25	294,089.28	218,882.77	284,236.09	326,967.46
Due from res've ag'ts	164,842.00	242,341.28	190,926.96	188,819.92	246,882.58
Due from nat'l banks	302,385.07	282,430.95	521,074.30	496,227.46	410,043.97
Due from State banks	152,153.21	148,211.06	90,127.84	131,225.99	109,918.08
Real estate, etc	178,063.50	184,096.46	204,412.78	224,195.43	220,356.27
Current expenses	40,827.55	28,674.80	43,290.42	13,224.17	20,087.83
Premiums paid	72,656.24	60,427.09	56,043.38	56,138.59	58,472.87
Cash items	21,770.71	19,281.03	30,908.49	34,767.75	23,226.83
Clear'g-house exch'gs	....	....	....	....	....
Bills of other banks	31,122.00	35,542.00	27,417.00	12,627.00	20,545.00
Uncur't & minor coins	363.10	250.20	290.01	341.50	258.80
Trade dollars	9,002.00	....	....	....	1.00
Specie	478,510.80	541,527.70	554,162.05	572,981.65	494,373.95
Legal-tender notes	22,345.00	31,700.00	32,828.00	22,131.00	51,120.00
U.S. cert's of deposit	....	....	....	....	....
5 % fund with Treas	17,851.50	18,112.50	17,100.00	16,520.00	17,812.50
Due from U.S. Treas	10.00	20.00	520.00	350.00	400.00
Total	4,782,351.77	5,066,479.95	5,447,830.96	5,990,617.03	6,254,199.11

WYOMING.

	7 banks.	8 banks.	8 banks.	8 banks.	8 banks.
Loans and discounts	$2,321,375.81	$2,315,220.90	$2,470,070.25	$2,490,790.61	$2,527,061.94
Bonds for circulation	198,750.00	223,750.00	223,750.00	223,750.00	223,750.00
Bonds for deposits	....	....	....	....	....
U.S. bonds on hand	....	....	....	....	....
Other stocks and b'ds	63,030.27	62,142.09	71,325.82	76,054.57	85,360.38
Due from res've ag'ts	232,055.09	146,259.90	167,181.43	222,103.56	107,676.52
Due from nat'l banks	212,091.25	117,229.06	140,959.86	110,263.91	76,632.44
Due from State banks	21,258.71	8,361.39	9,920.40	6,660.61	10,256.31
Real estate, etc	46,661.07	53,228.06	60,185.54	66,773.58	76,010.83
Current expenses	40,570.79	17,801.72	17,155.81	18,602.20	32,763.44
Premiums paid	23,227.78	22,825.56	22,521.90	22,396.90	23,876.90
Cash items	14,587.37	9,256.37	12,368.39	23,535.76	13,191.69
Clear'g-house exch'gs	....	....	....	....	....
Bills of other banks	27,505.00	35,750.00	27,211.00	17,018.00	15,234.00
Uncur't & minor coins	313.11	372.05	309.93	401.76	408.82
Trade dollars	....	....	....	....	....
Specie	310,073.08	279,421.10	256,663.74	265,008.48	236,016.15
Legal-tender notes	54,956.00	40,421.00	57,458.00	44,630.00	29,584.00
U.S. cert's of deposit	....	....	....	....	....
5 % fund with Treas	8,943.50	8,943.50	10,068.50	10,068.75	10,068.75
Due from U.S. Treas	3,210.00	700.00	500.00	1,100.00	....
Total	3,580,418.73	3,353,772.76	3,553,656.57	3,600,091.72	3,567,964.17

by States and reserve cities—Continued.

UTAH.

	7 banks.	7 banks.	7 banks.	7 banks.	7 banks.
Capital stock	$850,000.00	$850,000.00	$850,000.00	$850,000.00	$850,000.00
Surplus fund	302,750.00	328,250.00	328,500.00	371,000.00	373,000.00
Undivided profits	153,203.59	108,991.37	113,358.53	94,221.67	115,469.72
Nat'l bank circulation	294,630.00	280,570.00	285,970.00	208,530.00	292,130.00
State bank circulation	....	....	....	....	....
Dividends unpaid	1,140.00	1,574.00	1,541.00	2,186.00	1,276.00
Individual deposits	2,058,125.40	1,926,436.74	2,023,631.80	2,201,701.96	2,334,045.53
U. S. deposits	12,282.84	37,286.50	50,350.32	51,526.11	86,552.88
Dept's U.S. dis. officers	78,540.47	42,764.62	41,594.61	57,804.32	53,025.00
Due to national banks	56,630.57	26,980.07	43,048.23	37,190.48	67,116.94
Due to State banks	19,119.57	24,073.83	70,353.88	37,073.12	64,461.79
Notes re-discounted	....	....	14,242.50	11,202.50	23,756.00
Bills payable	....	....	....	....	....
Total	3,826,491.44	3,635,927.13	3,822,590.87	4,012,436.16	4,202,333.86

WASHINGTON.

Liabilities.	DECEMBER 28.	MARCH 4.	MAY 13.	AUGUST 1.	OCTOBER 5.
	18 banks.	18 banks.	18 banks.	18 banks.	18 banks.
Capital stock	$1,130,000.00	$1,130,000.00	$1,180,000.00	$1,230,000.00	$1,280,000.00
Surplus fund	155,450.36	190,077.02	199,077.02	229,456.93	233,456.93
Undivided profits	500,820.00	433,303.00	494,283.44	438,892.65	475,892.08
Nat'l bank circulation	350,480.00	354,720.00	341,225.00	341,850.00	350,540.00
State bank circulation	....	....	....	....	....
Dividends unpaid	240.00	480.00	310.00	1,490.00	440.00
Individual deposits	2,543,421.84	2,794,559.22	3,106,601.33	3,475,146.22	3,638,303.51
U.S. deposits	....	....	....	....	....
Dep'ts U.S. dis. officers	....	....	....	....	....
Due to national banks	50,821.29	81,296.13	58,266.82	110,968.83	135,240.48
Due to State banks	51,118.28	72,983.98	68,067.35	73,312.39	113,926.11
Notes re-discounted	....	....	....	....	....
Bills payable	....	....	....	....	20,400.00
Total	4,782,351.77	5,066,479.95	5,447,830.96	5,900,617.02	6,254,199.11

WYOMING.

	7 banks.	8 banks.	8 banks.	8 banks.	8 banks.
Capital stock	$953,550.00	$1,029,500.00	$1,055,000.00	$1,075,000.00	$1,075,000.00
Surplus fund	175,500.00	190,000.00	197,000.00	210,367.80	210,367.80
Undivided profits	215,806.71	140,755.55	153,693.49	141,273.10	180,369.55
Nat'l bank circulation	177,980.00	188,255.00	197,725.00	200,775.00	200,645.00
State bank circulation	....	....	....	....	....
Dividends unpaid	....	....	....	60.00	....
Individual deposits	1,012,561.62	1,633,994.91	1,783,113.06	1,718,461.95	1,697,281.62
U. S. deposits	....	....	....	....	....
Dep'ts U.S. dis. officers	....	....	....	....	....
Due to national banks	48,407.72	31,154.13	23,920.75	43,506.80	30,385.48
Due to State banks	14,609.94	8,613.17	4,537.86	14,016.34	15,900.69
Notes re-discounted	81,982.74	130,500.00	128,657.41	205,630.73	147,915.03
Bills payable	....	....	10,000.00	....	10,000.00
Total	3,580,418.73	3,352,772.76	3,553,656.57	3,609,091.72	3,567,964.17

INDEX.

	Page.
AMENDMENTS:	
To the laws relating to the national banking system	4
Salary of the Deputy Comptroller of the Currency, and enlargement of his duties	4
Officers of a bank not to constitute a majority of the board of directors	4
Revised oath of directors	4
Banks with branches can not retain them after entering the system	4
Method by which directors may resign their positions, and be discharged from further accountability	4
Relief to shareholders who do not assent to the extension of a bank	5
Relief in case of non-concurrence with directors as to appraisement of stock	5
Reducing amount of bonds now required to be deposited by banks	5
Modification of existing restrictions as to holding real estate	5
Surplus fund as a substitute for contingent liability of shareholders	5
As to custody and examination of plates and dies used in printing national-bank notes	5
National-bank notes as a part of the cash reserve of banks	6
Cashier's signature of circulating notes, how affixed	6
Repeal of provision requiring extended banks to deposit lawful money to retire circulation.	6
Provision as to profits arising from failure to redeem notes of banks extending their corporate existence, extended to other banks	6
Issue of notes of new design to all banks	6
Appropriation therefor	7
Plural offices of national banks	7
Sale of stock upon neglect or refusal of shareholders to pay assessment for the purpose of restoring impaired capital	7
Five per cent. redemption fund as part of the lawful-money reserve	7
Relief to banks of the obligation of keeping cash reserve against Government deposits	7
Investments in real-estate securities	8
Limit as to loans to individual, firm, or corporation	8
Penalty for loans made contrary to law	8
Responsibility of directors	9
Certification of checks	9
Usury	9
Penalty for failure of banks to transmit reports	9
Duties and responsibilities of examiners	9
New scale for reckoning assessment of examination fees upon national banks	9
Relieving banks of obligation to pay fees for preliminary and special examinations	9
Supervising examiners	9, 10
To reduce probability of failure of national banks for certain causes	10
Interposition of Comptroller in affairs of banks in voluntary liquidation	10
As to selection of agent of stockholders	11
Discharge of agents of stockholders	11
Duties of directors and officers of national banks that are in a position of insolvency	11
Discharge of receivers of national banks	11
Restoration to solvency of a national bank during receivership	11
Status of United States district attorney as to receiverships	11
Semi-annual tax on circulation	11
Protection of banks against discriminative State taxation	11
Criminal offenses	12
Use of the word "national" as a part of the corporate name by other than national banks	12
ASSESSMENTS:	
Shareholders	91
Cost of plates	107
Examiners' fees	108
BANKS. (*See* National banks; State banks; Savings banks; Private banks; Converted State banks; Loan and trust companies.)	

BONDS, UNITED STATES: Page.
Changes in law as to amount of deposit to secure circulation 5, 20
Deposited by banks organized during the year ending October 31, 1887 51
Minimum amount of bonds required to be kept on deposit by banks in operation October 5, 1887 66
Actually deposited and minimum required each year, 1882 to 1887 66
Outstanding interest-bearing bonds 68
Outstanding 3 per cent. bonds from August, 1, 1886, to July 1, 1887 69
Interest-bearing bonds the only legal security for circulation 71
Variations in market price 4 and 4½ per cents August, 1886, to August, 1887 72
Changes in bonds on deposit as security for circulation 73
Comparison for five years of bonds deposited as security for circulation 73–75
Additional circulation issued on 81
Highest and lowest amount of bonds on deposit to secure circulation 93
CAPITAL STOCK:
Of banks reporting during the year 2
Of national banks closed during the year 3
Of national banks organized during the year ending October 31, 1887 51
Of banks failed during the year ending October 31, 1887 52
Of banks to reach expiration of corporate existence up to the year 1901 60
Of banks the corporate existence of which will expire during 1888 61
Of banks organized in fiscal years from 1882 to 1887 .... 66, 75
Of banks organized during the year ending October 31, 1887, with capital of $50,000 67
Of banks organized during the year ending October 31, 1887, with capital of over $50,000 67
Of banks organized during the year ending October 31, 1887, with capital of over $150,000 67
Paid in during the year 70
Increase 76
Decrease 70
Impairment or withdrawal of 91
Reduction of 91
Amount of, 1886 and 1887 93
Variations in 93
Twenty-five cities (exclusive of reserve cities) having largest, with circulation, loans and discounts, and individual deposits 96
CIRCULATING NOTES:
Issued, redeemed, and outstanding, of national banks closed during the year 3
Issued to national banks organized during the year ending October 31, 1887 51
Amount issuable on bonds deposited 66
Minimum circulation 66
Possible maximum circulation 66
Circulation outstanding October 5, 1887 66
Decrease during the year 70
Banks without circulation 70
Retired since June 20, 1874 81
Issued to banks during the year 81
Amount of, 1886 and 1887 93
CLEARING-HOUSE TRANSACTIONS:
New York Clearing-House 102
Number of members 102
Comparative statement of aggregate clearings and balances for 1886 and 1887 102
Kinds of money used and amount of each kind, for 1886 and 1887 102
Gold certificates, Bank of America 102
Comparative statement of transactions of New York Clearing-House for thirty-four years 103
Clearing-house transactions of assistant treasurer United States in New York for year ending October 1, 1887 103
Comparative statement of the exchanges of the clearing-houses of the United States for October, 1886 and 1887 104
Comparative statement for last weeks in October, 1886 and 1887 105
Clearing-house transactions in thirty-seven cities of the United States for year ending September 30, 1887, and comparison with previous year 107
Percentages, exchanges, and balances, New York City 107
CLERKS IN THE OFFICE OF THE COMPTROLLER OF THE CURRENCY:
Names and compensation 46
CONCLUSION:
Suggestions received from various sources as to modification of present law, by which it is thought the system may be improved 118
Classification of plans suggested into propositions 118
General remarks on propositions 118–128

	Page.
CONVERTED STATE BANKS	56, 57
DECISIONS. (*See* Legal decisions.)	
In national-bank cases	133
Digest of national-bank cases	131
Digest of decisions in bank cases involving questions of practical banking	155
DIAGRAM:	
Grouping of main features of national banking system	93
DIRECTORS:	
Revised oath of	4
Officers of bank not to constitute a majority of board	4
Proceedings against, for losses and damages	91
Method by which directors may resign their positions, and be discharged from further accountability	4
Non-concurrence of shareholders as to appraisement of stock	5
Changes in law to establish antecedent presumption that directors know and consent to operations of bank	93
Protection to shareholders	92
DISSOLUTION. (*See* National bank failures, Receiverships, and Liquidation.)	
National banks closed during the year	3
In liquidation	3
Failed	3
Number of banks passed into liquidation since establishment of system	77
Number of banks placed in hands of receivers since establishment of system	77
Number of banks passed into liquidation by expiration of corporate existence	77
DIVIDENDS. (*See* Receiverships.)	
EXAMINERS:	
Accountability of directors	91
Scope of sections 5209, 5239, Revised Statutes of the United States	91
Duties of examiners	91
Conferences of	92
Reports of	93
Supervision	90
Examinations	92
Fees	90
Examinations at expense of bank	90
Assumption by the Government of such expense	90
Discovery of defalcations	90
Maladministration of directors, fraudulent entries on books, etc	90
Assessment for fees on national banks	108
EXAMINATIONS:	
Supervision	90
Territory, division of	92
Areas	92
EXPENSES OF THE OFFICE:	
Plates, printing, etc	47
Salaries of employés	47
EXTENSION OF CORPORATE EXISTENCE. (*See* National banks.)	
FAILURES. (*See* Receivers and Receiverships.)	
Of national banks during the year ending October 31, 1887	52
Causes of failure	52
FIVE PER CENT. REDEMPTION FUND. (*See* Redemption.)	
GOLD BANKS. (*See* National banks.)	
INFORMATION:	
Requirements of section 333 of the Revised Statutes of the United States	50
Number of national banks organized in each State and Territory during the year ending October 31, 1887, aggregate capital, bonds, and circulation	51
INTEREST-BEARING FUNDED DEBT OF THE UNITED STATES:	
Amount held by national banks	67
Maximum public debt	67
Interest-bearing debt October 31, 1887	67
Bonded debt for fiscal years from 1865 to 1887	68
Amount of 3 per cent. bonds issued, amount redeemed and outstanding from July 12, 1882, to October 31, 1887	68
Changes in debt from 1866 to October 5, 1887	73

INTRODUCTION: Page.
- Report submitted to Congress 1
- Requirements of section 333, United States Revised Statutes, in detail, as to Comptroller's report 1

ISSUES AND REDEMPTIONS. (*See* Circulating notes; Redemption.)
- National-bank notes issued and redeemed during the year 80
- Additional circulation issued during the year 80, 81
- Amount issued under act of July 12, 1882, during the year 81
- Circulation retired 81
- Duties devolving upon clerical force 82
- Issues of incomplete currency during the year 82
- Amount received from Bureau of Engraving and Printing during the year 82
- Amount canceled not having been issued 82
- Amount in vaults 82

LAWFUL-MONEY DEPOSITS. (*See* Redemption.)

LEGAL DECISIONS. (*See* Decisions.)
- Suggestions as to interstate commercial code 38

LIABILITIES OF NATIONAL BANKS:
- On dates of report during the year ending October 31, 1887 2

LIQUIDATION. (*See* Dissolution.)

LOANS:
- Classification of, in central reserve cities, reserve cities, and country 94
- In New York City for past five years 95

LOAN AND TRUST COMPANIES:
- Official returns from 38
- Capital stock, surplus and undivided profits, and deposits 39
- Official and unofficial 39
- Distribution of stock 39
- Gold, silver, legal tenders, and national-bank notes held 39
- Aggregate resources and liabilities, official and unofficial 40
- Aggregate resources, liabilities, and condition, from unofficial sources 41
- Number, capital stock, surplus, and undivided profits and deposits 42
- Distribution, number, and average par value of shares of stock 45

MORTGAGES ON REAL ESTATE. (*See* Amendments.)

NATIONAL BANKS:
- Summary of the state and condition of every national bank reporting during the year ending October 31, 1887 2
- Closed during the year 3
- Organization of branches 4
- Organized during the year ending October 31, 1887 51
- Aggregate capital, bonds, and circulation 51
- Organization of 55
- How organized, by whom they may be organized, and necessary steps 55
- Amount of bonds required to be deposited under original act and amendments 56
- Capital at date of organization 58
- Present capital and surplus 58
- Number that have gone into voluntary liquidation 58
- Number that have become insolvent 58
- Extension of the corporate existence of 59
- Number of which the corporate existence has been extended 59, 77
- Number organized under national currency act of February 25, 1863 59
- Number organized under national-bank act of June 3, 1864 59
- Number extended under act of July 12, 1882 59
- Number still in operation under original certificate of organization 59
- Number in operation October 31, 1887 59
- Number to reach term of corporate existence from 1888 to 1901, inclusive 60
- Number of which period of succession terminated during the year ending October 31, 1887 60
- Number of which corporate existence will expire during the year 1888 61
- Number organized during fiscal years from 1882 to 1887 66
- Number organized since establishment of system 79
- Number placed in liquidation 79
- Number which failed 79
- Number reorganized 79
- Gold banks 88
- Deposits, loans and discounts, cash, etc., 1866 and 1887 93
- Supervision of 90

NATIONAL BANKS—Continued. Page.
Aggregate capital, surplus, undivided profits, circulation and deposits, 1886 and 1887 94
Loans and discounts 94
Investment in bonds 94
Specie 94
Loans and discounts, United States bonds, and specie percentages 94
Organized under act of February 25, 1863, excluded from acting as reserve agents 98
Amount of reserve required 99
Redemption fund as a part of reserve 99
Examiners' fees 108
Taxation by States 108
NATIONAL-BANK CODE:
As proposed 12
NATIONAL-BANK FAILURES. (*See* Dissolution.)
Causes of failure 52
Surplus and undivided profits of banks failed during the year ending October 31, 1887 52
Liabilities at date of last report of condition 52
NATIONAL BANKING LAWS. (*See* Amendments.)
OFFICERS AND CLERKS IN THE OFFICE OF THE COMPTROLLER OF THE CURRENCY:
Names and compensation 46
ORGANIZATION OF NATIONAL BANKS:
Increase 47
Number of national banks organized in each State and Territory during the year ending October 31, 1887, aggregate capital, bonds, and circulation 51
ORGANIZATION AND EXPENSES OF THE BUREAU OF THE CURRENCY:
Increased labor devolving upon employés 47
Growth of the national banking system 47
Recommendations as to improvement in organization of Bureau 48
Clerical work performed in the office 49
Value of items representing clerical work 49
Comparative statement as to work performed and compensation paid, by years 50
PRIVATE BANKS:
Official returns from 38
Capital, surplus and undivided profits 39
Official and unofficial 30
Aggregate resources, liabilities, and condition, from official sources 40
Aggregate resources, liabilities, and condition from unofficial sources 41
Number, capital stock, surplus and undivided profits, and deposits 43
Number, capital, deposits, investments in United States bonds up to May 31, 1882 45
REAL-ESTATE SECURITIES. (*See* Amendments.)
RECEIVERS. (*See* Receiverships.)
Appointed during the year 52
RECEIVERSHIPS. (*See* Receivers.)
Number of banks failed during the year 77
Dividends paid 77
Number of banks placed in hands of receivers since establishment of system 77
Restored to solvency 77
Number of insolvent banks closed during the year 77
Total dividends, principal, and interest paid to creditors of insolvent banks 77, 79
Inactive 77
Names and location of banks 77
Total dividends paid creditors during the year 79
Amount of assessments upon shareholders 79
Amount collected from that source 79
Pending litigation 79
REDEMPTION:
Statutes in respect thereto 82
Five per cent. redemption fund 83
Deposits of lawful money 83
Amounts of national-bank currency received annually at redemption agency 84
Localities from which forwarded and percentages 85
Total amount of notes redeemed and mode of redemption 86
Of notes of insolvent national banks 87
Of notes of banks reducing circulation under act of June 20, 1874 87
Amount of notes of failed banks redeemed and outstanding since establishment of system .. 87
Of notes of banks in voluntary liquidation 88

REDEMPTION—Continued. Page.
Total amount lawful money deposited under act of June 20, 1874, on account of liquidating and insolvent banks, and under section 6, act of July 12, 1882 88
Amount deposited for redemption of notes of gold banks 88
Amount deposited under section 6 of act of July 12, 1882 88
Total amount of lawful money deposited during the year 88
By banks in liquidation 88
By banks reducing circulation, act June 20, 1874 88
By banks retiring old circulation, act July 12, 1882 88
Amounts previously deposited 88
Notes redeemed and destroyed without reissue 88
Notes redeemed and destroyed prior to June 20, 1874 88
Notes redeemed and destroyed since June 20, 1874 88
Notes of gold banks 88
Total national-bank notes received for redemption since establishment of system 88
Limit of term for deposit of lawful money by liquidating banks 88
National-bank notes received at Treasury during past year and percentages as to localities from which received 88
National-bank notes received monthly for redemption during past year by Comptroller of Currency and at redemption agency 89
National-bank notes received by Comptroller of Currency and destroyed each year since establishment of the system 89
Vault balances 89
Number of packages of national-bank notes received from Treasurer United States and from banks direct during the year 90
Charges for redemption of notes 108
REDEMPTION CHARGES. (*See* Redemption.)
REDEMPTION FUND:
Amount of 100
As a part of reserve 99, 100
REPORTS OF CONDITION:
Made by banks to office 93
Publication of 93
Number received during the year 93
Tabulation of 93
Abstract of 93, 120
RESERVE:
Act of February 25, 1863 96
Act of June 3, 1864 97
Act of June 20, 1874 97
Banks organized under act of February 25, 1863, excluded from acting as reserve agents 98
Act of March 3, 1887 98
Under which central reserve cities may be established 98
Amount of reserve required by national banks 99
State of 100
New York City 100
Amount of, in reserve cities 101
Amount of, in States and Territories 101
Summary 101
Movement of reserve in New York City, weekly, during October, for last eleven years 106
RESOURCES OF NATIONAL BANKS:
On dates of report during the year ending October 31, 1887 2
SAVINGS BANKS:
Official returns from 38
Aggregate surplus and undivided profits 39
Average par value of stock 39
Gold, silver, legal tenders, and national-bank notes held 39
Aggregate resources and liabilities 40
Distribution of shares of stock by States and geographical divisions, and deposits, number of depositors, and average amount due each 40
Aggregate resources, liabilities, and condition, from official sources 40
Aggregate resources, liabilities, and condition, from unofficial sources 41
Number, capital stock, surplus and undivided profits, and deposits, by States 43, 44
Distribution, number, and average par value of shares 45

SECURITY FOR CIRCULATING NOTES: Page.
Amount, in classes, of United States bonds owned by the banks pledged for circulation and public deposits 73
Comparative statement of amount of bonds on deposit from 1882 to 1887, inclusive 73
Deposited by banks organized during past five years 75
Minimum amount of bonds required, amount deposited, excess, and percentage of excess 75
Amount of bonds withdrawn and transferred to securities held for public deposits 76
Amount held, 1866 and 1887 93
Decrease in amount of bonds held by national banks 74
Decrease in amount of circulation 74
Increase of lawful money deposited to retire circulation 74
Bonds deposited by national banks organized during the year ending October 31, 1887 51
Minimum bonds required of banks organized in fiscal years from 1882 to 1887 66
Bonds actually deposited by such banks 66
Percentage of excess 66
Circulation issued 66
Changes in bonds 67
Inspection of bonds held in trust by the Treasurer of the United States 67
Validity of transfers 67
Amount 3 per cent. bonds issued, amount redeemed, and outstanding from July 12, 1882, to October 31, 1887 69
Redemption of 3 per cent. bonds from July 12, 1882, to October 31, 1887 69
Changes in 3 per cent. bonds from August 1, 1886, to July 1, 1887, amount called, redeemed, and voluntarily surrendered 69
Interest-bearing bonds required 70
Opinion of Attorney-General 71
Amount of 3 per cent. bonds voluntarily surrendered for redemption and replacements in other bonds 72
Amount of 4 and 4½ per cent. bonds purchased for sinking-fund purposes, and amount withdrawn from deposits to secure circulation by national banks 72
SEMI-ANNUAL DUTY:
On circulation 107
SHAREHOLDERS IN NATIONAL BANKS:
Number and par value of shares of stock 62
Assessment of shareholders 91
Protection to shareholders 92
STATE BANKS:
Official returns from 38
Number of banks 39
Aggregate capital 39
Surplus and undivided profits 39
Deposits 39
Unofficial returns from 39
Aggregate capital 39
Surplus and undivided profits 39
Deposits 39
Gold, silver, legal tenders, and national-bank notes held 39
Resources and liabilities 40
Distribution of shares of stock by States and geographical divisions 40
Aggregate resources, liabilities, and condition, from official sources 40
Aggregate resources, liabilities, and condition, from unofficial sources 41
Number, capital stock, surplus and undivided profits, and deposits 42
Distribution, number, and average par value of shares of stock 45
Converted 57
Number of 57
Capital at date of conversion 57
Present capital and surplus 57
Number that have gone into voluntary liquidation 57
Number that have become insolvent 57
STATE TAXATION OF NATIONAL BANKS:
Discriminative taxation 108
Restraining statute 108
Restriction upon the States 109
Purpose of Congress 109
Recent decision of the Supreme Court of the United States 109

SUGGESTIONS AS TO AMENDMENTS OF NATIONAL BANKING LAW. (*See* Amendments.) Page.
SUMMARY OF THE STATE AND CONDITION OF EVERY NATIONAL BANK REPORTING DURING THE YEAR ENDING OCTOBER 31, 1887 2
SUPERVISION:
Of national banks 90
Powers of Comptroller 90
Examinations 90
Compensation 90
TAX ON CIRCULATING NOTES 107
Total tax collected up to July 1, 1887 108
TAXATION OF NATIONAL BANKS BY STATES (*see* State taxation, etc.) 108

TABLES CONTAINED IN THE APPENDIX.

Contents of digest of national-bank cases 131
Digest 133
Digest of recent decisions in banking law 155
Propositions received from stated sources in relation to amendments to existing law by which it is thought the national banking system may be improved 165
Estimated population in each State and Territory, aggregate capital, surplus, undivided profits, and individual deposits of national and State banks, loan and trust companies, savings and private banks, and per-capita averages 175
Number of banks organized, in liquidation, and in operation, with their capital, bonds on deposit, and circulation issued, redeemed, and outstanding on October 31, 1887 176
National-bank currency issued, redeemed, and outstanding for the year ending October 31, 1887 177
Number and denominations of national-bank notes issued and redeemed and the number of each denomination outstanding on October 31 in each year from 1868 to 1887 178
Statement of monthly increase or decrease of national-bank circulation for the year ending October 31, 1887, and quarterly increase or decrease since January 14, 1875 180
Amount of national-bank circulation issued, the amount of lawful money deposited in the United States Treasury to retire national-bank circulation from June 20, 1874, to November 1, 1887, and the amount remaining on deposit at the latter date 181
National-bank notes outstanding, amount of lawful money on deposit with Treasurer United States to redeem national-bank notes, and amount of United States bonds on deposit to secure circulation 182
Number of banks in each State, Territory, and reserve city, with their capital, minimum amount of bonds required by law, bonds actually held, and circulation outstanding October 5, 1887. 183
Number of banks in each State, Territory, and reserve city, with capital of $150,000 and under, and those with capital exceeding $150,000, and amount of bonds deposited to secure circulation, October 5, 1887 185
Number of banks in each State, Territory, and reserve city with capital of $250,000 and under, amount of bonds on deposit to secure circulation October 5, 1887, amount required by proposed code (page 20), and amount which might be withdrawn upon adoption of code 187
Ditto as to banks with capital of over $250,000 189
National banks in voluntary liquidation under sections 5220 and 5221, Revised Statutes, dates of liquidation, amount of capital, circulation issued and retired, and circulation outstanding October 31, 1887 191
National banks in voluntary liquidation under sections 5220 and 5221, Revised Statutes, for the purpose of organizing new associations with same or different title, date of liquidation, amount of capital, circulation issued, retired, and outstanding October 31, 1887 200
National banks in liquidation under section 7, act July 12, 1882, with date of expiration of charter, circulation issued, retired, and outstanding October 31, 1887 202
National banks in liquidation under section 7, act July 12, 1882, with date of expiration of charter, circulation issued, retired, and outstanding, succeeded by associations with the same or different title, October 31, 1887 203
National banks placed in the hands of receivers, with capital, circulation issued, lawful money deposited to redeem circulation, amount redeemed, and amount outstanding October 31, 1887 204
Insolvent national banks, charter number, date of appointment of receiver, amount of capital stock, claims proved, and rate of dividends paid to creditors 206
Insolvent national banks, with dates of failure, nominal assets, amounts collected, claims proved, dividends paid, and dates of closing 210

	Page.
Insolvent national banks, date of organization, failure and closing, amounts collected from all sources, loans and disbursements, expenses of receivership, claims proved, dividends paid, and remaining assets returned to stockholders	212
Liabilities of the national banks and reserve required and held at three dates in 1884, 1885, 1886, 1887	217
National banks by geographical divisions in reserve cities and central reserve cities, condition at various dates from 1882 to 1885, inclusive; amount of reserve required, and amount held, etc	219
Average weekly deposits, circulation, and reserve of national banks in New York City by months in years from 1881 to 1887	229
State of the lawful-money reserve at various dates from October 1, 1881, to October 5, 1887	230
State of the lawful-money reserve by cities, States, and Territories October 5, 1887	232
Earnings and dividends of national banks for semi-annual periods from September 1, 1886, to September 1, 1887	234-240
Earnings and dividends of national banks by geographical divisions for semi-annual periods from September 1, 1878, to September 1, 1887	242
National banks in reserve cities, ratios of dividends and earnings to capital and to capital and surplus from March 1, 1883, to September 1, 1887	244
Classification of the loans and discounts of the national banks in the reserve cities and in the States and Territories October 5, 1887	246
Clearings and balances of the banks in New York City by weeks ending at dates given	247
Abstract of reports of condition of State banks, loan and trust companies, savings, and private banks, official and unofficial	249-294
Report of the condition of the National Savings Bank of the District of Columbia October 5, 1887	295
Distribution by States, Territories, and geographical divisions, number and average par value of shares of stock of State and savings banks and loan and trust companies June 30, 1887	296
Aggregate resources and liabilities of national banks from October, 1863, to October, 1887	299
Summary of the state and condition of the national banks on dates of report during year ending October 31, 1887	319
Condition of each national bank at close of business October 5, 1887	Vol. II

○

www.ingramcontent.com/pod-product-compliance
Lightning Source LLC
Chambersburg PA
CBHW030400230426
43664CB00007BB/673
* 9 7 8 3 7 4 1 1 5 1 5 7 6 *